B
GAVIN
B

Booth, T. Michael
(Thomas Michael)

Paratrooper.

$27.00

DATE		

BAKER & TAYLOR BOOKS

SIMON &

SCHUSTER

NEW YORK

LONDON

TORONTO

SYDNEY

TOKYO

SINGAPORE

PARATROOPER

THE

LIFE

OF

GEN. JAMES M. GAVIN

T. MICHAEL BOOTH and

DUNCAN SPENCER

SIMON & SCHUSTER
Rockefeller Center
1230 Avenue of the Americas
New York, New York 10020

Copyright © 1994 by Thomas Booth and Duncan Spencer

Designed by Barbara M. Bachman

Manufactured in the United States of America

10 9 8 7 6 5 4 3 2 1

Library of Congress Cataloging-in-Publication Data
Booth, T. Michael (Thomas Michael)
  Paratrooper: the life of Gen. James M. Gavin/T. Michael Booth and
Duncan Spencer.
    p. cm.
  Includes bibliographical references and index.
  1. Gavin, James M. (James Maurice), 1907– . 2. Generals—
United States—Biography. 3. United States. Army—
Biography. 4. United States. Army—Airborne troops—
History. 5. World War, 1939–1945—Aerial operations,
American. I. Spencer, Duncan. II. Title.
U53.G38B66 1994
940.54'21'092—dc20
[B]   93-42776 CIP
ISBN 0-671-73226-9

In memory of

Joe Gradzewicz:

Green Beret,

paratrooper,

father, husband,

friend.

He died too young.

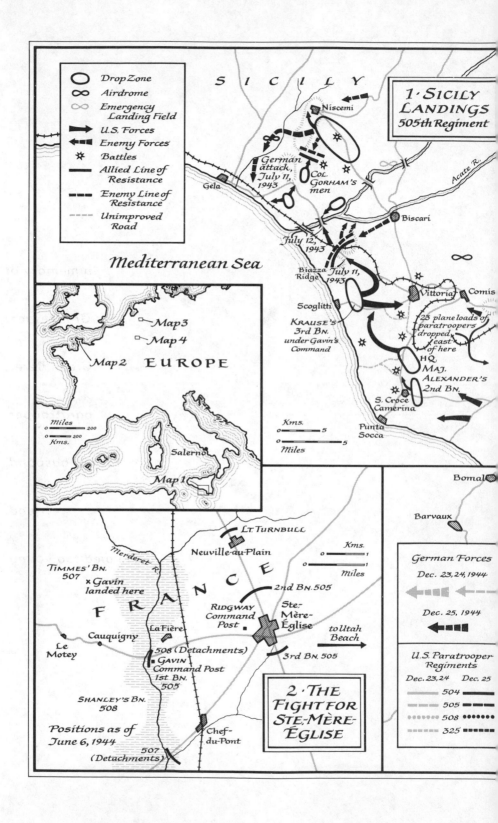

Legend:
- ○○ Drop Zone
- ∞ Airdrome
- ∞ Emergency Landing Field
- ► U.S. Forces
- ◄ Enemy Forces
- ✳ Battles
- — Allied Line of Resistance
- – – Enemy Line of Resistance
- ····· Unimproved Road

1 · SICILY LANDINGS
505th Regiment

SICILY

Niscemi

German attack, July 11, 1943

Col. GORHAM'S men

Gela

Acate R.

Biscari

July 12, 1943

Mediterranean Sea

Biazza Ridge July 11, 1943

Scoglitti

KRAUSE'S 3rd BN. under Gavin's Command

Vittoria   Comiso

25 plane loads of paratroopers dropped east of here

HQ. MAJ. ALEXANDER'S 2nd BN.

S. Croce Camerina

Punta Socca

Kms.
0 ———— 5
Miles
0 ———— 5

EUROPE

Map 3
Map 4
Map 2

Miles
0 —— 200
0 —— 200
Kms.

Salerno

Map 1

Bomal

Barvaux

LT. TURNBULL
Neuville-au-Plain

Kms.
0 ———— 1
Miles
0 ———— 1

TIMMES' BN. 507
×Gavin landed here

Merderet R.

2nd BN. 505

FRANCE

RIDGWAY Command Post

Ste-Mère-Église

to Utah Beach

Cauquigny
La Fière

Le Motey

508 (Detachments)
GAVIN Command Post 1st BN. 505

3rd BN. 505

SHANLEY'S BN. 508

Positions as of June 6, 1944

Chef-du-Pont

507 (Detachments)

2 · THE FIGHT FOR STE-MÈRE-ÉGLISE

German Forces
Dec. 23, 24, 1944
◄■■◄ ◄ – –
Dec. 25, 1944
◄■■■

U.S. Paratrooper Regiments
Dec. 23, 24   Dec. 25
———— 504 ———
———— 505 ━━━
•••••• 508 •••••••
– – – 325 ■■■■■

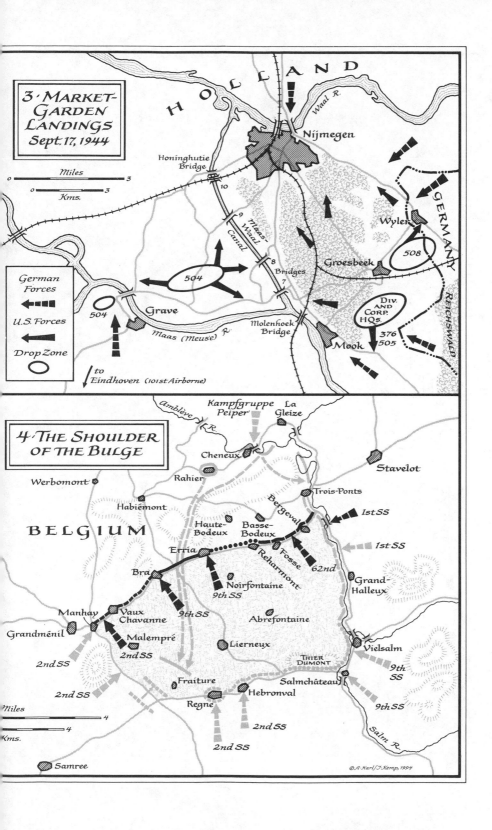

3·MARKET-GARDEN LANDINGS Sept. 17, 1944

HOLLAND

Waal R.

Nijmegen

Honinghutie Bridge

10

Maas-Waal Canal

9

Wyler

508

GERMANY

Groesbeek

8 Bridges 7

REICHSWALD

504

Grave

504

Maas (Meuse) R.

Molenhoek Bridge

DIV. AND CORP. HQs.

376 505

Mook

to Eindhoven (101st Airborne)

German Forces

U.S. Forces

Drop Zone

4·THE SHOULDER OF THE BULGE

Amblève R.

Kampfgruppe Peiper

La Gleize

Cheneux

Stavelot

Rahier

Trois-Ponts

Werbomont

Bergeval

1st SS

Habiémont

BELGIUM

Haute-Bodeux

Basse-Bodeux

1st SS

Erria

Reharmont

Fosse

62nd

Bra

Noirfontaine

9th SS

Grand-Halleux

9th SS

Manhay

Vaux Chavanne

9th SS

Abrefontaine

Grandménil

Malempré

Lierneux

Vielsalm

2nd SS

2nd SS

THIER DUMONT

9th SS

2nd SS

Fraiture

Salmchâteau

Hebronval

9th SS

Regne

Salm R.

2nd SS

Miles

Kms.

2nd SS

Samree

© A·Karl/J·Kemp, 1994

CONTENTS

1.

EVE OF FAME—

JUNE 5, 1944

Fierce fiery warriors fought upon the clouds,
In ranks and squadrons and right form of war. . . .

William Shakespeare, *Julius Caesar*

Bill Walton watched Brigadier General James Maurice Gavin gripping the door frame of the C-47 as it flew low over Normandy, buffeting through the cold air. Behind Gavin, Walton stood amidst a "stick" of eighteen paratroopers, straining under the weight of weapons, hooked by a thin static line to a jump cable. For the hundredth time, Walton, a civilian journalist, who had begged to get on the plane, cursed this stupid idea. Now he could clearly see his own death in a dozen different versions. The noise was a drug, overwhelming. Numbed by the clamor of laboring engines roaring, air sucking and screeching past the metal plane, Walton kept his eyes on the figure in the doorway and tried not to think.

Below, the land looked flat as cardboard, but Walton knew there were thousands of German soldiers down there, ready to kill him. There would be no support or protection. The clumsy transports had flown through the coastline defenses, flack rocking the planes. Preflight briefings had shown the tall poles, "Rommel's asparagus," the Germans had set up to smash landing gliders. The low beaches were bristling with guns and metal obstacles. But the planes droned on, dropping lower. The final stage of the European war, the invasion of occupied France and the destruction of Germany's waning military machine, would begin at the door where Gavin stood.

Walton was glad to be close to Gavin. Before taking off he had hoped for a big story for *Time* magazine on the man rapidly becoming a legend, but the hopes had dissolved and been replaced by fear. This was Walton's first jump. He vowed then and there never to do such a thing again if only God would spare him this time, if only the parachute worked! Walton felt himself pushed forward toward the wind-tortured door frame of the rocking aircraft. At least, he thought, the Germans would not expect them.

Then came the buffeting blows and the sound of metal spattering. Flack pinged and pattered, random jagged bits of metal meant to cut, wreck, and kill. There would be no surprise.

That night, all over Normandy, men jumped in a broad band behind the beaches, bent on many different errands of war. By the end of the next day, more than 1,000 men of the 82nd Airborne would be dead, wounded or missing. Many would fall into marshes and sink, or hit trees, where they would dangle to be murdered later. Some of the missing would be disabled, many with broken bones, and quickly taken prisoner.

Most of the men of the 82nd knew they were jumping into something very big, into history, like Crécy or Waterloo or the Cannae, but for days the tide of battle and uncertainty would cover these men. They would fight alone, almost out of touch with the seaborne invaders at first, not knowing the outcome of the invasion.

The Normandy invasion was Gavin's doorway to fame in battle. It captured the attention of the entire world and made Gavin larger than life. Looking for heroes, Americans found them in Gavin and his paratroops. The unforgettable images of the Normandy beach by *Life* magazine photographer Robert Capa gave Americans the picture of American boys storming ashore past wreckage, past even the corpses of their friends, but irresistible. Gavin's black-faced troopers fulfilled another fantasy: the elite, tough, warriors who fought by stealth and surprise, who put their lives at risk behind enemy lines. Gavin was their beau ideal.

Thirty-seven years of age on the night of the Normandy drop, Gavin looked about ten years younger. Throughout his life, until arthritis from a jump injury, and later, Parkinson's, stooped and slowed him, youth was his trademark. But not only youth, a particular brand of it. Lean to an extreme, his strength was of the sinew-and-muscle kind, the strength of endurance. He lived a Spartan regime, uninterrupted since early childhood, of heavy manual work, long-distance marches, simplicity of diet, and a belief in the virtue of physical toughness.

At the height of his powers the night he hurled himself out of the transport at the German enemy, Gavin had been preparing for this moment for twenty years. He had spent most of his waking moments thinking about his work and ways to improve it. He had read almost continuously about the great soldiers of history, and he had written out favorite aphorisms from their recorded statements for his own reference. Now the hoped-for opportunity had come.

Suddenly the green light came on, the signal to jump, and Gavin, soon to be the youngest Major General since George Armstrong Custer, left Walton with a last flashing image—the wind plastering dark cloth against the paratrooper's wiry arms, his form outlined by the naked light, both hands tensed on the alloy doorway. Gavin hurled himself forward and disappeared into the prop blast. Like a suicidal caterpillar the entire stick of eighteen men, automatons now, pushed forward, a sharp metallic sound marking each man's exit. "Don't push," Walton heard himself saying, "I'll go quick." Then he too reached the door and jumped into the black-and-white photo below. Twisted and tossed by the turbulence of the prop blast, his mind went numb, and then with a wonderful lurch, it all stopped. He was swaying, masterfully above the earth; silently, the canopy blossomed above his head. The ground approached fast, then Walton heard gunfire and saw tracers streaking across the ground, and the fear returned.

James Maurice Gavin—though sometimes obscured by the more renowned, elder generation of World War II commanders—was an innovative, brilliant, courageous leader who earned a special place in the annals of twentieth-century warfare. He was foremost a paratrooper—one of the first. He was the man who defined airborne concept, fought fiercely for its acceptance, and indelibly stamped his vision upon it. While other general officers shunned the risks, he jumped from so many airplanes with so many different parachutes—many of them still experimental— he earned the nickname "Jumpin' Jim." He also led the first American regimental parachute assault in history and from there went on to gain more combat jump stars on his Airborne wings than any other general in World War II—or since.

In many ways, Gavin was an old-fashioned soldier, as much a throwback as he was an innovator. In a century full of inconclusive warfare, Gavin was a warrior of the ancient tradition, a character he himself formed from the books he read as a child searching for a role model. He seized the image of the soldier for his own. Great captains, and he studied the lives of all of them, led from the front, never wavered before adversity, were relentless in their foes' destruction, were willing to suffer the awful hardship and the purifying glory of the fight.

The great soldiers—Caesar, Alexander, Napoleon, Lee, Jackson—were his inspiration, his guides through life, and he became uniquely like them.

Gavin's idealism drove him to extremes and destinations that gave him fame. It drove him from an obscure coal town to excel at West Point, when his preparation and background spelt only anonymity. He never forgot that ceaseless study was essential to soldiers, even in peacetime (his major criterion for any army post was always the quality of its library). The somewhat sentimental idea he held of an officer's integrity was played out at every level. It made him personally lead his men in the long, sleepless toughening marches and caused him to despise officers who lived and ate better than their troops.

In combat, it made him seem to be without fear. Often he took foolish personal risks, but his trust in his luck and his own capabilities proved sound. Time and again he made the correct decision and broke his enemy. He mastered the old ways and became a legendary pioneer of the new, a crackpot to his rivals, a visionary to his friends. For great captains the latest weapons, tactics, or forms of mobility are the engines that drive them to crushing and total victory. The same search for mastery led him to woman after woman as much for the conquest as the love.

He was a pure soldier in an era of political generals, but he was also an intellectual, a diplomat, an executive, and a writer. Buoyed by his rigid code, he stood above other men and sometimes magnetically drew them to him, more with lightning than thunder, more with grace than force, and more with intelligent calculation than bluster.

Gavin rose professionally at a time when American military thought was frozen in the theory of overwhelming mass, the legacy of Union General U. S. Grant, whose tactics personified the application of pure power. While Gavin's military peers studied how to dominate the battle-field with overwhelming numbers of men and machines, Gavin idolized the speed, the maneuverability, and the color of Stonewall Jackson. His thesis was contrary to the reigning orthodoxy in his own profession, yet he was proved right again and again.

In the twentieth century, particularly in America, the soldier had al-ready changed from Gavin's warrior ideal even as he developed himself. Somewhere between the shadow generals of the First World War, the political generals of the Second, and the police actions that followed, the warrior faded into anachronism. The impeccable gray Lee on his tireless horse, Traveler, amidst the smoke and flash of a desperate Gettysburg dimmed to be replaced by the smiling Eisenhower, well to the rear. Generals moved from the front of their men to be far distant from the noise and confusion of the fight—their lives suddenly too important to risk, and the logistical functions they represented too brittle for the sound and shock of battle. Decisions based on the seen yielded to the unseen, to reports received at communications centers and pins on maps. Victory and its totality grew indefinable. And with that the general at the front of his command evolved into the new sort, the sort who needed more of the skills of diplomacy than of the flank maneuver. Gavin became one of the last of his kind; and his life, so contradictory, becomes comprehensible only when he is understood in that light.

Battle, the dream of it and the consummation of it, escaped Gavin's grasp during the thirties and left him laboring in obscurity in his post—West Point promotionless army. Then the concept of airborne warfare suddenly drew fresh attention, thanks to pioneering by Russian and Ger-man military innovators. Gavin quickly grasped and helped to pioneer the new airborne idea for America. Its newness promised the opportunity for decision and a certain chance at combat in any war; it took him into something he truly could do better than anyone else.

Gavin's war, when it came, fulfilled his vision of lightning-fast maneu-ver and new technology and justified his years of preparation for combat. His theories of training were also justified, as his paratroop division, the 82nd Airborne, was recognized even by its enemies as the best infantry in the world, a bunch of "cold-blooded killers," as he put it. Promise was fulfilled—and as fast was dissipated.

Gavin left the battlefield for the peacetime army of the fifties and the politics of rear-echelon generalship that Eisenhower's committee leadership as Supreme Commander personified. Words and appearances now mattered more than deeds, but Gavin entered the fray with the absolutism with which he had fought in World War II—and he lost. On the battlegrounds of the Pentagon, he demanded total victory, and he never got it; for though he did not realize it then, its time had past. In the end, he did what he perceived any warrior must do in defeat. He ended it all for himself.

He was appalled by the army's performance in Korea, he was an early proponent of tactical nuclear weapons and enthusiastically planned for their use on a vastly expanded battlefield. But neither nuclear diplomacy nor police actions offered the absolute victory he saw as mandatory. The result was one of the nation's most famous battle leaders turning in the face of his friends and against government policy during the Vietnam War, working to reverse that policy, being considered a traitor by many of his colleagues in the army, and eventually leaving public life for a life of writing and business.

Questions followed in his wake, as colleagues watched his ascending star stall, yet he left them unanswered. While other soldiers adapted themselves to the realities of a highly political, cost-conscious Pentagon during the fifties, Gavin could not. Others, epitomized by his rival and counterpart, General Maxwell Taylor, could accommodate even to the quagmire of Vietnam. Gavin fought for new weapons and methods and for the army he believed in, and he lost. Warriors do not bare their souls, and to have answered the questions, he would have had to bare his. Yet, if only because he was indeed one of the last of his kind and so good at what he did, his story deserves telling, and the man deserves exposure to clearer light; for in an army long inundated with the belief that all success comes from overwhelming power, Gavin believed it came from the actions of individuals. And when all goes wrong, in battle or in a difficult peace, these are all a nation has.

2 .

B O Y H O O D

Through forty years of intermittent effort, bringing to bear all the influence of a war hero, an ambassador, James Maurice Gavin never discovered who impregnated Katherine Ryan of Kilmihill, County Clare, one day in 1906.

Worse, he was never sure that his mother was that same Katherine Ryan he had discovered after patient research into long-idle parish records in the west of Ireland, half-remembered accounts of aged people, and the subtle, polite secretiveness of the Catholic adoption agencies.

The old general never stopped chewing it over. Time and again he would begin his own story, "I was born on March 22, 1907, in Holy Family Hospital in Brooklyn . . ." and he would stop, unable to finish that simple sentence with "the son of . . ." It was a question he worked his entire life to answer.

He, who had won almost every contest in life, never won the fight to know who James Maurice Gavin was. He was never sure whether his real last name was Ryan, or Nally. He, whose life could be summed up in the word "control," had only chaos, misinformation, and doubt about his own history. Whatever his name truly was, it was not, he knew, Gavin, the name of the mining family who took him in as a foundling and brought him up in Mount Carmel, a bypassed Pennsylvania coal town.

He never even knew where his middle name, Maurice, came from, or he never told. As a child, his adoptive parents dubbed him Morris. He later erased Morris, a part of his practice of either romanticizing or demonizing his discordant youth.

Why should names and lineage bother him so? Perhaps it is the question of every successful self-made man: "Why me?" that leads to a scrutiny of forebears. His was a classic Horatio Alger success story, yet he felt uncomfortable with its cliché cadences. From early youth, Gavin felt that he was different from others and a stranger to himself.

Parochial school records of the small town of Killaloe, parish of Kilmihill, perched amid the stone walls and bare fields of County Clare near the headwaters of the river Shannon, record a Katherine Ryan born in Lacken, County Clare, December 28, 1883. She emigrated to America at the right time. This woman he thought to be his mother, but he never knew.

It was because Gavin always wanted to know the reasons for his own difference that he kept on with this inquiry, poring over orphanage records, probing the secrecy maintained by the hierarchy of the Catholic Church, seeking the help of influential friends like New York's Cardinal Spellman, hiring private detectives to try to pierce the Church's adoption code. Still his search ended in a silence he could not break, a mystery he could not solve. Gavin went to his grave not knowing who he was, where he came from, and perhaps most important to a man who fathered five daughters and no sons, the character of his own father and mother, or even a sketch of their life stories.

Gavin's story begins with that mysterious young expectant mother's sea trip from Ireland and continues in Brooklyn, New York, with a two-year-old orphan baby, farmed out to a working-class Irish immigrant family, but it ends in the stars.

James Nally Ryan, the child who it appears became James Maurice Gavin, was born March 22, 1907, at St. Mary's Maternity and Infant Home (now known as Holy Family Hospital) in Brooklyn. The birth certificate gives no indications of the baby's height or weight, no hint of the child's health, but gives every indication of instability in the baby's family situation. The full name of the child, on the original birth certificate, is altered; the middle name, Nally, crossed out with a single clear stroke of a pen. The father's occupation, listed as "laborer electrician," is also altered with a similar pen stroke, striking the word "laborer." The father's residence is set down as "unknown," the mother's as 692 Dean Street, Brooklyn (the address of the hospital). The mother's age is given at twenty-three, her name as Katie Ryan, birthplace Ireland; the father's age is given as twenty-six, birthplace also Ireland.

The attending physician, Dr. Eugene Cronin (then serving as an intern at the hospital), was interviewed by Gavin in 1941; he reported he could remember nothing in particular about the birth.

What is plain is that James (Nally) Ryan came unwelcome and unwanted into the world. If his mother was the Katherine Ryan he suspected, she was among thousands of other immigrants from the rural west of Ireland, a young woman in her twenties, dumped on the less-than-tender mercies of New York City, during one of the greatest waves of immigration this country has ever known.

With the help of a scholarly, interested elderly priest of County Clare, Gavin unearthed a house where Katie Ryan is thought to have lived and a school record for a Katherine Ryan (which indicates an outstanding scholastic record from grades two to six in Lacken National School in the town of Kilmihill). Katie Ryan, born in 1883, was first in her class in reading, spelling, geography, needlework, and second in arithmetic and writing. The record shows her name struck off the roll in March of 1897. Her next official appearance seems to have been in Brooklyn in 1907, ten years later, at age twenty-three. It seems to tally. Gavin's search of shipping records uncovered no proof of her passage; no memorial has been found of her death. But the assumption is that she arrived in New York harbor from County Clare.

If so, Katherine Ryan passed through without notation in the records of Ellis Island. Her life is a mystery. But it is certain that she spent the next two years in or near New York, that she was poor, and that she was forced to give up her child when he was two.

Almost nothing is known of the infant years of James Ryan. One source has it that his mother was permitted to remain for over a year at the hospital where he was born to take up training as a nurse—and incidentally to pay back the hospital for the costs of his birth and housing. There are no hospital records to prove this.

At less than two years the infant boy became a ward of the city of New York, "A minor child of Thomas and Katherine Ryan, who abandoned the said minor in the Angel Guardian Branch of the Convent of Mercy in Brooklyn, where the said child was maintained at public expense by the City of New York until February 26, 1909, when said minor was placed with your petitioners."

This bare account is found in the adoption language in 1917 documents through which James Ryan was legally adopted. The petitioners, the coal-mining family of Martin Gavin and his wife, Mary Gavin, of Mount Carmel, Pennsylvania, had no interest in accurate detail. No mention of a father by the name of Thomas Ryan was uncovered during Gavin's forty years of research and it would be very unlikely that Katherine Ryan, having had one child out of wedlock with the unknown laborer-electrician, James Nally, would shortly find a husband by the name of Thomas Ryan and then give up her child. Far more likely is the manufac-ture of "Thomas Ryan" for the purposes of decency and to fill in the blanks, and the fictional marriage, which legitimizes the birth.

Gavin's own memory begins with life with his adoptive parents in the small town in Northumberland County, Pennsylvania. The Civil War spurred industrialization, which led to the building of canals and railroads and to the founding of hundreds of eastern Pennsylvania towns that were little more than labor camps for collieries. The coal, in unbelievable amounts, lay at first near the surface, and later, as mining methods developed and even richer lodes of it were found deep underground, the labor camps became permanent, each one connected by rail to the main line east and west, and the mines themselves became stable. The mining towns were built, not as were other towns, over generations, but quickly and for a specific reason, with neither a future beyond the coal beneath, nor a past. Mount Carmel is one such town. The region's mines were served in turn by the waves of immigrants moving west—first restless New Englanders of Scottish and English descent; then the Welsh came from their own overcrowded mines in southern Wales to work new veins in America. The Irish followed, pouring in after the 1848 potato famine in Ireland. Then, after the turn of the century, arrived the Polish, the Lithuanians, and the Italians.

Mount Carmel is on the eastern edge of a mountain of coal, and thus it was among the first towns to be developed and was destined also to have a later role as a railroad town when the hinterlands farther west were mined. As a boy, Jim Gavin would wait for the afternoon trains bringing the newspapers, fresh from the presses in Philadelphia, to be eagerly read by miners returning from the early shifts at about 3 P.M.

The coalfields of Pennsylvania were in a boom period throughout Gavin's childhood and until after he left Mount Carmel in 1924. It was a place where a man could find good work if he could do it—no nonsense about training or education; not even the ability to read was required. In the world of coal, books were a luxury, things to be read at weddings and in church.

It was into this world of boom-time mining, cold outhouses, sediment-filled creeks, and the blight of gigantic piles of mine wastes called "tailings," plus the harsh winters and summers of the coalfields that James Ryan (Gavin) was brought.

"My first memory of boyhood," Gavin wrote in his old age, "was hearing my foster father, Martin Gavin, stirring about in the predawn hours of a cold winter morning. The house was quite cold with small drifts of snow on the inside windowsills. When we had gone to bed, fresh coal was placed over the remains of the fire in the stove and the stove was dampened, so the first task upon arising was to rekindle the fire. The heat went up the chimney through the upper floor where small outlets allowed some of it to escape into the rooms. Hearing my foster father go downstairs, I would follow him. Outside the snow was about a foot deep and drifting. He would finish his breakfast with a cup of black coffee laced with a jigger of whiskey. Then he would pick up his tin lunch pail, usually containing a sandwich, possibly a hard-boiled egg, and a small mason jar of coffee. Mason jars were plentiful in all of the homes because Mount Carmel was the first market for the Pennsylvania Dutch farmers, and all the miners' families did a lot of canning during the summer to tide them over the winter."

Though the Gavins led a simple life, it was not impoverished. Fuel cost them little or nothing. Gavin tells of gathering the winter's coal by hand from slag heaps and from the open seams visible even today on most road cuts and so-called open faces in Northumberland County. Another clue to the Gavins' status in the town is the fact that the boy attended the parochial school run by the Church, and only later, when times became harder for them, switched to the public school, where he was marked for success from the first.

The family lived in rented houses. According to Mount Carmel records, they moved a number of times on the same block during the period of Gavin's youth. The boy may have been an only child, but aging Mount Carmel residents recall a sister, a woman whom Gavin seldom mentioned to his family later and who was not in his own memoirs of his youth. A photograph survives of Jim Gavin and the putative sister.

Martin earned approximately $25 a week in about 1910, a good deal more than the average wage of $10 to $12 a week prevalent in the rest of the east at the time. It was enough to command at least a two-story frame house in the Irish "Dooleysville" and "Connorsville" villages at the edge of town.

The adoptive father is a well-remembered figure. In his last interview, Gavin said he liked him very much; he remembered Martin as "kind and generous . . . a God-fearing man," a first-generation Irishman who spoke with an accent. "Hard working . . . he was well liked throughout the town. He had no faults of which I was aware; he drank moderately except on Saint Patrick's day, which was a day to be celebrated with friends at the corner saloon. The strongest language that I ever heard him use was 'the curse of Cromwell on you,' and it was some years before I found out what that meant. He was a very gentle man and never raised a hand against me. When Mrs. Gavin beat me, he made it a point to leave the house."

Martin Gavin emerges from interviews with contemporaries as weak rather than kind, the sort of man who was the last hired for a job; his weakness, neighbors hinted, was gambling. But, though he was the only father Gavin knew, he was no role model for the young boy, whose reactions gradually hardened into a single wish—to do differently than his father.

If the mild Martin Gavin cuts only a barely coherent figure in Gavin's own recollections, the small, slight, dark-haired Mary Gavin is sketched with no shadings.

"My foster mother, Mary Gavin, was typically Irish and given all too frequently to invoking the intercession of the entire Holy Family and all of the saints while she lambasted me for some not-too-minor misdemeanor. Like many Irish, she was a heavy drinker and this combined with a proclivity to violence made mine a hazardous life . . . the Gavins did not hide from me the fact that I had come from an orphanage . . . I was full of curiosity . . . but all they would tell me was that I was eighteen months of age at the time."

Gavin tells how at the age of eight or nine he climbed to the attic of their Fig Street house and came across papers referring to him as "James Ryan" and mention of the Catholic Home Bureau in New York. But he put the papers back, and never asked his adoptive parents about the details of his background.

Gavin's resentment of Mary Gavin remained to the end of his life, and she seems to have embodied every negative cliché of the American Irish. "That slut," Gavin called her shortly before his death. Mary Gavin was known in the neighborhood, however, as a character of some strength and charm, capable of easy smiles. The eighty-year-old memories of Mount Carmel recall her friendliness, they recall that she told cards and took in boarders.

To Gavin, the cards and the boarding men, and most of all the female, solitary drinking, were unforgivable. He harbored suspicions that she slept with her boarders and ran some sort of a tarot business on the side and remembered that her drinking and dark rages continued throughout his childhood to the point that both Martin Gavin and the boy Gavin seriously considered leaving.

But that was years later; perhaps because Gavin was an orphan, his record of his early life reveals a boy who thought of himself and was thought of by his parents as different from other children. His adoptive mother, perhaps fearful that her own life was under scrutiny, often told the boy that others would try to take him away from them. Gavin writes that she insisted that he stay close to home while he was a child. "One problem was that Mrs. Gavin did not want me out of her sight. If she allowed me out of the house, she wanted to be able to go to a window or door and look out and see me. Her concern did not stem from any affection for me. I wanted her to show that she liked me, but this seemed out of the question. I do not recall that she ever put her arms around me or hugged me, but she certainly whipped me when I misbehaved."

One of the most curious recollections from Gavin's early school days concerns an essay he attempted to write about his mother, his real mother whom he never knew: "The third grade was my undoing. I was getting along very well in my studies, but at the end of the year the teacher assigned us to write a composition on the subject 'All That Glitters Is Not Gold.' I knew very well what the title meant, and I also knew that all that glitters was not gold; but I had a deep-seated preoccupation that I wanted to write about. I wanted to write about my real mother. She was very much on my mind; I envisioned someday finding her, and that when I did she would cry and I would see her eyes glisten with tears. Somehow, I had the idea that I could associate that event and the glitter in her eyes with the title 'All That Glitters Is Not Gold.' Of course, she wasn't gold; she was more important than gold, she was my mother. Starting with that theme, I wrote my paper about three times and each time could not bring it to a rational conclusion. I was obviously off the track and well beyond what the teacher had in mind, but not up to the ability to develop the idea. So the paper I turned in wasn't very good and I failed to get a passing grade."

The event proved to have more than passing significance. Because of the failing grade, Gavin was required to sit in a different part of the classroom with other students who also had failed to satisfy the teaching nuns. The Gavins reacted as well, deciding to remove their adopted son from parochial school to a public elementary school at Fourth and Vine Streets, halfway through the fourth grade. There he proved an outstanding student.

Another poignant episode remembered from preteen years was a visit one day from representatives of the Catholic Home Bureau, a woman, tall and "rather attractive" from the point of view of a ten-year-old, and a man. The setting was stiff and formal, an interview. Gavin, called into the sitting room at the end of the conversation, was asked by his foster mother if he would like to go with the woman. "I do not know what prompted my answer, but I was looking into the woman's eyes and I liked her appearance. I was aware that the Gavins did not want me to answer 'yes,' but some invisible forces were at play that I could not understand, so I did answer 'yes.' The Gavins were furious. It was the only time I can remember Martin Gavin being angry with me. They sent me out back. After the visitors left in a few minutes, they called me back into the house and demanded to know why I had said 'yes.' I really didn't know."

In Gavin's later years, this visit from the mysterious and attractive woman grew into an event of enormous importance. He felt that her remembered features resembled uncannily those of his youngest daughter, Chloe, who was graduated from Harvard and went on to become a corporate lawyer. Gavin became convinced that the woman visiting Mount Carmel that day was his true mother, who had come to reassure herself that her son was well and in good hands before she married or married again.

There are also hints from early youth of Gavin's lifelong craving for beautiful, successful women to fulfill his imagined ideal of his own mother. Not exactly an unusual psychological tack for a man to follow, but in Gavin's case it was combined with two characteristics of great appeal to most women—even as a boy he exuded a steely reserve and bristling danger that made him a ringleader of sorts among his neighborhood cronies, and yet he betrayed a hint that the tough exterior sheltered a deep strain of romantic sentimentality. Gavin was always to put women on a pedestal, while freely accepting their affection. As he put it in his diaries later, in manhood, "They are my solace."

It was Jim "Morris" Gavin's habit, as a schoolboy, to escape from his sometimes watchful, sometimes inebriated adoptive mother whenever possible, in spite of the fact that it would frequently result in a beating. Gavin recounts that she used a hairbrush and later "a piece of broomstick," and he recalled in considerable detail that she had an unnamed boarder create a leather whip. The simpler implements "did not seem to get the results that she wanted.

"She persuaded one of the boarders to go to the harness shop at the mine and get a cat-o'-nine-tails made. It was a leather strap about an inch and half wide, and about a foot and a half long. The upper part, about six inches in length, was left uncut, while the remainder was cut in quarter-inch strips. Grasping it by the small leather end, she hit me with it, and the whipping was very painful. She hid the whip where she supposed I could not find it, but I soon did. At the same time I found an opening in the wall of the house where a staircase had been cut through and partially boarded up. I dropped the cat-o'-nine tails down the opening between the walls, and that was the last seen of the whip. She was very upset when I couldn't find it.

"Sometime after that, when I misbehaved—I probably had taken some food out of the cupboard, which was forbidden—she said she had been talking to a neighbor and that she had a new way of making me behave. She said that the next time I misbehaved, she would wait until I had gone to bed and fallen asleep and then she would whip me. The first time this happened I had a very bad night since I was afraid to go to sleep, knowing what would happen, so I stayed up and walked the floor most of the night. By morning I was in very bad shape, but nothing had occurred. About a week or so later, she again told me that she would whip me for something I had done. Because she had not kept her promise the first time, I was careless and fell asleep. Sometime before daylight, I was awakened by her whipping me quite hard. The practice was not continued, however, and as I got older, she tended to beat me less and then only when she had been drinking."

Apocryphal or not, it reflects what Gavin wanted to say: he never forgave Mary Gavin for her abuse.

A boarder named Grant Whary, a powerfully built miner with coal-blackened, scarred hands, provided the role model Gavin was so restlessly seeking. A man set in his bachelor ways, he was a hunter who owned or borrowed two beagles, had his own gun, and was a naturalist "of Dutch background." Gavin notes in his reminiscences, "He was kind to me and usually took me with him when he hunted rabbits with his one or two beagles in the fall. When I did not go with him, probably on account of school or work, he would bring back a pocketful of wild chestnuts. He also brought back wild flowers for Mrs. Gavin, which she seemed to enjoy. In later years, I made it a point to bring her flowers, thinking she would like them, which she did."

Whary bought Gavin an occasional hard candy and also took the boy to the movies, where (in 1915, when Gavin was an eight-year-old) he saw a silent film, presumably a newsreel, about the war in the Balkans, and was impressed for the first time with soldiers, or at least with military organization. He noted: "I was very impressed with the masses of men that were being moved about and with the fighting itself. It seemed to be more movement than actual combat."

As soon as Gavin learned to read, he discovered history. He has recorded his first memory of school, which was a seminal experience for him, as it got him away from his home for the first time without accompanying punishment; put him in company with other children, which he relished; and began showing him the keys to his long self-education.

To his young companions, Gavin was automatically one set apart. They viewed him differently from themselves. He was the orphan, a natural mystery among the tight-knit large Irish families. Alone, he was fiercely independent, active, and aggressive; yet these qualities appealed to his friends and made him their leader.

Gavin had learned to work from an early age, not out of duty, but to get money and, with it, freedom. He learned the ways of business well. From his own account, Gavin had almost no leisure. He worked from the day he was old enough to pick coal. From coal picking and errand running, he graduated to remunerative jobs—as soon as he entered school. He did "boots" for miners, carrying and delivering the essential hard-worn footwear to shoemakers for repair and cleaning and back to the miners' homes.

He had a memorable career as a newsboy and also worked at other jobs. As a barber's assistant, he soaped the miners' week's growth of beard when they came to the local barbershop on Friday or Saturday to clean up for the one universal family event in the Irish mining community—Sunday Mass. But enterprise, not service, was his forte.

"As soon as I was big enough to carry papers and find my way around town, I got a job delivering the Philadelphia morning paper, the *North American*. By the time I was in fifth grade and had reached the age of eleven, I had both morning and evening routes, and I was the local agent for three out-of-town newspapers. By thirteen, I had cornered two Sunday routes and had a couple of boys working for me. . . . Carrying and selling newspapers was the most profitable job I had during my school years, but it was a rough life. One had to fight for the best corner on which to sell papers and to be ready at any time to fight for the papers and the routes. In our boyish fantasies, we all felt we had to look tough, even if we were not. So, at about ten years of age, I learned to smoke a cigar."

Gavin told how he learned to act quickly and decisively (and violently) in order to overcome disadvantages of size and strength from a fellow newsboy who was harassed by "one of the bigger toughs in town," who was attempting to take over routes and corners by intimidation. One winter evening as Gavin and his friend stood talking, the tough walked by, unaware of them. "He would have gone by because it was dark and he hadn't noticed us. Suddenly my friend, who was considerably smaller in size, dropped his papers, ran into the middle of the street and started swinging at the tough. In seconds the bully took off on the run. I was amazed and my memory of the incident still lingers after all these years. The smaller boy was in the right and had the courage to stand up for what he believed in," Gavin wrote of the incident. But there was a more practical lesson: A stinging attack to the flank or rear of an unsuspecting foe was to be one of the hallmarks of Gavin's tactics in war.

Gavin himself was not small; he was tall and lean and known for quiet demeanor and authority. He also clearly saw ways to maximize his business that others didn't, jumping aboard the trains during their few minutes' stopover at Mount Carmel and hawking papers through the passenger cars until the trains began moving. Furthermore, instead of making change for the three-penny papers he sold, he charged a nickel, making the transactions faster and much more profitable. He also learned to unload his unsold papers at the end of the day at the lobby of the local movie theater, where in return he got free admission for himself and his close friends. And the theatergoers could read the papers while they waited for show time. Years later he reminisced fondly of his first crush, Pearl White, in *The Perils of Pauline.* "Once you were caught in the coils of sin with the beautiful heroine, Pearl White, you'd had it."

He learned more of the military by watching prospective recruits drilling for service in World War I in 1917—all the while regretting he was too young to go and dreaming of the newsreels and the history books he had read.

The relatively carefree period of his youth ended with the eighth grade, when Gavin was about thirteen. He had outgrown newspaper hawking and assisting at the barbershop. He had avoided, with some skill, the fate of the "breaker boy," the child who shovels coal. He had begun to work at a local gas station from 3 to 11 P.M., a job that gave him freedom from home and the hope of moving up to the position of franchisee himself. This, of course, would mean the end of his education. He had enjoyed modest success at school. His parents had switched him more than once between the Catholic and the public school systems, in response to Gavin family economies and young Gavin's boredom and lack of outstanding work except in his best subjects—English and history.

In Gavin's telling, it was the public school eighth grade history course on the Civil War that first fired his imagination about the use of armies and the military techniques that brought success. He proved an analytical student; "I read everything that I could get my hands on, made small tents out of paper and created encampments of soldiers so that I could play war games, keeping in mind some of the battles that I had studied. Our teacher . . . put an outline of the Civil War on the blackboard that I copied on a typewriter. When she learned that I had done so, she paid me twenty-five cents for the outline. I read all the books I could find about the Civil War. I was intrigued by the way that generals such as Grant, Lee, and Jackson moved many thousands of men about in an orderly planned way. One could see from the battlefield sketches how platoons or companies were led, but moving armies seemed to require special skills. It was a mystery to me. Whatever it was, this skill had obviously been taught at West Point, since the generals were all West Pointers."

A lifelong habit was already in place at age thirteen. Throughout his life, Gavin typed information important to him on small sheets of paper and then stored them for future review. Unlike many military figures who suddenly remember to keep diaries (or order subordinates to do it for them) to memorialize their actions and thoughts when they become general officers, Gavin took memoranda to himself from his late teens on. His personal papers are littered with notebooks of these sometimes random jottings, notable for their order and focus.

At the end of eighth grade the crisis, which had been brewing for several years between the self-sufficient youth and the Gavins, finally burst. It started when Gavin, quite typically, decided to tell his foster parents that he intended to go to college and that he would arrange his high school courses with that in mind. "I wanted to go to college," he writes, "but the Gavins wouldn't even talk to me about it. They simply told me that when I finished eighth grade I was to continue to work and see if I could earn more than I was earning." To Gavin, this could mean only one thing—the path to the pits and a regular job as a miner.

About a year after the decision that Gavin was to leave school, when he was fifteen, he had a conversation with his father that was another turning point in his life. "Martin Gavin intercepted me as I was walking down the street to the house, and talked to me about conditions at home," Gavin wrote. "He said that he thought we should both leave her [Mary Gavin] and go someplace else. This did not surprise me, although his coming to me took me aback. Conditions at home were intolerable. As meals were not prepared now, the house was hardly more than a place to sleep, and even that was interrupted by her drinking and their fighting. He [Martin] had two sisters living in town and a number of other relatives nearby. It seemed to me that the solution to his problem was to go to live with them. . . . Each day, Mary Gavin's drinking seemed to get worse. I remember coming home from the filling station sometime after 11:00 on the night of March 21. (March 22, of course, was Gavin's birthday, the one fact of his personal history of which he was sure.)

"When I got home they were fighting, and as usual she was drunk. It was a very disagreeable situation for me to be in. They went to bed about midnight and I went to bed convinced that after midnight, on my seventeenth birthday, I would leave home."

Gavin had an intimate knowledge of the Pennsylvania Railroad's schedules; he knew that there was a 2 A.M. train for New York. Armed with the money he had on hand, Gavin rose quietly at 1:30, walked through familiar streets in the dead hours of the night, and boarded a train, $2.75 in his pocket (but with a nest egg in a local bank), never to return again to the protection of his family or to live in the only town he'd known.

3.

FROM PANAMA

TO WEST POINT

"I arrived at New York shortly after daylight on March 22, crossed the Hudson River by ferry, and landed at the foot of Liberty Street," wrote Gavin of the trip which was to change his life.

For the young runaway, New York was not only his spiritual home but also the city of anonymity, of immigrants and opportunity. Gavin was determined not to return home.

The first thing he did was send a telegram to his foster parents, telling them he was in good health but nothing more, thus insuring he would not be sought by the police. He spent the rest of the day industriously looking for work. He could hardly have come at a less auspicious time for an unskilled youth who needed immediate employment. The city was stuffed with recent-immigrant jobholders, and the Irish, his natural network, were already being undercut by hordes of eastern and southern Europeans. Southern blacks, too, were settling where they could in the city and competing for whatever was available at the bottom of the job market.

For different reasons, the army recruiting service was itself in bad shape, and the fact that the two even met, Gavin and the U.S. Army, the child and the mother, as he would later see it, is something of a miraculous coincidence.

After every major conflict in American history, the army has disappeared, and this was the case in the 1920s. World War I was over, and when the men flooded back they were welcomed with open arms—for a while.

Gavin discovered employers "weren't the slightest bit interested in hiring me since I was not trained." He himself was not interested in domestic service or kitchen work, and he could not compete with tradesmen and apprentices with experience. He was dismayed to find his own situation mirrored in the conversations of "a number of young men who were drifting about the city as I was."

He drifted for the better part of a week, but not without a plan. It's impossible to know what he thought in this period—the record is a void —but for most of his young life, Gavin had sought financial independence by doing the obvious and doing it better, harder, and longer than other youths. This had led to his success in cornering part of the news market at Mount Carmel. Like many young entrepreneurs without their own ideas, he had joined an existing structure. Even the experience with the gas station franchise fits the emerging pattern.

New York, however, had no network for him to fit into. No one there knew that Jimmy Gavin was a sharp and active customer, as they said back home. Besides, the skinny youth with the gray eyes didn't simply want employment. He wanted a job that would allow him to go to school in the evening.

Gavin may have had in mind joining the army all along. Certainly his hopes for success in the big city were faint enough without a prolonged period of struggle simply to survive. But one day in late March, he made his first contact with an army recruiting sergeant seeking recruits from a ground-floor office adjoining Battery Park.

That momentous meeting reads like a cliché—the underage runaway and the canny old recruiter—but like many clichés, it was based on fact. The army was looking for live bodies and didn't care much how it got them. The economy was good in the 1920s, and by 1924 World War I volunteers and career men, attracted by industrial wages far higher than the peacetime army could offer, had left it in droves.

The sergeant eyed the young potential recruit and listened to the boy tell of his plans—school, the future. The sergeant broke into a story he had heard hundreds of times before to ask his questions: any venereal disease? And what was the boy's age?

Gavin, though unsure about exactly what it was, quickly assured him about the former problem, but there was little he could do about his age. The myth of the young hero who lies about his age to join the service had resulted in too many recruits rejected after induction, added expenses, and a continuing problem for recruiters; so the army had expedients ready, Gavin soon found. He had passed his seventeenth birthday just days before and now was told that minimum enlistment age was eighteen —with parental consent. Gavin sagely decided to confess to the sergeant —but only to the fact that he could not get parental consent. ("I wasn't about to ask the Gavins," he noted.) So Gavin told the recruiter that he was an orphan.

The sergeant took him to the Whitehall building nearby, where to Gavin's surprise, a handful of other boys in precisely the same situation waited. The group was escorted to Broome Street and upstairs to a lawyer's office. The lawyer asked a few questions of the boys and signed papers making himself their guardian and gave the needed consent. All of them were accepted for induction.

"I couldn't wait to join up," Gavin wrote later in life, "and I held up my right hand in the Whitehall building on April 1, 1924. I have always remembered the name of the officer who swore me in because it was the same as a Civil War general,—Captain Buckner. He was the first captain of the U.S. Army, in uniform, too, that I had ever seen, and I was impressed." And without much further ado, Gavin, now recruit Gavin, was told to report for assignment—to Panama.

Gavin may have been satisfied with his first assignment in the organization that was to be his life's work, but it's doubtful. At the time, Panama was one of the army's four foreign posts along with "the China Station," the Philippines, and Hawaii. He may have made a favorable impression on his recruiting sergeant. Whatever the cause, Panama proved an extremely lucky posting for the young soldier-to-be.

Things in the "Panama Department" were not good. The strategic assignment was one of the anomalies of military life: the army had to be there in case the canal was attacked, but because the army was there, the canal would never be attacked. Mission fulfilled—with maximum frustration.

Conditions in the Canal Zone were either atrocious or paradisiacal, depending on your point of view. General Andrew O'Meara, a close contemporary of Gavin's who knew him well and commanded Panama himself during a distinguished career, has always held that Gavin was extremely fortunate to have Panama as his first posting.

In those far-off days there was no boot camp. The recruit training that had been necessary to handle the thousands of World War I recruits had vanished with postwar compression of the army. Recruits like the seventeen-year-old coal-town boy were shipped directly to the division and regiment where they served. Training began on the job, with the U.S. Coast Artillery, Fort Sherman, "Atlantic Side."

Service in the Canal Zone was "very pleasant" in the recollection of General O'Meara, but it was much less so for enlisted personnel. The army had in most places simply taken over the construction works and buildings from the last stages of canal building in the early 1900s and turned them into military facilities. Acquired by the United States for $40,000,000 in 1904, the Canal Zone is equatorial. The temperature averages 83 degrees, with fierce humidity during the long rainy season, April to November. The anopheles, or malaria, mosquito—which the garrison fought ceaselessly by "sanitation" measures like cutting underbrush and weeds, swallowing quinine, increasing drainage, and spraying oil on standing water—were so bad during the rainy season that troops were kept confined to nearby cleared areas known as "the Sanitized District."

From the army's point of view in those days, far worse dangers than mosquitos lurked in the Panamanian towns, in cities like Colón and Panama City "which rank with the world's worst in vice conditions" according to one 1926 report. The voluble, attractive, and omnipresent Panamanian whores inflicted the worst casualties. Venereal disease ran at a rate of about ninety cases per thousand men.

Along with venereal disease, malaria, drunken riots, and constant friction between the civil authority and the implanted U.S. military mark the little-noted record of the between-war years in Panama. But perception is everything. To Gavin the posting was a joy.

His memories of those days told something of the excitement that the youth felt, arriving as he did from late winter among the coal heaps, snow, and smoke of Mount Carmel and the prison of his relationships with his foster parents into the scalding sun of Panama.

There was the leisurely steamship voyage through the South Atlantic, around the Florida Straits and into the Gulf, a trip on which the sun grows stronger each day and the winds more kind, and clothes are gradually cast off.

The country seemed utterly foreign to Gavin, whose every sense was assaulted by new sensations. Most important, for the first time in his life, he was in a place of his own choosing, making his way among other men.

Gavin quickly caught onto army life. He was assigned to a 155mm gun crew "under a fine old Irish sergeant named McCarthy." The life was hard work, but McCarthy, though "hard as nails," took care of his men. Another primary figure from Gavin's memory of the first days in Panama was "our first sergeant, an American Indian over six feet tall and hefty . . . I learned to like and respect him." Duty was quixotic, much drill and practice but little of the real thing. The big guns were fired only a few times each year because of stringent peacetime economies, and exercises in the jungle could only be held during the dry season to avoid malaria. Gavin learned about soldiering at its most basic—the art of the garrison, unchanging drill, routine, punctilio, and inspections in the blazing sun, with an emphasis on details. "Every Saturday there was an inspection of the troops," Gavin wrote, "the barracks and the kitchen. I noticed that on those days there always was a huge pan of baked beans in the oven, and the mess sergeant would proudly open the oven door and pull the pan forward for the captain to inspect it, sniffing the delicious odor of freshly baked beans as he did so. Later I heard the first sergeant say that the reason they had baked beans every Saturday was because the captain liked them."

It was this first sergeant who first divined Gavin's intellectual ability, rare enough in those days when the army was competing with private industry and offering a wage of under $20 per month after deductions. Appointed battery clerk, Gavin soon noticed in the papers passing over his desk an opening for noncommissioned officers who knew semaphore. Gavin studied the flags, passed the test and made corporal in about six months. Already he was moving fast. Years later he noted that he reached corporal rank "rather young for a soldier in those days."

Gavin's discovery of the small base library allowed him to feed his imagination, and it became his refuge. While his fellow soldiers were reveling or sat in the barracks, Gavin was deep in Dodge's *Great Captains*, the sympathetic biographies of the world's greatest soldiers—Alexander, Hannibal, Napoleon—and their battles.

Gavin downplayed his scholarly side to his fellows. "I was always a bit concerned lest the soldiers in the battery find me reading such things. It was not for a private to dream of being a great captain, nor to dream of being a high-ranking troop commander either."

Duty ended at noon on Saturday, and the troops were released until Monday morning. Gavin stayed on the post and walked alone, much as he had done as a younger teenager in the Pennsylvania coal hills. "I went to look at all the fortifications, including the six-inch disappearing rifles and twelve-inch mortars. The mortars were surrounded by a high cement fence that could do little to stop an aggressive intruder. Beyond the mortars along the Atlantic Ocean was a trail. I followed it for about four miles and came to a small cabin called Outpost One. I continued on seven or eight miles from Fort Sherman, and came to an old Spanish fort on a hill known as Fort San Lorenzo. It overlooked the mouth of the Chagres River . . . I went down the hill to the Chagres and found along the bank, evidence of what once was a town. There was an abundance of broken china with a blue-and-white pattern, utensils, bottles and much evidence of human occupation. Actually, it was the site of the Spanish settlement of Chagres. I remembered from the pirate stories I had read as a boy that the pirate Henry Morgan had captured Chagres and Fort San Lorenzo in 1670. After that he and his buccaneers went up the Chagres, across the peninsula, and captured and sacked Panama City. Until then, I had no idea that the Chagres River was within walking distance of Fort Sherman.

"The following weekend I followed a railroad track to where I understood were some gun emplacements that I had not seen. They were located on very high ground overlooking the Atlantic and about four miles inland from the trail I had previously followed. The guns were twelve-inch barbettes [platform guns]. After looking at the gun sites, I went down the hills through jungle to this trail and returned to the post. Earlier, during my recruit training, our drill sergeant had taken us to a shack in the jungle that had been abandoned when the government took over the land for a fort. It was several miles from the fort and was surrounded by mango trees. I had never tasted the fruit and at first did not like it, but mangoes were such a pleasant change from our rations that we devoured handfuls of them. That particular location was near a trail around the bay that followed the track of the water pipe which supplied the post. I made it a point to walk along it for several miles as soon as I could."

If ever a junior general prowled the sleepy post at Fort Sherman it was

Gavin. He sought to imagine ways to invade and sack the place, as Henry Morgan had, with a small group of men. He would do it, not by the current theory of possibilities, but by a lightning raid from an unexpected quarter.

Gavin's early experience in this obscure post was for him a period of almost unalloyed pleasure. He had found his family at last, in the hierarchical and hidebound ranks. He had found much more, in fact, thanks to an overactive imagination. While other men may have seen the Canal Zone as a pleasant enough but boring post, Gavin saw duty there as his first practical education. He learned nothing that other soldiers did not learn—the operation of the gun batteries, mine planting, plotting and artillery practice, and the methods of running and organizing a military unit, from parade ground to paperwork—but he had never seen so much orderly activity involving so many men except in the movies. Instead of the griping and bingeing of enlisted life, Gavin saw a giant machine, perhaps flawed, perhaps rusty, but capable of improvement. And he longed to get his hands nearer the controls.

The summer of 1924 passed into fall, marked by Gavin's promotion to corporal. Whatever letters came for him from Mount Carmel he did not keep. Instead, he wholeheartedly took the chance to remake himself. He had rejected his foster family, and he was prepared to rationalize that action. "When I came to my decision to leave home, it was a hard one to make," Gavin wrote late in his life. "Young boys had done that before in Mount Carmel, but almost invariably they came back, having been unable to make it." More than anything, Gavin didn't want to be one of those who came back.

Meanwhile, an opportunity presented itself that was to make an enormous change to Gavin's future. Even before he made corporal, Gavin's American Indian first sergeant, "Chief" Williams, had realized Gavin was different from most other recruits and had made him his company clerk. Then when one of hundreds of routine memoranda that came through the post announced the availability of appointments to West Point, the sergeant called it to Gavin's attention: "You go up and take a look at it," he told him. Gavin had already come to his own conclusion about the Point. "The more I read, the more I became aware of the contributions made by West Point to our nation's history. If one were to be a soldier, that was the place to go. Such a possibility seemed far beyond my attainment."

But he did as the older man suggested. The memorandum offered, not a direct chance at an appointment to West Point, but a chance to compete for an army prep school that would filter out enlisted hopefuls for the next year's entering class. It was part of a program to capture officer talent from the youth in the enlisted ranks, and it had produced a small, but steady number of appointments to the fast track into the army's higher command cadre.

School started September 1, giving Gavin only two weeks to prepare. He passed the physical and attended, with about a dozen other young men, a school set up at Corazel. A month of preparation led to a written examination to discover those qualified to enter the full four-month course.

"The exam was a disaster for me," Gavin remembered, "In mathematics I had a very low grade because I had never studied the algebra that they asked us about." (In fact Gavin's switches from public to parochial school in Mount Carmel had allowed him to avoid algebra.) "I suspect that there may have been some question about us staying in school since we were so far below the minimum standard." Gavin was selected to continue in school in spite of his poor showing.

But as would happen over and over again in his career, the willing and hopeful boy found a mentor. Lieutenant Percy Black, of the Chemical Corps, took an interest. Black was a born pedagogue with a set method. He would arrive at eight in the morning and spend four hours with his charges, one each on algebra, geometry, English, and history. Four subjects, four hours a day, four months—then Black's method was that the last two months, from January to March, would be spent taking old West Point entrance exams for practice.

From the start, Gavin struggled to keep up with Black's heavy reading load. Thirty to forty pages in each subject were assigned each night. Unlike many good students, he had in his nature some dogged strain that kept him from skimming the material but, instead, insisted he master each page before going on to the next. From noon until midnight he was grinding at the books. "By February," he remembered, "there appeared to be a chance that I could make it."

When the big exam arrived on March 1, it was formidable. A four-hour written test on each of the four subjects was given, and this time reading, not mathematics, let Gavin down. Instructed to write a short composition on the theme of one of Shakespeare's plays, he simply blanked out. He hadn't really read the plays. He handed in an empty sheet. Lieutenant Black, however refused to accept the paper and insisted his favorite student write something—anything. Gavin wrote as much as he could remember of the plot of *The Merchant of Venice.* "I have always been grateful to Lieutenant Black for his insistence and have felt that this was what enabled me to pass . . . I was notified in late May that I had passed the entrance examinations."

Gavin was never to lose the sense of intense gratitude he felt toward the army for allowing him to accomplish this feat. It was far more important than anything else he had experienced as an enlisted man, for in the very short time he'd spent soldiering (actually from May until September of 1924), he'd hardly done more than basic training, plus the invaluable hours spent as clerk in the orderly room, to which he had added the weekends of wandering among fortifications that he suspected were already outmoded. In a way, the time of young James Gavin's setting out in life was doubly rewarding for him, for he would always have it in the storehouse of confidence, and as an ornament to his future reputation, that he had done it on his own.

James Gavin arrived at West Point by train after a sea voyage from Panama in the summer of 1925. He was three months past his eighteenth birthday, bleached gold by the equatorial sun, and lean as a sapling.

For Gavin, West Point's first months were a long grind to make up lost ground and establish himself among the leaders of his generation. To rise and change from hard paperboy and smart filling-station attendant to join the officers' mess is a worthy feat. That Gavin succeeded at West Point is part of his enduring story. But it was not easy.

One of the unusual aspects of Gavin's early life is that it had made him literally homeless—something that was his own doing. He refused the opportunity to return home between his separation from the regular army and his entry into West Point in the summer of 1925. He had cast off his foster family and adopted a new one with a fervor that never left him over the next thirty years. The army's rough and simple life, such a contrast to the civilian lives of some, was not new to Gavin.

He had traveled up the east coast, his small case of belongings beside him, through the railroad stations in Newport News, Washington, Philadelphia, and New York, without visiting Mount Carmel. In the case was a letter identifying him as a member of the West Point Class of 1929, with the scant details of his appointment by examination, his passport to a different social class than he had ever known. Almost alone among the swarms of young men arriving at Thayer Hall, Gavin already wore an army shirt and trousers and walked in the peculiar linear manner of a man who has been drilled.

As a functioning school for American military leaders, the United States Military Academy had recently completed its first century when Gavin arrived. When Congress had authorized its formation at West Point on the Hudson River on July 4, 1802, it was meant to be a center for technical instruction as well as the military arts, but by 1811, the new school was all but moribund as the nation faced the British again. The War of 1812 did not go well, and West Point officers were seen as disappointments. But Congress reacted, and the school was reorganized more or less along its present lines.

On July 1, 1925, Gavin eagerly embraced his new life. Like a camera, his mind recorded the texture and detail of that day in a portrait that stayed with him all his life. "[It] was a scorching day, too hot to be drilling in the compounds of the barracks at West Point. Not only drilling, but double-timing to the cadet store to get plebe skins, the new cadets' first uniform, to the barbershop for a military haircut; assignment to rooms, change into uniform, back to drilling; bracing with chins tucked in and stomachs sucked up; and back to drilling to be sure that we were ready to march to the mess hall at noon for our first meal. We were hustled about by the 'beast detail,' a group of First Classmen especially selected for the assignment, who were a sharp-looking lot. Precisely at noon, we were lined up outside the barracks and we stepped off smartly to the proper command. Someone was playing a joke on us, for the band that was playing for our march to the mess hall struck up 'Collegiate, collegiate, yes we are collegiate,' a refrain of the bathtub gin, hip flask and raccoon coat era."

After the no-nonsense but paternalistic world of the regular army, Gavin's shock at being plunged into this half prep school, half hallowed atmosphere heightened his reserve. It took him little time to realize that, in spite of the petty rules and absurd customs, he and his fellows were locked in cutthroat competition with one another for the prizes held out to those who achieved. As a private, he had received help and admiration and some salty advice from senior men, but at West Point that first summer he was considered a star—and a threat—by his fellow classmen until proven otherwise.

West Point's natural constituency in the twenties was white, middle-class, small-town boys, a disproportionate number of them from the South, plus a good number of sons of army officers. It was not then, nor is it now, a place for the rich, the artistic, or the socially registered. It is a place where conservative families seize an opportunity for a free and famous education for their sons and, today, their daughters.

The West Point of Gavin's day was less intellectually demanding than today's. Lucius Clay, class of 1918 and an instructor there during Gavin's West Point career, recalled: "I found the studies on the whole relatively easy. I didn't have to study hard or work hard, and I did an awful lot of reading on the side—which I could have done anywhere; Balzac, Dickens, Thackeray, Zola, Dumas and so forth . . . you didn't have to study to do quite well if you had a reasonable background." Gavin would have little time for "Dumas and so forth."

But neither was West Point in 1925 the torture chamber of the military caste that it had been a few years before, in the era of General Douglas MacArthur ('03), when plebes were forced to warm the toilet seats for upperclassmen with their bare buttocks on winter mornings, squat over bayonets, be hanged by their thumbs, hold rifles at arms' length until their muscles failed them, or suffer even more imaginative humiliations of unchecked hazing. It had just gone through a period of major reform, partly occasioned by a cadet suicide, and spearheaded by the recently departed Superintendent Douglas MacArthur. Hazing had been drasti-cally reduced.

Though Gavin had no "background" at all, his first crisis at West Point was a crisis of conscience. He recalls the first day at the Point as a time of "traumatic shock," and he envied the "cool and capable members of the beast detail." But as the afternoon wore on, he found things were more to his liking. "Finally as the day neared its end, we were formed up on the plain overlooking Trophy Point. Ahead of us was an impressive view of the Hudson River; we would see that view many times in the future and there were those among us who would come to love it. At the proper moment we raised our hands and were sworn in, thus beginning for me a career that was to extend for thirty-three years."

After swearing in, the cadets were conducted to a large room and given Personal and School History Sheets to fill in, and Gavin was immediately confronted with the lie about his age, a matter that weighed heavily on him, coming as it did only hours after forceful explanations of the academy's honor code. Instead of minimizing the matter (he was eighteen, a perfectly acceptable age for a West Point cadet) he put down twenty-one, because, as he thought then, if he had put down his true age, his enlistment would have been seen as fraudulent. He later said that he wanted to be of legal age to make his own decision to stay or to leave the academy, rather than risking any involvement with the Gavin family. The lie was part of his naïveté about the new upper realm he was entering. "There were also many questions about high school, college and participation in sports, all of which I had to answer in the negative. I must have appeared a rather poor prospect to anyone who read my entry form."

Gavin's conviction that he was below the salt at West Point stayed with him that summer, and he unobtrusively questioned some of his new friends about the mechanics of applying to college: where, for instance, examination for entrance could be taken, costs of tuition and the possibility of scholarships. He believed that eagle-eyed instructors would soon spot the discrepancy between the ages quoted on his honorable discharge from the regular army and his fact sheet. They never did, but the specter kept Gavin hard to the grindstone. "Not until I was doing very well did I feel comfortable in my status . . . in the beginning I knew that I had to study hard and to do as well as I possibly could, and I needed to do more than just simply pass."

Unlike the civilian cadets, soldier Gavin found plebe summer, with its hazing, strictures, petty discipline and the rest of the plebe system, fairly easy going. When September came, with the beginning of the academic year, the situation was reversed. He was "mentally prepared" for the strictness and sophomoric absurdity of the upperclassmen, but he was completely cowed by the academic work, for which he had no way of preparing. By contrast, most members of his class of 450 (soon whittled to 385 by attrition) had been solid high school students who found studying a welcome relief from the mindless drill and order taking. "I found it extremely difficult. They were reviewing subjects that we should have completed before we arrived, such as math and English. We were given 40–50 pages a day and I found it difficult to keep up. The only way that I could make it was to get up early in the morning, about 4:00 or 4:30, and study in the basement latrines where there was a light."

Gavin kept up this routine twice a week into the late fall, until he faced

December, the time of plebe class "writs," written examinations designed to weed out the academically unworthy or indolent. If writs were failed, a plebe had only a final "turn out" examination to determine whether or not he would be dismissed from the academy. Greatly to his relief, he passed through safely. But his class ranking was only 385th out of 450 for the first semester.

Better things were on the way. Second semester found him moving along "without too great difficulty," and the introduction of history at the beginning of his second year gave him an academic boost. It was a subject of lifelong fascination to him, and he found himself in the first section academically.

That spring of 1926 brought the Gavin family back into his life for nearly the last time, in extremely unpleasant circumstances. Gavin received a telegram from his foster mother, Mary Gavin, informing him that Martin Gavin had been shot and was hospitalized. Without explanation, she asked that he return to Mount Carmel. Gavin was able to get a three-day emergency leave to travel to Pennsylvania, where he found that his foster father had become engaged in a fierce quarrel with Grant Whary, the boarder whom the young Gavin had liked, and at some point a gun had been produced and Martin Gavin was wounded in the shoulder. The injury was a flesh wound and not serious, and Martin refused to press charges, so the police passed the matter off as an unfortunate accident.

There was little that Gavin could do to assist, but he visited his foster father to offer what comfort he could. Mary, however, seized the opportunity to heap Gavin with drunken reproaches. Why wasn't he home, she asked, earning a living to help the household and helping to pay the mortgage the couple had acquired when they moved a few doors from their old house on Fig Street? Gavin had no answer.

Instead, he inquired about the mortgage holder and found the note was held by the construction firm of E. R. Bastress. Gavin called on Mr. Bastress personally in his office and found not a brush-off, but a hearing from a man who regarded the cadet with respect, even with awe. "He became very much interested in what was happening to me and talked at considerable length about West Point, my studies there and what I intended to do after graduating. He told me that I should go into the Corps of Engineers and develop a useful career as an engineer officer. Under no circumstances did he think I should leave the Military Academy. He was sure that mortgage arrangements could be made with the Gavin family. I talked to Mrs. Gavin about it."

Bastress agreed to suspend payment on the note during Martin Gavin's recovery. Mollified, Mary Gavin subsided, and Gavin took the next train back to West Point. He would later rationalize his rather chilly reaction to the people he'd abandoned. "Actually, there was no way that I could be of financial help to the Gavins. Cadets were not allowed to have money. An account was kept in their name in the treasurer's office and cadets were paid $80 per month, against which they were charged for food, books, uniforms, etc. It was assumed that by the end of four years, they would have saved enough to enable them to go to their first stations and start their careers as second lieutenants."

Working hard to keep up with the academic pressure and finding it difficult, Gavin switched his attention to another area in which he could "do more than simply pass." He began to box. Gavin had been good with his fists in Mount Carmel and had sparred with a coal-mining boarder who had been a pro. He had also boxed in Panama; at West Point, with his wiry frame and ruthless concentration, he stood out.

Yet of all sports at the academy, boxing was the lowest on the social totem pole, early proof that Gavin had yet to develop a sense of social snobbery. The academy's social sporting set played polo; the institution had large stables, and riding was something that every officer was expected to master. Gavin became a good rider at West Point, and later an expert one.

Boxing made Gavin better known; he was not a shy or a timid cadet, but he had learned there was safety in silence. Then as always, he seldom spoke unless he had something important to say. A direct result of his boxing was an invitation by a first classman to spend part of the summer of 1926 as a counselor at a Catholic boys' camp, Camp Chippewa, on Lake George, New York. He eagerly accepted the offer, perhaps as a way to avoid a long leave at Mount Carmel. As it was he spent two weeks there before starting the counselor's job, a visit that proved a liberation.

This return, with Gavin well established at West Point, with his summer plans secure, was a two-week triumph. He joyfully walked his familiar wooded hills and visited his old friends as a returned hero might. "It had been hardly more than two years since I left home, the differences in my attitude and the attitudes of my former friends around town could be measured in light-years; in a way, conditions at home had not improved very much, but my own attitude toward them and my attitude toward the town and my many friends had improved tremendously."

Gavin may not have known who his real parents were, but at the right time, he had found another family, and he was to write, in as lyrical a statement as the prosaic Gavin ever made, of his gratitude to "my Spartan mother" West Point.

During Gavin's time at West Point, the institution was rolling uncomfortably, like a big sailing ship with no wind. Douglas MacArthur had set it rocking. MacArthur's career got its first big boost after World War I when he was named superintendent of the academy and confirmed in his rank as brigadier general while his fellow officers lost the inflated ranks they'd gained during World War I service. MacArthur was something West Point had never had before, an iconoclast who liberalized the course of study, checked hazing, modified the honor code and brought it under cadet control. He brought in more humanities while shrinking the formidable science-math curriculum. MacArthur instituted weekend leave for cadets, who could travel as far as New York, abolished "summer camp" training under canvas and substituted regular army training at Fort Dix in New Jersey.

Modern in outlook, (he was only thirty-nine and so handsome, commanding, and socially adept that underlings nicknamed him "god"), MacArthur had scandalized professors by inviting General Billy Mitchell, the promoter of air power and bombing, to lecture.

MacArthur was a fanatic for sports, and he impressed his ideas of sound mind in sound body on a man who was to have the profoundest influence on Gavin's later career, West Point's young athletic director, Matthew B. Ridgway ('17).

But most of the faculty were of an older school and resented MacArthur's academic changes, as well as his theatrical personality. The result was steely reaction, and MacArthur's normal four-year tour as superintendent was cut short in 1922. His replacement, General Fred W. Sladen ('90), was quick to restore the old order. But MacArthur had at least, in the words of Lucius Clay, "done an excellent job in bringing the military academy into contact with the real world."

Gavin returned from a happy camp counselor experience at Lake George fit, "richer by $100," and ready for anything in the summer of 1927. He spent his third year at the academy hard at work. Honors first came to First Classman Gavin in the summer of 1928 when he was appointed first sergeant of C Company and in charge of beast detail, his assignment to be a mirror image of those young men who had so impressed him on his arrival at the academy with their "cool and capable" handling of themselves. No more the rube without a high school diploma, Gavin himself had become one of the elect, selected not only for his knowledge but his address and demeanor to be an inspiration to the newcomers. He was soon to find that he had come to the notice of feminine eyes as well.

Gavin's relations with women are a part of his legend, and many came to idolize him as his star rose. He was a magnet for attractive women all his life, and, whatever the length, the intensity or the extent of the relationship, women were almost anxiously grateful for the time he granted them. He always seemed slightly puzzled by his conquests.

But his gift for charming women came from harsh beginnings, for Gavin's first romance proved a neophyte's disaster, resulted in a spoiled first marriage, and was a matter Gavin downplayed and sought to shroud in mist ever after.

Any mixing of the sexes had long been forbidden at West Point. One of MacArthur's innovations to the bleak social arrangements at the academy was to allow dances, or "hops," to be held during the warmer months. It was at one such hop in the summer before senior year that Cadet Garvin met Irma Baulsir, a summer student at Cornell, a resident of Washington, D.C., and a pretty, vivacious, fun-loving, well-brought-up brunette from an upper-middle-class background. Irma was the friend of a friend, a girl to "fix up" Cadet Gavin with a date. Gavin took to her immediately, and she to him, though from Gavin's side, the relationship was touched with a calculation (at least in his telling of it later) that does not show in the passionate letters he wrote to her at the time.

By now the tempo of life at the academy had become second nature to the young soldier. "For the first time, we were taking physical training, tactics and the maneuvers of small units," he wrote. "The training was quite exacting and demanding, but it usually ended at noon and we could spend the afternoon as we saw fit, playing tennis, canoeing on the Hudson, or just reading."

Into the pleasant atmosphere of the Hudson Valley in summer, Irma Baulsir came, returning in late summer, and again when she was invited to the "ring hop" in the fall. This was an invitation full of symbolism, falling as it did after the upcoming first classmen wore their class rings for the first time.

In the social etiquette of the day, cadets gave a miniature of the class ring to their girlfriends, not exactly as a signal of a coming engagement, but not far from it either. Gavin would later deny that he intended anything in particular in giving Irma Baulsir a miniature ring that evening, but she seemed to consider it a portent.

He and Irma corresponded almost continuously, and she saved all his letters. Gavin reveals himself in them as a florid, panting wooer-by-mail: "I am desperate to see you . . . not a thing in the world can keep me from being with you . . . when I am with you, darling, words fail me in attempting to express my feelings . . . I am hoping and living to see you . . . I have been infinitely happy with you, dearest, and want to be always."

If he seemed to use every cliché in the style book, perhaps it was only innocence and a desire to conform to the language of the Hollywood screenplay. He kept the pace up for a full year, filling his letters with minutiae of news between the sighs. One of the last of the series, however, from May 14, 1929, when his graduation was only a month away, squarely confronts the idea of marriage to Irma Baulsir. In it he reaffirmed his love for her and his desire to marry.

Later he wrote, "Giving Irma the ring caused much more excitement than I had anticipated. It was not my intention to marry her, and I was sure she understood that, since we had not even talked about the matter. However, her mother seemed to have ideas of her own."

Gavin, outflanked, outmaneuvered, and doubtless swayed by youthful lust, followed Irma Baulsir to Washington for Christmas holidays. His fate was sealed. The Baulsir family made wedding plans, and for the first time in his life, he seems to have been helpless to make his own course. "The situation seemed to be out of my control," he complained. And to give him some credit in his equivocal telling of this tale, he admitted always, "I wasn't opposed to the wedding, but had certain doubts about our compatibility; the prospects for a happy marriage seemed to be less than I would have hoped for." Gavin's misgivings were kept private, though, and the two were married at the end of the summer, on September 5, 1929.

So it was that all during Gavin's senior year at the academy, he was an engaged man. Scholastically, Gavin was assured. He finished about 100th in his class for the year, though his average standing for the entire four years would be lower; he was squarely in the great middle ground for West Point graduates.

Graduation came in June, and Irma was there. He was selected to represent his company in a riding competition as part of the exercises, and he placed well. He graduated 185th out of 299. In the 1929 edition of the *Howitzer*, West Point's yearbook, Gavin is remembered as a boxer and a man who had been a soldier before he became a cadet. There is also a photo of his company, and below it, an anonymous cadet has written: "They are just like the rest of the Corps with a few different ideals."

Gavin had created a new character for himself, a thing far more important to him than mere grades. No longer lost, no longer alone, he had used his four years to the maximum effect.

4.

UP FROM ZERO

Gavin faced his first decade of service as a career soldier, the decade when youthful achievement is first measured, with dismal prospects.

He chose the infantry as his branch of service, not the engineers, although the army engineers had the best assignments and received most of the funding during the 1930s. Alone among the army branches the engineers actually profited from the Great Depression, when President Franklin D. Roosevelt's public works programs emerged as part of the government's answer to widespread unemployment.

The top soldiers in each graduating West Point Class traditionally chose their branch of the service and their post. Cavalry was the province of the social elite in Gavin's day, many of whom were already excellent horsemen when they arrived at West Point. Engineering and artillery were the choice of the best mathematicians, with engineering preferred because in peacetime it translated directly into well-paid jobs. Infantry was for the rest, and for the real soldiers, the fighters, and those determined to remain in the profession of arms. It was also for those who knew that the fastest, riskiest way to military glory and promotion was by leading men on the battlefield. The infantry, the "queen of battle," was where the glory was won.

Years later, Gavin was self-conscious and rhetorical about his reasons for wanting infantry. "I went forth to seek the challenge, to move toward the sounds of guns, to go where danger was greatest, for there is where the issues would be resolved and the decisions made."

Not to mention that his grades were middling, his social standing nil, his horsemanship adequate, his pocketbook empty, and he disliked desk work.

With a pretty new bride by his side and behind the wheel of a new car, a gift from his in-laws, he headed west across the country, relishing the thought of visiting the famous Civil War battle sites in the Shenandoah Valley on the way. His sadness at leaving West Point was soon pushed aside by the adventure that awaited the young couple.

Gavin had been accepted at flight school at Brooks Field, Texas. Aviation was a new and revolutionary arm of the army. Gavin loved innovation (as a lifelong rule, if it was new, Jim Gavin wanted to try it) and he thought the new branch might be a place to pioneer and be noticed. Since boyhood he had been fascinated by the warrior's world of weapons, machinery, and technological innovation and had early idolized those military leaders who had used maneuver and stratagems to defeat their foes. He had noted, too, how apparently simple innovations won wars. And by 1929, with the recent advent of the machine gun, tanks, aerial bombs, and other new weapons, the science of deadly force was accelerating at a breakneck pace. While Gavin valued the tradition West Point had instilled in him, he valued innovation more. His fellow cadets took as gospel the lessons learned from the study of Union strategy in the Civil War and the study of the tactics of artillery preparation and massed assaults of World War I. Gavin viewed them with impatience and a contrary mind. Somehow, he knew that his future lay in adapting new ideas to the ancient science of warfare. The conclusion he had drawn at West Point was simple. Soldiers remain the same in all wars, subject to the same psychological stresses throughout history, but technology alters how those soldiers might best be used. He believed his would be a generation of swift movement and machines that would deliver the blow decisively. This is what attracted him to aviation.

But he failed flight school, and he seldom spoke about the experience afterward. Jim Gavin never liked or accepted failure. He wrote "The object seemed to be to keep graduated cadets from learning how to fly. . . . I was in a group of five that reported to Lieutenant Rodgers, who confidently told us that he would probably eliminate all of us. He advised us as a parting precaution not to start spending our flight pay right away. I loved flying . . . but love of flying wasn't enough. It was a lot of fun flying those open cockpit biplanes, but after a couple of weeks, I was told to report to my check pilot for probable elimination. He was busy, the weather was bad, and he didn't get to me for a couple of more weeks. By then I was so far behind the class that he was appalled. With a shake of his head and a "tch! tch!" I was sent on my way." The airman told Gavin that one either had it in oneself to be an airman or one did not. If one did not, then one should not worry over it. Gavin said, "I didn't."

He then applied for a post that was, as he put it, as far away from Texas as possible. That brought him to Camp Harry J. Jones near Douglas, Arizona, close to the Mexican border. Long considered a military backwater, Camp Jones was of questionable value for a young officer's career because it featured the all-black 25th Infantry. Gavin said, "Washington must have been so shocked by anyone applying for duty at that remote place that they approved it at once and I arrived just before Christmas in 1929."

The 25th Infantry at Camp Jones, led like every black unit of the period by white officers, was Gavin's first real contact with black Americans— there had been none in Mount Carmel. The army was segregated in 1929, and Gavin was expected to bow to custom. His diary says little of race relations at the camp; but for other reasons, it became a purgatory for the ambitious young officer. The post was a career zero. There were no settlers to protect, no warlike Indians, and no Mexican raids.

The army of the 1920s and 1930s was understrength. Congress had authorized a force of 225,000, later raised to 297,000. But the army did not reach this number until just before World War II. Instead, its strength fell to 131,254 by 1923. Ironically, the understrength army was stuffed with officers. An officer corps approximately twice the size of what had existed before the World War I buildup sweated and starved its way with Gavin through the 1920s and 1930s.

With too many officers, too small a force, and too little money, the United States Army was also ambivalent about its philosophy of war. The lessons of the past included the brilliant, successful maneuvers of Lee and Stonewall Jackson; the lightweight speed of the Indian-fighting army; the campaign of Sherman, whose doctrine was that war was total and a foe was best defeated by destroying his supporting nation, and these tactics had their supporters, but it was the doctrine of overwhelming force fed by powerful industrial might that attacked its enemy powerfully everywhere at once, as practiced by U. S. Grant in his victory over Lee, that held sway, despite the impasse brought about when two massive Grant-style armies faced each other in the trenches in the Great War. It was the philosophy of Grant that held sway.

Gavin was a Stonewall Jackson man then and always, drawn to the speed-and-maneuver school of battle and the belief that technology would create the weapons, particularly aircraft and motorized vehicles, to break through stalemates like the western front in World War One. He was out of step with the majority of army leaders.

Arriving at Camp Harry J. Jones, he was the lowest man in the eighteen-officer cadre running the 25th Infantry. Morale in the unit was low, and even Gavin's normally enthusiastic public voice was chastened. It was not the segregated troopers, however, who caused Gavin's frustration with his first assignment; rather, his Camp Jones diaries reveal that there was very little to do. The division had no duties other than training and no money to do it with. It was cheaper to organize basketball games and sports events than to expend ammunition and wear out equipment with training maneuvers. The army sat on its hands, counted the days until payday, hoped that things would not get any worse, and above all, prayed for war or crisis.

Douglas, Arizona, the nearest town to Camp Jones, was only a few miles from the Mexican border and 80 miles from Nogales, a town where American dollars were welcome and the laws of Prohibition were not in effect. The triangle of activity for the tiny group of officers to which Gavin belonged was between the town of Douglas, where they lived and played tennis, the camp where they worked, and Mexico, where they drank and whored. Gavin spent almost three years at the sun-blasted post, where the chief activities were staff beer busts, tennis tournaments, occasional marksmanship competitions, and very rare field maneuvers.

Arizona was perhaps the lowest point in Gavin's career. He watched his marriage crumble, partly from his own doing. Gavin engaged in at least one sexual affair while at the camp, perhaps more. His diary for August of 1931 contains this circumspect note: "I hope E. had a happy birthday. I love her more and more each day . . . suggested to Peggy [Irma] that it might be mutually beneficial if she took a vacation."

As Gavin and Peggy traveled east in the blistering summer of 1932, en route from Arizona to Gavin's new post at Fort Benning, Georgia, they drove over the same roads that carried thousands of the Depression's desperate job seekers in the opposite direction. It must have occurred to Gavin that in the hollow faces and strapped-up belongings of the stream of California-bound migrants he was seeing the life that he had escaped when he got to West Point. During the summer of 1932 the Depression had reached its cruelest depths. With millions of men out of work, and one third of the nation's children out of school, America was just short of collapse.

Gavin drove on, bound for the deep pine forests of Georgia, to the army's great shaker and grinder, the Infantry School. It was the way by which nearly all who aspired to lead in battle must go. It represented Gavin's main hope of shouldering his way ahead of his former classmates.

At Fort Benning, Gavin at last found the army he was looking for, an army that was actively seeking new directions and had started on a course of self-improvement.

They called it the "Benning Revolution." The changes are credited to George Catlett Marshall, then head of the school's academic department, who brought in another veteran of World War I and China service, Joseph "Vinegar Joe" Stilwell. Perhaps their sense of urgency sprang from attitudes acquired far from Washington. Both men agreed that the book of tactics, as it stood, should be thrown out and a new volume written. Marshall brought Stilwell to head the tactics department because he felt the "old China hand," contrary, argumentative, blunt, and always walking the fine edge of insubordination, was just the man to bring change. This change affected two hundred men, students and instructors at Benning during the revolution, who would reach general-officer rank and lead the army in World War II, among them men who would play an important part in Jim Gavin's future: Omar Bradley, J. Lawton Collins, Courtney Hodges, Matthew B. Ridgway, Walter Bedell Smith.

Their methods were simple, and simplicity, in fact, was the first principle of the change in philosophy. As if able to forecast the problems that would be theirs to solve in another decade, Colonel Marshall taught his subordinates that the only methods that would serve in training for war were those that could be transmitted in the shortest possible time to a large force of volunteers raised in a hurry.

While European armies taught their young officers the proper way to write orders, Marshall, and particularly Stilwell, decreed that orders be reduced to the minimum. Stilwell's creed for battlefield direction was simplicity itself: "Move, Shoot, Communicate." In practice, his methods meant young officers were left to figure out the details of an operation, with only general direction given from the top. "Throw out everything that doesn't make common sense," Vinegar Joe told his students. He was an enemy of complicated maneuvers and schedules, having discovered in the Great War and in China that the only sure prediction is that, sooner or later, the original conception of a situation will prove wrong.

Stilwell wanted to make every part of his training regime focus on effectiveness. He cared nothing for the student who handed in a perfect paper on protocol, on report writing, or the endless intricacies of administering a battalion or a division. What he cared about was how the student reacted when faced with a predicament—a trap, a quirk of geography, a breakdown in the telephone line to headquarters.

Gavin flourished under this instruction, and immediately took to Stilwell, whose nickname was derived from the acid critiques he would deliver on young officers' field exercises, scenes of humiliation carried out in full flair in front of contemporaries. One of the verbally wounded caricatured Stilwell rising from a vinegar bottle with an expression of infinite disgust on his narrow face. Typically, Stilwell was delighted with the drawing, which had reached a bulletin board, and he asked for the artist's autograph and the original artwork.

"He was a superb officer in that position [head of tactics], hard and a tough worker," Gavin recalled, "and he demanded much, always insisting that anything you ask the troops to do, you must be able to do yourself. I was skeptical about that at first but soon learned in the parachute troops how right he was."

Stilwell seldom appeared in chalk-talk classes at the base, leaving them to lower-ranking men. But when officers were in the field during the frequent war games and tactical exercises, he was never absent. Stilwell's way was to present the students with the most difficult problems he could think of, then judge how the young officers handled them in the field.

There is little doubt that Gavin began to adopt two of the most important trademarks of his own leadership while at Benning. One lesson Gavin absorbed was pure Stilwell: a belief that the leader must be as tough as, if not tougher than, the troops he is trying to inspire.

The second life lesson Gavin learned from Stilwell was in the matter of personal appearance and address. Stilwell made an art out of his unconventional appearance, as noted quickly by Gavin and others when they met him for the first time. His biographer Barbara Tuchman painted it vividly: "Stilwell in his World War I campaign hat and government-issue khakis which in a kind of inverse snobbery he wore without insignia or decorations . . ."

The campaign hat, bleached but clean, the wrap leggings from the "doughboy" days only added to the effectiveness of this unusual soldier whom George Marshall described as "a genius for instruction" after the first year of Stilwell's tour at Benning. Even within the regulations of the army, Gavin noted, there was enough room, at least in the officers' corps, for individualism of dress. Soldiers who served with them never forgot Douglas MacArthur's crushed hat, Pershing's black cavalry boots, Vinegar Joe's weathered "Smoky the Bear" hat, Colonel Marshall's riding crop. In each instance, the idiosyncracy enhanced the image of the man by subtly reminding the observer that, in the case of Stilwell, he had been at Verdun in 1918 when the Germans launched their last-gasp offensive, that Stilwell, like Pershing and Marshall, was a soldier of the old horse army tradition.

It was at Benning that Gavin first began to attend to the details of his own personal "look" that were to become so effective later: perfect physique and perfect dress, which later led to his nicknames "Gentleman Jim" or "Slim Jim." He had not yet come upon his own particular trademarks: the pair of perfectly polished brown paratrooper boots, the glider patch, and his M-1 Garand, but he was looking for them.

Gavin was the athlete, the rugged active officer for whom no hike was too long and for whom extra exercise was a regular habit. He was thin as a garden rake, with the whipcord sinews and lanky muscles of an Irish miner. But Gavin also dressed perfectly, spending extra money on the sharpest ties, waist-hugging pants, the best-tailored shirts, and always with double starch so that the points of his collars looked like planed pinewood and his shirt creases still stood out when the rest of the shirt was darkened with sweat.

Stilwell was closing out his four-year stint as head of the tactical section at Fort Benning when Gavin arrived in 1932. And George Marshall was just leaving, but he had put his stamp on the place.

Gavin toiled through the winter and loved it. Only two things marred his full enjoyment of the rigorous training. First was the uncertain state of the army, rocked with cutbacks. But when a further reduction of 2,000 officers was rumored in December 1932, Gavin wrote, reflecting his distaste for the "war crowd," that "hump" of junior officers who had stayed in in 1919: "Cut would be good."

The second sour note was the continuing disintegration of his marriage. Columbus, Georgia, a town that owes much of its livelihood to

Fort Benning, shared all the flimsiness, unpleasantness, raucousness, and general raffishness of every "base" town. And there was no dearth of pretty and available young women in Columbus, either the type suitable for a hasty, lusty weekend fling, or the girls determined not to leave town without a promising young officer as a husband and a future more secure than most.

Gavin was still as poor as a junior officer without a drinking habit could be. In spite of a few well-meant gifts from the Baulsir family, he could hardly afford to set Peggy up to take advantage of the social or recreational delights of inland Georgia.

Peggy Baulsir did not like either aspect of Fort Benning, and let her husband know it. The two of them motored haltingly "home" to Washington on December 23, 1932, for Christmas with the in-laws. Disconsolate over fitness reports that gave him only one superior, thirteen excellents and two satisfactory ratings, Gavin complained to his diary "yet I am given a general rating of satisfactory which is very disappointing." He played a little tennis and sat through the Christmas formalities.

Gavin should not have been disappointed with his ratings, for under Stilwell's high-minded influence, "superior" ratings, the ticket to choice of station and advancement, were about as scarce as gold nuggets after a gold rush. Complaints about the lack of top awards during the Stilwell days had caused so many disappointments and blighted so many young careers that they had reached the ears of Benning's commandant, General Campbell King, who suggested to Colonel Marshall on three separate occasions that he get rid of the prickly "Vinegar Joe." Tuchman notes "One cause of the animosity [Stilwell] aroused in some officers was the extreme strictness of his standards, which would not allow him to give a 'Superior' on an Efficiency Report unless he considered it thoroughly deserved. The result was that few officers under his supervision could go on to War College, whereas in the more routine Weapons Section 'Superiors' were freely given, easing the advancement of the recipients' careers."

Shortly after this Christmas leave, Peggy decided that she preferred the relatively comfortable and familiar family life of Washington to the honky-tonks of Columbus and the wooden barracks of Fort Benning. Whatever trepidation she might have felt at leaving her young and handsome husband alone in such a town, she countered by becoming pregnant in February.

Gavin, somewhat dissemblingly, glossed over her decision to remain in Washington. "Fort Benning and the Infantry School was a demanding institution. It left little time for family life . . . Irma decided in the early spring of 1933 to go to Washington to visit with her friends and her mother. She grew up in Washington, went to school at the George Washington University, and she had many friends in the city. I don't think that Army life was particularly to her liking. In any event, she went to Washington where I joined her for a brief visit in late May." In late May, Peggy was three and a half months pregnant.

But in the meantime, public events had intruded into Gavin's life.

The spring of 1933 was the whirlwind time of Franklin Roosevelt's One Hundred Days. The new President closed the nation's banks, and in rapid succession between March and June took the country off the gold standard, ordered massive federal relief, initiated the Civilian Conservation Corps, the Agricultural Adjustment Administration, the Tennessee Valley Authority and a dozen other important agencies to stem unemployment and provide jobs.

Part of Roosevelt's rush scheme to get paychecks in men's hands meant using whatever facilities and personnel were available for assistance. The army service schools were obvious and logical choices. Roosevelt simply closed them down in 1933 and sent their staffs and students to sites scattered around the country as leaders and instructors at the labor camps of the CCC.

The army, led by Chief of Staff Douglas MacArthur, achieved a minor miracle in its new role as shaper and molder of a mobile labor force; over a quarter of a million young men were enrolled, trained, and then shipped all over the country to man projects of the U.S. Forest Service in almost every state. Roosevelt gave these civilian recruits a better pay scale than privates in the regular army, $30 a month for CCC recruits, compared to about $18 a month for privates. In the end, more than two and a half million Americans wore the CCC uniform, and they planted two hundred million trees.

Army Infantry School was over for Gavin. The doors shut, and Gavin, always searching for troop command time, had to maneuver adroitly to avoid becoming one of hundreds of luckless junior officers who were doomed to spend the next half decade training recruits for Roosevelt's employment programs. He managed an assignment with the 38th and 29th Infantry Regiments at Fort Sill, Oklahoma.

Gavin's arrival at the isolated Oklahoma post, then commanded by Lieutenant Colonel Lesley McNair, coincided almost precisely with the departure of a well-regarded contemporary, Lieutenant Maxwell Taylor, who had shown early evidence of his astuteness in political maneuver by gaining appointment to the Command and General Staff School at Fort Leavenworth, Kansas. Taylor was one of the first lieutenants to be admitted under a new move to improve sagging army morale. The two men met briefly, without recorded comment.

Taylor, West Point '22, and Gavin, West Point '29, would become leaders of airborne divisions and lifelong rivals whose careers crossed for decades. Neither man liked the other; they differed completely in style. Gavin took a dislike to Taylor the first time he set eyes on him when Taylor had been an instructor at West Point.

General Lesley McNair, after whom the fort encompassing the Army War College in Washington is named, was America's foremost artilleryman, but a man whose opinions were so strong that American theories about the use of guns had veered out of line with those of the rest of the world during the peaceful 1920s and 1930s. Though later responsible for equipping American ground forces in World War II, McNair had never been in battle.

After the Civil War, American artillery development had lagged to such an extent that most American staff officers who participated in World War I were ashamed and embarrassed that the U.S. doughboys had to fight with foreign-supplied weapons, except for the excellent American Springfield rifles. Arms heavier than rifles and machine guns came mainly from French arsenals. America had led the world in the development of light weapons such as the Gatling Gun and mass-produced repeating rifles, as befitted the nation's preoccupation with border constabulary duties and its philosophy of a citizen army. Both tended to stress units that could be quickly trained, were light and mobile. Heavy artillery meant something else—the Navy.

As a result of exposure to the prolonged artillery bombardments of World War I, the army tried to reform its Ordnance Department, the bureau responsible for designing and producing weapons for the army. But one of the curious and oddly democratic decisions the planners made was to leave weapons design to the officers and their men. "This change proved less helpful, however, than might be assumed from the apparent common sense," notes Russell Weigley, the battle historian of World

War II. One result was that the tank—the most dramatic and effective new weapon of World War II—was regarded by the army as merely a protected machine-gun carrier. Tanks were not considered important enough to become a separate branch of ground forces (the 1932 army had only twelve tanks made after 1919), and as a result they were assigned to the infantry as an aid to foot soldiers. So when Gavin arrived at Fort Sill, there were no tanks. Instead he found cavalrymen assembling on Sundays for polo and artillerymen practicing with ancient French-made 75mm field pieces.

Thus while the Europeans built on the lessons of the trenches, which gave artillery a more important role on the battlefront, the American field artillery designers still favored movement over power. An army study of antitank weapons employed in 1914–18 had recommended a big 75mm cannon, which would have blasted through almost all World War II armor, but the army stuck to the lighter 37mm until 1944, and found it no match for the 75mm German antiarmor gun or the terrible 88mm that could be used as a tank killer, a field piece, or even an antiaircraft weapon.

Likewise, the hand-held antitank weapon, was invented by an American and improved by American rocket wizard Robert H. Goddard, whose "rocket gun" was ignored by the Ordnance Department in 1918. It was not until 1942 that it was rediscovered as the "bazooka."

So Gavin walked into a firearms museum in the summer of 1933. But it was at Sill that Gavin first undertook, in a serious and determined way, a study of strategy and the history of armed conflict. The Infantry School at Benning under Marshall and Stilwell had been all action and practicality, "Fort Sill, however, was quite different. It had an excellent library and I at once began to read and study books that I should have read years before. People assume that the cadets at the Military Academy read a great deal about war particularly Clausewicz, Liddell Hart, etc. In fact they do not."

While others led the genteel life of Fort Sill's rather pleasant round of shooting, polo, and parties, Gavin sat in the library, enraptured by the world of military theory. Still living a bachelor's life for his first months at Sill, he caught up fast on his reading, took notes, and distilled them onto library cards and three-hole notepaper to be assembled into a loose-leaf, green government-issue notebook he kept with him throughout his career.

The notebook reveals an intensely practical and analytical mind, which nonetheless could be touched by emotionalism. Many notes relate to famous speeches given before battle, such as Henry V's speech before Agincourt. Gavin kept an annotated page that contains the famous speech and these notes:

"Pre-battle talks to the troops generally include the following:

1. Our cause is a holy one.
2. There are enough of us to do the job.
3. The eyes of the world are upon us (i.e., the folks back home)
4. We will gain everlasting fame.
5. Living, or dying, you shall gain everlasting fame."

Among the authors who particularly impressed the young soldier was J. F. C. Fuller, who in Gavin's eyes, "saw clearly the implications of machines, weapons, gasoline, oil, tanks, and airplanes. To him the future war was a war of great and extensive mobility with decision making playing a very important part in every action and decision making at all levels of command. I read with avidity all of his writings."

Gavin's first child was born while he was a service bachelor at Fort Sill, and the circumstances show clearly the distance that had grown between him and Peggy. The day the baby was born was a national holiday, and not surprisingly, Gavin had chosen to make the holiday an "all-day hunt on the Sill reservation." His wife tried to reach him with the news but could not. She then tried a telegram. But the telegram was placed by a mailboy into Gavin's mail slot at post headquarters, which he didn't check until the following afternoon. "She was very unhappy with me, as was her mother also," Gavin noted grimly.

Peggy Gavin did join him at Sill, however, with the baby in tow; and the pair of them were still able to put on a good army front. She is remembered by officers there as an attractive woman, "not colorful or flashy," one put it. And she was rated "a good coat of tan," that is, a fine rider by General O'Meara, who served with Gavin then.

The army finally granted Gavin's wish for Philippine service in 1936, and in transit he paid his last visit to his foster father, Martin Gavin, at Mount Carmel. He found Martin much older, "totally lacking in education and too old for mining." Gavin felt pity for the man who had raised him and mediated his quarrels with his foster mother, whom Gavin didn't see during his visit. He attempted no reconciliation with Mrs. Gavin and would never see either of them again.

Gavin's tour in the Philippines gave him service in an entirely different world. He was assigned to a Philippine scout regiment, part of the tiny force under General Douglas MacArthur, then commander of the Philippines.

MacArthur's job was to build up Philippine forces so that they would provide a threat—on paper at least—to aggressive Japanese expansion. In truth, America had no practical plan to defend the archipelago, only a vague theory that Luzon could "hold on" until it could be relieved by the U.S. Navy.

Gavin was shocked by the state of the 20,000 U.S. troops stationed there ("Our weapons and equipment were no better than those used in the First World War"). He noted that maneuvers often consisted of practicing the retreat to the Bataan Peninsula, an exercise he thought ominous.

"Surely, I thought, there must be some Master Plan in Washington to take care of this situation," Gavin wrote. "The American people were not just sitting idly by, accepting this as inevitable and doing nothing about it. But there was no master plan."

While in the Philippines, sure that war with Japan was a strong possibility, Gavin thought briefly of learning the Japanese language. But the wisdom of the army intervened. In this case, his battalion commander warned him that ignorance was bliss. "He wisely counseled me against taking a Japanese course, telling me if I did so, I would spend (the next war) translating Japanese documents and interrogating prisoners."

The Philippines were of utmost importance to Gavin in other ways. It was here that he made two lifelong friends, young fellow officers William Ryder and William Yarborough. Both Ryder and Yarborough would cast their lot with the fledgling paratroop branch before Gavin and would encourage his interest in it. Yarborough's father, an army intelligence officer with the 31st Infantry Division stationed in Siberia in World War I, came home with stories and photos of Russian airmen, curious bundles on their backs, clinging to the wings of biplanes and then falling, floating to the ground unharmed under an umbrella of cloth.

Gavin developed a reputation for avoiding most personal conversations in favor of discussions of tactics. Ryder described him as "very private about his own affairs."

Yet he had his ways of being noticed. Gavin always loved tennis and riding, not unusual in the army then or now; but in the Philippines, he customarily played tennis with the British and worked his horses between noon and three, a time when commanders suspended training due to the intense heat. He loved both activities, but it was also his quiet way of being seen. And seen he was. His reputation for tactical knowledge, physical stamina, and fine leadership was growing. A friend recalled, "If you went through the regiment with a straw poll in which everyone could vote for competence, Gavin would have been identified as a real comer. . . . I think the military figures he read about appealed to him, not only his ego, but his sense of romance. I think Jim genuinely loved the army." With troops, Gavin always displayed a legitimate concern for their well-being. He had a reputation for knowing the troops: which ones were good at what, which had marital problems, were short of money, lazy, or short on rations. He made a personal effort to correct inequalities. His troops liked him for it, and his platoon consistently won interunit military competitions.

Gavin now had the "superior" ratings he had wanted. He left the Philippines with a stronger reputation and with the style that would make him a superb combat leader.

After a year and a half, he brought his family back to the United States to duty with the 3rd Infantry Division at Vancouver Barracks, in Washington State. It was the fall of 1938 and war loomed in both Europe and Asia. Mussolini had invaded Ethiopia, Civil War raged in Spain, and Adolf Hitler bloodlessly toppled his weaker neighbors.

It was a happy time for a young officer with his first real command. Gavin made captain and became commanding officer of Company K of the 7th Infantry Regiment. Excitement filled the air as the division gradually shifted to serious war preparation with numerous exercises. Gavin, meanwhile, took a course in public speaking.

Tensions in his marriage seem to have eased. He was no longer engaged in his marriage to Peggy, but the baby, Barbara, nicknamed "Babe," took a strong hold on his affections.

It took the first viewing of Gone With the Wind on a rainy day in March 1940 to bring Gavin to set down his thoughts about his troubled marriage. "I never expect to see a better movie," Gavin gushed, "I went to be stirred by the military and economic efforts of the South for a lost cause, to see on the screen the many things I have for years formed pictures of in my mind, particularly Sherman's splendid envelopment of Atlanta and march to the sea, and I saw a romance and subsequent emotional sequence evolve that so closely parallels my own that I was stirred to the depths. I have felt for some long time now that her refusal and my slowly growing and now definitely formed sexual indifference to her was perhaps peculiar to myself. Maybe I should sublimate myself to her personality and desires regardless of the intensity of their selfishness and be 'normal.' I have been unable to bring myself to it. I seek solace of a sexual kind, and solace is the word, elsewhere. I have not been unfortunate. . . . But it cannot go on forever, and I recognize that fact. Ultimately we will be an embittered even antagonistic couple. I see one solution; more children, of course if possible many more. Then . . . as we grow old we would have children and their children. . . . Would that I could start anew with someone who knows more of life and the sacrifices that one must make. The Babe is everything to me, everything. For her and her future no sacrifice is too great to make. . . . Never despair, there is always an out. A war would almost certainly settle all."

Gavin had at least two mistresses, "Belle" and "E," whom he mentioned to his diary during his tour with the 3rd Infantry. Their identities are unknown. Belle, he noted, "is a confirmed complete realist."

In 1939 Gavin suffered a detached retina in the right eye while playing handball at his new post, Fort Ord, California. At once—and without any impact, "I seemed to go blind in my right eye," he recorded. Gavin feared that the injury, whatever it was, would end his chances of serving in a combat division in a war he now felt certain must come. He wisely drove to Monterey to see a doctor not in his division, who concluded it was a detached retina. "He recommended I take 90 days sick leave, wear a dark patch on the eye, and take it easy, no exercise."

Such a prescription was unacceptable to Gavin. He left the eye to heal itself, which it did "after several months," during which he disguised the problem. "Otherwise, after spending a career preparing for war, there would be no war for me," he noted.

After a strenuous winter (1939–1940) "in a small tent on the sand dunes of the California coast," during which he worked his troops hard in tactical exercise and maneuvers and won some ambiguous notoriety in his quiet way by planting nasturtiums on two sides of his tent ("I got tired of looking at the scrub oak and sand around the tent . . . some of the young officers wrote home about it"), he was ordered to West Point as a member of the faculty in the Department of Tactics.

He loved the assignment, one in which he could study and read as he pleased and learn through teaching. While the radio reported the activities of the German Bund's rallies in New York, the annexation of Czechoslovakia, then the blitskrieg in Poland, Roosevelt promised no intervention. "Yet, there was great uneasiness in the military establishment," Gavin wrote, "We were convinced that a war was inevitable and we knew that we could not have been farther from ready for it."

As the Germans were slicing into France in the spring of 1940, the West Point faculty was trying to explain the circumvention failure of the Maginot line, the conquest of Fort Eben Emael, and the other wonders of the mechanized German attack.

"A quantum jump, technologically speaking, had been made by the Germans," Gavin recorded. He remembered dramatizing the situation in class by sweeping the red arrows off the old war maps of Europe onto the floor. "They were too small for this new kind of war," he told them. And his instruction proved successful. His classes were the highlight of a cadet's day. Gavin believed in "hands-on" instruction to keep cadet interest and used such aids as sand tables and war footage obtained from the British. He told his cadets they would be fighting Germans soon, and he had encyclopedic knowledge of German tactics and equipment. He even had the cadets learn vulnerable points and thickness of armor on German vehicles. His superiors regarded him as a "natural instructor," and the cadets who learned under him called his classes the most useful they had.

But outside the classroom, Gavin worried about something those cadets never saw. He had deep misgivings about the coming war. He believed that all the military establishment had in mind was to improve U.S. machines and methods in imitation of the German methods. "It would not be enough to copy the Germans," he wrote. "We had to strike boldly into the areas of innovation. From what we had seen so far, it was clear that the most promising area of all was airborne warfare, bringing the parachute troops and the glider troops to the battlefield in masses, especially trained, armed and equipped for that kind of warfare."

Gavin concentrated on a study of the German airborne assault on Fort Eben Emael, north of Liège, Belgium—a brilliant operation in which German paratroopers attacked the only weakness in a heavily armed fortress. Surprise, preparation and determined execution by well-trained men had short-circuited the battle. The affair was largely decided in minutes, through the fort's defenders held out for thirty hours. This, in addition to his long study of the Stonewall Jackson's tactics of maneuver and "penetration to the vitals of an opponent [that] paralyzed every fiber of his being," finally caused Gavin to take the momentous step of applying for airborne duty and parachute training in April 1941.

But Gavin's application met resistance. The West Point bureaucracy immediately blocked it, and when his request for airborne training arrived in Washington on February 20, 1941, attached was a memorandum that insisted that to leave, Gavin would have to find "an officer of equal ability ordered to this station." Additionally, the West Point superintendent personally wrote that Gavin, "so far as I know. . . . is not peculiarly fitted to this type of duty." Though the rejection was actually a compliment to Gavin's teaching skills, he was furious about it.

Gavin drove to Washington on a Friday evening after work to talk to a friend, Major William Kean, who worked in the Personnel Office of the Chief of Infantry. Several strenuous weekends of trips to Washington, and letters to friends like Yarborough and Ryder who were already in airborne, plus a résumé of stainless merit led West Point at last to relent. "I was ordered to Parachute duty in July . . . and graduated from the Parachute School in August 1941," he wrote.

But before he left for parachute school at Fort Benning, Gavin went to New York to begin a new phase of the search for his real mother. With the war and training looming and time short, Gavin hired the Burns Detective Agency to take over the case. They found that his place of birth was the Holy Family Hospital on Dean Street, Brooklyn.

When he went there personally, he was able to locate the ledger from 1907. He turned to the month of March and found the record of his birth. "There I was, big as life: born on March 22, 1907," he wrote. But his joy in the discovery turned to frustration when he rushed to the home address indicated—also on Dean Street. There was no trace of the house. The detective agency tried various leads, raising Gavin's hopes, but with no results.

The upshot was that Gavin became even more convinced that the mysterious female visitor who had came to the Gavin house in Mount Carmel was Katherine Ryan, his mother. But as he went off to war, leaving his wife and a little child, he still did not know anything about Katherine Ryan for sure.

However, he did believe he knew what World War II would be like and how to win it.

5.

THE AIRBORNE

IDEA

Graduation from Airborne School was the fulfillment of an old dream. Gavin had long suspected that he would need a new way and a new technology to bring his gifts to bear. At Airborne School his years of study, his fascination with modern tactics, and his belief in the power of new ideas would manifest themselves in something important. He would pioneer a fresh weapon that could change warfare.

Today, paratroops are no longer revolutionary. Their legend took shape during World War II; and the paratroopers, with their mystique of danger and ruthlessness, became part of American folklore, a symbol of the best in American soldiers. In 1941, that hadn't yet happened. Though parachutes had been around a long time, their use by infantry was something new. By Gavin's time aircraft and parachute technology had evolved from extremely modest origins to make large-scale airborne drops feasible.

Already common as a safety device in both airplanes and balloons, the parachute was first seriously considered as an attack device during World War I. Near the end of that war, army General William "Billy" Mitchell suggested the idea of vertical envelopment with parachute-dropped infantry as a way of breaking the stalemate of trench warfare, though at the time it remained little more than a suggestion. Aircraft technology was too primitive, and the war ended before anyone could give it a try.

Nevertheless, the idea had been born, and once a new weapon has been developed, it is only a question of time before it is used. Mitchell was a few years too early.

Immediately following World War I, many nations experimented with parachute-dropped infantry, but the Soviet Union was the first to employ mass drops, and though their efforts have gone largely unacknowledged in Western literature, the Soviets were the true pioneers of the concept. In the late 1920s and the early 1930s, spurred on by the development of large transport aircraft and a fear of the Japanese, the Red Army began effectively employing parachute battalions. The United States Army was aware of what the Soviets were doing, but, due to lack of funds and the between-wars malaise that stifled weapons development, army leaders showed little interest. That changed dramatically in 1940 with the German invasion of the Low Countries.

From autumn 1939 until spring 1940, the war in Europe was more words than action as the German Army, short on supplies following the invasion of Poland, settled into six months of inactivity, glaring menacingly across the border toward France. The still-mobilizing British and French were unaware of the German supply situation. At the time, the military world was unimpressed by the victory in Poland. The German invasion had been fast and thoroughly successful, but Poland's army was considered third-rate, and the Germans had been helped by a Soviet invasion from the east. They had not yet faced the best armies of the rest of Europe, the English and the French.

The French defense plan depended on a massive string of hardened-concrete fortifications constructed in the 1930s along the Franco-German border and named the Maginot Line after a French minister of war who died in 1932. Conventional wisdom said that their defensive line would be impregnable until the French Army fully mobilized. The Germans proved what conventional wisdom was worth that spring.

But the first thrust was north. Lured by Norway's long coastline on the North Sea and hungry for the Swedish iron ore pouring into the Norwegian port of Narvik, Hitler's divisions invaded Norway on April 9, 1940. Germany's success was immediate and complete. In spite of some British help, Norway's limited forces were devastated, and the nation capitulated at midnight on June 9.

Impressive though the German invasion was, most of the world still paid little heed. Norway's army was tiny, and her long coastline made defense a nightmare. The real battle, it was predicted, would come in northern France. It came quickly, and was concluded even faster than the battle for Norway.

The Germans came on with over 120 divisions, and they did not attack the Maginot Line. Instead, powerful German forces, led by their vaunted panzer divisions, struck at France through the Low Countries. A concentrated aerial assault dismembered their opponents' air forces almost immediately, often on the ground. When German tanks and infantry burst into Holland, Belgium, and Luxembourg on the clear morning of May 10, 1940, their main thrust came in an unexpected place, the Ardennes Forest, then thought to be too dense for armored units. Surprised at Sedan, the French Army was shattered in short order. Within ten days, German forces reached the English Channel at Abbeville, thereby encircling Allied armies to the north. Along the way, captured equipment and prisoners poured into the conquerors' hands due to the swiftness of the advance. On May 15, Holland was finished. On May 26, the British began Operation Dynamo, their desperate evacuation from Dunkirk. May 28 saw the end of Belgian resistance. Paris, which the Germans had not reached in four years of fighting in World War I, fell on June 14. On June 17, Marshal Pétain told the French people to cease resistance, and on June 22, the armistice was signed. Some 400,000 troops from the four armies on the frontier around the Maginot Line surrendered. The world has seen few such total victories.

What most intrigued Gavin and a few other like-minded military thinkers was the German invasion of Belgium. The Belgians too had built a fortress, called Eben Emael. Though not nearly as massive as the Maginot Line, it was placed strategically in a commanding position on the Albert Canal, and its stiff fortifications were garrisoned by over 1,000 men. It too was thought to be impregnable. For their thrust through Belgium to work, the Germans had to have it. They got it easily with a stunning surprise, using four detachments of parachute-trained engineers.

The Belgian defenders had thought they would have time to prepare for oncoming Germans. They had not expected their enemy to fall from the sky without warning. The fortress, largely out of commission after the initial German attack, which involved 41 gliders carrying 363 men, fell when reinforcements arrived on the second day. Even though the defenders of the fort had been on full alert for two hours, the attackers, approaching like giant bats in wide-winged observation gliders, landed with perfect precision in the gray predawn of 10 May. A group of 10 gliders came to rest on the roof of the fort itself, and within ten minutes the fort's artillery had been put out of action by determined glider infantrymen armed with satchel charges, grenades, and the element of utter surprise. Twenty Belgian soldiers were killed and 1,200 surrendered. Of German forces landed on the fort itself, 6 were killed and 20 wounded out of 96. The other German glider assault groups, assigned to secure the nearby Albert Canal bridges, suffered still fewer casualties. On 11 May transport planes dropped reinforcements by parachute. The Germans even made the elegant move of dropping 200 "parachutists" 25 miles west of Eben Emael as a diversion—straw dummies in German uniform, equipped with explosive devices that went off on landing to imitate gunfire.

As if to double the coup, German paratroops on the same day captured important invasion-route bridges across the Maas and Rhine estuaries, and Waalhaven airfield in Rotterdam.

The successful airborne assaults on Eben Emael and in Holland signaled the arrival of a new weapon. But its debut in World War II was inconclusive. Airborne strikes required a perfect execution rarely achieved in military operations. They were fragile, liable to be ruined by weather, by antiaircraft fire, bad timing, a fortuitious warning to the defenders, even an unforeseen local wind. The German method of seizing airfields to insure reinforcement passed the advantage to the defenders and proved extremely dangerous to the reinforcing aircraft. But airborne assault was born. An event the next year confirmed its striking potency.

In the spring of 1941, concerned for his exposed flanks as he prepared to launch his invasion of Russia, Hitler turned his panzers south and conquered the Balkan countries—capping the invasion with a dramatic defeat of British arms in Greece. To make their victory complete the Germans needed Crete. With its strategic position in the Mediterranean, it sat like a giant aircraft carrier that could not be sunk; it offered easy access to North Africa and the Suez Canal and made a launching platform for bombers striking Hitler's oil fields in Rumania. The British recognized the importance of the island as much as the Germans and, after the evacuation of their forces from Greece, fortified Crete with over 40,000 defenders, including two weak Greek divisions. The Germans countered this with a 22,000-man force; however, what was different this time was that, on the morning of May 20, 1941, most of this force arrived, not by sea, but by parachute and glider. The German paratroopers dropped this time not like spies, but onto heavily defended British airfields. A bitter daylong battle ensued that brought the Germans heavy casualties. The Rétimo and Heráklion airfields were successfully defended, but the airfield at Máleme was in the attackers' hands by nightfall. This enabled the Germans, by dawn of the second day, to begin pouring in airborne reinforcements and supplies. The battle ended on May 31 with the last of the British evacuations. It was a battle such as no one had ever seen. A major target had been taken by troops and supplies brought in solely by air.

The key to the German method was concentration and control. The first objective was a major airfield—in order to enable reinforcements to pour in. The paratroops were used to capture landing space, and heavier gear, artillery and infantry then could be brought in by glider and transport aircraft. During the operation, control of the air by the Luftwaffe was crucial. Thus while paratroop theory had envisioned the airborne troops as a shock force to disrupt and unhinge ground forces, the Germans were developing a true airborne strike force.

In fact, although the operation had succeeded, the German high command had mixed feelings about it afterwards. Their casualties had been frightful; 5,140 were dead, wounded, and missing out of an airborne force of 13,000; it had begun to look as if the fledgling weapon was no longer such a surprise to defenders, and in fact, Hitler would never use paratroopers on a major scale again. But to the outside world, and Gavin, the drawbacks were not immediately apparent. Rather, Crete seemed to herald the arrival of a new, sophisticated, and devastating force, and Gavin wanted to be a part of it. That is why he saw his graduation from parachute training in the summer of 1941 as one of the significant moments of his life.

Yet the fledgling airborne arm of the U.S. Army in the spring of 1941 was far from ready to emulate the Germans. At the time, no U.S. airborne force greater than battalion size existed. Such units that did exist were still working diligently to perfect the direction of training, and there was no established doctrine, no theory of how to send such forces into combat, nor were there enough troop-carrying aircraft available even if training and doctrine had been fully developed. The beginnings were humble and stilted. Though the army had been interested in parachute infantry for some time before World War II, limited funds kept the idea nothing more than a concept until Eben Emael.

Slightly more than a month after witnessing that stunning success, the army, at the behest of Chief of Staff General George C. Marshall, ordered the creation of the first, all-volunteer, parachute test platoon at Fort Benning, under the command of Lieutenant William Ryder. The platoon was to test in the wooded hills of Georgia whether the airborne idea was feasible and, if so, to begin developing it. Ryder and his men achieved their purpose admirably. They had fantastic success, feeling their way almost intuitively through a parachute-training course that they invented as they went along, with the help of an experienced Air Corps jumper, Warrant Officer Harry "Tug" Wilson. They had no fatalities, their equipment functioned well, and they managed to organize themselves efficiently after landing. While doing it all, they also set some of the high physical and mental standards in rigorous training that would become trademarks of American parachutists. When they were through, the army was ready to take the next step and expand the airborne concept into the airborne weapon. General Marshall immediately ordered the formation of the first parachute battalion, and in October of 1940, five months after Eben Emael, the 501st Parachute Infantry Battalion was formed under the command of Major William M. "Bud" Miley, a short feisty man who would soon become a major general and the commander of the 17th Airborne Division.

America was at peace, and any urgency to catch up with the new weapons of the European war was matched by reluctance to spend money on munitions. Within the army of 1940 and 1941, paratroop enthusiasts faced stringent peacetime budgetary and manpower constraints. The new branch remained grafted onto army ground forces, and planners had to face the fact that airborne operations—far more than others—required the cooperation of other military branches to be successful. Parachute infantry are of little use without aircraft piloted by trained pilots to give them lift. A desperate shortage of transport aircraft plagued airborne operations and airborne development throughout World War II because parachute training and parachute production moved much faster than pilot training and aircraft production.

In spite of the lack of lift capacity, airborne development continued.

New battalions were formed, and more men were trained. Credit for the development of this new wing of military power belongs to many; however, certain figures stand above all others for their contributions. Perhaps the most significant role was played at the very top by Marshall himself. Dynamic, farsighted, and extraordinarily capable, Marshall ultimately did more to shape the victorious American ground forces of World War II than anyone else, and it was he who acknowledged the need for and encouraged the growth of America's airborne arm in a time when many general officers considered the idea an expensive and unwieldy luxury.

Below Marshall, other men played significant roles. The officer directly behind America's fledgling airborne capability was then-Major William C. Lee, a member of Chief of Infantry General George Lynch's staff in 1940. Long before the Germans used paratroops in Belgium and Crete, Lee had been an ardent promoter of the airborne idea, though he was seldom taken seriously. Suddenly, after Eben Emael, Major Lee's ideas no longer seemed so radical, and Marshall selected him to set into motion America's own airborne effort. A soft-spoken, intent, lean North Carolinian in his early forties who had served in World War I with distinction and who was known for his physical energy, Lee became the driving force behind airborne. It was Lee who organized the test platoon. Then Lee established the 1st Provisional Parachute Group (later Airborne Command) and parachute training (ultimately the Airborne School) at Fort Benning. Procedures for training paratroops were still experimental, and large amounts of training apparatus were needed in record time. Every jump was a new experiment and each component of the individual paratrooper's equipment withstood tests and constant modification. Lee focused the effort, and provided strong hands-on leadership. He selected the best men he could find to flesh out his organization, while at the same time lobbying Washington for funds and priority. By combining many roles, he managed to generate an airborne arm with startling speed.

By the time Gavin arrived for parachute training in the summer of 1941, the airborne training area at Fort Benning was firmly established. Set up with the help of ideas and apparatus lifted from a captured German parachute-training manual, the school looked then much as it does today, down to the 250-foot and 34-foot jump towers and the howling, menacing instructors. Its cadre was drawn from the 501st Parachute Infantry Battalion—the first of only two parachute battalions then in existence.

Everything was in short supply, but the most dire need was manpower.

The army had a manpower ceiling, and it had been reached. Commanders of units then in existence did not relish parting with any men—let alone the dynamic men airborne recruited. Nevertheless, in July of 1941, the 502nd Parachute Infantry Battalion formed under the command of Major George P. Howell, Jr., swiftly followed in August by the 503rd under Major Robert F. Sink. Therein lay the real fruit of Lee's efforts. He was winning his battles in Washington for a fair share of what was available, making possible the accomplishments of paratroopers in World War II. It is why Lee is justly called "the Father of the Airborne."

When Gavin finished jump training, the force he entered was still experimental. Fifty years later, General William Yarborough described it this way: "We had lots of enthusiasm in those early days—and some great men—but nobody really seemed to know how the thing was going to actually work when we went to war." Gavin would supply some of the answers.

Gavin's early airborne assignments came in rapid succession. His first was as commander of C Company of the 503rd Parachute Infantry Battalion, just being formed at Fort Benning. It was his long-time friend William Ryder who, through Colonel Lee, had encouraged the Department of the army to override the West Point superintendent's rejection of Gavin's original airborne application. With that accomplished, Ryder and Yarborough helped him get what he wanted while doing what they thought was in the best interests of airborne itself. Ryder, at the time directing airborne training, and Yarborough, working directly for Lee as his chief of intelligence at the Provisional Airborne Group, both recommended Gavin to Lee as the right man for developing training and doctrine at the group. Lee followed the recommendations, and soon after becoming the Battalion Executive Officer of the 503rd, Lee transferred Gavin to be his S-3 (chief of training and doctrine). Lee did not then know Gavin well, but he would soon, and when he did, he became Gavin's mentor.

What Ryder saw in Gavin was the military mind needed to answer the many questions about how paratroopers should fight. Should airborne units be no larger than battalions and reserved only for special commando-type operations? Should airborne divisions and corps be created? What percentage of airborne troops should be glider troops and what percentage should be parachute trained? How should they be deployed—as the Germans had done, to first capture airfields, or were there other possibilities?

The answers needed to be found before facing the Germans in combat. All the years of studying and debating the latest in military thought were now about to combine to launch Gavin's career. His reputation as being absolutely dedicated to the "art and science of war" is what his friends saw as his greatest asset, and it was why Colonel Lee put him in charge of developing the art and science of the American paratrooper.

Captain Gavin was ecstatic. He had been an officer in the military for twelve years. Promotions had come slowly, and recognition had been minimal. On October 16, 1941, with his new assignment, he became a major, but even more importantly, he now had his chance. Few West Point classmates would be able to put their ideas on modern warfare into practice in such a way that those ideas might have a powerful effect on the war he was certain his country was on the threshold of waging. Suddenly, Gavin felt his "star was rising."

The Lee-Gavin "marriage" became a happy one. It should have been, because they were similar men. Both were serious and soft-spoken with reputations for no-nonsense demeanor and directness in their personal dealings. And each had a special gift he brought to airborne. Lee never ceased to surprise subordinates with his knowledge of how to cut through paperwork in Washington and somehow get what his paratroops needed. And he was in touch with everything going on within his command. Men remember him as being everywhere, not just for ceremonies and inspections. He had a way of just "popping up" and talking with NCOs and young officers so he could have an accurate picture.

In Gavin, Lee found the perfect protégé. Gavin was not only similar to Lee in mannerisms, concern for his soldiers, hands-on style of leadership, and convictions about the value of the paratrooper, he was also the innovative mind Lee needed on his staff—and he proved it dramatically over the next six months.

One of early airborne's biggest needs was a codification of the principles of how paratroopers would deploy and fight. One of Gavin's first actions upon arriving in his new office in the Provisional Airborne Group was to write FM 31–30, a manual titled *Tactics and Technique of Air-Borne Troops*. Captain Yarborough, S-2 (intelligence), had busily collected all the information he could on the German and Soviet airborne efforts, and his father, who spoke Russian, helped him by translating Soviet documents. In the short time he had been S-2, Yarborough had collected a great deal of information on how others were doing it. Gavin took advantage of it all. He wrote FM 31–30 from two sources: information gleaned from the Germans and the Soviets, and his own interpretation and innovation. The Russian contribution defined the art and science of parachuting, the German contribution, the training and combat employ-ment of the parachutist, and Gavin combined the two with his knowledge of the American Army to shape a uniquely American model.

Viewed today, the manual Gavin wrote is dated, but it is still a worthy document. The bulk of the book is devoted to parachute operations, train-ing, and the organization and equipment of parachute units. Here, Gavin's own view of modern warfare is clearly revealed. He believed that the war America was about to fight would be one of rapid movement with fluid "front lines," and that paratroopers, if they were to be successful, should be supremely self-reliant. He wrote, "The vital need for flexibility in parachute units demands that the smaller components be as nearly self-sustaining as possible. This, in turn, requires that each individual in the squad be capable of performing the duties of any other member of the squad." Paratroopers must be self-reliant and trained to fight on their own if necessary, because, unlike regular infantry who arrive at a battlefield organized but often become disorganized under fire, a para-troop force arrives in battle disorganized and must organize under fire.

Beyond the information on tactics, Gavin's book also details parachute training, how parachute units should be organized up to regimental level, what type of operations they can perform and the elements, such as surprise, that are needed for success. What he produced was farsighted, and it got him noticed. Years later, when asked why he thought his career in airborne soared as it did, he responded with a smile, "Because I wrote the book."

Elsewhere in airborne, others were making their mark. As the com-mander of the 501st, Major Miley set many precedents and shaped this first airborne battalion into an elite force. As a group the men of the 501st set an extraordinary record. Selected from the very best volunteers the army could then offer, their training and high physical standards were far beyond those of the regular army, and they formed the nucleus of men who would ultimately train and lead an airborne army into com-bat. It was they who created and cadred the original Airborne School, and when airborne expansion began in earnest, they formed the nucleus of experienced men in each regiment. They made other contributions as well. It was in the 501st under Miley that the silver parachutist badge, still worn by all who have graduated from Airborne School was designed by then-Lieutenant William Yarborough, Gavin's longtime friend, as were the jump boots and the jumpsuit.

Another airborne tradition that began in the 501st was the Prop blast. Prop blasts were celebrations for the newly inducted paratrooper consisting of a great deal of jumping off chairs, tables, sometimes even out of second-story windows, and more than a little drinking. The resulting hangovers were as legendary as the celebrations. Men in airborne units felt they were a part of something special, that they could do things other soldiers could not. Everything they did had a freshness about it because it was usually something few men had done before.

This applied to Gavin as much as it did to the lowest ranking soldier. It was the attitude the paratroops took to war.

In charge of developing doctrine for the airborne force, Gavin knew exactly what he wanted. Long a disciple of Thomas Stonewall Jackson and J. F. C. Fuller, Gavin envisioned a war of mobility, where victory depended upon the initiative of lower-level commanders far more than it ever had before. Of that period he later wrote, "I went to work at once in applying all the knowledge that I had gained in studying past operations. Concurrently with the development of doctrine, loading of aircraft, formations, operating procedures, we had to move as rapidly as technology and money would permit in the development of appropriate weapons, uniforms, combat rations, etc. In addition we had to develop methods of issuing orders and engaging in combat. Front lines, such as were known in past wars, did not apply."

FM 31–30 *Tactics and Technique of Air-Borne Troops* was the first book Gavin ever wrote, and perhaps the most significant. As a result of the manual, he received a great deal of attention, and the nature of his brand of soldiering became public. His insight had earned him leadership. His other qualities would make him an outstanding commander.

War in the Pacific had long been anticipated; nevertheless, when, on December 7, 1941, the Japanese devastated America's Pacific fleet in a surprise attack on Pearl Harbor, Americans were stunned. All Americans who heard the news that day remembered for the rest of their lives what they were doing when they heard it. Gavin was no exception. He wrote, "I was attending a movie in the town of Columbus, Georgia, with my wife and daughter Barbara, when the owner of the theater stopped the film and stepped on stage to announce the attack. I was shocked. We left to return to Fort Benning, expecting orders of some kind. To the contrary, all the aircraft we had been using for training were taken away and all of Washington's attentions seemed to be concentrated on the Pacific and the West Coast."

Instead of rushing off to war, America's paratroops simply returned to training as best as they could with limited amounts of aircraft. Gavin, who had been longing for war, would have to wait: for during the first few months, America was not in a position to challenge anyone. The army first had to gather its strength, relying on the nation's isolation and two oceans for protection, while it did. Volunteers poured into recruiting centers and factory assembly lines began increasing output.

In February of 1942, Major Gavin attended an abbreviated course at the Command and General Staff School at Fort Leavenworth, Kansas. This, the army's equivalent of graduate school, was a reward for fast-track officers. It qualified him for division-level staff work, and it allowed him to return to the Provisional Airborne Group, where he immediately set about designing the airborne division. He recorded, "In the spring of 1942 General Lee and I went to Headquarters Ground Forces in Washington to discuss the organization of our first airborne division. The Army Ground Forces was anxious that we get on with the creation of an airborne division as rapidly as we could. They stipulated however that it must not be a National Guard division because after the war it would go back to the state with which it was affiliated. Therefore, we were expected to select a division in the organized reserves, preferably one that had already finished all its basic training and was located near one or more airfields." The division selected was the 82nd Division, at Camp Claiborne, Louisiana. It was led by two officers who would go on to greatness, Lieutenant General Omar Nelson Bradley, commanding, and executive officer Major General Matthew Bunker Ridgway, and it had a distinguished history. Famous in World War I as the "All-American" Division (because it contained a resident of every state then in the Union), it fought the Great War under General Jonathan Wainwright—the same Wainwright who in 1942 fought his desperate battle in the Philippines against the Japanese. The nation most remembered the 82nd for the exploits of Sergeant Alvin York, the noncom who captured an entire German battalion by himself. Now it was to be America's first airborne division to see combat, and it and its commander, Bradley, would become famous.

But all that lay in the future. In 1942, the division fought hard to overcome its growing pains.

The frantic rebuilding process the army had plunged into and the arrival of the airborne idea brought the division temporary chaos. First it lost Bradley. High command considered him one of the army's top comers, so when the 28th Infantry Division began having organizational problems the army grabbed Bradley to straighten things out. Ridgway then inherited command of the 82nd. But the division needed to be relocated to a post near an airfield, so no sooner had Ridgway moved into the commander's slot than his division set off for Fort Bragg, North Carolina—where the army scheduled it for reorganization for airborne status along the lines of Chief of Army Ground Forces Lesley McNair's vision of what an airborne division should be, a conservative vision, based on a glider force.

Under the pressure of rearmament, the paratroop concept was fading in favor of the glider concept. Glider troops would enter combat in gliders towed by troop-carrying aircraft. McNair liked the idea and designated that each airborne division would have two glider regiments and one paratroop regiment. His vision of airborne operations was like the German model: the paratroop regiment jumped first and secured an airhead into which gliders poured reinforcements and heavier equipment. Gavin and Lee disagreed. They thought the airborne division should be mostly paratroop regiments, while gliders only hauled heavy equipment; but McNair's mind was made up, and the 82nd, and all the original airborne divisions, were constituted exactly as the chief of Army Ground Forces thought they should be. From the 82nd's viewpoint, that meant that two of three infantry regiments had to be converted into glider regiments. The other would simply be transferred out to make room for a parachute regiment.

Ridgway, the new commander, was a respected but highly traditional infantryman with strong ideas on how war should be waged. He had come to the division because George Marshall had personally promised him a command when Ridgway had been on his staff before Pearl Harbor. Forty-six years old when he took command of the division, he was intelligent and liked outdoor activities. Though he was balding, he looked younger than his years. Not a large man—5 feet 10 inches tall and about 175 pounds—he was solid as a tree trunk, moved with stiff military bearing, and was passionately devoted to staying fit. He was conservative and somewhat shy, a man some called "intense," and though he had a tendency to remain aloof from others, he was known for high integrity and loyalty to those he valued. Ridgway was not an airborne pioneer, but now that he was part of it, he was tireless in his efforts to make airborne viable. For if Ridgway was nothing else, he was a professional soldier in the classical sense. He liked life in the military, physical hardships never bothered him, and he had a powerful sense of duty. His latest "duty" was to make the airborne division a workable entity. The only way he knew to get the job done was to mold the division in his own likeness. In the process he would make the 82nd one of the elite army units of World War II, perhaps the best-known division in American history—but in 1942, he had a big new task before him.

First came the problem of reorganization. McNair wanted the spare infantry regiment made available immediately because he intended to create the 101st Airborne Division, which would be commanded by Bill Lee, by splitting off troops the 82nd no longer needed and augmenting them with parachute troops. At the time, the 82nd consisted of the 325th, 326th, and 327th Infantry Regiments, and Ridgway knew each of them well; he had been with them when they had gone through their basic training. Though he had preferences (he liked the 325 and the 326), he opted for fairness. Lee and Ridgway flipped a coin and Lee got the 327th along with elements of the other two regiments. Meanwhile, Ridgway got the 504th as his parachute regiment. Soon after, he went to Fort Benning to get his first look at the 504th and to make his first parachute jump, for he believed that if the division had to be airborne, he should be the first out of the plane. The jump, made after a crash training course, proved a success, though he never came to relish parachuting. But his first impression of the 504th was negative. He concluded that they seemed to know a great deal about jumping but had forsaken infantry tactics. Subsequent inspections revealed this initial impression to be accurate, and he relieved all the early battalion commanders. One of the replacements was Lieutenant Colonel Reuben "Rube" Henry Tucker III, a handsome West Pointer known for his athletic feats but weak in academics. He was diminutive in stature but possessed seemingly limitless energy, and he was a fine troop commander. Ridgway liked Tucker instantly, and soon after the regiment arrived at Fort Bragg, gave him command of the 504th.

Tucker was one of those characters who formed the paratrooper archetype. His almost foolhardy daring lasted throughout the war. But he got results. He built the 504th into one of the most celebrated regiments of the war, and remained its commander for the duration.

While Ridgway reshuffled the 82nd and built it into an airborne division, Gavin was building the regiment he had been assigned, the 505th, at Fort Benning. He got his command in August of 1942 and was soon made a full colonel. Among the airborne, his work in the Provisional Parachute Group had given him a strong reputation as a "comer"; parachute-trained officers were in seriously short supply; and his mentor, Bill Lee, thought he would make an outstanding commander. Gavin was intent on proving Lee right.

The 505th was the first parachute regiment to be built from the ground up. Soon after he took command, Gavin informed his officers of exactly what he wanted. "A number of us who had been junior officers—captains —a year earlier discussed at great length the training of the parachute troops. We decided that they had to be superbly trained physically if they were to do the things that were expected of them, but their mental condition was equally as important. In this respect, we decided that the old method of forcing individuals into a mold, while at the same time removing their personal identities as far as possible, had to be done away with. From the moment they joined the parachute units, we tried to impress on them what outstanding individual soldiers they were. We wanted to do everything we could to enhance their pride, and we sought to do so. At the same time, we wanted to train them just as thoroughly as we possibly could." Gavin believed the best way to accomplish his goal was through realistic mock combat exercises and long marches for toughening, and the 505th did both. He designed the mock exercises himself, and he led the marches at a blistering pace.

He had but one priority: combat performance. The 505th was his chance to show what he could do, and he approached it with a zealot's effort and demands. He was hardest on officers. In the 505th officers were required to be "the first out of the airplane door and the last in the chow line." Gavin thought he had the finest infantry on earth in the ranks of his battalions, and if properly led, trained, respected, and treated, they would be the instrument to prove his ideas correct. They would be the masters of modern combat. The building blocks were physical hardiness and mental toughness. After months of grueling training, in early 1943, he had a final test for them. "As we neared our time to leave, on the way to war, I had an exercise that required them to leave our barracks area at

7:00 P.M. and march all night to an area near the town of Cottonwood, Alabama, a march of about 23 miles. There we maneuvered all day and in effect we seized and held an airhead. We broke up the exercise about 8:00 P.M. and started the troopers back by another route through dense pine forests, by way of backwoods roads. About 11:00 P.M., we went into bivouac. After about an hour's sleep, the troopers were awakened to resume the march. It takes trained troopers to execute such a plan very well, since all of them were quite exhausted, and they had to remember where every item of equipment and the weapons were, and post security and move promptly at night. We marched all night and I remember, not long after daylight, calling a halt when we were about an hour's march from the barracks. I was at the head of the regiment and we fell into the ditches at the side of the road quite exhausted. I suddenly awakened and looked back and everyone was sound asleep. I got them on their feet and in a few moments we were on our way. . . . In 36 hours the regiment had marched well over 50 miles, maneuvered and seized an airhead and defended it from counterattack while carrying full combat loads and living off reserve rations."

But what struck Gavin more than anything else about his troopers was what happened after the exercise. They were no sooner back, with all their equipment put away, than he saw those same troops who had been without sleep for two days waiting in their dress uniforms for buses to take them downtown. To Gavin's eye, this meant the men were now ready for combat.

He didn't know where that combat would be, but his answer came directly.

In February of 1943, the 82nd Airborne Division was selected to deploy to Africa to participate in the invasion of Sicily. As with most things in World War II, the invasion was largely an improvisation, and it is still surrounded by controversy. The assignment of the 82nd to this task was a surprise. To the men within airborne in 1943, it was almost taken for granted, until the orders to Africa arrived, that the 101st would be deployed first. It was, after all, commanded by Major General William Lee, and it was thought that since he was the real "father" of airborne, he should be accorded the honor of leading the first division-sized airborne assault. However, when the decision came down, the 101st was not selected to go first. It is difficult to decipher exactly why it was the 82nd that was selected; but the logic at the time, which lingers still, was that because Ridgway was one of "Marshall's men," officers Marshall knew, liked, and trusted, he was picked over Lee, who had risen from obscurity with the parachute infantry concept. Politically, Ridgway outmaneuvered Lee, it seems. However it came about, relations between Ridgway and Lee were significantly cooler after the 82nd received first call to action; and from then on, there would be two groups within the airborne: the early airborne figures, who were considered to be "Lee men," and the men Ridgway nurtured, the Ridgway men. Gavin was a Lee man; however, in terms of his career, he was fortunate that his mentor lost the honor of leading the first assault, for it gave Gavin an early opportunity at combat.

One of the first problems facing the 82nd, now preparing for an actual operation, was that it had two glider regiments, but it did not have enough gliders to deploy both regiments into combat; to make it ready for the fight in Sicily, one of those glider regiments had to be replaced with a parachute regiment. In short order, the 326th transferred out, and the 505th and Jim Gavin transferred in. The 82nd would have to go to war with a slightly different composition than had been planned.

Gavin's unit was welcome at the 82nd. The division was going to be in combat soon, and whatever regiment Ridgway got, he did not have the time to work with it to make sure it was what it should be. It needed to be ready go. Gavin's unit, in Ridgway's opinion, was such a regiment, and he considered it to be one of the best. Ridgway sent a letter to Gavin at the time, confirming that good opinion, and the greeting the 505th got when they joined the 82nd reinforced it. Clay Blair described it in his biography of Ridgway: "The 505th may have been one of the best trained and most highly motivated regiments the army had ever fielded. 'They were awesome' an 82nd Airborne Division staffer recalled, 'Every man a clone of the CO, Gavin. Tough? Oh God, were they tough! Not just in the field, but 24 hours a day.' "

The 505th was as famous for its off-duty adventures as it was its on-duty performance, but Gavin was fiercely loyal to his men even through the worst of it. One of his troopers had shocked Fort Benning when he was arrested for having sex with a young lady on the lawn of the local courthouse. When an angry post commander demanded severe and immediate discipline, Gavin refused. He responded, "In view of the fact that that young man will be asked to give his life for his country in the next few months, I suggest we give him a medal."

If Ridgway was not impressed with the 505th's off-duty shenanigans, he was impressed with their intensity, their competence, and their leader, for by now, Gavin was recognized and respected throughout the airborne branch. He had found his place.

Gavin now had most of what he had wanted: an elite unit he himself had created, and the chance to prove his ideas in combat. But one area of his life remained turbulent: his marriage. Still searching for that perfect love, Gavin moved from woman to woman—as had become his habit— with complete disregard for Peggy's feelings. And their long period of pretending had led to bitterness, even hatred. Peggy and Barbara were with him at Benning, and he treated his daughter to all the love he had never had, but his relationship with Peggy was about over. He was even then thinking of divorce. Before leaving for Africa to prepare for the invasion of Sicily, he broached the subject with her, and they agreed that when he returned they would end the marriage. Meanwhile, the affairs continued. And, though he said good-bye to Barbara with some regret, he felt relieved to be leaving Peggy.

6.

SICILY

Gavin and the 505th Parachute Infantry Regiment joined the 82nd Division in March of 1943. Before the month ended, they received their alert for overseas embarkation and were restricted to Fort Bragg. This unusual measure produced a slew of AWOLs. They received harsh punishment. Some troopers were given time in the guardhouse, work detail, or made to wear fatigues with a yellow stripe painted down the back. Gavin knew his command; he knew his malingerers, but some of the men had compelling reasons, and he showed them leniency. Ridgway growled about the problem, and Gavin himself called it "a mess," but AWOLs did little to detract from his bright mood. He stood on the verge of deploying his troops in combat, putting his methods to the ultimate test. He believed his regiment ready to fight and scrawled in his diary, "The type of training that we need most is that we will get in the theater of operations. A few men killed, a few air attacks and an exchange of gunfire will do wonders to drive our lessons home." For the first time, Gavin felt the fever of battle.

At home, he let Peggy and Barbara know his time had come, and they showed less enthusiasm. Peggy and he had agreed that their marriage should end, but she still loved him and would until her death. Nevertheless, she maintained silence in public and even considered giving him a farewell party, but when the time came, the party never happened and he left quietly.

Just before they deployed, Gavin's 505th staged the first mass regimental parachute drop in American history, near Camden, South Carolina. It ended in tragedy. One of the 130 C-47s lost engine power and altitude;

it cut like a knife into the parachutes blossoming from the planes ahead. Three troopers died. Those who saw it never forgot it, but Gavin remained calm. Jumping out of airplanes was dangerous work. Accidents happened. The 504 scheduled a similar drop; but heavy fog on the drop zones made it impossible, and the troop-laden planes returned to base.

On April 10, Ridgway briefed Gavin, giving him all the information available on the upcoming mission, the invasion of Sicily. Though Ridgway's main concern was to execute the drop successfully, he took extra care to emphasize the importance of getting along with the British. Maintaining good relations with the sometimes prickly British was army policy. Ridgway knew it was not always easy; he had already visited North Africa himself and had found the British to be arrogant. Some of his resentment showed. To Gavin, he described the Americans now deployed as "always the tail of the British kite." Later that day, an ecstatic Gavin noted in his diary, "I was assured by Gen. Ridgway that the part of the 505 is a prime one. It is exciting and stimulating to realize that the first regimental parachute operation in the history of our Army is to be taken by the 505. It is going to be very tough to do well, but if we fail it will not be through lack of effort. I know the regiment will fight to the last man. They will fight as American troops have never fought before."

Anglo-American relations weighed on every American general then, for there was a constant tug for leadership that determined the course of the war as much as the quality of the troops and their equipment. Operation Husky, the invasion of Sicily, was a political and strategic compromise, as well as a blow at the overextended Wehrmacht. Americans wanted more control over and a bigger share of the fighting, but the British wanted to keep or expand what they already had, preferably by placing American units under British command. North Africa had been largely a British-led "show," and Americans were determined that Husky would be their show.

As Husky plans were perfected, friction between American and British strategists increased. American commanders remained true to their heritage of massive, frontal assaults. Men of Eisenhower's generation saw as their mission to assault the main body of the German Army across the strategically crucial northern European plain, using huge legions backed by irresistible firepower. Not possessing the industrial might of the United States, and unable to overwhelm an enemy with sheer resources, the English saw the situation very differently. Nor were the British confident about American manpower and industrial production. The flood of men, arms, and machines had not reached full strength in 1942 and 1943; until it did, the British were the experts on fighting Germans. They believed the German war machine would wear itself out in the wastes of Russia. Americans continued to press the British for a massive invasion of the northern European plain, and the British continued to resist the idea.

Then there was the Winston Churchill factor. Based on World War I strategy, he advocated a thrust through the "soft underbelly of Europe," believing it would cut off Eastern Europe from the possibility of Russian occupation while it would upset the Germans and allow the Allies to threaten a second front close to the heart of Germany.

Then there was the British Empire. Churchill saw it as essential to England's future greatness, and he wanted to wage the war in such a way as to protect the empire. Churchill lived in the distant future. He foresaw the emergence of a new world after World War II, and he wanted England to have her place in it. If the Americans and Russians assumed control of the largest war in world history, it would mean the British had been supplanted in their traditional role. No one had foreseen that in 1939, but by 1943 it seemed a distinct possibility.

These priorities were irrelevant to American officers. Therefore, Churchill sought to promote his interests by placing British officers into the highest levels of command. Another voice and perspective, every bit as urgent as Churchill's but never as influential, came from the leader of the Soviet Union, Joseph Stalin. The German military machine had overrun or destroyed huge portions of the Soviet Union's land area, citizenry, and military. Stalin held, with great justification, that the Russian Army had done more than its share to keep the Germans occupied. He wanted a large-scale invasion of Europe from the west to open up a second front, and he wanted it immediately. The invasion of Sicily was the compromise.

In 1943, Sicily represented a clearly defined, limited piece of Europe for the British and Americans to invade as an interim action while the United States built up manpower and industrial potential for the big cross-Channel invasion U.S. Army leaders wanted. The invasion of Sicily complied with Churchill's vision of the war, placated Stalin for the time being, offered a chance to knock Italy out of the war, and would provide valuable combat experience for American ground troops. The island was honeycombed with German air bases; its conquest would be one way to greatly relieve pressure from air attack on Allied Mediterranean shipping, which in turn held the British Empire together. Husky was scheduled for the summer of 1943.

The Germans, misled by their assessment of Churchill's mental processes and British intelligence's ruse of planting false invasion plans on the corpse of a phony British major done up to look like the victim of a plane crash into the sea and released from a submarine off the coast of Spain, feared an attack on the Balkans. They were not oblivious to the importance of Sicily and anticipated a diversionary attack there, but they continued to stake the bulk of their defenses against the expected main attack elsewhere. Thus, they allotted four divisions for the island's defense. Two of the four German divisions were in place in addition to the main force of twelve Italian divisions stationed in Sicily under the command of General Alfredo Guzzoni. The German divisions, the 15th Panzer Grenadier Division (motorized infantry) and the Hermann Göring Division (a Luftwaffe armored airborne division equipped with the latest Tiger tanks), were considered first-rate divisions. What particularly worried the Allies was that the Hermann Göring Division had stationed itself a mere 25 miles from the proposed American landing area, near an undistinguished west-coast town called Gela.

If Husky planning at the highest levels was political, the actual invasion planning was even more so. Planners were faced with a fundamental decision: American or English leadership. Here another compromise was reached, similar to the one in North Africa. The choice for the post of invasion commander was British General Sir Harold R. L. G. Alexander. Eisenhower, by then theater commander, who held the position more for his political than his combat skills, endorsed it. The British insisted upon it. Because of bad experiences in North Africa, British officers lacked confidence in the prowess of American arms. A popular joke held that the "Germans had their Italians, but the British had the Americans." In Africa, the theater commander, Eisenhower, was American, but where it mattered, in the field, British officers commanded. Eisenhower's choice of Alexander also appeased the British hope to be the force that defeated the Germans, a wreath they felt they had earned during four bloody years of war.

Naturally, different outlooks produced two distinct invasion concepts. The first, favored by Lieutenant General George S. Patton, commander of the U.S. Seventh Army, called for landing areas on opposite sides of the island to squeeze the Axis troops while Patton cut off their retreat to mainland Italy through the Messina Strait. Patton's II Corps would land at Palermo and drive east, while General Bernard L. Montgomery, England's hero from North Africa, would land his British Eighth Army at Syracuse and drive north. British leaders, particularly Montgomery, dismissed Patton's plan immediately on several grounds: they still distrusted American troops, they feared dire consequences for the divided forces, and they questioned whether there would be enough air and naval support for two separate invasions. Instead, they put forth their own plan. Montgomery would land in the area surrounding the Pachino Peninsula, near Syracuse, and Patton at the Gulf of Gela, on Montgomery's left, where he would perform a secondary role supporting Montgomery's flank and rear. Alexander, in operational charge, backed Montgomery, and the invasion went off according to this plan.

The politics of the airborne portion of Husky grew similarly complex. Lieutenant General Sir Frederick A. M. "Boy" Browning was the father of the British airborne and had made the British 1st Airborne Division with their jaunty red berets a household word in England. As the airborne advisor to Eisenhower, his plan for Sicily called for a largely British drop—with the U.S. 82nd Airborne playing a subordinate role. Under Browning's plan, England would supply the bulk of the paratroopers, while the United States would donate the troop-carrying aircraft.

Ridgway was incensed by the idea. Fearing Browning's influence on Eisenhower, he considered an American airborne voice close to Eisenhower crucial and sent for his trusted commander of division artillery and longtime associate, Brigadier General Maxwell Taylor. Taylor's mission was to influence Eisenhower to promote the American portion of the airborne invasion and gain a larger role for American paratroopers. Taylor faced a ticklish diplomacy in Africa. Most commanders felt Eisenhower's first priority was political, that American commanders should cooperate with the British. He went to the length of personally informing every general officer who entered his headquarters that this was his policy for Anglo-American relations—including Ridgway and Taylor. Sensing the political situation, Taylor went to the one influential, outspoken American officer who cared little about the politics of the British, Patton. Patton promptly demanded that two American parachute regiments shield his beaches on D day. The ensuing argument remained unresolved when the 82nd arrived in North Africa in May.

On April 29, 1943, Gavin and 5,388 officers and men left New York

Harbor aboard the *Monterey*, a former Matson liner, bound for North Africa. He wrote, "The entire convoy consists of twenty-three transports, eight destroyers, one aircraft carrier, and the battleship *Texas*. Total shipment, about 58,000 men. Destination: Oran. Object: murder. And the morale is very high."

Gavin's thoughts dwelt upon what lay ahead. Not yet combat tested, he wondered wistfully on the voyage over what it would be like and how he would do when he got into it. How would his men react to his style of leadership? He needn't have worried. One striking attraction he held for his regiment was his daring. At a time when normal static-line jumps were considered courageous, Gavin experimented with free-fall parachuting. If it was important to airborne operations, he wanted to be the first to try it—particularly if his troopers might end up doing it. Another attraction was Gavin's leadership touch. Often the technique of "hands-on command" (practiced by commanders who give orders, then watch to see that they are carried out) creates resentment among subordinates; Gavin, though he was definitely that sort of leader, was liked. From the time the regiment formed until it jumped into Sicily, he made it his practice to remain visible and to spend as much time as possible in the regiment's area, both during training and off-duty hours. He deliberately learned as many names as he could as he listened to and took action on as many military and personal problems as he could uncover. One former 505 battalion commander and staff officer remembered it as Gavin's "genius for finding excitement." In this way, Gavin built a regiment that really did owe its first allegiance to its leader. They may have doubted themselves, but they believed in him—and on almost any terms.

Though the 505th was destined to jump into Sicily, it first landed the old way, by ship, at Casablanca on May 10, along with other troops selected for the invasion. From there it moved to Oujda, a town in French Morocco, which none of the survivors can ever forget. Even today, troopers who lived in the "tent city" they constructed at Oujda remember it as the most miserable place they ever inhabited. Set amid dry and rocky desert, Oujda's temperatures often reached 140 degrees and the dust seemed inseparable from the air. Sandstorms, a mixed blessing because they gave some relief from the ever-present flies, came without warning almost daily; and they invariably reached their worst during mealtimes. Bad water, poor sanitation, and compulsory Atabrine tablets to fight malaria gave many dysentery. To make matters even worse, desperately poor Arabs attempted to steal whatever they could get from the American camps—including from freshly buried garbage and corpses of recently fallen battle dead. And there was absolutely nothing to do in the nearby town. Gavin too hated the place. He lived through it by making training his foremost priority once again, and when he did have time for recreation, he read books and showered his daughter with letters—though he wrote none to Peggy, he clearly knew she would read what he wrote to Barbara.

At the time the 82nd arrived in North Africa, the campaign there had just ended with the rout of Rommel's resource-starved Afrika Corps. Now that it was over, planning for Husky moved ahead rapidly. Patton, who cared nothing for British sensibilities, seemed delighted with the idea of having parachute troops help clear the resistance by landing inland from his invasion beaches. Even more important was his conviction that Americans should share the limelight, with himself as their leader. He remained intransigent, insisting that two parachute regiments from the 82nd go in behind the beachhead on the night of the invasion.

But what Patton wanted was militarily unrealistic. Any airborne operation would have to be limited because of the severe shortage of troop-carrying aircraft and gliders. At the time, there were less than 400 troop-carrying aircraft available in the entire Allied force—most of them American planes with American pilots—and given these constraints, no more than two parachute regiments could be dropped on that first night.

Yet Sicily would become the first major airborne assault of the war. Both commanders, Ridgway and Browning, wanted their troops to have pride of place in the assault. Their rivalry grew bitter. Ultimately, Eisenhower intervened and allocated aircraft himself, 250 for the Americans and the 150 for British. Browning felt Eisenhower favored the Americans because he had given them more aircraft. Ridgway thought that Eisenhower favored the British because he had given them "our" aircraft. As a result of Eisenhower's decision, on D day, Ridgway could deliver only one regiment, reinforced with a battalion.

Ridgway chose Gavin's 505th, recognizing Gavin's seniority in rank to Tucker and also that Gavin's regiment was in a higher state of readiness. The 505 would make the assault with the help of one additional battalion from the 504th. Gavin would be in command, and with the additional troops, the 505th Parachute Infantry Regiment became the 505th Regimental Combat Team. Their mission was to block counterattacks against Patton's landing beaches. The rest of the 504th would come in on D + 1 or D + 2 and land on drop zones secured by the 505th and 504's already deployed battalion.

The first problem was the shortage of gliders needed to deliver the division's heavy equipment and the 325th in a follow-up landing to reinforce the paratroops. Gliders were difficult to ship and required many hours to assemble. In addition, the British proposed a radical idea that required nearly every glider available. Even though it was then considered nearly suicidal to attempt to land gliders at night, General Hopkinson, commander of the British 1st Airborne Division, presented a plan for glider-borne troops to seize a major bridge, the Ponte Grande, at night, in support of Montgomery. Montgomery liked the idea, and, in spite of the acute glider shortage, it went forward. Every available soldier in Moroccan ports soon found himself working in a massive glider assembly line, and nearly 350 were assembled by invasion time. Glider pilots needed 100 hours flying time to be competent and those available actually averaged only 4.5 hours, but that failed to daunt Hopkinson.

Back in the 82nd, other problems loomed. The first and major crisis was that Patton insisted the invasion be scheduled at night. American pilots had little night training, and Ridgway and Gavin both feared disaster. Nevertheless, even though Gavin predicted that he and his men would be spread all over Sicily, the 82nd anxiously set about coordinating night training drops. The drops proved extremely dangerous and difficult to execute. Given the hardness of the ground and the strange desert winds, the division set a record for parachute injuries on the first drop and soon canceled further practice drops for fear of losing a large portion of the invasion force. Meanwhile, Gavin vehemently disagreed with Ridgway's wish to substitute the lighter mortars for bundle-dropped 75mm pack howitzers. Gavin always sought a technical advantage and felt his men needed the extra firepower and virtually demanded the howitzers. He got his way, but some hard feelings remained.

Gavin's private concerns increased almost daily. He thought the base was vulnerable to German air attack, and he became increasingly concerned with the entire concept of the Sicily mission. He wrote on May 16, "It is clear that the effort will be a very risky and costly one. It is nonetheless a typical parachute operation. The risks are great, but the rewards are greater. Many lives will be lost in a few hours, but in the long run, many lives will be saved. . . . Our training is to start tonight and from now on will be conducted mostly at night. We have one hell of a lot of work and not enough time."

Meanwhile, training for night operations posed many problems. Everything seemed in short supply. And British achievements in Africa led many officers to believe British methods best, and American airborne tactics were now being altered. Argument ensued over minutiae, such as which formation the planes should fly. The Americans favored echeloned formations and the British favored in-line trailing formations. Ultimately, each did it their way, but in the interim there was debate and disharmony, and energy wasted.

To add fuel to the fire, the 509th Parachute Infantry Battalion, which had already been in North Africa for six months and had made a badly dispersed combat jump in support of North African operations, had been grafted onto the 82nd. Its members, though American, seemed to have adopted the superior British view toward other American soldiers and vocally objected to being attached to the 82nd. Tired of hearing about British exploits, Gavin privately commented on May 21, "It is annoying to encounter these officers who because of the recent British successes in this theater must continually extol the merits of the British system, especially contrasted to ours. Even the British admit that with even numbers and material the Germans would not have been beaten. A year ago it was the Germans who everyone wanted to emulate. Compared to the Germans our organization was wrong, our staff was wrong, and fighting technique worse. Now it's the British. It is high time that the American system be given some credit. Our soldiers, especially our parachutists, are as good as any. If they lack anything, it is effective leadership." Gavin feared that the British would succeed in taking over the airborne portion of the invasion. If they did, he would lose the chance he now had to prove what the 505 could do.

In early June, Gavin complained about the difficulties of coordinating aircraft because they were being held under theater control. Ridgway answered his complaint by making him coordinator of the "entire show." In his diary, he moaned, "I will never learn."

Also in early June, Gavin met a New York woman, named Miss Sigman (she later died at Anzio), at a dance held with some army nurses. Though he found her a bit coy, he enjoyed her company.

For the next month, Gavin's diary entries remained a mixture of wishful optimism and dire pessimism while he worked hard to maintain a calm facade for his men. Intrigued with an experimental parachute that could be jumped either static line or free-fall, Gavin decided to try it in the free-fall mode. Unfortunately, instead of using rubber bands to stow the bundled lines when packing the chute, as the designers had specified, someone had substituted string because rubber was in short supply. Gavin's chute malfunctioned and he only got the reserve out at the last possible second. Ridgway, who never understood Gavin's obsession with jumping, promptly grounded Gavin from all further jumps until after the invasion.

Undaunted by the malfunction, Gavin turned his attention back to the invasion and told his battalion commanders exactly what he wanted. "Your priorities are as follows; first get every unit tactically intact to its DZ; second, get every unit tactically intact on Sicily; third, get every man on Sicily. There will be no refusals. Dead or alive, every man will jump. There will be no ships returned unjumped. If no other choice is left, I expect them to jump on Sicily and fight to the last man or the last round of ammunition. Some ships will get lost, but no matter what or where they are [the men] must and will fight. All refusals get either a Purple Heart or a decent burial." In contrast to those spirited words, he commented a few days later, "This goddamn stuff is getting serious. . . . Talked to Bill Yarborough today. He asked me if I expected to get back to the States from this alive. Told him I didn't. I shouldn't do that. Optimism is a characteristic of any commander worth a damn. Still the picture looks bad. As a matter of fact, I actually expect to live through it, probably and very likely wounded but not killed. I will have to be completely killed to be stopped." Then, after all his trepidation and gloomy predictions, he went on to finish this entry with, "We are in for one hell of a fight. I love the prospects but feel as scared as I did on my first jump. It is going to be exciting."

In training, Gavin had the 505 march long distances with their full complement of ammunition, grenades, and other equipment. Few had realized how heavy their combat loads would be, and he swore that he would continue this in the future, so the men would grow accustomed to the weight.

On June 10, at Gavin's insistence, he and his staff successfully flew the proposed air route for the Sicily drop. Antiaircraft fire was light, but en route, Gavin endured his first air raid at one of their stops. He noted it in his diary, saying, "At about 10:05 we were hit with an air raid of nice proportions, thus breaking a record of years of never having heard a hostile shot."

It was also the first time he had ever seen British combat troops up close, and he gave them high praise. "They are splendid-looking soldiers, tough, tanned, clean, hair cut, etc. I would be the last to say this of British troops, but they are at this writing the best looking troops that I have ever had the pleasure of seeing. The British attitude was very interesting and amusing. Compared to us, they are like professionals and we amateurs. We are sweating, tense, trying hard at everything we attempt. They are relaxed, appearing indifferent at times, no pressure, and everything seems to be getting done in tip-top shape." After the flight, he was optimistic once again. "The DZ's are O.K. and we will hit them. We are going to do a good job."

Gavin believed in intelligence and rehearsal almost to the point of obsession. For years, he had been studying the German Army. He thought he knew it as well as any man alive. In the weeks leading up to the invasion date, he also pored over the maps of the projected drop zones in Sicily. Now he intended to use it all to his advantage. In preparation for the jump, Gavin had his men set up mock targets similar to their actual objectives, and he increased his presence among his troops, leaving as many administrative tasks as he could to his staff. Perhaps the men were bored, having waited so long to get to combat, but in the last two weeks before their deployment, they grew tense. Gavin wrote his daughter, "This afternoon we are, among other things, having a sniper contest. Fun. These youngsters are getting to be good shots. Regrettably, in the past few days they have practiced on some menacing looking Arabs. It makes them mad to get shot and we should stop it. It is difficult to sell international good will to a private soldier."

As he made final preparations, he had three battalion commanders in the 505 he trusted a great deal: Arthur F. Gorham of the 1st Battalion, Mark Alexander of the 2nd, and Edward C. Krause of the 3rd. Also Charles Kouns, commanding the 3rd Battalion of the 504th. All of them had proven themselves in Gavin's eyes—though he had some reservations about Krause, who had always been the most "gung-ho" of the group. Krause had his men shave their heads on the eve of the invasion and thought the other battalions should follow their example. Gavin worried over Krause's almost too "hard-core" attitude, but thought he would be a good fighter.

Yet, with the problems that had already surfaced in the weeks leading up to D day, the airborne portion of Husky had a future that promised disaster. Clay Blair described it: "Seldom in modern warfare had there been such an ill-prepared force on the eve of battle. The Americans, with virtually no night jump training, were to be delivered by pilots with the least experience in combat and who were grossly undertrained in formation flying and navigation. . . . The stage was set for a military disaster."

For the troopers of the 505th Regimental Combat Team, the road to Sicily began at Kairouan in Tunisia, more than 1,000 miles across the top of North Africa from their old home at Oujda in French Morocco, where they had been transported to board their planes at sunset, 10 P.M. on July 9, 1943. Simultaneously, a massive convoy corkscrewed west through the Mediterranean toward the invasion beaches, against heavy seas and high winds. Their mission (as described in the 82nd Airborne Division after-action report) was to land during the night D − 1/D in an area north and east of Gela, capture and secure high ground in that area, disrupt communications and movement of reserves during the night, be attached to the 1st Infantry Division effective H − 1 hours on D day, and assist the 1st Infantry Division in capturing and securing the landing field at Ponte Olivo. Colonel James M. Gavin was in overall command of the combat team and, in addition to his 505th P.I.R., he also had attached the 3rd Battalion of the 504th P.I.R., the 456th Parachute Field Artillery Battalion; Company B, 307th Airborne Engineer Battalion, a signal detachment, a medical detachment, and other assorted personnel to include naval gunfire forward observers. Their planned drop zones were located just north and south of an important and heavily defended road junction 7 miles east of Gela.

Before they left, each man received what was called "a poop sheet," which contained a personal message from their commander:

SOLDIERS OF THE 505TH COMBAT TEAM

Tonight you embark upon a combat mission for which our people and the free people of the world have been waiting for two years.

You will spearhead the landing of an American Force upon the island of SICILY. Every preparation has been made to eliminate the element of chance. You have been given the means to do the job and you are backed by the largest assemblage of air power in the world's history.

The eyes of the world are upon you. The hopes and prayers of every American go with you. . . .

James M. Gavin

The darkened planes, as they took off that night, appeared pregnant in the moonlight, their bellies hung thick with equipment bundles. The troopers waited with faces blackened with burnt cork, uncomfortable and laden like dark beasts of burden. Strapped in parachute harnesses supporting both main and reserve parachutes, they carried their full complement of ammunition, grenades, knives, gas masks, rifles, entrenching tools, rations, bayonets, ropes, canteens, flashlights, and other assorted equipment. Many carried explosive charges, and some had a ponderous anti-tank weapon known as the bazooka. All of them felt nervous. Many of them suffered dysentery. None of them knew exactly what fate held for them in the next few hours. All of them hoped to return. None of them knew that the Hermann Göring division awaited them. To protect code-breaking security, higher command neglected to warn them about the panzers.

Because the pilots had little experience, the air plan was simple. Flying east from Kairouan, the pilots would continue in a straight line until they sighted a powerful illuminated signal from Malta designed to tell them to turn. From there, they would swing north to Sicily. If all went according to plan, they would sight the Malta turning beacon on their starboard (right) side.

Gavin himself appeared calm as he boarded his aircraft. There was little left to say, and he had pushed worry past him now. He wanted some quiet time to himself on the plane, yet even before takeoff he had two interruptions. First, an airman stuck his head in the door to inform the young colonel that the winds on Sicily were blowing at around 35 miles per hour. That was 20 miles an hour faster than was considered safe for training jumps, but this was not a training jump. There was nothing he could do about it now.

Right behind the airman came a man from staff, staggering under the weight of a bulging barracks bag. The man informed Gavin that the bag contained the proper paperwork for the handling of prisoners of war.

Gavin said, "O.K.," and waved him good-bye. The plane taxied down the runway, and Gavin pulled out a book to read. Soon after taking off and reaching the ocean, he had his S-1, Captain Alfred Ireland, make the paper-laden bag the first jumper to exit that night.

Though no one now knows what was on Gavin's mind that night in the darkened C-47, some of the men who flew with him had some indications. He talked little during the flight, but before taking off, he had two concerns. The first was that the planes would not hold formation and get them to Sicily. The second was that his men would not be able to regroup on the drop zones. Gavin also wanted stealth on the drop zones. Before departure, he had given instructions that no one would refuse to jump—if they did, they would be thrown out anyway. Also that, in the darkness, men should favor the knife over their other, noisier weapons. He wanted these instructions carried out.

Sometime after taking off, Gavin put down his book and searched for the lights of Malta. He never saw them. Keeping the alarm off his face, he walked back to his old friend Bill Ryder, who was along as an observer and a spare battalion commander in case one was needed, and said, "I think we're going to have some problems here. I think we're off course. Bill, I want you to look after Beaver Thompson [a *Chicago Tribune* reporter on the plane who was to jump in to cover the story] on the drop zone. You know he has no weapon, so you look after him and get him up to me as soon as you can."

Ryder reassured Gavin he would take care of Thompson, and the young colonel went back to looking out the windows for signs of something recognizable. He never saw anything. Due to the high winds they swept past the important landfall at Malta completely.

Finally, the pilot decided he had flown far enough and turned in the direction of what he hoped would be Sicily. About an hour later they spotted the flash and the smoke of preinvasion bombing in the distance. At least, Gavin thought, they had found Sicily. By then he had ordered the jumpers to prepare and stand hooked up, with all combat gear, in case they had to jump from a damaged plane. They waited that way for some minutes. First out the door, Gavin leapt powerfully into the night. The prop turbulence caught him, then the brutal opening shock snatched and jerked him, and a comfortable silence replaced the throbbing noise of the aircraft. He had no time to enjoy it. He saw the ground coming up quickly and felt a sharp pang in one leg. The landing hurt—the weatherman had been right about the winds. They had slammed him down hard. Gavin shook himself and found his leg hurt, but after he freed himself of his parachute harness, he succeeded in walking, so he ignored the pain.

There is a strange high after a parachute landing. He still wasn't sure he was on Sicily, but he was alive, and battle loomed imminent. His war had begun. Years later he remembered it as the most significant moment of his life and said, "Combat—at last. After a lifetime of preparation, I was on the threshold of battle. As a young second lieutenant I joined the infantry out of the conviction that its combat role would be a decisive one. I liked troops and I liked the infantry; by joining the parachute infantry I could get as close to combat as one would wish."

It would get harder than even Gavin anticipated. Since he had been first out the door, he knew his troops should be scattered behind him, so he immediately strode back in the direction the plane had come, looking for them. He soon found his S-3, Major Ben Vandervoort, and his S-1, Captain Ireland, who also had a bad leg. From there, the three searched for any other friendly faces in the darkness, found a few, and in short order had collected a band of about twenty, some of whom had been injured by rough landings. Ryder, who was trying to find a now lost Beaver Thompson, was missing with the reporter. Years later, he recalled, "That was how I came to spend my first night in combat running from bush to bush calling, 'Beaver, Beaver.' "

It slowly dawned on Gavin that from all indications, his band was isolated. He suddenly realized how very wrong his situation was. The area in which he had landed was quiet, but he saw tracer fire and explosions in the distance to the northwest. Wherever the bulk of the regiment he meant to lead was located, it clearly was not here. He had no idea where he was, he had no real command, and the only signs of combat he saw were at least 20 miles away through what he assumed was hostile territory teeming with enemy. He did the only thing he could think of for a soldier to do, he took off on foot in bright moonlight toward the distant gunfire.

He had to get to the scene of the battle—wherever it was. This was his first chance at combat, he had a regiment to lead, and he was determined to lead it. Always a vigorous marcher, Gavin took off cross-country fast, avoiding the roads in favor of olive groves surrounded by ancient stone walls. An hour later, he saw his first live enemy soldier.

His little band had just come to a narrow dirt road. They had paused behind a stone wall at its edge in preparation for crossing it, when suddenly a lone Italian soldier in baggy pants approached, whistling to himself in the moonlight. When the whistling got close, Gavin put an eye up, pointed his carbine and said, "Alto!" The Italian stopped.

Vandervoort charged from a break in the wall with a knife in one hand and a .45 in the other, rasping, "I'll take care of him!" Gavin did not exactly know what Vandervoort meant, so he responded, "No, let's get the hell out of the middle of the road. Let's get him over into the shadows and maybe we can get some information out of him." As he later wrote, at that time he still felt "some doubt as to whether we were in Sicily, Italy, or the Balkans, although the odds strongly favored the first." He hoped to find out from his prisoner.

Surrounding the soldier, they tried questioning him on which direction Palermo or Syracuse lay. But the Germans had spread many paratrooper atrocity stories among the Italians, and the now wild-eyed man looked too petrified to speak. Vandervoort interceded with another, "I'll take care of him." He holstered his pistol, grabbed his knife, and reached for the man's fly. The Italian, convinced that all the stories he had heard were true, groaned, "Mama mia, Mama mia!"

When the knife reached his crotch, he screamed a scream, Gavin remembered, that "could be heard all the way to Rome," deftly grabbed the blade of Vandervoort's knife, and pulled the American to the ground. Seconds later, the now bloody-handed Italian was running up the road like an Olympic sprinter. Gavin described it: "I don't know how he did it, but one second he was with us and the next he was gone. I was madder than hell. I asked Vandervoort, 'What in hell did you think you were doing?' "

The S-3 remained mute.

Figuring they would now be beset with angry Italians on all sides, Gavin led his group off into the night as fast as they could move. His troopers did their best to keep up in spite of their jump injuries, but most proved unable to stand the pace. Dawn revealed only six of them left in Gavin's patrol; nevertheless, he pressed on.

Daylight brought serious trouble. Lacking a covered approach, Gavin led his people to an exposed hilltop. At the crest, bullets flew from the scrub brush to their front. Gavin fell flat. Realizing that the only way out of the situation was to fire and maneuver to real cover, he tried his carbine. It jammed. He cleared the weapon and tried again. It jammed again. To his left he saw Vandervoort had the same problem. Gavin fired single shot. Captain Ireland's Thompson submachine gun, however, worked, and he cut down a nattily clad officer, apparently Italian, who made the mistake of standing. Lying by the brush, Gavin saw his lead trooper ahead, already dead in the first volley. He had been nearly on top of the enemy's concealed position. Mortar fire suddenly fell among them, and with it, Gavin realized they had made contact with at least a platoon-sized element in a defensive posture. They had to get out of the kill zone. He ordered the others to retreat while he covered them. They worked their way back over the crest, then covered Gavin as he low-crawled behind them. Now in safe defilade, the little band moved back down the hill—fast.

Still determined to find the rest of his command, Gavin and his group circled around the hill where they had met the Italian ambush, thankful the Italians had not pursued as the Germans surely would have. Their situation grew more precarious. Gavin heard the sounds of spasmodic fire from several directions, and he could not tell by the sound who was doing the firing. With only five men, and two worthless weapons, he had to avoid enemy contact, but Sicily's open country left them highly visible. Realizing that he needed darkness to move effectively, he ordered his men to stop in the cover of well-concealed irrigation ditches. Years later, he described his desperate mood, "I wanted to survive until dark and then strike across country again to the combat team objective. It was the high ground north and east of Gela, and there, with the help of God, I hoped to find troopers and an enemy to fight."

In his ditch, he should have slept, but he did not. It was one of the darkest moments of his life. Last night's exhilaration at entering combat had died. A lot was at stake for Gavin then. On a personal level, he had botched his first chance. It was a bitter blow for a man who wished above all to prove that the paratroop concept was more than a gallant abstraction. Gavin and his four parched troopers helplessly awaited sunset.

When it came, they resumed their exhausting march. He recalled, "It was a relief to be moving instead of sitting and worrying." Soon they found a small detachment of wounded 505 men under the command of Lieutenant Al Kronheim. The men could not move, but they could hand over their functioning M-1 Garands (Gavin kept one of those Garands for the duration of the war), and Gavin gave them all the tiny battle group's morphine Syrettes. The group moved on. Finally, about 2:30 A.M., a sentry challenged them from a 45th Division outpost. They had reached American lines 5 miles southeast of Vittoria. He had picked up some stragglers, and had eight troopers with him then.

In Vittoria, Gavin commandeered an unguarded jeep, packed his men aboard, and went in search of troopers rumored to be nearby, moving toward Gela. What he found was a large portion of the 505's 3rd Battalion in foxholes in a tomato field of no particular tactical value, just awakening as he arrived. He found "Cannonball" Krause, their commander, sitting on the side of a foxhole with his feet dangling. He too had just awakened. Gavin asked what they were doing.

Krause explained that he had landed near there, organized the men, and had about 250 present.

Gavin curtly asked what Krause had done about his objective. Krause replied that he hadn't yet done a thing.

Gavin ordered Krause to get the men up and moving toward their objective, took a platoon of 307th engineers commanded by Lieutenant Ben L. Wechsler and led them off in the direction of Gela. No sooner had the little column rounded a bend in the road, than a motorcycle with a sidecar occupied by a German officer zipped into view and screeched to a halt. Surrounded, the officer threw up his hands, shouted that he was a medical officer, and demanded passage. Since there were grenades in the sidecar, Gavin didn't buy the story, and the first live German soldiers he had ever seen went rearward under armed guard. Another mile down the road took Gavin to a railroad junction, equipped with a small cottage for the crossing keeper. Just ahead jutted a 100-foot-high ridge covered with burnt yellow grass and surrounded by olive orchards.

Years later, Gavin explained that at the time, he was not sure if Biazza Ridge was tactically important or not; at the time he scarcely noted the name; but since its height dominated the surrounding territory, he ordered Wechsler to deploy his platoon and seize the ridge. Suddenly, bullets whizzed from the hilltop. Ignoring them, the platoon formed a skirmish line and moved forward through the olive groves. The firing grew in intensity. Gavin sent a messenger back to Krause, ordering him to bring his men forward fast and to be ready for serious contact.

With Gavin moving among the troopers, the platoon took the ridge, but once on top, they regretted that they had done so. The German force had been pushed down the back side of the hill, but they were supported by a much larger element from below. The platoon now faced fire from several directions. Men had fallen during the advance. Others fell now, even as they tried to dig in. Leaves and olive branches snapped from the trees as if mowed by a scythe. Survivors remembered the air being full of the sound of swarming bees—only the bees were machine-gun and rifle bullets. Wechsler fell, badly hit. The men dug harder and faster, but the ground proved too rocky to dig even a hasty firing position. The platoon could no longer maneuver and was pinned down. Gavin crawled rearward to fetch help. The situation looked desperate, and Krause's men needed to come on—now.

Once clear of the worst of the firing, Gavin crossed the railroad junction at a run. Still no sign of Krause. Momentarily Gavin met Major William Hagen, the battalion executive officer. "Where's Krause?" he demanded.

Hagen shrugged and responded that Krause had gone to the rear to apprise the 45th Division of the situation but that the battalion was close behind. Gavin was angry. To him, the only place for a commander was with his troops. Anything else was unacceptable. Any private soldier could have served as a messenger. Now Gavin gambled. He suspected the units on the hill to be German; what their strength really was, or what their intentions might be, he could not tell. One thing was clear. The enemy's actions proved the hill was key terrain, and he had decided that the Germans were not going to have it. Confident his troops could face whatever was there, he told Hagen to order his battalion to drop their packs and deploy to throw the Germans off the ridge. Hagan had roughly 250 paratroopers, and along the way, they had also picked up a platoon from the 45th Division, part of a company from the 180th Infantry Regiment, and a few sailors who had come ashore during the landings.

Now the men of the 3rd Battalion proved what they could do when properly led. Seeing the desperate situation of the beleaguered engineer platoon on the forward slope, they came through the olive trees fast and hard, delivering all the fire their M-1's could give. Some of them fell, but they continued to come. Soon their ranks broke over the crest. Like the well-trained infantry they were, they continued attacking through their objective, over the German positions, and down the reverse slope in the precise manner of a textbook assault. Then they wavered and stopped.

The forward slope of the ridge became a firestorm. This was not a patrol, not a platoon, and not a company. This was a powerful German force, and the paratroops, for all their élan, realized they were seriously outgunned. Large-caliber mortar and 88mm artillery fire ripped the hill.

Even worse, Tiger tanks rumbled into view, spraying machine-gun fire and more 88mm rounds. Gavin ordered his men back to the reverse slope, where they dug in as best they could in the hard shale surface.

Tactically, Gavin's situation could not have been more precarious. The first prisoners interrogated revealed these Germans were a unit of the Hermann Göring Division which had been driving toward the sea. Suddenly Gavin understood the situation. By luck and a fine eye for terrain, he had happened onto the 45th Division's exposed flank. What he had before him was a German column bent on exploiting the gap. He now held the hill; however, the hill itself could easily be out-flanked and hit from the rear.

Gavin counted his resources: he had two 81mm mortars, a few engineers in reserve, and bazookas for the Tigers. Bad news came fast. The only real antitank weapon they had were the bazookas, and although he had been told that they would stop German armor, they did not. Bazooka men risked the fire on the forward slope to take on the Tigers, but their rounds only bounced off the front plates of the tanks. Gavin realized that when the Tigers came, they would smash through his force easily. They hadn't charged up the slope yet, and he wondered why. He felt thankful for his luck. Then more luck came his way. A 75mm pack howitzer from the 456th Parachute Artillery arrived and then another one. Gavin knew they couldn't stop the Tigers head-on, but by placing them on the reverse slope, they could be aimed to shatter the thin-skinned undersides of the tanks when they reared up to breach the stone wall that ran across the ridge line. He positioned the guns to have maximum effect. Then he told his troopers what he wanted. The howitzers would do what they could with the tanks, and the bazookas that remained could try side or rear shots when they came through, but his infantrymen would remain in their positions no matter what. He knew that after the tanks came on, his troopers would need to confront the German infantry trailing them. Gavin knew that the tanks would not long survive without their infantry support, so one way or another he reasoned he could end the fight here.

He interrogated some prisoners through an interpreter. They confirmed his suspicions. This column's mission was indeed to break through American lines to smash the beachhead. Surprisingly, several of them complimented his men. They wanted to know if they had been fighting the Japanese before this. They had never seen troops fight this hard before. In their experience, unsupported infantry always scattered in the face of Tigers and concentrated fire.

And concentrated the fire proved to be. German shelling increased in intensity as the day wore on and they brought more batteries to bear. The concussion of the shells grew so severe that Gavin found his prostrate body bouncing into the air with the hits. He placed his palms flat on the ground in the push-up position and held himself inches off the earth to absorb the shock. Then the Luftwaffe entered the fray, and Messerschmitts dove down from the clouds. The troopers braced themselves for the bombs they expected to come, but none did. Instead, they fell on the unoccupied cottage by the railroad junction to their rear. Gavin smiled. The pilots must have thought that the command headquarters was in that cottage. In most cases, they would have been right, but this was not most cases. He and his staff sweated among his troopers' foxholes while the planes returned several times that day and blasted the cottage. No bombs hit near Gavin.

The continuous shelling brought more and more casualties, and Gavin saw the situation grow increasingly desperate. Where was the help Krause had gone rearward for? Some troopers who had heard there were elements of the 505 in this direction had wandered in; however, they had no word from the 45th Division, and they had no radios with which to contact them. Captain Ireland volunteered to go to the rear to find out what was going on.

Gavin spent most of the afternoon moving among his men to check their positions. Then a Tiger poked its 88 from between two buildings to their front, inching forward enough to bring the gun to bear. The artillerymen decided to chance taking on the tank—even though they had no armor-piercing ammunition—and quickly dragged one of their 75mm pieces forward. Just as they had set it up, the Tiger fired and shattered the earth before them. Gavin, standing to their left rear, found himself knocked heavily to the ground by the concussion. The troopers ran, then steadied themselves, and manned their gun once again. Their first shot hit the Tiger. Though it did not disable it, the tank backed to its concealed position behind the building.

To their left, Gavin heard other Tigers growling their way through the undergrowth. Expecting the main assault, he turned to dig a firing position. Then two troopers, armed only with rifles, suddenly charged up the back side of the hill, driving an Italian armored personnel carrier. They asked Gavin's permission to drive the carrier at the German lines. They had the idea that they could scare the Germans into thinking that the Americans too had armored support. The young colonel advised them against it; they went ahead anyway. Gavin watched the vehicle flop over the spine of the ridge, to be almost immediately shattered by a direct hit. The two dead men inside remained there for the remainder of the day, an obscene reminder that this was no exercise.

Krause arrived, obviously panicked. Gavin saw tears running down his cheeks as he told Gavin that his battalion was finished. Gavin calmly told him that they would stay there and fight, using the infantry without support if need be. Sensing that Krause was badly distraught, he sent him to the rear. Gavin would continue to command the battalion himself.

Just before evening set in, a naval ensign with a radio arrived to call in naval gunfire. Now the situation turned. Two hours after the naval gunfire began falling, Lieutenant Harold H. Swingler, a former professional boxer, brought up a large number of troopers he had collected elsewhere, and six Sherman tanks came on right behind him in response to Ireland's calls for support. Gavin decided to counterattack. Every able man joined in, cooks and clerks included. Buoyed by their tank support and the fierce barrage from the fleet, the paratroops surged forward and down the hill. The Germans gave as they closed. Two hundred yards behind the original German positions Lieutenant Swingler discovered a Tiger with its crew standing outside it, not expecting an American assault to reach them. Swingler tossed a grenade. The Germans died where they were, and the 505 captured its first German tank. The attack rolled forward. Soon the troopers stood among German machine-gun pits. Most of their occupants had already run. Next, they reached the mortar pits that had been raining shells on them all day—their crews had run too. The Germans, Tigers and all, withdrew under the weight of the assault. Gavin was surprised. He had expected them to stand. Instead, when his troopers had closed, the Germans had handed them a dramatic victory. Despite his exhaustion, he was exhilarated. He had just won his first battle.

Gavin remained up front with his troopers until satisfied that they were well dug in and ready for a counterattack. Then, he wearily moved his command post off the ridge to an olive grove beneath it. There he dug a fighting position and lay down. While digging it, he noticed tremendous firing break out in the direction of the beach. It didn't involve him, so he continued with his labors. The ridge, now known as Biazza Ridge, remained in 505 hands, and Gavin, content that it would stay that way, finally slept. When he awoke, he felt hot sunlight.

.   .   .

The paratroopers' story in the invasion of Sicily is a diffuse tale. There were some large battles, like Biazza Ridge; however, much of what happened in Sicily took place in small-scale engagements, where tiny bands of widely scattered troopers took their own initiative and engaged enemy units any way they could. Gavin's part of the overall battle was only one example. There are many others.

As he woke that morning after the Biazza Ridge action, Gavin could reflect that his ad hoc battle plan seemed to be working. The men were to engage and disrupt the enemy through any means they had at hand. For the most part, they followed those instructions. All over the island, American paratroops cut phone lines, ambushed patrols, and sprang from cover on an unsuspecting enemy. Often, Gavin found his men had no idea where they were, nor even if the invasion had been a success. Yet, alone, scared, tired, and possessed of limited resources, they fought on anyway. Many of their stories can never be told, for many died in isolation, but their actions impressed the Germans, who reported they had been hit by several paratroop divisions.

The stand on Biazza Ridge proved much more than a trial by fire for American paratroopers; it was crucial to saving the invasion. Major General Paul Conrath, the commander of the Hermann Göring Division, had logically positioned his force on the night of the invasion near Caltagirone. It was far enough from the sea to avoid naval gunfire, yet it was within easy reach of potential landing beaches. The division had already rehearsed what to do if an invasion came. Conrath organized two main battle groups or Kampfgruppen for a pincer counterattack to flank the invasion beaches. On the right, one battle group was to attack through Niscemi across the Ponte Olivio airfield and over high ground known as Piano Lupo to smash the beachhead. The left group had the same objective but would attack over Biazza Ridge. Gavin's stand ended the left group's hopes of breaking through and, the night before, others of his unit had destroyed the right thrust, when scattered troopers who had Piano Lupo as an objective waged a desperate struggle against the panzers.

Unknown to the German commander, Gavin's regiment had been scheduled to jump directly in the path of his right thrust, and some had made it. The haphazard drop itself was a blow to the defenders. The little knots paratroopers who missed drop zones and struggled on in the dark often appeared to the Germans to be proof of a massive paratroop landing. It was chance that placed Gavin and his men on Biazza Ridge that day, and it was chance that spread other troopers all over the region, cutting every phone wire they could find. Conrath had wanted to jump off as soon as the landings began but with all the phone lines cut, he faced major communication delays, and the counterattack began late. The German right column was repeatedly hit from the air and scattered as it moved toward the beaches. Allied planes devastated its troops, and its lower-level commanders were inexperienced and sometimes panicked.

And not all the Americans were spread like crumbs in the wind. Some landings went according to the letter of the plan. Landing close to his correct drop zone, Lieutenant Peter J. Eaton, of the 3rd Battalion of the 504th, had organized an element of nearly platoon size. Then they spotted two Italian vehicles pulling antitank weapons. After ambushing them and capturing the guns, they mined the road, dug in the guns, and waited for anything else that might come by. When Conrath's men came down that road with a tank in the lead, the paratroops knocked out the tank and scattered the column.

Lieutenant Colonel Arthur "Hardnose" Gorham, the tall taciturn leader of the 1st Battalion of the 505th, also landed near his correct drop zone but without most of his men. He and one of his company commanders, Captain Edward M. Sayre, scoured the area and collected about one hundred troopers. He had them dig into a hillside that covered the Niscemi-Gela road. Just after dawn, a German armored column heading toward the beaches appeared on Gorham's road. Gorham signaled hold fire. When the Germans closed, he hit them hard from the side. When given a flank shot, the bazookas worked reasonably well. They quickly destroyed or disabled four tanks. The German infantry, trapped in the open without support, were slaughtered by Gorham's hidden guns. The survivors fled pell-mell. A German retreat turned into a full-scale rout. Satisfied he had halted the German counterattack, Gorham promptly moved out his men to what had been his primary objective: fortifying Piano Lupo.

Later, Gavin wrote of Gorham and his small band, "Actually, Colonel Gorham and his small group of troopers and the lieutenants of the 504 accomplished all the missions of the entire regimental combat team. It was a remarkable performance, and I know of nothing like it that occurred at any time during the war. Sadly, in the fighting the following morning, Colonel Gorham engaged a tank with a bazooka and he himself was killed."

After the failures of the first day, a furious General Conrath decided to renew the attack with more vigor. This time, the panzers took Piano Lupo. However, their moment had passed. The veteran 1st Infantry Division lay in wait for them, Patton himself called in naval gunfire on the column, and their assault forces scattered. The paratroopers had bought the seaborne invaders the extra twenty-four hours they needed.

Elsewhere on Sicily on jump night, another element of the 82nd found its maiden battle. Mark Alexander, commander of the 505's 2nd Battalion, told Lieutenant Colonel Cerny, commander of the 64th Troop Carrier Wing, that his main worry was that the paratroops would be scattered in the winds. An intense man who tolerated no nonsense, Alexander told Cerny, "If you do nothing else on D day, make darn sure you drop us together."

He had this on his mind when he boarded his plane that night, and he watched for all the checkpoints carefully en route to the drop zone. But like many others he had seen nothing but moonlit ocean. Then suddenly the word came from the pilot to get the men ready. The stick shuffled tensely into line; he placed himself in the door. The green light came on and Alexander felt pressure from the men behind him, blindly pushing forward. Grabbing the supports about the door tightly, he held his men back. Something was very wrong here. The green light was on, but all he saw below was ocean. Shouting commands, he forced his way back into the airplane, unhooked his static line and ran forward to the cockpit. An embarrassed pilot explained that they had been anxious, that the navigation was flawed, that the estimated time had run. Alexander cursed him out.

Finally, with ground below, the green light came on again, and this time they jumped. As soon as Alexander leaped out, he realized there had been another mistake. The powerful wind grabbed his chute, and when he looked down, he saw with shock that he was about to land. They had been flying too low. He landed hard, then the wind picked him up and tossed him against a stone wall. He felt a blow and fell unconscious. When he awoke, tracer fire from five pillboxes streaked about the drop zone. But Alexander's men did what is often considered a military impossibility: They formed under fire. By dawn, they had taken the pillboxes, but with twelve dead and many wounded, and they were pained at the discovery that these were the wrong pillboxes. They too had been badly misdropped.

With dawn, Alexander had some good news. The troop carrier, by the merest chance, had accomplished what he asked; he had 425 soldiers ready to fight, including elements of the 456th Parachute Field Artillery and one of their 75mm pack howitzers. By midmorning, their number had swelled to around 525. But though they had been dropped together, they were 25 miles east of Gela. The reason they had been dropped too low was that the ground here was 250 feet higher than the correct drop zone. They had been dropped in high winds at 300 to 400 hundred feet, resulting in many jump injuries.

Now Alexander made a decision. He remembered from briefings that an enemy shore battery was located at Marina Di Ragusa, a small town on the coast not far from where they had landed. He decided to attack it on the march back toward Gela, but on approach, found it to be a strong concrete structure. He directed the crew of his lone howitzer to shell it. Armed with only thirty rounds, the gunners began to pound the structure with high explosive. Luckily, white flags fluttered above it, and the Italian garrison surrendered just before Alexander was to launch an assault.

Knowing his men were exhausted from the all-night battle with the pillboxes, Alexander had his battalion dig in for the night. Then, as darkness fell, they took sporadic sniper fire. A young lieutenant knew Morse code and signaled a British cruiser off the coast with a flashlight, requesting naval gunfire. With naval shells whistling overhead, the snipers soon gave up. The next morning, Alexander formed up his troops and began the long march to Gela. En route, they took the town of Santa Croce Camerina against light resistance, a free gift to the 45th Division whose objective it was. They made it to Gela that night.

The paratroopers were faithfully gathering, painfully walking to their objectives. But command jitters had begun almost immediately after the first drop. Soon after daylight on July 10, D day, Ridgway landed by boat on the 45th Division's beachhead. He made his way immediately to Major General Troy Middleton's corps headquarters, hungry for any information on the fate of his troops. Middleton had none for him. No contact with Gavin had been made. Ridgway was concerned. Gavin, who had landed some twelve hours before, should have made some radio contact by now. Desperate for news, Ridgway got a jeep and an armed bodyguard from Middleton and drove to the front lines. Finding nothing there, he went through the front lines. Soon a Messerschmitt came after his jeep.

He hit the dirt, and the Messerschmitt gave up. Now frantic, Ridgway continued to drive forward into what should have been enemy-held territory. He found no enemy but did find a paratroop captain with a broken leg, propped against a tree, but the captain knew nothing. Ridgway pushed on but located only stragglers—none of whom knew where Gavin might be or the fate of the mass of the paratroops. Fearing half of his division might have been destroyed, he returned to the beach and advised Patton to cancel the 504th's drop, which had been planned for that evening. Patton agreed.

On the next day, the 11th, Conrath's panzers launched their furious attacks on the beaches, and Patton demanded the rest of Ridgway's force. Ridgway followed orders, and the remainder of the 504th took off that night into a major tragedy.

Axis bombers had been pounding Gela all day on the 11th (twenty-six raids were counted), and the antiaircraft crews ashore and on the ships were jumpy. Ridgway, General Bradley, commanding II Corps, and several other commanders therefore made doubly sure to notify all naval units that paratroopers would be flying over that night. With more favorable weather than the night before, good results were expected. At the time of the appointed drop, Ridgway waited on the drop zone, ready to greet his men. Five minutes ahead of schedule, the first planes arrived and paratroopers spilled out right on target. Then things went wrong. Two Axis bombers flew over the fleet and dropped their bombs. Right behind them came the transports at the same altitude. Somewhere, on one of the ships or ashore (no one really knows to this day), a nervous gunner fired a burst at one of the transport planes. Every other gunner in the Gela area followed his example, and suddenly the sky filled with crisscrossing tracers and exploding flak. Mark Alexander, then marching with his battalion on the coast road just east of Gela saw clearly the Allied markings on the C-47s in the navy's searchlights, but the sailors kept on shooting. Of the 145 C-47s approaching, 60 took serious hits. Twenty-three planes crashed into Sicily or the sea. The slow, low-flying aircraft were perfect targets. Powerless to stop the fusillade, Ridgway could do little but look on as planeload after planeload of his men fell out of the sky. Reuban Tucker, the 504th's commander, had been in the third echelon when the firestorm broke. His pilot had been unable to find the drop zone in the smoke and flames. Tucker ordered him to turn the plane around and to keep trying until he could. The pilot found the drop zone, and Tucker jumped safely. Over 1,000 holes were counted in that airplane.

Others proved not so lucky. Bull Keerans, the assistant division commander, had been in one plane, not to jump but to see his men off. He perished when his aircraft crashed into the sea. Tucker's executive officer, Leslie G. Freeman, survived by the merest chance. His plane took several direct hits and spun out of control. The troopers inside, flattened by centrifugal force holding them in the plane, were unable to jump. The plane crash-landed, and stunned men crawled out of the wreckage, eleven of fifteen wounded.

Finally, the slaughter ended. The drop, like Gavin's, had been scattered due to the friendly fire. The toll from the friendly fire was first hushed up and later never accurately fixed. Estimates held that 229 paratroopers and 90 air crewmen became casualties; 81 paratroopers and 60 airmen died. Recriminations continued for weeks. Ultimately, higher command blamed the fact that the Germans had dropped paratroops near British lines that day, and a German bomber attack had just preceded the arrival of the 504, confusing antiaircraft gunners in the fleet and ashore.

Ridgway was heartbroken, but he decided that there was little to be gained by fixing blame. Rather, he concentrated on the lessons that could be learned from the mistake: not to fly over anxious invasion fleet gunners again if possible, or to do so only if a strict cease-fire order remained in effect during the appointed drop time.

The next morning, July 12, Ridgway had to report to Patton that of the more than 5,000 paratroopers who had jumped into Sicily, he had but 400 under his operational control. From the point of view of airborne command, the drops had been catastrophic. He still did not know about Biazza Ridge and other critical actions his men had fought. The 325th was scheduled to drop by glider that night. After what happened to the 504th, Ridgway canceled the operation.

When Gavin awoke in his foxhole on the morning of the 12th, Biazza Ridge was still in 505 hands and all was quiet. Then he noticed his leg hurt. His shin was cut, red, and swollen. After being treated at a nearby aid station, he was informed he would get a Purple Heart. It embarrassed him.

Returning to the ridge, he saw the unburied bodies of more than fifty dead paratroops scattered on the stony field. In addition to the dead, Gavin lost more than one hundred wounded. That day, they patrolled forward but found little to report, and General Bradley issued orders to limit their movement until the big picture became clearer. On the morning of the 13th, Gavin met General Patton to discuss the operation.

Gavin liked Patton. That morning the old cavalryman stood on high ground overlooking the beaches with his ivory-handled pistols on his hips. He could only be American, and unique at that. Patton offered Gavin a drink from a large silver flask and beamed energy. He said he planned to make history in Sicily. The British were too much in the limelight. To Patton, the time had come after the landing. When his forces had stabilized the beachhead, Patton savagely counterattacked the Hermann Göring Division and continued to press inland. Unwilling to be relegated to protecting Montgromery's rear, the infuriated Patton flew to Tunis to confront Alexander over the Seventh Army's role in Sicily, and having won that political flight, he never let the Germans on the island rest again. If Montgomery was going to drive to Messina, then Patton would take Palermo.

The pursuit toward Palermo, some 200 miles, was made by the 2nd Armored Division, the two regiments of the 82nd, and elements of the 9th Infantry Division that had been consolidated into what was called the 39th Regimental Combat Team. It was an easy test compared to Biazza Ridge. Veteran German troops had been brought to the east to oppose Montgomery. The enemy forces remaining in front of the 82nd and the other American units were Italians who had no great interest in fighting. When the advance jumped off on July 19, the 82nd lacked motorized transport. The paratroopers faced a footslog of 150 miles to their objectives of Trapani and Castellammare. For the most part, they were unopposed. At various points, the Italians fired token volleys to assuage soldierly honor before surrendering or running for the hills. Gavin described this odd half war: "The usual action of the Italians was to fire a few shots, rifle and machine gun, cause the advance guard to deploy, and then surrender as soon as pressure was brought to bear on them. It made for treacherous action. Even the white flag could not be trusted. There was always the possibility that Germans would be strengthening their defense. Some Germans were captured."

On July 22, 1943, the 505th Parachute Infantry reached Trapani. The last leg of their advance was by truck. Gavin noted, "The only hazards en route were the fruit and caramelos thrown by the Sicilians." Though they did receive some heavy artillery fire at the edge of town, Gavin deployed his troops, and they advanced faster than the Italian artillery could adjust fire, so they received no serious casualties. His honor satisfied by the artillery barrage, Admiral Alberto Manfredi surrendered the town and its 5,000 man garrison that day to General Ridgway. The 82nd's job invading Sicily was nearly done.

Trudging on foot, they had covered the 150 miles through difficult terrain, against sporadic resistance, with such speed that it astonished even Patton. Some officers grumbled that their progress slowed during the march not because of enemy fire, but because of the posturing of Ridgway and his staff. Ridgway was new to combat then. He still felt he had something to prove, and he had often prowled the front of the road march to Trapani. Not to be embarrassed, his staff had followed him. At least one battalion commander at the time complained that his maneuver against enemy positions would have been greatly eased if the general and his staff had not been in the way. Years after the battle, many soldiers still remembered it.

According to Gavin and his intimates, Ridgway exhibited odd behavior at several points during the march. Perhaps it was the fact that he was not a true paratrooper and his subordinates were. Or it might have been the hours he had spent on D day not knowing where his command was or what it was doing. Whatever the reason, he behaved, they thought, unreasonably on at least two notable occasions, summarily relieving Bill Yarborough, an airborne pioneer and one of Gavin's closest friends and mentors, for allowing his men to eat lunch—thereby drawing an ambush attempt by the enemy—and also threatening to relieve another successful battalion commander, Warren Williams of the 504. Gavin was shocked at the treatment of these officers and the rages that presaged it. Throughout his career, he would feel that American generals were far too eager to dismiss subordinates for single errors of judgment.

Ridgway recommended Gavin for a Distinguished Service Cross for the stand at Biazza Ridge and later delivered it personally. He also informed him that he was to be considered for a general's star. Gavin had proven himself in Sicily—not just to Ridgway and his troops—but also to the higher levels of command. Patton and Bradley now knew Gavin, and they thought him to be one of the best young commanders in the theater.

In his diary, Gavin noted several lessons learned. He believed that his troops had performed well, justifying their high reputation in training. In Trapani, he wrote, "We have learned many lessons in the past few weeks, foremost of which is the basic fact that there is no substitute for discipline. It must be iron. The troops themselves, once having been in combat, want it; but it must be exacted from them. Parachute troops are extremely courageous and love to fight. They will take on odds gladly. The Germans are good fighters but can be beaten badly especially if outsmarted and attacked when they least expect it. Surprise is costly to them always whereas a paratrooper will fight anytime. American marksmanship is far superior to any foreign. In fact, the impression most of us get is that other troops do not shoot accurately for a kill every shot. Instead, they appear to fire area fire even with their rifles. The best defense is to attack. . . . All men must be able to march long distances with combat loads. . . . Loud talking, certain to be the first in the fight troop leaders, are sometimes the most unstable officers in combat. The quiet types are frequently more valuable because of their emotional stability. Quiet confidence, deliberate orders, and quick decisions, are necessary even in situations where defeat is apparently certain. Troops respond and reflect it in their behavior. An officer can show caution but not fear. Even caution should be tossed to the winds sometimes when the moment appears opportune. Troops will follow a daring, confident leader anywhere. Nine times out of ten all that they need is someone to say, 'Let's go.' " In Sicily, Gavin had shown himself very capable at saying "let's go."

Yet combat in Sicily changed Gavin. He had always been sensitive. This had manifested itself in the concern he had shown for his troops when he was a lieutenant and by his hostile reaction to the arrogance of some of his fellow officers. It revealed itself in his constant worry over his own inadequacy. Army leadership manuals in Gavin's day warned against scurrilous NCOs and troops; only later did they emphasize the supportive and understanding officer. Yet what Gavin did worked because it was genuine. Troops will always uncover the truth. If an officer is truly primarily interested in his own career and acts concerned simply for his own benefit, the troops sense it.

Gavin's Sicily experiences are particularly illuminating. In ordering his men to hold Biazza Ridge, he was ruthless. Though very much a neophyte in battle, he saw a critical moment that required instant decision. He seized that moment and committed himself and his men to stopping the

Tigers if it took the last trooper. The men he'd trained performed without question. He was usually beside them, sharing their fears, sweat, suffering, and then he saw that the dead were buried. He would never lose his sense of shock and horror when members of his command lay dead on hard-fought ground. Thirty-five years later, the image of their bodies still haunted him, and he remarked upon it in his own tale of the war. He wrote Barbara in the wake of his Sicily experiences that after the war was over he wanted to join a monastery somewhere and be a monk with no more of the death and destruction about him ever.

Gavin would again order his troops into firestorms against impossible odds. He would again mourn their losses. But he developed one trait that remained with him forever after Sicily: He never wasted troops if there was any way of avoiding it. A change in Gavin began in Sicily. His Civil War images of toughness and heroism were tempered, and he cared for his troops in life as well as in combat.

Sicily was the Allies' first large-scale airborne operation. It neither doomed nor boomed the concept of airborne warfare, but rather left it essentially untested. There were too many anomalies about Sicily: the wind, the terrain, the "friendly fire" horror, the dubious fighting qualities of the Italian units. While the experience taught a number of lessons, it also raised as many questions.

Gavin had made two important discoveries. First, the bazooka was an ineffectual weapon that could not stop a German tank unless the gunner was either very lucky or had a clear shot at a tank's points of vulnerability. This was serious, for it meant that paratroops would be helpless before German armor, and that greatly limited their combat utility. Gavin did not bury the question. At Piano Lupo, he had found dead bazooka men with their just-fired weapons ground into their bodies by tank treads. Correcting the situation was impossible because the United States had no better weapon. Almost as soon as the Italians surrendered in Trapani, he had his troops out training again, and he particularly emphasized bazooka training. Using captured German tank hulks, he had his men probe them for vulnerable points. Meanwhile, out of respect for the hazards of the bazooka men's job, he had special patches with crossed bazookas made and distributed to all his gunners. It was all he could do.

From the viewpoint of higher command, Sicily left important unresolved issues about airborne's future. Once Patton liberated Palermo, he turned east and charged for Messina, Montgomery's objective. The Germans reacted swiftly, and soon he found himself funneled by rough terrain into disadvantageous positions. He contacted Ridgway about possible airborne drops to flank the Germans; however, Troop Carrier Command feared that dropping troops over concentrated German forces might lead to a disastrous loss of aircraft, so the idea was shelved. Instead, Patton staged two brilliant amphibious flanking maneuvers, which resulted in his reaching Messina before Montgomery.

Following the campaign, the airborne concept again came under sharp criticism. The first question was whether paratroopers made a crucial difference. Many observers considered the drops absolute folly. The problems with the 504 drop were obvious, and the 505 drop had scattered paratroops all over the island with wasted casualties as a result. The British drop had been even more disastrous.

The mission of the 2,075 British airborne troops was to seize the critical Ponte Grande bridge behind Montgomery's beaches. They intended to do it with gliders. Bucking the high winds in their gliders, the British lift did a good job of locating Syracuse, but things went sour quickly. Syracuse became alive with searchlights and antiaircraft fire. Panicked pilots released gliders too early, and most of them splashed down into the sea. Of the 137 gliders that left Tunisia, 54 actually landed on Sicily, and 4 landed on their correct drop zones. Of 2,075 men only 104, under the command of Lieutenant L. Withers, reached their objective. They succeeded in dismantling the explosive charges the Germans had set to blow up the bridge and repulsed one counterattack; then they came under a daylong attack. Nearly out of ammunition and reduced to eighteen men, Withers finally found himself surrounded by a battalion and surrendered on the afternoon of D day. Fortunately, the troops from the British 5th Division arrived only minutes after the surrender and retook the bridge before it could be blown. The 1st Airborne had saved the bridge and would carry the battle honors. But they had taken nearly six hundred casualties. Many were drowned in the drop, and it seemed like an excessive price to pay for a single bridge.

Ponte Grande was not the last action for British airborne troops in Sicily. They had one more battle to fight, and it well may have been the most unusual airborne action of World War II. In the days immediately following Montgomery's landing, his effort to push the Germans across the island bogged down. The Germans were determined at the very least to bottle him up, for if they were going to withdraw from the island, they would have to do it through Messina, and they could not let Montgomery have it. The critical line of defense for the Axis was along the Simeto River just south of Catania. The key to that river was the Primosole Bridge. On the night of July 13, paratroopers from the British 1st Airborne Division, Brigadier General Gerald W. Lathbury's 1st Parachute Brigade, took off from Tunisia to take that bridge and thus outflank and unlock German defenses.

The Germans too considered parachute operations. The mastermind behind the German airborne effort, General Kurt Student, had two airborne divisions at his disposal and urged Hitler to use them at once. He felt certain that, if they dropped a large force on the Allied beaches, they could wreak enough havoc to turn back the invasion altogether. Hitler dismissed the idea, but he did feel that a parachute brigade dropped in friendly territory near the Primosole Bridge would do much to stiffen the line along the Simeto River. The fighting prowess of the German paratrooper remained widely respected. That idea went ahead, and 1,817 German *Fallschirmjaeger* (paratroopers) from the 1st Parachute Division prepared themselves for a drop near the Primosole Bridge on the night of the 13th into the same drop zones then under consideration by the British.

Forewarned by the fate of the 504th on the hazardous business of flying over invasion fleets, the British took a great deal of care to ensure that the British paratroops did not meet a similar fate. Unfortunately, one of the merchant ship captains unloading supplies for the invasion had not been briefed on the intended drop that night and his ship opened fire. As before, all the other ships off the beachhead followed his example and another disaster ensued. Eleven aircraft either fell from the skies or sustained such damage that they aborted. The 113 surviving planes continued on—though now wildly dispersed. Once again, paratroops landed all over Sicily, but 39 planeloads came down on or near their drop zones. They actually might be counted as the unfortunates, for theirs was a wild reception indeed.

By an extraordinary coincidence, the Germans had been winging toward the same place at the same time.

The German troop carriers had done a somewhat better job, and the German paratroopers, who had landed one hour earlier, had hit their drop zones with pinpoint accuracy. They had just unpacked their bundles and organized for movement when they heard the Allied C-47s overhead and saw parachutes spilling out. Fortunately for the English, the Germans at first felt confusion. Was it possible that this was an airborne assault on the same drop zones they had just used? Thinking that the chances of that were entirely too remote, they decided that these must be reinforcements and held their fire. Then the British landed, and weapons began crackling across the drop zone. Now both sides milled in confusion. Neither had expected to find the other. What made matters even worse was that their uniforms looked very much alike in the darkness. Soon, when realization hit, the fighting became a wild melee of close-quarter battles all around the drop zone. Casualties mounted quickly on both sides; but somehow, a small detachment of around two hundred Englishmen slipped away and secured the bridge. They did not hold it long. The Germans launched a vengeful counterattack, and the British paratroops were forced off half of the bridge the next day, in spite of repeated calls for fire from an offshore cruiser. The survivors were saved at the last moment by the arrival of British tanks.

The butcher bill for the battle at Primosole ran to about nine hundred paratroopers. Montgomery questioned whether it was all worth it and, labeling the missions "failures," canceled all future airborne operations.

Americans too agreed that the British drops had been failures, and they conceded that the 504th's drop had been a total disaster. They judged Gavin's drop a success. Patton believed that Gavin's force had speeded his advance inland by as much as forty-eight hours. Bradley felt that the dispersion of the paratroopers actually might have helped things. It was because they seized the initiative and attacked, destroyed, or harassed whatever they could find, that the Germans became badly confused and convinced they had been hit by several parachute divisions.

Paratrooper Joe Swing, having been sent by Marshall as an observer, recommended that the Airborne concept be shelved because of the disastrous drops. Within the 82nd, opinions were divided between paratroopers, Gavin and Tucker, and nonparatroopers, Ridgway and Taylor. Perhaps because he found commanding a dispersed paratroop division so vexing, Ridgway concluded that Troop Carrier Command had proven it could not do the job without considerably more training. He believed that parachute regiments should be withdrawn from airborne divisions and used solely for commando-type raids. The division itself would only air-land or stage glider assaults and then only in daylight. Gavin, on the other hand, (and Tucker agreed with him) felt that the airborne division should be left as it was; however, he thought Troop Carrier Command should devote far more attention to training, particularly night training. He also suggested that C-47 formations be augmented with B-17 Flying Fortresses that could provide electronic navigation capabilities and defensive firepower. Going a step further, Gavin thought new modified transport planes with more sophisticated navigation equipment, armor, and their own defensive weapons should be developed. Finally, Gavin suggested that a new specialized unit known as pathfinders be attached to airborne divisions. Pathfinders would incorporate specially trained troops and pilots who could find the drop zones and mark them with lights and beacons for the mass drop that followed swiftly behind.

Naturally, since giving up the parachute regiments would have cost Ridgway two thirds of his command, he did not tell higher command his true feelings. Instead, he recommended that Troop Carrier Command improve its training, that improved antitank weapons be given to paratroops, and that more aircraft be made available so the division was not committed piecemeal again.

At the highest levels, opinions were divided. Some, like General Lesley McNair, who was in charge of activation, training, and evaluation of new divisions, favored eliminating the airborne division or at least shrinking it. Others, like Marshall, still favored the airborne experiment as it was. Whatever their perspectives, Sicily had given the airborne concept a very rough delivery.

Gavin, though, had benefited greatly from the invasion. Sicily was a career maker. Years later, Bradley's aide, Colonel Chester "Chet" Hansen, remembered the Gavin he met on Sicily as a young man cutting an extraordinary figure. He was tall, sharply turned out in his paratroop uniform, and he was always unshakably in control. Even today, the memory of Gavin's troops brings Hansen to smile and shake his head. The "crazy aggressive characters" as he calls them, had dropped all over the island but had not, as saner men might have done, elected to go into hiding. Rather, the crazy characters had, though they often felt confused and lost themselves, brought even greater confusion to the enemy. If an enemy military vehicle came down a road, they attacked it. Wherever they found power substations, telephone poles, or small enemy units, they attacked and destroyed them, too. Hansen remembered them as "popping up all over the island for weeks." He also remembered General Bradley's opinion of their commander. Bradley thought Gavin to be one of the best young commanders in the theater.

Ultimately, Gavin achieved all his objectives in Sicily. Militarily, the unit he had trained had done the nearly impossible in simply recovering from the chaos of the night drop. In addition, they somehow had accomplished their mission. Gavin's unit was in stark contrast to almost every other airborne unit. His image and his reputation were indelibly printed on the mind of every general officer on the island who mattered. He had captured the imagination of his troops and his superiors, as well as of the press.

7.

I T A L Y

The Germans committed elements of four divisions to the defense of Sicily, a measure of their complete distrust of Italian troops. By mid-August, when they felt certain the battle would not go their way, they evacuated these troops and large numbers of Italian troops. More than 100,000 Axis soldiers successfully fled across the Strait of Messina to Italy. Years later, Gavin criticized the planning of the Sicily invasion on the grounds that the Allies might have bottled up the retreating Germans with an amphibious assault and through proper use of Allied supremacy at sea. He faulted Eisenhower and his remoteness from the battlefield (he was in Africa during the invasion) for allowing the Germans to escape, and he would find more fault in the future. Unlike many Americans who fought in World War II, Gavin was not an Eisenhower fan.

In the summer of 1943, with combat in Sicily behind him, Gavin's thoughts returned to his career, primarily his general's star. From Trapani, he once again deluged Barbara with letters and kept his diary updated. At first, the division expected to be sent back to Africa, where the 325th still remained. By August, Gavin had settled into the realities of Trapani. Fearing that the troops would contract diseases from the local women, Ridgway authorized the opening of an official whorehouse where the ladies received daily inspections from the division medical staff. Ridgway, a very moral man, made the mistake of inspecting it himself. He left disgusted, commenting, "They're just like animals!"

Gavin noted in his diary, "Opened the recreation building. Rates at 25 lira per piece. About 325 pros administered. Had the Battalion C.O.'s talk to their men about it today to be certain that they understood that they were not expected to patronize the place. It is not required."

But the place amused Gavin, and when reporter Jack "Beaver" Thompson came to see him in Trapani for follow-up stories, Gavin drily asked him if he would like to see his house. Thompson said that he would like to see how a colonel lived, so Gavin took him, and an astounded, blushing Thompson found himself surrounded by three Sicilian beauties as soon as they stepped in the door. Gavin simply smiled.

Meanwhile, Gavin continued to itch over his promotion. "I went to G-1 and asked him to let me know if General R's recommendation on my Brigadier General was bounced back for any reason. If it does not go through I am going to look for a new home. I have organized, trained, and fought this regiment over a period of a year and a quarter. It is a satisfying accomplishment in itself. Continued carrying on in this same spot only means that I am blocking the advancement of deserving officers in the regiment and I am becoming stalemated myself." He plotted ways to improve his record. Gavin had treated Beaver Thompson well not only because he liked the reporter, but because he also understood the importance of good press to a young officer. He commented in his diary that he thought highly of Thompson then said, "Our continued association may be to our mutual gain."

On August 9, Gavin received his Distinguished Service Cross, and it made him introspective. Somewhat embarrassed, he said of it, "I feel that many of the fine boys now buried on Biazza Ridge are much more entitled to decorations than I am. It will nevertheless be nice to have and of considerable help professionally." Once again, he debated in his own mind what an effective combat leader should be and thought he knew. "There is only one way to fight a battle or a war; I am more than ever convinced. Fight intensely, smartly, and tough. Take chances personally and in matters of decision. Nothing ventured, nothing gained never was more applicable. Most people become too mesmerized by the holocaust and the danger to be promptly and energetically aggressive in a fight. That moment, the initial moment of indecision, should be made the most of. Hit them quick and hit them hard. Keep the initiative even on the defensive. Most men do not think. They merely do as they are trained. That is O.K. If they thought, chances are they would do nothing or spend all their time figuring out fancy plans. The leader should think and he will if he is battle trained and has any guts at all. Having decided what to do the machine starts instantly to put his thoughts and plan into execution. Close with them and kill them. Clausewitz says, 'Overcome their will to fight.' Perhaps that is better."

On August 14, three days before Messina fell, Gavin received his first briefing on Avalanche, the plan for the invasion of Italy at Salerno, the place fated to be the next test of his ideas. At the time, the mission called for the 82nd to jump to hold high mountain passes inland from a projected landing at Salerno. It was a classic paratroop role, a blocking attack to shield the invasion from swift enemy reinforcement. That plan would change, not once, but several times.

The invasion of Italy was another political compromise at the highest levels. After Sicily, Eisenhower had planned a small-scale attack across the Strait of Messina to prevent German artillery on the mainland from shelling Sicily; but it soon grew into something much larger. True to their Grant traditions, the Americans wanted to turn the full attention of the Allies to the invasion of Normandy as soon as the guns cooled on Sicily.

The British, led by the persistence of Churchill, still preferred the idea of attacking Europe through her "soft underbelly." Italy, the British believed, was vacillating and might well be knocked out of the war if the Allies invaded her coasts. This would force Hitler to divert more of the Wehrmacht from the Eastern Front, thus satisfying Stalin's demands. Churchill got his way. The American proviso in the bargain was that Avalanche be kept small so that forces earmarked for Normandy the following year would not be thrown in and possibly wrecked. This included most of the units that had fought in Africa and Sicily.

The plan was rather simple and involved shared responsibilities. To the south, Montgomery's British Eighth Army would leap directly across the Strait of Messina and capture Reggio di Calabria. To the north, another landing would be staged by Mark Clark's largely green Fifth Army at Salerno, which was picked because it was as far north on the Italian boot as land-based fighters could reach. After Sicily, fighter cover over the landing beaches had become a top priority. It played to the Allies strength, and against the Luftwaffe's growing weakness, and the weather was usually suitable. Eisenhower also considered a landing closer to Rome but quickly discarded the idea because it would not enjoy enough air cover for the beaches. From Salerno, the Allies would drive over the mountains to Naples—thereby gaining the famous deep-water port to support future operations that would lead to the conquest of Italy.

Perhaps it was because the American mind-set remained fixed on Normandy, or because of inexperience, but through a series of bad decisions and poorer judgment, Avalanche became an operation that the American army seemed bent on losing from the start. This puzzle becomes clearer if seen from both German and American points of view. On the German side, there existed some dissension: what to do about Italy? The commander in southern Italy, Field Marshal Albert Kesselring, felt confident of winning a defensive battle. He felt that he knew Allied intentions and that Italy greatly favored the defenders. To the north the German tank genius Field Marshal Erwin Rommel commanded a powerful force; he believed attempts to defend Italy ridiculous. He claimed the boot could be invaded amphibiously nearly anywhere, and once it was, all forces below the invasion would be cut off. He advocated writing off southern Italy and forming an impregnable defensive line along the Po River in the north. There the mountainous terrain and the river could form a nearly impassable barrier that the Allies might spend years trying to breach. Kesselring's view prevailed, although Hitler kept the forces divided to be able to meet a threat in either north or south.

What Kesselring did in preparation was known. The Allies heard of each move he made because they had broken German codes and read most of his radio traffic. They knew, for instance, that he anticipated an invasion at Salerno, and that the Italians did want to get out of the war (they had just deposed Mussolini). Kesselring also knew the range of Allied fighters and planned accordingly. He deployed a panzer division and a parachute division near Rome to send the Italian government a message and to be ready to move against an attack on beaches near the city. About 43,000 Germans waited ready near Rome.

Far to the south, Colonel General Heinrich von Vietinghoff Genannt Scheel took command of the newly formed German Tenth Army, which answered to Kesselring. It had six divisions, five of them panzer and four of them including the newly refitted Hermann Göring Division, veterans of Sicily. Two of the Tenth Army divisions were deployed at Salerno to back up the Italian troops stationed there. Kesselring's plan was relatively simple. If the Allies invaded from the south, at the toe or the lower boot, he would order the two divisions there to fight a delaying action, retreating until they reached the more defensible area just south of Rome. There in the vicinity of the Volturno River, all eight of Kesselring's powerful divisions would dig in and make further rapid advances too costly for serious consideration.

If the attack came at Salerno, six of the eight available divisions would rush to meet it, and the two retreating divisions from the south would join in the defense directly.

On the Allied side, Mark Clark's Fifth Army consisted of the British X Corps under Lieutenant General Richard L. McCreery and the U.S. VI Corps under Major General Ernest J. "Mike" Dawley. The 82nd Airborne Division was also committed, given to Clark to use as he saw fit, though it was to be returned in ample time for its role in Normandy the following spring. The invasion date of Avalanche was set for September 9, 1943. The divisions in the two corps Clark commanded had seen some combat prior to Sicily but one, the 36th, was completely green. Only the 82nd was considered a "top" division, though some of the others had seen some action in Africa with mixed results. In total, between Montgomery and Clark, the Allies had mustered nine combat divisions for the invasion. This meant that they, on paper at least, possessed roughly equal strength to the forces Kesselring mustered, provided Rommel gave him no assistance.

Due to the number of panzer divisions, the German defenders had more firepower. The Allied advantage derived from the fact that the American divisions would be supported by a naval armada and all the available airpower. Kesselring mustered 1,500 aircraft of all types in the Italian theater, not including Italian forces. On the hoary theory that three times as many attackers are needed to overcome a defender, the Germans felt confident. The balance of forces before the invasion promised a difficult fight for the Allies from the outset; Allied bumbling made it even more so.

The forces for Avalanche quickly assembled in Africa for the invasion, the 82nd Airborne with problems of its own. Several missions were planned for the division in support of Avalanche. As new orders arrived, they were immediately changed. Each time, the division adjusted its training requirements to meet the new mission. Gavin first planned to jump into high mountain passes to "shield" the beachheads, but higher command aborted this and replaced it with an operation code named Giant I that required both amphibious and airborne forces to land at Capua, 40 miles north of the Salerno beachhead, on the Volturno River. The two parachute regiments, led by Gavin, would drop near a key road junction and block all German movements through the area and destroy all the bridges over the river. The 325th would land amphibiously at the mouth of the Volturno and march overland to meet the other elements. Then the navy discovered the mouth of the river was unsuitable for amphibious operations because of reefs and shoals, so they canceled that portion of the operation, but planning for the parachute drop was continued. Clark's headquarters optimistically thought that relieving forces from the beachhead would reach Capua within five days.

Ridgway considered the plan insane. Gavin, who would command and do all the planning for the airborne portion of the mission, was philosophical. His self-confidence precluded objections. He would do what higher command required.

The 82nd returned to Africa August 20 and 21 for rush training for their assault. Ridgway had wanted weeks to train. He would get days. Gavin did not worry over it. After Sicily, he believed his 505 could do anything. Further, his pathfinder idea had taken hold and pathfinder training was coming along nicely. In practice drops, the planes reached the correct drop zones with a better than 90 percent success rate. He did not even mind returning to Africa. He wrote on August 17, "Glad to move. Africa may be much hotter and not quite as comfortable as here, but a change is good for the [troops'] morale. They have a feeling they are going somewhere and the war is moving along."

But the details of the training were messy, not to his liking. "At this stage things are in one hell of a mess," he wrote. The more he knew of the Volturno mission, the less he liked it. Would the Italians fight? Could his troops hold as long as they had to? He was not at all sure that they would have enough ammunition. He wrote, "At best, however, a lot of us are not coming back from this show."

Meanwhile, the 82nd was being considered for one of the oddest missions of the war. On September 2, Gavin and several other ranking officers in the division flew to Syracuse, Sicily, for a high-level, secret meeting on a new plan, code named Giant II, a drop to seize Rome. Shortly after the Italians deposed Benito Mussolini, the new government, under Marshal Pietro Badoglio, contacted Eisenhower to open negotiations on Italy's withdrawal from the war. The 82nd's mission was to hold Rome with the cooperation of the Italian Army units there and protect the new government from the Germans. The Italians promised that they could hold certain airfields around Rome and neutralize German resistance as the paratroopers dropped.

Ridgway, ever cautious, did not buy it. Gavin did. He felt intrigued by the dash and the highly public glamour of the mission and went ahead planning and coordinating the drop. Ridgway's misgivings grew steadily. Intelligence informed him that the Italians feared the Germans; and because the Germans were already suspicious of the Italians, they had reduced supplies of ammunition and fuel to Italian units so that most were no longer mobile or able to fight for long.

Nevertheless, planning went ahead and on September 3, the Italians signed a secret armistice with Eisenhower with the understanding that an American airborne division would drop on Rome to protect the King of Italy and the Badoglio government from the Germans. Badoglio would announce Italy's withdrawal from the war on the night of September 8, just as the paratroopers arrived and the invasion fleet approached Salerno. At the highest level—Eisenhower, Churchill, and President Roosevelt himself—this plan met hearty approval. Italy was out of the war, and the troops at Salerno would only have to face German resistance.

But Eisenhower, Churchill, and Roosevelt did not have to make the actual jump on Rome. Ridgway, Gavin, and Taylor did, and only Gavin liked it at the outset, though he liked it less and less as he planned for all that could go wrong. After meeting with the Italians for over ten hours, Ridgway wrote for the record, "During these conversations the deep rooted fear of the Italian representatives of German armed forces became more and more apparent. They would give no assurance of their ability to withstand a German attack, or even to guarantee complete elimination of German anti-aircraft defenses in the Rome area or the approach corridors by which the airborne forces had to reach the airfield." Ridgway faced an internal political problem. All the people at the highest levels wanted the Rome drop. Ridgway believed it meant the destruction of his division; however, it might be the end of his career to voice his objections. To his credit, he voiced them anyway.

The defenders in Italy expected a significantly stronger invasion force than the one scheduled to land at Salerno, and General von Vietinghoff busily installed mine fields, built up stong points, and prepared bridges for demolition to slow the invaders. When he heard of the Italian surrender September 8, he ordered the 26th Panzer Division, then assigned to delay Montgomery, north. Then he waited.

For some time the Germans had prepared for Italian treachery and were not surprised when it came. They also expected the invasion on a beach nearer Rome. Ridgway's pessimism grew with his lack of trust in the Italians; he had to plan for the worst. How long could the light infantry of the 82nd, if they even reached Rome, hold out against determined attacks from the forces the Germans had available? Ridgway demanded that before they drop, some Americans be smuggled into Rome to see the situation firsthand. With this approved, he selected his acting assistant division commander, General Maxwell Taylor, and the intelligence officer from the 52nd Troop Carrier Wing, Colonel William T. Gardiner, for the risky mission. The machinery of invasion was already in motion, poised for landings at Salerno on the 9th.

Departing on September 7, Taylor and Gardiner's trip was high adventure. At 2:00 A.M. they left Palermo in a fast British patrol boat headed for the open sea, wearing American uniforms so they would not be shot as spies. As dawn broke, they hove to with an Italian corvette, the *Ibis*. In his luggage, Taylor carried a clandestine radio. He had been instructed to use secret Italian channels to reach high command, but since neither he nor Ridgway trusted these, he carried his own radio for backup. The corvette docked at Gaeta that afternoon. The Italians doused the Americans' uniforms with salt water and treated Taylor and company like captured airmen while marching them down the gangplank. A military car took them from the dock to the outskirts of the city where they transferred again, into an ambulance with frosted windows, for the leg to Rome. Through slots, Taylor scanned the countryside as they went. He noticed, with foreboding, that the closer they got to Rome, the more Germans he saw. Once in Rome, he found the Italians far less enthusiastic than those he had met in Sicily. On the early morning of September 8 he met with Badoglio himself and discovered that the Italian leader, once he learned that Allied forces intended landing as far from Rome as Salerno with only nine divisions, opposed Giant II altogether. He also informed Taylor that he had no intention of making the "Italy withdraws from the war" speech he had guaranteed Eisenhower he would make that evening. He suspected that the Germans might devastate Rome if there was trouble. Taylor concluded that if the 82nd jumped in, they would jump to a quick death. Giant II would be a disaster. He sent word of the situation on his clandestine radio that day. That night he left Rome on an Italian aircraft and flew to Eisenhower's headquarters.

Eisenhower was incensed. He wanted the armistice announced before his troops hit the Salerno beaches the next day. He radioed Badoglio that he would make the announcement himself that night if the Italians did not. Still Badoglio wavered. Eisenhower broadcast the announcement at 6:30 P.M. Finally, just before 8 P.M., Badoglio himself got on the radio and made a similar announcement. Italy was out of the war. But, unknown to the Allies, the Germans were not disturbed by the defection.

The paratroopers of the 504th were loading into their transports on the afternoon of September 8, ready for the night assault on Rome. They did not know what Eisenhower and Taylor had decided, that Giant II was canceled. When they got the word, several planes already had paratroopers on board and waited with engines running. Five years after the war ended, Gavin had a close-up look at how the Germans had been disposed about Rome. He concluded the drop would have been a failure. But in 1943, he simply unpacked his combat kit, returned to preparing for the Capua drop, and noted in his diary, "Just before take off the entire mission was called off. . . . Germany, in anticipation of this move [the Italian withdrawal from the war] had already heavily reinforced the German garrisons in and around the city of Rome. It was well that we did not jump. . . . Any Airborne effort made beyond fighter support is impossible with our present air transports, they are clay pigeons."

The 82nd was in the odd position of the designated hitter, always on the ready, never knowing when the call would come. All Gavin could do was wait. The 504th was scheduled to deploy first next time, so Gavin calculated he was due a layoff. He commented that they needed the training time and wondered how the men waiting off Salerno would do. He did not, on September 11, expect to find out firsthand.

On the night of September 8, Mark Clark's huge armada was closing on Salerno, and several serious mistakes had already been made. Clark and troops under his command were about to pay for them. The beaches, immortalized by the poet Longfellow as a "Blue Salernian Bay with its sickle of white sand," were ideal for landing, but also ideal for defense, something the attackers ignored in their planning, for in the vain hope of surprise, they ordered no preparatory artillery barrage. Backed by higher ground, overlooked by mountains, the landing areas could be easily defended even by an inferior force. And even if the landings succeeded, 40 miles to the north of Salerno runs the Volturno River, a natural defensive barrier the enemy could easily exploit to protect movement north.

To the south, Montgomery and his enemies moved as if in a set-piece drama. Montgomery opened his attack on Calabria on September 3 with a massive preliminary air bombardment and artillery barrage, and as per plan, the Germans had let him move north while skillfully mining roads, sniping, burning bridges, and employing all the methods of skilled rear-guard action, at which they were masters. Montgomery's ponderous offensive methods made it easy for them to buy time cheaply. Meanwhile, the bulk of the two panzer divisions fell back on Salerno as planned.

Next, Clark himself stumbled. The night before the landings, September 8, Clark let his troops know that the Italians had withdrawn from the conflict. As an understandable result, they felt the landing would be unopposed. At 3:00 A.M. of September 9, as they boarded their landing boats, they were psychologically unready for the German divisions that had smoothly and efficiently moved into the vacated Italian positions on the beach. To compound that error, Clark's plan of attack was faulty. The beachhead ran 20 miles long, and he decided to use all of it rather than concentrating his assault force at critical points. He ended up with a 25-mile front with a 7-mile gap in its center, between the American and British forces. In that gap flowed the Sele River, so not only was there a gap between his assault elements, but also a natural obstacle. Clark compounded these negatives by refusing preliminary naval bombardment of the beaches, claiming guns would only alert the enemy to his arrival. Montgomery's invasion had already alerted the Germans that someone was coming, and Kesselring expected there might be an attack on Salerno anyway. How Clark thought that German reconnaissance would miss his giant invasion armada steaming north under sparkling skies when every longshoreman in North Africa knew of their departure remains a mystery.

The landing went badly before a single boat reached the beach. The Germans, not in the least taken by surprise, first shot off flares to illuminate the approaching landing craft, then they announced over loudspeakers in English, "Come on in and give up. You're covered." The men in those first boats were from a Texas National Guard unit, the 36th Infantry Division. They were totally new to combat. Clark had picked them because he had helped activate the division and believed it would give a fine account of itself. It did, and because it did, the invaders hung on, in spite of all their commander's errors, through a day of murderous fire.

But they did it under horrible conditions inflicted by the veteran 16th Panzer Division, freshly refitted after rough service on the Eastern Front. Fortunately, on that first day the Germans had their own reverses. Thinking that the Allies might hit Salerno, they had left a single panzer division there to delay the assault until the strength of their other seven divisions could be brought to bear. General Sickenhius, the commander of the 16th Panzer Division, had built eight strong points from which he would hold a 30-mile front. He knew his division would suffer, but it would achieve delay.

Salerno's defenders had been alerted to the impending invasion the previous afternoon, and reinforcements already streamed their way. But, as soon as the firing began, Italian refugees clogged the roads, and the reinforcements were themselves slowed. There was also the unusual problem of disarming elated Italian soldiers hurrying home in the wake of Badoglio's announcement. That was accomplished, but the 16th Panzer and its one hundred tanks had a frenzied and anxious wait as Clark's armada approached. Nevertheless, when the landing craft finally appeared before their guns, they plied their trade with professional dexterity.

Churning in toward the calm silver beach in their boats, 36th Division soldiers expected to walk ashore and assume the role of occupation troops. They quickly found themselves under heavy fire. The naval historian Samuel Eliot Morison compared German defenses at Salerno with those at Tarawa in the Pacific, a slaughterhouse for Marines. As soon as they came within range, artillery salvos tore into the defenseless fleet of tiny boats. Soon mortar fire joined the artillery. Then, when the boats had closed to within 300 yards, the Germans lashed the attackers with small-arms and machine-gun fire; many died before they ever disembarked from their landing craft. And German fire from the veterans of defensive warfare on the Russian front proved horribly accurate.

Just after dawn, the Allies tried to land tanks. The Germans hit four of the six tank-bearing landing craft, and the other two withdrew. Ashore, soldiers hugged dunes and sparse clumps of grass, scarce on the bright sand, for protection. At first, progress was minimal. Most soldiers sought simply to survive and counted themselves lucky if they had made it to the beach at all. In spite of disorganization during the first hours, individual groups recovered and began to move inland. Soon squads, then platoons, then haphazard companies moved as well. One infantry regiment, the 141st, remained pinned on the beach for the rest of the day. The others inched, crawled, and grappled their way to high ground. They found the Germans spread thin on that first day, in spite of the accurate deluge of fire they had produced. The Americans exploited the immediate advantage; officers and NCOs shouted and kicked their men forward.

Men responded, growling that it could not get worse than it already was. The assault force sought to win a respite and wait for reinforcements and artillery if they could just silence the guns before them. They were wrong.

With dawn came the Luftwaffe. Never, before or since, was a beachhead pummeled from the air like the one at Salerno on September 9. Planes swept the narrow beaches with bombs and machine guns for hours. Troops looking for sanctuary lay stunned. There was no safe place on the Salernian sands, for Kesselring had boasted that this landing would not succeed. "The invading enemy in the area Naples-Salerno and southwards must be completely annihilated and in addition thrown into the sea," he proclaimed. He had six more divisions rapidly closing on the fray.

By day's end, little Allied artillery had landed and the beach was still under direct German fire. But at last the naval force standing offshore began using its heavy guns on the defenders. The fleet supplied the invader's artillery. Gunners on Allied ships lobbed tons of high explosives at German positions. But even that was not as effective as it might have been. German fire had played havoc with Allied communications, so much of the Naval guns' fire was unaimed and ineffectual. Still, the soldiers of the 36th Division had clawed doggedly toward the German weak points, and in many cases, succeeded in reaching them, though with heavy casualties. Several miles inland, a few American troops had even reached and held some high ground about Capaccio. The British assault troops, their numbers decimated, had gained little.

Clark had delivered a fantastic military opportunity to the Germans at Salerno. Kesselring had enough—but barely enough—force available to defeat the Allied invasion. If Hitler released Rommel's troops to reinforce him, a disastrous Allied defeat was a certainty. Kesselring asked for them. Hitler refused. Rommel wanted to keep them. Kesselring would have to do with what he had. He thought it might be enough, and it nearly was.

The Allies continued blundering. Eisenhower's headquarters had approved a plan for invading Taranto, at the heel of the Italian boot, at the same time as the Salerno landing, believing this second invasion would reinforce Montgomery's largely unopposed drive north, divert and confuse the Germans. Supported by the guns of two battleships, five cruisers, and a destroyer screen, 3,600 veteran British troops from the 1st Airborne Division made the landing, as planned. They took Taranto easily on

September 9 because they were unopposed. Fine veteran infantry that would have been invaluable at Salerno was diverted for a nearly worthless sideshow, as was the firepower of the capital ships that supported it. Meanwhile Clark's forces took the main weight of the German defense.

As day followed day at Salerno, Clark's original invasion plan revealed its myriad flaws, and German strength steadily increased. Too weak at any one point to increase their toehold, Allied troops spread on the wide beachhead found themselves wired in by an iron perimeter of panzer divisions, seasoned infantry, and German paratroops.

The panzers hammered away, intent on splitting the Allies and splashing them back into the sea. Clark committed every man he could muster to hold back the Germans. With the steady stream of naval gunfire over their heads, they succeeded in hanging on, but the Germans grew stronger each hour, and Clark had nothing left to commit. He called for reinforcements.

Alexander offered to land parts of the 82nd, using some landing craft Montgomery had used. On September 13, the 325th and the 3rd Battalion of the 504th boarded them and headed for Salerno. Alexander reminded Clark that he still had the rest of the 82nd available. Clark wanted them to drop inland of the invasion to cut off more German reinforcements on September 11 or 12. But Ridgway did not receive the message until the 12th, then planners could find no suitable drop zones where Clark wanted the paratroopers. On the 13th, the Salerno beachhead reached its first crisis.

Powerful panzer forces crashed through the thin line and nearly reached the sea as the German armor encircled unit after unit and GIs collapsed under the weight of superior fire. Allied casualties mounted, the situation became unstable, and Clark had to concede his invasion was failing. He ordered preparations for an evacuation. Major General Troy Middleton, commander of the American 45th Infantry Division, seized the moment, decried the evacuation, and told Clark, "Put food and ammunition behind the 45th. We are going to stay here."

While Clark and others considered evacuation plans, the Germans sliced through portions of the 36th Infantry Division's line, almost reaching the beach. Clark's front had collapsed. Now it became a fight of individuals and small units. Some defiant GIs simply refused to leave. Antitank and artillery gunners stood fast and fired salvo after desperate salvo at the German tanks. Well-directed naval gunfire pounded the exposed enemy. The day closed on desperation, as Clark's battalions nearly cracked.

Eisenhower at last ordered all forces available to come to Clark's aid. The Allied navies sent every ship they could find, belatedly including the force from Taranto. Air forces also responded, and the Germans now found themselves attacked by heavy bombers. Alexander beseeched Montgomery to speed up his advance and sought landing craft to transport armored and infantry divisions now in Africa and Sicily to Salerno. Some were found, and the troops began moving.

Still, another panzer assault like the one that day might finish the invasion. Clark needed help soon. Bill Yarborough, Clark's airborne planner suggested where he could get it. They would bring in elements of the 82nd that night. Clark needed the 82nd, and he needed it now. Not trusting official channels, he hand-wrote a summary of the situation at Salerno for Ridgway: The 82nd was to drop a regiment into the beachhead that night to bolster the defenses. He gave the message to a reconnaissance pilot, Jacob R. Hamilton, to take to Ridgway. He instructed Hamilton to give it to no one but Ridgway himself. Hamilton took off on a makeshift runway and reached Sicily about 1:30 P.M.

Gavin met the pilot, who insisted on talking to Ridgway. Ridgway was not there. He had flown north to talk to Clark about the 82nd's inland drops. Fortunately, his plane was still within radio range and was immediately recalled. As soon as Ridgway landed, Hamilton handed him the message. Aware of the high drama of the moment, Ridgway sent a magnificently appropriate and quote-worthy response back to Clark, "Can do." Hamilton took off immediately to let Clark know Ridgway was coming and made a landing on the beach runway in spite of strafing by the Luftwaffe.

To plan and coordinate a regimental jump in a few hours is a major feat under the best of circumstances. The 82nd staff faced some of the worst. They had no time to recon the drop zones. They would have to depend solely upon their new pathfinder devices, and they would have to be ready to organize under fire if navigation erred. Their only sure guide was to be the men on the ground, who would illuminate the drop area with a large T made of flaming 55-gallon drums. To avoid another Sicily disaster, Ridgway radioed Clark and personally demanded that all antiaircraft fire be held from 9:00 P.M. until otherwise directed—no matter what was flying. As if forewarned, the Germans launched an air raid, but

Clark's soldiers and sailors endured it without shooting back. Five minutes later, the drone of the C-47s rose from the horizon, then they came in low and fast. Fifty pathfinders jumped and set up radar homing beacons on the flaming T for the main body to follow.

Eight hours after receipt of the order, the planes of the main body were airborne; the operation had been so hurried, many of the pilots were briefed next to their planes, holding flashlights to see their maps. Nonetheless, the drop proved a spectacular success. As promised, the flaming T marked the drop zone, a half-mile long. The main body homed in on the beacons set up by the pathfinders, and suddenly, almost exactly at midnight, 1,300 paratroopers filled the sky, and cheers erupted from Allied positions. As if on peacetime maneuvers, the troopers landed on or within a mile of their drop zone. They received no friendly fire from the silent ships. Tucker assembled his regiment ready to fight in less than an hour after the last plane went over. He went to Clark personally. Clark told him, "As soon as you are assembled, you are to be placed in the front lines."

Tucker answered, "Sir, we are assembled and ready now." Clark sent the 504 to reinforce the depleted 36th Division. Tucker marched his men at the double and had them in place and ready by the time the sun came up. Ever to be called "the Little Colonel" after this fight, Tucker told his men he had no intention of retreating. Gavin noted, "The regiment that had jumped the first night, the 504th, had had little sustained combat in Sicily; it was commanded by a tough, superb combat leader, Colonel Reuben Tucker, probably the best regimental combat commander of the war. He seemed eager to get into combat, and as the troops prepared to load the airplanes, he drove by in a jeep, speaking to each planeload. His message was brief: 'Men, it's open season on Krauts, you know what to do.'"

The arrival of the 504th had a powerful impact on the beleaguered forces at the beachhead. The dramatic midnight drop, the confident paratroop swagger, and Tucker's feisty attitude renewed their comrades' sense that they could survive and overcome. The next day, when the panzers again came clanking at the beachhead, Tucker and his men were there to prove what they could do. They yielded no ground, and Gavin always thought their arrival the decisive turning point at Salerno.

On the next day, September 14, Mark Clark canceled the 505th's jump at Capua and ordered them to join their sister regiment at Salerno. The Germans again hammered powerfully at the beaches, and Clark believed the 505's deployment at Salerno would be far more critical than for an inland drop. On the night of the 14th, the 2,100 men of the 505th boarded their C-47s at Sicily. Gavin did all he could to prepare. He knew what awaited them at Salerno, and worries dogged him as he boarded his plane, the lead pathfinder plane. The night was clear and the moon shone brightly; he felt little could go wrong with the navigation, but he superstitiously kept watch out the windows. At last he saw a whitish peninsula below, rimmed by ocean, and the red light came on in the plane. Gavin stood his stick up and waited in the door. He knew the drop zone should be illuminated with another great T. No welcoming marker appeared. After what "seemed like forever," Gavin remembers spotting a white beach bisected by a river. Still there was no T. Suddenly, the green light came on, and in spite of his apprehensions, he leaped out into the prop blast. Then, like magic, the T suddenly came aglow beneath him. They were in the right place, silently floating down in a placid darkness. The drop on Salerno would be remembered by surviving troopers of the 505 as the easiest combat jump of the war. Like the 504's the night before, their drop was accurate, all but seven planeloads of the troopers landing squarely on the T. As they assembled, the sound of artillery filled their ears, and out in the bay, an ammunition ship that had burned for days suddenly exploded, illuminating the sky and shore with a dancing, eerie light.

It took Gavin only forty-five minutes to form his regiment and report ready for combat. Then came an easy assignment. Trucks awaited the troops, and they took them to nearby Monte Soprano, where the soldiers dug in. For the 505 and Gavin, Monte Soprano turned out to be the quietest spot they had yet seen in combat. The Germans did not strike there. They busied themselves elsewhere. So did the 504th.

On the morning of September 15, Ridgway, minus his staff, landed amphibiously into an uneasy situation. Mike Dawley, the VI Corps commander, seemed to have lost his nerve. Clark made Ridgway Dawley's deputy corps commander, hoping the stern and somber paratrooper would restore confidence. On September 16, the Germans tried for the last time to penetrate and smash the beachhead. Panzer groups struck Middleton's 45th Division, which was finally fully landed, and others moved toward the British. The British had been able to land an armored division, and their tanks repelled the attack on that front. Troy Middleton's 45th Division did the same to the panzers on their front. The beachhead stabilized.

After landing, the 504th took defensive positions 3 miles from Paestum, southwest of a town called Albanella. There they awaited a tank attack, which they repulsed with alacrity with flank shots from bazookas and supporting tank destroyers. Tucker patrolled aggressively, and soon the 504th knew what lay in front of them for several miles. The important German position in the area was the high ground about a town aptly named Altavilla, heavily fortified because from it long-range guns could spot and hit targets up to 15 miles from the beachhead. A green battalion from the 36th had tried taking it by assault, but was thrown back with heavy casualties. Tucker, eager to attack, thought he could take it. Ridgway agreed, believing the Germans were tiring (they had in fact thrown in their last reserves, and Rommel stubbornly refused to lend aid). Both men felt it was time to begin offensive operations; so he gave Tucker a tank destroyer battalion and orders to go ahead.

So on the morning of September 16, the regiment marched forward unopposed, 5 miles from their positions, through mountainous terrain to Albanella. At noon, in Albanella, Tucker gave the order to take Altavilla and the two hills directly behind it, hill 424 and hill 415. The 1st Battalion, under the command of Lieutenant Colonel Warren Williams, would assault through Altavilla and take 424, and the 2nd Battalion, under Major Dan Danielson, would take 415. To succeed, they would have to advance over an open valley floor, so Tucker ordered a wait until darkness. The objective they were about to attempt to seize, unbeknownst to the attackers, was a German artillery practice range. Every inch of the valley was ranged and charted like a shooting gallery. Tucker did not know enemy numbers, but he knew that the Germans were well dug in on commanding heights.

At twilight, the battalions moved forward. By a lucky chance, an American observation plane flew low over the advance and dropped a note to Williams as his men moved. The plane had seen German machine gunners in positions directly to his front, waiting in ambush. Williams deployed his men to flank the machine guns and routed the Germans. Then the attackers ran into a mine field; Williams' radio operator tripped a Tellermine that stunned them both.

Meanwhile, Tucker and his command group had moved between the two advancing elements, but alert German artillery soon found their range. To avoid it, Tucker led his men forward. Soon they were challenged by an American voice. It was a forward patrol from Danielson's battalion. Tucker's command section inadvertantly had become the front line on Hill 424. German artillery opened up to their rear, firing toward the beaches. Tucker in a moment realized he was behind significant German battle formations, trapped by his own advance. He set up a command post anyway. At once the battle became heated. Tucker was surrounded and had few options. His 1st Battalion had gone to Hill 415 instead of Hill 424, and the 2nd Battalion was elsewhere. Units became confused and a melee at close quarters between surprised Americans and Germans broke out. Tucker had to find and then direct his battalions in darkness and under fire. By dawn, they managed to take the hills, but once there, found German artillery and mortar fire was vicious and accurate, the worst they saw at any time during the war. The Germans had each fold and hollow of the terrain already targeted; enemy infantry assaulted the hills again and again—four successive times on the first day alone. However, possessing good fields of fire and the high ground, Tucker's men fought them off repeatedly with steady rifle fire German survivors called the most accurate they had ever faced. German casualties grew as battalion after battalion ran into Tucker's rifle sights. The paratroopers suffered steady artillery fire that often hit their positions, but the survivors continued to fight.

Alarmed at the seriousness of their situation, Ridgway finally ordered Tucker to withdraw. But Tucker responded, "Hell no! We've got this hill and we are going to keep it. Send me my other battalion." Ridgway did. Ridgway ordered the 3rd Battalion, held in reserve, to join Tucker on the 17th. Then he ordered army artillery units and the offshore ships to help with barrages against German positions, pounding them with heavy shells. On the 18th, the Germans withdrew from the rim of Salerno. The 504 still held its hill, and Tucker and two of his men won Distinguished Service Crosses for their actions at Altavilla.

Gavin would later praise the action as the moment the 504th made its reputation. In Italy, the 82nd Airborne Division suffered 1,605 casualties, of these the 504th accounted for 1,106. Many fell at Altavilla.

The German attacks on September 16 marked the end of General von Vietinghoff's resolve to throw the Allies back into the sea. His resources had run low, and if he continued attacking the beachhead, he knew Montgomery's advancing British forces would soon outflank him. When he withdrew from the 504th's advance on September 18, he withdrew across the entire front and fell back on his original plan to form a defensive line south of Rome.

Through their code breakers, the Allies again knew German intentions. The Germans wanted to use Rome as a tool of attrition. They would retain it as long as possible, costing the Allies as many casualties—and themselves as few—as they could in the process. For this purpose they planned to place their forces behind the Gustav Line, a line of complex defensive fortifications stretching across the Italian boot. To get at Rome, the Allies would be forced to assault the Gustav. During their retreat, the Germans planned to make the port of Naples useless by blowing up all port facilities and sinking hulks in the famous harbor to create supply problems for the invaders.

Alexander's plans shifted with this intelligence. He calculated that if he vigorously pursued with Clark's Fifth Army on the west coast and Montgomery's Eighth Army on the east, the Germans would not be able to finish fortifying the Gustav Line; the twin armies would stick to the easier coastal areas and, supported by naval artillery, would enfold the Germans from either side. Unfortunately, immediate and vigorous pursuit could not be mounted. Clark's army had been badly mauled at Salerno; the German defenders less so. And there was resistance among the troops; a mutiny by a group of British reinforcements who thought they had seen enough combat in Africa resulted in 139 men court-martialed and sentenced to twenty-five years in prison. The attack northward did not kick off until late September, giving the Germans several days and freedom to create delaying obstacles.

The Allies did move toward Naples, which with its fine port and airfields around Fossia, to the east, offered the best base for the attack toward Rome. But here the Allies were to learn how doggedly the Germans could harry an advancing army. Skillful delaying tactics worked well in the mountainous terrain, and Allied infantrymen had to fight for each hilltop, to discover the foe had vanished only to reappear at the next.

The 82nd next participated in a large attack to break through the mountains on the Sorrento peninsula to reach Naples. The plan called for the 82nd to smash through the Chiunzi Pass, then held by Lieutenant Colonel William O. Darby's Rangers (a highly trained commando type unit), and then on to Naples.

The fight for Chiunzi Pass was vicious, but the Germans had no intention of making their stand there; as the troopers closed, the Germans withdrew. The weight of the 82nd's assault had convinced them further resistance would be too costly.

The next day, Gavin saw Naples in the distance from the heights of Sorrento; the wondrous bay and islands were covered with a deep pall of smoke from the burning waterfront facilities. Ridgway ordered Gavin to the assault. The paratroopers advanced down the slopes without opposition in a strange, peaceful silence. The Germans had withdrawn completely. Word spread rapidly that the city was abandoned. Except for the heavy throngs of cheering Italians in the towns along the way, the road to Naples lay wide open and so did the way for Mark Clark's divisions to launch their coastal move north.

On the morning of October 1, Jim Gavin's 505 reached the outskirts of Naples. Early that morning, while with his advance guard after a full night, his S-3, Major John Norton, came up from the rear. Norton relayed to Gavin remarkable orders. The dusty column was to wait at the outskirts until a "triumphal entry is organized," per order of high command.

Gavin had never seen a "triumphal entry." Visions of Napoleon's victory parades from illustrated books swam in his head. Ridgway then informed him that General Mark Clark would be arriving and Clark and Ridgway would enter the town at the head of the column. Gavin would be honored by being assigned to lead the forward elements. Ridgway had sent a man into the city to coordinate the march route. The Italians were to stay off the streets and assemble at the main square.

As Naples was the first major Italian city liberated, the press and photographers quickly gathered. General Clark planned to make an appropriate "conqueror's speech," and there would be a photo and a question-and-answer session. What Clark and Ridgway did not know then was that Clark's first city liberation would go as badly as his first landing, at Salerno.

At midafternoon, the column moved into smoking Naples and wound its way through vacant narrow streets to the noise of scattered gunfire and Luftwaffe strafing, even shooting down one German fighter. They reached Garibaldi Square without incident, but without cheers, either. The triumphal entry never happened; there were no delirious Italians in the square as there had been along the roadsides beyond the city. There was no one at all in the square. Clark called it "a ghostly city." For the benefit of the press, Clark delivered his speech to the advance guard, and the press snapped some pictures, but the Italians never materialized.

Neapolitans had wanted to cheer, but when police had cleared the streets as instructed, the populace expected Clark to come to Piazza Plebis-cito, where conquerors traditionally came. That was where the crowds went. With the "triumphal entry" a bust, the 82nd turned to occupying the city while the heavier regular infantry divisions moved forward to pursue the Germans.

Gavin found a city in chaos. The Germans had ruled Naples with brutal directness; anyone resisting them was executed, collaborators were rewarded. As a result, there was now a witch hunt for collaborators. Some of the gunfire that had made troopers wince as they entered the city was from retreating Germans, but a lot of it was from Italians settling scores. Also, Naples had been heavily bombed by Allied planes, and the Germans had destroyed anything that was left they thought might be useful to the Allies, particularly on the waterfront. Naples was a gutted city, its rubble still smoking.

Ridgway divided up the city among his regiments into occupation zones. The random shooting continued, and he wanted it stopped. In his zone, Gavin immediately asked local police how they dealt with the vio-lence. They shrugged. Italians are high-spirited people, he was told. Not willing to accept that, Gavin announced to the chief of police that any Italian found armed near where a weapon had just been discharged would be shot by American troops. Minutes after his announcement, Gavin heard a gun discharge. He snatched up his Garand, and charged out from his command post, gathered a platoon of infantry and charged to the site. They didn't find the shooter, but they did make their point. Shooting stopped in Naples that night.

The next day the troops began the major chore of restoring the city. Not only had the docks been systematically destroyed, but the railway, communications and telephone centers, and fuel depots lay in ruins as well. The Germans had set mountains of reserve coal afire, to smolder for weeks. They had set booby traps wherever they could, and they had planted several large bombs, armed with timing devices, around the city. The Americans found most of the bombs. Two, they did not. About a week after the occupation, one exploded under the post office and, four days later, another under a building used as a barracks, killing several Italians and eighteen Americans. A 1,700-pound bomb was found under Ridgway's hotel headquarters and defused just minutes before it was set to go off.

On October 4, Gavin and his 505th were sent from Naples northward to lead the drive to the Volturno, to secure bridges essential for further progress up the Italian boot. The effort was a scaled-down version of a more ambitious plan to penetrate German defenses, and Ridgway stubbornly opposed it. Clark proposed that the entire 82nd be assigned to lead VI Corps across the river. Ridgway, like Gavin, a believer in command from the foxhole, immediately went to the front to study the ground over which Clark would send his troops. He saw a wide plain leading to the river, behind it on high ground waited the Hermann Göring Division, well dug in. Ridgway was appalled, likened it to a World War I assault, and objected strenuously. He believed the attack would needlessly destroy his division, and again he endangered his career by protesting; nevertheless, he submitted to the orders.

Gavin ordered Mark Alexander's 2nd Battalion to seize the small town of Arnone on the Volturno River and the five canal crossings that led to it. The 1st Battalion would wait in reserve, while the 3rd remained in Naples for police duties.

The 2nd Battalion resolutely attacked on October 4, and by the next evening had taken the five canal bridges, with only one bridge damaged, but the British proved reluctant to deploy their tanks until infantry routed out anything that might destroy one. German resistance was heavy, and the area liberally sprinkled with mines, and the troopers found the Germans willing to fight hard for Arnone itself; nevertheless, after a sharp and bloody two-hour battle amidst intense German artillery fire and stout counterattacks, the battalion took Arnone on October 6. During the attack, Alexander had called for British tanks and received none, so he had demanded all the artillery the British had. That he got, and the concentrated artillery fire helped break the German counterattacks. Then the panicked enemy broke and retreated, partially blowing a section of the Arnone bridge. Having reached their river objective, the 505 contented itself with stopping further enemy movement with artillery, but Alexander did send patrols across the river and requested permission to secure a bridgehead, which the British tank commander, Brigadier H. R. Ackwright denied. On October 8, the 505 returned from Arnone and resumed occupation duties in Naples. They had forged the way to the river, and on October 14 British forces were across. Having delayed as long as they liked, the Germans fell back to prepared positions farther north.

During the fight, Gavin had not prowled the front as much as usual.

He was in the process of turning over his 505 to his executive officer, Herbert F. Batcheller, because back in Naples, Ridgway had promoted Gavin to brigadier general and the job of assistant division commander. On October 10, Ridgway himself pinned on Gavin's general's stars, in front of a division headquarters formation in Naples.

Though happy about the promotion, the attack to the Volturno troubled Gavin. They had had to fight alongside the British, who refused to attack without everything perfectly in place, even if the situation called for fast action. British tanks might have saved his battalion a great deal of sweat in Arnone, but the British refused to use them until it was safe and the tanks were no longer really needed. He wrote, " . . . typical British attack methods. There are many things about their technique that I admire, but their attack tactics are not among them. Their employment of armor was a great disappointment. They are reluctant to take losses, but when they do lose, they die well."

Gavin's reward for his battles in Sicily and now in Italy, besides the bright star on either shoulder, was to be included in the planning of the decisive operation of the war, the long-awaited Normandy invasion. Though Ridgway was the senior airborne man, he recommended Gavin because of his personal, detailed expertise on what paratroopers could and could not do. Gavin was considered the point man, the one who could be expected to do the impossible—or die trying.

Normandy, still only a figment, hung like fog over the Allied campaign in Italy in 1943, exerting more influence than the persistent defensive strategy of the foe. Because the army's top minds throughout that year remained focused on Normandy, the Italian campaign was fought as a sideshow. Gavin noted the lack of urgency and focus in late October, "It is evident that if Rommel wanted he could counterattack and drive the Fifth Army one hell of a long way back. They are very tired and have no fresh troops in sight. The number of divisions present are barely enough to cover the front leaving wide gaps between units. If the German counterattacked in force at any one point he could really roll them up."

This caused an ironic crisis for the 82nd. The division was already designated as an Overlord (invasion of Normandy) unit. Yet the Italian campaign continued inconclusively, an expensive slog up an extremely defensible peninsula, a type of warfare that absorbed troops like a sponge, and the 82nd, an elite, highly trained and specialized unit, would be doubly wasted crawling through the rocky ambushes of Italy.

While the 505th had spearheaded the first crossing of the Volturno, the Germans had gained time to fortify the Gustav Line, and they fell back onto it. Here they would stop retreating, and the Allies would be held far south of Italy's prize, Rome. To add to Clark's troubles, the weather turned against him. His divisions faced difficult terrain for assault, and Italy's winter rains came. And arrayed in deep defensive positions, the Germans fought on with patience and ferocity. Clark would not reach Rome for another eight months, and then only after the agony of Anzio and Cassino.

Mark Clark wanted Rome and planned an amphibious invasion to outflank the Gustav Line to get it. The place he picked for it was Anzio. Now where would he get the troops? The obvious choice for the assault was the 82nd. It was one of the best divisions in the theater and was sitting in Naples on occupation duty. Predictably, Clark requested it, and he nearly got it. At the SHAEF level, where all eyes remained on Normandy, a compromise was reached. The 82nd would go to England to prepare for Overlord, but it would leave behind one regiment reinforced with artillery to bolster Clark. Tucker's 504 drew the duty.

When Clark got the 504 at the end of October, he sent the regiment forward immediately as regular infantry. In this incongruous role the men of the 504 wrote one of the 82nd's proudest chapters in Italy. They took objective after objective in difficult terrain, under difficult conditions. Gavin visited them at the front in early November and found them far ahead of their flanking units, undaunted by Germans on three sides of them. He noted, "Tucker doing well on his front. Parachute troops are making a name for themselves with the Germans." And they were. It was the 504 that earned the name "Devils in Baggy Pants" from the Germans who faced them. German commanders characterized them as barbarians and spread the rumor that they were criminals freed from U.S. prisons only to fight. But there was no glory for the 504 in Italy, just continuous fighting and casualties. They continued their mountain campaign until after Christmas. Then the regiment was pulled out in preparation for a landing at Anzio.

British General Alexander's headquarters conceived the plan. It called for a series of frontal attacks at the Gustav Line, while VI Corps landed at Anzio. Behind Anzio is a coastal plain, with the Alban Hills rising dimly 20 miles in the distance, and Rome only 30 miles to the north. The landing operation was code named Shingle and its commander was Major

General John P. Lucas. He had at his disposal one American infantry division, one British infantry division, a British tank division, an attached infantry brigade, some Rangers, the 509th Parachute Infantry Battalion, and the 504th Parachute Infantry Regiment from the 82nd.

D day was January 22, 1944. The landing force was to drive swiftly forward and capture the Alban Hills overlooking Rome, which, Alexander hoped, would make Kesselring withdraw and give the Allies the city. Mark Clark saw it differently; he remembered Salerno. He instructed Lucas to show caution and first establish a strong beachhead that could withstand violent German counterattacks. Then he could initiate offensive actions if he thought them possible.

Anzio was a gamble. By Christmas, Rommel had been sent to France to prepare for the cross-Channel invasion the Germans knew must come. Hitler made twenty-five divisions, some from the Balkans and some from Rommel's old command, available to Kesselring for the defense of Italy, while the Allies had but eleven. High Italian mountains eliminated the possibility of maneuver, and the war became one of attrition. The principal German defensive strong point along their Gustav Line was Monte Cassino, a mountain crowned with an ancient monastery. It looked impregnable to the Allies, and its taking proved one of the costliest victories of the war. The 36th and 34th divisions were thrown against it and nearly destroyed. Clark believed that Cassino could be avoided altogether if the German line could only be outflanked. The outflanking could be done amphibiously, and that was Anzio's purpose.

Clark lacked the necessary men to do it by the book, but with Eisenhower preoccupied with Overlord plans, the Mediterranean Theater fell under British command. And Churchill demanded the fall of Rome. Anzio would go ahead.

At first, all went well. The invaders achieved surprise when they came ashore on the morning of January 22 to a quiet beach. It felt, on the shore, more like a training exercise than an invasion. By noon, the beachhead was already 3 miles deep and 15 miles wide.

But Kesselring reacted fast. Units from all over Italy that were not already in combat streamed toward Anzio, including a German parachute division stationed in Rome. Lucas waited. His troops did little that first day but sit on the beach and dig defenses, nor did any aggressive moves follow on the next few days. Thus Lucas gave the Germans the Alban Hills to his front, and they soon rained shells down on his position from above. Anzio became another quagmire for Allied hopes. Four months of paralysis followed, of continuous bombardment and stinging German counterattacks, while the troops dug in deeper and deeper in the beachhead and endured a merciless pounding. Anzio became an unforgettable nightmare.

But again, the 504th, in an amphibious landing, added to its reputation.

While the 504th fought in the mountains and dug in at Anzio, most of the 82nd was with Gavin in Sicily, training and perfecting pathfinder techniques. Since Gavin felt accurate navigation was the key to airborne success, he monitored their progress constantly while working his way into his new job as assistant division commander. The rest of the division was learning what the 505 already knew, that Gavin might turn up anywhere.

But soon after Gavin became ADC, George Marshall contacted Ridgway and requested an officer with combat experience and vision to be the airborne advisor for Overlord planning. Ridgway gave him Gavin. He told Gavin of his new post on October 31. Elated, Gavin wrote, "He [Ridgway] has recommended me to go to UK as advisor on airborne matters for the coming show. It is to be a job on General Marshall's staff. Upon arrival of the Division I am to return to it. This is opportunity with a capital "O." I am going to work hard. . . . General Ridgway was nice enough to tell me that ultimately he wants me to get the division. I am a bit young for it."

On November 17, Brigadier General Gavin left Italy for England, and the 82nd Airborne Division, minus the 504th, sailed for Northern Ireland, where they would begin refitting and training for the invasion of Normandy.

8.

A I R B O R N E

P L A N N E R

Having urged the invasion of the northern European plain upon the British for two years, the Americans made it clear in 1944 that they would wait no longer, although they still needed British cooperation.

England would be the staging area, and the weight of English troops could be decisive. Yet it was not a foregone conclusion that the Americans would get what they wanted. "Though Winston Churchill breathed fiery defiance and vengeance as soon as the British army had returned from Dunkirk, his design for invasion was always one that would be applied only after a combination of aerial bombardment, nourishment of anti-Nazi resistance within Europe, and closing a ring of peripheral attacks around Hitler's empire had so undermined the enemy's strength that the invasion would simply be the coup de grace." He didn't feel that had happened by the fall of 1943, when the Americans demanded a decision.

Memories of the Somme died hard. Rough treatment in France and Africa and the guarantee of a fierce fight for France added to British reluctance. There was no clever way to execute a large-scale amphibious invasion, not at least in Europe in 1944. It could be fought only one way, frontally. The troops that invaded Europe would have to charge from the sea into well-designed and powerful German defenses. That meant high casualties. It meant political cost and a repeat of the national heartbreak of 1916. Salerno was another reminder, as was Tarawa in the Pacific. The British wanted fewer casualties, and they did not want Overlord. Overlord was forced upon them by the Russian and American governments. The Americans sought decisive battle, to destroy the enemy's forces. The Russians wanted to weaken German forces arrayed against them in the East.

In May 1943, the British agreed to the invasion for the following year. Overlord was officially born. It was intended to hurry a decisive war-ending engagement the Americans believed they could win with superior numbers and matériel. That fall, Churchill attempted one last time to get the Americans to postpone the invasion until a year later, the fall of 1944, to continue Mediterranean operations. Only Stalin's insistence weighted the balance in the American favor, and Overlord proceeded.

The British tried to maintain as much control as possible. The politics of the invasion grew dense. Naturally, the British wanted the overall commander to be British.

By the beginning of 1944 the Americans, too, had fought the Germans, and they had earned some victories. American production and manpower had reached the point where their input of men and matériel in the future would vastly outweigh the British. At the Quebec conference in August 1943, Churchill brought with him General Sir Alan Brooke, the man to whom he had promised command. Roosevelt balked. The commander would be American, and it would be America's first soldier, Chief of Staff of the Army George C. Marshall. Then came a change of mind. Marshall was too indispensable to Roosevelt as chief of staff. FDR simply could not spare him from Washington. Eisenhower was a logical second choice.

Still, the British persisted. If the overall commander was American, then, the commander of the ground attack should be British. Montgomery was brought back from Italy to take the job. He was England's hero, and even though notorious for lack of diplomacy and ponderous in his methods, he was considered England's ablest general. Once the assault on the beaches was over, Eisenhower would arrive on the Continent, and the American generals would gain equivalent status with Montgomery as commanders under Eisenhower. All of this made for an odd command arrangement from the very beginning, and, politically, it created a permanent committee, not a leader.

Gavin arrived in London on November 18, 1943. It was the first time he had ever been there and the first time in his life he had been an important man. His spirits soared with the spirit of the undaunted old city. He had an important job to do, and he knew how to do it well. Gavin took planning seriously, but he also hoped, after a year of war, to relax a little. And he liked London. The London of 1943–1944 remained blacked out; Londoners had suffered, and the "grim resolve" of 1940 was still there, but now, after victories in North Africa and the Mediterranean, it seemed that the Allies were winning.

Gavin loved walking. From his billet at Grosvenor House (later he was given a one-bedroom apartment at 18 Berkeley Street) he wandered incognito, like a college boy on holiday. He scrambled through bombed buildings, and he saw how rationing and shortages stripped down the shelves in the shops. But London was a rich city compared to Naples, and the people he met were friendly. He felt a special energy about the city. Uniformed men and women scurried about at work or on leave, and nightlife careened at a mad pace. London was a romantic place in those days. It seemed to live up to every cliché, gallant, wry, and fun loving. It had been a point of pride to be out and about when the bombers came, and the smoky pubs remained constantly full—as did the restaurants. Good dinners could still be had, for a price, and Gavin ate out often— though he complained at the expense of it all. On his second day in town, he met someone to show him where the best dinners were. Her name was Val Porter, and she was married.

General officers were assigned their own drivers, often young women, and vehicles by the British government. Eisenhower's "chaufferette" was Kay Summersby, and their affair is documented—at least by her. Valerie Porter was Gavin's driver. The first day he met her, he commented in his diary how lovely he found her. The day after that, he took her to dinner, and from then on his diary is full of entries about how he felt about her. She was from an upper-class British family and spoke with the "Ox-bridge" accent of the officer corps. Standing about 5 feet 6 inches, she had reddish-brown hair, a slim, athletic figure, and is remembered admiringly as magnetically attractive. Gavin pursued Val Porter with the same intensity he had shown on Biazza Ridge—though he kept the affair second to his duties. She became his main London diversion.

The day after Gavin arrived in London, he reported to his new boss, Major General Ray W. Barker, a large, gruff man, at COSSAC (Chief of Staff to the Supreme Allied Commander) located at the Norfolk House. It was there that the planning for the invasion took place. Much to

Gavin's surprise, Lieutenant General "Boy" Browning, the well-known British airborne leader, awaited him with General Barker in the high-ceilinged wood-walled spacious office. This was top level indeed. It turned out to be not a good beginning. Browning discussed several things with Gavin, but the chill came when Browning commented that he thought Ridgway's amphibious landing at Sicily, as opposed to jumping in, was "badly done."

The insinuation was unmistakable—that Browning, and perhaps others, thought Ridgway a coward. Gavin came immediately to his chief's defense. It was his first meeting with Browning and his first conflict. Actually, Gavin was on the lookout for Browning before he ever arrived. He had noted in his diary on November 17, "Before my departure General Ridgway warned me of the machinations of General Browning, stating that he was intelligent, charming, and very close to Mr. Churchill. Further that he was unprincipled and ruthless in his efforts to align every operation and every piece of equipment to the complete benefit of the British Empire at our expense. Worse still, he had completely taken in General [Bill] Lee who thought his word was law. This is just about entirely true and Browning must be handled cautiously but firmly."

But Gavin went on to note the positive side of a potential relationship with Browning. His concern for his career had become more active with his new assignment, and Browning had some ideas about what the next war might be like that powerfully interested him. "I am aware however," Gavin wrote, "that he is thinking beyond this war to the creation and maintenance of an international airborne force. I am especially interested in it, and I believe he will head it. This is not the time to alienate his friendship. The officers of the army of tomorrow must be international minded. I have thirty years of service ahead of me. I must see beyond the next battle whether I get clipped in it or not."

Nevertheless, he remained cautious. He said of the meeting, "Talked to him [Browning] for quite a while. He is smooth as ever and quite generally distrusted by American high commanders. Afterwards, General Barker said referring to him, 'Oh yes, he is quite an empire builder.' I still think a lot of Browning. We can go a long way together." That view would change; but then, at the outset, Gavin was excited just be in London and at the center of things.

His excitement faded fast. Within three weeks he had already tired of life as a staff officer. His days were filled with meetings, and he found too many difficulties he could not attack head-on. The first was the mission itself. Airborne plans for the initial assault phase of the Normandy landings (code named Neptune) were modest, and there were some who doubted they had a place in the operation at all. Only battalion-sized drops from the 101st—and none from the 82nd—were envisioned, and they would have little significance to the landings themselves. They were projected for an area behind Omaha Beach, the area most suitable for tanks.

Gavin had seen lightly armed paratroopers struggle against tanks before, and he wanted the plan changed. This took him to Lieutenant General Omar Bradley's office. Bradley commanded the forces landing on Utah Beach, and he remained a strong proponent of airborne operations. Thirty years later, Bradley's aide, Chet Hansen, recalled that that was one of the big reasons Omar Bradley succeeded so well as a commander in World War II, because he knew what his subordinates could do, and he gave them missions they could accomplish. His subordinates in turn respected and trusted him. In Bradley, Gavin found an ally. They created a new plan that helped Gavin in several ways.

Because the area behind Utah Beach is marshy, troop movements could be easily channeled by the terrain. Bradley and Gavin saw this on their maps. Even if Bradley broke out and away from the beaches easily, the maze of obstacles, irrigation canals, swamps, streams, and bridges might cost him more than the beach assault itself. Thus Bradley insisted as part of planning that he would not land on Utah Beach unless substantial airborne forces landed behind the beach defenses and helped him take and hold the critical transportation centers and bridges. Paratroopers, he argued, would also block German reinforcements coming to the beach.

Bradley's scenario helped enlarge the drop. It was aimed at terrain Gavin thought favored paratroops and involved both the entire 101st and the 82nd. Gavin liked even better that Bradley's plan helped forestall a plan of Boy Browning's to corner nearly all the available troop carrier aircraft to lift the British airborne divisions for a drop near Caen.

Meanwhile, the meetings dragged on. Often the British would bring to the conferences one or two individuals who deliberately obstructed progress. However, the British would only send them out if an equal number of Americans left with them, usually someone essential from the American delegation.

Gavin fretted. Despite Bradley's new plan, airborne power and effect still depended on influence. Who would control the most aircraft? Who would have overall airborne command? Browning tirelessly pursued this and made clear he meant to have mostly American aircraft, with American pilots and British paratroopers. Who would drop where with what support? When would the drops be? These and a thousand other issues rested on the table, and each required negotiation. Irritations grew. Gavin found one friendly British officer, confided in him, then discovered that the same officer went back to Browning and told him everything. Gavin noted in his diary, "Keep the upper hand is the watch word. . . . I am at the moment persona non grata with General Browning. . . . I have never seen such a command as this. . . . Before an order is published everyone must be queried. . . . In some measure, large or small depending on the circumstances, squabbling, jealousies, politics, and self-aggrandizement are rampant. God, to get back to the soldiers! This however is an education."

By Christmas, he wrote of Browning, "The situation regarding Browning looks particularly bad. There is no doubt that he is doing some long range planning, planning that will ultimately encompass the entire Allied airborne effort well into the peace beyond the war. . . . He is still endeavoring to get control of the entire allied airborne lift."

Other problems arose. The 52nd Troop Carrier Wing had gained a great deal of experience in dropping paratroopers over Sicily and Italy; and after the successful drop at Salerno, the troopers had confidence in the wing. The 82nd wanted to remain mated to it. But in England, higher authorities, particularly General Brereton, specified that they would be mated with newly arrived wings, even though those wings had had no night training.

Brereton, a short, vain man who habitually referred to himself as "Lewis Brereton" rather than using the pronoun "I," had excelled as a political soldier before the war, but he ran into trouble during the first few days of American involvement, when his B-17 bombers were largely destroyed on the ground in the Philippines. After that disgrace he had been sent to India for some time, then resurfaced in England to command the very large American Ninth Air Force. To Gavin's annoyance, Brereton saw air power as the "end all" of modern warfare. Ground battle was obsolete. The way to beat Germany was from the air by wrecking her cities and industry, thus destroying her production and morale.

Brereton's boss, the commander of all air forces in England, was Air

Chief Marshal Trafford Leigh-Mallory, famous for his part in the Battle of Britain. The British had long been engaged in night bombing raids on German cities, terror raids designed to destroy German morale. Flying at night, they could avoid the bulk of the Luftwaffe, which flew by day; the German night-fighter wing was not yet a major concern.

Brereton and the Americans believed that the German economy could be destroyed through pinpoint bombing at important "choke points" that every modern economy had to have, such as ball bearings and fuel. Without necessities like these, the Germans could no longer fight. To achieve this, the Americans had to bomb by day, using heavily armed bombers, such as the B-17, and fighter escort, within the fighters' limited range, to ward off the Luftwaffe. In practice, the air force suffered severely in 1943 daylight raids and the concept was under attack. Then, to complicate Gavin's fight for lift to drop his forces, the P-51 Mustang fighter arrived. With long-range fuel tanks that could be jettisoned, the fighters could escort all the way to the target. By the winter of 1944, massive daylight air raids struck Germany. Not only would they destroy important German targets, but the Mustangs would lure out and destroy the Luftwaffe.

The men who held such theories were no friends to the airborne arm. Neither Leigh-Mallory nor Brereton cared much for supporting ground operations or accurately dropping paratroopers. Brereton was willing to listen to Gavin's call for ground support and training time for troop carrier pilots, but his mind remained elsewhere. His fighters were taking on the Luftwaffe. Leigh-Mallory, too, would listen to Gavin, but he had his own special political agenda: retaining and promoting British control. Before Neptune, Leigh-Mallory informed Eisenhower that he was convinced that glider troops attempting to land at night would meet with disaster. He predicted that British drops would go well; however, American paratroopers would suffer terribly. By his reckoning, American glider troops would take 70 percent casualties, and paratroops would take at least 50 percent.

Recalling meeting with Leigh-Mallory, Gavin wrote "I sensed in Leigh-Mallory a real lack of confidence in the American glider troops' ability to do things we were confident they could do. . . . It was puzzling; he knew nothing about parachute combat, yet he was telling us that we would be ineffective. . . . I was a bit afraid that he might recommend that we not be employed in an airborne role, which to us would have been catastrophic."

Gavin sought to forge a plan for air support with these difficult men. It was at times maddening, but in the end, he got the 52nd Troop Carrier Wing moved to England with the 82nd.

The top commanders, Eisenhower and Montgomery, had not yet arrived in England when Gavin joined the planning team. As a result, men schemed without benefit of policy from the top. Finally, like a Caesar returning in triumph, Montgomery returned from Italy to crowds of English admirers, England's first hero of the war. With him in charge, planning took a serious turn. Gavin and Bradley remained stalwart supporters of the American theory of the coming battle, and Gavin's dislike for Browning grew more intense. For obvious reasons, Browning thought there should be a unified airborne command and he should head it. He ran into resistance from an unlikely source, Brereton. When Browning proposed a combined Allied troop carrier command, Brereton refused. Troop carrier aircraft came under his authority, and he refused to give them up.

Meanwhile, a stone-faced Gavin sat through the meetings, muzzling his impatience in public and telling his diary, "I wish to hell that tomorrow were D-day. It is the waiting that is bothersome, not the fight itself."

Despite his ennui, Gavin managed to leave his stamp. Since airborne was young, standard operating practices and terminology varied widely and bred confusion and delays. For instance, the place where the parachutists jumped was called a "jump area" in the American Army and a "drop zone" in the British Army. In December, after much haggling over what it would say, Gavin published "Training Memorandum on the Employment of Airborne Forces." This document cleared up a lot of the differences between services and divisions over what would be called what and how it would be done in Allied airborne units. Yet each line had to be negotiated. As Gavin later wrote, "Everyone wanted to discuss, alter, criticize, and contribute to it." It galled him to endure all the petty controversy, but it was necessary if the British and Americans were to work together. Finally, on February 16, Gavin returned to the 82nd, which meantime had come to England. He was relieved. He had feared he had become a cog in the planning process and that the process would not let him go.

Gavin went back to troop command, always his first love, but the airborne planning for the invasion was far from over. The final plan and exact dispositions did not come into being until just days before the actual jump. From Gavin's front-row seat, it seemed that perhaps the biggest miracle of the Normandy invasion was not so much that it worked but that the British and Americans managed to work together long enough for the vital details to be resolved.

On February 16, the 82nd Airborne Division, (minus the 504th, still locked in combat at Anzio), moved from Northern Ireland, where it had been stationed since November, and arrived in the north of England, in the Leicester-Nottingham region. Gavin joined them. SHAEF immediately asked for him back. Ridgway, with Gavin importuning him, refused. Happily, Gavin set to work.

The division had changed in his absence, and there were many new questions to consider. Thanks to Leigh-Mallory's objections, and some unsuccessful trial runs, the night glider drop for Normandy was scratched. Only paratroopers, plus a few gliders loaded with heavy equipment, would go in at night. The glider troops would follow at sunset the next day. This made more aircraft available for parachutists, and some independent regiments were assigned to the 82nd and the 101st. The 507th, under the command of George V. "Zip" Millet, Jr., and the 508th, commanded by Roy E. Lindquist, became parts of the 82nd. Now the division had four parachute regiments—though one was still in Italy—and one glider regiment. The glider regiment also swelled. The 325 had been a two-battalion regiment, but for Overlord, a regiment of the 101st was divided and the 325th acquired one portion, so that it grew to three battalions. Gavin and Ridgway both worried about the training and leadership of the new regiments and resolved to watch them closely, taking severe measures, if necessary, to ready them. To speed their preparation for combat, veterans from the 505 were sprinkled into their line companies.

Ridgway, then engrossed in higher-level meetings, chose Gavin as the man in charge of final training. Gavin relished the task and, as was his custom, made training intense. All the regiments immediately set out on marches through the English countryside, sometimes tramping 20 miles. When they thought they were going to get a break, Gavin would appear with a difficult mission to be executed immediately. After spending a sleepless night on the exercise, Gavin led the march home. Through it all, Gavin did his best to appear where trouble started. His form soon became familiar. He now addressed the soldiers he met as "son," and the men instantly picked out his tall, lanky, long-armed profile. Commanders who had not dealt with him before soon found themselves off balance.

Gavin's old 505th was proof that even the best-trained regiments were not above reproach. When he had left the 505th, Gavin had been replaced by his former regimental executive officer, Herbert F. Batcheller. Gavin had been disappointed with Batcheller's performance on Biazza Ridge, where he had seemed "jumpy," according to Gavin's notes. But men often improved in command. To give Batcheller his due, to be under Gavin's nose and in charge of his favorite regiment was an impossible situation. Gavin watched the 505th closely—and within three weeks of its arriving in England, he found fault. In field problems, the two new regiments outperformed the veteran 505. Officially, that was why Gavin recommended that Batcheller be relieved. The reason ran deeper; it was not just Biazza Ridge. Gavin noted on one occasion while the 505th was in the field on an exercise, Batcheller was with his girlfriend. Gavin was incensed that a man would choose a mistress over his regiment, even for a day. Neglecting troops was one sin Gavin would not forgive. On March 16, 1944, Gavin wrote, "The 507 and 508 both look better to all appearances right now than the 505th. I spoke to General Ridgway this evening about relieving Batcheller; recommended [William E.] Ekman to take his place. . . . It would be disastrous to continue counting on Batcheller. I have never told anyone of his behavior on Sicily, neither on D-day nor at Biazza. I had hoped he could do the job when put on his own." Ridgway followed the recommendation and relieved the unlucky man and appointed the executive officer from the 508th, Lieutenant Colonel William E. Ekman, to command the 505th. Ekman had never been in combat, and he would face a regiment that had two combat jumps and was notoriously cocky and prone to discipline violations. To make for a truly inauspicious beginning, he began his first speech to his new regiment with a slip of the tongue, "Now you men of the 508th . . ." A friend commented years later, "It's a wonder he lived beyond that night."

Gavin wrote, "That is a tough spot for Ekman, but I'm sure he can handle it." Ekman was a disciplinarian, and Gavin liked him, partly because he had modeled himself on his chief. He was calm, bright, extremely knowledgeable about things military, he moved everywhere in training, and he seemed tireless physically. Veterans remember that he did pull together the regiment, but he did it sensibly and fairly. Ultimately, he performed well in combat and won the respect of the 505th and Gavin.

With Ekman in charge of the 505th, Gavin turned his eyes to the inexperienced regiments. He did not like Millet and wrote him down as "lazy, soft, indolent, lacking leadership necessary for combat." Gavin believed that Millet was not nose to nose with his men in training. He was seldom to be found near his troops, and he seemed primarily interested in his regiment's athletic teams. But Gavin felt reluctant to be the "hatchet man" himself. He noted, "There will be lots of bad feeling if Millet must be relieved. . . . There will be many SNAFU affairs in the 507 as long as Millet is in command. This is a vicious system. It will turn against the hatchet man if he is not careful. If you do nothing, many lives might be lost needlessly and your unit will not function satisfactorily. . . . If you kick a man out you make many enemies." Of the third new commander, Lindquist, Gavin thought he had gathered an excellent staff, but he did not respect the man's leadership ability. He seemed too remote from his troops. In time, however, Gavin warmed to him and gained confidence in him.

Gavin's method was to locate trouble spots with his personal radar, and when he found them before the regimental commander, which was often the case, that commander slipped in Gavin's estimation.

The new commanders at first failed to note that Gavin's information usually came from the troops, not from the command structure, which gave him a head start and usually, a shortcut to a solution. To get there before Gavin took a very dynamic and active officer. Good regiments, Gavin believed, begin with a commander knowing his troops. Having accomplished that, he felt all it took was decisiveness in combat to gain victory.

Officers and men who found themselves on his wrong side seldom forgot the experience. Gavin's voice never went up an octave, and he controlled his temper in all things; but his eyes reflected his moods, and his subordinates hated facing their wrath. Speaking quietly, Gavin would calmly outline such faults as he had located, but the hard gray eyes revealed his intensity.

To be a regimental commander under Gavin could be difficult. He did not think like most military commanders of his day. The key to Gavin's leadership, for as long as he wore a uniform, was his troops. He evaluated his military units by watching individual soldiers intently. Did they have all the equipment they should have? Were they technically and tactically proficient at what they were doing at that moment. Did they get their mail? Were they treated fairly?

Some officers adopted British habits and class distinctions. Sometimes they lived better than their soldiers and seemed not to care. Privately, Gavin commented, "This fast growing habit of officers putting their troops in tents then getting themselves a fine house in a nearby village burns me up. At present, every regimental commander has himself a house while his troops are under canvas, then we wonder about accusations of officers being aloof, unapproachable, and unsympathetic. I don't like the mud and rain anymore than anyone else, but neither do the troops. Someone is losing their sense of values, maybe their perspective." Gavin believed that there were no bad regiments, just bad commanders; and he very much liked and saw tremendous potential in the troops in the 507 and 508. "It is very refreshing to work with troops fresh from America, enthusiastic and anxious. They listen and hang on every word, and as far as I could observe, try to do exactly as they are told. The battle-hardened veterans of the 505th are by now calloused. The 507 and 508 appear to lack the technical proficiency of the 505th, but what they lack they more than make up for in their zeal and interest in doing the correct thing. They will do all right."

The focus of his diary entries during this period in Britain is squarely on the commanders of the new troops. To be certain of the status of all units under his command, Gavin kept an exhausting schedule. His diary reveals nights when he worked until evening, caught a train to London to visit Val Porter, got back to Leicester at 4 A.M., and set out to evaluate training by 6 A.M. He never missed troop training and preferred arriving unannounced and without a bevy of staff officers. Whether it was a rifle range or a mock perimeter in the dank English countryside, he found it, talked to troops, and discovered their difficulties. Accounting for equipment particularly irritated him. Gavin believed that any unit destined for combat must have every piece of its fighting equipment available and ready so that each trooper had an equal chance of surviving. To his irritation, he continually found troops and units without important pieces of gear such as ammo pouches, spare uniforms, and the all-important serviceable extra pair of socks. After finding insufficient numbers of bayonets and other essentials in the 3rd Battalion of the 505, he noted, "Strange thing and one most of us have long since learned. That is that a unit commander will repeatedly profess complete equipment and weapons status for his unit yet a showdown will show up many deficiencies." Gavin increased the frequency of equipment inspections to ensure readiness.

He took just as much care with his own readiness. Running, (and to his troops' dismay he often ran back from training), relieved his tension and prepared him for the ordeal he knew was coming. He ran almost daily and methodically kept track of his times. Jogging past the ancient stone houses and the deep green of the countryside helped him keep his busy life in perspective. Ridgway once made the mistake of running with Gavin. Gavin noted the day afterwards, "General Ridgway was very badly stove up after our last jaunt. Sometimes it is difficult for a formerly active man to realize that he is aging. I expect to have the same difficulty myself." Gavin's other source of relief from the grind of his job was his London love life. His need ran deep. Even though he lived far from London now, he still visited Val whenever he felt satisfied his work was done in Leicester. She also came to see him. "Val is a problem but grand. . . . There is no one who can cause me more damn concern and discomfort at this moment. That must be corrected," he wrote. But the affair grew more serious. In April, he speculated, "I have always figured that the woman I married next would be very active in athletics, music, theater, and have many and diverse interests. It is odd that Val so completely meets every standard that I have had in mind yet she is not especially interested in any of the above. Because of the war and its social deprivations I have come to feel that a woman's honest complete and full love is more important than anything, recognizing the fact that biological sex is a very transitory attraction and that a permanent union must be based upon something more permanent than sexual attraction."

The 82nd was completely segregated, as was the entire U.S. Army, but black service units were stationed in the Nottingham area, and racial prejudice among his men annoyed Gavin intensely. Shortly after the 82nd arrived in the vicinity, a black soldier knifed, but did not kill, a paratrooper. Paratroopers plotted revenge, and because of Gavin's relations with the soldiers, he immediately heard of the plot. He felt he had to confront the problem squarely, and Ridgway supported him. "Several near riots in town last night," Gavin wrote, "English people, especially the lower classes, do not discriminate in any way. In fact they prefer the company of colored troops. The colored troops have been in this community for almost a year and they are well entrenched. Many are living with local English women. With the advent of the white troops, frays and minor unpleasant encounters have occurred in the local pubs and dance halls. American whites resent very much seeing a white woman in the company of a colored soldier. Here they almost see them in bed with them. Last night the 505th had its officer patrols armed." Gavin declared Leicester "off-limits until further notice."

Gavin was ahead of his time in race relations, but he would not tolerate troops preparing for combat devoting energy he felt should have been focused on the Germans, to racial conflicts. The problem was never fully resolved. The off-limits policy ended soon and fights continued until the division left Leicester.

Gavin knew the target of the Allied landing in Europe was to be the beaches of Normandy; he sought to know the area blindfolded and reviewed every bit of intelligence he could find on that bland, low coast. What he uncovered worried him. In France alone the Germans had at least major parts of fifty-six divisions. With that huge troop concentration, far more than the invading force could muster, Gavin wondered who was planning to invade whom.

Close study of aerial photographs identified a new, specifically antiairborne defense erected by the Germans. Intelligence called it "Rommel's asparagus." Simple, but deadly, stout poles, 12 feet tall, by the thousands were dug in on potential drop zones. Some appeared to be connected by wires that doubtless activated mines. The simple devices would wreak havoc with landing gliders, and serious damage would be done to paratroops landing at night. Gavin also noted increasing numbers of weapons pits dug in about the fields where Rommel's asparagus rose the thickest. He saw that the Germans were not only aware that airborne was to play an important role in any coming invasion, but that already the enemy had trained and prepared to meet it. This led him to adjust their drop zones to avoid the defenses, but shifting drop zones gave advantages to the enemy, for it forced the attackers away from the most favorable areas. With a month left to go, Gavin wrote, "I am getting anxious as we get closer."

Gavin felt certain the next fight would be a tough one, and in April, he increased his already intense level of activity. Above all else, he wanted Millet gone, and he stated his views to Ridgway, who disagreed and kept him. An angry Gavin wrote on April 10, "This afternoon General Ridgway gave me for comment a letter that General Howell sent him recommending the retention of Millet as regimental commander of the 507th. Too bad that we are at odds. I no doubt am making many enemies in this army by refusing to retain or condoning the retention of inefficient unit commanders. I cannot see any other course. Many lives are at stake. If a unit commander does not have it, I do not see how in the world I can keep him. I have been a bit ruthless and I have hurt many people, but I have had many people killed too." The next day, he settled the issue with Ridgway. He noted, "It looks as though he [Ridgway] may take him into his first fight. Poor Zip [Millet] is in a hell of a sweat, and I am sorry as hell for him. An officer should stay away from high troop command unless he is especially fitted for it and supremely confident." But there were other officers Gavin liked very much. He commented often on Vandervoort, Norton, Alexander, Ekman, and Winton. He believed there would be enough of them to see the regiments through—if the pilots got them to their drop zones. The Normandy invasion would be the largest airborne drop ever attempted, and practice drops in England had indicated that many of the green pilots might not make it.

As the northern European spring came swiftly on, more important changes seemed necessary within the 82nd. Gavin's old friend and mentor Bill Lee suffered a heart attack in February. He had begun having heart problems as early as 1941, but he had concealed it. Finally, on February 8 while on a field exercise, he suddenly collapsed with severe chest pains, and doctors sent him directly back to the States. Ridgway recommended Maxwell Taylor as Lee's replacement, and the recommendation won approval. Taylor informally took command of the 101st Airborne Division on March 8 and became its commander officially on March 14, 1944. Taylor had been carried on the 82nd Airborne Division's roster as the division artillery commander, but he had seldom trained or been with the division since it arrived in Europe. Instead, he had been detached from the 82nd on various planning staffs.

Taylor's language ability, plus the fact that he was a friend of Ridgway's, as well as a favored protégé of General "Vinegar Joe" Stilwell, led to a wildly varied pre-World War II career as a diplomat-soldier, serving in China, Japan, and South America. Socially adept, attentive to superiors and highly intelligent, he had risen rapidly after service as a personal assistant to America's top soldier, General George Marshall, in Washington. Unlike Gavin, Taylor had little interest in parachute operations or jumping and had won his jump wings through only a single training drop at Fort Benning, though he would jump at Normandy. Still, Ridgway wanted him for his staff abilities, and by 1942, Taylor had been made commander of the 82nd Airborne's field artillery. As such he joined the costly assault of Sicily only in the relatively calm second week of the battle, landing by ship in the company of a young battalion commander loaned to the 82nd by the 9th Division, Lieutenant Colonel William C. Westmoreland.

But Taylor's daring secret mission to Rome in September of 1943 won him fresh laurels. He also participated, shortly afterwards, in an Allied attempt to set up an Italian government in exile; this mission brought him into close contact with luminaries such as U.S. State Department advisor Robert Murphy and future British Prime Minister Harold Macmillan. Lee's heart attack gave Ridgway the opportunity to advance Taylor further, to command of the 101st. It was Taylor's first real combat test. It was also the first time he and Gavin stood face to face as rivals. Taylor outranked Gavin, but there was little comparison between the training and combat experience of the two paratroop leaders.

Though they have been lumped together as mutually supporting comrades-in-arms by historians, the Taylor-Ridgway-Gavin relationship was an odd one. Taylor and Gavin were never particularly good friends at the best of times, and came to loathe one another after World War II. While Taylor was in the 82nd, he and Gavin worked together but remained distant. Gavin's attempts at forbearance are almost palpable when he noted in his diary on the day of Taylor's departure from the 82nd: "Taylor went to London today to take over the Airborne section in SHAEF [Supreme Headquarters, Allied Expeditionary Force]. It is expected that he will shortly get the 101st, General Lee's Division. A long time ago I had figured out that the place for me at this stage of the game was on higher staff. That may have appeared correct at that time but it seems as clear as can be that the place for me now is with this division. I am certain that Bradley will give Ridgway a corps soon. I may be fortunate enough to get the division although I will certainly be rather young, and there will be lots of clamoring for it. I do not ever want to jump and fight the division for anyone else. . . . Sorry to lose him [Taylor] in many ways although it gives me an opportunity that I hope to be able to make the most of."

Gavin had seen staff work, and he had seen combat. He preferred combat. He preferred it in itself, and he preferred it as his own best route to reputation. The coalfields of Mount Carmel still lived for Gavin, and they fueled his ambition for recognition. But he increasingly understood how army careers were created by staff work and by personal association with the top brass. It caused ambivalence in his relationship with Ridgway. He was usually the respectful, honored son, but sometimes a petulant brat who must have his own way. Ridgway respected Gavin's professional ability and results but did not see him as the ideal of a perfectly rounded soldier, a mold his classmate Taylor seemed to fill. While Gavin and Ridgway worked well together Gavin felt uncomfortable with Ridgway's aloofness.

On April 25, he wrote, "Working with General Ridgway leaves me frequently with a feeling of not doing well enough or not doing the right thing. One rarely experiences a complete feeling of satisfaction. . . . I believe that he likes more personal attention than I give him." Gavin himself mused over the relationship at the time—almost with tongue in cheek. On February 16 he reported, "Walked home from the office for dinner accompanied by General Ridgway. General Ridgway in a good humor. Had a feeling he would not have been displeased to find me faltering at his pace. He takes considerable pride in having walked many people off their feet. It is unfortunate in some respects that we are so god damn much alike." Years later, Bradley's aide Colonel Chet Hansen remembered the Ridgway-Gavin relationship as "odd." Gavin had risen very fast because he was supremely competent—not because he was anyone's protégé, and he was certainly not Ridgway's protégé. Hansen said, "I wouldn't call Gavin anyone's man. He was very much his own man. Now he was Ridgway's protégé to the extent that he was his Assistant Division Commander, and I'm sure Ridgway recommended him for command of the 82nd. . . . I also thought there was a little competitive relationship between Gavin and Ridgway. They were both gentlemen who had great confidence in themselves."

Self-confidence in different areas of command might have been one of the problems. Gavin came to the 82nd as a paratrooper. Ridgway was not a pure paratrooper. He did jump, but reluctantly. What few knew at the time was that Ridgway had an injured back and worried that jumping might irritate it. When he had made his first jump shortly after he had discovered that the 82nd was about to become an airborne division, he had wondered even then why he was doing it. On the eve of Normandy,

Ridgway had four jumps to his credit. His fifth and last would be in Normandy. Gavin, on the other hand, seemed willing to jump from anything with anything and had thrown himself out of an airplane scores of times.

Gavin's troops respected that, and so did higher command. He had now made two combat jumps and his third was fast approaching. At all levels (except perhaps in the eyes of the British) he embodied American paratroop expertise in Europe in 1944. Ridgway signaled his approval when he created a special command arrangement for the Normandy invasion. He divided the division and gave Gavin command of all three parachute regiments, calling it Task Force A, while he retained command of the glider regiment and various supporting elements. A third part of the division, Task Force C, under Brigadier General George P. Howell, was assigned to land at the beachhead and reinforce the paratroops by driving inland. Howell had commanded the 507 and 508 together as part of an independent brigade. Also assigned to the beach mission was Colonel Edson D. Raff, who had commanded the 509th Parachute Infantry Battalion that had jumped into North Africa. He had written a book after the action and become a minor army celebrity as a result. Considered to be cocky, he had difficulty finding a command. Ridgway refused to give him command of a parachute regiment and instead gave him the far less glamorous job of landing on D day with roughly two platoons of 325 men each and 21 Sherman tanks, to streak from the beach to reinforce the 82nd inland.

Gavin was ecstatic when all the command relationships had been worked out. Ridgway's decision to give him command of the parachute regiments gave him a deep sense of satisfaction. Now he was in charge of his own invasion force. Ridgway perhaps believed the gloomy prognostications of disaster for the paratroops and felt his deeper responsibility was to command the division, rather than risk death at its cutting edge. But Gavin knew his was the star role.

By the end of April, Gavin resembled a man reviewing his will. He tried to settle his personal life before he left for the invasion, now scheduled for early June. The major change was Val. As he devoted more time to the coming operation, jealousy flared. Sometimes he would call her late at night and get no answer, which drove him to fury. He reacted by abandoning the idea of marrying her. His diary relates: "I have never let myself get so one-tracked before. It gets painful at times. Called again

this evening at 2030, no reply. I've got to decentralize, and right now."
At the end of April, Gavin took an attractive woman named Ethel Steiger
to dinner and a dance that Val surely would have heard about, and Val
spoke to her husband about a divorce. Gavin responded by reaffirming
his love for her. Still, his true feelings were filled with confusion. He
worried over her wealth and his lack of it. He also thought she would
never adjust to life in America. Finally, two weeks before he was to jump
into Normandy, he reached a decision. He wrote, "I am still entirely
unsatisfied about her [Val] continuing to go about so and about to give
up on it." He decided to cool the affair, and as the invasion approached,
thought less and less about her.

The grand mission the 82nd Airborne Division had planned for all
winter was daring and as dangerous as could be conceived—to drop south
of the strategic port of Cherbourg, at the neck of the Cotentin Peninsula,
near a town called St.-Sauveur-le-Vicomte, create confusion behind German defensive lines, divert reinforcements, seize bridges, and if possible
split the defenders so that some were isolated at the tip of the peninsula
near Cherbourg. The 101st Airborne Division was to land closer to the
beaches, near Ste.-Marie-du-Mont. It would attack and take the causeways leading inland from Bradley's forces landing on Utah Beach. This
would stop the Germans from reinforcing the beaches and it would make
Bradley's breakout from the beaches easier.

Ideally, each force would help the others, tanks and motorized columns
would pour ashore and swiftly make their way to link up with the paratroopers fighting to hold onto the strong points behind the lines that
surprise and good organization had enabled them to take.

The 82nd would cut off the Cotentin from the main German forces,
making it easier for the Allies to take Cherbourg, which they needed to
sustain further operations. Gavin liked certain elements of the plan instantly. The marshy ground, canals, and rivers that honeycombed the
countryside would force German armor onto roads and bridges, making
tanks less mobile and more avoidable. But far more appealing, the bold
nature of the exploit promised the success that would give airborne units
the recognition he felt they deserved.

As he pored over intelligence photos, Gavin found more and more
Rommel's asparagus on their proposed drop zones; and an infantry divi-
sion had built impressive firing positions in the vicinity of all the planned
DZs. Gavin wondered if the Germans had read the Allied plans. They

seemed uncannily aware of what was coming and were doing everything in their power to prepare a deadly reception for paratroopers.

In fact, Field Marshal Rommel did anticipate an airborne threat, though opinions differed within the German high command where it was most likely to come. One German plan proposed dropping paratroops over the Allied marshaling areas in England on the eve of the invasion to break up Allied preparations. Throughout the Atlantic Wall (as Hitler called his coastal fortifications), German commanders spent precious aircraft time trying to anticipate Allied airborne actions. They held mock antiparatroop exercises and published a pamphlet titled, "What Every Soldier Should Know About Airborne Troops," which eventually found its way to Gavin's hands. He called the pamphlet excellent. It was a handbook on how to fight against paratroopers and described their weaknesses in detail. The German 243rd Division, stationed in the area in which the 82nd would drop, published several memos on what to do in the event of an airborne assault. "All echelons of the German 243rd Division had gone to work with imagination and vigor. They established static sentinel posts and lookouts at critical points, and they began regular antiairborne patrols. They held frequent antiairborne training exercises and alerts and, as far as possible, took every step they could think of to meet and destroy the threatening attack," Gavin wrote. In mid-May, Rommel moved another division, the 91st Infantry, into the area of the projected 82nd landings.

The Allies were then maintaining a detailed, massive deception, complete with mock staging camps and phony equipment dumps, to persuade the Luftwaffe that they would land at Calais, where German defenses were the strongest but the Channel was narrowest. Hitler believed it for most of the winter. Then he suddenly changed his mind and seemed to have second thoughts. He had a feeling that the Allies would land in Normandy and he ordered defenses there augmented. Above Rommel in the Wehrmacht hierarchy stood overall commander Field Marshal Gerd von Rundstedt. The two fought over how to repel an invasion.

Von Rundstedt thought it would be best to defend flexibly, to allow the Allies to land, then, as soon as they were out of naval gunfire range, trapped, to his thinking, beyond the beaches, he would smash them with his panzer divisions. Rommel disagreed. He feared Allied airpower would ruin the field marshal's defensive equation, that the tanks would not be able to concentrate or to move to utilize their guns, nor would the defenders be able to deploy their antitank guns effectively for demoralizing "Pakfront" tactics. The invasion, Rommel argued, must be stopped on the beaches. In the end, they compromised. Not all German forces were committed to the beaches, but many were. And a large mobile mechanized force of the Germans' best troops remained in reserve. Neither general was satisfied.

The defenders had other crises to handle. The Allied air offensive in the winter of 1943–44 had produced a surprising result. Though it had not significantly destroyed German industrial production, as American planners predicted (1944 was Germany's peak production year for munitions and weapons), the streams of bombers did cripple the Luftwaffe. In a sense, Germany's air force was destroyed by its own success, for the nearly unlimited supply of targets that the Allied bombers presented gradually used up more German aircraft than the factories could produce. In addition, the P-51 Mustang proved a superior fighter, and the Luftwaffe became so diminished that by the spring of 1944 the Allies possessed secure air superiority.

SHAEF took full advantage in the weeks leading to invasion. All strategic bombing of targets within Germany was temporarily halted, and all Allied air resources hit France—though to preserve the Pas de Calais subterfuge, they did not single out Normandy. Immediately, German forces in France found they had little or no daylight maneuverability. Rail lines, roads, and canal traffic received nearly constant air attack.

Unable to end the fierce air attacks, Germany was also weakened by the dire situation in Russia. In the summer of 1943, the Wehrmacht had launched a final offensive on the Eastern Front with the aim of stunning the Russian Army at Kursk. It failed. The Russians, undeterred by dreadful losses, continued to press westward with the largest army in world history. The Germans were more and more anxious to slow its advance as it approached East Prussia; fierce defensive battles were draining the country of reserve manpower. Their resources in the west were thin, many units in France having lost men and machines to the Eastern Front. Von Rundstedt's order of battle showed more than fifty divisions on paper, but in combat power and mobility, these were far below the levels of a year or two before, and several of those divisions were made up of unwilling East European troops. Some of the divisions in the Cotentin were static divisions, designed for coastal defense and equipped with little equipment for mobile warfare. What vehicles they did have were vulnerable from the air.

But in England, the invaders were unconvinced of their foes' weaknesses. They saw a formidable array of forces before them; when the German 91st Division was reported near the secret landing areas of the 82nd, Leigh-Mallory charged into Eisenhower's office to deliver his dire predictions about the fate of American paratroopers personally. The Germans apparently knew details of the landing plan, and Ike considered canceling the drops. Bradley insisted that he must have paratroopers before him when he came ashore and proposed a new deployment. The 101st would drop where planned, but the 82nd would be dropped nearer to the beaches in the vicinity of a small critical road junction at Ste.-Mère-Église. They were to land on both sides of the Merderet River, seize Ste.-Mère-Église and hold the critical bridges across the Douve River, block Germans moving through the area, and be ready to advance when ordered.

Parachute forces were to land the night before D day (D −1 in Army parlance) and glider forces were to land at sunset on D day and on the morning of D +1 because the Allies feared the heavy losses in night landings that Leigh-Mallory kept harping on. The 82nd would be reinforced by Raff's Sherman tanks (notably weaker in firepower than the German Tiger and Panther), which would land on D day on Utah Beach and charge inland from there. The combined parachute elements of the British 6th Airborne Division (which would drop between the British beaches and Caen) and the American 82nd and 101st Divisions were to drop simultaneously.

On the morning of May 25, 1944, the seaborne forces of the 82nd, Task Force C, left Leicester for their ports of embarkation. On Saturday, May 26th, Gavin was informed of the new changed mission; this made the 82nd's last hours in England frantic as the staff went to work to put it all together. Omar Bradley visited the division on May 30th and had dinner with all its unit commanders. Afterwards, Gavin said, "He [Bradley] is still confident as ever that we will swamp the German. It is difficult to fully share his optimism although one really wants to."

The day after that, the division moved to airfields around England. Gavin traveled from field to field to talk to the men before they left. He said, "I certainly had a lot of fun. At this stage they are lots of fun to talk to. Finally evoked some spontaneous cheers after twenty years of waiting. Their morale could hardly be improved upon. With God's help, they will do their job well and return. . . . They will do a good job and it is just as well. Either this 82nd Division job will be the most glorious and spectacular episode in our history, or it will be another Little Big Horn. There is no way to tell now, but they are going in and they will, I am certain, do a hell of a good job. It is regrettable that so many of them have to get lost, but it is a tough business, and they all figure that parachutists have nine lives."

The 82nd had trained hard in England that winter. They had staged one mass exercise and countless field problems. Though by the end of May, Gavin believed the troops were ready to go, he still worried about the troop carrier aircraft. The rain and fog of England caused drop after drop to be canceled. When they did go, often parachute battalions ended up scattered, and exercises did not go as planned as a result. But at least there was lift. Normandy was to be the largest drop yet in the history of Allied airborne, primarily because finally, for the first time, the Allies had enough planes and pilots.

Five days before they took off for France, Gavin wrote his own feelings. "I want to come back from this one, much more than I have ever wanted to come back before. I am not as uneasy about going in as I have been before. Although it is certain to be a hell of a rough fight, those of us who have been there before are all a bit more certain of ourselves and of our ability to handle anything that develops. There are not so many unknowns this time. It is the unknowns that bother the new soldier." Then, the afternoon of the day he left England, he wrote, "I expect this to be my hardest fight. . . . They [the troopers] will do well as is becoming American parachutists." At this point his main worry was whether they would hit their drop zones.

The invasion was scheduled for June 5. High winds, cloud, and rough water forced a postponement, and with sketchy weather reports, Eisenhower made the decision to go the next day, June 6, 1944, the last opportunity for favorable tidal conditions until June 19. That afternoon, Eisenhower, with aides, drove to the 101st Division's headquarters. He had originally wanted to visit the 82nd, but Ridgway and Gavin both felt he would only distract their men and had asked him not to come. When Eisenhower arrived at the 101st, he had just finished the mournful task of writing the official news release that was to be distributed if the invasion failed:

"Our landings in the Cherbourg-Havre area have failed to gain a satisfactory foothold and I have withdrawn the troops. My decision to attack at this time and place was based upon the best information available. The troops, the air and the Navy did all that bravery and devotion to duty could do. If any blame or fault attaches to the attempt, it is mine alone."

The weather was clearing after a day of clouds, just as weather experts had predicted, and the operation was finally irrevocably on. Eisenhower wandered among the groups of troopers in the final stages of preparing for the short airlift to France. They were blackening their faces, hyperactively cheerful, and clearly ready for action. That evening, Maxwell Taylor walked with Eisenhower to Taylor's assigned C-47. There the SHAEF commander shook his hand before walking back to 101 headquarters to watch the lumbering cargo planes rev, race, and trundle off into the clearing dusk.

Uncertain but exhilarated, Gavin's paratroopers made their uneasy last preparations at Cotesmere, sensing that they were on the verge of one of the most dramatic moments in American history. They were scheduled to land minutes behind the first elements of the 101st. In all, 378 planes boarded heavily armed groups of paratroops at airfields across the south of England on the evening of June 5. Gavin himself was unaware of Eisenhower's visit to his rival, but by then he was sinking into his own jumper's fatalism. "When you hear the roar of the engines turning over and you move down the runway and become airborne," he wrote, "you realize at that moment there is no turning back. Then your total faculties are concerned with survival, and that means carrying out things you have been trained to do as well as you possibly can."

9.

OPERATION

NEPTUNE

On June 6, 1944, after three years of strategic struggle, the American Army got the massive cross-Channel invasion it had wanted. The hope was for a decisive collision with the main German battle formations. Once Eisenhower's invading troops had broken through the German defensive perimeter, he would have a stable base into which he could pour his superior resources, to flood and drown the German Army with men and machines.

Because of its high drama, its significance, and its scale—the largest seaborne invasion ever mounted—the invasion in Normandy is one of the most closely examined moments in history. As a result, the success of Overlord now carries an air of inevitability. That was not the view from the ground that day, however—nor from the air. Success in Normandy was not a foregone conclusion, and the outcome of World War II was far from decided.

By 1944, on paper, the Allies seemed to have little to fear. As military logistical scholars have meticulously detailed, modern mechanized war is decided less on the battlefield than in the factories of Detroit, the Ruhr, the Saar. From 1939 to 1945, the Axis powers produced 51,845 tanks and self-propelled guns (of which 46,857 were German) to the Allied total of 227,235; 73,484 German mortars against 657,318 Allied mortars;

674,280 German machine guns against 4,744,484 Allied weapons; and the Germans managed to manufacture 179,694 artillery pieces to the Allied production total of 914,682. The Allies held preponderant, almost geometric, advantages in aircraft, fuel, trucks, manpower, and other necessities of modern warfare.

The Germans, on the other hand, had the crippling drain of the Eastern Front, a war somehow everywhere slighted by Western historians, but in reality the arena of the main military effort of the German Army. In 1944, the Germans had lost the initiative in the East. Critical shortages meant that German commanders at once committed everything they had to the front. Because of this, even when temporary advantages appeared, the Germans did not have enough reserves to exploit them. Russian production and manpower, plus enormous amounts of American aid simply swamped them. Historians have not questioned the superiority of the German troops and their battlefield leadership; however, that tactical superiority meant virtually nothing in the face of Allied resources.

Yet smaller forces have defeated larger, better-equipped forces, and many variables were in play aside from production. For instance, Allied armor was produced in enormous quantity, but German armor proved far superior on the battlefield. This meant that the Allies, particularly the Americans with their Shermans, needed an edge in numbers to engage German Panthers and Tigers in combat with some equality. And the numbers take no account of the advantages of shorter and shorter supply lines, of defenders fighting on their own soil, a nation fighting for its existence.

Ironically, Overlord offered the Germans something they badly needed, a chance for a definitive victory. The invasion provided the opportunity to place superior forces on the battlefield against inferior Allied forces.

The Allies could hurl great strength against the Germans, but the problem was that they had a limited number of landing craft with which to bring that strength to the beaches. The best they could do, given their landing craft and aircraft limitations, was to deploy little more than five infantry divisions, three armored brigades, and three airborne divisions in the initial attack. The Germans had fifty-six divisions available in France, even if many of these were green, over-age, or understrength; eleven were panzer divisions. If they reacted swiftly and decisively, the Germans had the opportunity to concentrate forces in Normandy against those assault waves attacking across exposed beaches and throw them back into the sea.

The chance for a mighty feat of arms existed here for them, a feat that might cause an Allied disaster, prolong the war, and possibly lead to a negotiated settlement or a unilateral treaty with a single enemy of Germany. The Allies had much to lose if Overlord failed.

Gavin was aware of all this when he boarded his plane the night of June 5, 1944. He knew too just how hard the Germans had been working to defend against an airborne drop into the very area where the 82nd was about to jump, and how much armor they had available.

Jim Gavin landed in France, hard, in an apple orchard approximately 2 miles from where he was supposed to have landed, though he didn't know that until an hour later. At first, he had no idea exactly where he was.

Checking that all his parts worked after the hard collision with the ground, Gavin got out of his harness. About him tree branches hung low, and among the scattered blossoms, cows grazed in the moonlight. Gavin's aide, Lieutenant Hugo V. Olsen, had landed nearby, and Gavin and Olsen "rolled up" their stick, collecting other members in short order. All the members except one were accounted for. Gavin heard heavy firing in the distance, and knowing he was not where he should be, moved out toward it, as he had done in Sicily, with the fifteen men he had collected.

It was a calm, damp, mysterious spring night; that Gavin would always remember. The Cotentin Peninsula in Normandy is difficult enough to move about in at best; at night and with the danger of ambush everywhere, it was treacherous. The land lay in a checkerboard of ancestral fields surrounded by steep fences and walls, some overgrown, some neglected, the characteristic hedgerows of rural Normandy. These walls proved fortresses: piled with dirt and brush, often heaped in stout mounds up to 20 feet high, covered with trees and tangled undergrowth. The Germans had already fortified the hedgerows with pre-dug firing positions; Gavin found several unmanned rifle and machine-gun pits scattered about the edge of the apple orchard. To move in such country was doubly dangerous, then. Dug in, nervous Germans were scattered about the hedgerows, fingers on the trigger, all alerted by antiaircraft fire and the racket of the low-flying transports.

The Germans were waiting, silent, in position. Lost paratroopers had to move, and their crackling through the underbrush invited vicious close contact with a concealed enemy waiting in ambush. Nevertheless, Gavin had to risk it. He had to find the rest of his troops.

Right off the orchard, they found a small, worn tree-lined country road. Gavin moved his men along the two sides of it, each man moving in a crouch, weapon at the ready. Gavin, too, had his M-1 ready, for he was now a rifleman. Then, about 400 yards down the road, Gavin saw what looked like a wide expanse of water. On closer inspection, he found it to be a very watery marsh. Out in the water, they saw equipment bundles. Gavin wanted them retrieved, for he knew they contained critical gear—machine guns, bazookas, radios. Some of his force went after them. A red light began flashing across the swamp, then a blue one, the first an assembly marker for the 507th, the second for the 508th. Gavin sent Olsen out to contact the regiments and, if possible, get some information about where they were. Confused by the wide waterway, he was unsure of his location on the map. More troopers joined Gavin's party (by now numbering about forty), and the general helped retrieve bundles.

Olsen soon returned with news. He had found a railway embankment on the far side of the marsh. Suddenly, Jim Gavin knew where he was. Checking his map, he found but one rail line in the area. They had overflown their objective by several miles, and they were now about 2 miles north of the La Fiere bridge over the Merderet River, a 505th objective. The Germans had flooded the Merderet, thus the wide, lakelike area, which had been hidden from aerial reconnaissance because the high grass disguised it as solid ground. Now what should have been a small river was a thousand-yard-wide lake. The 508th men on the other side had told Olsen that they were moving out to La Fiere. It was the nearest objective they knew of.

Meanwhile, the troopers with Gavin were having little success collecting bundles. The water was too deep and the bundles too heavy, but still more men had arrived. By now, over a hundred had joined them, but these were 507 men, most of them green to combat. Their commanders had told them to black out all rank insignia, so no one knew who the officers and NCOs were. As a result, they were disorganized, unsure of themselves, and many of them kept falling asleep. The shock of the jump had left them exhausted. As German fire built, the troopers took cover in the hedgerows. It was almost impossible to organize under those conditions. Gavin was frustrated. With dawn approaching, he still had no idea what had happened to his command, and he had accomplished virtually nothing.

Gavin was told that a glider containing an antitank gun was down in the swamp in the direction of La Fiere and decided it was time to move for it. He led the troopers he had forward. The glider was there, and so were the Germans. They had machine-gun and rifle positions covering the deserted glider, and as Gavin and his troops neared it, the German troops fired. The Americans ignored it and kept closing, but the closer they got, the heavier came the German fire, and to his dismay, Gavin found his troopers did not shoot back. Amidst the whisper and snap of fire, he jumped from man to man to try to get them to use their weapons, but such unseasoned troops did not yet know that the best protection from hostile fire was suppressive fire, and he had little success. Several of his men fell wounded, and still the troopers did not return fire. Gavin decided to withdraw across the swamp from his blocked position, gather what additional troops he could find, and attack La Fiere. He would have to leave his wounded behind.

Gavin waded into the marsh to lead the withdrawal; wading deeper and deeper into the water, the paratroops saw the Germans gathering on the bank, kneeling or standing as they shot at the helpless Americans. But the distance was too great for accuracy. The troopers deployed a wide interval apart and held their weapons above their heads, but every step was difficult. High grass under the water twisted and grabbed at their legs; daylight increased steadily to expose them. Several troopers fell; bullets whined past Gavin. All they could do was move on. Finally, exhausted and cold from the frigid waters, they reached the railway embankment on the other side of the swamp, out of range of enemy fire. Gavin gathered his force to move toward La Fiere along the rail line.

Then Gavin had his first good news of the morning. After about a 2-mile advance, he found the 1st Battalion of the 505th. "About a half a mile from the LaFiere [bridge] I came across the 1st Battalion of the 505th Parachute Infantry, organized, under control, and already launching an attack on the LaFiere bridge. It was a most reassuring sight." The troopers, whose unit commander, Major Frederick Kellam, though alive then, was one of the first officers killed that day, had coolly reorganized and were ready to move off in the attack.

· · ·

Gavin's vision was limited to a few acres of swampy French farmland and a rail bed; it was as well he could not see the whole picture of the early hours of invasion. The drop had been part success, part disaster. Yet because of its incoherent and dispersed nature, no single eye could assess its effect. Individuals and units wandered isolated, or fell into small battles with the defenders. For the first few days, in fact, few units of the 82nd reached their objectives as standard military units. The dispersion of the Sicily drop had happened again. Paratroopers of the 82nd and the 101st were scattered all over the Cotentin, beginning with the first elements that jumped, the pathfinders of both the 82nd and the 101st.

The pathfinders had taken off from England about 10 P.M. on the night of June 5. Their specially trained pilots took a circular route to the drop, both to avoid the fleet below and to approach their targets from an unexpected side, the southwest. Along the way, things went seriously wrong. The planes encountered little antiaircraft fire, but as soon as they reached the Cotentin, they found themselves in thick, turbulent clouds. The clouds cleared just as they reached the drop area, but by then the pilots had grown disoriented and only two pathfinder teams hit their drop zones.

About a half an hour behind the pathfinders, came the 101st Airborne Division, with 485 aircraft, 52 gliders for heavy equipment, and nearly 7,000 paratroopers. They too hit the clouds, and soon their formations became wildly dispersed. The paratroopers of the 101, shouting "Bill Lee" as they exited their planes, landed all over Normandy, some on their drop zones and others as much as 8 miles away. Carefully laid plans fell into disarray.

The 82nd, in 377 aircraft, 52 gliders, took off behind the 101st at about 11 P.M. on June 5. They formed in the air efficiently enough and headed for the Cotentin. Then navigation problems and local weather, the same factors that had plagued the earlier lifts, affected them, along with some additional dangers. German antiaircraft batteries had sounded the alarm, and they peppered the low-flying planes, which were already tossed about and lost in the turbulence and fog.

The lead C-47s carried the 505th and General Ridgway, making his fifth and last parachute jump, and fared best. Their mission was to drop between the Merderet River and the town of Ste.-Mère-Église, to secure the town, the La Fiere bridge, and the bridge at Chef-du-Pont, while forming blocking forces near the towns of Neuville-au-Plain and

Beuzeville-au-Plain. They were ordered to link up with forces of the 101st, which should have been between Ste.-Mère-Église and Utah Beach itself. Like all the planes before them, the 505th's transports ran into the clouds and bucked and twisted their way through blindly. Like the others, the paratroops were dispersed, but not so badly. About half of them landed within a mile of their drop zones. Another 350 landed within 2 miles of their zones, but the rest of them, around 600, came to earth scattered as much as 14 miles from their targets.

The 508th, with Gavin's plane, followed the 505. It was supposed to secure the opposite side of the Merderet, facing the 505th; however, drop accuracy was even worse. Its men were so badly dispersed that the regiment never formed elements larger than company size—and most units remained platoon size. Some men landed as far as 20 miles from their drop zones. Some went into the sea and drowned. One company landed almost intact—but they hit Utah Beach. Many 508 troopers landed in the marsh of the Merderet, and some drowned. Nearly all the regiment's equipment landed in the swamp, and it was nearly all lost. From the time it landed, the 508th was never able to organize well enough to fight as a regiment.

The 507th followed close behind the 508. Its mission was to capture Amfreville and secure the La Fiere bridge across the river from the 505. They were no less scattered than the 508 had been. However, George Millet hit the drop zone, and he had about forty men there with him. After collecting all the men he could find, Millet organized a force of over four hundred and attacked Amfreville. But unknown to Millet, Amfreville was the closest 82nd objective to the newly arrived German 91st Division, and the unlucky troopers found themselves instantly and viciously counterattacked, cut off, and surrounded. The rest of the regiment came to earth too badly dispersed to organize into groups much larger than platoon size.

Much as in Sicily—though they were not dispersed nearly as badly—small bands of paratroopers did what they could in the night to orient themselves. What no one had foreseen was the effect the hedgerows would have. Once on the ground, the paratroopers found they had tumbled out of the clear sky into a maze. Every field seemed treacherous. Every hedgerow threatened the wink of rifle fire. Officers were as confused as their men, because no one could see far enough through the hedgerows to identify significant terrain features. Sound was blocked or distorted just as vision was. The hedgerows hid the sounds of firefights, and when they did not, they made them sound deceptively near or far. Paratroopers found each other as often by luck as by design.

Paratroopers, with no idea where they were, chose their route instinctively. They tended downhill, so most of them, like water, flowed downhill into ravines and draws. It was there that they found the friendly faces of other men with similar inclinations. It was there they formed into ad hoc squads, platoons, and companies, under leaders they had never seen before that night, and it was from those places that decisive military action began. Gavin's lake along the Merderet was one such place. There were others.

Time and retelling have obscured how random was the emergence of the battle groups. Gavin's own recollections of action that day are of organized units and certain actions, and historian after historian followed this pattern. In fact, it was never that simple. Kellam's 1st Battalion of the 505th, a group that figures prominently in Gavin's retelling of the action, was at less than half strength, and it had among its ranks members of other battalions and regiments.

On finding Kellam's group, Gavin assumed that the La Fiere fight was underway, and he was informed that the men would have their objective shortly. He had no reason to doubt this. All seemed to be well, and Kellam appeared in control and confident, though his executive officer was already dead and Kellam would be shortly. Gavin, with a scratch force of over two hundred 507 and 508 men, moved to help him. The bridge at La Fiere was critical because it spanned a stream that could make a formidable German defense line. Gavin wanted to make sure it was taken. There were other objectives and possibilities; the bridge at La Fiere was one way across the Merderet, but there existed another bridge near the town of Chef-du-Pont. That too was critical. Squatting in the hedgerows, he made two plans based on one premise. With his now sizable force he could help in the La Fiere bridge action and also attack the Chef-du-Pont bridge, if he moved his men to the other side of the river.

Gavin's first thought was to find boats at nearby French farms and sneak across. That would give them mobility; they could even surprise enemy forces defending the other side. He dispatched Lieutenant Colonel Arthur Maloney to see if boats or a path through the swamp could be found; Maloney's patrols along the river succeeded only in exhausting themselves, finding no path and no boats. Foreseeing a maneuver like this, the Germans had destroyed them all.

Gavin decided to try his second plan. Chef-du-Pont was not that far from La Fiere, and a Frenchman had told him that there were no Germans in Chef-du-Pont. Maloney's men were still scattered, looking for boats, but Gavin still had a hundred men and Lieutenant Colonel Edwin J. Ostberg of the 507th to command them. With this force, he would move on Chef-du-Pont in case it was not in American hands, and from there perhaps they might cross and double back on La Fiere.

Lacking communications with anyone but men he could see and talk to, and having no idea who was where, Gavin correctly assumed that Chef-du-Pont was untaken and unassaulted.

When his small force reached the town, they found a train moving from the railway station. Gavin ordered it assaulted. German troops aboard scattered and sprinted for the bridge as soon as his troopers fired. The train contained nothing but empty bottles and Normandy cheese. From this encounter, Gavin moved his troopers to the river and found its banks strewn with prepared German rifle pits and machine-gun nests. Flooding had made the Merderet very wide at that point. Rising water had turned the bridge and approaches into a causeway almost a mile wide, with an island by the bridge in the middle. Though the prepared defenses along the Chef-du-Pont side were unoccupied, the island in the middle of the causeway was bristling with Germans. As soon as his force reached the bank, rifle and machine-gun fire met them. There would be no easy crossing at Chef-du-Pont. Gavin saw both his impromptu plans thwarted, so he ordered Ostberg to assault to take the river crossing "whenever it would be feasible." German positions looked stout, and Gavin intended for the assault to take place that night (the 6th). Ostberg, a determined man, had other ideas.

Gavin wanted to see what had happened at La Fiere; so, with his familiar M-1 rifle in hand, he left Ostberg to secure the bridge at Chef-du-Pont while he and aide Olsen went back to La Fiere. There he found Lieutenant Colonel Mark Alexander, executive officer of the 505, and ordered him to take command of the 1st Battalion of the 505th and the other troopers on the La Fiere side of the causeway, replacing the fallen Kellam.

While Gavin footed north, trying to unlock the tactical situation facing him, an unfortunate incident occurred back at Chef-du-Pont. Impatient and bent on seizing the bridge, Ostberg moved troopers closer to the bank. Suddenly, a nearby German rose to surrender. A tired trooper shot him. Another German repeated the act, and he too was shot before anyone could call cease fire. Now the Germans, who might have surrendered en masse, found themselves unable to retreat down the causeway and unable to surrender. They would fight to the last.

Even though the arched bridge and the defended island lay a little over a hundred yards from the closest cover, Ostberg organized a charge. Running at the front of his men, he led about fifty brave paratroopers straight into German fire. As soon as they reached the arch of the bridge, the colonel and five of his men were cut down by a stream of machine-gun bullets (Ostberg survived his wounds only to be killed later in Holland). The following troopers, seeing no tactical advantage to their position, withdrew. Then Maloney, having been sent by Gavin to take command, arrived with his tired crew. Maloney organized a second charge. It too was stopped at about the same point with roughly the same effect, though Maloney survived unwounded. Now he tried stealth. They crawled onto the bridge approach and fought at close quarters from one foxhole to the next with grenades and rifle fire. The battle raged inconclusively all afternoon; in the midst of it, Maloney and his men were recalled to La Fiere. Command at Chef-du-Pont passed to Captain Roy R. Creek, and the stalemate took a bad turn. On the opposite end of the causeway, the stubborn Germans wheeled up a field piece, and now the crouching troopers—after Maloney's withdrawal they numbered just over thirty—endured direct artillery fire. It got worse. After the gun opened fire, Creek looked to the rear of his position to discover a German platoon deploying for an assault.

But as death or surrender threatened, help came from an unexpected direction.

An American glider carrying a 57mm antitank gun, lumbering in on schedule, landed amidst Creek's position. It seemed miraculous. The troopers quickly turned the 57mm on the field gun across the river and scored a direct hit. Next, they turned it on the still-forming infantry to their rear and broke their ranks with a few shots. As they did, a reinforcing American platoon arrived. The crisis had passed. Just as the sun set, Creek discovered a position north along the riverbank that offered a perfect field of fire to hammer the remaining Germans on the island. Within ten minutes, the island fell. Creek now had half a bridge, thirteen dead, and twenty-three wounded. The other end of the causeway loomed a distant 700 yards away, and from all appearances, the Germans still held it strongly. For the time being, Creek and his troopers would have to be content with half.

Meanwhile, trouble came elsewhere. Because of the hedgerows, the small crossroads town of La Fiere did not fall easily or swiftly, though it was weakly defended by only one German platoon. The Americans assaulted with more than a battalion, but such was the defensive position and the valor of the defenders, it held all morning. One obstacle to the taking of La Fiere was American disorganization. The separate parts of several forces were unaware of each other; the hedgerows and the lack of radio communication led several American paratroop elements to assault the town piecemeal. It finally fell in the early afternoon, and A Company of the 505th took up positions on the riverbank on the right side of the road overlooking a causeway similar to the one at Chef-du-Pont. Captain R. D. Rae, commanding a mixed batch of 507th and 101st Airborne men, held the left. Other 507 men had already crossed the river, and Rae and Captain John J. Dolan, commanding 505's A Company, saw others over there; but it was a long way off.

An old military maxim says that the best way to take a bridge is to attack both ends at once. The La Fiere end, which had been defended, was duly attacked. The 507th on the other side had been ordered to hit a place called Cauquigny (nothing more than a bombed-out church), which would have secured both ends. And elements of the 507 did as ordered. Many American paratroopers passed through Cauquigny that morning, and all of them were looking for a fight. The reason most of them did not remain was that there was no fight to be had at Cauquigny. The Germans had not defended it.

Very little happened as it should have on the west bank of the Merderet River. The two regiments that should have landed there had not. Only three significant groups of U.S. troops had formed. The first, under Millet, had been cut off and battered by the German 91st Division, racing for Ste.-Mère-Église. The second was under the leadership of Lieutenant Colonel Charles J. Timmes, commander of the 2nd Battalion of the 507th, who had been nearly drowned in the marsh where he had landed when the wind grabbed his chute and dragged him and his equipment through the water. When he came to rest, he was near the same rail line Jim Gavin had discovered the night of the drop. He guessed his location to be near Amfreville and he was right. That night, he moved about collecting such men as he could, and at dawn arrived in Cauquigny with a band of thirty. Hearing gunfire from the direction of Amfreville, Timmes abandoned Cauquigny and moved toward the noise via a cross-country route. Along the way he picked up more men; at Amfreville, large detachments of the German 91st Division waited, entrenched, and as Timmes got close, they responded with heavy fire. Timmes saw he was overmatched and began a fighting withdrawal, hedgerow to hedgerow, with the Germans in pursuit. Finally, he and his men reached the same orchard Gavin had left the night before.

There, with their backs to the marsh, they dug in in a defensive perimeter. Turning to fight, the paratroops were still under fire but it was no longer heavy. Though a line of retreat remained open through Cauquigny and back over the river, Timmes would not be driven completely from his unit's assigned area. Charles Timmes and his band would make their stand in the apple orchard amidst the carpet of blossoms. It was not long before heavy German forces moved in to surround him. Cauquigny remained free for the taking.

Lieutenant Colonel Thomas J. B. Shanley, also had a considerable force assembled on the east side of the Merderet. Shanley and his battalion were the one battalion of the 508th that was dropped somewhat intact, though their assembly took time. When, at dawn, he had collected as many men as he could, Shanley found himself not far from the bridge at Chef-du-Pont. As they moved to fortify the east end of it, they ran into superior numbers of Germans, and withdrew to a hill known as Hill 30, which was the high ground on that side of the Merderet and Shanley's original objective. Along the way, he picked up more troopers, and by the end of daylight on D day, he had more than half a battalion under his command and stood on his assigned high ground. What he did not have were the approaches to the Chef-du-Pont causeway or sufficient force to take on the Germans who held it. In fact, he faced serious German pressure just holding his own position. Artillery soon found the range of his foxholes, and machine-gun fire raked his force. He and his men prepared for a siege, and the vital bridge and causeway, a top objective for the paratroopers, remained in German hands.

The bridges of the Merderet soon proved the focus of raging battles between the outnumbered paratroopers and the defending Germans, and larger numbers of men from both sides moved toward them. Gavin's command was splintered, but of all the deadly firefights swirling between groups of frightened men near the small rural bridges and the flooded riverbeds, the fiercest was for the causeway at La Fiere: that battle fate gave to Gavin as his lot.

On the morning of D day, another force that had helped take La Fiere crossed the La Fiere bridge and passed through Cauquigny. Again, they did not stop. But Colonel Timmes, in the apple orchard, was having second thoughts. Sensing he might have overlooked something, he sent a ten-man patrol under the command of Lieutenant Louis Levy to Cauquigny to fortify it. Levy did so, and waited. That morning several American paratrooper bands passed by, but none of them stayed. They all sought objectives elsewhere. Levy, without radio or further orders, kept anxious watch.

When the 505th began fortifying the riverbank at La Fiere, they sent up the designated signal. Orange smoke was to signal friendly invasion forces, and when the 505th popped orange smoke, on the west side, a relieved Levy on the east side responded with orange smoke in reply. To the 505th it signaled all was well across the bridge. Surely the 508 or the 507 was there in force. They did not know that only ten men and a lieutenant held the bridge.

But a German battalion with tank support approached Levy's little group without benefit of signals and found little opposition. Levy and his ten fought bravely—they succeeded in disabling three German tanks— but were soon crushed. The practiced German troops thus quickly turned the situation to their advantage and at the end of D Day, the Americans found themselves blinking with fatigue, but holding only halves of the two vital bridges they had been dropped to capture.

Elsewhere things were better. The critical town in the 82nd's area of operations was Ste.-Mère-Église, the transportation hub for the area, the meeting of all local roads. Holding it meant German reinforcements to the beaches would be severely disrupted. In the early hours of the morning of D day, it fell easily to Lieutenant Colonel Edward "Cannonball" Krause's 3rd Battalion of the 505th and became the first French town liberated in World War II. Krause had learned from a drunken Frenchman, who gaily offered to guide him, that only one enemy platoon remained there. The Germans had thought the fight was over hours before and, as a result, they were completely surprised.

Krause found an ugly sight. Dead and wounded paratroopers lay on the streets, some hanging from telephone poles, buildings, and trees. One man dangled from the church steeple throughout the night and saved his life by feigning death. A house fire that night had confused some pilots, who dropped their sticks of 505 men right on Ste.-Mère-Église. The Germans had killed most of the unfortunate troopers before or just after they hit the ground.

Thanks to Krause's windfall, by noon on D day, Ste.-Mère-Église became the center of 82nd Airborne operations and a target of German wrath. Not far from Ste.-Mère sits the small town of Neuville-au-Plain, which planners hoped Lieutenant Colonel Benjamin Vandervoort's 2nd Battalion would fortify to block approaching Germans.

But command bungling canceled the plan. Without enough working radios (most had ended up under water) to clarify positions, Lieutenant Colonel William E. Ekman, the 505th's commander, ordered Vandervoort on to attack Ste.-Mère-Église instead, not knowing Krause had already taken it. Vandervoort, who had broken his leg on impact wheeled into action on a cart pushed by troopers. Though he did as Ekman ordered, he had the foresight to send a platoon on to Neuville-au-Plain just in case. Vandervoort arrived to find Krause in charge of Ste.-Mère-Église and joined him in the town's defense; but behind them, three German battalions, apparently bent on recapturing Ste.-Mère, came at Neuville-au-Plain. The platoon there, under Lieutenant Turner B. Turnbull, somehow held all afternoon. After losing more than half his men, and seeing Germans closing on both his flanks, Turnbull felt doomed but determined. Finally, just before dinnertime, a relief platoon covered his retreat back to Ste.-Mère-Église.

Gavin, by midafternoon, had returned to the La Fiere bridge, where the situation had deteriorated badly. As he approached, retreating troopers rushed past, saying the Germans had broken through, formed a lodgement on the eastern side, and a withdrawl had been ordered. Aghast, Gavin ordered them to turn back and found Colonel Roy Lindquist, the ranking man, who had a small reserve of about eighty. With the Lindquist group behind him, Gavin double-timed for the causeway while sending a runner for Maloney's men from Chef-du-Pont. Gavin arrived at the causeway, ready for a fight but instead found that one had just ended.

That afternoon, the same German battalion that had scattered Levy's little band launched an armored attack across the causeway. The 505th's A Company under the command of Captain John J. Dolan dug in at the western end of the causeway and took the attack head-on. The Germans led with a powerful barrage of mortar and artillery fire, then they came on with two French Renault tanks, infantry running in their wake. Dolan's men, supported by two bazooka teams, squatted in formerly German rifle pits.

The bazookas did their work on the thinly armored French tanks; both stopped after a close-range duel of bazooka rounds and point-blank cannon fire. The German foot soldiers, now without their shield, were exposed and cut down or routed back across the causeway by accurate American fire. Dolan's men still controlled the approaches to the causeway, and success bolstered their confidence. The Germans returned several more times, but the paratroopers kept driving them back, though their artillery barrage never ceased. By morning, it had cost Dolan six more men.

Gavin had arrived in La Fiere just after the German counterattack, still thinking of offensive operations. A look at the new enemy positions across the river convinced him that would be suicide. The Germans seemed to have no intention of yielding the other side and were staunchly entrenched. He wondered if the paratroopers could hold on. At best he hoped for a stalemate. There was nothing he could do at either causeway, so he moved back from La Fiere toward Ste.-Mère-Église. He established a command post more or less equidistant from the two bridgeheads. His awkward position baffled him. He had no idea what fate had held for the paratroopers on the other side of the Merderet. He had no radio contact with Utah Beach; therefore, he did not know if the landings had succeeded, or even if they had commenced. He had no jeep or truck to shuttle between his two critical bridgeheads. However, he did have radio contact with division headquarters, so he knew of events in Ste.-Mère-Église. Ridgway had set up his command post, but the town was under siege from several points now that the Germans realized they had lost it.

Division headquarters obligingly sent Gavin a jeep, and he succeeded in raising Shanley, across the river. Shanley had little good news to share, but at least Gavin knew some force across the river was still fighting. As night fell, he decided that he had done all he could. He lay down to rest. For a blanket, all he could find was a parachute laid across a dead trooper. He could not bring himself to use the shroud, but soon found a camouflage net, lay down against a hedgerow to give himself shelter from artillery fire and shivered himself warm. A runner soon brought a summons from Ridgway's staff. Gavin walked with Olsen through the full moonlight to Ste.-Mère-Église only to find that the message had been in error. Ridgway was asleep himself and annoyed at the visit. Frustrated and weary, Gavin trudged back to his command post and resumed his rest.

This trivial incident marked the beginning of a coolness between Ridgway and Gavin and rankled in both men for years, in spite of the fact both were no doubt blameless: Commmunications are the first thing to be lost in the chaos of combat. Ridgway later would maintain that a distraught Gavin had come to ask for permission to withdraw from La Fiere that night, an implication Gavin resented.

Dawn of June 7 found the 82nd in precarious possession of a triangle of French soil. Time was against them, for unless relieved, and unless the overall invasion plan worked, there was no chance for them. Ridgway had gathered only about one quarter of his division. The Germans had tanks, superior numbers, and vastly superior firepower. The 82nd's position was anchored by corners resting on La Fiere, Chef-du-Pont, and Ste.-Mère-Église. The division's lower echelons had no assurance of an advance from the beachhead. Soldiers' rumors spread that the invasion had failed. Ridgway and Gavin, however, knew better, retained their confidence, and ignored them. They were going to hold what they had no matter what—especially Ste.-Mère—even if the invaders on the beaches were flung back into the sea.

The Germans had not finished with La Fiere. On the morning of the 7th, after a two-hour mortar barrage, they launched a final attack on the bridge with all they had, and this time four French tanks led the way. Once again the valiant bazooka teams fought their duel, now helped by a lone 57mm gun to their rear. The combination wrecked the first tank, and that stalled the others. But it gave the Germans a steel shield of wrecked tanks just 35 yards from Dolan's lead platoon, under the command of Lieutenant William A. Oakly. The Germans zeroed in their mortars on the ground and kept up small-arms and tank fire. Oakly was badly hit almost immediately and dragged to the rear, where he died just a few hours later. Sergeant William D. Owens, leader of the first squad replaced him. Owens found himself in a desperate situation. More than half his men had fallen already and the survivors had little ammunition. His machine guns fired so fast they quit from the heat. The company first sergeant grabbed the wounded and threw them back into the fight.

Owens, a quiet Detroit punch drill operator, stood his ground and ran from man to man, redistributing ammo from the dead and wounded. His gunners were dying, so he took over their machine guns. Later he said, "The artillery shells and mortars were coming in like machine-gun fire. I don't know how it was possible to live through it. Then the infantry came on again and we gave them everything we had. The machine gun I had was so hot it quit firing. I took Private McClatchy's BAR, he had been wounded earlier, and I fired it until I ran out of ammunition. Then I took a machine gun that belonged to a couple of men who took a very near hit. They were killed. The gun had no tripod, so I rested it across a pile of dirt and used it. With this and one other machine gun and a 6omm mortar we stopped them, but they had gotten to within twenty-five yards.''

Then abruptly, the Germans called a halt. Owens was down to fourteen men. He kept firing and yelling for them to hold on. He had no radio because his radio man had taken a direct hit from a German 88mm gun, so he sent a runner to Dolan describing the situation and asking for orders. His answer came back in writing. It said, ''I don't know of a better place than this to die.'' Owens passed the message, and the survivors hung on. Suddenly, the Germans raised a flag with a red cross. Firing tapered off, and ceased. They indicated they wanted to evacuate their wounded. Their nonwounded went with them. One platoon had broken the back of the last German attempt to regain the bridge at La Fiere, and now Gavin could plan his own attack.

Gavin had a small mobile reserve. During the fighting, as pressure came at the critical points, he kept moving Lindquist and a scratch bunch to the rescue. Both he and and Ridgway wondered how long they could hold, for German infantry, armor, and artillery continued to threaten Ste.-Mère-Église.

Unknown to the airborne commanders, help was on the way; the armored task force under Edson Raff had landed on D day as planned, and Raff launched them toward Ste.-Mère with all the speed the armor could make. But 2 miles from Ste.-Mère, the Germans had constructed a strong point of infantry and 88mm cannon. Not only did it stall Raff's column, it also overlooked the landing zones designated for gliders scheduled to land on D day. The 88s hit four of Raff's armored vehicles (three of them Sherman tanks), then as the sun set, came new disaster. The gliders came on, winging toward a double death trap. The field was too small for proper landings, so most crash-landed heavily. Those who survived came under immediate fire from the Germans' 88s, rifles, and machine guns. Shaken glider infantry were helpess to defend themselves as they fought to get out of their flimsy craft. In minutes, the landing zone was strewn with crashed gliders and dead and dying glidermen, while Raff could only look on helplessly. His tanks and infantry fired and did what they could, but they had little effect. The Germans continued to shoot, stopping only with darkness. Then survivors crawled from the field toward the protection of Raff's tanks. Raff's stunned force remained at the landing zone for the night.

Elsewhere, glider landings were just as disastrous. Casualties and German fire were heavy. Ridgway's vulnerable glidermen were fated to die by the hundreds in Normandy before they could even fire back. However, those who landed near Ste.-Mère-Église not only added to Ridgway's desperately thin force, they also brought news that the invasion had succeeded. Help was coming.

The 82nd still had no radio link with the outside world, but one patrol had got out word of the paratroops' predicament. On Utah Beach the commanders knew the situation, and as soon as Major General "Lightning Joe" Collins landed on D +1 and heard, he ordered a reserve tank battalion, the 746th under Lieutenant Colonel D. G. Hupfer, forward to break through.

On the morning of D +1 German forces launched an assault on Ste.-Mère-Église, preceded by an artillery barrage and supported by self-propelled guns. Vandervoort's troopers resisted with verve. They had been holding against the Germans for two days and their confidence ran high. They yielded no ground except to evacuate wounded and readjust fields of fire. At noon, the 8th regiment of the 4th Infantry Division under Colonel James Van Fleet arrived along with Hupfer's and Raff's tanks. Behind came the jeep of VII Corps commander General Collins himself. With the tanks and the help of the 8th Infantry, Vandervoort's paratroopers counterattacked immediately. German troops in the Ste.-Mère-Église area were decisively thrown back southward that afternoon. The liberation of the town was final.

The cost to Dolan's A Company was high. Conventional military practice judges that a unit should be withdrawn from combat after 25 percent casualties. Dolan's company lost sixty-six dead or seriously wounded and had twenty-three additional wounded men still fighting. This unit would remain in almost continuous combat for another month. Counting men still fighting, that meant Dolan's company was at less than 30 percent strength until lost troopers showed up later and bolstered it to nearly 50 percent.

With the arrival of the armor and the 8th Infantry, the 82nd's hold on the Ste.-Mère-Église–La Fiere–Chef-du-Pont no longer seemed tenuous. But Millet's group remained encircled, Shanley's and Timmes's forces remained under severe pressure on the other side of the river, and the 82nd had not achieved its objectives. The bridges remained blocked, one end of each held by strong German forces. Both Ridgway and Gavin found the situation infuriating. They were determined to relieve the forces across the river, and they had a plan. Ridgway would break the deadlock with his fresh 325 troops. On the morning of D + 2, the 505th, with elements of the 325th in support, assisted by the 8th Infantry, attacked north toward Montebourg to expand the area the division already held. Meanwhile, Ridgway ordered the 1st Battalion of the 325th to use a fortuitously discovered sunken road that led across the Merderet between the two causeways to attack across the river near Timmes's force to relieve them. They intended to then smash the Germans at Cauquigny. Simultaneously, Lindquist was supposed to assault over the Chef-du-Pont causeway with 507 and 508 troopers to relieve Shanley. Millet's force would attack toward the 325 men and in the process break out themselves.

The 505's assault to the north proved difficult. The troopers and glidermen advanced rapidly against heavy, determined German resistance, hedgerow to hedgerow. However, the assisting 8th Infantry was not able to make such progress, stalling the overall attack.

For the assault across the Merderet, Ridgway allowed his lower-level commanders to make their own decisions on details. Trouble began with Lindquist's group at Chef-du-Pont, where Shanley was ordered by radio to clear out the opposite end of the causeway before an attack was attempted. Shanley responded, sending a twenty-man scratch patrol forward. That patrol, led by Lieutenant Woodrow W. Millsaps, fought one of the hardest engagements of the invasion.

Everyone considered Millsaps an eccentric, but this night he proved pure warrior. His men moved easily off Hill 30, but as they approached the head of the causeway, they struck machine gun after machine gun. At first his column buckled. Some men tried to run, but Millsaps steadied them under heavy close-in fire at night. They kept moving toward the machine guns, methodically destroying them with grenades and accurate fire, hedgerow after hedgerow. Then they reached a road junction near the causeway, where three machine guns plus riflemen waited. Again, Millsaps urged his men on and again they destroyed the German positions. Millsaps himself was knocked down three times by German grenades, but neither he nor his men hesitated. They had entered a killing frenzy; each man was alone, paying no notice to those who fell. They fought on and killed until the Germans broke before their charge.

Finally, they reached a farmhouse. The nearest hedgerow was thick with Germans. The enemy fired flares, but instead of taking cover against the lights, the Americans charged, firing, killing all who did not flee the apparitions outlined in the harsh light and black shadows of the flares. When they reached the farm, they found no enemy, but there were animals in the barns. They killed them too. Only when the last animal died did they stop firing. When the smoke cleared, they had damaged the German defenses, but Millsaps had only eleven men who could still fight. They dug in about the farm while Millsaps hurried to cross the causeway to tell Lindquist to attack at will. One man volunteered to go with him, a Sergeant William Kleinfelter, so they took off together along the causeway. Some Germans were dug into its shoulders. Millsaps killed them with his bayonet. Then he noticed that Kleinfelter lagged behind. The sergeant said he thought he had been shot. Millsaps examined him. Kleinfelter had been shot six times. The young Lieutenant took the sergeant's weight and they made it to Lindquist's position. The causeway was ready. Millsaps's force had cleared the main resistance. It now needed only a final charge by Lindquist's force to relieve Shanley.

But Lindquist decided not to mount the attack. He had seen what the fixated Millsaps had not, that artillery was falling near the causeway. Lindquist feared shells would hit the trucks he planned to send over and block the bridge. After all his effort, Millsaps felt mortified and begged Lindquist to go. His prodding proved futile. Lindquist would remain where he was. Just before dawn, Shanley withdrew the survivors of Millsaps's charge. Their efforts had been in vain. A military advantage had been gained through horrible sacrifice. Lindquist chose to throw it away. It would be another whole day before he sent a relief force across. Meanwhile, Shanley's men—low on food, water, ammunition, and medical supplies—sweated in their foxholes under constant German punishment.

The 325 made its move along the sunken road. The battalion commander, Terry Sanford, drew up a detailed plan that gave each company separate objectives on the other side of the river.

The operation began well enough. As Sanford's men crossed on the sunken road, they drew not a shot. But as soon as they reached the first hedgerow, German machine gunners found their range, and as each company took off for its assigned task, it disintegrated. The troopers advanced, but the fight became confused amidst the hedgerows. Companies lost contact with one another and the fight grew desperate and at close quarters. Ridgway, watching from across the river, remembered it as one of the most intense combat actions he saw in the war. It proved fruitless, and the men of the 325 ended up in retreat, joining Timmes beneath the apple trees. During the withdrawal of one platoon, the huge Private First Class Charles N. DeGlopper stood defiantly as rear guard, covering his friends with his BAR until he was killed. He was the largest man then in the 82nd. Those who were there remember the last sight of him, his 6 feet 7 inch, 240-pound frame illuminated by the flickering muzzle flashes of his weapon, still firing in spite of several wounds. When he finally fell dead, his comrades had made it to safer ground. He received the Congressional Medal of Honor. But this action too had been in vain. The Germans still held Cauquigny, the causeway remained useless to the Allies, and a battalion of the 325 now sat bottled up with Shanley.

Millet had attacked toward the Timmes force as instructed and succeeded in breaking out. However, in the darkness, his forces became divided, and he himself stumbled into a German bivouac site and was captured. His men did not succeed in breaking through to Timmes or Shanley. Ridgway made Art Maloney the new commander of the 507th. Gavin, in wry relief over his fellow officer's capture, noted in a letter home, "Zip probably likes cabbage soup and black bread."

With the dawn of D + 3, June 9, Ridgway faced difficult decisions. His night assaults—which had not been Gavin's responsibility because of their command structure—had been humiliating failures. Now General Joe Collins suggested that his newly arrived 90th Division be used to force the La Fiere causeway. Ridgway refused to consider it. He was far too proud and too determined to let others do what had been assigned to him. He discussed it with Gavin. Gavin agreed. The 82nd would do the job. Yet the situation was growing more difficult by the minute. The Germans also knew that Cauquigny was key ground. Gavin wrote, "I got the details of the failure of this attack [the failed 325 assault] at daylight, and by that time the situation at the bridge was becoming desperate. We could not lose a moment in forcing our way across and rescuing troops on the other side, and German strength was obviously building steadily."

1

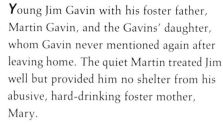

Young Jim Gavin with his foster father, Martin Gavin, and the Gavins' daughter, whom Gavin never mentioned again after leaving home. The quiet Martin treated Jim well but provided him no shelter from his abusive, hard-drinking foster mother, Mary.

Jim Gavin's West Point graduation photo. Never happy as a child, Gavin "created" himself while at the academy. In later years, he referred to the academy as "my Spartan mother." He is buried there next to the Old Cadet Chapel.

Jim Gavin and Irma (Peggy) Baulsir's wedding photo. Gavin, then bound for pilot training, is wearing Air Corps brass. After washing out of flight school within a month, Gavin entered the infantry and remained there for the rest of his career. He seldom spoke of his failure in pilot training.

2

3

*P*eggy Baulsir Gavin with daughter Barbara in their apartment in Washington, D.C.; 1944. Peggy endured the poverty, frequent moves, and Gavin's numerous extramarital affairs during his peacetime service, but the marriage did not last. Gavin seldom wrote Peggy during World War II, but he showered Barbara, the object of most of his affection, with near-daily letters.

*P*aratroops jump from an early version of the C-47 in 1941, about the time Gavin completed jump training. Jumpsuits and jump boots had not been invented when this photo was taken.

*B*y 1942, the airborne idea was growing fast, and VIPs visited regularly. In this Fort Benning inspection, Field Marshal Sir John Dill (holding the swagger stick), the ranking British officer in Washington, and Army Chief of Staff General George C. Marshall (examining soldier in second rank) inspect a platoon of paratroops. Brigadier General Bill Lee, the "father" of airborne, stands between Dill and Marshall.

British Prime Minister Winston Churchill and
Marshall visited the 82nd at Fort Bragg on March 24,
1943. The 82nd staged a demonstration of glider
landings, and Gavin's 505 provided the color guard.
Left to right: Marshall, Field Marshal Sir John Dill,
Churchill, U.S. Secretary of War Henry L. Stimson,
and Lieutenant General Robert Eichelberger.

The 82nd jumps for a demonstration in Oujda in
North Africa in early 1943, just prior to its combat
jump into Sicily. The hard ground caused record
numbers of jump injuries, so after this the 82nd
seldom jumped while in North Africa. Cargo bundles
had white chutes to make them easy to locate.

Snapshot taken in July of 1943 at
Kairouan, just before the Sicily
drop. Gavin confers with battalion
commanders. Left to right: John
H. "Beaver" Thompson (Chicago
Tribune reporter who jumped with
Gavin into Sicily), Major Ben
Vandervoort (back to camera),
Major Mark Alexander, Gavin, and
Lieutenant Colonel Herbert
Batcheller. Though outwardly
confident, Gavin often wondered in
his diary how he would do when
the shooting started.

10

Troopers of the 504th embark on a C-47 for their drop into Sicily on July 11, 1943. Just hours later, many of them died in one of the worst friendly fire disasters in history.

11

After the first regimental combat drop in American history, Gavin established temporary headquarters on Biazza Ridge in Sicily, pictured here. Elements of the Hermann Göring division lay just beyond the ridge line. The troopers had been badly dispersed in the drop, but Gavin's successful defense of the ridge began his legend.

Lieutenant General Mark Clark (right) with Major General Matthew Ridgway, 82nd Airborne commander, in Naples, on their way to the failed liberation reception.

12

13

Two of the 82nd's greatest fighters: newly promoted Assistant Division Commander Brigadier General Gavin (left) with Colonel Reuben Tucker, commander of the 504th Parachute Infantry Regiment, in England right after the 504th returned from Anzio in the spring of 1944. Tucker was one of the best and most aggressive regimental commanders in World War II and always seemed happiest when in combat.

Three of the finest division commanders of World War II meet in Normandy. Left to right: Matthew Ridgway, James Gavin, and Manton Eddy. Eddy built the 9th Infantry Division, then in the process of capturing Cherbourg, into one of the premier divisions of the war until, after he left to become a corps commander, it was mauled in the Huertgen Forest.

14

An American machine-gun position in a Normandy hedgerow. The Germans fortified the hedgerows into formidable defensive complexes that had to be taken one by one.

15

*E*tienville, photographed just after it was secured, one of the last objectives taken by the 82nd in Normandy. This was the town's main thoroughfare.

16

*A*n aerial view of troopers loading into their planes in England on September 17, 1944, for operation Market-Garden, the airborne invasion of Holland. Elements of three divisions jumped that day, making it the largest airborne drop in history.

17

*G*avin, now division commander, briefs his staff and regimental commanders on Market-Garden. Left to right, seated: William E. Ekman, 505, and Robert Weinecke division chief of staff; standing: Walter F. Winton, Jr., G-2; Rube Tucker, 504; Alfred W. Ireland, G-1; Francis A. March III, divisio artillery; Albert G. Marin, G-4; Gavin, at map; Charles Billingslea 325; John Norton, G-3.

18

Gavin greets Field Marshal Sir Bernard Law Montgomery, the mastermind of the tragic defeat in Holland, after Market-Garden ended.

The Nijmegen bridge, spanning the Waal River. It was the largest and last bridge to fall in Market-Garden, but to take it, the 504 had to mount a daring daylight river crossing into the teeth of German defenses while the 505 and British troops fought their way through Nijmegen house to house.

Gavin with General "Boy" Browning in Holland. Gavin cracked his spine during the jump, but only his awkward posture betrays the pain. Browning was a famous paratroop pioneer in England, but Gavin thought he was out to build his own empire and never quite trusted him.

*T*roopers of Gavin's 82nd march through a shattered Nijmegen.

*A*s the battle rages on in Arnhem and Nijmegen, Gavin confers with British General Sir Miles Dempsey on how to break through.

*A*s he had done in North Africa, Gavin mounted a jeep to address his troops in Sissonne after Market-Garden.

A famous picture of Gavin carrying his familiar M-1 Garand during the Battle of the Bulge just after leaving the 508th, then engaged in heavy close-quarters combat, to head for another trouble spot. During the battle, Gavin seemed to be everywhere as he juggled men to meet German threats from several quarters at once.

25

26

German tanks like this Tiger were impervious to the 82nd's bazookas, and the Germans threw hundreds of tanks into their Ardennes offensive. Allied troopers often fought them with German weapons.

Ridgway, XVIIIth Airborne Corps commander, confers with Gavin, 82nd commander, during the Bulge. Ridgway, a no-frills, pure soldier, had as his familiar trademarks the grenade taped to his web gear, seen in the picture, and his Springfield '03 rifle.

27

Gavin in an impromptu headquarters during the Bulge. In battle, he was never far from the scene of the greatest crisis. He fervently believed that a commander's place was at the front, where the action was decisive.

Some of the last German prisoners taken from the battle for Huertgen Forest. By 1945, German soldiers were beginning to look either very old or very young.

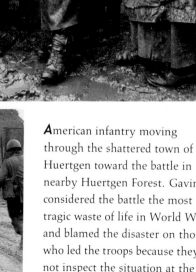

American infantry moving through the shattered town of Huertgen toward the battle in nearby Huertgen Forest. Gavin considered the battle the most tragic waste of life in World War II and blamed the disaster on those who led the troops because they did not inspect the situation at the front themselves.

Cologne as the 82nd saw it in 1945. Despite the near-total destruction of the city, the twin spires of Cologne's famous cathedral, seen here in the distance, remained undamaged.

31

32

Concentration camp inmates liberated by the 82nd Airborne Division at Woebblin Concentration Camp. Gavin was horrified by the camp. He made the Germans lay the emaciated corpses of inmates in the center of the nearby German town of Ludwigslust. Then he forced the entire population of the town to march past the bodies and to bury them. The large building in the distance is the palace in Ludwigslust, where Gavin set up his headquarters and accepted the surrender of General Kurt von Tippelskirch's 21st German Army Group.

33

34

Gavin and Soviet Marshal Georgi Zhukov
review the Allied victory parade through the
ruins of Berlin.

Jim Gavin and Marlene Dietrich. Rumors
about them abounded. One wild account even
had him jumping into the Battle of the Bulge
to save her. Actually, it was more of a fling
than a romance, but Gavin did locate and
rescue her mother in Berlin.

35

Gavin in Berlin with
Eisenhower (Bedell
Smith is behind
Eisenhower).

36

Gavin with Gen. George S. Patton in Berlin at the end of the war.

At the head of his 82nd Airborne Division, Gavin leads the victory parade through New York City. It was suggested that he ride in a car, but Gavin would not hear of it.

Review for Eisenhower. Left to right on the reviewing stand: Gavin, Eisenhower, Ridgway, and Lewis H. Brereton. Brereton, like most air force officers then and today, was obsessed with strategic bombing and placed a low priority on Troop Carrier Wing. He ended up commanding it, though, as commander of the First Allied Airborne Army, a complex joint command invented by Eisenhower.

Gavin attends the Army-
Illinois football game in 1948,
shortly after his wedding, with
his second wife, Jean, and
General Maxwell Taylor (left).
Significantly, Taylor and Gavin,
lifelong rivals, are not seated
side by side.

40

Gavin as army head of research and
development under Eisenhower. This
photo was taken in January of 1958, just
before his retirement.

Gavin with Jacqueline Kennedy and the
newly inaugurated President John F.
Kennedy and Vice-President Lyndon B.
Johnson. Gavin and Kennedy were
friends; Gavin and Johnson were not.
Kennedy appointed Gavin ambassador to
France.

41

42

Ambassador and Mrs. Gavin in Paris on the day he announced his resignation as U.S. ambassador.

The Gavin family. Left to right, seated: Pat, Gavin, Jean, Line; standing: Chloe and Caroline (Jean's daughter by her first marriage).

43

44

Gavin became interested in painting while in Italy and continued the pastime until he became too sick to hold a brush. For a man who never received formal training, he did fine work.

45

Gavin, while at Arthur D. Little Co., talks with Wernher von Braun during a visit to NASA's George C. Marshall Space Flight Center. He had worked with von Braun when he was head of army R&D, and Gavin always respected the master engineer's talent—despite the fact that von Braun had been a key man in Hitler's V-2 program. They became close friends.

Portrait of the chairman of the board of Arthur D. Little.

A retired Gavin in 1984, already feeling the effects of Parkinson's disease. He is surrounded by modern-day 82nd Airborne paratroops with their distinctive berets. Due to the worsening of his disease, he seldom appeared in public after this.

Ridgway gave the mission to Gavin. He was to force a crossing and drive the Germans back westward toward Amfreville. For the mission, Ridgway augmented Gavin's already stretched forces with the 3rd Battalion of the 325, under the command of Lieutenant Colonel Charles A. Carrell, and one company of 507 paratroopers commanded by Captain R. D. Rae. This unit had been defending the La Fiere side of the causeway since D day and had been severely punished by the Germans. In support Gavin also had the use of the 90th Division's artillery, what artillery the 82nd itself could assemble, and twelve Sherman tanks. They scheduled the attack for the morning of June 10, D + 4.

Psychologically, the 3rd Battalion was hardly ready for the task they had drawn. The objective looked daunting from the far shore. The Merderet was 500 yards across at that point, and the men would be silhouetted without cover on the causeway as they charged its length. To make matters worse, this battalion had been part of the 101st and was given to the 82nd at the preinvasion reorganization. Carrell thought Ridgway and Gavin were going to sacrifice the transferred battalion. His attitude was infectious, and the troops had little enthusiasm for the mission.

Gavin himself was uneasy with it on the morning of the attack. To get a closer look, he took the commander of 90th Division artillery, John M. Devine, and crawled out onto the causeway as close as he dared for a better look. Devine recalled that they drew a lot of fire, but Gavin seemed not to care. Gavin precisely pinpointed targets he wanted hit to the artilleryman. Meanwhile, Olsen lined up the tanks to give direct fire support on any targets across the river they could find. By the time Gavin ran crouching back from the causeway, it was 9 A.M.

A spring morning calm fell over the placid Merderet waters—it might have been a pretty, deep green landscape, with the hump of the bridge the focus, except for the German fire that raked the American positions.

But Gavin saw no scenery; he worried over the glidermen of the 325. Their commander had made it clear that he thought the causeway charge stood little chance. To hedge his bets, Gavin called over Art Maloney and Rae, both men he trusted. Maloney looked the part of the warrior that day. He was a huge man, 6 feet 4 inches tall, and about 240 pounds. That same morning, a close artillery round had sent a large fragment his way, to rip his helmet and gouge a deep wound in the side of his head. Maloney, who could have honorably stood down from the action, had his head bandaged, and found a new helmet. Gavin noticed with pride how tough

Maloney looked, with his hulking form and blood-streaked stubble of red beard.

Gavin gave brief instructions. He told Maloney to have Rae ready to charge instantly if the 325 assault faltered. He wanted them to "yell their heads off" and attack through the 325 in order to carry the faint of heart along. Then he had Maloney stay near him when the assault began so he could relay the command.

Rae, joined by Maloney, walked back to brief the anxious troopers. They took the news hard, for a glance showed every man they would be under fire from three sides for 500 yards of hard running. Maloney told them they owed it to Timmes and his men. They would give it a try.

Gavin ordered the 325 glidermen to move into jump-off position, taking advantage of a walled road that afforded a covered approach to the causeway. At 10:30, artillery, small arms, and tanks cut loose at the Germans' positions on the west bank. Fire was vicious and accurate. Gavin thought it seemed the whole shoreline caught fire. Stunned Germans jumped from their positions with bleeding ears to charge across the causeway and surrender. The barrage ceased and a short lull followed. They had planned to end the barrage with smoke to shield the charging troopers, and Gavin waited for its welcome sight. It never came because the artillery batteries had none.

Carrell and his men also saw no smoke. Then the Germans recovered from the barrage and began firing. The wall shielding the glidermen vibrated with the impact of bullets, and German artillery and mortars pummeled the causeway and the shoreline.

Gavin, crouching on a rise to the rear, waited for the glidermen to come into view as they charged forward. They didn't. Incensed, he ran to Carrell, by the wall, shouting "Go! Go! Go!"

Carrell yelled back, "I don't think I can do it!"

Gavin stopped in his tracks and asked, "Why not?"

"I'm sick," Carrell responded.

Gavin's voice fell almost to a whisper and he said, "O.K., you're through." In Carrell's place, Colonel Harry Lewis, the regimental commander, appointed the battalion S-3, Arthur W. Gardiner, to command.

Gardiner ordered his new command to move, and they did, but not as they should have. Most of the lead platoon took off, but as the next group moved up, a man fell dead in the gap in the wall, a bullet through his brain. The men behind him froze. Their platoon leader had charged the causeway and was not there to press them forward. As a result, the initial assault consisted of about three squads, thirty men. They charged into the combined weapons of the better part of a German regiment. Al Ireland, Gavin's S-1 with the 505 and a longtime friend, remembered it as a "firestorm of shell and whining bullets." Yet that first bunch of glidermen did not waver. Legs pumping hard, they charged on and reached the other side, miraculously, nearly intact. It was not until they had made it across that they realized that no one followed them. Still they pushed on and began rolling up German positions relentlessly in a series of sharp actions at close quarters.

Soon other glidermen overcame their shock and, with officers and NCOs urging and kicking them, moved forward. Accurate German fire cut many down. Others simply lost their nerve and lay in the road ditches. A few brave men fought to rally the others. As Gavin watched, the causeway became strewn with the living and the dead. Many men withered into frozen immobility, as if by recoiling they could somehow avoid death. Gavin knew it was the moment between success and failure. He, Ridgway, and Maloney ran out onto the causeway and urged the men on—Maloney bellowing in his deep voice, Ridgway setting a calm example, trying to move a disabled tank blocking the way. Troopers remember Gavin telling soldiers, "Son, you can do it." All three officers were without cover, yet the Germans hit none of them. The forward observer for the artillery, crouching in his foxhole, was stunned when Ridgway appeared to thank him for the good barrage that had preceded the first wave. Gavin, seeing more glidermen on the causeway than across it, knew it was time for Rae to charge.

He turned to Maloney and told him to bring on Rae. Maloney signaled, and together they led about ninety troopers in a mad rush onto the causeway. Now the wrecked tank proved a serious obstacle. Dead, wounded, and men who sought cover filled the space behind and beside it. The wreck offered respite to shocked soldiers who could find nothing to move them on. Rae, Maloney, and their men charged the tank like a football line. Kicking, prying, and pushing, they manhandled men out of the way and broke the jam, and their charge rolled on. Paratroopers ran, fired, and reloaded and ran some more. The wave of olive drab carried forward until it swept into the German embankment. With them went many glidermen who had also been trying to get through, and now the causeway and the bridge—though wounded and dead clogged its gutters

—filled with running, shouting Americans, sweeping around the wreck and on forward.

Gavin had long known that Germans hated close-quarters combat, and when the wave of Americans hit them, they withered and began surrendering in droves. Within half an hour the first crust of resistance on the far side of the river had melted. Behind the charge, Ridgway and others managed to move the wrecks from the road with the help of American tanks; and Gavin led his twelve Shermans across the causeway, a rough job because they had to clear the way of large numbers of wounded and dead soldiers, whom Gavin remembered as lying "stretched head to foot."

Many who were there, including Gavin, give Rae and his troopers credit for carrying the day, and they did break the attack loose, but they had help. The small contingent of glidermen had gone first and grappled in the teeth of the German defenses, so when Rae's assault came, German fire at the causeway had slackened somewhat. Rae's arrival consolidated a toehold at Cauquigny, but surviving Germans beyond that toehold fought desperately on to contain the breakthrough, and the glidermen and paratroopers trying to push beyond Cauquigny west toward Amfreville ran into stiffer and stiffer resistance.

Once the tanks crossed, Gavin returned to the causeway and continued pushing men forward. They needed every man possible to strengthen their assault. A sergeant pulled his laden jeep to a halt beside Gavin. He asked if any vehicles had crossed. Fire still swept the causeway, and the sergeant was not eager to brave it. Gavin asked him what he had in the jeep. On hearing the response, "ammunition," Gavin told him "to get the hell over there."

With all the available men and tanks across, Gavin went to Cauquigny himself around noon. There he found glidermen and paratroopers still routing the last resolute Germans out of firing positions and learned his forward troopers had expanded the bridgehead fast, having now relieved Timmes's and Shanley's positions. He headed for Shanley. He had to know what shape the glidermen and paratroopers were in after hanging on alone. He needed them now to expand the bridgehead.

As he moved gingerly along the riverbank he found a dead paratrooper, still in harness, hanging from a tree. After the vicious action, the sight angered him deeply. The Germans had shot the helpless man, rather than capturing him as the professional code dictated. With his rage came determination to push punishing offensive operations.

He found Shanley's unit battered but still game. Now Gavin had two battalions of 325 men, Rae's troopers, Timmes's men, and Shanley's men. With this considerable force grouped on the east side of the river, and the causeway taken, he set off to find Ridgway on the La Fiere side of the river to make plans for pushing forward. Gavin wanted his troops pushing westward against the Germans as relentlessly as possible to expand the bridgehead and to beat back the Germans from the counterattack he knew must come.

German battle doctrine dictated swift counterattacks upon the exhausted, disoriented men inevitably found at the end of a successful assault. The Germans stayed with doctrine and hit back hard late that afternoon, as Gavin conferred with Ridgway. The Americans started breaking as early evening arrived; a radio message from the 325 commander, Lewis, told Gavin the new bridgehead was collapsing. He broke off his hurried conference with Ridgway and ran back across the river to the command post of the 325th. Already he saw panicked men streaming rearward away from the incessant stutter of German guns, and when Gavin reached the command post, chaos ruled. Harry Lewis, the new regimental commander, had collapsed from shock (no one knew it then, but he had cancer and died just months later). Medics gave him an injection and evacuated him to the rear. In his place Lieutenant Colonel Herbert Sitler, the regimental executive officer, took command. Gavin found Sitler at recently taken Cauquigny, preparing a withdrawal. Losing his temper, Gavin asked what he was doing. Sitler responded, "I can't hold."

Gavin's eyes became icy gray slits and he told the shaken colonel before him, "We are going to counterattack with every resource we have—including you, regimental clerks, headquarters people, and anyone else we can get our hands on with a weapon." Sitler blanched but did as he had been ordered.

Then Gavin located Maloney. The giant, somehow unscathed in the charge, stood calm and ready for instructions. The two ran back to the causeway, where Gavin left Maloney, saying, "I want you to stand on this bridge and don't let any man by."

For the second time that day, Maloney, this time holding a thick broken tree limb in his hands, stood in the road and forced men back into battle. Gavin remembered it as a magnificent sight. Maloney, bellowing defiance vowing, "no one was going to get by him." Then Gavin headed for the front lines, farther west of the bridgehead where his units had pressed on. He had made his decision. The 82nd would not be moved back. Now his place was with the forward elements.

He had already memorized the terrain. To his rear lay the Merderet and La Fiere. To his front, beyond Cauquigny, lay the tiny crossroads of Le Motey, the logical point for a German counterattack and the last town before the center of German resistance at nearby Amfreville. He sent an armored car to tell Shanley to prepare to counterattack on his flank, then with his characteristic long stride, he set out cross-country for Le Motey and flung all the soldiers he could find forward into the fight with the words, "Where are you going, son? We're counterattacking and we need you up there." Le Motey was where the fight would be, and he knew Robert Rae and his troopers would be nearby.

He soon found out why men had buckled. The last fresh regiment of the German 91st Division had thrown itself into the advancing glidermen and troopers. German fire had mounted as they closed on the bridgehead. Their gunners sprayed machine-gun bullets at Gavin as he moved across a grain field just west of Cauquigny, cutting stalks about him "as though by a giant invisible scythe." Intent on reaching Rae, he low-crawled forward. He found Rae bogged down under the German machine-gun and mortar fire and ordered him to move on Le Motey before the Germans took it. Rae had a radio, and Gavin gave instructions over it to his other dispersed units. Rae's, Timmes's, and Sanford's units would all attack toward Le Motey with the 90th Division's 155mm howitzers in support from the other side of the river. The attack went forward, and Gavin stayed in the ranks to be sure it did. As instructed, Rae took Le Motey, and the Germans characteristically fell back as he approached, but well-placed machine guns increased his casualties, and as soon as Americans reached the town, the 90th Division's howitzers mistakenly shelled it, driving the Americans back.

An angry Gavin ordered the barrage lifted, and once more the American attack surged forward against vicious German fire from beyond the town. But as sunset drew near, the Germans realized their counterattack had failed, and badly bloodied, they gave under the pressure and fell back toward Amfreville to prepared positions among the hedgerows. Gavin, satisfied he had countered the German move, went to scout other units' progress now that Rae had regained the initiative. To Rae's rear, he found an 81mm mortar section withdrawing. He turned them around and sent them to Rae. Elsewhere, he found the situation had stabilized. Soldiers of the 325th, some with tank support, had counterattacked as ordered, and they too had blunted the German attack. The 82nd was not going to yield this ground. That night, the 90th Division arrived and relieved the 82nd. The roads to the beach now ran clear of Germans, and American tanks and infantry plowed inland. The Wehrmacht had lost its chance to concentrate superior forces against the beaches. Pressure from Allied air forces prevented the defenders from reinforcing at the decisive moment, and every day, thousands of Allied troops streamed into Normandy.

The Germans had yielded the beaches and the low Merderet country principally because of the double blow dealt them from behind. The initial "crust" of enemy behind Utah Beach, caught between strong forces coming ashore and the stubborn resistance of the paratroops, had been ripped up badly, and the survivors could only now regroup to form a line of resistance in the hedgerow country.

Gavin had every reason to expect that their Normandy fight was over. Airborne doctrine called for paratroopers to be withdrawn once they had accomplished their missions. The 82nd had done that by securing the bridges across the Merderet. By most standards it should have been withdrawn. Its line companies had suffered horrible casualties (some of them were at below 50 percent strength even after all the strays came in), and most of its artillery and vehicles had been lost in the drop. But a new phenomenon was at work. Higher command found the airborne divisions indispensible once the weakness of "regular" infantry divisions became apparent in France. The 90th Division, given the mission of pushing quickly north and west to seal off the Cotentin Peninsula, bogged down immediately in hedgerow-to-hedgerow fighting. General Joe Collins committed his reserve, then he informed Bradley that he still needed the 82nd. The paratroopers were the best infantry he had, and he wanted to keep them. Ridgway raised no protest, and Collins got what he wanted. The 82nd was to attack through the 90th Division westward along the Douve River, crack the hedgerows, and take the road junction at St.-Sauveur-le-Vicomte for the green infantry following. From there, the 90th could jump off in a last westward lunge toward Barneville and Portbail along the coast, and the Cotentin would be cut in two, isolating the Germans holding the critical port of Cherbourg to the north. With but a single day's rest from the causeway battle, the 508 swung into the attack on June 11 and the rest of the division on June 14. The fighting turned bitter when the Germans turned each hedgerow into a fortress, and twice, confused American artillery shelled paratroopers who were not supposed to have advanced as far as they had. Aggressive paratroopers now knew that the best way to beat the Germans was to fire and maneuver, to rapidly close on the enemy, and he would usually surrender. It worked, and the 82nd made rapid progress, but losses ran high once again. The 507 alone lost 192 men in just two days of fighting.

Those last days of Normandy combat became so costly because the landscape reduced the fight to a cruel game where the attackers had to charge across open fields before concealed defenders. Gavin continued to command from points forward. He wrote in his diary, "I continued to visit each battalion command post daily, and whenever circumstances permitted, the company command posts. The high-velocity artillery and mortars exacted a daily toll, but the German was unable to use his artillery in mass as we use ours—probably for lack of ammunition." On one such forward visit, Gavin himself was almost killed by one of his own men.

On June 17, Private Mike Tadusiac of the 505, an assistant machine gunner, sat in a hedgerow late at night next to a gunner called Azy. They had heard Germans moving about the hedgerow to their front and feared a night attack. Suddenly, Azy heard rustling and they spotted two figures moving to their front. Tadusiac whispered the password but received no reply. Azy still wasn't certain he should shoot, so he cocked his gun and tried the password again. This time the figures halted and replied. The figures approached, and the two privates pointed their guns away from the figure, aghast. It was Gavin and a staff officer. He had been out, as was his habit, walking night positions. Gavin complimented the gunner for being alert and moved on. Tadusiac never forgot; he survived the war to recall, "That's how close Gavin came to being shot by Azy and me."

On June 16, the 82nd reached a badly bombed out St.-Sauveur-le-Vicomte. The Germans chose not to defend it, so the 505 marched in that evening unopposed. Thus conscripted to bolster other troops, the 82nd played a vital role in helping cut off the Cotentin. The terrain past St.-Sauveur-le-Vicomte had fewer hedgerows, and two days later, the 90th division reached Barneville and the Atlantic. Cherbourg was now cut off, and the 82nd rested on the defensive near St.-Sauveur-le-Vicomte. Along the way, they had mauled the better part of four German divisions— including the hated 91st, which had shot defenseless paratroopers caught in trees.

Now Bradley turned his forces simultaneously to the north to seize Cherbourg and to the south to punch out of the hedgerow-checkered Cotentin Peninsula and into the open country beyond, where rapid movement could give the Americans the advantage. Collins's VII Corps would strike north, and the new VIII Corps, under Major General Troy H. Middleton, would punch southward. Bradley gave Middleton the 82nd to use as needed, and Middleton ordered that it assist with the breakout from the hedgerow country by providing the main punch in the center. Ridgway was happy to oblige to please higher command; Gavin voiced strong misgivings. By the end of June, when this order arrived at the 82nd, the division was badly understrength. In many of the combat companies, actual strength totaled around 50 men or less (one company mustered just 12); there should have been over 150. At least two of Gavin's regimental commanders protested the attack order, feeling that another attack might decimate the regiments and make it necessary to rebuild them from scratch, a process that would take several months. Gavin concurred and took the issue to Ridgway.

Ridgway was unbending. The division jumped off on July 3 as planned. Gavin's protests and Ridgway's insistence that they continue attacking fueled ill feeling between them. Gavin felt Ridgway was wrong, that he did not know his own men. Gavin believed that command included understanding that all men have limits. There was no reason to send the 82nd forward again. There were many units available for the job, and it was long past time when the paratroopers should have been withdrawn and the division rebuilt. He felt Ridgway was simply trying to please higher command. Yet the breakout attack went off well. The desperately understrength companies reached all their assigned objectives. Airborne was beginning to get a reputation for performance. Higher command was once again impressed by what those "crazy characters" could do. Gavin's fears were also confirmed. The final attack, through heavy rain from a bridgehead at Pont-l'Abbé, carried them to the outskirts of La Haye-du-Puits with such speed that the other divisions were left lagging, and higher command had to halt the paratroopers out of fear for their exposed flanks. But the hedgerow fighting once again proved costly. Understrength regiments became more so, and several battalion commanders fell, including Maloney, Shanley, and Alexander. Other notable leaders such as Lieutenant Louis Levy, who had held Cauquigny so tenaciously with his ten men, died in this final attack. When the 82nd Airborne

Division finally pulled out of the front lines to return to England, sixteen of its original twenty-one regimental and battalion commanders had been killed, captured, or wounded. In total, the division lost 46 percent in killed, wounded, and missing, but total casualties do not reflect the decimation of the division's infantry companies, whose men had done most of the bleeding. Most of these companies left Normandy, when the division was officially relieved of combat duties on July 8, at below 30 percent strength.

Losses like these have paralyzed many divisions; however, throughout the Normandy campaign, the 82nd never lost combat effectiveness in spite of them. And somewhere, during the desperate night actions and the bloody slog through the hedgerows, legend descended on the division. If their exploits had not been widely reported before, they were after Normandy. Though their dead lay strewn from St.-Mère-Église to Amfreville to La Haye-du-Puits, their deeds and rakish air captured the American imagination at a time of one of the nation's greatest successes. And above them rose the image of lean, handsome, and articulate Slim Jim Gavin. He had long been known to higher command. Now the press took him, and Gavin became a public figure. Already he had achieved more from his war than he had planned back before Sicily, but now he wanted more still. He wanted sole command of a division, and he was about to get it.

By July 11, Gavin was settled back in Leicester, England. Ridgway had become the darling of higher command in Normandy, and rumor had it that he would get a corps. Gavin waited to see if that meant he would have the 82nd.

10.

MARKET-GARDEN

After Normandy, the press made paratroopers seem larger or better than everyone else. Their exotic dress, their jumping generals, and the image of the solo airborne liberator caught the public fancy. The Germans feared them and hated fighting them. Gavin noted in a letter home after Normandy that, "These parachutists have been nothing short of remarkable in their fighting. Admittedly I am very biased, but I believe that the violence and savagery of their combat technique is without parallel in our military history. The Germans fear them now and give them lots of elbow room."

The mystique of paratrooper toughness grew much more from good training and technique than sheer bravado. The World War II paratrooper was indeed a courageous fighter, undoubtedly the best regarded soldier of the European Theater of Operation. Yet courage, the great essential in combat, is nothing without ideas. Gavin, an assiduous student of his own experience in the field, became a master at the application of "fire and maneuver" because it was army doctrine and because he thought it would work.* When he actually met the Germans in combat, his faith in it was reinforced, and by applying fire and maneuver ruthlessly, he discovered the German soldier's key weakness: a dislike of close-quarters combat.

Gavin was often surprised to find that, in general, the closer a unit

---

* "Fire and maneuver" involved two units, one of which would close on the enemy, pin down defensive troops with suppressive fire, and the other would close and destroy the enemy at close quarters. Gavin's troops used this tactic at La Fiere and elsewhere; it did not prove effective in all units, however, as it requires extremely aggressive infantry. The 1st, the 3rd, and the 9th Infantry Divisions were also fine aggressive divisions.

maneuvered, the less accurate became German fire. He made it dogma for the paratroopers to assault the Germans viciously and relentlessly. So when the Germans counterattacked his bridgehead at Cauquigny, he himself counterattacked immediately. Time and again he would find that captured German troops expected American infantry to retreat before determined assaults. But when paratroopers stood and themselves coun- terattacked, Germans either surrendered or withdrew. Gavin's troopers employed these tactics frequently as they battled through the hedgerows and took objectives others had said were hopeless.

The paratroopers' tough training led them to trust their leaders and each other. One trooper spoke for many when he recalled Gavin: "He was a person that you would follow anywhere. He would jump with the troops, and he wasn't afraid to be with you at the front lines."

Paratroops were also physically superior to many other U.S. units, and by that stage of the war, to the Germans they fought, thanks to Gavin's ruthless physical training and long night marches. No wonder paratroops soon became the sort of troops that corps commanders hate giving up.

As established, paratroop artillery was inferior; airborne divisions pos- sessed far less firepower than conventional infantry divisions, because their primary weapons were the pack 75mm howitzer and the short- barreled 105mm howitzer, the best a glider could carry. But the para- troops were not overly enamored of guns because they believed, with George S. Patton, that, "The poorer the infantry, the more artillery it needs."

On July 17, after a two-day London leave, Gavin woke in Val Porter's welcoming arms to be summoned by Matthew Ridgway. In a cramped office in a Nissen hut at Braunston Park, Ridgway informed him that he was moving up to take command of an airborne corps and Gavin would get his second star and take command of the 82nd Airborne Division. It was the job he had worked toward all his life.

Eisenhower had created the XVIII Airborne Corps to include the 82nd, Maxwell Taylor's 101st, and the newly arrived 17th Airborne Division under the command of old airborne hand Major General William M. "Bud" Miley. Eisenhower envisioned a larger airborne galaxy, a joint command called the First Allied Airborne Army (FAAA). This would consist of the XVIII Airborne Corps and the British 1st and 6th Airborne Divisions plus the Polish 1st Parachute Brigade. Troop carrier commands would also come under FAAA. The man in England most certain that he should command FAAA was Boy Browning, and to this end he pressed tirelessly but without success. His reward was the deputy commander position, and for the chief, Eisenhower selected Lewis Brereton. He was selected because Bradley, incensed over the disastrous drops by Brereton's Ninth Air Force, blamed Brereton's fixation with strategic bombing for his neglect of Troop Carrier. Bradley reasoned that the airman would be less distracted without the bombers and airborne drops would improve. Eisenhower listened to Bradley, and Brereton, who hated this new command away from his beloved bombers, got the job. In this way, Eisenhower, who loved joint commands because they gave him somewhere to slot pesky British generals, manufactured two command layers above the 82nd that had not existed prior to Normandy, just as Jim Gavin took command. The Eisenhower system of surrounding and layering authority was to cause Gavin difficuties.

Throughout June and most of July, the battle in Normandy raged on inconclusively; but no complaint about the slowness of the advance could take away the triumph, or disguise the fact that Hitler had failed to seize his spectacular chance on the Normandy beaches.

On the tactical level the American Army had run into unexpected trouble in the *bocage* (hedgerow) country, a place where massive superiority was less effective. The Germans, through harsh experience in Russia, were the masters of the fluid defense and defense-in-depth, tactics that often lured frontally attacking forces forward only be destroyed with sharp counterattacks at the moment of their imagined victory.

On the other hand, Allied air superiority was near absolute. Mustangs and Spitfires roamed the skies above Europe with impunity. The Germans found it nearly impossible to move reinforcements or supplies by daylight, except in heavy downpours or morning fog.

Early Allied priorities for the days immediately after the beach landings in Normandy were clear. In order to beat the Germans arrayed before them, the Allied armies had to get their superior flow of supplies and replacements to the front. Two towns became critical. The first was Cherbourg, the major port at the tip of the Cotentin Peninsula. Without it the Allies would be forced to bring in supplies over the beaches, or through the problematic and temporary "Mulberry" artificial harbors, which had proved susceptible to damage from northerly storms. The second prize was Caen, a lowland city a dozen miles from the coast on the river Orne, the rail and road hub of the Calvados region. It had been Montgomery's

D day objective, though he had fallen far short of it. Cherbourg fell at the end of June, before Caen, in part due to the effectiveness of the airborne landing that had helped seal it off, though credit justly went to resolute attacks spearheaded by the 9th Infantry Division. What broke the defense was American naval and air power. Nothing the Luftwaffe could do lifted the rain of steel. Battleships and lesser vessels pummeled the port from the sea, and the Americans organized a carpet bombardment to blast a hole through German defenses. But the destruction inflicted by the Allies, plus German sabotage, left the harbor facilities shattered. It was weeks before Cherbourg functioned as a port.

Caen was a case of even more delay and stalemate. By the end of June it still had not fallen. The area around Caen was good tank terrain; the Allies had concentrated their armor there, and so had the Germans. Here the imbalance of numbers was matched by imbalance of quality. Though the British did indeed have more tanks than the Germans opposing them, the superiority of the German tanks evened the odds.

The Americans, under Lieutenant General Omar Bradley, had to fight their way through the *bocage* country to reach Cherbourg, so far fewer tanks prowled the hedgerows on both sides in terrain that favored the defense. Small gains cost heavy casualties, and advance after advance slipped and stumbled after limited success. Because the Allies had limited docking facilities for unloading ships, they could not bring to bear their superior resources, either in the Cotentin or at Caen. And since the battle for Cherbourg was fought on a peninsula, the Germans there were able to concentrate their resources in a limited area. As a result, the Allies' advantages evaporated.

What Allied commanders had most feared seemed about to happen: a stalemate like that nightmare of World War I, a situation the Germans longed for, hoping it would lead at least to a negotiated peace.

Supply and manpower shortages shadowed every Allied plan. Stalemate threatened disaster for both Churchill and Roosevelt. (Roosevelt was running for reelection and wary of bad news involving high casualties.)

Eisenhower was again at the edge of his nerves. None of the American commanders, certainly not Gavin, had imagined how bad the hedgerow country could be for the attacking force. A breakout could solve all the worries.

When the breakout came, in late July, it was the work of Omar Bradley. The plan was for a concentrated attack on a narrow front, an idea at odds with American military wisdom but in tune with the realities of the territory and forces. Following carpet bombing of an area 7,000 yards long at the critical point of the St.-Lô–Périers road, two waiting infantry divisions were to rush in to subdue the stunned German defenders and keep the way open for armored divisions to drive toward the ports of Brittany, Avranches, at the root of the Cotentin Peninsula; St.-Malo; and the greater prize of Brest. Operation Cobra, as it was called, was a success. Suddenly the Allies found themselves with immense possibilities for movement and attack.

Lieutenant General George S. Patton's newly activated Third Army slashed across Brittany, isolating several German divisions around the ports, then wheeled northward and started a dash toward Paris and beyond. Meanwhile a German counterattack intended to seal the Allies in Brittany failed, and the retreating remnants of the counterattacking panzer force were decimated at the Falaise Gap.

Suddenly, the Allies met success after spectacular success. Patton raced for Germany, and Montgomery sped toward the Low Countries. By the end of August, Belgium had fallen to Montgomery.

Celebrations began in England and the United States. From all appearances, the German Army was defeated. The Wehrmacht had been unable to mount significant resistance to advancing Allied forces since Normandy, and they showed no sign of fresh vigor. As September arrived talk of ending the war by Christmas was widespread.

When the sweep into France began, the question of supply ports remained unanswered. Cherbourg functioned, but its shattered docks and cranes meant that much matériel still came in over the beaches. Antwerp had fallen to Montgomery intact after his speedy push north, but it, too, was useless until the Schelde Estuary leading to it was secure. Not only did the Germans control the 54-mile island-studded approach, but the German Fifteenth Army, now routed from France, was retreating through the estuary, from island to island, and willing to fight for their survival. The largest port in Allied hands remained only a propaganda asset.

An unsettling situation arose. As Allied supply lines through France grew longer, supply shortages multiplied. Everything, particularly fuel, was scarce. Eisenhower wished to exert pressure on the enemy everywhere but soon found he did not have the wherewithal to sustain it. The

Germans retreated faster than he could advance, and the Allies, like a giant stumbling over its own feet, could not move fast enough.

In early September, Eisenhower's two most noted commanders, Patton and Montgomery, each had hatched plans to end the war quickly. Both disagreed with Eisenhower's broad-front strategy and called for the single thrust deep into the enemy's rear area. Each thought his command should be the one to execute it. It became Eisenhower's decision. On September 1, George Marshall, in response to a public outcry about the huge American armies in Europe being still under the field command of British General Montgomery, had ordered Eisenhower to go to the Continent, and assume the position of ground commander.

Ike complied. Montgomery, sensitive to the motive for the move, suggested that he remain ground commander under Eisenhower's overall command. Though this was rejected, Montgomery continued to gather all available resources to knock Germany out of the war with his own plan while his divisions sat outside of Antwerp. By early September of 1944, he had swept aside the supply shortages and logistical realities and was sure not only that he could smash into Germany, but that he could charge to Berlin. Eisenhower scoffed at the notion.

On September 10, Montgomery arranged a conference with Eisenhower. The Germans had begun launching V-2 rockets on England. Aside from the heavy damage they wrought, the rockets were effective terror weapons, psychologically damaging to weary British city dwellers. Their launch sites were believed to be in western Holland. Montgomery believed, if all available resources were given to him, he could thrust through Holland, turn east, and smash into Germany, and in passing eliminate the mobile terror rockets that air power could not find.

It was a daring concept. The major objective in the quixotically named Market-Garden was the bridge that crossed the Lower Rhine at a town called Arnhem. If Montgomery took that bridge, then he would have outflanked the main German defenses and could crash into the Ruhr Valley, the industrial heartland of Germany. The problem was that Montgomery's forces were then 64 miles from Arnhem. In between was a very watery Holland. To get to Arnhem, Montgomery's armored forces would have to pass down a single road through the towns of Grave and Nijmegen, passing over at least five major bridges on their way. In many places the single road they would be compelled to use was narrow and raised high above the countryside so as to perfectly silhouette their vehicles for German gunners.

Impressed by the potential rewards of the plan, Eisenhower had made the First Airborne Army under Brereton and Browning available for whatever Montgomery wanted to do with it. These troops had been idle since Normandy, and back in the States, George Marshall was vehemently pushing Eisenhower to find some use for them. Montgomery proposed to drop three airborne divisions to clear the way for his assault and hold the bridges until his armor could reach them. The airborne portion of the assault was dubbed Market. According to plan, the 101st would be dropped in the vicinity of Eindhoven, nearest the British jump-off point; the 82nd would be dropped near Nijmegen, and the British 1st Airborne Division would jump into Arnhem. In Garden, the ground portion of the assault, the British Second Army's XXX Corps under Lieutenant General Brian G. Horrocks would charge up the road and reach Arnhem in about two days.

Eisenhower was intrigued. The plan answered Marshall's demands for using an airborne force, solved the V-2 rocket problem, and provided a way to smash into Germany. Montgomery well understood his man when he proposed the plan to the Supreme Commander. As a military thinker, Eisenhower was pure U.S. Grant, but he usually put his politics before his tactics. Montgomery made Market-Garden too politically neat to resist. Eisenhower gave his approval. Patton's army would be halted in its drive toward the Saar, for lack of supplies, and Montgomery's clearing of the Schelde Estuary would wait. Market-Garden would take priority.

In retrospect, Eisenhower's acquiescence in Montgomery's plan seems out of character and illogical. Allied armies had outrun their supply lines; therefore the sine qua non in the late summer of 1944 was to gain a port quickly. Montgomery was in the right position to do just that—if he had been so inclined—by clearing the way to Antwerp. Furthermore, the ground under the path of Montgomery's proposed attack was veined with canals, rivers, and bridges between XXX Corps and Arnhem; and at any one of them even a precisely timed assault could be stalled. All the Germans needed to wreck the plan was one determined stand or one demolished bridge, and they could trap the isolated airborne divisions, which could not be extracted once they dropped.

Market-Garden was approved because Allied commanders had come to believe the war was all but won. To base a plan upon such an assumption was a major misjudgment. The British Army under Montgomery had another urgent concern. England was literally running short of replacements. The army in France was the last great army she could field, and Churchill insisted that Montgomery not take heavy casualties.

Then there was Montgomery himself. Every Allied commander considered him to be competent; however, he was also notorious for being slow and ponderous on the offensive. They described him as "the master of the set-piece battle." He believed in husbanding resources and organizing meticulously until his troops went into battle with a preponderant superiority of numbers and equipment and moved from phase line to phase line in a "tidy" manner. It worked, but it certainly was not the prescription for a mad motorized dash 64 miles through difficult terrain to reach Arnhem.

Eisenhower's assent to Market-Garden was one of his most serious tactical blunders of the war. Montgomery's call for Market-Garden was based more upon his own vanity than his appraising logic. The only real option at the time was to give Patton gasoline for his tanks and trucks while Montgomery secured Antwerp. But behind every large decision in war there is usually to be found an impure mix of motives. Behind Market-Garden lurked the vanity of one man and another's desire for consensus. Eisenhower urged Montgomery to move forward with all possible speed.

Germany had been handed an opportunity, and they were not idle or unappreciative. Hitler had fired Gerd von Rundstedt in a fit of recriminations over the invasion, but amidst the deterioration of the Western Front, he brought him back on September 4 and placed him in command of all armies in the West. It was not an enviable job. The situation held little promise for the Germans. So far, more than 300,000 German soldiers had died, fallen wounded, or been captured. By von Rundstedt's own estimate the Allies had a 20-to-1 superiority in tanks, 25 to 1 in aircraft, and 2.5 to 1 in artillery pieces. And besides the troops already lost, an additional 200,000 soldiers remained cut off in isolated garrisons holding Channel ports.

A Prussian professional at the end of a long career, von Rundstedt determined to do what he could. His first concern was the gap in German defenses in Holland. While he marveled over Montgomery's inactivity in the face of opportunity, von Rundstedt found ways of turning the situation around.

The German Fifteenth Army, with 80,000 men, sat trapped at Calais. Von Rundstedt began withdrawing it with a hodgepodge of ships via the

Schelde Estuary in the first days of September. Fate favored the Germans, as they conducted the withdrawal with two ancient freighters and a fleet of small barges. The Allies knew of it because the voyage took place partly during daylight, and Allied aircraft swarmed in to attack but missed the ships. Yet despite the Allies' having absolute control of the sea, no naval action slowed the night evacuations, and the small armada went unmolested. Eisenhower's headquarters did absolutely nothing—nor did Montgomery, whose front lines were but a few miles from the evacuation route. The evacuation succeeded, and von Rundstedt had gathered a considerable force for operations in Holland.

In Germany the high command ordered Colonel General Kurt Student to organize the First Parachute Army to defend the Belgian-Dutch border. Actually, the army contained only a few thousand trained paratroopers. Of the total force of about 20,000, most were raw recruits, convalescents, and old men recruited at the last minute. Hitler assigned this force to defend the Albert Canal, behind which Montgomery's troops had stopped.

Even as Student's troops began fortifying the canal on September 5, a huge mob of dispirited German troops clogged Holland's roads. They were still retreating pell-mell before the British and had no intention of fighting anyone. To the Dutch, the day would be remembered as *Dolle Dinsdag*, "Mad Tuesday." What began as a slow trickle of troops on September 2, turned into "a mad exodus." The Dutch were jubilant. The battle they had anticipated would not come. The Germans were leaving on their own.

Then Major General Kurt Chill, commander of the German 85th Division, seeing the situation on the roads, stationed his men at critical junctions and bridges, gathered stragglers, and organized them into makeshift units to form a firm line of defense along the Albert Canal. The Germans were about to have good fortune in Holland.

Lieutenant General Wilhelm Bittrich's II SS Panzer Corps had been fighting long and hard. It needed some time to refit and receive replacements. Field Marshal Walther Model, the man now in charge of ground forces in Holland, decided that Arnhem would be a nice quiet place to send the division for refitting. They began heading for the area on September 5 and 6. Model liked the quiet little town of Arnhem so much, he set up his headquarters there.

Montgomery was correct in his September 4 assessment of the situation in Holland; the German front had split open. But, by September 10, while his troops remained at Antwerp, all that had changed. The panic-stricken flight had ended, and the Germans were reorganized. He had given them the time to do it.

Back in Leicester, Jim Gavin was a busy man. He had watched that Allied dash across France with interest, and airborne missions had come and gone. Whenever planned, they were canceled just as fast. In at least one case, Allied forces had advanced so fast that they overran the drop zones on the day of the drop, making it unnecessary. On August 16, 1944, he gained sole command of the 82nd Airborne Division from General Ridgway. He was not yet a major general, but the promotion orders had been requested, and when they came in in October, he would be the youngest major general since George Armstrong Custer.

While he waited, Gavin built the division in his own likeness. The men he selected for key positions were all Gavin men, original 505ers, with one exception, Bob Wienecke, whom Gavin made chief of staff. The rest of the staff were men he had watched as they had come up, and he considered them to be the best. Al Ireland was his G-1 (personnel), G-2 (intelligence) was Walt Winton, G-3 (plans and operations) was John "Jack" Norton, and G-4 (supply) went to Albert Marin. All were in their twenties then. Gavin said, "It was unquestionably the youngest division staff in the European Theater of Operations. It was also a very able, dedicated, hard-working staff." Gavin's appointments were notable for one absence. He named no assistant division commander. Rube Tucker was an obvious choice, but Gavin noted Tucker's regiment's poorly handled paperwork. Gavin might also be fairly accused of holding back the one officer who matched him in aggressiveness and daring. There could not be two Gavins in the 82nd; but he salved his conscience by saying he could think of no one else he wanted. With this omission, the division would enter its next combat without an ADC. Years later, Norton criticized the decison, saying it was one of the few mistakes he ever saw Gavin make. Had Gavin been killed, the unclear line of command succession could have led to confusion, even tragedy.

August was full of speculation and warning orders about anticipated missions. On Sunday, September 10, while Gavin visited Valerie Porter in London, the phone rang; he was to get to Brereton's headquarters as soon as possible. He drove as fast as he could but arrived late to find Browning conducting a meeting; also in the room were Max Taylor of the 101st, Major General Robert E. "Roy" Urquhart of the British 1st Airborne Division, and various top troop carrier commanders. The meeting concerned a mission called Market-Garden.

Gavin reflected that Browning finally had his command. He would lead Market-Garden, landing with his staff in gliders attached to the 82nd. The division was scheduled to drop near the towns of Nijmegen and Grave, where it would secure several bridges and the high ground between Nijmegen and a town called Groesbeek.

The 101st Airborne would drop near Eindhoven, and Urquhart's 1st Airborne would drop at Arnhem, to be joined later by the Polish 1st Parachute Brigade. By taking these towns and the bridges in and around them, the three airborne divisions would open the way for Montgomery to punch his way into Germany. Gavin immediately had the obvious misgivings. Holding until relief came was nothing new, but depending upon British troops to charge 64 miles down one road in a limited time was too daring.

Gavin knew this drop would be different from the others. Because the Allies no longer feared the Luftwaffe, they would jump in daylight. Glider regiments would be in the initial assault for the first time, and the numbers would make it the largest airborne attack in history, far larger than the D day operation.

British intelligence anticipated enemy resistance to be "negligible." It was thought that the German Army was finished, and Browning referred to the whole thing as "a party." Gavin felt uneasy when he left the meeting. Following his preaction habit, he went to British intelligence personally to see what they knew about the region.

The 82nd's mission was to capture and hold a triangular piece of occupied Holland. At the apex of the triangle sat the city of Nijmegen, with a large bridge that spanned the Waal River. This bridge was the 82nd's northernmost objective. From that bridge, the road led straight north 11 miles to Arnhem. Below Nijmegen was Grave, the left point of the triangle, where a bridge spanned the Maas or Meuse River on the German/Dutch border. The base of the triangle was formed by a road which led from Grave to the towns of Groesbeek and Wyler, which was within Germany. Between Groesbeek and Nijmegen heavily forested high ground ran along the German border. Each leg of the triangle was approximately 10 miles long, and within it, Browning expected Gavin's division to seize a total of eight bridges while blocking almost certain German counterattacks from the forests around Groesbeek. Aside from the panzer units suspected by Dutch intelligence to be near Groesbeek, Nijmegen itself contained at least a regiment, and the Nijmegen bridge was nearly 2,000 feet long and prepared for demolition.

As Gavin studied the area, he realized that he simply did not have enough troops to fulfill all the missions assigned. On September 14, he discussed this with Browning, and the English general directed him to leave the Nijmegen bridge alone until he had accomplished his other objectives. The Nijmegen bridge was the largest bridge, but it was also farthest from the advancing British XXX Corps. If the 82nd failed to seize the lower crossings, or German armor was not destroyed in the forests about Groesbeek, there would be no need of the Nijmegen bridge.

Gavin had qualms about leaving the Nijmegen bridge alone, so he decided on his own to detach a battalion, as soon as he could spare one, to seize it. Gavin viewed it this way, "The big Nijmegen bridge posed a serious problem. Seizing it with overwhelming strength at the outset would have been meaningless if I did not get at least two other bridges: the big bridge at Grave and at least one of the four over the Canal. Further, even if I captured it, if I had lost all of the high ground that controlled the entire sector, as well as the resupply and glider landing zones, I would be in a serious predicament. Everything depended upon the weight and direction of the enemy reaction, and this could not be determined until we were on the ground. The problem was how much could be spared how soon for employment on the bridge."

In front of his men, he never let on that he had serious doubts about what Montgomery had planned, but his doubts ran deep. As the Allies had dashed across France, he and his staff had kept a careful watch on troop movements, which were the natural subject of everyday analysis. He knew the commanders involved.

On one of his trips to London that summer, Gavin saw Allied supply statistics at Eisenhower's headquarters, and he knew the Allies along the German border had severe fuel and ammunition shortages. Montgomery's forces had been given priority on all logistical support. Gavin considered this intolerable. He had seen Montgomery in action since Sicily, had little respect for his methodical generalship, and serious misgivings that Montgomery would quickly fight his way to Nijmegen—let alone make it to Arnhem. Ireland recalled that as they prepared to board aircraft for Holland, all the officers had serious, though seldom-voiced, doubts on that issue. Gavin had full confidence in the ground commander, Horrocks, and always considered him to be the best type of British soldier, a man who would do his best to get there; but he did not believe the enemy completely beaten, nor that Market would be the "party" Browning had predicted.

His diary entry before leaving for Holland was dour to the extreme: "The flak in the area is terrific, the Krauts many. It looks very rough. If I get through this one I will be very lucky. It will, I am afraid, do the Airborne cause a lot of harm."

Operation Market-Garden began on Sunday, September 17, 1944. The Allies kicked it off with massive aerial bombing of German flak installations and airdromes, in case the Luftwaffe showed some life. Pathfinders followed the bombers, and all but one crew hit their drop zones and set up their beacons. When the paratroopers took off, they flew in two distinct serials. The 101st flew to the south, over Antwerp, and the 82nd and the British 1st Airborne Division flew a northern route. Altogether, more than 1,500 troop carrier aircraft rushed northeastward that day.

Gavin, in charge of a third of that aerial strike force, carried a burden of doubt over and above the problematic rendezvous at Arnhem. There was not enough lift to move all three divisions and the Polish brigade to Holland on D day; actually there was only enough to move about half the required force. The others would be air-ferried in later. To avoid pilot fatigue, Brereton forbade the pilots to fly more than one mission per day. As a result Gavin would not have the entire 82nd ready to fight when he landed, and bringing in the others depended upon the weather in England and Holland remaining favorable. He also had misgivings over the mission of the British 1st Airborne. Because of German flak around Arnhem, drop zones were nearly 10 miles from their objective. Although they had treated the situation cavalierly, a matter of a few hours movement, Gavin did not think it so easy for them to fight their way to the bridge, particularly since, in daylight, they would lose all chance for surprise.

Gavin was also uncomfortable under Browning's command. During an earlier operation, planned and later canceled, Gavin had noted Browning and his staff at work. He wrote of it, "General Browning shed considerable of his professional aura and under pressure became the disheveled frustrated officer that most of us are in combat. . . . He unquestionably lacks the steadying influence and judgment that comes with proper troop experience." It did not help that once again a British commander led a majority of American troops. Gavin wanted Ridgway, a man he trusted.

But he did not worry about an enemy concentration at Arnhem because he had no inkling of its presence: for once, his contacts in the Dutch underground and his own nose for intelligence had not been keen enough.

Ironically, Market-Garden leaders, including Montgomery and Eisenhower, were aware panzers had gathered at Arnhem, and Gavin would have paid dearly for the foreknowledge. Eisenhower's staff had known about the 9th and 10th SS Panzer divisions' presence at Arnhem and had informed Montgomery of the situation. With the evidence of decoded German messages in hand, Ike's chief of staff, Bedell Smith, had come to see Monty personally to urge him to strengthen the Arnhem element. Monty and his staff dismissed the warning, still believing that the Germans to their front were finished.

In the air about Gavin on that beautiful fall morning of September 17 were the 450 planes that carried much of the 82nd. The first-wave units included the 505th (with whom Gavin flew), the 508th, the 504th, the 307th Parachute Engineer Battalion, and the 376th Parachute Field Artillery. Eighty Gliders containing the division's 75mm guns, non-parachute-qualified staff, and thirty-eight gliders' worth of Boy Browning's FAAA staff followed the parachutists. All flew unharassed to converge over the pathfinders' beacons. The 504th landed in two drop zones south and north of the Grave bridge. The 508th landed between Groesbeek and Wyler, and the 505th and the headquarters section landed between Groesbeek and Mook.

In the vicinity of this drop zone Gavin had been warned to expect panzers gathered in wooded terrain at the German/Dutch border. As a precaution, he sent the entire artillery section to land there, to be ready for the tanks. The 504 was to seize the large 1,500-foot Grave bridge and the smaller 50-foot bridges spanning the Maas-Waal Canal. The other regiments were to hold the high ground against the expected German counterattacks, while the 505 assisted the 504 with taking the bridges over the canal.

For the drop, Gavin had given a unique order. To save airplanes and protect Browning's follow-on command section from antiaircraft fire, he ordered his troopers to grab their parachute shroud lines and steer toward antiaircraft batteries they saw while descending, in order to knock them out immediately. The order is remembered as a supreme test of paratroop mettle.

One man, Private Edwin C. Raub, became enraged when enemy anti-aircraft fire ripped through his canopy; he steered as ordered straight for a gun. Landing close to it, he charged, dragging his parachute behind him, his tommy gun blazing. He killed or captured the gun's crew, then blew up the gun with plastique. Similar acts were reported elsewhere as the regiments hit the ground.

Gavin wrote of the fatalism of some of his veterans on this jump, for few men expected their luck to hold forever. For some, this was a fourth combat jump. "They had been through many difficult battles, and many of them had been wounded, some several times," he wrote. "I knew practically all of the survivors personally, and I knew what went on in their minds. They were well aware of our heavy combat losses in the past, and to ask them once again to jump into combat more than fifty miles behind the German lines in broad daylight was asking a great deal." There were no refusals recorded that afternoon; during the last hours before the drop, Gavin sought out his "old-timers" in order to personally reassure them that it would all be O.K. They appreciated his gesture, but many of the troopers who had followed him into Sicily, Italy, Normandy, and now Holland would go no farther than the bridges and fields southwest of Arnhem.

General Ridgway, too, had felt a nostalgic pull that day, and he had come to say good-bye to the 82nd that morning in person. For all he knew, this was the last large airborne action of the war; yet it was Browning's show, and Ridgway now was held to the role of an honored spectator. Unable to stay behind, he hitched a ride on a B-17 Flying Fortress and circled the battlefield at about a thousand feet for the better part of the afternoon. The drop was a spectacular sight, never forgotten by the tens of thousands who witnessed it. Thousands of parachutes filled the sky over Holland in the largest daylight combat drop in history, and even Ridgway was impressed by the sheer numbers and the display of military power.

Gavin's plane ride to Holland proved more eventful than he had hoped. They took off just after eleven o'clock that morning, and once airborne, he saw what seemed like an infinity of troop carrier planes and gliders in every direction. Zipping above and below them flew the fighters, their pilots looking for threats from the air and on the ground. Once the planes reached the Continent at the normal 1,000 feet of drop altitude, he busied himself looking for landmarks. The first one he saw was the Grave bridge. It was reassuring, distinctive. From there he could follow the flight plan exactly as it unfolded under him. Flak was heavy, but ineffective; Hugo Olsen, Gavin's ubiquitous aide, described the flak as sometimes darkening the sky, but the C-47s trundled along as if undisturbed. Gavin had his men ready themselves to jump as if it didn't exist.

The green light glowed. He had seen all the landmarks, and he jumped without hesitation, buffeted by the prop blast, until, suddenly, with a painful wrenching jerk, his canopy opened. The planes had been low and the descent was momentary. The parachute blossomed—and then he hit, his parachute still oscillating. Gavin just had time for his mind to record that enemy fire looked heavy. It was a bad, hurried landing. When he hit, he felt something rip in his back, and a painful electric jolt went down his spine.

There was little time to do anything but roll, get out of harness and take cover. Fire from several weapons came from the trees bordering the drop zone. Gavin pulled out his .45 before he even got out of harness, then he got his M-1 Garand out from under his reserve chute, replaced his pistol, and ran for the trees. A young engineer captain stopped him with, "Sir, I just killed two Germans in those trees, and there's a bunch more over there." Gavin ran on.

His planned command post was about a mile away through the same trees, marked on the map by a dirt road crossed by railroad tracks. He summoned a few men from the engineer battalion to be his infantry and plunged forward onto the road. The engineers moved slowly because they knew there were Germans about. But Gavin was in a hurry, so he and his Dutch advisor, Captain Arie Bestebreurtje, scouted ahead. The road dipped: in places it sunk between 8-foot banks, heavy forest, and thick undergrowth, so they could not see to either side. They were about five minutes down the road when suddenly, a machine gun opened fire just above Gavin's head. Bestebreurtje was on the opposite side of the road, so Gavin leaped up the embankment in the midst of a burst of reactive shots to get the gun. He was too late. The gunner lay dead and the assistant gunner was sprinting for safety. Bestebreurtje had saved Gavin's life with quick shots from the hip. He nodded thanks and the little group hurried on through the forest.

Gavin, always enamored of the technical aspects of battle, would relate the incident matter-of-factly: "If they had placed their gun in a position overlooking the road that Bestebruertje and I were following, they could easily have made casualties of us."

Commmunications were soon up and working after they arrived at the command post. For once, Gavin achieved contact with all three of his regiments almost immediately; however, both of the division's long-range transmitters had been ruined in the drop, so he had no hope of reaching XXX Corps.

Later that day Browning's headquarters loaned him one, but except for the first contact, communications proved troublesome throughout the operation. Holland's high water table soaked up radio signals and proved a radioman's nightmare. Incongruously, the public telephones still worked in some cases, and over the telephone, Bestebruertje made contact with the underground. In the first hours, the underground was able to tell Gavin that things seemed O.K. in Arnhem, and XXX Corps was already pushing north.

All seemed well in the 82nd's zone at Nijmegen those first few hours. Much to his relief, Gavin found his troopers well concentrated. His regiments had landed intact and ready to fight as regiments. More good news came immediately. The 504 had taken the massive Grave bridge intact; then captured the town of Grave itself. Opposition was light; the first step of the way was opened for XXX Corps coming from the south.

German demolition crews blew up two of the three smaller bridges across the Maas-Waal Canal in troopers' faces, but the third fell intact when 504 and 505 men attacked both ends at once. Now Gavin focused his attention on the large bridge (code named Bridge #10) located along the direct route between Grave and Nijmegen. Gavin thought this bridge the most important of the canal bridges, the only one he felt certain would bear the weight of armor. The 508 stormed it, but when the enemy blew the adjacent railway bridge, the blast badly weakened it. Yet as his men dug in for the night, Gavin felt satisfied. Each of his battalions had landed well, and 82nd had captured the bridges necessary to get XXX Corps to Nijmegen. That night he planned to capture the still-standing Nijmegen bridge, if the Germans did not blow it before he got to it. He didn't know then that Field Marshal Model in Arnhem had already ordered that it not be blown. Sitting atop his two panzer divisions, he wanted to keep it intact so they could counterattack across it.

Gavin's optimistic mood was not entirely shared by the other airborne division commanders, who had fared worse. In Arnhem, the British drop had hit the correct drop zones, and the paratroopers and glidermen organized quickly. Then, as the German divisions nearby responded to their visitors, things began to go wrong. The commander of II SS Panzer Corps, General Wilhelm Bittrich, was a bright, battle-seasoned soldier with an intuition for fluid situations. As soon as reports came in that paratroops were landing at Arnhem and Nijmegen, he immediately attempted contacting his commander, Field Marshal Model, at the other side of Arnhem, and General Student south of Eindhoven. But the phone was dead. Lines to Student had already been cut by paratroopers to the south, and Field Marshal Model, having been practically under the British drop zones at the Tafelberg Hotel near the town of Oosterbeek, had unceremoniously evacuated his headquarters, shouting that the paratroopers were dropping in a raid to get him. This left Bittrich temporarily on his own.

He reasoned that the drops were intended to cut off the retreating Fifteenth Army, after which the Allies could smash into Germany. To cut off the Fifteenth Army, bridges at Nijmegen and Arnhem would be critical. He alerted the 9th and 10th SS Panzers and sent the 9th in the direction of Arnhem and elements the 10th in the direction of Nijmegen with orders to take and hold the bridges at Arnhem and Nijmegen at all costs. By guessing right, though for the wrong reason, Bittrich alerted the panzer divisions that Montgomery had dismissed, an action that would cause untold trouble for the Allies.

The British 1st Airborne drop zones were unfortunately placed too near a German training battalion. The commander rightfully surmised that the British would head for the bridges, so he threw his troops in to slow them down. The British fought their way through this contingent swiftly but with unusually heavy casualties. By afternoon, 1st Airborne commander "Roy" Urquhart had sent three battalions toward the Arnhem bridge by three different routes, but only one had made it. The others had discovered the presence of panzer divisions and were engaged miles from the bridge. The battalion that had made it, Lieutenant Colonel John Frost's 2nd Battalion of the 1st Parachute Brigade, had only taken one end of the bridge, the north end. Their attempts to reach the other side had been bloodily repulsed.

Urquhart actually knew little of all this. Like Gavin, he was discovering that communications in Holland were tricky. Urquhart's signals section had erred. They had assured him that their radios would work fine, but now they could not reach the bridge from the drop zones (which also had to be held for follow-up missions and resupply), nor could they reach XXX Corps, nor Gavin at Nijmegen. By late afternoon, the signals mess had actually worsened; he had no communications with anyone, and he had no way of getting more than one battalion to the bridge. By then the panzers had cut off the route Frost had taken.

Montgomery had created a meticulous timetable for Market-Garden. Knowing that paratroopers were only light infantry, he and his staff realized that they would not be able to hold indefinitely. The longer they remained isolated, the weaker they would become, while the Germans grew stronger. The timetable dictated that XXX Corps must reach Eindhoven by nightfall on D day, Nijmegen on D + 1, and Arnhem on D + 2. In the face of confident theories about German resistance, this seemed a reasonable schedule.

In fact the only thing that XXX Corps did on schedule was launch its initial attack northward. At exactly 3:00 the afternoon of the 17th, XXX Corps struck at German defenses north of the Albert Canal. Progress proved less than promised. The attack began with a 350-gun rolling barrage to precede Horrocks's armored spearhead. And the fire did seem to devastate the Germans immediately before the tanks. Then the fire lifted, and suddenly, the devastation proved illusory. Like moles, the Germans quickly clawed out of dug-in positions and hammered back with their redoubtable 88mm antitank guns and Panzerfausts. Nine British tanks took direct hits and caught fire in the first two minutes, and their hulks made the narrow road impassable. The British fought back with small-arms, artillery, and tank fire, but German fire continued. Then one tank crew forced a captured German to ride on the back of their tank to pinpoint antitank positions. That helped reduce the fire, but now British troops lay stalled, dug in near the road and in its ditches. German machine guns and rifles tore into them cruelly, and the armor that followed could not punch forward because the road was clogged with shattered hulks.

The British called in Typhoons to bomb the enemy out and break the deadlock. The air attack came in fast and low; their bombs coupled with British tank fire trapped Germans in the target area. Survivors broke ranks and surrendered. Suddenly the defense broke, but by the time the British moved the hulks and Horrocks's men rolled forward again, XXX Corps was hours behind schedule.

Behind this German defensive line lay others, laid out with the usual meticulousness, further slowing the advance. XXX Corps, having expected to cover the 13 miles to Eindhoven in two to three hours, by day's end had covered 7, and Taylor's 101st Airborne at Eindhoven remained unrelieved. Student had guessed correctly and fortified the line of advance of XXX Corps, the same line the British assumed would be lightly defended. British intelligence registered embarrassed surprises that day. One incident alone illustrates how badly they had blundered in their assessment of enemy intentions and morale. As a group of German prisoners marched down the road past Horrocks's armored column, the leader of the assault element, Colonel J.O.E. "Joe" Vandeleur, spotted one of them suddenly toss a grenade he had concealed into an armored car. British soldiers immediately cut down the German at point-blank range, but the damage was done; the men inside the car all lay dead or badly wounded. Vandeleur shook his head, thinking that defeated soldiers from a demoralized army do not show such spirit.

At Eindhoven, General Maxwell Taylor's 101st Division had performed a nearly perfect drop. Like the 82nd, the 101st had early success. The northernmost bridge at Veghel fell quickly. Next came the two bridges across the Wilhelmina Canal to the south, one near the town of Best and one near the hamlet of Son. Both offered a way north to Nijmegen. Unknown to Taylor, the Best bridge, thought lightly defended, was close to Student's headquarters, where numbers of Fifteenth Army troops, recently evacuated from Calais via the Schelde, were re-forming. Only a company was sent to deal with Best, and it was stopped far short of its objective by surprisingly powerful German forces. Eventually the bridge was blown, adding to the pressure to take the Son bridge, on the alternate route. Colonel Robert Sink, commander of the 506, led his men there, and they moved rapidly with no opposition until they reached the town of Son. There they found Germans but decided to attack; the Germans let Sink come to within 50 yards of the bridge before it exploded in their faces. Several of Sink's paratroopers swam or rowed in commandeered boats across the river to avenge themselves, clearing out the Germans and digging in a bridgehead. They then improvised a wooden footbridge so the rest of the regiment could cross. But their deed couldn't change the fact that the advance would be further delayed; there were now no bridges on the best route across the Wilhelmina Canal.

. . .

Gavin spent an anxious night at his command post outside Nijmegen. He had heard rumors of reverses and slowdowns, but since communications with XXX Corps and Arnhem remained down, he had no solid information about other forces except reports from excited Dutch resistance fighters. He was in a good deal of pain from the jolting he'd taken on landing and assumed he'd torn muscles as he struck and rolled. (It would be weeks before he saw a doctor and discovered he had two broken vertebrae.)

As he tried to sleep, a train suddenly roared by, heading from areas already held by the 505. This surprised and alarmed him, and he tried to leap up to investigate, but his back failed him; he finally levered himself upright with a tree branch. He was furious that the train, clearly run by the enemy, had slipped through 505 territory. He ordered the next one stopped with bazookas. His troops were now in a static, passive stance; they had achieved all of their objectives except the bridge at Nijmegen, and though spread thinly, they held the assigned bridges and the drop zones for the next day's drops.

One battalion of the 508, sent to make a night try for the Nijmegen bridge, found far stouter German resistance than expected. The reports sent back to Gavin caused concern. Radio traffic gave him the impression that there were panzers in Nijmegen, a disquieting thought.

He had read the radio conversations correctly; there were indeed panzer troops in Nijmegen. Units of the 10th SS Panzer Division (known as the Frundsberg Division) under Brigadier General Heinz Harmel already waited in the town, defending the bridge. More of the division was on its way, though because Frost's paratroopers held one half of the Arnhem bridge, the Germans had to move their vehicles across the river on makeshift ferries, slowing the move south.

Two companies from the 508 succeeded in nearly reaching the Nijmegen bridge that night anyway, but they came under heavy fire from armored vehicles and heavy weapons. Their commander decided that whoever was defending the bridge was far too powerful for the small band of paratroops, so he withdrew. Pulling back, he collided with Germans who had moved to outflank him. These Germans, like those to his front, had armored vehicles and powerful weapons. The 508 men withdrew again in another direction. Most of the force succeeded in breaking off safely, but one platoon, sent to destroy what was suspected to be the bridge's detonating device, was cut off from the rest of the division and remained isolated for two days.

Suddenly, Gavin's so-far faultless execution began to waver. He wrote of it, "This encounter with 88's, heavy mortars, and stout German resistance at the southern end of the Nijmegen bridge was the first indication to us that something had been amiss in the intelligence briefings given to us before we left England. This was not a broken German army in full retreat. The Panzer Grenadiers we killed fought hard and were well equipped. Those we captured were tough and confident. The Germans were in far better condition to fight than we had realized."

The Germans met with an extraordinary piece of luck on that first day, had Model only recognized it. A glider crash-landed not far from General Student's headquarters. The glider's occupants were killed, and detailed plans of the entire Market-Garden operation were found in the wreckage and taken to Student by a German patrol. Student's study of the documents enabled him to hatch a plan he thought could wreck the whole attack. But when he tried rushing the plans to Field Marshal Model, the messenger took ten hours to get there. German communications had been badly disrupted too.

In any case Model glanced at the plans of Market-Garden and dismissed them. He believed the chain of events was too perfect, that they were an Allied plant, and never bothered to share them with von Rundstedt or Bittrich. Bittrich had formed his own plan. He ordered the 10th SS Panzer to Nijmegen to blow up the bridge, believing, if they did so, the Allied plans—and by now he had figured them out fairly accurately—were finished. But Model insisted that the bridge be left intact so he could counterattack over it.

The German high command now realized the significance of the attack on Holland, and von Rundstedt decided to gamble. The Allied advance toward the Rhine had to be stopped somewhere, and he suspected that units elsewhere along the front would not attack while attention focused on operations around Nijmegen and Arnhem, so he began moving troops and resources from other parts of the front to Holland. He had guessed Eisenhower's logistical mess and intended to use it to his own advantage. In addition, his local commanders tried desperately to do all they could do. Fifteenth Army troops joined the fight, and scratch units under commanders with initiative threw in everything they had. It proved to be quite a lot.

Dawn of the second day found Gavin and the Allied airborne force facing a tide of bad news and new problems. Al Ireland, Gavin's G-1, remembered the surprise and shock of that second day in Holland: 82nd headquarters was unbelieving; resistance seemed to come from everywhere, and it stiffened all day. The crisis was no longer just the SS Panzer troops at the Nijmegen bridge. Germans attacked simultaneously from several points of the compass. To the east of Gavin's perimeter, the 504th, clinging to the captured bridges and the 10-mile-long Grave-Nijmegen highway, found German troops persistently infiltrating across the length of the corridor the Americans were supposed to hold open. It was even worse in the 505 and 508 zones. Here dawn revealed several German scratch battalions made up of air defense, communications, and medical personnel, and even convalescent wounded, firing at the drop zones near Groesbeek Heights, the very areas in which the rest of the division's artillery was supposed to land that morning. A resupply drop was also scheduled there, ammunition that 82nd Airborne Division guns needed more each hour.

German forces poured from the Reichswald Forest just behind the drop zones. The town of Wyler, the anchor for one corner of the 82nd's area, was threatened. The 508 found they could not take and hold it against steadily increasing resistance. Attacks on Wyler, on German soil, seemed to elicit fresh fury; the Germans defended it tenaciously.

At division headquarters that morning, there was only one question. Where are all the Germans coming from? Without a clear idea of what the division was facing in Nijmegen, Gavin headed his jeep for Lindquist's headquarters at dawn. He found Lindquist in serious difficulties. The Germans attacking from the Reichswald had overrun the drop zones; his defenses were weakened by the battalion he had sent to Nijmegen. Gavin knew the drop zones had to be cleared; he ordered Lindquist to retrieve the battalion from Nijmegen and throw it into the fight, though it was exhausted from a night of fighting in Nijmegen and the long round trip. The bridge, now surrounded by German armored forces, seemed of less importance; there was nothing the paratroopers could accomplish there.

From Lindquist's headquarters, Gavin went to Ekman's 505th. It also faced an assault. As Gavin arrived, the Germans were preparing to attack Groesbeek, and Ekman was short of men. The regiment held a tenuous 7-mile line, but to conceal the gaps, Ekman ordered patrols between units to create an illusion of fierce activity while uncovering enemy probes.

Gavin left, feeling the 505 could continue to hold. However, he needed men to clear the landing zones and took an engineer unit from the 504, which was holding the bridges on its side of the triangle. Gavin led them to the drop zones, but their added weight was not enough. By eyewitness accounts the troopers were outnumbered five to one as they made a determined assault. Making no headway, they launched a bayonet charge, but to little effect. Casualties were high; one of the most loved officers in the division died that afternoon. Captain Anthony Stefanish had been the heavyweight boxing champion of the division, and was known for his humor, toughness, and devotion to his men. Just before he died of wounds, he whispered "We've come a long ways together. Tell the boys to do a good job." Stefanish's words swept through the regiment and stiffened their determination, but it was useless; the Germans did not crumble.

Gavin had failed. Stunned, he waited, but due to fog in England, the gliders that were supposed to come in at 10 A.M. did not arrive overhead until 2 P.M. Gavin's men held only one side of the landing zones. To his horror, and unable to stop them, Gavin watched as the vulnerable gliders took heavy fire from the moment they lumbered down toward a landing. Every German near the landing zone with a rifle poured bullets at the clumsy aircraft. Some glider pilots peeled away from the fight they saw raging beneath them and landed wherever they could. Others bore in regardless. Gavin braced himself to see his men destroyed in droves. But instead of milling in confusion and helplessness, the artillerymen burst from the landed gliders, guns blazing. Spontaneously, many men ran to join them and laid down a stream of suppressive fire on the Germans while others hauled equipment out of the gliders. Gavin wrote later of the action: "A highly creditable performance and one that I never would have thought possible as I watched them approach the landing zone." The artillerymen recovered over two thirds of their guns, and some of them were soon blasting at the German positions.

With the arrival of the additional artillery, Gavin had far greater firepower, but he still lacked the infantry numbers to deal with growing German strength. The 325 was due to arrive the next day, and without them the 82nd was spread thin. That afternoon he established contact with XXX Corps. He now knew about the Son Bridge and the failure at Best. XXX Corps had got through Eindhoven, but they would not be going farther than Son for now—not until their engineers got a bridge built across the river. They were not coming today, and they might not come the next day either. Gavin would simply have to hold with what he had.

The next day (D + 2) dawned with the battle undecided at the drop zones. Gavin's men were low on ammunition. Their success was partly due to the German obsession with attacking at the 82nd's strongest points. Had the Germans simply bypassed the strong points, they could have smashed into the defenders' flanks and cut the corridor held by the airborne troops. Yet, Gavin found they assaulted the same places frontally and repeatedly. This tactical error gave Gavin the chance to concentrate his strength.

Though the SS troops in Nijmegen were first-rate soldiers, the soldiers attacking the drop zones were clearly low-quality infantry. Gavin described his firsthand experience with them. He ran into an enemy group while traveling in his jeep and in the process got caught in the open. "I stopped the jeep, jumped out and took a firing position, leaning against the corner of a building. I fired from a standing position and had a good field of fire. To my amazement the German infantry came on, walking in a line about 5 yards apart, carrying their rifles in a position we call high port. I started firing, beginning with the man on the left. At this time they were about 300 yards away and I had excellent targets. I rapidly picked off one after another until I was about halfway down the line. At that point the German soldiers seemed to realize they were being fired at with live ammunition, and the remainder of the line hit the ground at once. I was amazed at their behavior. To cross an open field in the face of enemy known to be in the area was foolish. I was surprised, as I always was in the war, when the German infantry appeared to be very poorly trained."

Gavin did not have enough men to mount a resolute attack on the Nijmegen bridge. For that he counted on the elements of the 325 that were scheduled to land that day. But amidst delays and shortages, there was good news: XXX Corps had reached the Grave bridge. This gave Gavin British armor and infantry support, and he felt confident he could handle whatever the enemy threw at him. So he decided to make another try for the bridge at Nijmegen without the 325. He now had portions of the 504, since they were no longer needed to hold the other bridges in force, and the British loaned him one of their battalions, which freed up one of his favorite colonels, Ben Vandervoort, and his battalion from the 505 for the job of attacking the bridge. Gavin knew there could be no drawn-out struggle for this objective, for Market-Garden was seriously behind schedule, and the British 1st Airborne Division had been fighting alone in Arnhem for three days. Every minute lost meant soldiers dying unnecessarily in Arnhem—and unnecessary losses angered Gavin.

The earliest the 505 men could strike into German positions in Nijmegen would be that night or the morning of D +3, September 20. If they succeeded, that would ultimately yield one end of the bridge. He knew that a simultaneous attack on both ends would be devastating, so he planned to send part of Ruben Tucker's 504th across the river by boat to try to seize the bridge swiftly and intact. Both commanders involved, Tucker and Vandervoort, were the pride of the division, and Gavin had confidence in their troops. He proposed the plan to Browning and Horrocks and they approved. Boats were lacking; the only boats available were in convoy far back behind the British van. They would bring them up, but it would take time and a great deal of ingenuity.

The German reaction to the invasion was still gathering momentum. All along the corridor, the struggle intensified. In many places the road to Arnhem was littered with burnt-out and blasted hulks. The 101st, realizing that a powerful German element faced them at Best, threw more and more troops into battle there (ultimately more than a regiment), and was just able to hold the corridor open. So frequent were the German attacks that they now called the road, "Hell's Highway." So often was the road assaulted and cut, then reopened, that bulldozers and tanks were permanently assigned to roam its length, pushing wrecks out of the way. Traffic jams ran back for miles and sometimes took hours to unsnag. Hitler authorized one of the Luftwaffe's final mass raids on the clogged road. Eindhoven took a heavy pounding under the weight of a two-hundred-plane raid. Another two hundred aircraft went after troops and vehicles jamming the corridor, causing more chaos. The trucks with the boats got to Nijmegen, but not quickly.

One of the jeeps clogging that road carried Matthew Ridgway, a man without a command. He reached Eindhoven just as the air attack came in and left town quickly because of it. Several times he was stopped when enemy raiders cut across the road as he tried to get to Nijmegen where he heard a desperate fight for a bridge still loomed. Ridgway wrote: "I soon found myself blocked on every road. Great fires were burning everywhere, ammo trucks were exploding, gasoline trucks were on fire, and debris from wrecked houses clogged the streets."

Bad as the fiery corridor looked, British delays enraged Ridgway. Along the corridor he encountered a stalled British tank column. Informed that the road ahead was swept with small-arms fire, Ridgway waited to see what they would do. After forty minutes, they had done nothing, so Ridgway pushed on himself and got through the area without incident. In his own account of the war, Ridgway criticized the British acidly for not moving fast enough. He wrote, "I have always felt, and still feel, that the sluggish actions of the ground armies in that campaign were inexcusable."

Yet as Ridgway fumed and tried to get through to Nijmegen, and Gavin plotted how to take the Nijmegen bridge, no one knew exactly what was happening in Arnhem. By D + 3, the British paratroopers had got no closer to relieving Frost's single battalion on the Arnhem bridge. And disaster after disaster had befallen Frost's survivors. First there were failures of communication. Then on D day, General Urquhart, the man everyone depended upon to be a steadying influence, had been cut off from the rest of his division with his 3rd Battalion as they fought to get into Arnhem. On the next day, he and two other officers were cut off from the rest of the battalion by Germans now swarming everywhere, and hid in a Dutch attic. For thirty-nine hours the commander of the Red Devils, as the 1st Parachute Division was called, commanded nothing.

The Germans were unrelenting. Bittrich believed the key to it all remained the Nijmegen bridge. He urged Model to let him blow it. Model doggedly refused and insisted Bittrich hold on to it. Bittrich was in no easy position himself. The only way to get troops to Nijmegen was over the Arnhem bridge or by ferry. Ferrying proved too slow. With XXX Corps breaking through to the south, the British would be able to build up forces far faster than he could in Nijmegen. Thus both German commanders turned their energies to the eradication of Frost's battalion, which hung on doggedly to the north half of the Arnhem bridge.

Frost had no intention of yielding, nor had he a choice. A German armored battle group attempting to crash across the bridge had been reduced to scrap metal, and Red Devils had infiltrated most of the Arnhem neighborhoods surrounding the approaches to their side of the bridge. Over the next two days the two SS divisions hit Frost's paratroopers hard. Fighting was house to house and room to room. As soon as they could find targets, the Germans concentrated their artillery. The relieving force, the rest of the Red Devils, continued fighting to reach Frost, but the panzers would not permit it. The Germans stood like an immovable barrier between the rescuers and the beseiged. On D + 1 Frost's troubles intensified. The Germans bolstered their panzer divisions with a tank battle group reported by the Dutch underground to contain fifty tanks, some of them Tigers. By that same evening, a 150mm gun hurled 100-pound shells at Frost's headquarters, located in a brick house next to the bridge, and other German batteries switched to white phosphorous shells to start fires. Still the obstinate Frost hung on through the night.

The next morning, Urquhart finally escaped from his attic. A self-propelled German gun had been parked right in front of the house where he had been hiding, but a small group of Red Devils had fought their way through to the street, and to their surprise, liberated their general. At headquarters he found nothing but doubt and frustration. His division, still stuck 9 miles from Arnhem at their original drop zones, was being slowly ground to pieces; and XXX Corps had not reached Nijmegen.

In Arnhem on D + 2, the 10th SS Panzers' commander, Colonel Harmel, demanded Frost's surrender. He refused. His officers acted as if they misunderstood the German request. They told the German envoys, "Get the hell out of here. We're taking no prisoners."

The Germans now had tanks to spare, but they hesitated to use them en mass in the streets of Arnhem because even lightly armed paratroops have shoulder-fired antitank weapons that can destroy a Tiger with a shot to the lightly-armored rear. So the fighting went on from house to house. Frustrated, Colonel Harmel ordered his artillery to level every building occupied by the British, and they blasted what had been impeccably neat two-story stone houses into piles of rubble. Whole walls collapsed, then the interiors sagged, and finally the structures fell in upon themselves.

Then the tanks came. The lightly armed paratroops had little left but small arms to oppose them with. At close range, the Tigers and Panthers blasted buildings floor by floor. Still the British did not crack but fell back block by block to the bridge. German tankers watched as the sides of buildings crumbled, exposing British troops inside. The British simply scrambled out and fought from the rubble. In his headquarters by the bridge, Frost was now helpless. He had defiance, but little else. Even air supremacy could do nothing for him now. He could reach no one by radio who could call for air cover, and fog had grounded much of the Allied air forces in England.

. . .

Local partisans' reports and occasional messages from Urquhart's head-quarters told Gavin a consistent story: the British in Arnhem were desperate. At 3:30 P.M. on Tuesday, D +2, Gavin flung Vandervoort's battalion at Nijmegen bridge. The boats were not available, but it was hoped that the troopers with tank support might break through and take it themselves.

Vandervoort's troopers rode into battle on the backs of more than forty British armored vehicles and reached the center of Nijmegen near the bridge approaches fairly easily. Then the regiment split, half for the big highway bridge and the other half for a railway bridge that ran near it. Both wings met furious German opposition as they closed on the bridges. High-velocity 88s, self-propelled guns, and well-placed machine guns blasted the tanks back, and the troopers raced for cover. Both attacks stalled just 400 yards from the bridges. Air cover remained grounded, and artillery support remained concentrated on keeping the corridor open. Vandervoort directed his men to take the city house by house.

The British in Arnhem, almost in sight, would go unrelieved for another day, while XXX Corps and the 82nd tried fighting their way through Nijmegen.

When he had stood with maps covering the walls, Montgomery, using the metaphors and clichés of lightning assault, had spoken with almost airy confidence of taking Berlin, of smashing to Arnhem, of dashing over bridges. Now the battle was about to begin its fourth day. For most of the men sweating and scraping for survival in that corridor to Arnhem, Berlin was a forgotten abstraction and Arnhem an impossible dream. Most men in Market-Garden concentrated their lives on the hedge, tree, road, building, or field directly to their front. Each one had to be fought for, each one held its own peculiar terrors, and every man knew that hostile territory lay on three sides; if they survived the particular hazard of the moment, there were more ahead.

Gavin learned the morning of D +3, the fourth day of Market-Garden, that the boats had not arrived, and one truck carrying them had been destroyed by German fire. The others were somewhere in the hard-pressed column grinding northward.

In Arnhem that morning, Frost was down to his last 150 or 200 men. The fight, he knew, was over. There was little ammunition, many of the men still fighting were wounded, and he had no antitank weapons left.

Frost himself was wounded. Still the survivors fought on, but nothing could stop the onslaught, as the Germans methodically destroyed block after city block.

Meanwhile, Gavin worried. The 325 would not fly D + 3 either. Airfields near London remained fogged in. An artillery barrage hit the disputed landing zones near his headquarters, and two German combat teams struck out of the Reichswald Forest toward the thinly held 505 and 508 area. The radio crackled with reports that German forces were hitting the rest of the corridor. Field Marshal Model's planned counterattack was launched Wednesday, September 20. Reinforcements had been gathered from other areas of the front, where American Army units now sat with little ammunition and less gasoline. General Student had received a constant flow of reinforcements from the Fifteenth Army. Model himself felt confident that he could pinch off the thin arrow of invading forces aimed at Arnhem.

Gavin's troopers could not hold in the face of the attack at the Reichswald Forest drop zone. They were forced to abandon it while Gavin was working with Colonel Rube Tucker to try to cross the Waal River. He left Tucker in charge and raced for his headquarters. With the assault over the river about to start when the boats arrived and his own lines breaking, this was the moment that would decide the issue. The 82nd would hold at the drop zone and take the bridge, or they would not. If they failed in either, Market-Garden would be without two essential bridges and a means of resupply. They would be trapped while the Germans encircled and destroyed them.

Ridgway, impatient to know the situation in the 82nd's area, suddenly showed up at Gavin's headquarters and was waiting when Gavin arrived. This was no time for military courtesies and briefings; since Ridgway had no operational role, Gavin abruptly gave him over to Walt Winton for a briefing and turned to the saving of his position. Ridgway, always proud and stiff, stood fuming and would later demand a reckoning.

Gavin ignored everything but the crisis. His first reaction was to go to Mook at the southern corner of his tenuous triangle, where the 505 was reported to be holding. He found Mook had been overrun, his own troops giving way. Gavin wrote, "As I arrived . . . a tremendous amount of small-arms fire passed overhead. About twenty-five yards from the railroad overpass a paratrooper was in a foxhole with a bazooka. He seemed a bit shaken and he was all alone. . . . By then the town was overrun and the Germans were upon us." Gavin immediately sent a runner for reinforcements from the British Coldstream Guards. He turned to the railroad embankment and saw a cow walking up the side. When it reached the crest, impacting bullets shook its body and it flopped back down. He moved to the top of the railroad embankment and began engaging Germans pouring from the town ahead, firing his M-1. It was the best way he knew to steady the men. Troopers along the embankment saw or heard about their commanding general joining the fight and they steadied; the German battle groups wavered under accurate fire, then fell back to Mook. Soon Ekman launched a counterattack and retook Mook.

Gavin rushed on to the 508th section at Beek on the northern corner of the triangle, nearest the Reichswald. Their situation, too, was critical, but they still held. Here the Germans had backed their infantry with armored vehicles, half-tracks with 20mm antiaircraft guns trained against Gavin's infantry. This unit needed reinforcements but he had none to summon. He ordered Lindquist to hold, period. Then he moved about among the troops to spread such encouragement as he could. Darkness saved them; the Germans seldom attacked in darkness, preferring to maneuver in the light.

While Gavin ran to crisis points on his perimeter, Tucker's 504th went about its job of crossing the Waal River to take the opposite end of the bridge. In the city of Nijmegen, Vandervoort's battalion and British armor and infantry crept forward house by house against the German positions, but when afternoon came, they still had not broken through to the bridge.

One mile downstream from Nijmegen, to the northwest, Major Julian Cook, the commander of the 3rd Battalion of the 504 could do nothing but wait for the boats to come. He was the man Gavin and Tucker had charged with the river crossing. When Gavin had first suggested the crossing, Browning and Horrocks had thought it crazy, and the fact that they approved it is a measure of their desperation. Skeptically, one of the British officers had asked Tucker if his men had had any small-boat training. Calmly chewing a cigar, the Little Colonel, responded, "No, they're just getting on-the-job-training." None of this reassured Cook. That morning he had gone to the top of a tower at a nearby power station to survey the opposite bank of the Waal. A young captain with Cook wrote in a letter home: "When we reached the top of this tower, and had a glimpse of this scene which is indelibly imprinted on my mind forever,

I felt rather funny inside. I think everyone else did too although no one said a word—we just looked. . . . What greeted our eyes was a broad flat plain void of all cover or concealment. The first terrain feature which would offer us assistance was a built-up highway approximately 300 yards from the shore against the bank of which we would get our first opportunity to get some protection and be able to reorganize. . . . We could see all along the Kraut side of the river strong defensive positions, a formidable line both in length as well as in depth—pillboxes, machine gun emplacements and, what was really wicked looking, one or two old Dutch forts between the place where we were landing and the two bridges."

Cook's uneasiness was not completely alleviated by the support assembled for the crossing. The British had lined tanks up along the river to give covering fire, and all the artillery support that could be found was massed on the embankment.

A smoke screen was prepared to shield the attackers. Still the river stretched a full twelve football fields from one bank to the other. Cook's men would be nakedly exposed while out there paddling their clumsy boats, and there was nothing he could do about it. Originally, the plan had called for a night assault, but now Gavin and Tucker figured that the British in Arnhem could not hold until dark. The attack had to go as soon as the boats arrived.

It had now been postponed several times, and having been set for 1 P.M., was postponed two hours again because the elusive boats had still not materialized. The men clearly saw the obstacles across the river, and the longer they waited, the more time they had for fears to build, for willpower to seep away. Cook had tried to lighten the atmosphere with jokes while they waited. Finally, at 2:30 P.M., British aircraft bombed the Germans across the river hard, and the bank seemed to disappear behind a screen of dust and smoke. Twenty minutes before jump-off time, the trucks with the boats pulled up.

The boats, unloaded with frantic haste, did little to inspire confidence. There were twenty-six of them, 19 feet long, with a plywood floor and canvas sides. They were once equipped with paddles, but most of those were missing, so the troopers prepared to flail along with rifle stocks. There were not enough boats for the whole battalion; two waves were improvised. The engineers manning the boats would have to return for the rest of the battalion. Two companies, H and I companies, constituted the first wave. They jumped off on time, but the period of surprise was brief. The Germans quickly sighted the boats, recovered, and focused every gun they had. The Americans fired smoke as planned, and it at first helped, but a breeze dispersed it all too soon. The little fleet moved slowly forward amidst a spatter of small-arms and artillery fire pocking the surface. A man in one of the boats later wrote, "As we came into the open the weight of our boat seemed imponderable; our feet sank deep in the sand. We must have caught the Krauts by surprise because for the first 100 yards there wasn't a shot fired from the enemy side of the river. Then all of a sudden all hell broke loose. . . . Jerry opened up with everything he had. . . . As if in a rage at our trying anything so drastic, he was pouring everything he possessed at us. And behind us our second battalion and the ten tanks were blasting away for all they were worth."

Troopers on the bank watched boats that had been there one moment simply vaporize with direct shell hits to leave nothing but flotsam the next moment. Boats that did forge out into the stream often spun out of control or zigzagged because their crews had had no experience with rowing. Small-arms and shell fire ripped the ranks of the oarsmen, and the flotilla seemed to scatter. Yet the troopers came on. The British tank battalion commander wrote that when the boats finally made it to the opposite shore, "Nobody paused. Men got out and began running towards the embankment. My God what a courageous sight it was! They just moved steadily across the open ground. I never saw a single man lie down until he was hit. I didn't think more than half the fleet made it across." Boy Browning said of that day, "I have never seen a more gallant action."

With the first wave landed, the troopers from the 307th engineers turned their craft about and went back to pick up the second wave. Only eleven boats made it.

While the surviving boats, now emptied, turned back, the men who had reached the far shore charged into the featureless no-man's-land of the bullet-swept ground before them. The same young officer who described the German defenses noticed a transformation. "Many times I have seen troops who are driven to a fever pitch—troops who, for a brief interval of combat, are lifted out of themselves—fanatics rendered crazy by rage and the lust for killing—men who forget temporarily the meaning of fear. . . . However, I have never witnessed this human metamorphosis so acutely displayed as on this day. The men were beside themselves. They continued to plow across that field in spite of all the Kraut could do, cursing savagely, their guns spitting fire. Troopers charged Germans wherever they saw them. In less than a half an hour, the dike road was secured, and the Germans who had survived fell back to their next line of defenses. Frenzied troopers plowed in right behind them. After the torment of the boat passage, nothing could stop them; rage and fear joined forces. With brutal efficiency they dug the Germans out, and without stopping to rest or regroup continued their rampaging assault. They fought through fields, orchards, and houses back of the embankment under the fire of machine guns and anti-aircraft batteries hammering at them. . . . " By late afternoon, they had reached the railway bridge and secured one end of it. Yet it seemed the attack had finally lost its momentum. Exhausted troopers found the highway bridge, the real prize, too heavily defended.

Then the Germans, at the end of their tether, collapsed first on the Nijmegen side, then on the steep embankments leading to the bridge.

The 505 had continued its relentless attack in Nijmegen. Colonel Ben Vandervoort, would later write an account of it. "The troopers fought over roof tops, in the attics, up alleys, out of bedroom windows, through a maze of backyards and buildings. The tanks were the firebase providing covering fire and blasting strong points. Where feasible, tanks served as bulldozers, smashing through garden walls, etc. A tank cannon thrust through a kitchen door really stimulates exodus. . . . In the labyrinth of houses and brick-walled gardens, the fighting deteriorated into confusing face-to-face, kill or be killed show downs between small momentarily isolated groups and individuals." In this way, they fought their way ever closer to the bridge.

Perhaps it was the shock of Vandervoort's assault to their front, or it might have been panic caused by the men who survived the boat assault, or a combination of the two. German resistance suddenly ebbed. Where there had been room-to-room fighting in Nijmegen and bush-to-bush battles across the river, on some silent signal the Germans retreated over the Nijmegen bridge. Many of them abandoned their guns to flee. The 504 men fired furiously at the retreating figures—260 bodies were found on the bridge alone, plus wounded and prisoners. By dusk, the 82nd had the Nijmegen bridge. The enemy had waited too long; attempts to blow it had failed. Alert troopers, or perhaps Dutch underground members, had cut the wires. When the troopers inspected their prize closely, they found it had been defended by thirty-four machine guns, two 20mm antiaircraft guns, and an 88mm cannon.

Now British armor poured across. Exuberant 504 men greeted them with whoops and leaps. One trooper kissed a British tank. Arnhem lay 11 miles distant. But the column slowed, then stopped alongside the road. Crews clanged open hatches, clambered out, lit cigarettes. Exhausted paratroopers became furious. They had fought so hard to open the corridor, the way now lay open to the the isolated 1st Airborne Division. Why weren't the tanks advancing?

Perhaps most angry of all was Rube Tucker. The British had stopped because they had none of their infantry support with them. They said they could go no farther until their infantry caught up from Nijmegen. Gavin recalled that by dawn the next day, while XXX Corps still sat in the bridgehead, Tucker was so angry he could barely speak. He wanted to fling what was left of his battalion at Arnhem, but it was not possible. The 82nd was spread far too thin already. It was XXX Corps' job to get to Arnhem. They did not get it done that day.

The tankers were doggedly following orders. Some wanted to move up the road, but British command had made the decision to stop. Caution was the key. The road beyond Nijmegen ran high above the flat land, leaving trucks and tanks in stark relief. It was thought the most exposed, vulnerable section of the advance. The narrowness of the route and German attacks had cut the British off from fuel and ammunition. Their leaders preferred to wait, to clear up the logjams. But the American troopers, having cleared the way, watched incredulously as the autumn day wore on.

By the time the tanks moved, it was too late. The next morning, September 21, The 9th SS Panzer Division overwhelmed the last survivors of Frost's battalion in Arnhem. Without food or ammunition, their numbers decimated, they had done all that mortal men could. In the end, there was no coherent surrender. Colonel Frost, badly wounded, was evacuated by SS men from a burning building under a flag of truce on the night of the 20th. Scattered small bands of Red Devils tried to fight on all that night; but by morning, these few remaining men were either dead, evading capture, or prisoners of war.

Urquhart's main body was nearly finished too. No longer able to raise a group large enough to assault, they simply hung on in a small pocket on the north side of the river. Attempts by XXX Corps to break through were thwarted, and a drop by the Polish 1st Parachute Brigade was a failure. On D +8, the ninth day of Market-Garden, XXX Corps had given up trying to rescue the 1st Airborne. All they were able to do was reach the riverbank across from Urquhart's pocket, which the Germans turned their full efforts to destroying. Meanwhile, German jetfighter aircraft made their debut over the skies of Nijmegen, dropping cluster bombs on the city and the 82nd, a measure of their determination to destroy Market-Garden, and a total shock to men who had never seen or imagined such a thing as a jet aircraft.

On the night of September 25, the survivors who were able swam or used small boats to cross the river under cover of darkness to rejoin their countrymen. Urquhart came across by small boat, and the British troopers completed the evacuation by the morning hours of September 26, all of it under vicious German fire. When he mustered his men that day, Urquhart found that of 10,005 men he had brought into Arnhem, 2,163 live Red Devils had returned across the river to safety. The British 1st Airborne Division had been destroyed, and Urquhart, though he tried, was unable to reconstitute it before war's end.

Market-Garden was over, a dismal failure, a thing now to be played down in the Allied communiqués, an operation best overlooked. The town of Arnhem did eventually fall, but it was not until the following spring. By then, the Germans had ruthlessly starved and squeezed the Dutch in occupied Holland in retaliation for their cooperation with the Allied thrust and their continued underground resistance. Total Market-Garden casualties amounted to approximately 17,000 on the Allied side alone—of which 1,432 came from the 82nd Airborne Division. No accurate count has been made of the number of Dutchmen who froze or starved or were killed that winter in revenge. The Germans, too, lost heavily. An accurate count is difficult, but most figures place their losses in excess of 10,000 men, 3,300 of which fell at Arnhem.

Montgomery claimed Market-Garden was 90 percent successful and maintained that Eisenhower had not thrown enough equipment and military manpower behind him or it would have been 100 percent successful. The Germans claimed complete victory, a boast closer to the truth, for the operation was an Allied disaster, and top Allied leaders privately admitted it. It gave the German Army a heartening victory, a proof that the Allied host was not invincible. Everywhere along the western front, the news stiffened the German resolve to fight to the end. The affair in Holland gave the Germans time. The army that had been staggering and unable to reorganize itself after Normandy got the breathing space it needed elsewhere while all Allied resources flowed into Holland. Units that had had no hope of resting and refitting reorganized and re-armed and returned to the front. Finally, the diversion of force into Market-Garden seriously delayed the opening of a Channel port, and supply shortages remained a serious worry until late November, when Montgomery finally succeeded in opening Antwerp and supplies flowed in.

Market-Garden proved how joint ventures could crack at the seams, in spite of the best training and self-sacrifice by both British and American troops. The stubbornness and pride of Montgomery, the compliance and political nature of Eisenhower, proved a deadly combination for the men who were fed into a plan that presumed, without any foundation in intelligence data, that the German Army was crippled. Paratroop valor was wasted, except to buttress the deep pride survivors felt.

If mistakes were made at the top, they were exposed at the bottom, where the German Army fought with its usual competence and ferocity at a time when every man must have suspected the end was near. The Germans who fought in Market-Garden were a mixture of rear-area and top-line troops. Ill-equipped, often hungry, bombed relentlessly, and up against the best soldiers the Allies could field, they fought on in a sacrifice that was meaningless except to them. All the indicators about them pointed to their nation's defeat.

The significance of the airborne invasion of Holland, above all else, was ironic; Market-Garden, the operation intended to shorten the war, prolonged it.

Shortly after the Nijmegen bridge fell, the fog evaporated from the skies over English airports, and the 325 flew in to support paratroopers of the 82nd. By then, true to the nature of the whole operation, it was no longer critically needed. September 20 had been the day of decision for the Germans. If they could have cut the corridor, they might have brought troops forward to encircle part of the invading force, but they contented themselves with Arnhem and stalemate.

Gavin's personal problems with Ridgway continued. Left by the young commander at the height of the battle, Ridgway angrily returned to Eindhoven. Gavin sensed the gravity of the strain, and at first decided to prostrate himself like a penitent son. In his first entry after Market-Garden, Gavin wrote in his diary how proud he was of what his men had accomplished, then said, "I am afraid that General Ridgway has resented our success. . . . Unfortunately, I am in a tug of war, right in the middle. In the heat of the third day's fighting, General Ridgway visited my command post and when not immediately approached left in a huff later writing a letter demanding an immediate explanation. Such a lack of trust and confidence between his and my command can only do us both and our units harm. I have therefore asked that I be relieved of command of the division and assignment to his corps, the XVIII. This is a big step but a necessary one at this point. We cannot continue to serve in a strained critical atmosphere." And indeed, Ridgway's letter had been harsh. It was three curt paragraphs. In the first, Ridgway described Gavin's ignoring him. Paragraph 2 read, "No apparent effort was made to contact your Corps Commander, nor in any way to acknowledge his presence, which was completely ignored. No explanation has since been received." Paragraph 3 ordered, "You will at once submit a written explanation of this apparently flagrant breach of military courtesy."

Gavin having decided on the gesture, then played his own game. Rather than apologizing in his letter to Ridgway, Gavin began, "I am somewhat uncertain whether this statement will convey what is expected as an explanation, since I was, until receipt of the basic communication, unaware of any breach of military courtesy." He then went on to outline the military situation, then said, "I was sure you would want the correct picture when I talked to you. Under the circumstances, I was not desirous of appearing in a consultative role, nor did I want to appear unconcerned with the extremely critical situation that was now obviously almost out of hand. Knowing your usual understanding and appreciation of such combat conditions and, in addition, taking the liberty of assuming that a more friendly understanding existed between us than apparently actually did exist, I asked my Chief of Staff to extend to you my apologies for having to rush off." From there he continued his description of the fight and ended the letter with the request that he be relieved of command on the basis he described in his diary.

Ridgway had a big ego and Gavin's rivaled it. Gavin knew before he wrote the letter that Ridgway would not accept his resignation. At all levels, Gavin was considered one of the truly outstanding officers in the theater, and though Market-Garden might have failed, the performance of the 82nd was acknowledged as brilliant, considering the conditions. In his diary, when Gavin spoke of his resignation, he also spoke of his proficiency as a commander and his paratroop expertise: "I know airborne operations as well as anyone in our service," he wrote.

If Ridgway had accepted the resignation, higher headquarters would have been outraged. The older man simply wanted his pound of flesh. In his heart, he had not let the 82nd go yet, and he might have harbored some resentment for his rising subordinate.

The resignation flap evaporated when Ridgway acted as if Gavin's non-apology was an apology. Gavin and the 82nd remained in Nijmegen for two more months under British control. Gavin yearned to be returned to American command, but Montgomery did not want to give up the 82nd, so Gavin's troops remained under fire and in foxholes, cursing higher command. Each week his already bloody division got bloodier. Each week his frustration mounted. Once again the basic principle of relieving airborne troops immediately after they had achieved their goals had been violated. On October 27, Gavin wrote, "I am getting tired of the front. Six weeks without relief is a long time." Finally, in mid-November, the division left for France. Unfortunately, many of those "old-timers," the ones he had taken to Africa, were not able to return to France with their comrades.

Legend grew in the wake of Nijmegan; one incident in particular swept the front. Looting was forbidden in Holland and elsewhere, and Gavin, aware of his troopers' somewhat roughnecked reputation, went to great lengths to see that it did not happen. But Private First Class Robert Beckman, a young bazooka man of F Company of the 505, ran out of socks after some four weeks in the foxholes near Nijmegen. Barefoot in his boots, and unable to get socks from his supply sergeant, he went searching for some on Dutch clotheslines. As he entered an off-limits backyard, Beckman was surprised by Gavin, who was walking alone, on some forgotten errand. Gavin asked for an explanation, Beckman pulled one of his badly chafed feet out of his boots and showed it to the general. Gavin agreed that it was a problem but told him to stop looting and get back to his unit. Beckman complied. The next morning a sergeant from division headquarters appeared to personally deliver Beckman his socks. Beckman, thus immortalized, died weeks later in fighting near Ambrefontaine, Belgium.

11.

THE BULGE

Badly scarred after Market-Garden and the weeks of stagnant fighting after it, the 82nd went into reserve. Four hundred and sixty-nine crosses marking 82nd graves remained in Nijmegen, 640 troopers remained missing, and 1,933 of the living had new Purple Hearts to show for having been there. Early in November the division was ordered to old French Army cantonments at Suippes and Sissonne near Reims, and many an old soldier breathed a sigh of relief. Gavin made his headquarters at Sissonne.

Suippes was an old French Army post, used by the Germans when they occupied northern France. It was in the Champagne country of broad meadows cut by rivers and dotted with stone chateaux and little peasant villages. Line upon line of grape vines stood bare in their winter dress on the tan soil. For the troops, life at Sissonne had a touch of luxury. The town was nothing special, the women few. But there was plenty to drink and the French bistros were indulgent to the Americans, even though the Military Police were not.

Gavin wrote of Sissonne on November 28, "Troops of the division raised so much hell that at the request of the base commanding general, General Thrasher, all of our troops were restricted. Jumped right into the affair and had a meeting of all unit COs . . . the trouble seems to center in three things. There is no way to get a girl of easy virtue, all houses are off limits and guarded, food cannot be bought in town anywhere; champagne can be bought by the bottle anywhere, anytime."

Gavin raised some hell of his own in this period, slipping off to Reims and London for dinners and dalliance. "A most enjoyable night with Valerie," the diary reads. "Had a wonderful time, just what I needed."

242

New men streamed into the division, and Gavin, still believing the German Army had not been beaten, turned his attention to training immediately. "No champagne this night" one November diary entry reads. He quickly set up a rudimentary jump school to raise up standards of "airworthiness," and he led the men on his patented long marches for fitness. General Ridgeway's XVIII Airborne Corps headquarters was in nearby Épernay. Most of the seasoned men were given furloughs to Paris, where, Gavin wrote drily, "they made a good impression." Gavin got a laugh from comments about the fine appearance of his troopers, one of which triggered the response, "Alert? Damn right they look alert. You're looking at the survivors."

In spite of the reappearance and resurgence of the German Army in Holland and elsewhere, Allied high commanders were already thinking of a final victory they believed to be close. Gavin's initial impression was that airborne divisions would remain in a state of readiness to seize bridges across the Rhine for the final offensive into Germany in the spring, and the idea gave him occasional gloomy forebodings: "Chaplains are very much concerned with the attitude of the men towards continued operations," the Gavin field diary records. "They do not want to go to the Pacific feeling that they have already done more than their share. The four-jump people are sweating out any more jumps feeling they have used up all their luck. I understand exactly how they feel. I feel the same way myself. They have always done a fine job, but now their ranks are thinning, many of them are banged up from combat and hardly fit mentally or physically for further parachute operations, yet they have no other prospects. It hardly seems right, there should be some way out other then being killed or wounded."

In the meantime, the "big push" of Allied armies against the entire front of German defenses could carry on with someone else's son taking the chances.

Suippes billets were built of solid gray stone, a regular barracks with a mess hall, running water, intact windows, and perhaps most important, a complete lack of the rumbling and nighttime flash of artillery. There were even regimental movies in the chapel. Such things were to be relished doubly now, for each man nursed a hope, which grew every day, to survive to go home. War is a particular soldier's neighborhood—the whole picture is never seen, not even by generals with maps, and only partly by historians. To 82nd soldiers, particularly the four-jump men, their neighborhood was measured as much by their lost friends as the enemy they killed. None of them knew, as November gave way to a far colder December, that still ahead of them lay perhaps the worst fight yet, the Battle of the Bulge.

Sergeant Joseph Tallett of Levittown, New Jersey, a bazookaman, was a relative newcomer to the 505th, having joined it just after Normandy, but his initiation into combat in Holland had been severe enough that he too now hoped for little more than a safe return home. But on December 17, while walking across the center of Suippes compound on the way to watch a movie, his combat-tuned instincts told him his hope might not be fulfilled. Off to the east, he saw a curious flickering on the horizon, like heat lightning, but as cold as he felt in his jumpsuit (the 82nd had not yet received its issue of winter uniforms), he knew it wasn't heat lightning.

Shaking off the foreboding, he joined his friends amidst the crowd of noisy, smoking soldiers settled into creaky, narrow wooden chairs in the chapel while a film flickered in black and white on a small screen. Men talked and joked too loudly and smoked too much, though none of them mentioned the lights in the sky. When they came out into the hard night air, Tallett again looked instinctively to the east. Stars shone, and on a sector of the eastern horizon, where the Aisne country became the Ardennes Forest, the flickering continued.

Tallet would survive the battle named "The Bulge," and live to tell of what it was like during the last great German offensive. But he'd never again believe so strongly that the enemy was finished.

The lights were still there in the sky at 3 A.M. when the regiment, rudely rousted out of its bunks, assembled. "Get out of the sack," the sergeants screamed. "You ain't reserve no more. The Krauts have launched an offensive . . ."

Tallett collected his bazooka and field kit and joined others throwing equipment into the open stake trucks, called cattle cars. Sleepy and cold and complaining about their lack of winter coats, they set out on French and Belgian roads toward one of the most remarkable battles in the annals of the war.

At First Army Headquarters at Spa, Belgium, the lights in the east were brighter, and there army staff officers nervously ground out their cigarettes, calculated and estimated, rifled through intelligence reports, pored over neglected maps, and answered phones to hear repeated in different ways the same message: German infantry and armor had been on the move since nightfall, sometimes advancing by searchlight, placing an intolerable stress on a thin Allied line.

The Ardennes had been a tranquil place where both sides held static lines—almost as if in tacit agreement not to cause trouble on either side, for the ground was famously difficult. Particularly quiet was the Loes-heim Gap, a 7-mile-wide corridor that led from Germany to Belgium through the Schnee Eifel (Snow Mountains). The German Army had used the gap as an invasion route in 1870, 1914, and 1940, but high command had rejected it as a place for more offensive operations.

When the Germans had used a similar route for the 1940 invasion that had begun the deluge that defeated France it was for precisely that reason —contrariness. But that was 1940. In 1944, American planners accepted the common wisdom that the Germans would not now risk precious tanks in the Ardennes, not without an air force to support them. Some intelligence officers thought that the Germans no longer had the combat power for any but local and short-lived offensive actions. They were in a defensive posture, fighting the Russians in the East, the Americans and British in the West, and hoping for stalemate and negotiation. If the Germans planned a counteroffensive, it would surely come along the Roer River, where hydroelectric dams could be used to create widespread flooding.

So quiet had been the Loesheim Gap that it was used as a break-in ground for green divisions fresh from the United States, and a rest area for battered and tired divisions. On December 16, the freshly minted 106th Division under the command of Major General Alan W. Jones was stationed there, next to the 99th Division, to familiarize itself with war-time conditions. To bolster his force, Jones had the 14th Cavalry Group also stationed in the gap and under his control. These green troops sat in the Ardennes Forest of pine, larch, and spruce, amidst snowy Christmas card-looking hills, trying to settle into a routine. Having been there just four days, they had no idea what all the movement across from their lines on the night of December 15 meant. Because they were supposed to be in a quiet sector, all of the VIII Corps units were stretched thinly over a vast area of timberland, river bottoms, and upland pastures. The 28th, for example covered 23 miles of a front that would be the main axis of the

German attack. So thin were their fronts, that none of these divisions had formed continuous defensive lines. They instead depended upon isolated strong points.

Working with complete secrecy and on the personal orders of Hitler, the German general staff had developed a plan that used every factor of the terrain and the battle situation—and turned it to a fresh and unexpected advantage.

While the American and British top command bickered over the general strategies to be employed to end the war, the German staffs responsible for the defense of the shrinking Third Reich had far fewer options. They had skill won of hard fights over four years of constant movement, and they had an organization equal to almost any calamity. But they had so little in terms of supplies of tanks, trucks, fuel, manpower, and munitions that the fact that they were able to contemplate a risk-filled attack is a monument to their resourcefulness.

Hitler's plan—similar to the lightning attack of 1940 that had routed the French and led to Dunkirk—was to concentrate the heaviest and best of Germany's tank and motorized forces and strike into the heart of Belgium, toward Antwerp. The Germans would seize the great port, splitting the British Second Army, Canadian First Army, and U.S. First Army to the north away from the U.S. Third Army to the south, while bypassing heavily defended areas. By breaking a huge hole in the Allied front, Hitler thought the attack would produce panic and create that most unsettling situation for soldiers, the knowledge the enemy is behind you and you are cut off from the safety of the main body of friendly forces. It was conceivable under this plan that the huge Allied forces to the north —the British, the Canadians, and the two U.S. armies, First and Third— could be surrounded, cut off from their land supply routes and treated to a new Dunkirk.

But the Germans did not plan a finale. They had no objective beyond the capture of Antwerp. The single stunning blow had nothing behind it because Hitler believed a decisive victory was enough to force the British to sue for peace and collapse the alliance. Then he could turn the entire Wehrmacht to the East. Few of the experienced commanders to whom Hitler's "masterstroke" was explained believed it could work. Field Marshal Gerd von Rundstedt, cautious, conservative, two wars in experience, and Field Marshal Walther Model, a genius for improvisation who'd survived many impossible situations on the Eastern Front—the men responsible for implementing the plan—pointed out to Hitler that Germany simply did not have enough men and machines to carry out such a gigantic swoop of 300 kilometers, and with no air support to speak of. These senior generals suggested a smaller coup—such as a pincer attack at Aachen, where most of the First Army's troops were deployed, to shock the Allies into a defensive posture and allow Germany to concentrate on the far more desperate and fearful defensive battle against Russia.

After the fact, German Major General F. W. von Mellenthin, a staff officer privy to the German planning for the Bulge, summed up: "I do not think that those responsible for the detailed staff work connected with this operation have received adequate credit. The Wehrmacht achieved a surprise every bit as staggering as the one in the same area in May 1940, and under normal conditions of war and with reasonable equality of force we would have won a very great victory. . . . Tactically speaking, the Ardennes breakthrough was the last great achievement of the German General Staff, a stroke in the finest traditions of Gneisenau, Moltke, and Schlieffen.

"Of course, from the strategic aspect, this offensive was a desperate gamble and proved a very great mistake . . . yet it must be admitted that [Hitler's] will power and resolution were certainly commensurate with the magnitude of his aims. . . . In Hitler's favor it might be said that desperate situations demand desperate remedies and that pure defense never won a war. But at the end of 1944 Germany had no chance of winning the war and the only sane course was to concentrate on keeping the Russians out of our eastern provinces and to hope that even at this late hour there would be a cleavage between the United States and Russia."

Once reconciled to Hitler's thinking by the still-fierce force of his personality and mind, the military men applied themselves to the problems with fervor. They sought to capitalize on several advantages that together enormously helped their battle plan. First was the weather and, tied to it, the German Army's expertise at night movement.

Facing almost total Allied air superiority, German daytime movements were perilous except in snow, fog, rain—weather that kept fighters and bombers grounded. As a result the Germans had become expert at making large, complex movements at night and then waiting during daylight hours under camouflage. Similarly, the Allies had come to depend heavily on air reconnaissance. December, the time of the invasion, was also a time, the Germans well knew, when the weather could be counted upon to be at its worst, and the shortened days would minimize Allied flying time.

The second advantage was the locale, which the German staff felt confident could support swift tank movements and over which they had already rolled in 1940, an advantage doubled by the Americans' naive opinion that the route was unsuitable. The Germans also counted on skills won in three winters of fighting in the East, where they had learned the difficult art of moving machines in snow, ice, and mud.

The third advantage was the element of surprise. Hitler accompanied the announcement of his plan to a small circle of staff planners with a demand that each man sign a document submitting himself to drastic punishment for any leaks, radio silence was to be enforced, and no mention of this plan was allowed over the telephone. As a result, the American intelligence services, by this time nearly totally dependent on air reconnaissance and their Ultra code breakers, were totally fooled. To add to Allied confusion,the Germans planned to drop a body of paratroopers behind the American 1st and 9th divisions to the north of the main point of effort. They quickly formed a commando group, led by SS-Obersturmbannführer (SS Lieutenant Colonel) Otto Skorzeny, who was personally anointed by Hitler to gather a force of English speaking volunteers, dress them in the uniforms of captured Americans and send them through American lines to cut telephone lines, seize the Meuse bridges, and create havoc. They were well armed and equipped. They even used captured American jeeps and other vehicles, though some rode German vehicles painted with the familiar American white star. Desperate, determined men who could expect nothing but death by firing squad if captured, they created far more disturbance than their numbers warranted because news of them spread rapidly once the invasion began and forced the nervous Allies to take extreme countermeasures.

With mounting tension, the German commanders prepared their trap. Planned first for November 1, later postponed to Dec 10, and then to the 16th. For once delay proved a blessing, for the weather worsened. True to his reputation as a relentless scraper-together and assembler of fighting units out of whatever human material was available, Model had gathered about 275,000 men, 1,900 heavy guns, 1,200 tanks and 950 transports and other vehicles into the Ardennes Forest. Allied air reconaissance had not noted their movements.

Psychologically, the moment was right as well. Eisenhower's broad-front campaign to push the Wehrmacht back to the German border had stalled. After a month of indifferent Allied success, small gains with heavy casualties, in a kind of inch-by-inch contest that greatly favored the defenders, the Allies were impatient and baffled. They knew their foe could not win, but daily they met German sacrifice and ferocity that made attacking troops wary. Now that bafflement would have added to it an element of terror.

Three German armies gathered unseen: the Sixth SS Panzer Army in the north, the Fifth Panzer Army in the center, and the Seventh Army in the south. A butcher's son and Nazi zealot (a dramatic contrast to the educated aristocrats normally associated with high command in the German Army), SS General Josef "Sepp" Dietrich, commanded the Sixth SS Panzer Army. His career had been pushed by Hitler personally. The center German force, Fifth Panzer Army, was commanded by Lieutenant General Hasso von Manteuffel, a veteran of the fearsome tank battles in Russia in the winter of 1943. The southernmost element in the assault force, the Seventh Army, was commanded by Lieutenant General Erich Brandenberger. But it had no tanks at all and contributed only by keeping the southern American divisions, including the 28th, the 4th Armored, the 26th, the 80th, and the 10th Armored, the 4th and the newly arrived 5th, heavily engaged and preventing their use elsewhere.

The "defeated" enemy launched a concentrated artillery barrage across the entire Ardennes region in the early morning of Saturday, December 16, 1944. And out of the darkness their squat tanks and the waves of gray-coated soldiery came on right behind the barrage. Surprised and faced with massive armored and infantry concentrations, the green troops of the 106th and 28th Infantry divisions actually made a good accounting of themselves on the first day, but by the 17th, they were outnumbered, outflanked, cut off, and on the run. The Germans poured through the hole under heavy clouds that kept the Allies most potent weapon, air cover, on the ground.

Gavin was dressing for dinner at the officers' mess the evening of the 17th when the call came through from First Army. It was almost time to think about Christmas. As resplendent as he ever got, in semiformal evening wear, Gavin was starched and correct.

On the phone the excited voice of XVIII Airborne Corps Chief of Staff,

Colonel Ralph "Doc" Eaton, told him that in the last fifteen hours, since the predawn of December 16, the Germans had opened a heavy and successful offensive against the thinned out Allied lines in the Ardennes. Tanks were pouring northwestward. American units had been surrounded and captured. With Generals Ridgway and Taylor out of the theater (Taylor was in Washington at the War Department; Ridgway in England at Airborne Corps training headquarters) and their return delayed by the weather, Gavin was temporarily in charge of the XVIII Airborne Corps. Eaton informed Gavin that higher command wanted two divisions, the 82nd and Taylor's 101st, to be ready to move by dawn on the 19th, on orders to be issued. Gavin then ordered Eaton to alert the acting commander of the 101st, Brigadier General Anthony McAuliffe to prepare the 101st for movement, hung up the phone, and choosing to keep the news to himself until after the meal, went to dinner.

Gavin had first heard of the "trouble in the Ardennes" on the 16th, when it was thought to be a "small penetration." As a commander in reserve, he could only reflect gloomily on the thinness of U.S. forces in the area and the lack of nearby reserves that could quickly be thrown into a defensive battle. News came in over the radio all the next day. Now it was about "serious penetrations."

At 8 P.M. Gavin assembled his staff in the old barracks's war room, where the large-scale map of the Ardennes area and the latest teletype bulletins covered the walls. As Gavin and his staff tried to deduce from bulletins, geography, and logic where the German attack would concentrate, Eaton called again. Gavin was to report immediately to General Courtney Hodges at First Army Headquarters at Spa and move the two airborne divisions as fast as possible toward Bastogne, the central road junction in the area of the German penetration.

Gavin ordered troopers recalled from Paris leaves and the 82nd out at dawn ahead of schedule. He ordered Taylor's paratroops of the 101st to follow as soon as they were ready. Destination for all was Bastogne.

By 11:30 P.M. that same night, dinner forgotten, Gavin was in an open jeep with his aide, Captain Hugo Olsen and the 82nd's administrative officer, Colonel Al Ireland. The trio armed themselves as heavily as was practical; Gavin had with him his trusty M-1 Garand. They drove the 200 kilometers like wary cavalry. Gavin specified the open jeep for all-round visibility and trouble readiness, in spite of a cold light rain and a far longer ride due to downed bridges. They finally arrived half-frozen and soaked at 9 A.M.

They made their way into General Courtney Hodges's war room and found the old soldier looking very weary indeed. Gavin had served with him in the Phillipines in the 1930s and Hodges was, at fifty-eight, one of the oldest men involved in the battle. The general had had a difficult forty-eight hours and was giving orders to draw back the command post to Chaudfontaine. "Things in an uproar," Gavin jotted in his war diary, "the Germans about 10 miles away and coming on."

From where Hodges sat, everything had happened too quickly, and now the situation was desperate. His First Army had received the brunt of the German penetration. Some American soldiers had turned and fled, others had struggled valiantly but ended up surrounded by fast-moving armored spearheads. To First Army's left, things were better but only because the Germans had not chosen to concentrate their attack near Aachen, where First Army's leftmost forces stood to the northeast of the city. But on the right, where the rest of his troops were deployed along his hundred-mile front, chaos reigned. No one had fresh intelligence, and few that day knew where the German attack was going. The VIII Corps, consisting of most of the green or weakened units, had been hardest hit and was not holding its defensive line. Those that had held were surrounded in pockets, connected only by radio to higher command.

Hodges and his staff, with Gavin's assistance, gradually formed a plan based on the sound conventional theory that the best way to stop a sharply concentrated armored offensive is to threaten its flanks, or cut the invading spear at its roots. For this to work, the shoulders of the penetration had to become strong points that could be used as a springboard for counterattacks into the rear of the invaders, and the Germans had to be slowed down. Since Bastogne was the critical road junction in the area and the brunt of the assault seemed targeted toward the northern sector, Bastogne and the northern shoulder had to hold. The generals at First Army headquarters, sharing the now theater-wide belief in the fighting prowess of paratroopers, gave Gavin both: Bastogne to the south, with its convergence of seven major roads, and Werbomont on the north, where a dominating hilly mass and a little river, the Amblève, would supply a natural advantage to whomever held it. The Amblève is not wide or deep, but it has the steep banks and bluffs that are the despair of tank commanders and the hope of riflemen on foot. Men can easily splash across the Amblève in countless places, tanks must find bridges.

But who should go where? Since Werbomont was farther away, and the 82nd had moved out first, Gavin decided on committing his own division to Werbomont and sent the 101st on to Bastogne.

The separation of the two divisons would later upset Ridgway who wanted the 101st and the 82nd to fight in the same sector. But Gavin could not have known that, for Ridgway was at that time scrambling by plane and jeep to get back to his corps from his unfortunately timed visit to England, as was luckless 101st commander, Maxwell Taylor, who fretted out the critical hours of the Battle of the Bulge, trying simply to get to the fight.

Now sure of the situation, Gavin raced south and west by jeep toward Werbomont to establish his new headquarters. Then he began a daylong reconaissance of the projected path of the German advance, crossing clear down to Bastogne, then back to his headquarters at Werbomont. Though he did not know it, Ridgway was following roughly that same route, rushing back to XVIII Airborne Corps headquarters at Épernay, then down to Bastogne, then back to Werbomont to set up his new headquarters for the divided XVIII Airborne Corps near Gavin's own.

Gavin arrived back at Werbomont about the time the first of his truckloads of 82nd troopers rolled up in the darkness. He had had another hair-raising drive across country, this time under the nose of the advancing German forces. While making arrangements for the 101st at Bastogne during the afternoon, he had heard radio messages about a powerful battle group led by Joachim Peiper, a twenty-nine-year-old lieutenant colonel and a favorite of Sepp Dietrich. Dietrich had chosen Peiper to lead the offensive because of his determined daring in tank battles on the Eastern Front. His shock troops were drawn from an elite, ruthless group, the 1st SS Panzer Divison, Leibstandarte Adolph Hitler.

With volunteers clinging to the sides of his 146 tanks, Peiper charged forward against little opposition into the valley of the Amblève with half-tracks full of fuel and shells. He had scored double coups: the first by finding and capturing intact a dump of 50,000 gallons of fuel at Büllingen and the second by forcing a crossing over the Amblève at Stavelot. Peiper forced American prisoners at Büllingen to fill his fuel tanks, and rushed on to capture the Stavelot bridge. On December 17, he struck fear into the defenders by slaughtering American prisoners of war. His troops rounded up fifty prisoners at Büllingen, nineteen near Honsfeld, and those plus another 150 from a lightly armed 285th Field Artillery Observation Battalion were herded into a field near Malmédy and quickly machine-gunned (86 died, the rest feigned death or recovered from wounds to tell the tale of the "Malmédy massacre"). Peiper pushed on, spreading havoc and blazing the path the main force would follow.

As Gavin jumped out of his jeep at Werbomont, Peiper was roaming free, seeking another river crossing, this time over the Salm, so he could head for Werbomont. Engineers foiled him at the town of Trois-Ponts by blowing the bridges, but he found a bridge at Cheneux and raced on. Gavin, of course, knew nothing of the tank leader's reputation or his plan, only that a tank force had been driving behind the disintegrating First Army front for almost two days. What he did know was the little Lienne Creek, which ran through the village of Habiémont, was the only natural tank obstacle between the panzers and Werbomont and Huy, the logical crossing of the Meuse and the high road to Antwerp, which he had now deduced was the German objective.

Determined to allow the Germans no northern progress in his sector, Gavin spent a fevered night getting his freshly arrived troops in defensive positions around Werbomont for the battle that he was sure would come the next day. In spite of the rumors, the refugees, and the traffic-clogged roads, the men of the 82nd had yet to see an opposing German, but Gavin had secured Werbomont and that night snatched what badly needed sleep he could get on the floor of the farmhouse headquarters.

At first light, Gavin heard from his operations officer, Colonel John Norton, that Peiper had been stalled again by the destruction of the vital bridge at the hamlet of Habiémont by engineers of the First Army. True to his belief in assessing critical situations firsthand, Gavin drove through his own division's positions in the early morning half-light, parked out of sight, and, rifle at the ready, walked ahead to the bridge in the absolute silence of a winter dawn. "I felt as though I were in no-man's-land. There is a peculiar stillness and lack of activity beyond one's front lines until you encounter the enemy. Combat veterans sense this condition quickly . . . they become intensely cautious and listen, seemingly with every pore of their bodies."

Gavin found ruined German vehicles and several German bodies, but no clue of how many of the enemy made it to the Werbomont side of the Lienne Creek. There was nothing else. Where was Peiper?

The day revealed that this subunit of Peiper's force had crossed, fought briefly with Americans of the 30th Division, and rejoined their leader, possibly with American prisoners. Wherever the remainder of Peiper's panzers had gone, they seemed no longer to be in the 82nd's area.

Gavin drove back to his headquarters, where he found that General

Ridgway had arrived and set up his own headquarters nearby. Gavin's temporary command of the XVIII Airborne Corps was over, but he had accomplished much by placing the two airborne divisions where one held the critical road junction, and the other could halt the 1st SS Panzers from driving north.

Ridgway was at his best during the Bulge crisis, and he moved decisively as soon as he established his headquarters in a two-story farmhouse near Werbomont. The battle was now three days old, and the situation had become clearer. The Germans had penetrated deep and wide, but the battle-hardened 2nd Infantry Division and elements of the 99th Infantry Division tenaciously held the extreme north shoulder near Butgenbach, and two more fine veteran divisions, the 1st and the 9th, were even then streaming into that area as reinforcements. Americans also held the town of St.-Vith with two infantry regiments and a portion of the 9th Armored Divison, directly in the path of the Sixth Panzer Army. Brigadier General Robert Hasbrouck's 7th Armored Division was reinforcing St.-Vith even as Ridgway set up his headquarters. This left an undefended gap between St.-Vith and Butgenbach. If the gap could be filled, St.-Vith would become a formidable obstacle to the German advance.

But filling the gap would not be easy. True to their doctrine of following the course of least resistance to achieve penetration, the German Sixth Panzer Army now flowed into a 10-mile corridor between Butgenbach and St.-Vith. This slowed them down severely by reducing the area for maneuver but it offered a route, which Peiper had blazed, through which they might break into the open. Hodges and Ridgway now threw the 82nd Airborne Divison, the 3rd Armored Division, and the 30th Infantry Division, under Major General Leland S. Hobbs, into that corridor, directly into the path of the advancing Sixth Panzer Army. All the forces at St.-Vith now came under Ridgway's control. St.-Vith stuck like a dagger into the vitals of the German advance, and at its base, Werbomont was the key town in the region. What was clear to Hodges and Ridgway, was that if St.-Vith and the corridor could be held, Ridgway could thrust that dagger straight through the German offensive once the front stabilized. Gavin had already secured Werbomont.

Ridgway now ordered the division deployed fan-wise and forward in the direction of Vielsalm and Trois-Ponts to link up with units on the north corner and St.-Vith. The 30th and elements of the 3rd Armored Division deployed to the left to link up with St.-Vith. Ridgway and Gavin were determined that Peiper and the follow-up forces would not use that corridor. Gavin spent the day of the 19th preparing for the onslaught he knew would come. Good defensive positions for his troopers and artillery were critical. Unlike the 101st at Bastogne, they had no tank support, and German armor was vulnerable only to heavy artillery shells, flank shots, aerial attack, and rivers or deep ravines. He found ideal rugged defensive terrain along the Salm River and deployed the 508 to the rough terrain between Baraque de Fraiture and Salmchâteau, the 505 along the Salm River between Bergeval and Vielsalm, the 504 to the Trois-Ponts region, and the 325 on a wide front that extended from Grandménil well to the west.

Most World War II U.S. infantrymen, particularly lightly armed parachutists, had little to deter tanks, the bazooka having proved almost useless against the front armor of the Tigers and Panthers. But by this stage of the war Allied high command conveniently overlooked that. So accustomed were they to successes by the 82nd against German armored formations, they believed Gavin's crazy characters would somehow make do in spite of the fact that the Bulge represented the most formidable concentration of armor the Germans had ever hurled at American infantrymen. Against the rumble of those tanks, many Americans had panicked already. The frozen ground often making it difficult to dig quickly, soldiers on the move felt completely exposed to the gray metal monsters. All of Gavin's long and loud grumbling about the ineffectiveness of the 2.36-inch recoilless rocket launcher (bazooka) since the Sicily landing seemed to have been unheeded, for it remained the 82nd's primary anti-tank weapon. But the Germans had learned the principle of the armor-piercing shaped charge and had improved on captured U.S. bazookas. Gavin had seen the improved German versions, known as Panzerfausts, and since then had been in the habit of gathering them and arming his 82nd units with them. Truckloads of these captured tank destroyers went everywhere with Gavin's men.

As dawn broke on the 20th, Gavin was in heated conversation with Colonel Reuben Tucker of the 504th in a hamlet called Rahier. Ridgway's orders had been obeyed as far as possible amidst rumors and confusion. The 82nd still had no real idea exactly where the enemy was, but Belgian civilians had told Tucker that 125 vehicles including about 30 tanks had rolled northeast through the town in the direction of the neighboring town of Cheneux.

Gavin reasoned that this was one of the Peiper tank force columns that had been stalled at Habiémont and now sought another bridge strong enough for tanks. Logically, they must still be at Cheneux. Peiper had been found and in a town that, if seized, would disrupt German movement throughout the area. Gavin ordered Tucker "To move into the town of Cheneux without delay and, conditions permitting, to seize the bridge." Gavin concluded at the time that "if 125 armored vehicles engaged the 504 in the country around Rahier we were in for some anxious moments." Taking plenty of Panzerfausts with him Tucker moved on Cheneux. "Any ordinary infantry regiment would want at least a battalion of tanks in support before it attacked, but Tucker's idea was to attack the Germans and take their armor away from them," Gavin wrote in his battle memoir, *On to Berlin*. "He figured he would then have his own."

Gavin let Tucker have his way. But the 504's audacity ended in a wasteful, bloody battle. Tucker's scouts first ran into a motorcycle patrol then an infantry company supported by armor and light artillery a half mile west of the town. A fierce daylong fight ensued, but the advance elements of the 504, charging forward amidst trees that German artillery had shattered into deadly splinters, drove the company back to the town. The Germans too knew the importance of the bridge at Cheneux, and they recognized that these paratroopers were far different fighters from the inexperienced units they had met in the first hours of the battle, so they made a fortress of the village with their 20mm flak guns, an antiaircraft weapon with bursting shells that could be used to terrible effect on infantry. Still, the 1st Battalion of the 504 succeeded in establishing a headquarters on the outskirts of the town.

The Germans had good reason to be conservative, for the clouds above the Ardennes had broken momentarily that day to allow Army Air Forces Thunderbolts to shoot up parts of Peiper's force near Cheneux. Light spotter planes had also been able to trace their activities, so the German tankers sought the stone walls of the hamlets for concealment until nightfall.

A nightlong standoff ensued, with both sides seeking shelter from shells and bullets. Gavin had ordered Tucker to attack and destroy the German forces in the town and capture the bridge, and Tucker was determined to achieve this. After the sun rose on December 21, Tucker flung two companies in a World War I style frontal attack across a field in front of the town. The Germans waited, armed with machine guns, flak guns, mortars, and light artillery, but the paratroopers came on anyway in skirmish-line formation. Two waves of determined men fell immediately, their remnants forced to retreat. Then, belatedly, Tucker brought up two tank destroyers—cannons mounted on tank chassis—and concentrated on the German guns.

The third assault wave refused to be denied, and the surviving para-troops fought hand to hand, some climbing on the flak wagons to hack the crews to death with jump knives. The German panicked and fell back, and the paratroopers, swarming forward to the bridge, dug themselves into the ditches at the outskirts of town.

Tucker meanwhile had already sent a flanking battalion to attack the remaining Germans from the rear. While the tank destroyers and infan-trymen assaulted from the south, the flanking force labored for six hours over rough terrain to hit the Germans from the north. The bulk of the German force had escaped by the time the flankers arrived, but they killed or captured the entire German rear guard. Few of the SS men surrend-ered, most of the rear guard preferring to fight to the end.

Tucker had lost 225 dead and wounded, mostly from the first and second assault waves; he'd captured fourteen motorized flak guns (the troopers now called themselves the 504th Parachute Armored Regiment) and some howitzers, but no tanks. Gavin took pride in the unit's accom-plishments, but some historians have considered the frontal attacks sui-cidal. Gavin commented with restraint: "It had been costly; the Germans were well equipped and gave us a good fight." But his comment hid frustration at Tucker's tactics. Publicly, at least, Gavin did not express regret at loss of life when it showed the aggressive spirit of his troopers, and when an action ended in success for one of his favorite officers. In fact, the battle had a larger significance. Kampfgruppe Peiper was now stalled near Stoumont and pressured from three sides. Elements of the 3rd Armored Division had fought their way to the outskirts of Stoumont on one side, 30th Division men had hit the other side, and Tucker's troopers had stopped further penetration through Cheneux.

But the issue of Trois-Ponts remained. It was where the Amblève and Salm rivers merged, and the point where the 1st SS Panzer Division sought to cross. As the 504 had closed on Cheneux on December 20, the 505 had arrived at Trois-Ponts, where they found engineers commanded by Robert B. Yates, remnants of the retreating First Army forces, still holding the town. The bridges were already blown, the reason the frus-trated Peiper had not crossed there already.

It was becoming a question of getting to the next bridge before the

Germans, or ambushing them on the way there. Ekman's 505 expanded the Americans' hold on Trois-Ponts and demolished the other bridges in the area.

For the first time during the battle, the troopers were ahead of the game. Ekman assigned Vandervoort's 2nd Battalion of the 505 to hold Trois-Ponts. They knew to a close certainty that Peiper's tanks were nearby, and logic argued that other German forces would try to force the Trois-Ponts bridges to spring them, so they set a trap and waited through a long winter day. Vandervoort deployed D Company to the forward side of the Salm river to cover the Stavelot road, and on the night of December 20–21, at about 3 A.M., a German armored vehicle appeared as expected. Well-placed flanking bazooka fire hit and destroyed it. Another vehicle followed an hour later and struck mines placed where the wrecked German armored car narrowed the road. But at daylight heavier forces appeared, starting with a reconnaisance by infantry. Later fierce, screaming infantry supported by four or five tanks stormed directly into the machine-gun and rifle fire of the 505. This was the 1st SS Panzer Division, and through sheer determination and weight of numbers, they forced D Company back to the river, but the company held. One young German taken prisoner after the attack said that the frontal attack had been used against Americans since the start of the offensive and had always worked before. He was shocked by the German failure.

Now the 505 and 504 were both in critical positions. If they could keep the 1st SS Panzer occupied, Peiper would remain unsupported, trapped, gradually losing the men and machines of his battle group. On the 22nd, the ferocity of panzer attacks increased, forcing the 505 to abandon its forward positions, under the weight of ever heavier concentrations of tanks, for the relative security of the other side of the river, a natural barrier against armor.

Even after this tactical retreat, a scramble under fire across the shallows of the Salm river, Colonel Vandervoort remained confident the Germans could not cross in the face of blown bridges, and the fire of 57mm antitank guns. The 505 stood on the west bank of the Amblève from Trois-Ponts to Grand Halleux, blocking the Germans' westward progress. Gavin was there assessing the situation firsthand. General Hodges wanted to know the results of this fight immediately, for if the 1st SS Panzer could be held, Peiper would be alone and cut off. Vandervoort held until, finally, the badly bloodied panzer division gave up on Trois-Ponts on the 23rd.

. . .

On December 21, the frigid weather had turned worse. Damp fog that had clung close to the ground rose and formed a low cloud out of which snow fell. The temperature plummeted ever lower, and digging a foxhole became nearly impossible. Meanwhile, the Germans at last concentrated their attention on obliterating the defenders of St.-Vith. The compelling reason was that the town sits on the only rail line westward from the Ardennes, a vital prize for a German Army that still depended on horse-drawn transport for most basic war supplies. It was also, like Bastogne, a vital road junction, and the heroism of the American forces who fought there has been often overlooked.

St.-Vith was a refuge for all sorts of American battle flotsam left in the wake of the breakthrough—elements of the shattered 106th Infantry, 28th Infantry, and 9th Armored, the 14th Cavalry Group and the 7th Armored, rushed down from the north, which was the most intact and powerful. Its commander, Brigadier General Robert Hasbrouck, became de facto leader of the defending forces when the senior general in the horseshoe-shaped defense line around St.-Vith, Major General Alan W. Jones, fell into depression from the shock of losses his division had suffered. Among the soldiers of the 106th overrun by the Germans was his own son. Jones was shortly afterwards relieved of his command and suffered a major heart attack.

Hasbrouck, surrounded by Germans on the 20th and finding the units collected in the pocket little battle worthy after their ordeals, had sent a message to Hodges's chief of staff at V Corps headquarters, requesting permission to withdraw from St.-Vith before they were cut off. Hodges consulted Ridgway, and the aggressive paratrooper urged an attack by the 82nd, the 30th Infantry Division, and elements of the 3rd Armor, to relieve St.-Vith. Hodges concurred with Ridgway.

Precisely at this point in the unfolding drama of the battle, with a large American force apparently besieged, British Field Marshal Montgomery, who had been steadily promoting his theory of a unified command (himself at its head) and a single thrust attack, struck a responsive chord with the man who bore ultimate responsibility for the outcome of the defensive battle, Supreme Commander Dwight D. Eisenhower.

Montgomery seized upon the crisis in the Ardennes to cable British Prime Minister Winston Churchill, asking him to pressure Eisenhower and renew requests that a single commander be named to handle the Ardennes crisis. Though Montgomery's own troops were far from the battle, and his own advance toward Germany had slowed to a stop, he roundly criticized the American handling of the German attack, derogated the American command structure, and suggested he be put in overall command. Eisenhower, his political senses working overtime, agreed, but only halfway, giving Montgomery command on all forces north of the Bulge, including Ridgway's XVIII Airborne Corps, and therefore Gavin's 82nd.

The decision infuriated most American generals, most of all Bradley, who, as Twelfth Army Group commmander, was over both Hodges and V Corps commander Major General Leonard T. Gerow and would be stripped of a large part of his command. Hodges, whom Eisenhower secretly felt was uninspiring in a crisis, was mortified. Gavin, who would never forget Holland, wanted nothing to do with Montgomery.

Bradley was only able to swallow the arguments of his chief by sensibly voicing the hope that giving Montgomery what he wanted would perhaps persuade the haughty British general to commit his own reserves to the battle. Bradley bore the humiliation with his usual grace, but others like Lieutenant General Walter Bedell Smith, Eisenhower's chief of staff, could not restrain their anger.

Montgomery took a perverse pleasure in belittling U.S. management of the war zone; as he was admired by the lower echelons of troopers for his charisma and courage, so was he genially hated by all but a few of the American brass for his heavy arrogance and unshakable egotism. He came into the battle zone of St.-Vith like a schoolmaster ready to "set straight" a bunch of eager but oafish colonials.

He dumped scorn on Ridgway's agressive plan to reinforce the bastion at St.-Vith and suggested instead that Ridgway tell Gavin to pull back northward, away from the Germans, to safer, shorter lines. "After all, gentlemen," John Eisenhower quotes him as saying in his Sandhurst drawl, "you can't win a big victory without a tidy show."

The Americans were outraged, not only at the thought of a retreat over ground that had been hard fought for and was soaked in places with the blood of paratroops and their First Army colleagues, but also because Montgomery's plans revealed deeper fears about the strength of the German's attack. Courtney Hodges's ardent protests made Montgomery relent, at least for the moment.

Gavin was to learn of the import of these changes of high command only later. When he did he noted, "Field Marshal Montgomery at a press conference very kindly told the world that he ordered the division to withdraw after it had saved the 7th Armored, 106th and 28th Divisions." St.-Vith forces hung on until the 22nd, then withdrew with Ridgway's blessing under fantastic German pressure.

Gavin's start to the week before Christmas—during which the threatening cloud and freezing temperatures produced ample snow—was spent dealing with crisis after crisis on the battlefield, as his paratroopers fought to stop the German columns and prevent them from outflanking the entire division. Having failed to crack the 504 or 505, more fresh panzer divisions tried slicing through or around the 508 and the 325.

And amidst the continuous assaults, the weather became devilish—1944 is remembered as the worst winter in Belgium in forty years—because it would neither freeze hard enough to allow tanks to travel over frozen ground, nor thaw enough to let men get warm. It particularly hampered the thinly clad paratroops who had not been issued winter uniforms. Gavin tried to rotate his front-line troopers by thirds, so that some men could at least try warming themselves by fires in ruined houses and barns. The fires drew bullets, but the lack of winter uniforms meant inevitable frostbite without them.

The addition of snow, in some places thigh-deep by Christmas, made the scene resemble the worst time of World War I, the winter of 1916. Gavin mused over the sight, late in the battle, of green troops hesitantly struggling up to their new posts, some towing makeshift sledges, "wearing long overcoats, black rubber overshoes, carrying full field packs and all the equipment, weapons and impedimenta they believed a combat soldier should have . . . by contrast the 82nd was still in its old, faded jump suits, wearing long johns to be sure, but carrying only the essentials for fighting."

On the afternoon of the 22nd, Gavin got his first taste of what was to come. Scouts spotted about a hundred German vehicles, including twenty-five tanks, coming from the south to enter the town of Ottre near the positions held by the 325. The force gathered in the shelter of the hamlet of Joubieval, and as was the Germans' habit, prepared to lay up for the night among deserted stone houses; but American artillery concentrated on them and pounded them into the surrounding woods.

The Germans fought back to destroy their tormentors, counterattacking an outpost of the 325 and forcing the troopers to retreat as night fell. Gavin knew that the new enemy, identified as members of the elite Führer Begleit Brigade of the 2nd SS Panzer Division, wanted the road bridge in nearby Petit Langloir and would not be able to concentrate its armor in the area without it. In the dark an engineer team led by Major J. C. H. Lee, Jr., crept behind German sentries with a heavy load of explosives and blew up the bridge even as the Germans used it.

Overwhelming force came against the 325 the next morning, and the 9th SS Panzer Division had appeared before the 508. Gavin released his last reserves, a battalion of glidermen, to counter the threat to the 325. German infantry and armor took the town of Regne on his right flank, then lost it to a vicious counterattack by the 325. That night a German officer on a motorcycle rode into the town, assuming it was still under German control, only to be captured by glidermen. He had with him the plans of the 2nd SS Panzer Division for an assault through Werbomont to Liège. They intended on attacking through the 325 area. Knowing his glidermen were badly stretched, Gavin ordered the weary 504th, still bottling up Peiper and holding off the 1st SS Panzer Division in the northern part of the battle area, to leave a thin line facing Peiper's position and send the rest south to meet the new threat. The 508 was becoming ever more heavily engaged by 9th SS Panzer Division.

The confusion wrought upon the Germans by the channeling of their attack had abated, and the three Panzer divisions now knocked at several of Gavin's doors. He had to fight a miniature three-front war on the defensive, with the German threatening at the north, south, and center of his position, and the Germans kept trying to outflank the 325. Gavin anticipated each threat, but his division front now ran for 25 miles against pressure from hundreds of tanks and the best infantry the German Army had left. By December 23, the far flank held by the 325 looked particularly bad when he checked it himself. "At that time, Billingslea's regiment was deployed with riflemen 100 to 200 yards apart, very little antitank defense, and a serious threat was developing near the [Baraque de Fraiture] crossroads. I went to the town of Fraiture and proceeded from there to the crossroads. I encountered such a tremendous volume of fire that it was suicide to go any further. Small arms fire was ricocheting in all directions. Interspersed with this was artillery, mortar, and tank fire."

The Baraque de Fraiture crossroads fell that afternoon after a pitched battle. Forty-four of the 116 soldiers the 325 had sent to hold it managed to successfully withdraw.

Gavin's right flank was crumbling, and he had no more men to fill the breach. He jumped into his jeep and headed for the headquarters of Maurice Rose's 3rd Armored Division at Manhay, where the next strike on that flank was anticipated. Could he count on the 3rd's tanks if the Germans folded the flank completely? Gavin found no one at Manhay or any Americans anywhere near where the 3rd Armored Division was supposed to be protecting his flank. He wrote in the official after-action report, "At this point it was evident that there was nothing to prevent the forces from entering the rear of the division area." What Gavin did not know then was that Montgomery had ordered General Joe Collins's VII Corps to prepare a counteroffensive directly into the teeth of the German attack, rather than attacking through St.-Vith as Hodges and Ridgway had advocated. Actually, he wanted Collins to attack from the front to place additional forces between the Germans and the Meuse so he wouldn't have to send British troops to do it. The 3rd Armored had been ordered to join Collins's corps, so those units not engaged had already left. Angry, Gavin drove back to corps headquarters at Werbomont, where he found Ralph "Doc" Eaton, Ridgway's chief of staff. Gavin wanted support, especially tank support. Eaton told him he had none to give. Gavin wrote of the encounter, "To my amazement, the Corps Chief of Staff showed no reaction whatever."

Words, though now unrecorded, passed in the encounter. Eaton later called Gavin "A goddamn Black Irishman, looking out for number one." He blasted Gavin for his lack of gratitude to Ridgway, who had promoted Gavin to command his favorite division. Clay Blair, Ridgway's meticulous biographer states that Eaton was curt with Gavin that day. He intimates that there was jealousy between Gavin and Ridgway. Aside from the argument over Ridgway's Holland visit, the young, handsome Gavin and his dashing 82nd received much press, and Gavin, as always, courted it. Eaton saw Gavin as disloyal. But the fight seems less a display of disloyalty than Gavin's natural anger over the possiblity of losing his position —or even his division—because support he had been promised was not there. Though Ridgway and Gavin had long been distant, James Gavin had always had the gift of concentration. In a crisis as severe as that which faced him that December 23, it is doubtful personal animosities were an issue. Gavin was a proud division commander with a long reputation for calm under fire, and he would not have appeared personally at corps headquarters to ask for help unless he believed the situation was serious. He was one strong flank attack away from disaster, he knew it, and he could do virtually nothing about it without support. Eaton's reaction to his request makes his anger understandable.

Profoundly alarmed, Gavin could do little more than tell the 325th to extend its position and hold on while he moved more of his 504 troopers away from Peiper's front to cover the division command post. And Ridgway did react to Gavin's desperate situation. Forces retreating from St.-Vith were badly battered, but they were the last that Ridgway had. He threw the 7th Armored at Manhay, and on the morning of the December 24, Combat Command B of the 9th Armored under Brigadier General William M. Hoge reported to Gavin, telling him his troops were too exhausted to fight a sustained action but were at his command. Fortunately, the front remained relatively quiet Christmas Eve morning—by Bulge standards—and the right flank stabilized. It's clear that Gavin would have relished battle that day, so confident was he in the training and toughness of his troops; but as it turned out, morning brought not the sounds of attack, but an order from Montgomery's command post to preapare to withdraw. The plans sketched out would draw the 82nd's sector of battle back to where they had first deployed after arrival at Werbomont, back to their starting-line days and many lives before. It would be a shorter, easier line to defend. A withdrawal of the defenders at St.-Vith also had been ordered.

Decisions had been made further up the chain of command, decisions that may have saved Gavin's troops from a likely fight to the finish, even annihilation. General Ridgway, on orders from above and in accordance with Montgomery's view that the St.-Vith pocket made for a "messy" battlefield, informed Gavin that they would "tidy up" the lines by withdrawing from the positions Gavin now occupied.

Montgomery made of it an opportunity to rub in his superior judgment (he had wished the retreat two days earlier, part of his "tidy up the battlefield" idea) by sending a grandiose authorization: "They can come back with all honor," he wrote. "They come back to the more secure positions. They put up a wonderful show."

When Ridgeway had made a last visit to the St.-Vith pocket, he had found exhausted men, tanks and vehicles mired in the mud, dozens of heavy guns, which would have to be abandoned, and large dumps of gasoline that would be eagerly used by the Germans if the retreat became rout. It became one of Ridgway's finest moments. He acted forcefully, summarily relieving the despondent General Jones of his overall command and installing Hasbrouck, visiting the suffering troops on the perimeter, urging calm and order. But Ridgeway's wish, that the retreat be accomplished that night, proved impossible. The mud and confusion precluded night movement.

Then, fortuitously, with the dawn of the 23rd, the weather front suddenly pushed through to the east, dropping the temperature still further, enabling the tanks, half-tracks, and towed viehicles to move. Best of all, clear skies permitted Allied aircraft to swarm into the area for the first time in several days, making it impossible for the Germans to move armored forces. About 15,000 men, one hundred tanks, and seven 155-mm howitzers and tow vehicles retreated successfully; remaining guns and stocks of gasoline were destroyed. These were the units that saved Gavin's right flank.

The 82nd Airborne withdrew from its positions the night of Christmas Eve, 1944. By this time, Gavin fully understood the need for a withdrawal, but part of him hated the idea. He wrote later. "By dark the last of the St.-Vith forces had passed through the 82nd and except for a few abandoned and damaged vehicles and artillery pieces in our area, there was no evidence of their transit. But a withdrawal is never a pretty sight. Intuitively, I felt I did not want to start a withdrawal of my own in the wake of what we had just seen."

Gavin also knew that the tactical retreat would not sit well with the troopers, who had taken as true writ the boast made by the division after Normandy, "No ground gained was ever relinquished." Paratroopers also felt loath to retreat for fear wounded might be left behind to be maltreated by the Germans, as had occurred in Sicily, when captured troopers had been murdered, and in Normandy, where troopers had been shot while hanging helpess, entangled in trees.

It would be the first retreat in the division's history. He hated to do it, and Ridgway hated ordering him to do it. "He [Ridgway] had unbounded faith in the 82nd; he believed it was a wall of steel that would hold no matter what the Germans threw at it." Gavin wrote in his diary, "This has been an experience the like of which I hope I never have again. It will be invaluable to me in future years." His troopers, too, hated it. "The

fact is that the troopers did not like to withdraw in front of the Germans.
. . . Rather than withdraw, if the troopers had had their way, they would
have much preferred to attack. Besides, they knew they had beaten the
Germans in every tactical engagement so far, and they did not see why
they should not resume the offensive."

But the bitter pill was swallowed Christmas Eve. Gavin would never
forget the details of the scene. "It was a very cold, bright moonlit night.
The snow was packed on the few hard-surfaced roads, and it crunched
when one walked on it. I was out most of the night with the troops during
the withdrawal." First he went to the 508, which alone of the retreating
regiments was attacked during the maneuver, when the 9th SS Panzer hit
it in force. They fought their way out, and at about 10 P.M. Gavin turned
his attention to his "own" regiment, the 505. This time his affection for
his old regiment almost cost Gavin his life. Driving in an open jeep in the
bright moonlight, he first ran into a platoon of paratroopers patrolling to
try to find a reportedly large group of Germans well behind the American
forces. One trooper in a jeep had seen Germans taking cover and acting
evasive as his vehicle approached and had sped on, outnumbered. Another
had claimed his jeep was shot at and damaged while he was out repairing
telephone lines.

The mysterious force was some of Peiper's remaining tankers and infantry but without their machinery, which had slowly come to a halt
from lack of gasoline. So desperate was Peiper's fuel situation that the
Germans tried an abortive unmanned parachute drop—which landed German supplies not on Peiper, but on the bemused troopers of the 505.
Peiper, with about 850 men (out of over 5,000 he'd started with in his
Kampfgruppe) left the tanks, hid by day and fled southward on foot by
night to rejoin whomever he could find still advancing west. But to do
this, he had to pass through Gavin's forces, then themselves in the act of
retreating. But for a miracle of chance and Gavin's continuing luck,
Peiper's men might have killed or captured Gavin as he drove the moonlit
roads. Gavin, determined not to get sidetracked away from the withdrawal, left investigation of the incidents to the 505 patrols, and Peiper's
escaping Germans did get into a brief shoot-out with the 505. In the end,
both forces sucessfully retreated through one another amidst sporadic but
sometimes violent close-quarters firefights.

The Germans seemed emboldened by the Americans' tactical retreat.
They promptly attacked near the just-vacated 82nd Division southern

wing and overran and destroyed nearly an entire regiment of Hasbrouck's retreating 7th Armored Division. One regiment of the 9th SS Panzer Divison stayed in close pursuit of the 508 and hit them hard just as they settled into their new positions. On the 27th the rest of the 9th hit the 504 at Bra and the 508 again in front of Erria, and the 62nd Volksgrenadier Division assaulted the 505 and was repelled with little difficulty. "The German division was roughly handled by the 505th. It was a poor division, not well trained," commented Gavin.

The 508 faced sterner stuff. "The Panzers came in screaming and yelling in a mass attack," Gavin remembers, "there were far more Germans in the attack than we had ever seen before. The 504th stopped them in their tracks." (One batallion of the 508, was overrun and had to counterattack in the morning to retrieve its position.) Gavin surveyed the battle area in daylight. Sixty-two German bodies lay in a single field before the machine guns at Erria, where the 508th had counterattacked. Once again Gavin listened as youthful Nazi prisoners told interrogators that they had tried the costly frontal assault because it had worked before against Americans in the Ardennes.

In the days after Christmas, the German Ardennes offensive exhausted its supplies and reached its limits. The withdrawal and the last attack on the Salm spelt the end of the first part of the Bulge for the 82nd and Gavin. During ten days of almost continual battle, the division had lost 76 officers and 1,618 men, 185 German prisoners were taken. Gavin noted in his diary on December 31, "Our Army has a hell of a lot to learn, but at present these airborne troopers of this division are making monkeys out of the Germans opposing them. They are better trained and far superior combat soldiers. The German has better armor, Panzerfausts, mines."

It had not been a bloodbath for the Americans, and it had been a singular triumph for Gavin, though not in the press. When the two divisions, the 101st and the 82nd, had first deployed, it had been Gavin who had decided which would go where. A spur-of-the-moment decision had sent the 101st to Bastogne, and there, cut off and encircled, the Screaming Eagles became immortalized by the press as the "Battling Bastards of Bastogne," while the 82nd's desperate duel with three panzer divisions to hold the northern shoulder of the Bulge had gone unnoticed. The surrounded 101st became America's heroes, for its energetic defense, assisted by a ragtag assortment of survivors from ruined units, and for one of the war's most famous messages: "Nuts!" Brigadier General Anthony McAuliffe's answer when asked to surrender the city by German Brigadier General Heinz Kokott. If the Bastogne story needed any more glamour, that was supplied by the attack from the south by the flamboyant Patton and his legendary drive to reinforce the defenders.

Yet many students of the battle conclude that it was the tough and unglamorous action of units like the 82nd at the shoulders of the break that destroyed the German plan. Time and the maps of the battle, which show the Bulge reaching its greatest extent to the south, have caused many to forget that the Germans were trying to push north. It was their failure to crack the northern shoulder that caused the Germans to fail in their thrust for the Meuse bridges and Antwerp, forcing them southward. The northern shoulder was where the weight of Sepp Dietrich's panzers was supposed to break through, and that was where the 82nd had met them.

The significance of the part played by the 82nd was that Gavin's force, in an emergency, was thrown into a role for which it was in no way trained and equipped, with no armor, no effective tank defenses except captured Panzerfausts, and little artillery. Yet the 82nd had dramatically outfought the enemy. They had withstood the assault of four of von Rundstedt's best remaining divisions and had wrecked the northernmost and quickest German route to Antwerp.

The 82nd had also provided a shield behind which divisions that never should have been facing the German assault or that were badly damaged at St.-Vith, could find safety. Now, without a pause, the 82nd would go onto the attack.

At a time in the war when the United States had a preponderance of matériel might—more trucks, more tanks, more howitzers, more planes —Gavin's paratroops enjoyed few of these advantages in battle against the Germans, and they were at a severe disadvantage against enemy panzer divisons. Yet they were consistently effective. After the Ardennes, they were considered the troubleshooters for any action that demanded speed and determination.

Shortly after Christmas, with the German fury spent and the 82nd holding new, quieter lines, Gavin was invited to First Army Headquarters by First Army Chief of Staff General William Kean and commander General Courtney Hodges. The mood was congratulatory, relaxed. All there knew that von Rundstedt's gamble had failed. The weather had broken, aircraft flew again. From the air, tank tracks etched on the deserted and snowy fields of the Ardennes stood out like accusing pointers. The tide was receding and the advantage was all to the defenders.

Equal in rank with most of the other men but far junior in years, Gavin was somewhat surprised to hear conversation "return again and again to Montgomery, Patton, and the daily newspaper *Stars and Stripes*." He also felt surprised at the ignorance of front-line conditions his fellow generals exhibited. He heard firsthand some of the violent resentments and jealousies that had come near to splitting the Allied forces into two warring camps—something Hitler would have welcomed above all. But to the top officers of First Army that evening the complaints were two: that Montgomery had seized the headlines by his access to the British press (as *Stars and Stripes* duly reported) and that Patton had stolen the headlines with his frequent aggressive proclamations, which always made good copy.

Gavin knew well the importance of publicity and its uses. It was part of the fabric of his makeup, part of his theory of command, one reason he carried his M-1 with him everywhere.

But at this point in his career, Gavin *believed*—in the army, in the U.S. cause, and in his superiors. Though he would sometimes complain of Ridgway's ambition, he called his boss "Undoubtedly the best combat corps commander in the American Army in World War II." It was only after the Bulge, after his first real experience in coordinating actions with other large units in a crisis, that it began to occur to him that some above him might have feet of clay and might be blinded by desire for glory and advancement.

Patton, that slightly larger-than-life figure who had staged the "relief" of Bastogne by turning around his tank forces and charging, like the cavalryman he was, toward the beleagered city from the south. Patton, always ready with the bloodthirsty quote and resplendent with his polished helmet, jodhpurs and twin ivory-handled revolvers, was a lightning rod to reporters and cameramen and every story sent two jolts of electricity—one increasing the pride and morale of Patton's own men, the other raising prickles of resentment among his West Point peers.

It was never clear how best to handle the press. Showboats were despised, and men who quietly declined to be interviewed—men of deep reserve like Courtney Hodges—often found they were considered less able to "inspire" their troops.

Of course First Army command knew that it was their troops that had stood the shock and held firm. "Yet, when *Stars and Stripes* arrived daily, it was full of stories about Patton and his Third Army and how the defenders at Bastogne were winning the battle," Gavin would write. The story that stuck in all craws was the one about Patton and the chaplain. Patton had ordered a chaplain to write a prayer for good weather. And when he had written the prayer, it found its way directly to a prominent box on the front page of *Stars and Stripes*.

Almighty and most merciful Father, we humbly beseech Thee of Thy great goodness, to restrain these immoderate rains with which we have had to contend. Grant us fair weather for the Battle. Graciously hearken to us as soldiers who call upon Thee that, armed with Thy power, we may advance from victory to victory. And crush the oppressions and wickedness of our enemies, and establish Thy justice among men and nations. Amen.

Patton's direct line to the Almighty was too much even for the glacial Hodges.

First Army staff went directly to *Stars and Stripes* and insisted that a seperate First Army edition be printed. And so it was.

12.

THE ROAD

TO BERLIN

The Allies followed the Ardennes offensive, the last lunge of a badly wounded German Army, with a counteroffensive as inevitable as it was ponderous. Montgomery, still empowered by Eisenhower to manage the northern sector of the Bulge, mounted one his characteristic slow, phase-lined, cautious advances.

On December 22, with the concurrence of Field Marshal Model, Von Rundstedt had asked Hitler to halt the offensive. Hitler had refused. The Germans continued attacking even as Patton's forces relieved Bastogne on December 26, and the weather cleared, allowing Allied aircraft to pound German columns mercilessly. The master stroke was now a calamity. Hitler called a halt on the 28th but would not order a retreat.

The Germans had concentrated all the resources they had. Every day of battle, the straining animal that was the German Army grew weaker as its strength leaked into the winter. After December 26th, measured in gallons of gasoline, in tanks that could move, in men without wounds, in artillery shells, the Battle of the Bulge was over—and perhaps the war. Only the nerve centers, where German staff officers pored over situation maps and weighed alternatives, still functioned efficiently. There pale men continued giving orders that others struggled to obey, trying to salvage something.

In the Allied armies the feeling was very different indeed. Commanders knew the offensive had badly hurt the Germans. Omar Bradley, furious over Montgomery's elevation to command of the northern half of the Bulge, had prodded Monty to launch a counteroffensive to coordinate with Patton's even as the weather cleared on December 23. But Bradley found Montgomery would not attack anything "until he was certain the enemy had exhausted himself." Bradley called Eisenhower to put pressure on Montgomery to attack but got no satisfaction there either. Then Montgomery overstepped himself and publicly asserted that he should be commander for all Allied ground forces. Eisenhower finally decided to sack him, and Monty, like it or not, relented. He was now forced to assume the offensive. The attack would begin January 3, 1945. First Army would attack from the north, and Patton's 3rd Army would attack from Bastogne, but Monty did not have in mind a daring penetration designed to cut off German Bulge units but something far more methodical.

Gavin chafed to get on with the attack but hated Monty's plan. "The Army's attack plan was based on a huge turning action, pivoted on Stavelot. It was as though a huge stable door were being closed. The movement of the divisions would be controlled by phase lines." Monty believed in his "tidy battlefield," and he made certain that in this attack, no division would advance faster than another. The Germans were the masters of the quick counterattack, and Monty wanted no one exposed.

Then there was the snow. Many inches had fallen during Christmas week, and now the Ardennes was nearly impassable. Coupled with Monty's doctrine, it made for exactly the sort of ponderous warfare Jim Gavin had taught himself to avoid at all costs. Gavin wrote, "It was frustrating, indeed infuriating, to watch the Germans begin to move weapons into position . . . where we could not interfere with them except by artillery fire. We knew they would be there once we resumed the attack." Gavin, correctly, felt that deep attacks through the German defenses, particularly from the north shoulder of the Bulge, would panic the stalled German divisions farther to the west and probably cut them off, much as Bradley's plan had envisioned.

Gavin felt his paratroopers had more honors yet to win. The Bulge had reinforced his long-standing faith that their training and morale made them capable of nearly anything. He also knew the foe well. The superior discipline and experience of the German soldier still made him formidable, but he still hated close-quarters combat, the very thing Gavin's troops were the masters of.

And he felt they had truly invested something, because the Bulge had already cost the division heavily. By December 31 the division had taken 1,694 casualties, and no replacements arrived to fill the vacancies. As a stopgap measure, the 82nd received the 517th Parachute Regiment, an independent parachute regiment that had been fighting elsewhere in the Bulge, to somewhat bolster the ranks. As usual, the bulk of the casualties had been in the infantry companies, the fighting teeth, and some companies swung into the offensive way below half strength. The support units, nearly half of division strength had lost little by comparison.

On January 3, the 82nd jumped off into the attack. Gavin, typically, stayed as much as possible with his forward units. One officer of the 517 (since this unit was new to the 82nd, Gavin spent a lot of time with it) recalled, "How he found the time and energy to be constantly with his front line troops and still direct the overall activities of the division was a mystery. He did it with outstanding success." And it almost got him killed on several occasions. But his spirits rose with the action. He jauntily noted in his diary, "Came close to getting shot at Grand Halleux when I had to dive into one of our foxholes to avoid a Schmeisser that was squirting in what a quick estimate led me to believe was my direction." Then he bemoaned the weather. "Conditions have been very rugged. Temperature about 18°F. Snow, wind. It is amazing how these lads live sometimes."

By this time of the war, Gavin had come to believe that appearing at the line like an ordinary soldier lent him a kind of protection. The Germans, he reasoned, seldom fired at single figures because of the almost certain reaction from numerous comrades. He also had an unhealthy scorn for German marksmanship. "It is an interesting fact that the Germans would rarely attack one person with such a weapon as a machine gun unless he was very, very close to them, and I never saw them display rifle marksmanship skills at any distance comparable to that of the Americans," he wrote.

Gavin's attack, because of the temperature, the snow, and limited "phased" objectives dictated by Montgomery was an odd and inconsistent drama. On the first day, the 82nd slogged its way through the snow into hard fighting but swiftly overran the remnants of the 62nd Volksgrenadier Division and the 9th SS Panzer Division, bagging 2,400 prisoners.

Then, after a few short days, they were halted by higher command because they had reached their phase line and had to wait for other units to catch up. Gavin noted of the 62nd Volksgrenadier Division in his diary, "One regimental CO, Col. Franke, of the 190th committed suicide, his adjutant surrendered. He was guilty of advising his troops against taking prisoners, so it is just as well that we did not get our hands on him."

Next they moved virtually unopposed through heavy snow and tall trees to get to the heights overlooking Thier-du-mont and Vielsalm. As he drew up, Gavin saw the ground he'd been forced to relinquish back in December. From his vantage point, Gavin saw an unbelievable sight: a German truck column toiled toward them unaware. The 505 allowed it to approach then hit it with devastating fire in close quarters and captured all the surviving Germans. The troops revealed that they had been in corps reserve and had been sent to bolster the 9th SS Panzer Division, which no longer existed.

Gavin knew now that the enemy was in disarray and rankled even more at the limitations of the phase lines. Perhaps it was his impatience that caused his next near brush with death as he roasted a 517 lieutenant for lingering in a pit in the open. While he administered the motivation, a German mortar crew emphasized the point by zeroing in on the pit. Gavin drily told them that if they stayed there, they'd be killed anyway and without accomplishing anything. The lieutenant never forgot Gavin's words that day and reminded the general of them when he saw him after the war. "Lieutenant, get off your ass and get going!"

The next day he again checked the 517 and found a mine field with a cottage next to it. Smoke came from the chimney, so he crossed the mine field to check the cottage. Inside were a dozen troopers drinking coffee and getting warm with no guards posted. Gavin quickly chased them out, then while recrossing the mine field, he became the sole point of interest for a German 20mm flak gun. "They were shooting at me and missing, with the projectiles ricocheting off the trees and off the road. They had apparently let me go by the first time," he noted laconically.

January 8 found Gavin ever more impatient. "We finally were allowed to resume the attack," he noted. But bad news came with the renewed offensive. Ben Vandervoort of the 505 had been seriously wounded in the head, a shell fragment having passed through his left eye severing a nerve. "He had been commanding a company and then a battalion since Sicily," Gavin noted, "and the veterans among us believed the chances of his luck running out were quite high." Vandervoort survived, however, and lived to an old age.

Yet Gavin never relented from exposing himself to fire. The day after Vandervoort was evacuated, while observing a platoon of the 325 in a heavily forested area, Gavin again came under fire. Earlier, Gavin's aide, Olsen, had been wounded in the left leg in close proximity to the general. Now accurate artillery fire wounded him in the right leg. The same burst severed a trooper's leg completely just feet away while the frozen ground erupted and the tops of fir trees showered down. Gavin's diary recorded, "I was very lucky. The boy between Olsen and myself had his leg severed just above the knee. I put a tourniquet on him, and to our surprise we saved his life. Olsen gave him the morphine. His leg flew across the road, and for a moment, Olsen thought it was his." Olsen recovered and was back by Gavin's side within a month. Meanwhile, the offensive ground on.

In this stop-and-go battle, the 82nd faced a German force struggling against extinction. But Hitler ordered a battle of attrition, and attrition bled Gavin's forces badly, thanks to German gunners and Montgomery's phase lines. The Germans adapted to the phase lines. They became obvious on German maps, and the defenders had ample time to place defensive strong points in strategic locations. The defenders had all the advantages. Wounded men frequently froze to death while awaiting evacuation. One battalion of the 517 had only 110 of its original 839 effectives by January 10. It was so bad, that Gavin withdrew the battalion, and it was soon deactivated.

The 82nd pulled out of the attack on January 9, after reaching the Salm. But after warm food and some rest in the area of Chevron and Pepinster, they returned to the line on January 28 to be paired with the fine 1st Infantry Division to break through the Siegfried Line, the concrete-and-steel fortifications erected as a permanent barrier to the invasion of the Reich. The snow slowed progress severely. "[It] had become so deep that the attacking formation, usually a battalion, would have a lead man wade through the snow, which was then waist deep, for fifty yards or so, to be replaced by another man." But when they reached the Siegfried Line, the much-vaunted fortifications turned out to be mostly abandoned.

Ridgway exulted in the sight of the predawn attack on Hitler's border defenses. It was the final stage of the war, and he had planned his own surprise. The Germans were used to heavy artillery bombardment before an attack, this time Ridgway ordered total silence when the paratroopers set off into the snowy fields at 4 A.M. They attacked in muffling snow, no artillery or covering fire, an unheard of risk attacking rigid defenses. "I don't think any commander has ever had such a magnificent experience as to see these two splendid divisions [the 1st and the 82nd], both veteran outfits, at their highest state of combat effectiveness, attacking side by side. It was a joy to see . . . like two great race horses drawing head to head to the finish line," Ridgway wrote.

The shock was complete; the troopers captured some Germans deep in their bedrolls, but the rate of advance remained slow. An impatient Eisenhower called it off on its fourth day, January 31, after just 10 miles of penetration. This mortified Ridgway, but Eisenhower, backed by Montgomery, felt the effort futile because of weather and resistance.

Gavin made his final attack on the morning of February 2 in spite of the fact that he knew the offensive was over. The assault carried the division 2 miles into concrete "dragon's teeth," tank defenses. Then inescapable orders arrived for the division to prepare for an offensive elsewhere. The 10-mile advance was hailed by Ridgway as "near heroic," but Eisenhower was willing to forego the heroism for better weather and faster movement. "It was a very rough deal," wrote Gavin at the time, "Five days of attacking through country entirely devoid of roads and even in many cases, trails. Deep snow hampered all movements throughout and the Krauts resisted quite bitterly. Fortunately, after the first day we had him on his ass, and it was simply a case of going fast enough to keep him there."

Gavin felt furious that the Army did not exploit the 82nd's penetration. "To our dismay and disbelief the penetration into the Siegfried line at Udenbreth was not exploited. In fact the entire 1st and 82nd sector was taken over by the 99th Division as a holding mission. The background is that Field Marshal Montgomery obtained the go signal to launch an attack with the British and Canadian armies and the 9th U.S. The U.S. 1st is protecting its southern flank. Thus the build-up is to be abandoned and much of our sweating and losses were in vain. Difficult to explain this sort of thing to the troops. It is surprising how influential Montgomery is. . . . We have got to learn to take risks to gain combat successes. Nothing ventured, nothing gained was never more true."

Having been called to a crisis in the Bulge, the 82nd was called to another one: to help secure the Roer dams and trap fleeing German forces who could (and did) open the floodgates. The idea was for the Americans to take the dams before the Germans flooded the Roer Valley and created a significant obstacle for the final advance into Germany. The rise of freezing water flooded the Roer basin, delaying a complex Allied operation, Grenade, which was to send the U.S. Ninth Army across the Roer and into the flat beet and wheat fields leading to the Rhine and beyond.

The 82nd fought in vain to prevent the flooding during the first two weeks of February 1945, but the action brought Gavin face to face with the grisly results of the bloody and wasteful fight at the Huertgen Forest, where German defenders had nearly destroyed the 28th Division the previous autumn.

Gavin being Gavin, and believing that combat commanders should always reconnoiter the battlefield personally, set off into the Huertgen as soon as he arrived. He walked into a melting graveyard of the 28th Infantry Division with growing dismay. As Gavin walked, scrambled, and rode his heavily used jeep over the steep ridges, slippery trails, and through the somber trees of the Huertgen, he saw evidence of a military disaster—a bloody stalemate where troops had died and disappeared in the snow, where wounded had been abandoned to freeze to death, where he knew sound tactics had been abandoned, and where thousands of Americans had died facing well-concealed and hardened defensive complexes of concrete bunkers and pillboxes. It was a mass graveyard, and unretrieved rotting corpses littered the forest where they had fallen months before.

The day's reconnaissance seared its images into his memory: "Our orders for the following day were to attack across the Kall River Valley from Vossenach and seize the town of Schmidt. By now most of the snow had melted; there was only a small patch here and there under the trees.

"I proceeded down the trail on foot. It was obviously impassable for a jeep; it was a shambles of wrecked vehicles and abandoned tanks. The first tanks that attempted to go down the trail had evidently slid off and thrown their tracks. In some cases the tanks had been pushed off the trail and toppled down the gorge among the trees. Between where the trail begins outside Vossenach and the bottom of the canyon, there were four abandoned tank destroyers and five disabled and abandoned tanks. In addition, all along the sides of the trail there were many, many dead bodies, cadavers that had just emerged from the winter snow. Their gangrenous, broken, and torn bodies were rigid and grotesque, some of them with arms skyward, seemingly in supplication. They were wearing the red keystone of the 28th Infantry Division, 'The Bloody Bucket'. . . .

"I continued down the trail for about half a mile to the bottom. There a tumbling mountain stream about six feet wide had to be crossed. A stone bridge had been over it, but had long since been demolished, and a few planks were extended across the stone arches for the use of individual infantrymen. Nearby were dozens of litter cases, the bodies long dead. Apparently, an aid station had been established near the creek, and in the midst of the fighting it had been abandoned, many of the men dying in their stretchers. Off to the right, about fifty yards, a hard road appeared. Across it were about six American anti-tank mines. On this side of the mines were three or four American soldiers who had apparently been laying the mines and protecting them when they were killed. About ten feet away was a string of German anti-tank mines. On the other side of the mines were three or four German dead—a dramatic example of what the fighting must have been like in the Huertgen. It was savage, bitter, and at close quarters." As Gavin cautiously surveyed this scene, he wondered how it could have happened, why this isolated and relatively worthless piece of real estate, too steep and precipitous for anything but forestry, became the grave site for so many Americans? Why had they attacked through this terrain rather than bypassing it? Why had they fought through it tree by tree? Why had no commander ordered these brave men scattered about the forest floor properly buried? Modern World War II historian, Russell F. Weigley echoes Gavin's 1945 sentiments: "An army which depends for its superiority on its mobility, firepower, and technology should never give battle where those assets are at a discount; the Huertgen Forest was surely such a place . . . the motives for fighting in the Huertgen remained largely negative."

Repeated attacks against stout German pillboxes, concentrated artillery fire, exhaustion, and cold badly mauled several divisions and two in particular, the 9th and the 28th. And because of the weather and the terrain, the Army Air Forces could do little to help. Lack of real knowledge of terrain, and the inherited World War I habit of following one disastrous frontal attack with another had culminated in a military disaster. Gavin hid his mounting fury as the 82nd moved in under cover of darkness. Years later, he remembered vividly comforting a young replacement who stood struck with terror and about to vomit at the sight of the bodies about him: "He began to turn pale, then green. . . . I talked to him, calmed him a bit, and assured him that we never abandoned our dead, that we always cared for them and buried them, I knew his state of mind."

Climbing from the bloody valley, Gavin walked to the high ground where the roads were. It was the route by which the battle could easily have been bypassed. You could drive straight down to Schmidt in a jeep or a tank in minutes. "The following morning I went to Lammersdorf and met the commander of V Corps [General Leonard T. Gerow] and the Commander of the Division whose headquarters was in that town. Obviously the attack on Schmidt should have been made straight down the ridge from Lammersdorf. Lammersdorf and Schmidt are connected by a paved road; the terrain was a mixture of woods and open farm land, good tank country, and it would have been a much simpler tactical undertaking than crossing the Kall River. The question in my mind was how in the world they had ever gotten involved in attacking across the Kall River Valley? Why not stick to the high ground, bypassing the Germans in the valley, and then go to the Roer River? I raised this question with a corps staff officer present, but he brushed it aside. I asked why in the world they had attacked through the Huertgen Forest in the first place, but apparently that was a 'no-no' question. . . .

"I noticed that the corps commander and the division commander were bent over a map. The corps commander occasionally drew a short line, a quarter to a half of an inch, with a blue grease pencil. It represented an infantry battalion, and he was suggesting to the division commander a tactical scheme by moving battalions about. I had the strangest feeling when I realized how remote they were from the realities, from what it was like up where the battalions were. The thought crossed my mind that the disaster that had befallen the 28th Division might have had some relationship to the lack of understanding in higher headquarters of what the actual situation on the ground was. It turned out to be true, as I later learned."

Gavin's disapproving analysis of the Huertgen battle became a subject of an infantry course later, to teach young officers how not to approach such military problems.

After the shock of seeing the neglect those infantrymen in the forest had been shown, he noted in his diary, "Much of their tanks, jeeps, weasels, arms, etc., abandoned. Their wounded and dead left on the ground now rotting. If only our statesmen could spend a minute hugging the ground under mortar fire next to a three months old stiff! We just simply have got to stop wars!"

Following Gavin's meeting, the 82nd pushed down to Schmidt and on to the Roer River within twenty-four hours and with few casualties. Next they were to cross the fast-moving and turbulent Roer. Perhaps it was the picture of the dead in the Huertgen gullies, perhaps it was the attitude of his fellow commanders, or the evil, ghost-ridden atmosphere of the place, but for the first time, Gavin did not long for the moment of decision.

German guns overlooked the point where his men were to cross, and the artillery had already zeroed in on the embarkation points. Obviously the crossing must be at night. They would ferry troops across in rubber boats, by cable, until they had enough men to establish and hold the bridgehead, a shoestring operation, but possible. He still didn't like the idea, and he rehearsed it. "I began to experiment with rubber rafts in the Kall River near the Roer, and it was disastrous. The river was flowing so fast that it tossed the rafts around like corks and the rafts collapsed and the troopers were thrown overboard into the icy water."

But once again his luck held. For the first time, Gavin avoided an operation. As he told the story, an eager young division commander longed to try his troops with the daring plan, and at an XVIII Airborne Corps meeting, spoke with envy of the 82nd. Gavin quietly saw that he got his way. "We were delighted to give him the mission," Gavin wrote. The crossing of the Roer proved a costly and difficult affair, but not for the 82nd. By that time, the paratroopers were on their way back to their former homes at Sissonne and Suippes for a rest.

The role of the 82nd, beyond jumping into combat, now stood well defined in the minds of higher commanders. The division's reputation had grown so that it—along with a few precious others like the 1st, 2nd, 4th, and 9th Infantry divisions; the 101st Airborne Division; the 2nd and 4th Armored divisions—would be used wherever decisive action was needed, theater fire fighters. Gavin himself became increasingly disdainful of the regular infantry he saw in the late stages of the war. In mid-January, noticing the reluctance of troops feeling the war would be over soon, he wrote, "If our infantry would fight, this war would be over

by now. . . . American infantry just simply will not fight. No one wants
to get killed, not that anyone does, but at least others will take a chance
now and then. Our artillery is wonderful and our air corps not bad. But
the regular infantry, terrible. Everyone wants to live to a ripe old age.
The sight of a few Germans drives them to their holes."

On February 10, 1945, long weary of waiting for Montgomery's authorization to jump off into the Germans in the Bulge offensive, he wrote,
"It seems to me that it takes two different temperaments in this army.
One is for regular ground divisions and a different [one] for an airborne
division. The airborne trooper gets furious, impatient, and finally disgusted with the vacillation and delay in getting going in a ground fight
with ground units. They take forever to plan and stage a show and then
they get nowhere when they start. The analogy of hitching a racehorse
to a plow is no fallacy."

Soon after they arrived back from the Huertgen, they were forced out
of some of their valuable space in their stone barracks to make room for
a hospital. A happier Gavin recorded, "190 nurses, they are rather welcome. . . . Met a Lt. Peggy Knecht of 242 at the propblast and dragged
her to a movie last night. Rather interesting." But the rest of February
was hard work training replacements, reequipping, and reorganizing. Rumors with some truth to them flew about a Berlin drop. They called the
mission Eclipse, and it was under serious consideration. Finally, Eisenhower scratched it when he decided to let the Russians get there first.

Gavin marveled at the political maneuvering in the midst of ending a
very bloody war. "How in the world can it be arranged for the Russians
to wait at one street while we load up and jump a week later? Even now
they are close to Berlin," he told his diary on March 12. "I'd sure like to
live through combat jump five. I believe that five are as many as one man
should be given. Beyond that is too much. . . . There is a drain on the
courage of a man that cannot be replaced."

As if to prove his point, he jumped a few days later with the 508 and
watched in disbelief as a C-47 transport lost a propeller, dove into the
parachutists from the plane ahead, and carried six of them to the ground.
Gavin immediately jumped again after the crash. "Thought it a good idea
to jump with the troops in the P.M. and did so uneventfully," he noted
laconically. "Marlene Dietrich here Tuesday. A bit demanding and expectant and in a way surprisingly unattractive. Had an interesting conversation with Mrs. Ernest Hemingway [Martha Gellhorn, war correspondent

and later Gavin's mistress] . . . she was particularly interested in my political views." A few days later, Gavin's view of her had changed dramatically. "March 22: Well, Miss Gellhorn turned out to be quite a person. I have never met her likes and would just as soon not in anyone else. She took the damn place apart. It was wonderful. There will be no more visits with her here." There would be personal visits with her elsewhere though, and with Marlene.

Meanwhile, the spring of 1945 became an increasingly political time for Allied generals. They had awakened to the fact that they would go into the history books. Montgomery was naturally at the heart of it. During and after the Ardennes offensive, Monty's voice rang loud through the press with disdainful remarks about American generalship. He painted himself as the hero who had saved the bungling Americans in the Bulge. Then he had sent an infamous letter to Eisenhower demanding command of all ground forces because, he said, "I am so anxious not to have another failure." Eisenhower had nearly relieved him.

So angry were the American generals who had directed the Ardennes fight that they became determined to overshadow Monty's lavishly planned, publicized, and supported final offensive with spectacular successes of their own. They hoped these would bleach away the annoying stories of Monty rescuing the inept Americans with wise battlefield counsel amidst the chaos of the Ardennes attack. The resentment reached clear back to Army Chief of Staff General George Marshall, who cabled Eisenhower directly about the Montgomery demands: "Under no circumstances make any concessions of any kind whatsoever."

For such successes, Eisenhower and his most trusted commander, Omar Bradley, would have to reach for the Rhine, for the Elbe and make sure that the troops who first reached each milestone were American. This required troops who were willing to risk their lives in the spring of 1945, when almost everyone on both sides knew the end was a matter of time. They needed men who would risk being the last men killed in the war— airborne troops.

But now Gavin had real questions on how airborne troops would be used. The Huertgen haunted Gavin at his comfortable billets at Sissonne. He wrote, "It was into this that the 9th Infantry drifted on September 19. In less than four weeks the division lost 4,500 men, one casualty per yard gained. This was not the worst loss, however. The 28th lost 6,000."

Gavin's greatest fear was not the past, but the future. "I think it is fair to say that little was learned from it and less understood. It had been our Passchendaele." With the conviction of a political innocent, Gavin remained outspoken all his life in his blame of the senior officers who allowed Huertgen to happen. Now, sitting amidst the politics of impending victory, he suspected that he might be a less than full-fledged member of the political army. Gavin always believed mistakes offered something for the future. Huertgen was the worst mistake he saw in World War II, because it was senselessly caused by poor leadership. Gavin wanted the thing to be fairly studied and blame assessed. It never was— at least, not until many years after the backslapping of victory ended, and then not loudly.

Then too, he saw the war differently from many other general officers and now realized it. He fumed at what he thought was complacency and timidity. After the war ended, he always remembered the Market-Garden failure, the unexploited Siegfried Line breaching, and the indecisive political behavior of Eisenhower over how to beat the Germans. He summed it up with: "By mid-1944 most of our military decisions were made on the basis of absolute certainty not to fail; ultimate success appeared inevitable and could wait. This attitude seemed to permeate the lowest of commands, and venturesome, skillful tactical schemes were rare indeed. Methodical phase-line-by-phase-line attacks were preferred. The thought often occurred to me that a 'Stonewall' Jackson would have been given short shrift as a tactical commander. He probably would have been relieved for falling back or giving up ground."

The proposed Berlin drop focused Gavin's perspective more on the present, though, and he had some misgivings. "It was a sobering prospect, especially to the veterans with four combat jumps." The "old-timers" had been sweating since Normandy.

Under the plan, the 82nd would land two parachute regiments south of Tempelhof airfield while a third took the airfield itself. The total airborne assault force would be two American airborne divisions and one British airborne brigade. After some training, Gavin decided that the mission was indeed possible, and he thought his troopers just might pull it off. Still, he was pleased when it was canceled. He understood it as part of the politics of upstaging Montgomery.

He kept on training his division to prepare for whatever else might come, and he listened to the rumors. The final fall of Germany was to be Monty's show. Eisenhower had already approved a massive effort, that included the 17th Airborne Division, to force a crossing into Germany. American units not expecting to be part of it, like the 82nd, had much to speculate on. Under consideration then was the removal of men who had been wounded or had served a long period in the war zone. These men would be sent home first. Eminently fair, it would wreak havoc with the 82nd, Gavin knew, because the bedrock of his troopers' efficiency, morale, and skill, rested with the longtime troopers and noncommissioned officers who had made multiple jumps and learned the arts of war firsthand. There were many such men in the 82nd, and they would be the first to leave the battle zone if those with the highest points left first. Then there was Japan: pressure already mounted to get the best units to the Pacific to prepare for the invasion of Japan.

On March 7, Gavin was invited to Reims to dine with Eisenhower and several senior airborne officers. (Also present but unmentioned in Gavin's recollection of the evening was a coguest of honor, General Maxwell Taylor of the 101st.) Eisenhower war biographer David Eisenhower notes that the purpose of the dinner was to talk "about airborne operations in the American sector to gain a Rhine bridgehead."

The two young airborne division commanders and rivals put on their shining best for Eisenhower, but Gavin, the younger, would not forget that history was made that night, because in the midst of the meal, Eisenhower received a call from Omar Bradley, relaying the news that General Courtney Hodges's First Army had seized an intact bridge at Remagen, an isolated Rhine city deemed of little import, south of Bonn.

The news caused elation at the dinner, for not only had Americans made the first crossing and gained an invaluable route across the wide river, but also now the possibility was suddenly open for the "broad front" instead of grudging support for Montgomery's northern attack on his single axis. Here was an American success to tell the world. It was clear then to Gavin that a new horizon had appeared for action to end the war and to upstage the ponderous Montgomery.

Instead of hesitating or conferring, Eisenhower forgot for a moment his ingrained caution and approved Hodges's plan to anchor the bridgehead. He ordered Bradley by phone, "Hold on to it, Brad. Get across with whatever you need, but make certain you hold on to that bridgehead." He suggested moving four or five divisions across the bridge immediately. By next morning, Eisenhower had turned pessimistic and cautious once again. He had already made up his mind on Monty's crossing, and he wanted all forces to close on the Rhine in a broad front before he exploited any crossing. Bradley, meanwhile screamed for support so he could drive on into Germany.

On March 23, Montgomery's fully orchestrated Operation Plunder, including the airborne assault, Varsity, came off successfully. American casualties were comparatively light except among the 17th Airborne Division paratroopers who jumped to secure the opposite side of the river for Monty's bridgehead. Gavin, who had never before seen an airborne operation he wasn't fighting in, grabbed a lumbering C-47 to go watch from 2,000 feet. Other notable spectators for the 10 A.M. assault were Prime Minister Churchill, Eisenhower, and British Chief of Imperial General Staff, Field Marshal Sir Alan Brooke. It may have been the last time people could gather to view the spectacle of a modern battle. Gavin was horrified by the weakness shown in this daylight exercise of his chosen method of warfare, "At one point I counted 23 transports or gliders going down in flames, trying desperately to make it back to the west bank." The low-flying, slow-moving transports were fat targets for the veteran antiaircraft gunners, skills honed by years of battling the bomber stream. Most of the burning transport craft were C-46s (19 of 72 were lost that day), not fitted with self-sealing tanks; in contrast the C-47 formations lost a far lower percentage of aircraft. The C-46 proved to be a flying death trap when hit, as leaking fuel flowed toward the fuselage from the wing tanks. It was never used again as a troop carrier, on General Ridgway's orders.

Flak accounted for most of them. If there had been an opposing air force, there would had been carnage. While the troops who crossed under artillery and small-arms fire in assault boats escaped almost unscathed, 44 transports crashed (of 1,696) and 159 airborne troopers of the new U.S. 17th Airborne Division died (522 were wounded, 260 missing, of whom many were recovered). Gavin found himself wondering from his seat beside the C-47's window if it was all necessary, if ground troops could not have done it as well at far less cost. And he concluded again that the elaborate "set-piece" battle calling for enormous amounts of preparation, matériel, and men was a relic.

Gavin would also realize that these few minutes of spectacular airborne assault (17,000 paratroops in two hours) were the high point but also the death knell for the airborne concept he had fostered and mastered. How much longer would it be possible for fleets of slow-moving aircraft to assemble and stream toward a target in broad daylight? One weapon, the 88-mm flak gun, had accounted for most of the damage to the transports and gliders. Another superior and ruinous weapon that the Germans had at hand (but didn't use), the Me 262 jet, could have wrought havoc with the airborne landing. New technology had appeared during World War II: jet aircraft, V-2 rockets, massively improved vehicles, assault rifles, and much more. Even then, he pondered how that technology might change future battles, and his sixth sense told him that World War II might be the last fight of its kind.

The 82nd soon returned to the fray. Their station was on the west bank of the Rhine, centered on Weiden near the old cathedral city of Cologne, which had been flattened except for the mighty cathedral, which, Gavin noted, had been mainly spared, even to its windows. Officially, the 82nd remained in strategic reserve. They filled a portion of the line, but orders dictated that they not enter sustained combat. However, on his way to Cologne, Gavin spoke with Lieutenant General Gerow, now commander of the 15th Army, who instructed him to patrol aggressively while locating and identifying German units across the river. Gavin drily reassured Gerow that being aggressive would not be a problem.

What was a problem was that for the first time since Italy, Gavin found himself in an administrator's role. Part of Gavin's charge was somehow dealing with a camp containing 10,000 Russian prisoners of war whom the Germans had left behind. Gavin was fascinated by the Russians, finding them a "spirited lot" who had organized their POW camp thoroughly, giving it a unified command and regular briefings on the war situation on hand-drawn maps. They begged him to let them loose to take revenge on the citizens of Cologne. Gavin, with the aid of an interpreter, was forced "to harangue the crowd for about an hour" from the hood of his jeep to explain to the Russians why he simply could not have rioting, looting, and mayhem. "The displaced persons, slaves really, are quite a problem," Gavin wrote, "especially the Russians, who love nothing better than to beat up or rob a German. Next to burning his home to the ground or robbing and looting, they like this best." It was a static situation for a division accustomed to movement, with only patrols to run, and the river intervening between the Americans and the enemy. Trouble with the troopers at once began over fraternization with the local women, something utterly forbidden by higher command, who feared that innocent American youths might be easily corrupted and seduced by

Nazi propaganda. Curiously, General Patton was convinced of this point, and when Gavin told him that what was going on was not fraternization in the sense of political fraternity but a simple call of nature, Patton spluttered, "Gavin, you're as nutty as a fruitcake."

Anxious for activity, Gavin thought it would be interesting to test various antitank weapons on a few of the numerous German tanks, some of them the formidable late-model Tigers, which the Germans had abandoned on the wrong side of the Rhine. He was gratified to find that the captured Panzerfaust, his favorite from the first, was "by far the best weapon." Yet it would take someone of his sanguine spirit to use it properly. He admitted it worked best "if one was ready to wait until the tank was within approximately fifty yards." Others preferred more dangerous games during this twilight war. Colonel Reuben Tucker, the ever-brash commander of the 504, who had been crossing the river nightly on patrols to capture prisoners, decided that it would be easier to patrol, if instead of making the tiresome and risky crossing of the fast-flowing river, they simply seized a German town on the other side and used it as a strong point. Tucker's crossing of the Rhine April 5–6 was a success; and with little resistance, Tucker cleared the town of Hitdorf and prepared to establish himself there. The Germans, however, were nearby in great force (some 325,000 trapped in what was called the Rose pocket) but in a passive posture, waiting for the end while holding their ground. They took violent offense at this daring raid and reacted as if this were another major Rhine crossing, hurling in first an artillery barrage, then an assault force, and when that was driven off, the 504's opposite number, the German 3rd Parachute Infantry Regiment drove the Americans to the last houses before the water. Tucker's troopers withdrew with one officer and five enlisted men killed, and in high spirits, claiming 150 Germans dead. This was the kind of action Gavin always condoned for morale purposes, but he got a roasting from his corps commander, Major General Ernest Harmon, who told Gavin that part of his job was to keep the 82nd intact—no casualties—for the next airborne assault. Gavin thought he meant Berlin. Years later General Harmon told him that the assault that high command had in mind for the 82nd was the mainland of Japan.

Not even Ridgway knew what was planned for the 82nd, for he had persistently asked for Gavin's division (and Taylor's 101) for the Ruhr campaign. Already they were, in a way, helping him by tying up Germans across the river; and, as Gavin chafed to go, it became a massive roundup that ensnared 317,000 German troops, including 25 generals, 200,000 slave laborers, and Field Marshal Walther Model's four-door Mercedes-Benz convertible (which Ridgway gave to Omar Bradley). Model, who deserves credit for refusing to obey Hitler's final orders to destroy Germany's industrial heartland, committed suicide April 21 after surrendering. Meanwhile Gavin fumed on the "wrong side" of the Rhine.

As Montgomery's advance to the north continued at its slow pace, the American high command devised the final plan for the destruction of Germany. Originally, it was to be Monty, attacking from his spectacularly gained bridgehead, who shattered Germany and drove to Berlin. He intended on taking American units as he needed them to flesh out his own drive. But American commanders had bridgeheads of their own, Bradley at Remagen and Patton to the south—and they were keeping their troops engaged to justify not giving them to Montgomery's plodding, phase-lined attack. Under pressure from his own generals to turn them loose, Ike changed his mind and, convinced that the closer Russians should crack the hard defenses of Berlin, he opted for a broad attack that used all the bridgeheads and had its main thrust forward the Dresden-Leipzig area. Along the way, Patton's southernmost forces would cut off the Germans from entering the feared "National Redoubt" in the Alps, a —mythical as it turned out—vast fortified refuge in which Hitler and his most dedicated troops supposedly planned to carry on the fight indefinitely. Marshall supported the plan and gave it his blessing on March 27, 1945. American units flooded Germany shortly thereafter, while in London, Churchill fumed over the Allies' giving Berlin to the Russians.

The northern thrust and the sealing off of Denmark from the Russians was Monty's task, but by mid-April he was way behind the rapidly advancing Americans in the south, and it appeared the Russians would reach the Jutland Peninsula first, while he sat on the Elbe. Through every channel of communication available, including a face-to-face blasting, a furious Eisenhower prodded Montgomery to get moving. Monty retorted that he needed additional units to get the job done. Eisenhower informed Monty that he would be given the XVIII Airborne Corps. The Supreme Commander had selected Ridgway, who had just finished shattering Model's Ruhr pocket, for another important and glittery milestone of conquest: the crossing of the Elbe below Hamburg to isolate German forces on the North Sea and Baltic coasts. Bradley immediately spoke personally with Ridgway to impress upon him how important it was to seal off Denmark first and offered him any units he needed. Ridgway did not forget the young commander that he often treated as a son, and to whom he gave respect, preference, and even on occasion his jealous rage. As his biographer Clay Blair records: "his first choice was almost a foregone conclusion, the 82nd Airborne. It was no longer required for strategic reserve or occupation; it could move faster, it was still Ridgway's first love and he wanted it under his command in what would certainly be the last operation of the war." He got Gavin. He also wanted and got the 7th Armored Division, the 82nd's frequent teammate during the Bulge battles. Additionally, high command gave him the 8th Infantry Division and the 6th British Airborne Division. Though plans for the crossing put British units across first, Ridgway was not planning to stand still and allow the British to proceed at their usual pace. Bradley had made it clear he believed that only a rival American force that would threaten Montgomery's triumphal march to Berlin could speed the British field marshal along.

April 29 was set as the Elbe crossing date. That same day Gavin was directed to assemble the 82nd at Bleckede. Giving his men no time beyond what it took to disembark their vehicles, Gavin got his troops moving into the attack. The 505 would cross during darkness in collapsible wood-and-canvas assault boats, no life preservers provided, and secure the opposite side of the river; then work would commence on the bridge. Gavin, peering through binoculars at Germans digging defensive emplacements 1,000 yards away across the water in the fading afternoon light thought the plan "marginal." But timing and preparation proved the key. Swarming across in the light boats at 1 a.m., the 505 confidently made short work of the Germans in their foxholes. Amphibious vehicles and engineers who started to build a long pontoon bridge for tanks followed right behind as the 505 quickly consolidated control over the ground around the landing site—a peacetime ferry port—but at daylight the Germans began furiously bombarding the engineers and their bridge-building teams from farther east. Sensibly, some of the engineers proved loath to lose their lives in the war's final days and took certain shelter under the east bank. It led to one of Ridgway's best-known exploits. The general strolled out onto the pontoons that had been laid in place, amid the falling shells, to prove that artillery rounds landing in the river did little damage —their shrapnel burst harmlessly underwater—meanwhile telling the engineers, "I don't see why an engineer shouldn't get killed the same as a doughboy." This won him a second Silver Star. (He also ordered heavy American guns to knock out the German batteries.) The engineers finished the bridge in thirteen hours and another, smaller bridge in a little more than six, sacrificing thirty-two dead and wounded. The engineers later disputed this, Ridgway's version of the story, saying that they had been working when Ridgway made his appearance, but the story has passed on into Ridgway legend.

The day the 82nd crossed the Elbe, Hitler and his wife Eva Braun committed suicide in the *Führerbunker* in the heart of Berlin.

"Reached the depths the day before on a reconnaissance in Hitaker when I came across a pig eating a dead Kraut. The noise that he made was more bothersome than the act. I could hear it at lunch. I have seen enough of war for a lifetime," wrote Gavin as he realized the war was nearly over. A few days earlier, April 13, he'd felt far differently: "I want to get to the Pacific," he wrote, "As this thing approaches a wind-up, I realize that I will have a frightful peace. Fighting and excitement have become my daily sustenance, I miss them after a while. I will die as a quiet civilian."

With his troopers, meanwhile, Gavin raced eastward all day May 1, hearing rumors that the Russians, advancing westward, were close ahead. The next morning, as was his habit, he wheeled out at dawn to find them. Bouncing along in the open jeep was like a joyous romp: "the fields were freshly green and flowers and chestnut trees along the road were in full bloom. The roads and streets were deserted," he wrote. But as he proceeded, a half mile ahead he saw the unmistakable bucket helmet and leather coat of a German soldier on a motorcycle. The German cut off the road, aware of the jeep. Gavin ordered his driver to give chase; and kneeling over the jeep's windshield, he began firing with his M-1. Gavin —who never hesitated to kill a German when he had the chance—missed this time. Something made him hesitate to kill this man. "We soon overtook him, and as he caromed into a ditch beside the road, we took him prisoner. He was the last German in the war we were to see running away." Now Germans gave up singly and in units as fast as they could. Gavin ran into "large groups of Germans in patches of woods on the horizon. They seemed to be milling about indecisively and to be not particularly desirous to fight. It was an eerie sight for those of us who had fought for more than three years all the way from Africa, for the mere sight of the bucket helmet meant certain death unless one reacted instantly and instinctively, taking cover and firing. So, taking our lives in our hands, we drove right up to them. They wanted to surrender." So anxious were they to avoid capture by the Russians, that as the day wore on, Gavin's jeep steered unharmed through a great stream of them, "young and old, crippled and wounded, robust and ailing, men and women, but mostly men, were trying to get through the town to get to our rear." Gavin stopped, as ordered, to "take" the unresisting town of Ludwigslust.

It happened by the chance of war but became one of the defining events of Gavin's later life. The town was small and chaotic, crowded with German soldiers and civilians fleeing the advancing Russian Army, with which Gavin's far-ranging scouts had already made preliminary contact. The town was notable for an exquisite palace, the home of the Mecklenburg princes. It had already been suggested to him as a suitable headquarters. Gavin was well aware that the meeting with the Russians would be historic and would happen momentarily. There were to be other surprises, however. The first was a trooper who came up to him and said "Sir, there's a German general looking for you." Gavin, fresh from the chase of the fortunate German motorcyclist, wore his usual paratrooper's jumpsuit as he stood in the town square with his rifle slung over his shoulder and his tin helmet on, "looking like any other GI in the 82nd except for the two stars on my collar and on my helmet."

Duly the general appeared, "Rather haughtily, I thought, and a bit threadbare, but otherwise impeccably attired in the field gray uniform of the Wehrmacht. It was set off by the red collar tabs and insignia of a general and an Iron Cross dangled at his throat. When I told him I was the American General, he looked at me with some disdain, saying I couldn't be; I was too young and did not look like a general to him."

Gavin quickly persuaded him he was who he claimed. The general then announced that his superior, General Kurt von Tippelskirch, commander of 21st Army Group, wished to talk terms of surrender. Gavin said von Tippelskirch should meet him at the palace at eight. Further fantasies played out in real life before Gavin's eyes that day.

There were the Hungarian cavalry regiments, both mounted on "splendid" horses, who urged Gavin to let them fight with him against the Russians. There was the parking lot with 2,000 German vehicles, 125 half-tracks and trucks, thousands of small arms and machine guns that materialized when Gavin gave the word that prisoners were to surrender their arms and equipment if they wished to move to the rear. And there was the trooper who found a concertina. Standing by the side of the road, he serenaded the column of defeated Germans with "Lili Marlene." Tears rolled down their cheeks, but the 82nd troopers only laughed.

Then there was the return of the lost troopers. Five 82nd troopers who had been POWs, four of whom had been captured in Sicily and one in Italy, suddenly strolled into 82nd lines. They had been held in East Prussia, but their panicked guards had taken them west to get away from the Russians. Then suddenly the guards disappeared and the troopers found themselves on their own. In one of those fantastic coincidences of war, the first Allied soldiers Bill Grisez, Dick Rooney, John Rinkovsky, Garcia, and Lindsey found were 82nd troopers. A happy Grisez said at the time, "The first free Yank we saw was a Sicilian veteran from the same gang we jumped with. He told us we'd missed the show at Salerno, Volturno, Anzio, Normandy, Holland, the Bulge, the Siegfried Line, and the Elbe." But these five had their own story to tell—having been moved throughout camps in Italy and Germany, then enduring a 500-kilometer hike to get back to American lines.

That evening, as the rapid advance approached the Baltic coast and the effective sealing off of Jutland, Gavin found himself accepting the surrender of a complete army group, more than 150,000 men, at a polished table in the palace, underneath oil paintings of family members that hung on damasked walls yet untouched by the war. Von Tippelskirch wanted only to make it known he was surrendering to the Americans and not to the Russians. Incredulously, he asked Gavin to tell the Russians to halt their advance. "Of course, I had no control over what the Russians would do," Gavin noted; so he offered only to accept an unconditional surrender. The German accepted the bargain, a surrender document was typed, and the man and his staff were coldly but correctly sent to the rear and into captivity. Uneasy troopers and staff members looked on with obvious dislike in their eyes. Enemies such as these could never really be friends.

The English-speaking owner of the palace appeared in Wehrmacht uniform and asked if he could spend the night there. A hardened Gavin replied that if he spent the night in American lines it would be as a prisoner of war. The man asked him if he would take good care of the palace. Gavin asked him if he knew how much care the Germans had given Coventry, and the German retorted, "No, but I know what the Allies did to Cologne." Gavin responded by describing exactly how abused Cologne had been, then he sent the man on his way to captivity. Gavin spent the rest of the night in a sumptuous bed in one of the palace's principal rooms. But he was disturbed at dawn by a messenger with news that the mayor of Ludwigslust and his wife and daughter had committed suicide at the town hall. The event puzzled Gavin, who had firmly warned his troopers against "the abuse of German civilians."

Two days after the suicides, Gavin discovered the hidden horror that had hung around the mayor's neck to his death: Woebblin concentration camp was his secret shame. The camp was not an extermination plant like Auschwitz and Buchenwald. There were no gas chambers or crematoriums. It had been hastily built when the Eastern Front had cracked in 1944 to take thousands of political prisoners whom Hitler had ordered moved. It held about 4,000 prisoners, not all of them Jews.

But in the last three months of the war, food, as well as almost every other commodity, had been in scarce supply. Under the Nazi system of provincial leadership, mayors of towns were responsible for maintaining emergency stores of grain, tinned goods and other essentials for the support of their districts, and were answerable to the Gauleiters, the Nazi overlords of the district. In the case of Ludwigslust the mayor had simply starved the poor wretches in the Woebblin camp to maintain his level of food stocks.

When Gavin heard rumors of the camp, he drove immediately to it. "One could smell the Wobelein [sic] Concentration Camp before seeing it," he wrote, "and seeing it was more than a human being could stand. Even after three years of war it brought tears to my eyes. Living skeletons were scattered about, the dead distinguishable from the living only by the blue-black color of their skin compared with the somewhat greenish skin taut over the bony frames of the living. There were hundreds of dead about the grounds and in the tar-paper shacks. In the corner of the stockade area was an abandoned quarry into which the daily stacks of cadavers were bulldozed. It was obvious they could not tell many of the dead from the living."

Gavin, as the absolute master of the town of Ludwigslust and the surrounding territory, confronted the people of the town in the most direct way possible with their participation, either active or passive, in the starvation of a large percentage of the inmates at Woebblin.

This he did by forcing leading citizens to dig graves and bury dead victims in orderly rows in the large park before the palace where he maintained his 82nd Airborne headquarters and occupation forces head-quarters. Close to 1,000 deaths were laid to the camp. He also forced the entire adult citizenry, plus a good many of his German officer prisoners, to observe conditions in the camp and witness the burial ceremonies.

He publicized the events by arranging for a French film crew to film the entire affair, including shots of the prisoners, the guards, the towns-people filing past the open graves, while paratroopers stand guard. Gavin's pale face seems incredibly young and untouched amid the horror.

The film shows better than any words the contrasts, the unreality of conditions that human beings had hardly ever seen before; and it recorded emotions so strong that it is a mercy the film is black and white and silent, except for the French narration. The German soldiers stream into captivity, broken men with lost expressions, some smiling vacantly, some staggering as if drunk or on the edge of collapse. They are just men, from grandfathers to sixteen-year-olds, humanity in ruins. Some hold themselves with a stoicism and weary strength. Raw rage, on the other hand, hatred and disgust, fills the faces of the townsfolk who are forced to endure being filmed and to watch the end result of their allegiance to Hitler's regime, however passive it may have been. There are faces in that film that do not bear watching, and they are not only the now-familiar faces of the starved victims, but the faces of their captors and tormentors. They, too, seem destroyed in a different way. One of Gavin's daughters, Line Lewis, recalled that Gavin had from time to time showed that film to his children and that he never failed to cry.

"One Jewish boy named Paul was from Budapest. He had been thrown into a concentration camp at ten and four times he had been to the gas chambers and four times they had withdrawn him at the last moment," Gavin wrote. "One was Peter G. Martin, a sixty-seven-year-old Paris works manager, who two years earlier had made the mistake of ques-tioning Nazi politics. We found a Dutch boy who had been taken shortly after our landings in Holland in the fall of '44 for being in disagreement with the German occupation in Holland. We made the mistake, at first, of getting black bread and cans of meat from the warehouse and delivering them directly to the camp. The inmates stormed and clawed the wagon and stepped on each other in the stampede as they fought for food. One frenzied man got up off his sickbed, the lousy straw that they slept on, ran a few yards, and dropped dead of convulsions. We stopped the distribution of solid food, and as quickly as we could organize it, hundreds of cots were placed in a hangar at a nearby airfield. Doctors were brought in and intravenous feedings began. It was a sad sight and I went by the hangar almost daily until the people were ready for more solid feedings and movement. The dead we buried in the park in front of the palace, where we required the leading German citizens to dig the graves and place the bodies in them. The entire population of the town was required to attend the burial service."

13.

THE RUSSIANS

Within twenty-four hours of the discovery of Woebblin, Gavin met his first Russian near the town of Grabow. It was another grand spring day, May 5. Two days later, General Eisenhower and the high command watched Colonel General Alfred Jodl put his signature to a document of unconditional surrender in a red schoolhouse at Reims, SHAEF forward headquarters. The war officially ended May 8, the surrender becoming effective on May 9, at 11:01 P.M.

Gavin was speechless. "This is it. . . . One doesn't know whether to cry or cheer or just simply get drunk," he wrote.

American dead, among almost 600,000 official casualties in Europe, numbered 135,576; other Allies had lost 60,000 dead, with 179,000 official casualties, figures that should make clear America's contribution and her cost in the battles of the West. A huge American army, over 4.5 million troops—61 U.S. combat divisions plus 30 other Allied divisions, stood at rest.

News of the surrender meant that German soldiers for the first time since the summer of 1939 were on their own. They chose to surrender to the nearest Allied unit, the practice in the West, or flee west in uniform or otherwise; surrender to the Russians was not something German soldiers did voluntarily.

Between the fronts, that unknown territory without people, the thinning slice of German land left between the weight of advancing armies, Russian and Anglo-American, confusion, folly, danger and joy all reigned.

There were senseless killings, drunken accidents, reported Russian acts of revenge and rapine. And there was simple silliness, the actions of men who have become so used to war and fear that the absence of deadly danger makes them dangerous. For suddenly masses of men—Germans, Russians, Americans—most of whom had none of each other's languages, were face to face, most of them bristling with weapons and all filled with bitterness of some sort.

The confusion and unreality of those May days, between the death of Hitler in his bunker April 30, which signaled the end of serious resistance by the German Army, and the restoration of order by the conquering Allies a month later can hardly be imagined now, almost fifty years later. On the ground, it was like two waves meeting, at first tentatively, then jostling together and, almost as suddenly, parting again. Few who went through the uncertainty, the hope, the terror and the wildness in the midst of hundreds and thousands of fearful, vengeful, or victorious soldiers will forget it.

Leonard Linton, a young 82nd Airborne translator fluent in both German and Russian, kept a diary to inform his commanding general about one man's madcap journey though Ludwigslust the day before Gavin arrived.

"Their surprise was extraordinary," Linton wrote Gavin of the Germans he met as he sped eastward in a jeep, "one or two started literally shaking from fear, some jumped up at Prussian style attention. This was an attitude I had already become very used to, caused by intense propaganda that US paratroopers usually committed atrocities. . . . Addressing the mayor [of Ludwigslust], who was the ranking official there, I told him in strong terms that he is to continue running the town in strict discipline, and that I hold him personally responsible for any and all matters that are contrary to our regulations. I kept them standing, addressing them harshly and accentuating my statements with my folded carbine. I asked about the little castle's utilization for our commanding general and the best house where we would install the offices and billets for the military government.

"I told the man [at the castle] we are taking over the place and to remove the several tons of files cluttering all the nice rooms in something like two hours. When he told me that this is humanly impossible I told him that the windows were big enough for our men to throw out everything. . . .

"I continued driving and on leaving Ludwigslust had nearly a collision with the first two drunk Russians I saw riding wildly in a brand new liberated German military Volkswagen. They were deliriously happy to kiss and embrace a Russian-speaking American. Luckily for me their vodka bottle contained only a tiny mouthful, which they forced me to drink literally at gunpoint. They did not know the names of any towns but waved to Grabow in response to my question where their outfit is. I asked them to lead me there. We could not get their Volkswagen into reverse, so we pushed it around by hand and off we went.

"Just on entering Grabow they ran out of gas but would not leave their car. There was a lot of loose shooting going on by staggering Red Army soldiers and officers. . . . There was what appeared to be a discipline breakdown and dangerous wild small-arms shooting into the air and at random targets. I saw no Germans whatsoever. I returned to Ludwigslust and miraculously met up with my commanding officer that evening. We were engulfed by a mass of Germans, from generals, naval personnel, civilian and concentration camp inmates in their striped clothing; they kept streaming westward. My CO questioned many (via myself) and we tried to keep the stream flowing until we went exhausted to our new billet for a few hours of sleep realizing for us the war was over."

Linton's CO would not wait for the Russians to come to him; wanting as usual to see for himself, Gavin, in his jumpsuit, rifle at the ready, headed east in his open jeep, driven by a noncom and accompanied by Captain Hugo Olsen. As they rolled into the open square of a small town, he heard firing. He was about 4 miles east of his front near Ludwigslust, at Grabow.

Gavin remembered the scene focused on a keg of wine surrounded by soldiers. The hogshead was shot full of holes by the Russians' rifles, and the men caught the flowing wine in their helmets and drank until they fell down or wandered, shooting whatever they fancied, into the side streets. As Gavin watched, a soldier smashed in a shop window with his rifle butt, stepped through the broken glass, and picked up a blue dress.

"I understand why the Germans do not want to surrender to them," Gavin noted, "they kicked in store windows, looted. . . . Drunks swooned about the streets flagging down vehicles. Their military courtesy was unusually good. . . . I would [as] soon fight them as anyone. The quantity of U.S. equipment in their possession was remarkable."

The meeting with the Russians dissolved into fragments, all moving too fast, all too different from the harsh logic of battle: the vision of a packed troop truck full of Russians coming toward Gavin's jeep, now properly adorned with a general's flag. It was veering slowly, deferentially, off to the side, until its wheels mounted a high bank and it gracefully toppled over to spill its human load in a tangle of legs and bodies onto the road. And the Russians laughed when Gavin stopped to ask if he could help.

Gavin's mission was simply to find who was in charge, "so I continued to the next small town, a couple of miles away. There on the main street were two very prim looking, Tartar featured, stocky, tough soldiers guarding the front of a building. They had Russian Tommy guns slung across their chests and looked at me rather menacingly. I inquired about the nearest Russian headquarters; that building turned out to be the Command Post of the Russian division commander I was looking for (CO of the Fifth Guards Cossack Division). I went into the living room of the house and introduced myself. Maps were spread on the table and I went about explaining our disposition. The thought crossed my mind that this must have been what it was like in 1939 when the Russians met the German Army in Poland. I suppose I thought along these lines because the Russians acted distrustful, as though we were combat enemies."

What Gavin wanted was to coordinate the dispositions of troops so the two armies didn't shoot at each other. He achieved that and prepared for a return to the United States, but before that eventuality the 82nd readied for another mission—to be the first occupation troops for Berlin. On May 5 the division was ordered back to Sissonne, and then to Épinal July 3 for special training for the occupation.

Gavin, meanwhile, faced an intense personal crisis, having been told the army planned to send him back to Texas to head a bond drive there June 10. He could leave the division to others safely now, but did not want to. The public relations mission came with its own reward—two weeks leave in the States, a prize most troopers would have risked death for. "It is hard to believe after all this time. My feelings are mixed. I do not want to leave the division at this time. Dominating all else at this moment is worry about P. [Irma/Peggy Baulsir Gavin]."

Gavin, badly bitten by Martha Gellhorn, was half in love with her, as well as continuing a relationship with Valerie in London. But the Gellhorn romance, with a woman who was a celebrity herself, both as Ernest Hemingway's wife and a popular writer for national magazines, was widely whispered about and was sure to have come to his wife's ears.

Throughout the war he had used the device of writing to his daughter to send news home to the long-suffering Irma Gavin, and by that means had kept his contact with his family without ever actually addressing his relationship with his wife.

The American trip was personal torture as a result. He dutifully returned to Washington where he visited his wife and daughter. "They were fine," is the total of the diary notation.

While in Washington, he got a taste of his new status as celebrity and hero. He called on General George Marshall and President Harry Truman ("both delightful to talk to"), and attended a tea with Secretary of State Henry L. Stimson.

He then returned to Mount Carmel, after a tryst in New York with Gellhorn ("A remarkable person") to a hero's welcome "A Hollywood homecoming," he wrote, and then disappeared to Long Island with Gellhorn, to her summer retreat on Fire Island, [on the beach for] "several days with Martha at Point of Woods—a delightful place, the first real vacation."

By July 3 he was back with the division at Épinal, France, without having resolved his personal future. The fate of the division was also uncertain. "Talked to Gen. Ridgway about Pacific prospects. Appears to be little chance. I am to go to Berlin and that's that. The division was slated for demobilization." August 2, he was there.

The division was chosen for this sensitive but highly visible duty for interesting reasons. It was Ridgway's wish of course—a kind of reward for his favorite soldiers, who he knew would be squarely in the public eye as the American press homed in on the greatest story of their lives, the victory over Germany. But it was no snap decision. Long before, a part of Bradley's reasoning for plans to use the division in the aborted air assault on Berlin included their unique combination of menace and polish. He felt it was vital to make an overpowering impression on the bomb-battered city and its defenders and instructed Gavin to have his troopers ready not only to do battle for Tempelhof airfield, but also to have with them their best uniforms.

It was a tack Gavin had always taken as a troop leader, and throughout the war the 82nd had striven to be the best dressed—or at least the "smartest"—unit on any battlefield or in any barroom. Like their leader, they sought to win every brawl, but appear minutes later unconcerned and unmussed. Ever since the first drop in Africa and increasingly with every airborne operation, the brown, highly polished jump boots had been the envy of other "straight leg" infantry units.

Early in the war, Ridgway made a policy stating that only jump-qualified personnel, that is troopers having made five jumps, could wear jump boots or jump wings—the only exception being men who had made a combat jump. By this formula, one combat jump equaled five training jumps. Glidermen, who matched the paratroops in almost every way, certainly in sangfroid, did not get their boots until later in the war, when Charles Billingslea, the first paratroop commander of the 325, took over the regiment after Normandy. When he got the command, paratroopers jokingly hung conventional infantry footwear all over his jeep. The 325 suddenly began sporting jump boots immediately after that.

During the serious business of occupation of an enemy country filled with a bitter and defeated people, Gavin came up with another device in tune with the 82nd's reputation and his own canny self-taught instinct for public relations.

He had his trusted officers select about 170 men—a company—stipulating that all be highly decorated and over 6 feet tall. These men, resplendent with honors, would be presented to visitors, newspaper people, and at all of the numerous ceremonial functions inherent in peacetime military life as the "honor guard" of the division. As an added flourish, Gavin ordered them to sport white silk scarves at the neck and white boot laces cut from parachute shrouds, and he allowed white gloves and pistol belts. Even a critic of troops as severe as George Patton said when he saw this group, "In all my years in the Army and of the honor guards I've seen, the 82nd Berlin honor guard is the best."

Gavin's men won praise as an occupying force during the summer of 1945. But many of them, and particularly Gavin, realized they were suddenly without a job. The smart honor guard rang hollow beside the planned and abandoned Berlin drop.

There was work, important work to be sure. The city had to be reorganized, for the "unconditional surrender" terms had stripped it of its Nazi government. There were thousands of bodies rotting in the subway system where Berliners had fled to avoid bombardment in the final, hellish days of April and May. There was barely enough food to provide a rationed daily diet for the population that remained. There was so little coal that Gavin ordered trees from parks and forests to be cut down and stored against the winter.

Complex and baffling to an outsider, these were problems not unlike those facing the commander of a division of soldiers—problems of shelter and food and supply and health and burial—and he had the men and the method to do these basic jobs, or organize the Germans to do them by themselves. The occupation was run under stringent and severe guidelines (Joint Chiefs of Staff Order No. 1067) which prohibited any economic help or help to rebuild Germany's economy. The directive was unworkable and gradually was put aside; it called for the occupying Americans to make the Germans solve their own logistical problems, not offering aid of any kind unless to "prevent starvation or widespread disease or such civil unrest as would endanger the occupying forces."

But the drift of political details that he saw daily, and the gutting of his division were bigger problems. "The Army, from a strength of eight and one quarter million in 1945, was reduced to less than 2 million in 1946," he noted dryly. But the way it had been done—by the point system, Gavin would say, "came close to destroying the military establishment." The reason was that points toward release from service were awarded for length of service, days in combat, awards and decorations. The better you were as a soldier, the earlier you left. "Soon," Gavin wrote, "it began to cut into the very bone and muscle of the organization."

And the politics thickened. After the riotous welcome and the drinking and the exchange of vodka-laced dinners had thawed relations between the Russians and the Americans in Gavin's sector, there came a chill from the East. Even before he was assigned the Berlin occupation, Gavin noticed a change in the attitude of his Russian counterparts. ". . . As the days went by, I noticed that the senior Russian generals were accompanied by their political commissars. The Russians began to behave a bit more quietly and more seriously and . . . in fact almost became unfriendly," he wrote.

Gavin assumed that this was the result of deliberate policy. Discomfited by it, he was far more upset that the United States had not formulated a policy of its own concerning Berlin and relations with the Russians. (Gavin would later learn from a Russian division commander he had befriended that the Russian officers' cool behavior was dictated by political commissars. The Russian general actually apologized to Gavin for his unfriendly behavior.)

Gavin's sure touch with troops plus the practical knowledge he had gleaned from a youth spent among coalfields and railroads brought the division new praise from SHAEF's top generals and swarms of visiting dignitaries, all of whom wished to see the ruined city and the remains of the Nazi monuments. For him it was a relaxing, prideful time, a time for picking up his romance with Marlene Dietrich, whose mother he arranged to slip from the Russian zone of occupation to the Allied side. Celebrity continued to crowd in on him. The diary entry for August 10 reads, "News of the first atomic bombing still crowds everything else off the front pages. It is frightening and unbelievable in its implication. Last night [photographer] Bob Capa brought Jack Benny and Ingrid Bergman by the house for supper about 2300. Had a nice time. She is lovely."

Gavin had become a soldier because, as he often repeated, he wanted to be where the decision was made. He had excelled at soldiering, now he began to see that the decision so firmly won in combat, could be lost without follow-up in the forbidden world of politics. Long before the subject became a bone of contention with scholars and historians, Gavin had begun to feel serious doubts about U.S. strategy at the end of the war. They never left him and would, in the end, be one more factor that would estrange him from the inner circle of top thinkers on U.S. foreign policy.

Gavin the paratrooper could not understand, for instance, why the SHAEF generals, led by Eisenhower, had not simply insisted on moving on Berlin in the war's last weeks, taking the surrounding German lands from the Baltic to Prague, which lay before the American Army.

He knew that it would have been the 82nd's and his personal assignment to capture Berlin as the leading edge of the paratroop operation Eclipse, which was designed to take the Berlin airfields and quickly land tons of supplies, guns, machines, and reinforcements. He had been "confident it could be done and regretted the decision that came in late April to cancel the operation."

The decision was not simple, Gavin knew. Competing interests pushed Eisenhower and his staff from several directions. Montgomery wanted the glory of the job, but he had proved glacial in his movements (or "pachydermial" as one famous memo put it). The War Department in Washington, on the other hand, had no single focus. It was still fighting a draining war with the Japanese, which might require, as General Douglas MacArthur predicted, an invasion of mainland Japan. There was in the spring of 1945 no assurance that the atomic bomb would work, that it would be ready, or that America would choose to use it against a civilian target.

The young general's thoughts were crystallized by an event in early

July, shortly after he took over as military commander of the American sector of the city. A parachute regiment, bound for duty with the 82nd in Berlin, had left by train from Magdeburg and somehow was switched off the "corridor" to Berlin to be lost in Soviet territory. Gavin personally commandeered a lightplane and went looking for it.

He found the lost troopers, and immediately arranged for their return, but the view from 2,000 feet gave him an awareness of the exposure of the Germans' greatest city, "clearly subject to Soviet control." Gavin felt that the defense of the Berlin corridor was a military impossibility and wondered how Eisenhower's staff had ever contemplated such an arrangement. He knew that the American broad-brush plan for the ending of the European war had been simplicity itself: invade at Normandy, push east with two powerful groups, one north, one south, reach the German border, and make the final conquest an envelopment of the Ruhr. Berlin had not even been considered until the capture of the bridge at Remagen. That had made the Rhine crossing possible for General Courtney Hodges's First Army, and Eisenhower had cautiously exploited that opportunity.

From that point on, the Americans were able to act independently of the British at their own pace and with their own objectives. Wrote Gavin: "It was the surprise crossing at Remagen that for the first time suggested the possibility of a plan other than that of reinforcing Montgomery and giving him the mission of seizing Berlin. It posed the possibility for Bradley and his army commanders to make an early thrust to the east. . . . Less than two weeks after the crossing at Remagen, [Bradley] spent two or three days at Sous-le-Vent, [a seaside mansion near Cannes] in a private meeting with General Eisenhower. That meeting enabled them to hammer out all the details of how they would bring the war to an end. Once the Ruhr pocket was taken care of, they would then move forward rapidly to the Elbe, hold on that river line, advance on the right toward Leipzig to break up the German armies, deny them the opportunity to establish a redoubt, and meet the Russians."

The plan had the benefits of simplicity. But it was a military plan, based in the practicalities of the day and the hour and the balance of forces. Gavin alone saw that there was no political plan. As David Eisenhower asks rhetorically in his grandfather's autobiography about the hush-hush conference at Sous-le-Vent: "What were Allied objectives?" and he cannot give an answer.

In fact the most important events of the Cold War in Europe—the disposition of Germany among the Allied victors and the subsequent "Iron Curtain" announced by Winston Churchill, fell into a strange black hole of diplomacy.

Partly, this was due to Franklin Roosevelt's final illness, partly to Eisenhower's lack of a clear political idea to present, partly it was due to Roosevelt's practice of excluding the U.S. State Department as foreign policy advisor, and partly it was due to the sudden, profound shift from attention on military matters.

And partly it was caused, as Gavin came increasingly to think, by the weakness and insularity of the State Department. Gavin was correct at least in this, for during the Roosevelt presidency the State Department had remained a branch of the government still in the hands of an entitled group of career diplomats from the best families, the best schools, but with few new ideas. Such ideas as they had were anti-New Deal and self-protective. It was natural for Roosevelt to leave them out and organize his new programs through other agencies. But when he died, the State Department heads were in no position to persuade Truman that they should formulate a plan for Europe.

So in the end Berlin was Eisenhower's decision to make. The other decision makers, from Roosevelt to Marshall to Robert Murphy, the State Department's official advisor to SHAEF, did not take a strong line on the matter. Eisenhower was convinced the possibility existed that the battle for Berlin would be costly, even to the extent of 100,000 lives, and after that, it might still be ceded to the Russians in a political deal. As Omar Bradley told David Eisenhower, "A heavy price to pay for a prestige objective, especially when we've got to fall back and let the other fellow take over."

Gavin felt that the State Department had fallen down badly on this vital decision. But Berlin was lost long before the final battles. Acquiescence to Russian control of large portions of Germany, including Berlin, went back to 1943 when far-ranging plans for the occupation of Germany were formulated by the Chief of Staff to the Supreme Allied Commander (COSSAC). Even before the Teheran Conference, contingency planners assumed Berlin would be deep within Soviet territory by the end of the war. Such plans, purely hypothetical, in this case slowly grew solid and gained stature because no one in leadership had alternatives.

At Teheran, where the only State Department official present was

Charles Bohlen, then acting as interpreter, the time was ripe to forge Berlin policy. It was, as Eisenhower's grandson and war biographer wrote, "the decisive moment." The Allies did not address the issue, choosing instead to avoid topics that would split the coalition.

Such vital details as a signed agreement for free access to the city of Berlin were never seen to, and as a direct result the Soviets came very close to seizing the city in 1948, and only the courage of the top soldier on the scene, General Lucius Clay, prevented it. But from 1944, the United States in the form of SHAEF had the power, the position, and the control and failed to use it. It was Eisenhower's greatest blunder. He simply accepted the status quo, believing sincerely that it was time to "bring the boys home."

To Gavin, this was profoundly wrong. From the ground where Gavin stood and the dinners he attended, it was obvious that the Russians were unified, their minds set on a clear agenda, to keep whatever military gains they had made and get whatever other territories they could.

As senior member of the Kommandatura, the governing body for the city of Berlin, Gavin had a brief but powerful exposure to a few of the men who would run postwar Russia. "I noticed that when Marshal [Georgi] Zhukov came into a room, everyone disappeared. I was invariably left standing, drinking and talking to him by myself. Such was the degree of fear that he seemed to cause among his subordinates. He apparently had the right of life or death and didn't hesitate to use it in combat to get results."

Zhukov was the Soviet's outstanding general at the end of the war; he had been Chief of the Russian General Staff in 1941 and suffered through the worst parts of the German invasion, but he had survived to command the four army groups that surrounded Field Marshal Friedrich Paulus's Sixth Army at Stalingrad in the early months of 1943, and had gone on to command the Russian center, the Ukrainian and Belorussian fronts in 1944–1945.

On April 7 President Roosevelt had sent his permanent military governor for Germany, Lieutenant General Lucius D. Clay, to SHAEF headquarters in Paris. It was Roosevelt's last important appointment, for the President would die at Warm Springs, Georgia, five days later.

Clay was a brilliant West Point engineer and New Deal administrator who would become the hero of the Berlin Airlift in 1948. Clay, like Eisenhower, received no political direction at all from the State Department. "It never occurred to me that they had anything to do with it," the brusque, authoritarian Clay, a complete Washington insider, told his biographer Jean Edward Smith. Clay and Gavin both got to know the dominant Russian military figure. Zhukov became friendly with the top Americans, General Eisenhower and General Clay, and created the same impression on these men as he had on Gavin. "Personally, I found him to be a very warm, intelligent and witty man. He loved to tell stories. At the same time, I could see he was one of the toughest individuals I had ever encountered," Gavin noted.

Gavin felt that a great opportunity was being lost before his eyes. "The problem was not on the battle front but in Washington," Gavin concluded. "President Franklin Delano Roosevelt had been his own Secretary of State, and when he became incapable of making decisions, action originated neither in the White House nor in the State Department."

If politics bothered Gavin, and his own future remained uncertain, the spring and summer of 1945 was a personal rejuvenation, a plunge back into vibrant, full-time life after three years of a suspended death sentence. Like most paratroopers, he went a little wild.

Usually intensely curious and interested in people with wider experience than his own, Gavin naturally gravitated to journalists, both because he genuinely liked them and because of the flattery that was completely natural between writers and their subjects. Correspondents like John "Beaver" Thompson and Bill Walton liked and admired Gavin because he was—charming and brave, stern and determined by turn, and a brilliant success at arms. Gavin returned that goodwill by giving them access to him and his troopers, quotes, transportation, even parachute drops into action if they had the nerve (Walton and Thompson both had.) The circle was completed when the journalists produced excellent insider stories of combat operations to thrill their editors and the public.

During that spring, while the 82nd trained for occupation duty, Gavin socialized with soon-to-be-famous journalists like photographer Robert Capa, radio's Charles Collingwood and others. Capa was a friend of writer Ernest Hemingway, then himself still on the upslope of fame. Hemingway was still married to Martha Gellhorn but was also accompanied by his current mistress and later fourth and final wife, Mary Welsh.

Hemingway's glittering acquaintances included Marlene Dietrich, who had been with the troops throughout 1944 and had enjoyed a tremendous popularity. Dietrich was a phenomenon, because of her Prussian birth, her remote and yet available sensuality, and her combination of hardiness and glamour. Often traveling in an open jeep, living on tinned hot dogs, and performing without makeup men or artfully placed lights—and frequently in or near the battle zone—Dietrich, forty-five, approached morale building with the zeal with which Gavin, thirty-eight, engaged the enemy. It was inevitable the two would meet. Yet when they did, while Dietrich was touring for the troops and the war was still raging, Gavin was not particularly impressed. But in Paris, they met again—more sympathetically.

By the spring of 1945, Dietrich had settled into the habit of staying at the Paris Ritz Hotel, where Hemingway stayed. Sometimes she was with another famous lover, General George Patton. Hemingway, who had been hearing about Gavin from Martha Gellhorn, "invited the general for drinks."

It must have been an unusual table. Cocktails could hardly have been necessary with Gellhorn and Mary Welsh sparring over Hemingway, Gellhorn eyeing Gavin, and Dietrich also taking in the trim young soldier with the stars on his shoulders and the neat gold pin under his tie.

Welsh was immediately impressed, but the other two women were instantly possessive. Army press liaison officer Colonel Barney Oldfield, a close friend of Gavin's and a ceaseless promoter of the 82nd Airborne, who had among other jobs that of Dietrich's protector, recalled: "Both were strong women, tenaciously determined, probably in the land of the Amazons, and [acted like] opposing warlords. There was always the impression that each resented the other and denigrated her. To Gellhorn, Marlene was 'that actress,' while Marlene thought of her as 'that writer.' These two women jousted for the attention of General Jim Gavin."

Gavin, never one to hesitate with a decision at hand, chose Dietrich and made off with her to his rooms that night, to begin an affair "conducted with the utmost discretion," Dietrich's biographer Donald Spoto writes, ". . . and continued with Dietrich following him back to Germany."

Throughout her USO tour, Dietrich had sought the help of the high-ranking officers to rescue her mother, Wilhelmina Dietrich von Losch. When Gavin went to Berlin as the occupation general in charge of the American sector, he sent an officer to the address Dietrich had indicated to find the sixty-nine-year-old woman, who was living in dire circumstances with an older sister with hardly enough to eat. Gavin made sure

she was well supplied with rations, and arranged for a reunion at Tempelhof airfield with Marlene Dietrich on September 19. The mother had not
seen her prodigy since 1931. She had gone through the war believing that
her famous daughter had been killed in the London blitz and the propaganda programs she'd broadcast in the summer of 1944 were only re-
cordings.

Gavin was so smitten with Dietrich that only a fierce storm kept him
from the funeral when her mother died of heart failure in November
1945. And Dietrich would continue to believe. She frequently told listeners that whatever happened in love, "when I devote myself to someone,
no one can undo it."

Irma Baulsir soon heard of the affair through a New York gossip item
about a "certain young general." She called it, on top of the gossip about
Martha Gellhorn, the death knell to the marriage. "Who can compete
with Dietrich?" she said.

The end of Gavin's Berlin summer came with Dietrich's departure for
Hollywood, with military pride and pomp, and a near-disaster for his
beloved division. Eisenhower established a Berlin headquarters for Clay
and his Berlin Office of Military Government, United States. To usher in
the new military overseers of the U.S. Zone, Gavin staged a Tempelhof
airfield military review in Eisenhower's honor in September. Gavin had
become increasingly skilled in staging such events. The maneuvers of his
perfectly turned out troops, including the towering honor guard, were
followed by precision drops of a parachute battalion and the landing of a
dozen gliders, which swooped down from the sky. Eisenhower and Walter
Bedell Smith, Eisenhower's chief of staff, were so dazzled that they suggested that he repeat the review for Marshal Zhukov a week later.

Gavin, of course, complied and sent an invitation to the marshal who
replied he would be delighted to come with twenty-eight members of his
staff. "Fortunately, I was living in the former home of German Gen.
Walther von Brauchitsch, [the former Wehrmacht commander in chief,
dismissed by Hitler for failing to conquer Russia in 1941] and we had a
dining room large enough to accommodate the group," Gavin wrote. He
had also arranged to lunch that day with a Russian division commander,
whom he assumed would join the Zhukov party.

But so sincere was the terror that the Russian marshal inspired that the
division commander fled, mumbling excuses, when he learned who was
the guest of honor. "I saw him out on the lawn, visibly quite agitated,"

Gavin wrote, "and when he learned that Marshal Zhukov was in the house, he actually trembled. He would not enter the house under any circumstances. With apologies, he departed." The review was a huge success, except for one minor point: General George Patton was upset Gavin hadn't told him Zhukov would be wearing his full military honors.

It was Clay's plan to replace the military field commanders with a separate military government and governors who would report directly to Eisenhower and not up the usual chain of army command, bypassing the army staff system. By the time the 82nd left Berlin, Gavin had his fill of parade duty, though he was to write, "the morale of the division had never been better by summer's end in 1945. Not only had it performed well after Berlin, but it had proved to be an outstanding occupation division. Airborne warfare was entirely new in the U.S. Army, and we were certain that there would be an Airborne division in the postwar army. We were sure, too, that it would be the 82nd."

Gavin could reasonably expect that he, with his four combat jumps and the increasingly important assignments the war had brought him, would get his reward. But he was almost upstaged by an equally determined and far more politically adept rival, General Maxwell Taylor of the 101st Airborne.

In the midst of preparing the division for return to the United States, Gavin learned in a brusque cable that the 82nd was to be deactivated in Europe. This was bad, but worse was to come. Gavin was told that the 101 would be retained as the airborne cadre, the only division to return to a permanent home and a continued existence. "I couldn't believe it," Gavin recorded, "The only division to be kept on active duty was the 101st, which was a splendid division, but it had seen far less combat than the 82nd. The 101st did not get into the war until June 1944 in Normandy, and by then the 82nd had fought through Sicily and Italy. We were told the 101st was to be brought back to march up Fifth Avenue in a victory parade. This came as a shock to all of us."

Gavin knew that a month before the telegram, Taylor had been appointed superintendent of the U.S. Military Academy, West Point, a career plum which carried with it great influence and a signal that the appointee is a candidate for U.S. Army Chief of Staff. Taylor, cultured, good looking, and perhaps the only Army general fluent in Japanese, was also skilled in public relations; the 101st Division's Bastogne battle had been fought almost to a finish before Taylor, visiting Washington on airborne matters, had joined them, but Taylor's name was inevitably linked with that story. He had also personally knocked on several Washington doors to make certain his 101st remained on active duty.

Gavin might keep his counsel when in disagreement with Bedell Smith or Eisenhower, but this was different. With the straightforward anger of wounded loyalty, Gavin went to General Matthew Ridgway to ask a favor. He knew he had only a couple of weeks to work before the decision and the relatively minor matter (in the eyes of army high command) would soon be set in concrete.

Ridgway came through for his favorite. The senior airborne commander, officially impartially loyal to his two airborne divisions, wrote a thundering memorandum to Army Chief of Staff George Marshall, pointing out that the "82nd has participated with honor in two wars, the 101st in one. . . . One division has lived to 27 years, the other 3. . . . Personalities of former and present commanders should not be factors in arriving at a decision, which should be based solely on records, in and out of combat. . . . Retention of the 82nd will be accepted by the Army as a just and proper recognition of its service. Inactivation of this Division will be viewed as a grave injustice to the many thousands of living and dead who contributed to its achievement."

Ridgway cleverly recommended that both divisions be retained on active duty, the 82nd first.

Armed with this broadside, Gavin pulled every string he had in his possession to get favorable publicity. He called on John "Beaver" Thompson, the courageous *Chicago Tribune* reporter who had jumped into Sicily; writer Bill Walton of *Time* and *Life* magazines, a veteran of the combat jump into Normandy; Charles Collingwood, and Martha Gellhorn. All agreed to do their bit, and it worked.

Gellhorn told the audience of the hugely popular *Saturday Evening Post*: "[He is] the outstanding student and innovator of airborne warfare. . . . To his men, he is one of them. They believe in him because he always jumps out of the lead plane first, because he is serene and cheerful in combat, because he drives them relentlessly and gets results of which they are fiercely proud, because he has dignity, but no pomp, and any man can be sure of his consideration and his justice. They also like the cocky way he wears his hat."

Though Gellhorn's *Saturday Evening Post* piece came out after the final decision was made, the successful battle with Taylor on the field of persuasion marked a turning point in Gavin's life. Though he could hardly have known it then, he would never ride his jeep forward to survey a battlefield at daybreak, grip his rifle in excitement and fear, or steady troopers under fire again.

The 82nd shipped home on the *Queen Elizabeth* in December.

He would have his parade. And like an embodiment of all America's wartime wishes for a perfect American warrior, James Gavin would step out ahead of his division (at least all who volunteered to march in the victory parade in January 1946) to be idolized by the nation, reviewed by New York Governor Thomas E. Dewey, New York City Mayor William O'Dwyer, and General Jonathan Mayhew Wainwright. Gavin swung, slim and erect, up the pavement in the cold, through the arch at Washington Square, disguising the pain from his broken vertebrae, as well as the pain he felt for the dead; 60,000 men had passed through the division, and many of them were gone and more were wounded and crippled. He would march with his enviable luck intact, but with only twelve of his true peers, men who like him, had made all four combat jumps. He was a hero, and almost a national figure. The war had made him "Slim Jim, Gentleman Jim, Jumpin' Jim." But the war would also always define him as the pure combat leader.

Gavin would plunge immediately into the problems of a man formed by war, suddenly at peace. There would be many more parades, for which Gavin had a natural talent, and more politics, for which he had little.

14.

JEAN

It was January of 1946. Gavin was at the glorious pinnacle of his excellent war, when he stepped off on Fifth Avenue to lead the remnants of the gutted 82nd in the victory parade. He was transformed from the coal-town orphan boy into a most admired man, not only for the past, but for the future.

His youth, courage, and bearing seemed to promise new leadership for the army and perhaps even for the nation. The image of the brilliant young general who had dropped from the sky behind the lines in Sicily, Italy, Normandy, and Holland, who had often almost alone salvaged glory from impossible situations by his personal heroism; the liberator of Woebblin, the commander of Berlin, whose division was the best, the toughest, the proudest and among the most battle worthy of the victorious World War II forces—that image would never fade for Gavin's admirers.

But there's a secret about all great soldiers, and particularly American soldiers; they can be a positive embarrassment to the national psyche in peacetime—witness America's ambiguous attitude to its veterans. But in that important year of Gavin's life, 1946, none of this was as clear as it is now. It was in the background, though—and it was something that Gavin, the archetypical warrior, did not really understand. He would write of 1947 "The Army didn't know what to do with me." And he was right. Because he had been such a fighter, he had risen fast. But he was so young, and so many older generals lingered about . . . What should the army do with this young fighter of unproven political prowess in peace? Not exactly sure, it would leave him at Fort Bragg with the 82nd for two more years.

So as he marched up Fifth Avenue, that moment of triumph and glory carried with it some sense of loss. There was literally nowhere to go from there. There was no war, and his youth made his immediate future uncertain, but that was O.K. He wanted to try some new ideas, and the 82nd could once again be his implement, though this time, the battle would be in a new arena.

Sent back to Fort Bragg immediately after its proud show in New York, his division quickly changed under the pressures of peace. In a year or so, by 1947, there would be fewer than two hundred men in the 82nd who had jumped with him into combat in Europe. To fill the gaping holes left by men leaving the service, the remnants of the 13th Airborne Division and one of the army's most unusual units, the all-black 555th Parachute Infantry Battalion (known as the Triple Nickel) became part of the 82nd. The Triple Nickel had been parachute trained but was sidelined from combat in Europe and trained as fire fighters and stationed in California to wait for Japanese firebombing of Western forests.

So the 555 had jumped to combat forest fires. There was institutional racism involved, of course. Gavin immediately assessed the men of the unit, noting "they had splendid physiques and were in fine physical condition." But their status and lodgings brought Gavin a first minicrisis.

The 555 lived in tar-paper shacks and later in a wooden dormitory about a mile from the division area at Bragg. Gavin had dealt with official army segregation before, but now he was not a junior officer but a very famous general. "When I at once toured the facilities with the battalion commander, I was appalled. Their swimming pool was a muddy pond, without beaches and having little shelter where one could change clothes. The buildings were in a poor state of repair. It was obvious that these black troops were going to be treated as second-class citizens in the 82nd if their living conditions were not improved. I pondered what to do in order to get them closer to the 82nd."

Gavin's action, when he took it, resembled others he was to take: he addressed the problem with his own simple, very public solution, ignoring higher command and army policies in a way that raised eyebrows in Washington. "I finally decided that there was only one way to handle the situation, and that was to integrate them into the 82nd Airborne Division without delay, making them part of the division and sharing with them the decorations which the division had brought back from Europe," he wrote. "But how to go about it? If I were to write a letter, it would have to go through the corps and Army Ground Forces headquarters before reaching Washington. My idea was so far removed from what the Army had been doing up to then with its black soldiers that I was sure it would be highly unlikely to be approved."

Yet he knew the army would quickly find out and hoped they would see his integration policy as the prerogative of a single division commander. Further, Gavin gave orders that the battalion should join the 505, his own former regiment, one over which he had complete control (it was widely said in the hyperbole of those glowing days that if Slim Jim had asked the 505 to jump out of their air transports without parachutes, they would have obeyed to a man). Gavin was sure the 555 would prove themselves; but only after a time of training with the 505, during which they would remain a separate, segregated all-black unit, would Gavin go up the line of command to ask permission to allow the black troopers to integrate the regiment and then the division.

Washington stung Gavin with an icy rebuke after he called on the Army Chief of Plans and Operations in the Pentagon in the spring of 1946. He was asked, "Do you intend, General, to have the 555th wear the French and Belgian Fourragers, and the Dutch Order of Orange-Nassau that the division earned during the war?"

Gavin told him, "I certainly do, and they will earn them by their high standards as soldiers." There was no more discussion or open opposition to Gavin's plans, much to his surprise. The army apparently intended to make Gavin learn his own lesson, but the only lesson he learned was that the black troopers were excellent soldiers and paratroops.

The fearsome reputation of the division was still very much alive and kept so in some unusual ways. At Fort Bragg, for instance, they honed their smartness and punctilio to a fine degree, even in such matters as the maintenance of the lawns of the division area, where, instead of the usual demure "Keep Off the Grass" warning, the 82nd posted signs reading "Achtung! Minen," complete with skull and crossbones. Too, the 82nd's reputation led to a constant stream of high-level visitors who had to be shown training exercises.

Gavin had often told himself that a soldier's greatest mistake is to keep fighting the last battle. He had to look to the next one. The day Gavin had witnessed Montgomery's massed crossing of the Rhine, he realized that airborne operations, as he knew them and practiced them, were no longer possible against a modern opponent. He had written the book on airborne operations and now he found it outdated. He resolved to write a new book and began studying new tools that could overcome problems of mobility, stealth, and speed with innovative methods, such as deploying troops into battle with helicopters. Jim Gavin did not wait long after the guns fell silent before he began planning his next war.

Amid the change that peace brought to Gavin's life was another, personal change. He was a man totally ready for a new start, a new relationship. When he returned with his division to Fort Bragg, North Carolina, his new relationship was waiting for him.

Women intrigued James Gavin all his life.

He sought relentlessly to solve their mystery and was both pursuer and pursued throughout a romantic career that, to his admiring troops and fellow officers, was as much a part of his mystique as his battlefield legend.

Though he confided in his diary and memoirs almost obsessively about his foster mother, Mary Gavin, and his "real" mother, Katherine Ryan, the mysterious Irish immigrant girl he spent years trying to trace, Gavin spoke or wrote little of the many transitory women in his life. In his frequent diary entries concerning the women he referred to as his "solace," or by other masked or endearing terms, they are mentioned only by first name or by initials.

It was Jim Gavin's fate to be able to enter relationships as easily as he could leave them, in most cases without bitterness, and usually leaving behind women grateful for the handsome general's attention. The war made him a celebrity, and with that distinction had come acquaintance with other celebrities and affairs with Marlene Dietrich and Martha Gellhorn.

But the central relationship of his life was his marriage to Jean Emert of Knoxville, Tennessee, a stunning petite blonde divorcée almost twenty years his junior. She was, like him, on the rebound from an unhappy marriage when she first met Major General James M. Gavin in 1946.

Jean had heard plenty already about James Gavin from her sister Aileen, who had married an officer of the 82nd, Colonel Melvin Zais, who as executive officer of the 517 Parachute Infantry had fought in southern France and the Champagne campaign. A few years apart in age and similar in outlook, Aileen and Jean had grown up in a conservative, comfortable middle-class family in Knoxville, Tennessee, the daughters of a local banker. They were expected to go to college and to marry Southern businessmen. Yet both were to be wives of army generals.

Aileen led the way. She married Melvin Zais (who later achieved notoriety for ordering costly assaults at Vietnam's "Hamburger Hill") before
World War II, and settled into a life of career-army wifehood. Her
younger sister Jean had married Aaron Chester Duncan, a young Army
Air Corps officer, at the age of nineteen. At the end of the war, he left
the army to become a cosmetics salesman, and after a time, the two
settled into separate lives.

Aileen's husband had risen as a wartime paratroop officer even as her
sister's marriage fell apart. Peace found the Zais family stationed at Bragg
with the 82nd.

When Jean's husband left for New York to begin training for Chanel,
leaving Jean behind in Knoxville, she went back to her parents' home,
where her daughter Caroline was born, and later, after her divorce, enrolled at the University of Tennessee to study nutrition and institutional
management.

Gavin was by then in a peculiar marital situation himself. He and
Peggy had agreed to remain married for the duration of the war for the
practical reason that divorce would have meant a serious hardship for her
and daughter Barbara. Yet when Gavin returned to the nation's cheers,
wearing two stars and clearly destined for higher rank, Peggy began to
have second thoughts about becoming a single woman. She had lived
through a war of rumors about her husband's romances, during which
time Gavin's primary interest in his family lay in his relationship with
his daughter; yet in spite of their long separation, Gavin's national fame
made her reconsider the marriage.

The result was a bitter standoff between the two. Gavin considered the
marriage finished. Now he wanted out and was willing to make financial
sacrifices to get out. But it was not until after Peggy had driven a hard
bargain with Gavin that she retreated to Florida for their six-month
separation. It was perhaps Gavin's only abject retreat. A measure of his
desperation was that he did not fight the settlement arrangements suggested by Peggy Baulsir's lawyer and in fact hired no lawyer himself,
which was to prove costly from a financial point of view. As a result,
Gavin would be left with a lifelong alimony burden.

While there were no public fights, Gavin's unhappy situation was well
known to high and low at Fort Bragg. Gossip about his private life was
relished to the full.

Jim Gavin's youth made friendships with fellow general officers, who
tended to be older, difficult. As a result, many of Gavin's friends were of

lower rank. Gavin and Zais were friends, and Aileen Zais liked Jim Gavin. The name of "General Jim" was a constant in conversation in the house, always spoken with admiration and pleasure. "They were always raving about General Jim this and General Jim that," Jean Emert Gavin remembered.

Having seen Gavin at a division review, she next met him and Peggy formally at a cocktail party for staff members and wives, at the general's official quarters, and then again at a supper she attended with Aileen and Mel Zais, where she was the dinner partner of William C. Westmoreland, then a rising young officer Gavin had first noticed when Westmoreland commanded an artillery unit in Sicily. The two evenings were pleasant but nothing more. At that time, she didn't know that Jim Gavin would soon be single.

Jean went back to Knoxville, the fall and winter sped past, and she returned to Bragg in May 1947 to once again visit Aileen. The occasion was the marriage of one of Gavin's staff officers, Woody Long. Army friends planned a picnic celebration at McCeller's Pond, a local park area, and Aileen Zais arranged to have Jean invited. This time, both she and Gavin were single.

As the guests stood about in groups at the cookout, Gavin came over to the group where Jean stood and asked her directly, "Are you one of the spare parts?" She was taken completely aback, not aware that the division slang applied that name to units that were not directly attached. "I don't know what you are talking about," she responded. Gavin took time to explain to the blushing blonde. This was their first conversation.

Gavin had a plan. After the party, he invited a few of his closest friends to his house in the division area, known as his "cabin," to hear a record then making the rounds, a 78 by jazz singer Dorothy Sims. Gavin asked Jean to ride with him to the party. At the end of the evening, Gavin asked her if he could come to the Zais house to see her the next day. "He asked me if I'd like to take Caroline out for an ice-cream cone," she recalled, "and that was sort of the beginning." They drove in Gavin's new convertible with the top down, Gavin in civilian clothes, toward Fayetteville, and set tongues wagging.

Jean Emert Gavin remembers her paratrooper's courtship vividly. They had one date by parachute, when a detachment of the 82nd dropped into the Smoky Mountains near Gatlinburg. He said he'd give her a call after the jump and he did, though there was still another woman who had flitted back into Gavin's life.

Martha Gellhorn, who helped create Gavin's shining image with her dispatches, visited Fort Bragg in May. When Gavin and Peggy separated, and he, as if to announce his bachelorhood, moved into smaller quarters, Gellhorn helped him redecorate his new home. Jean later noted that she had to live with Gellhorn's tastes in draperies and slipcovers for several years as a result because they couldn't afford new ones.

With Gellhorn gone, and having spent some time now with General Jim, Jean felt serious interest in the tall, quiet man. And Jim Gavin's interest in her now seemed high. Through the summer of 1947, he deluged her with phone calls and letters. Things took a turn when she decided to fly into Raleigh-Durham airport in response to a Gavin invitation. As usual, she sought the hospitality of the Zais home, but this time dropped a bomb. "Don't bother to pick me up at the airport," she told her sister, "Jim will do that."

"Jim will do what!?" She remembers her sister blurting out. From that point on, she became his special relationship.

Jean had conquered her many rivals. "Actually," she reflected, "it wasn't so difficult. Deep down, James really wanted a family. And the other women, they wouldn't have worked in the army, not for his career. I knew enough to know that he didn't want someone who was going to be a bigger star than himself."

Nineteen forty-seven was the summer of decision for both estranged couples. That summer, the two divorce decrees, his and hers, came through a day apart, on August 7th and 8th. Tongues began wagging anew as Jean became General Gavin's usual date. She was twenty-four years old, just older than many of the children of the army families the couple circulated with. Gavin was forty.

In October, Gavin asked Jean to be his date at West Point for a football weekend. She remembers her mother lecturing her about the propriety, but she went with him to New York anyway. Jean stayed at friends' apartment, Gavin at the Waldorf. They went tea dancing at the Sherry Netherland. She thought it was tea they meant to order, but Gavin laid on martinis. They danced and a waiter asked her "was she sure" when she ordered a second martini. "He seemed to be warning me against the older man I was with," she laughed, recalling the evening. Gavin gave Jean the full treatment. He took her to Club 21 with Charles Collingwood and Robert Capa. Then on to another spot. Everywhere in New York Gavin was recognized by headwaiters and hotel doormen, even by people on the street.

At El Morocco, Gavin was immediately accorded the hero treatment; he had celebrated there the night of the Fifth Avenue parade. Jean remembers well the moment Marlene Dietrich "sailed in with a couple of guys in tow and came flying across the room and—I had my head down and I don't think she saw that he had somebody with him—and she said, 'Darling, I haven't seen you in so long' and she started giving him the big hug and kiss, and suddenly I lifted my head up, and she looked, and the great Dietrich looked flustered." Coolly, she spun on her heel and turned away.

In the morning, they drove up the Palisades Parkway, had lunch at Bear Mountain, and arrived at West Point in time for the Washington and Lee Football Game. He acted like any cadet with his girl, showing her where he had lived on the autumn-glorious campus. Gavin called in none of the privileges that his fame and rank could have brought him, humbly filing into the class of '29's allotted section of the stadium.

Later, they walked the famous Flirtation Walk above the Hudson, hand in hand, where cadets traditionally propose marriage. At a convenient bench, he did just that. "I realized later, he thought about this a lot. West Point meant so much to him," Jean recalled. Gavin later told her that the proposal had to be perfect—to fulfill his vision in the only place he felt was home. He had premeditated it, writing, "The highlight of the visit, indeed the whole purpose, was for me to propose to her." Jean remembered it as "a very sentimental and romantic moment for both of us." The quiet Gavin wanted his actions to speak loudest.

She accepted him. "Are you serious?" she asked.

"Of course I'm serious," Gavin replied.

He saw in her a refinement of the vision he had formed of a general's wife, and unlike his previous match, he had no doubts about this one.

Gavin gave Jean no ring, however, but celebrated with a visit to 504 World War II commander Ruben Tucker, then teaching at the Point. Gavin said nothing about the proposal, and Jean, although bursting with emotion, followed his lead. At Christmas, Gavin repeated another West Point custom and presented Jean with a miniature of his class ring.

Gavin had been concentrating on the happy prospect of founding a new, permanent Gavin family that would include children. But soon, his attention returned to his career. George Catlett Marshall had retired and Eisenhower now ran the army. He believed young generals who had commanded a combat division should have time as a chief of staff of an Army, and Gavin, in early 1948, was selected to join Lieutenant General

Walton Walker's Fifth Army in Chicago. Jean and he had agreed to keep their marital plans a secret, both feeling their divorces were still too fresh, until he came up for his next assignment. His orders to Chicago were the signal for the announcement.

Jean returned to Knoxville in the glow of love. Her mother questioned her. "Are you sure you want to do this? He's quite a bit older than you." And her banker father disapproved. "He thought James was too old." He told her in the bluntest way that he thought his youngest daughter was making another mistake.

Jean was undaunted; she felt liberated. She felt that her first marriage had been doomed and now the way was clear to put things right. In the end, the young couple had their way. The Emert family succumbed to Gavin's charm and their daughter's happiness.

Jim Gavin reported to the Fifth Army's Hyde Park headquarters in April. He married Jean on July 31, 1948. It was a quiet ceremony, and they spent their honeymoon night, for that was all it was to be, at Gatlinburg, a place of some romantic import to the couple. Then they picked up baby Caroline and drove to Fort Sheridan, where they took residence in a general officer's quarters on Scott Loop in what Jean recalls was "an arc of a house on the shores of Lake Michigan."

Jean's arrival at Fifth Army was celebrated with a reception for the newlyweds hosted by General Walker and his wife at the officers' club at Fort Sheridan. She remembers the long drive from Knoxville with two-and-one-half-year-old Caroline, the scramble to find a babysitter, the worries about clothes, impressions, people's names. Unfortunately the new babysitter was late that night, so they arrived at General Walker's reception about twenty-five minutes late.

Army style, the officers and wives had been lined up from the precise minute of 2 P.M. both outside and inside the officers' club. "I felt like I was walking a gantlet," Jean remembers, noting that she seemed to be far younger than any of the other senior officers' wives. Later she heard General Walker saying to Gavin, 'There is really no excuse, General.' "

The mortification could have wilted a more fragile Southerner, but Jean was anything but fragile. "I wished the floor would open up and swallow me . . . but I truthfully tell you that I was never late one single time again to one official thing until we left the army—and never in the diplomatic corps. I learned the hardest lesson any poor army wife ever learned."

She chose to recall also Gavin's kindness afterwards. Later when he took her aside, "He exercised the most incredible restraint. He simply told me, 'Darling you must be on time.' " She knew enough about her new husband to know that from him, that amounted to a reprimand.

She was beginning to learn her new role would be demanding indeed. Army wives in those days had their station. Whatever reflected glamour would shine on her, it would illuminate only a very traditional woman's role, the general's wife: always groomed and correct, ready to entertain five or fifty guests on a moment's notice, and acutely aware of the friends and foes of her husband's career.

Peacetime was a letdown. Gavin's ambivalence about war no longer bothered him, but he had to find a place in the new postwar order. He would always have a job with the army, for that is the reward of war heroes. Most are killed slowly, by peacetime jobs that are the antithesis of their wartime great deeds. Some find they can do both war and peace, both the truth of battle and the compromise of politics, and they make it to the top again. Gavin saw this as his new challenge: finding a place within the hierarchy of the political army.

The freethinking among Gavin's admirers, who were legion, thought that he was a shoo-in for Chief of Staff of the Army, the pinnacle of the profession. Yet getting to Chief of Staff would be an entirely different thing than fighting his way from cadet to colonel to major general. For one thing, if he were to become a full-time staff officer, there would be no more fighting and no more jumping out of airplanes. The army's version of the "Peter Principle" was that men got advancement for great deeds in battle only to find that the skills that fostered them were no longer needed, but that skills of an entirely different character were.

For Gavin the comedown was particularly cruel. After only six months in Chicago, he received a Pentagon assignment in planning. From a mansion in Berlin astride the continent of Europe, his word law to thousands, to find himself crammed into a two-bedroom apartment in Arlington, Virginia, rent $89.75 a month, with a baby and another on the way, and alimony payments was a comedown indeed. His pay barely covered basic expenses. He used their one car to commute to the Pentagon, one among dozens of striving general officers in a political army. And Jean Gavin was left to sit on the stoop of an airless brick box on Wellington Street in the stifling heat of July.

1 5.

PEACE—AT A

YOUNG AGE

When Gavin left the 82nd, he realized that this was a moment to make or break his career. The army has never liked specialists, and his service with the paratroops made him seem like one. He commented somewhat sadly, "I left the 82nd in March 1948. We had a farewell review of the Division and I do not believe it had ever marched better. We estimated that in the more than six years I was with the division, it had processed through its ranks about 60,000 soldiers—the killed, wounded, missing in action, and the many thousands who were discharged and returned home. We made a quick survey of how many paratroopers were still with the 82nd who had been with it from the beginning and had made our four combat jumps in Europe, and we found that there were 24. We took their picture; they do not look like a very friendly lot, but they exuded confidence and sureness."

Gavin's time in Chicago lasted less than a year, little more than a ticket punch on the way to higher command. The Fifth Army was an "on paper" unit that commanded an array of active and reserve units scattered throughout the West and Midwest. His life there was ceremonial and educational, because he had never held—or wanted—a job so far from the field, but to find himself amidst a shell organization was at first galling.

A tight budget (only $325 a month after alimony), long days, but the general and his wife would go into Chicago to listen to jazz and occasionally visit the Wine Garden Restaurant, owned by a former 82nd trooper.

Only Sundays were sacrosanct from routine and work. Even then, custom intervened, and normal leisure activities became impossible. Visitors such as General Robert E. Wood, in the nineteenth-century tradition, made a procession of Sunday "calls" on fellow general officers they wished to meet.

Jean Gavin remembered. "In those days people still came and called on Sunday afternoon. They'd bring their little cards with them and leave them in the silver tray in the front hall. Twenty minutes. You called on the staff, on a new general officer, particularly if he had a new wife everyone was curious about."

After two months, Gavin was detailed to Fort Monroe, Virginia, for three months of weapons evaluation with a group assembled there. Somehow he had found the time, between the wooing and winning of Jean and running a division, to put together his first book, a treatise on the future of the parachute force with which he would be forever linked. *Airborne Warfare*, printed by the Infantry Journal Press in 1947, was aimed at a highly specialized military audience, but it reveals how Gavin envisioned the next war would be fought, and incidentally foreshadowed his own role as a developer of weapons and systems to fight it.

Gavin's thinking can be summed up in two words: more mobility. He had learned two paramount lessons from World War II: the first was that nothing could replace on-the-ground eyeball leadership of troops. But the second was that true mobility, on the ground or in the air, was the most essential element in combat. Mobility meant machines, planes, trucks, armored cars, and a fairly new toy, the helicopter.

He did not believe that air power's most important task was to drop explosives on targets from 10,000 or 20,000 feet, however good their aim. Tons of artillery rounds had been thrown on defenses in Europe so that there seemed not a square foot in which a creature could live. But the defenders were always up and shooting back when the assault came. His experience in Berlin had also taught him that modern cities were far more resistant to heavy bombardment than planners thought.

Normandy, he wrote, was the fullest extension of sea power. "Then, the Allied powers, using hundreds of seacraft of all types, invaded the Continent of Europe. The sea was used to the fullest. It is significant, however, that part of the invading forces were transported by air. It was significant because that battle saw sea power at its peak. Air power was just beginning. And this is the critical point we have now arrived at and this is the competition we are in. This medium that envelops us we must use. We must imagine, design and develop the means for using it. . . . Air power is now the deciding element in modern war, and by air power is meant every contribution to waging war that man has created and that can be flown. Men, weapons, ammunition, food, bombs, missiles, and all that it will take to fight a future war must fly."

As he sought to carve a new direction for himself, Gavin was defining himself as a rebel, even before he achieved a decision-making place in the army's planning apparatus. Most of his contemporaries thought airborne was an anomalous concept, born at a developmental time in air warfare, doomed to remain nothing but a slightly odd experiment—armies dropping out of the sky. Gavin was seeking to distill from paratroop experience the essence that made airborne tactics work. The war had been an awakening for him, and far from wanting to fight it over, he wanted to project it into the future. Privately, to Jean and a few close friends, he was willing to state another real ambition—to become Chief of Staff of the Army, in emulation of two of his life's ideals as soldiers, Pershing and George C. Marshall.

Gavin was surprised to find his little book no more than a subject of polite conversation among his peers; true, he had filled most of the volume with a recounting and critique of the operations of the 82nd and an assessment that for future wars, airborne troops in larger numbers and in ever swifter delivery machines would be needed, and the primary preoccupation of American military thought in the postwar period was the stunning new weapon called the atom bomb, which threatened to blow out of the intellectual water any developmental theory for warfare. So perhaps his surprise was unwarranted.

The bombs that fell on Hiroshima and Nagasaki created utter chaos in the upper reaches of military leadership. Here was a development that took even the forward-looking Gavin aback, because it changed not only the method of making war, the means of making war, but also the war itself, which had become, in one stroke, a noncontest that by its very nature could not be won. Among the confusion and upsets that a world-destroying weapon brought was the sudden obsolescence of all that he had come to believe. It would take him several years to retrench and discover that the black humor of the superweapon was simply this: by its nature, it destroyed all previous theory and thinking about war; but by its nature, it would never again be used.

However, unlike most who studied the awesome possibilities of the atom bomb, Gavin felt sure that there could be a defense against it, just as there had been a defense mounted against every other revolutionary new weapon. Gavin found himself isolated in an intellectual battle; for he belonged neither to the "bomb" school of annihilation, nor to the anti-bomb school, which felt atomic weapons should be treated like chemical and biological weapons, anathema to civilized soldiers. Fortunately, he was used to intellectual isolation as a paratrooper. "As the war came to an end," he wrote, "the U.S. strategic bombing survey was appointed to move in the wake of the advancing armies and assess the results of our bombing efforts. The findings were reported in over two hundred detailed reports. They were never, in my opinion, given the recognition they deserved." So as the bombing advocates eagerly embraced their new weapon, they also chose to ignore the hard evidence that the saturation bombing of German cities had not substantially altered the course of the war. German production had continuously risen as Allied bombing raids had wrought ever more destruction.

American strategic bombing advocates, such as Major General Curtis "Bombs Away" LeMay, believed all they had to do was knock out certain critical "bottleneck" segments of German industry. The famous raids on the Schweinfurt ball-bearing factories were the perfect example. Ball-bearing production was a specific, absolutely necessary segment of industry on which almost all the machinery of warfare depended, so ball-bearing plants were pummeled mercilessly, but it simply had not worked. Aircraft losses ran too high and the effects did not stop the production of ball bearings. "One of the most interesting aspects of our bombing effort" Gavin wrote, "was that German production increased in the same ratio as our bombing effort until late in 1944," when the ground armies were pounding the shrinking boundaries of the Reich. Gavin was early and clear-sighted in these ideas.

Gavin's reaction to the atom bomb was not to be swept away by it, but to face it through "dispersion." "Never again may troops concentrate as they have in the past. For example, a buildup similar to that for the Normandy assault would suffer a most disastrous scorching if caught under an atomic bombing or missile attack," he wrote in 1947. "In the same manner the defending force opposing such an attempt as the Normandy assault would have to remain continuously dispersed or they would be practically wiped out without a foot being set on shore."

Only when the forces came into contact and there was a chance of both being wiped out by the same nuclear weapon, could soldiers be concentrated in the old way. A curious paradox, it seemed, that generals would be forced to lock their troops in World War I style trench combat to deter annihilation. In such a situation, a retreat by one side out of the nuclear kill range could be the brilliant and devastating move. Just so was the military situation thrown on its head by the bomb.

To his credit, Gavin did not recant. And of course he was proved right in the end. Though his principles of dispersion were never tried in battle, he grasped immediately that deterrence was more important than delivery, and that under the bomb's long shadow, war methods could continue their development. The atomic bomb altered very little in the arms race except its expense, since after Nagasaki, no new weapon ever has been used. Therefore war could continue as before.

The key to the future, Gavin maintained, lived in airborne forces. Perhaps one reason thinkers of his day did not seize on his idea immediately was because by 1948 the term airborne meant one specific thing: paratroopers. But to Gavin, the master paratrooper, the term actually meant the projection of military might through the air. Airborne force could be projected rapidly, thus allowing American armies to get in close proximity to the enemy—and away from nuclear bombs. He also foresaw America's role in limited nonnuclear police actions, and he believed that the rapid projection of military power would prove decisive. He wrote, "The nation that in the future has the best trained and equipped airborne forces has the best chance of survival. . . . The knowledge of a well trained airborne army, capable of moving anywhere on the globe on short notice, available to an international body such as the United Nations, is our best guarantee of a lasting peace. And the nation or nations that control the air will control the peace." Full of innovations made possible by rocket science, the helicopter, and advance air technology, his thinking had already predicted the army that would fight Operation Desert Storm in the 1990s.

If Gavin's book did not divert the military from its atomic mesmerization in his own time, it did have one important effect: it labeled him for good as an intellectual in an organization where intellectuals held little real power. For Gavin, however, it held a certain double advantage. Gavin would not have to prove his valor or his ability to lead men, two qualities which the army prizes above all others and believes intellectuals lack, and it eased his way into a field of true interest, weapons development. When the army, in reaction to the dawn of the atomic age, set up a new organization called the Weapons Systems Evaluation Group (WSEG), with one top officer from each of the services in a board of directors arrangement, he eagerly agreed to be a part of it. Perhaps the sounds of the guns were no longer the place where the decision was made, but Gavin hurried into the future with that belief. Weapons development intrigued him nearly as much as their employment, and this area would dominate the remainder of his military career—again making him a specialist.

General John E. Hull and Dr. Philip Morse of the Massachusetts Institute of Technology were to be cochairs of WSEG. "The group had in its ranks some of the best scientists in the country, and could draw upon the scientific community for help when needed . . . it came at one of the most critical times in our Defense Department's history. First there was the atomic bomb, then jet planes and missiles . . . an argument was raging in Washington and throughout the country about the meaning of the atomic bomb. Did it mean the end of land warfare? Was it the ultimate in air power, as Duhay and Billy Mitchell had foreseen? I did not think so," wrote Gavin a little blankly, "In summary, our promethean achievement left us in intellectual disarray."

Gavin early in his contact with the "other" side of the army, the Washington side, admitted that he had a lot to learn. Almost the first thing he learned after joining WSEG and moving Jean and three-year-old Caroline to Washington (by that time Jean was pregnant with Patricia Gavin, who would be born September 28, 1949), was that the three services were engaged in a heavy turf fight over the bomb, which seemed to dictate the future of the military.

Every source seemed to indicate that the United States (aided by its allies and conscripted German scientists) had at least a five-year head start on the only other entrant in the nuclear "race," the increasingly hostile Soviet Union. (In fact the Soviets detonated a nuclear device in August of 1949). In the meantime, lulled by illusions of invincibility, the services seemed determined to wage a war of their own over control of the bomb.

The fledgling U.S. Air Force, split away from the U.S. Army Air Forces under the National Security Act of 1947, was the big winner. Not only had the atomic weapon been delivered by air, the *Enola Gay* raid had imprinted on the minds of all who envisioned it, the picture of the single, tiny, all-powerful aircraft carrying in its belly the unanswerable victory. And though the bomb was expensive, the plane was relatively cheap, the men who would guide it few, and the distances, thanks to aircraft carriers and foreign bases, manageable. A few expensive bombs and planes to carry them would be far cheaper than massive armies, so the air force looked financially attractive as well. From a controversial novice at the beginning of the war, aircraft had become the king of weapons by the end. Particularly at odds was the navy, the most traditional and convention bound of the services, which held out against the air force for its own share of the weapon. The army seemed to have no place in the new nuclear arrangement, so it would take whatever the other two services would give it, which goes a long way toward explaining why the American Army was so dismally prepared to fight exactly the war the navy and the air force were so certain would not come again, in Korea.

One of Gavin's primary responsibilities at WSEG was exploring the possible development of tactical "battlefield" nuclear weapons. As was his habit, Gavin wished to see for himself. He was ordered to the Nuclear Weapons School at Sandia AFB in Albuquerque, New Mexico, where he learned the principles of fission. Later, in 1951, he would witness the explosion of a 50 kiloton bomb at Eniwetok, a small Pacific island where Gavin sat about 10 miles from ground zero. The day before the moment of fission he had visited the experimental bomb field, which was littered with sacrificial objects of the experiment. "Radiating out from ground zero for several miles were containers of animals—dogs, pigs, and mice. The dogs were used because their circulatory systems were analogous to that of a human being; pigs because of their skin's sensitivity to radiation and burns; and mice for continued laboratory biological tests. All types of weapons then in use were deployed at varying distances. The wings of aircraft, the fuselage, and various components were also placed at known distances in varying profiles. Houses, aircraft hangars and smaller buildings were erected at calculated distances from ground zero."

He and his WSEG group toured this macabre scene, and returned twenty-four hours after the blast. "Our backs were turned to the bomb, and when it was detonated we could feel the shock as well as the heat. We then turned around and observed the cloud as it drifted skyward. About twenty-four hours later we were allowed to return by jeep to the blast area to see for ourselves the results of what had taken place."

Gavin plunged into his new work at the Pentagon, commuting after long hours to his tiny apartment in the Virginia suburbs—"3130 Wellington Road, Park Fairfax, $89.75 a month," Jean remembers—where Jean dealt with another pregnancy, then a new baby and a four-year-old. There was no chance of quarters in Washington, even for a distinguished general. "It was on the top of this rise in Arlington," Jean recalls. "It was cheap and available. My God it was hot. And I was so pregnant. And I can remember sitting out on that little stoop on the hot summer evenings, and we'd walk down, trying to get a breath of air. It was miserable."

Occasionally they were able to play "six holes—no more"—at the nearby Army-Navy Club course and go to the dances, dinners and socials that are a constant there. The social life left plenty to be desired. Jean was called upon to provide hospitality on her husband's meager salary. "I served Gen. John Hull Mexican cooking—it was the only thing I could afford." When Patricia Gavin was born, Gavin used the medical services at nearby Fort Belvoir because they were free. "Suddenly a big vase of flowers appeared in my room and I thought, 'How sweet of James to do this,' and I read the note. It was from the commanding general of the hospital." He had sent flowers because Jean Gavin was the only general's wife who had ever had a baby in that hospital.

Occasionally, the Gavins and friends would drive to the nearby Civil War battlefields, a lifelong Gavin passion. "They would walk and walk . . . at Sharpsburg he knew what everyone was doing at every moment," Jean remembered.

No longer did Gavin have to deal with staff work. As it was an interservice group, there were no command duties. There were trips to Eniwetok and weapons-testing ranges. Gavin was profoundly interested in his work. "He had five or six books open at a time, he read everything he could get his hands on," she recalled. But politics did not interest him in the least at this point in his life. Even the constant shop talk of army officers seemed to pall. "James was kind of isolated over in the E Ring of the Pentagon . . . but he did not bring his work home. I don't know whether he thought I didn't understand it or wasn't interested."

Gavin remained in grade—as a major general—for a long time, a fact that often caused Jean discomfort. "The army being as it is, James sat in grade . . . but many junior to him [in rank], because they were older, passed him right on by." He had been the youngest, now let him remain the youngest forever, she fumed. The problem was there were not many lieutenant generals. Brigadiers in plenty, major generals a good few, lieutenant generals, a geometrically reduced few. The trouble with a pyramid, they would joke, is there is only one point.

Others were making progress, oblique, but perhaps better progress than Gavin's, toward the top. One was his longtime rival, and eventual bitter enemy, Maxwell Taylor, commander of the 101st Airborne. Far from being comrades-in-arms, these two men were as different as chalk and cheese though doomed forever to be identified with each other as commanders of the two most famous airborne divisions. Most contemporaries date their rivalry back to the time in 1945 when the 101st, with Taylor's prodding, was selected as the airborne division to remain on the active list—until Gavin outmaneuvered him to get the army to keep the 82nd instead—but their dislike for one another went back far in time, even to West Point.

Though the two men behaved with the cordiality expected of general officers—they could smile and chat and sit across from each other at dinner—Gavin's animosity for the pluperfect, handsome, and fluent Taylor was intense. Taylor, for his part, chose to ignore Gavin, much as he did others he felt could not help him forward.

But Army officers working for the Army Military History Institute taped Gavin's personal assessment of his rival: "When I was a cadet at West Point," he began, "and when I was a first classman, I was made first sergeant to the C Company when the young plebe class came in. . . . and so on.

"And I'll always remember . . . one day . . . the plebes all [were] lined up. . . . One or two of them looked like they weren't going to make it. They were a little shaky . . . they weren't responsive; and I was a little bit worried about them. Maybe we were working them a little too hard. . . .

"And in walks this very trim, smart looking officer, resplendent, and clothes well pressed, sabre at his side, which they wore in those days. . . . And he was Lieutenant Maxwell Taylor; he was normally one of the instructors in the language department and he was put in charge, for the summer, of a company, and he wanted to know if things were going well, and I said 'yes.'. . . and he walks off and that is the last that I saw him. . . . He was absolutely cold and impersonal. He wasn't interested in the troops at all. He was just interested in himself, in being protected.

"So from that time on, I've always had the most personally interesting relationship with Maxwell Taylor. He is a brilliant man. Very intelligent, has a capacity for languages, good memory. Ambitious, terribly ambitious, so ambitious that he is almost ruthless in trying to satisfy that ambition. He has a very interesting intelligence. It's sort of . . . sort of superficial and brittle. I've never known General Taylor to ever think through a new concept and a new thing and say, 'this I believe, and this is the way it's going to be next year, from what I've studied.' He isn't that kind of thinker at all. It's an unusual sort of a thing. He's almost . . . a drawing board soldier. He comes up to all specifications, except the capacity for creative thinking, thinking through new concepts.''

But while Gavin was theorizing about the use of tactical nuclear weapons, the development of faster and bigger air mobility systems, and the problems of the next war, Taylor had secured the vital career post of superintendent of the U.S. Military Academy at West Point. In September of 1945, when appointed, he was the second youngest man ever to hold the post. Only Douglas MacArthur was younger.

Earlier that summer, however, Taylor had made a gaffe before his troops that only highlighted the difference between the fanatic bond the 82nd felt for Gavin and the cooler feelings the 101 troopers had for their commander. As recounted by Taylor's biographer Douglas Kinnard, Taylor toured his division as the war in Europe ended to raise their spirits after it was learned they would be redeployed to the Pacific Theater in spite of their Bastogne heroics. Of course this never happened, thanks to the atom bomb, but as Taylor toured the units, he gave a booster speech, ending it with, ''We've licked the best that Hitler had in France and Holland and Germany. Now where do we want to go?''

The troops, accompanying their shouts with boos and catcalls, yelled ''HOME!''

16.

THE FORGOTTEN

WAR

During the summer of 1950, United Nations forces who had been hastily thrown into the fight, fell back before North Korean infantry spearheaded by Russian T-34 tanks. Most of the U.N. troops were members of the American Eighth Army under Lieutenant General Walton Walker, and in turn under the direction of overall allied commander in the Far East General of the Army Douglas MacArthur. The United States military establishment, locked in debate over the use of nuclear weapons versus conventional forces, found itself in further disarray. Gavin and colleague Major General Kenneth Nichols converged on the Pentagon office of General Matthew Ridgway.

Ridgway, then deputy to Army Chief of Staff General J. Lawton Collins, listened as the two men argued that he should recommend the use of nuclear weapons against the invading North Koreans. "It would have been militarily inexcusable to allow the 8th Army to be destroyed without using the most powerful weapons in our arsenal," Gavin wrote, "yet we almost did so!"

Gavin's radical counsel was disregarded. Neither Ridgway nor Collins was a believer in the radical new battlefields Gavin foresaw. The Eighth Army rallied in a defensive perimeter around Pusan. The war slowed to a bitter contest for ground. The predictions of pronuclear generals went unrealized. The bomb existed, but the political situation, the potential involvement of the other nuclear power, the Soviet Union, and world opinion guaranteed America's nuclear arsenal would remain unused.

Korea remained from start to finish a conventional war, fought with traditional weapons. The cliché about soldiers always fighting the last war became the new reality. In Korea, the United Nations forces fought a Korean and later a Chinese army with World War II weapons and methods, and in the early days, many of the weapons were poorly functioning World War II surplus.

Jim Gavin, still working in WSEG on developing tactical nuclear weapons, felt increasingly frustrated as the world's most technologically advanced nation was denied the use of its scientific prowess, wrote off the lessons of 1941–45, and allowed the enemy to dictate the shape of the battle. He noted with disgust that his least favorite World War II weapons, the 2.36-inch bazooka and the carbine, were still on the battlefield and still ineffective.

Gavin's calls for reforms, in military journals and in *Airborne Warfare*, had been ignored by a strategic nuclear establishment. Over and above believing the entire army needed a technological overhaul, he also denied the belief that large strategic nuclear bombs capable of destroying whole nations represented the future of warfare. He thought tactical nuclear weapons capable of securing an immediate battlefield advantage far more feasible. He envisioned, not bigger bombs with nuclear warheads, but smaller nuclear bombs, to be delivered by rockets or artillery shells, or even fired from hand-held bazookalike devices.

It was as if he had become too farsighted. His vision of the future battlefield was not shared by politicians, ordinary people, or the mainstream of general officers. His urgings for a complete rethinking of the military establishment that deemphasized large-scale nuclear destruction shows just how far from Pentagon thinking he had veered. He called for divisions completely deployed by helicopter (he had experimented with this concept when still with the 82nd in Fort Bragg), and in 1947 he had called for lightweight armored vehicles and new types of aircraft to deploy them into battle. It was a period during which his inquisitive mind led him all over the world, into conversations with scientists, engineers, and generals, ever convinced that air mobility was the key, that small nuclear weapons would be used in battle, and that commanders should be ready for them. He even became allied with that brilliant but controversial opponent of the hydrogen bomb, Robert Oppenheimer, who once said of Gavin, "He was one of only about ten men with whom I could speak in shorthand."

During the crucial first years of peace, Gavin's logical analysis of tactics and strategy for winning the next war lessened his influence and hurt his career. He believed that never again could a nuclear-equipped nation back another nuclear-equipped nation into a corner and threaten it with annihilation. Wars must now be limited. None of this was popular in the late 1940s and 1950s. In the battle for interservice supremacy, it was the air force with its planes, then the sole delivery mechanism for nuclear weapons, that trumpeted the nuclear future loudest. Gavin later commented that the idea of tactical nuclear weapons "ran contrary to the basic theory of strategic air power enthusiasts; that an all-out air offensive was the only sound tactic and that any diversion to defense was a waste."

Most historians of the period agree that the U.S. force that met the Communist threat in Korea was the worst trained, worst equipped American Army of modern times. The first forces to meet the North Korean advance had never expected to be locked in sudden desperate combat in a treeless, mountainous country unsuited to American mobility. They were occupation troops rushed from Japan, accustomed to the warm regard of their former foes. Occupation troops in Japan knew little of hard training and a great deal of soft billets, good food and luxury far from combat or even realistic tactical exercises.

Gavin, by nature always eager to be where the most progress was being made, had faced the end of World War II with a decision and a judgment. He had decided that in a period of peace—and he could not imagine that a new war could start within five years of 1945—the key place would be in planning. This was, he had learned, the one place that could correct the ills of the peacetime army.

Like few general officers in history, he was in the right place and ready to "grow with the country" in nuclear tactics and strategy. The only problem was that he was wrong. He was wrong about the acceptability of his bold theorizing about tactical nuclear weapons.

Gavin later thought that he might have been too preoccupied with the nuclear battlefield. But all his career he had seen officers "atrophy" as time tucked their war into the past, and he was determined not to become one of them. "In the intellectual climate of the Pentagon following World War II, one had to show that one could live with nuclear weapons—either that or simply go out of business." Gavin hated the idea of massive retaliation. His tactical nuclear weapons research had been his way of becoming conversant with nuclear weapons while studying alternatives to the air force's vision of "doomsday."

Always the practical soldier who needed to touch, taste and feel the scene of conflict, he soon became completely disillusioned with the purely apocalyptic defense system the country had erected since World War II. Yet military men in America are paid to think the unthinkable, and Gavin was doing just that. "For better or worse," he wrote, "we had to face up to the fact that the teachings of Lenin were Soviet policy once again, and that according to that policy either we or the Soviets would survive, not both."

Reading voraciously as he always had, but now with better access to materials and more time, Gavin decided on his own that the inevitability of the next war was inherent in Russian actions and strategies. He had read everything he could get his hands on about the Russians, from a line-by-line study of hundreds of translated speeches and news articles, to detailed photo analysis of Russian military parades. The question bothering him was: can an all-out war with the Soviet Union be limited to less than global destruction? Tactical nuclear weapons at first suggested to him that it might be.

But history turns on the details of the day. The facts were that the atom bomb had been an enormously expensive project; and already it was the property of the air force, if only because a B-29 Superfortress had delivered the attack on Hiroshima on August 6, 1945. And from that point on, the air force and the theory of strategic atomic bombing dominated the thinking of weapons planners and diplomats as it would for many years.

The crushing logic developed and steamrollered opposition: America's security depended on bombers—big, fast, and long range enough to deliver the bomb—and supporting aircraft to protect them. It was an updated version of the daylight bombing of Germany. Air force planners who pointed to the potential of the German V-2 technology that produced the unmanned rockets that flew fast enough to avoid defensive efforts, were silenced. The critics who knew that the massed bombing raids of German cities had failed in their objective were few—and besides, the atom bomb was a new weapon.

Then came Korea. "In a short time, it was obvious that air power, despite its great promise, was doing little to stem the tide of the Korean Communists in their southward march," Gavin wrote. The invasion came in June, and within a month the resisting U.N. forces had retreated into a hardening defensive line outside Pusan that could be traversed by jeep in a single day.

Gavin was ordered by President Truman's secretary of defense, Louis Johnson, to "take three scientists to South Korea to visit the combat troops and find out what science could do to assist the ground forces." Gavin's team was superbly credentialed. It included Dr. Charles Lauritsen, Sr., a nuclear physicist from the California Institute of Technology; Dr. William Shockley, a Nobel Prize winner for discovery of the transistor effect and who later became controversial for his studies of race and culture; and Dr. Edward Bowles, an electronics expert.

Though the presence of so much brainpower must have been daunting, Gavin was equal to it. He showed them, firsthand, what they did not know, traveling by jeep and on foot to forward areas where they could see units hard pressed and outnumbered. He also took them to Inchon, the site of MacArthur's brilliant landing which completely reversed the course of the war, until the Chinese invaded.

As a result of this trip, a study group, VISTA, was assembled, under joint service leadership, to study the use of the new weapons in the "limited" war that Korea represented. "The project was well worthwhile and soundly conceived," Gavin wrote. Among the leading scientists in the group were Lauritsen, and Dr. Robert Oppenheimer. Because Korea had renewed the possibility of minor wars, they sought a minor atomic bomb. But so great was the aura and mystique, the awesomeness of atomic power, that the project ran into political trouble right away.

Paranoia about Russian spies discovering U.S. atom bomb secrets was well founded. Dr. Klaus Fuchs, one of the team that developed the first atom bomb during the Manhattan Project in 1944–45, was also an assiduous passer of secrets to the Kremlin, and now the Russians had tested an atom bomb. Gavin himself noted "I have no doubt whatever that the Chinese moved confidently and skillfully into North Korea, and, in fact, I believe they were able to do this because they were well informed not only of the moves [General] Walker would make but of the limitations on what he might do." Many scholars have concluded that all messages sent to MacArthur, dittoed to allied military chiefs, were passed through the British embassy in Washington and directly over the desks of H. A. R.

"Kim" Philby and his fellow defector Guy Burgess, who were first and second secretary. A third possible conspirator was Donald Maclean in London.

Now suspicion was aimed at Gavin's VISTA and centered on the enigmatic Oppenheimer, whose ambivalence about a weapon potentially suicidal for mankind was so profound he had turned from having been the leader of the Manhattan Project to being the focal point of opposition to the hydrogen bomb. Air force SAC boomers viewed such doubts as blasphemy. "Enthusiasm of the Air Force [for VISTA] began to wane when it was realized that increasing emphasis on tactical air support and tactical airlift would conflict with Air Force views on strategic air power. At the same time, the Air Force began to suspect the views of Dr. Oppenheimer. An Air Force observer who was present at a VISTA session and heard Dr. Oppenheimer expound his views went out of the meeting and called his boss in the Pentagon, an Air Force general, and remarked that Oppenheimer must be either a Communist or a Communist sympathizer, since he was attacking the Strategic Air Command. . . . Dr. Oppenheimer's work with VISTA came under closer scrutiny." In the early 1950s a suggestion, a whisper of suspicion was all that was needed.

Gavin's trip to the battlefield at Inchon had led to a curious discovery. The press and staff gathered around the victorious General Douglas MacArthur at Kimpo airfield, one of the key targets of the Inchon invasion plan. While the group of visitors remained with the great man on his day of undeniable triumph, Gavin wandered off to examine the physical aspects of the airfield. Perhaps he felt curious about Korean air operations, which had appeared so feeble against the Americans. To Gavin's amazement, he found "an elaborate arrangement of hard stands and revetments all around the airfield. They were as good or better than anything I had seen in the airfields of Europe in World War II. Obviously some sophisticated thinking had gone into the planning, and much labor and effort had been expended in anticipation of using the airfield by a modern air force. Either the North Koreans were wasting their time, which seemed unlikely, or a first class air power was about to intervene in the war." Gavin told historian William Manchester that he laid his findings before MacArthur's intelligence officer, General Charles Willoughby, a longtime MacArthur staff officer. Gavin told the German-born Willoughby that this kind of hard unambiguous intelligence was taken very seriously during the war in Europe. He extrapolated from it that the

Chinese were not only considering moving to help their allies in the peninsula, but had already prepared to do so. "The preparation of Kimpo is a sure indication that this is what they are going to do, and when they are ready, they will come in," Gavin told Willoughby. But this report was shelved.

And in a small way, Gavin, too, was shelved. In his account of the Korean War, Clay Blair, describes how Ridgway took command in Korea in the wake of MacArthur's removal by President Truman, on April 11, 1951, and notes that Ridgway brought with him all those he most trusted. His old friend Gavin, the man who had much to do with Ridgway's World War II successes, was deliberately not brought. Blair writes, "During the war the Ridgway coterie had formed the opinion that Gavin was not sufficiently grateful for the unstinting support and promotions Ridgway had gained for him and he was an egocentric publicity hound, intent on displacing Ridgway as 'Mr. Paratrooper.' "

Blair is not the only historian to ask why Gavin, the superb battle commander and the greatest of the younger generals of World War II, the master of troop training and effectiveness, was not summoned to new and more important jobs during the Korean conflict.

Whether the "Ridgway coterie" liked Gavin or not is moot. Ridgway himself liked Gavin, and that is precisely why Ridgway selected Gavin to be his G-3 (chief of operations) right after Korea, when he became Chief of Staff of the Army.

The real answer to why Ridgway didn't take Gavin to Korea is a bit more complex. Part of it lies in the army's ironclad protocol of command: there was no place for him. The generals who had served in unglamorous staff support roles during World War II had precedence for the Korea fight, and Gavin, after his experiences with Fifth Army in Chicago, seemed destined for higher things than another division, which is what his rank suited him for. But even more important was the question of Washington's priorities. As the Korean war dragged on, the Washington establishment kept its eyes on Europe. Planners suspected Korea to be a diversion. The real action might take place in central Europe, with the Soviets launching an all-out invasion. Europe, then, was the place for the first string. Gavin was definitely first string, so he left WSEG directly for Italy.

So Gavin's influence on Korea, that "police action" that cost 54,246 dead (33,629 on the battlefield), was peripheral. It was, however, his blooding in the difficult and shadowy maneuvers of Pentagon politics. He would return for more shortly.

Meanwhile, he went to Naples, a town he had liked since his World War II triumph there, to work under Admiral Robert Carney in charge of newly forming Allied Forces, Southern Europe. And Jean, who would soon give birth to another baby girl, Aileen, was pleased. Though she noted that the navy equivalent to her husband's army command had both a villa and a yacht, she and her husband lived well, too, in "a comfortable new apartment" in a recently constructed building on Via Orazia, with "a wide terrace that overlooked the famous postcard scene of the Bay of Naples showing Vesuvius."

Gavin took up a long-desired pursuit while in the glamorous but quiet assignment in Naples: he began painting. Later he recalled that it was the beauty of Naples that inspired him to paint, and though his first efforts were mediocre, he stayed with it and even took professional lessons during his next assignment, in Germany. He painted the rest of his life, and his work soon improved.

But he remained first and fundamentally a soldier, and a soldier who now had real expertise in the field of nuclear weapons. He had stopped on the way to Naples to call on General Eisenhower, then NATO commander, to urge the stepped-up testing of nuclear realities on combat formations. He urged Eisenhower to place a top scientist on his staff, and Eisenhower responded by appointing Gavin's WSEG colleague Dr. H. P. Robertson.

Gavin was not about to just bide his time with Allied Forces. The navy had complained that they had no theater command in Europe, and in spite of the fact that a Soviet invasion spelled primarily a land campaign, the navy got its way and this Southern European command was the result. Gavin had the job of making a land war make sense for sea-minded officers and found it frustrating. He found the naval officers sensitive to all the publicity MacArthur had received in World War II, and he commented, "Admittedly, they did not know Fulda Gap from Brenner Pass, but that didn't disturb them." He went about his new position as was his custom, wearing out jeeps and drivers to see situations firsthand. By jeep, and not command car, he immediately toured the Southern European Theater. "I visited all the mountain passes in northern Italy to familiarize myself with the terrain and its limitations on military movement. I also visited northern Greece and drove by jeep from Lárisa to Salonica all the way across Macedonia and Thrace to Turkey, thence south to the Dardanelles where I crossed the narrows." Along the way he had dinner with the king and queen of Greece, met the Greek general staff, and visited the prime minister of Turkey.

In December of 1952 orders came for him to proceed to Germany and assume command of VII Corps. This was his first troop command since the 82nd, and it was a three-star position.

Eagerly he packed up Jean and the children and moved them to Stuttgart, Germany, his new headquarters. VII Corps had a band and a color guard awaiting his arrival, but the amenities ended quickly. Always the unconventional warrior, Gavin now launched into radical experimentation and a "housecleaning." Because the Pentagon worried over what the Russians might do in Europe while Korea dragged on, Cold War tensions grew greatly in the aftermath of the Berlin Airlift and nuclear stockpiling by the world's two "superpowers" (a new word in the 1950s). National Guard divisions had been sent to Europe to hold the line. American arms had continued occupying Germany after World War II as just what their name implied, occupation troops. Now that had changed. VII Corps was not an occupier but a defender, and Gavin found the two National Guard divisions, the 28th and the 43rd Infantry, little prepared for their task of defending half of Germany. Gavin wore out more jeeps and drivers. Once again, wherever a field problem took place, he showed up unannounced and with few of the usual general's followers. When not in the field, he checked motor pools, arms rooms, and unit training schedules. Old airborne hands smiled. They knew well his "nose for trouble," but for the uninitiated, the omnipresent Gavin whirlwind was staggering. Then he began staging alert after alert (one right in the middle of a dinner Jean cooked for his staff, for which she had difficulty forgiving him) and found several to be disasters when he changed the areas in which units were to deploy from those that had become their routine. Then came the new emphasis on night training and battalion, company, and platoon training. He tutored his battalion commanders exhaustively, then, to find out how good they were, he tested them individually and reluctantly relieved one colonel. The year after he left, seven battalion commanders were relieved when the traditional tests were reinstated. He noted years later, "I was very disturbed by this. Our senior commanders must be better troop trainers and learn that the responsibilities of command consist of training subordinate commanders as well as troops. It is very easy to relieve men of command, but it takes hard work to make a subordinate commander in any position into a good combat commander."

He also set about making sure VII Corps was properly integrated. This included higher headquarters where white officers were deliberately excluding black officers. They claimed that black officers were not up to the responsibilities. Gavin responded that was because they had no training. He immediately demanded they be trained, and he integrated all higher headquarters, personally selecting black officers with the help of a former 555 Parachute Infantry Battalion man, Bradley Biggs.

Once troop standards began approaching what he wanted for them, and integration was well along, Gavin began experimenting with dispersing troops for nuclear attack. He obtained what he thought were successful results. Others, outside the corps, looked on with amusement. Conventional army wisdom still did not include innovative tactics for dealing with tactical nuclear weapons.

Throughout his time in Europe, Gavin served as a nuclear expert at numerous conferences and war games, notably those organized by his World War II sometime-commander Field Marshal Bernard Montgomery, then deputy commander at Supreme Allied Command Europe (SACEUR) under General Alfred Gruenther.

Gavin attended every war game and conference Montgomery held. "A number of us called them 'The Field Marshal's School for Dull Generals,' " he wrote. He remembered the last one he attended vividly. "We were assembled in the conference room in SACEUR headquarters outside of Paris. As I recall, all of the major generals and higher-ups and officers of equivalent rank in the Navy were in attendance. The Field Marshal and the four-star generals sat in the front row while we lesser lights occupied four sides of the conference room. In the middle was a huge relief map of Europe from the Scandinavian Peninsula to the Mediterranean in the south. Field Marshal Montgomery equipped himself with a school bell which he rang to commence the exercises, and he had a box of cough drops that he would offer to anyone who developed a cough. His talks could be quite amusing, but they were very serious too. In the last exercise I attended the question came up about the tactical use of nuclear weapons. 'Was it possible?' he asked with raised eyebrows. My Air Force colleague said, 'No, nuclear weapons were only to be used by the Strategic Air Command.' I knew better than that. Otherwise, why were we doing all that testing in the Pacific against tactical targets? Perched high in the

bleachers in the top row, I said that it was perfectly feasible to use tactical
nuclear weapons against tactical targets. Furthermore, if adequate research were conducted and we could bring the yields down to fractional
yields, we could have tactical weapons to use on many military targets as
well as against airfields, etc. Aircraft could use them against ground
targets as well. My friends in the Air Force were very unhappy with me,
but we had a good discussion.''

One who took notice of the kibitzer was Montgomery. He asked Gavin
to come to his château for a personal visit in December 1953 in the last
days of Gavin's broken-up time in Europe. ''He also invited Dr. Vannevar
Bush, (the top scientist engaged by the armed services to help with planning and research after World War II and a man who had been with the
committee that sought alternatives to the use of the Hiroshima bomb)
and British Major General Sir Richard Gale, a top World War II airborne
commander who had landed in Normandy.

The château was frigid, heated only by a small fire in a downstairs
sitting room. The thought of this overnight visit with the older war hero,
in the circumstances, fascinated Gavin. The tiny group dined without
benefit of wine—Montgomery neither drank nor smoked—and afterwards gathered before the fire.

''I was interested in the form the discussion took. The Field Marshal,
supported by Gen. Gale, was of the opinion that troops should deploy in
time and not in space in order to defend themselves from tactical nuclear
attack.'' To Gavin, this was an old argument, already passé in the new
world of the nuclear battlefield.

The Montgomery argument went back to Napoleon, dictating that an
attacking force must time its arrival on the battlefield in such a way as to
be able to attack without exposing itself to the enemy's defensive measures for long.

Gavin, who had been mulling these problems for years, responded
vigorously. ''I argued that they had to be dispersed at all times with
adequate communications and weapons . . . this was to be a way of life on
the nuclear battlefield. If the enemy had good intelligence with modern
reconnaissance aircraft, troops dispersed in time alone would become ex-
ceedingly vulnerable at any one point when their location could be de-
tected.''

But the discussion did not resolve the question. Dr. Bush, knowledgeable about the developments of missiles, sided with Gavin and favored an

entirely new method of troop dispersal and assembly by aircraft. But the British stuck to their arguments. "What disturbed me about that evening, as well as the Field Marshal's school conduct earlier, was that none of those present really had seen nuclear weapons fired or had any idea of what the effects were, except what they had read, and that is quite different than personal observation. They seemed to be trying to rationalize slight modifications of old tactics to meet this new phenomenon without understanding the phenomenon itself."

Dissatisfied, Gavin left, with barely enough time to return to his short-duty station at Stuttgart and say his farewells. He was once again headed for the army's peacetime battleground, the Pentagon. Ridgway was now Chief of Staff, and he wanted Gavin as his chief of operations.

Jean and the children packed once more. Gavin's family had expanded rapidly since the end of the war. Besides Barbara, his daughter from his previous marriage to Peggy Baulsir (living with her mother in Washington) and Jean's Caroline, from her previous marriage, he had daughters Patricia, four, and Aileen, two. Jean was also six-months pregnant.

As the dirty March snow of Stuttgart melted, Gavin and his family, laden with bouquets from the obligatory military review of corps headquarters, took the train to Frankfurt in a light rain. It had been nine years since Gavin stood with his M-1 rifle in hand, looking into Germany for the first time, as a conquering American soldier.

He knew he faced a crisis at home with the army but felt up to it. "It was one thing to oppose massive retaliation as a matter of principle, or as a philosophical or moral concept, but we had to propose alternatives that were acceptable and militarily sound. . . . Perhaps 'massive retaliation' was oversold by the politically powerful and the Army was undersold. The tactics and equipment of World War II and Korea were inadequate for the missile-space-nuclear age. Greater strategic and battlefield mobility were in order. Vastly improved communications and more tactical fire power were needed. Since the tactical theater of NATO was all of western Europe, its central nervous system, the command's communications network, had to be updated and expanded and made more responsive. Finally, the potential of the helicopter had to be developed as a matter of highest priority."

In the spring of 1954 Gavin was, at forty-seven, still very much a young man. His carriage remained ramrod straight. His hair was thinning, but his waist would never really change from its waspy look. Vigorous games of handball and tennis kept it that way. It was his misfortune to be at the prime of life and at the top of his powers as he returned to Washington.

An older man might have more easily fit in with the "live and let live" of the post-Korea Pentagon, the Defense Department that spent most of its time defending itself. A younger man would have held back and adjusted to his superiors. But that was not Gavin's fate, nor his way.

17.

TILTING AT WINDMILLS AT THE PENTAGON

Gavin's brief Stuttgart posting had brought him back to troop duty at last. "I felt, deep inside, a sadness that I would not return to troop duty," Gavin wrote. But he was now, at the Pentagon, about as far from the sound of the guns as a top commander could be. Here he would fight once more for the modern army he believed in.

Since 1948, he and Jean had gone through four moves in four years—"all unexpected," he would write later. His return to Washington put him once again in play on the field of power within the army. He welcomed the opportunity and felt determined this time to fight for new ideas as doggedly as he had fought for his beloved division and what, for him, it had come to represent. And he was in the right position, wearing two hats as chief of plans and training and chief of research and development.

His nuclear views had further moderated, and he considered the antinuclear people as simply unrealistic. So many people in and out of the

346

military were aghast at statements about the nuclear battlefield encompassing the whole of Europe. Now, instead of urging nuclear bazookas, howitzers, missiles, and ballistic missiles, he urged new generations of conventional weapons and space-age technology. It was back to his constant theme of war: rapid movement and striking power.

"To come back to G-3 (plans and training) once again was a stimulating prospect, and I looked forward to it very much indeed," Gavin wrote. "All my years of troop duty, the nuclear weapons school, my work with the Weapons Systems Evaluation Group, and my service with NATO would bear fruit. . . . The functioning of the Army staff pivots about G-3."

No matter that the Pentagon was profoundly uninterested in new machines like Gavin's favorites vertical takeoff and landing (VTOL) aircraft and new families of helicopters, or weapons systems like "fighter gunships that could engage and destroy armor and heavy vehicles." Gavin wanted to revolutionize the way America fought "limited" wars like Korea. Most of his peers were convinced there would never be another such war. Gavin found even that subject so politically sensitive that few spokesmen for the Pentagon dared mention "small tactical nuclear weapons" as a possibility. No matter that missiles were considered unnecessary under the "nuclear shield" supplied by the air force's fleet. No matter that the country and the new president, rid of the Korean involvement at last, felt that another world war would mean the end of civilization, and limited war could never be decisive. Gavin thought otherwise and knew there were men who would listen. He had a long card in his hand: Matt Ridgway was Army Chief of Staff and the necessary link to the Joint Chiefs of Staff and policy.

In fact Gavin seemed, on cursory view, well positioned politically. Ridgway was his chief, and Dwight Eisenhower his commander in chief, both of whom held him in high regard. His cordially disliked rival, Maxwell Taylor, had served as West Point superintendent for two years, and by 1949 had Gavin's old job as commander of the U.S. sector of Berlin. In 1951 Taylor returned to Washington as assistant in charge of operations and training to Chief of Staff of the Army General J. Lawton Collins, and gained his fourth star. Taylor visited Korea to evaluate the potential of the Republic of Korea (ROK) forces. He had gained a spot in the Korean War as it neared its close and General Eisenhower won the 1952 election. Taylor was chosen to follow Lieutenant General James Van

Fleet as Eighth Army commander. The war had by then become a bitter standoff, and Taylor's mission was to fight defensively while long armistice negotiations ground on. Gavin, it appeared, was among colleagues who would at last listen.

Gavin also stood directly in line behind Taylor, his senior by six years in age, for a real shot at Army Chief of Staff.

The strange five-sided building which is the heart and symbol of America's military was a pasture when Gavin first came to Washington as a young officer, but because of World War II it became a colossus. In a way it marks the coming of age of the American style of war—a style marked more by machinery than by men, a style of bigness that is overwhelming, as if by sheer power of numbers America could swamp its foes. The Pentagon is the architectural symbol of the victory of massive, all-fronts material war, the War of Grant and Eisenhower, over the more intellectual warfare waged by the Lees, the Guderians, and the Gavins of military history.

The Pentagon in which Gavin was to make his fight for a singular future for the army was a place of parties and factions and arguments, of allies and enemies, in a time when careers were marked by two of America's most dubious wars, Korea and Vietnam.

There, in five concentric rings and five floors lay the other army, the army that moves by paper, by prestige, by persuasion and politics. It was an army that Gavin had tasted briefly as he put forward his plans for the army of the future, and it was an army he was determined to master on his way to his natural goal, which was to become Chief of Staff, the top man on the second floor. (The army occupies the second floor, the air force the third, and navy the fourth.)

Gavin returned to the Pentagon without Korea but not harmed unduly by having missed it. As an outsider, he had avoided all blame for the blunders, the lack of preparedness at the beginning of the war, and the breakdown of policy and coordination between civil and military powers, which had led to General Douglas MacArthur's dismissal.

Now in the 1950s, the Pentagon was the right place to be, but a man needed a cause, a theory, a weapons system, a group of friends on the right committees of Congress to prevail. Some survived without having a cause or a theory, by merely avoiding being wrong, by carefully calculating the power struggle among the lieutenant generals and admirals, chieftains who circulated like courtiers. They all waited for the same thing, the next step closer to the top of their profession, Chief of Staff.

When Gavin was sent to Italy during the summer of 1951, revisiting the city he'd helped liberate in 1943, his future seemed undimmed. His job, a complete anomaly for him, was to serve as chief of staff for Admiral Robert Carney, a pleasure-loving gentleman sailor who had lived like a sea lord, waited on by a total of twenty-two Filipino servants gathered during the war, and availed himself of the motor yacht and the wonderful pleasures of one of the world's gayest, brightest cities as top man at Supreme Headquarters Southern Europe Command.

Those who had known Gavin in Naples noticed a change in him. He then wore impeccably tailored civilian clothes when off duty, (from Naples' finest tailor, Caggula, who was regularly sent for by Egypt's King Farouk), visited Naples' elegant cafés, usually accompanied by the stunning Jean. The Gavin reputation as a war hero, liberator of Naples, and intellectual, got him instantly noticed and commented on. In the Pentagon, he had a growing reputation as the up-and-coming brain, the man who championed the helicopter. Joe Napoli, a State Department employee who knew the Gavins while stationed with SHAEF, remembers Gavin as a reticent, extremely elegant man, so reserved he might be deaf. With him at this command, Napoli remembers, "were a number of Airborne officers, Lieutenant Colonels and Colonels, who would have laid down their lives for him."

He was working on new plans for a mobile cavalry force that would replace the airborne's, expanding its overspecialized and rather uniquely limited role in the future. Gavin saw a way to save both the future of airborne forces and revive a vital element of the army that had lost its function. He combined the two things in a concept called "sky cavalry."

The way Gavin saw it, the entire function of cavalry in battle—skirmishing, patrolling in force, retreating while delaying major enemy forces, diverting, and reconnaissance—had been subverted by the introduction of "wheeled" horses, including tanks, armored cars, half-tracks, and other vehicles. In reality, the cavalry had become as slow as the infantry. With everyone mechanized, cavalry no longer had the advantage of speed or mobility. He was livid about the way army forces had been used in Korea and felt the stalemate there and the tactics that led to it (with the important exception of MacArthur's brilliant flanking assault at Inchon on September 15, 1950) were responsible for a near disaster.

Cavalry, he argued, was the eyes of the army. But somehow, the entire concept of the mobile, lightly armed force had been lost. "All the soul-searching in the world and the most brilliant cerebrations, will not conjure up tactical success in cavalry action unless the means of achieving it are provided to cavalry commanders. They do not have the means today. They are roadbound. Even assuming they will be fortunate enough to fight in countries where roads are numerous, they are no more mobile than the mechanized infantry divisions they are expected to screen from the enemy."

When the Chinese escalated the Korean War after Inchon and swept down from the north in November of 1950, the resulting debacle embodied some of Gavin's worst fears about how war could be waged. The Chinese masses had avoided the roads, or used them at night, and hidden hundreds of thousands of men in the hilly, difficult countryside between the two prongs of the northward-thrusting U.N. forces. After his visit to Inchon, he had foretold such an invasion, but he had also seen that even in a stunning victory, MacArthur's invading soldiers and marines simply did not know how profound their victory was. They went forward not knowing that nothing was left to resist them. MacArthur's Inchon victory could have been complete, Gavin argued. "Memory can become idolatry of things past and close our minds to the meaning of events. We quote the preachings of [Basil] Liddell Hart and [J. F. C.] Fuller in the twenties, as though mere repetition would extend their validity into the present. We run the risk of forgetting that it is not what was said and done, but why it was said and done that is important. In the meantime, one of the most, if not the most critically evolutionary periods in military history is upon us."

Gavin continued to believe technology paramount and that the nation that had it would enjoy an enormous initial advantage. World War II had revealed how mistakes in U.S. armaments policy—the slow development of artillery equal to the Germans' all-purpose 88-mm cannon, the inferiority of the bazooka and the Sherman tank, among others—had been overcome only by the enormous advantages in numbers and resources. The next war, he was convinced, would be against Russia, whose resources he believed to be as limitless as those of the United States, or in another limited conflict on the Soviet Union's periphery. Perhaps it would not be an all-out nuclear exchange. If not, then the need to update and modernize U.S. weapons systems was all the more important.

These ideas came together in his mind in the early 1950s: He had seen the greatest and fastest development of his own weapons arm, the airborne force, and he knew, by the day he witnessed Montgomery's vast

Rhine crossing in the spring of 1945, that parachute assault would never again take place in such mass and concentration. It was only because of the lack of a German air force and the disorganization of German "buzz bomb" attacks that the crossing had succeeded.

He had also seen air power in the form of the fighter and the fighter bomber bring an end to the apparently unstoppable blitzkrieg apparatus of tanks, dive bombers, and motorized infantry. Like no other soldier, he had understood that tanks were already dinosaurs at the end of World War II. In the Ardennes, he'd witnessed the monster Tiger, crouching like a terrified beast in a stone farm building to avoid the deadly air assault of fighter bombers.

He had come out of the war believing that new vehicles for aerial combat would soon be developed, among them cargo planes with detachable pods to carry heavy equipment, parachutes big enough to drop heavy artillery and vehicles, and futuristic craft to bridge the gap between air and land or sea. None of these ideas seemed any more than pipe dreams, except for the development of one neglected machine, the helicopter. Another solution, the VTOL aircraft, which in theory could fly fast, hover, and land on a baseball diamond presented engineering troubles from the first.

But the chopper and its permutations—yet to become the "fighting gunship" Gavin dreamed of in the early 1950s and the most important attack vehicle in the Vietnam War that Gavin hated—was a mass of contradictions. Considered slow and vulnerable to enemy fire, it was more of a military gadget than anything else, in the 1940s. Its engineering was complicated, particularly the highly stressed hub where the blades are attached, and one slim steel shaft bears the whole weight of the pod and motor, not to mention the crews. Failures of helicopters were frequent and disastrous because of the lack of ability to glide.

Gavin combined the threads into a concept that was to define his own future and career and would have a great influence on future development of America's conventional war methods. "The more I pondered the operations, the more I became convinced that in carrying out their role, the airborne forces were performing the traditional cavalry role. They blocked enemy movements, thus enabling our offensive main body of troops to develop its attack relatively unhindered. They provided timely information on enemy dispositions and actions. They supplied raiding forces to capture objectives such as Fort Eben Emael and Corregidor. Their outstanding deficiency was their lack of adequate mobility once they landed by parachute or glider. In fact, they were no longer cavalry.

"The conclusion seemed clear. We had to develop vertical takeoff and landing vehicles and helicopters. With an adequate research and development program we could restore the cavalry arm to its proper role. I proposed that we bring into being a high mobility force of VTOL aircraft with scout vehicles well equipped with sensory devices and long range communications, fighter gunships that could engage and destroy any armor and heavy vehicles, personnel carriers for moving large groups of riflemen, heavy logistic support with VTOL vehicles and the command vehicles that could control a battlefield of over a thousand square miles. In addition to developing an arm with significant military differential over the infantry, we had to develop a family of small tactical nuclear weapons. And finally, we had to move rapidly into the challenging world of missiles and space."

This, it turned out, was a lot more than the Pentagon was willing to do, and it was perhaps Gavin's growing blind spot that he was unable to understand why. He never did understand how Washington worked.

To the military mind, the theory made little sense. War is, after all, a formal game in which both sides agree to join. There can be no battle unless the combatants agree, which is why it is rather quaintly called "giving battle," like a gift. Gavin was part of this old-fashioned tradition and was completely comfortable with the notion of battle courtesies, frequently commenting that the Germans had given him "a good fight," even when that meant the destruction of hundreds of his beloved paratroopers. It was not until he had seen the atrocities at Woebblin that he was able to muster hatred of the Germans, though he had killed them willingly: It was part of the profession of arms. Had he not sung, as lustily as any, the chorus of the old West Point ballad that ends with the wish "to die a soldier's death beneath a soldier's blow"?

Korea, he said now in 1954, was a mistake—but not because the president and the Joint Chiefs of Staff had refused to use nuclear power against the invaders. It was a mistake, he said, because the army had forgotten how to fight infantry actions; somehow, Gavin said, between the blitzkrieg and the bomb, the army had forgotten the role of cavalry.

But in suggesting that the cavalry be resurrected in airborne guise, Gavin managed to offend both the tankers, who had inherited the cavalry tradition and become weighed down in heavy metal and road-bound machinery, and the air force, which had bet its entire budget on ever-larger bombers.

He had also unwittingly taken himself out of the circle of advisors to whom the president listened on matters of defense. Eisenhower, the superb coalition general, wanted to run things by consensus, through groups of advisors. Himself one of the few soldiers who was a good politician, he despised politicians as a breed and chose his cabinet instead from the successful leaders of business, the generals of capitalism. Warriors had their usefulness, but needed to be kept carefully in check. In the Eisenhower White House Gavin had the reputation of a warrior.

Gavin noticed immediately the difference in the atmosphere of the Pentagon he returned to: "I made my way around the E ring to the office of the Chief of Plans, Operations, and Research. The Pentagon had changed very little, but the strategy of the Department of Defense had changed dramatically. The long corridors were lined with paintings of battle scenes and portraits of the chiefs of the services of past years. There was a cathedrallike calm about the outer E ring that belied the intense discussions which frequently took place in the offices off the ring." The "honeycomb," as Gavin called it, was quiet with a kind of murmur. It was the sound of the armed services retrenching.

Gavin had an utterly ambivalent view of Eisenhower. He felt loyalty to him as his wartime chief, but he had no faith whatsoever in his military acumen and felt he had not spent enough time at the front commanding troops to understand the dynamics of leadership. The terms of praise he used for Eisenhower were faint damns, calling him "sensitive and thoughtful . . . his strongest suit was his patience." Gavin came to think Eisenhower had made a number of serious blunders in his handling of the war and that he had compromised himself by his relationship with Kay Summersby, his driver and confidante, a relationship that, surprisingly, given his own affairs, enraged Gavin. "A general simply doesn't walk about with an attractive young lady in his company in the presence of many thousands of troops whose wives and sweethearts are many miles away and whom they may never see again," he sputtered in a 1981 note.

Worst of all for Gavin, he believed Eisenhower turned his back on the army when he became president, ruthlessly cutting its budget and setting up a man who knew nothing about military affairs, Charles Wilson, as his defense secretary. For once Gavin was in league with the angry and red-faced older generals. "When he picked . . . Wilson to be Secretary of

Defense," Gavin wrote, "Eisenhower knew that he did not need a Secretary of Defense. He would be his own Secretary of Defense."

Eisenhower quickly disappointed those military men who had confidently thought that the old soldier would take care of the army. The navy could continue to propose ship-building programs and adapt its vessels to new conditions; the air force was in the ascendancy, but the army was the unwanted stepchild, its only apparent purpose to wield air defense missiles.

Eisenhower in fact had never met "Engine Charlie" Wilson, the chief executive of General Motors, thought to be the highest paid executive in America ($201,000 in 1952 dollars) at that time. He was picked on the recommendation of Lieutenant General Lucius Clay, the able postwar administrator of Germany. The Chairman of the Joint Chiefs of Staff was Admiral Arthur W. Radford. Radford had been navy commander in chief in the Pacific. But Eisenhower felt strongly that a man with experience in Asia should replace Omar Bradley, who had served two terms as chair of the JCS. Radford believed utterly in massive retaliation and in stockpiling nuclear weapons; he did not believe in stopping each Communist threat piecemeal. He had met and impressed Eisenhower when the president-elect took a whirlwind tour of Korea at the end of November 1952.

Radford was one of the group that repeatedly urged Eisenhower to intervene in the French struggle for a place called Vietnam—with atomic weapons.

Gavin acted from the habits that had worked for him as a troop leader. He would work longer, march harder, and argue more persistently. This was his way. He would be at his office at 7:30 A.M. and return to Jean and the girls at Fort Myer by 7 P.M. Saturdays, he considered "a good opportunity to catch up." And his staff men soon grew accustomed to the sight of the lean, intent general who always kept his door open.

Like few other military leaders, Gavin made a point of including the younger men during his deliberations. He wanted them to feel that they were a part of the decisions he reached and he knew that he would win their loyalty and their self-interest this way. Gavin soon attracted a new coterie: "I soon found that some senior officers from other staff sections would come to talk to me about our policy in view of those of the Chairman of the Joint Chiefs. The Chairman, Radford, insisted upon total support of his views, and, of course, of the official policy of massive retaliation . . . as he explained it 'a bigger bang for a buck.'" Soon this coterie met on Saturdays for informal discussions.

Eisenhower's philosophy developed from his thorough study of the theories of Dr. J. Robert Oppenheimer, whom he'd made head of a presidential advisory group to counsel him about strategy in the arms race. Oppenheimer had also chaired the Atomic Energy Commission. He convinced Eisenhower that a nuclear war could not be waged, particularly after October 1953 when the president had to acknowledge at a press conference that the Soviet Union had tested a hydrogen bomb.

Eisenhower agreed with Oppenheimer that the stockpiling of nuclear weapons no longer made sense in a situation that placed America and the Soviet Russia in the position, pointedly described by Oppenheimer in an article in *Foreign Affairs*, of "two scorpions in a bottle, each capable of killing the other, but only at the risk of his own life." Eisenhower's belief in this theory and the actions that naturally flowed from it—principally a search for a workable disarmament policy—set him at odds with many at the Pentagon and the State Department who believed the Russians incapable of honoring any agreement that would compromise their military might.

For Gavin, the result was a murky policy which at once assumed that future conflicts would not be nuclear and, at the same time, assumed that the threat of nuclear war would prevent all future conflicts. It made no sense to Gavin.

His Saturday group took shape in the E ring quite openly. Persuasion in secret was never Gavin's style. "The colonels coming in to see me, the group varying from two to half a dozen, were among the brightest on the Army staff. We were concerned that witnesses before Congress, for example, and staff officers in conferences with the other services, might not be fully informed of the implications of the present policy and of what the Army's alternatives were. I therefore took the responsibility upon myself as G-3 to have an occasional meeting with members of all the staff sections in a small auditorium in the Army's area of the Pentagon. Those in attendance numbered about 80–100 staff officers. These were good free-wheeling sessions intended to bring our thinking together. General Ridgway was aware of the work we were doing in G-3 and of the positions that we were developing for him and for the Army."

Though the meetings were anything but secret, Gavin's motives were soon under attack. He was seen as a lightning rod for officers in reaction against official Department of Defense policy. Though it is difficult to credit it now, in the early 1950s a deep fear and paranoia about disloyalty attached itself to any dissent from an ill-defined standard of loyalty.

Though Gavin was well aware of the witch-hunting activities of Republican Senator Joseph McCarthy, like Eisenhower, who gradually came to detest McCarthy, he believed firmly that the army, and particularly the officers' corps, was above suspicion and loyal almost to a man.

"To some," Gavin wrote, "being against massive retaliation was seen as an attack against the Strategic Air Command and a possible sympathy for Communism. You could therefore be expected to be accused of at least disloyalty. So we agreed among ourselves that we must be completely honest and above board, and must do nothing in secret or behind closed doors. The papers that would come from our deliberations should be made available to everyone. Finally, the Army Chief of Staff must approve of what we do or direct our efforts into other channels."

At the same time that Gavin was gathering his meager forces to do internal battle for the future of the army, he was beginning to see serious and crippling faults in the organization of the Joint Chiefs of Staff (JCS), the place where the president gets military advice and overall command of the armed services really happens. While he had previously thought that competition between the services was a good and healthy by-product of the system, he now concluded that the structure of the JCS made the mission of the individual chief impossible, like that of the man who, the Bible assured him, "cannot serve two masters."

At the time of the Korean Armistice, Eisenhower asked his service chiefs to review strategic policy. The result was a set of strategic scenarios that would cost billions. The fiscal managers of Eisenhower's administration were astonished, for they had hoped for big reductions, from $42 billion to $36 billion.

The reason for the large defense projection was that the services envisioned new threats to strategic goals being met in similar ways to Korea, i.e., with conventional forces. A cheaper defense budget could be realized, argued JCS Chairman Radford, if Eisenhower would make clear that he intended to use nuclear weapons from the start of any conflict. In this Eisenhower agreed. Out of a budget compromise arose the policy known as the "New Look." America would base its defense policy on massive retaliation.

The New Look effectively locked massive retaliation into policy because it was cheap in comparison with a combat-ready army with modern weapons and transports.

But there were deep internal difficulties. In the first place, the only service really satisfied with the New Look was the air force. Costs had to be cut for the other services, much to the dismay of Ridgway—and, even more, Gavin.

In addition differences among the services proved impossible to resolve. The problems were too deep to be resolved by consensus.

Gavin, as deputy chief of staff, and some others, notably Ridgway, desired to rethink military strategy.

18.

THE INDOCHINA

CRISIS

They called it the Indochina crisis in March 1954, and from the army loyalists' point of view, it exemplified how the policy of massive retaliation hamstrung the United States. If a problem wasn't big enough to risk blowing up civilization, America's armed services couldn't deal with it.

The French war in Indochina didn't fit the strategic plans. It wasn't Russia, or even China, it wasn't cities. And it was the opposite of a modern war. This contest was between the irregular troops of the North Vietnamese Communists, the Vietminh, who wanted their own nation, and French regulars defending a shrinking colonial empire.

But the United States had a stake in the fight of the French to preserve their colony against Communist aggression and had followed the State Department's doctrine of containment with a stream of dollars for years. Ever since the Truman administration, the United States had sought to counter Communist moves in the peninsula which seemed aimed not only at Vietnam, but also Cambodia and Laos.

When Eisenhower came to power the American treasury was supplying foreign aid amounting to one third of the cost of the French garrison, and the air force had two hundred technicians stationed there.

When in November 1953, the Vietminh's able general Vo Nguyen Giap responded to a deliberate lure—the French had dropped 15,000 paratroops behind Vietminh lines, had built an airfield there for resupply and practically begged the Vietminh to offer battle for it—the world was transfixed by the drama.

The place, Dien Bien Phu, had little importance, but when the siege opened at the end of the second week of March, the world and the French Army suddenly realized that the battle had deep significance.

From the Pentagon, Gavin watched and read with grave fascination as the teletypes clattered and the story unfolded: how Giap had gathered 100,000 peasants to manhandle big 105-mm field guns up almost impossible jungle slopes to positions overlooking the French base. How artillery harassment had made the landing field almost unusable and exposed a basic French battle error, their failure to seize and defend the overlooking hills; how supply by parachute either landed in Vietminh territory if dropped from safe altitudes, or if dropped more accurately, from lower altitudes, risked the loss of the aircraft to antiaircraft batteries; how the French artillery was soon partly out of action.

The French begged for more American help, particularly heavy air strikes, which could destroy the Vietminh guns. For the French, the ploy of baiting the Vietminh into an old-fashioned battle was proving worse than a tactical blunder. It proved they had mistaken the military capabilities of their adversaries, and if they failed, the French were finished in Indochina. "The senior French General in Vietnam, Gen. Henri Navarre, . . . seriously underestimated the Vietminh and from the outset his prospects were not good. . . . As they came to realize the vast stakes involved, the French sent the chief of the French Armed Forces Staff, Gen. Paul Ely, to Washington." Gavin recorded that Ely, arriving March 23, met immediately with Eisenhower's vice president, Richard Nixon, Admiral Radford, General Ridgway, and CIA director Allen Dulles. "Sobered by the experience in Korea, the Americans were quite pessimistic about what would happen at Dien Bien Phu. But Gen. Ely persisted in his belief that a military solution could be achieved, and he particularly sought U.S. air support."

Radford, who seemed the most suggestible, took the French general to see Eisenhower "who left the General with the impression that Admiral Radford was to furnish the French with whatever they needed to win the battle." Eisenhower's biographer Stephen Ambrose gives another view of this meeting, stating that Eisenhower and Dulles "had a series of meetings with Ely . . . finally, Eisenhower agreed to furnish the French with some C-119 Flying Boxcars that could drop napalm which would burn out a considerable area and help to reveal enemy artillery positions."

Eisenhower also told Ely (as revealed by Ambrose from an unpublished portion of Eisenhower's memoirs) that the "US could not afford to send its flag and its own military establishment and thus to engage the prestige of the United States" unless it expected to win.

Radford, however, helped Ely concoct an air-raid plan—possibly with atomic bombs—to crush the Vietminh surrounding Dien Bien Phu. But Allen Dulles learned from U.S. ambassador to France Douglas Dillon that the French believed the raid, named Operation Vulture, was being planned with presidential approval. Eisenhower recoiled and quickly snuffed the operation.

Other ambitious intervention plans were flying around the corridors at the Pentagon, Gavin recorded. Not long after General Ely's visit, the army was told by JCS to prepare plans for a landing in Haiphong in northern Vietnam, followed by a major offensive on Hanoi. Much of the work fell on G-3 Gavin and his staff. In spite of the nature of the plan, a perfect test case for the kind of highly mobile, powerful, and quick-striking conventional force Gavin had championed, he felt deeply disturbed by the risks. "I was very troubled with what we were about to do," Gavin wrote. "I had a tremendous amount of planning experience in World War II, but more importantly, I had extensive combat experience. So I knew that it is easy to start a battle, for that matter, a war, but it is something else again to bring it to a satisfactory end. I pondered the prospective attack with increasing concern. Because of my earlier experience in the Philippines, it seemed to me that we would have a difficult time in the event of a fratricidal war in Vietnam, where many northerners were intermingled with southern troops. There the rain forest, rice paddies, and mountains constituted an environment in which military operations could be very costly in lives. Furthermore, after a long experience as a colony of France—a condition that the French seemed most reluctant to change—many Vietnamese of all ranks had sympathy with the Vietminh. They would be willing to fight for liberation from the colonial power, but not for a continuation of the status quo."

Gavin had read deeply and felt that Ho Chi Minh must have strong military backing from China, and thus that the Chinese would have invested their prestige and will and "under the circumstances . . . it was very likely that China would not welcome our arrival in the Tonkin area up against the Chinese border. It seemed to me likely that in a short time we would be at war with China itself."

Gavin saw the heavily armed sortie potentially turning into a fight "in a very difficult environment against a force with almost unlimited manpower."

Ridgway was the logical man to turn to with these doubts, and when he talked with the Chief of Staff, Gavin found Ridgway "felt very strongly about the matter and also opposed it." Ridgway told Gavin to prepare a paper outlining the cost and consequences of the operation. The heart of the memorandum still chills with its accuracy:

SUBJECT: Military Consequences of Various Courses of Action with Respect to Application of U.S. Military Force in Indo-China

3. What are the military consequences of intervention of U.S. ground forces in Indo-China?

a. U.S. ground intervention in Indo-China carries with it a risk of initiating general war.

b. The Soviet Bloc would have succeeded in further dissipating U.S. Military power.

c. During the period D-day to approximately D + 9 months, the general posture of the Army would be at its worst since World War II.

d. Army divisions in FECOM (Far East Command) would be reduced to four. This will result in increased risks in that area until replaced by effective divisions about D + 7 months.

e. Decisions must be made by 15 April 1954 in order to have forces in place by the end of the rainy season in Indo-China.

f. Nine National Guard divisions must be called into Federal service.

g. The Army's three-division ready force for NATO will be employed in these operations and the force cannot be reconstituted in the U.S. until D + 6 months.

h. End FY 1955 strength required: 1,942,000.

i. Terms of service of all Army personnel must be extended nine months—Congressional action required.

j. Immediate resumption of production of critical items will be required to permit logistical support of combat operations in Indo-China.

Gavin sent the memorandum out over his own signature, hoping it would help sound the death knell to the incursion plan. Yet he knew that at the Pentagon, military adventures in search of glory sometimes had a life of their own.

Gavin committed himself to taking any risk necessary to scuttle the plan, but he soon found rumors spreading that his motives for opposing it were suspect, that the real reason was that the army's training, planning, and combat readiness were not up to the task. Since Gavin had been intimately associated with these aspects of army leadership, his own competence was placed on the line in the Pentagon gossip mill.

Meanwhile Gavin's memo went to Secretary of Defense Wilson. Ridgway, to be sure that the memo did not languish there unread, for Wilson was famous for simply not hearing what he did not wish to hear, took a copy to Eisenhower. The planning of the expedition into Haiphong went on, but without support from the top. Thus began Gavin's struggle against U.S. involvement in Vietnam.

Radford's rapid changes of enthusiasm continued to mystify Gavin. When the Joint Chiefs took up the plan, he was surprised to find that the navy—which after all would be responsible for the transport, initial artillery support, landing, and resupply of the invading force, was demanding that Hainan Island and the Chinese airfields there be seized by a marine division before the Seventh Fleet could perform a landing. Though it made sense to seize the huge island, which sits like a guardian fortress southeast of Haiphong, it would be an act of war against China. Was the navy turning thumbs down by making an impossible demand? Gavin thought not. "Although Gen. Ridgway was strongly opposed to the plan, Admiral Radford wanted to carry it out, or at least to make an air strike against the Vietnamese forces at Dien Bien Phu. He said it would bring the siege of Dien Bien Phu to an end in one afternoon's work. Ridgway opposed the introduction of U.S. air power in any form."

Gavin's disillusionment with the doctrine of massive retaliation became complete. "I was very curious why Radford, who had originally opposed the strategic bombing of cities and any signs of an exclusive reliance on strategic bombing, had changed his mind completely when he became Chairman of the Joint Chiefs. Now, he was a strong advocate of massive retaliation, going so far as to tell me that the Army should prepare for the withdrawal of all our forces in Western Europe . . . a complete denial of our obligations to NATO. But now, while enthusiastically embracing the policy of massive retaliation, he suddenly decided that we had to make a major amphibious attack against Haiphong."

Later a senior naval officer told him the navy hoped to retain Hainan for use as an airbase after the operation. Gavin marveled, "Thus the United States would propose going to war with Red China because the Chairman of the JCS thought the Navy should have a naval base on the Asian mainland!"

Dien Bien Phu fell May 7. Eisenhower's response had been solemn warnings about the fall of dominoes, one toppling the next. "You have the beginnings of a disintegration that would have the most profound influences." But he would send no bombs or troops. And when hawkish John Foster Dulles, Eisenhower's Secretary of State, and Radford both met with Eisenhower in the first week of April, Eisenhower said Congress would have to approve any military action. It was the old soldier's way of closing off the possibility.

That fall of 1954 saw the founding of SEATO in Geneva, the most hopeful result of the Dien Bien Phu debacle, and the partition of Vietnam into two countries at the 17th parallel was foreboding. Gavin himself flew to Vietnam via Okinawa, after stopovers at Tokyo and Eighth Army headquarters in Korea; he landed in Saigon. During his crowded few days there he gained the impression of strong backing for his continued opposition to U.S. involvement in the area. He stayed with General Michael O'Daniel, U.S. head of mission (there were still advisors in the country). He found that his host's wife had been spending her days trying to assist "thousands of refugees" who were streaming south from the Vietminh-controlled north. He dined with the defeated French General Paul Ely and the future president of South Vietnam, Ngo Dinh Diem. What they discussed is not recorded.

Gavin was appalled by social conditions in South Vietnam. "I was struck by the role played by the various Vietnamese sects. Each was powerful in a military sense, well armed and so established in the corrupt Vietnamese society that they could elicit funds to provide for all their needs. These came from their control of gambling, drug traffic, import-export tariffs, prostitution, and just about every source that one can imagine. I talked to a number of American civilians who were occupying various business positions in Saigon, and their stories of corruption and bribery were disturbing."

"Vietnam was no place in which to get the U.S. Army involved," Gavin wrote. "I knew that our position was going to be a difficult one and that it would take great skill on our part to avoid getting caught in a war, while through our aid program, we gave sufficient help to South Vietnam to enable them to bring about peace and live in harmony with the North."

He left for home after a sentimental stop in Manila, with its happy memories of harsh training with the Philippine scouts and of his parachute mentor William Ryder. But from Manila the military transport took him east to Eniwetok, the site of early nuclear tests. The plane rumbled over the place where one of the first test bombs had been exploded—Shot Bravo. What had been a coral island was now "a vast, deep, clear blue, water-filled crater . . . the fireball spread close to the earth and consumed the island in a fine aerosol that blew downwind over 200 miles. From the test we learned for the first time how rapidly and extensively radioactive clouds could travel around the earth carrying the isotopes of fission. The nuclear cloud had left in its wake radioactive fallout that could be measured in people who were exposed to it . . . each new event enhanced our knowledge of the nuclear bomb and of the many problems associated with it, such as the fallout and the extensive damaging effects of radioactivity. It also impressed upon me how much we did not know."

Seeing the Bravo crater once again spurred him to seek more data and ask more questions about his own vision of the nuclear battlefield. For at this point in his career, Gavin was convinced that there would be another full-scale war, probably with the Soviets and probably in Europe, and that nuclear weapons would be used, and that he would play a role. But as he recalled how he had seen the rather crude bomb atomize rock into "aerosol" when he had observed the experiment in his WSEG days, some of the planning in which he had been involved gave him pause.

He knew, for instance that under the plans for massive retaliation, the air force put a high priority on striking Soviet airfields that had been built or improved in the satellite countries facing Western Europe. The air force plan was to "take out" these airfields with 20 megaton hydrogen bombs so that radiation poisoning and gigantic craters would render them useless. This, plus bombing of other targets as retaliation for a Soviet strike, was expected to cause about 425 million casualties, not only in Europe, the Balkans, Greece, and Turkey, but also as far away as Southeast Asia. Even Japan, subject to fallout carried by westerly winds from planned hits on airfields in eastern Siberia, would be affected.

"Although I had been living with the problem for a long time, I realized that many people did not seem to be concerned about it. I did not see how any nation could launch a war with any prospect of winning it under those conditions," he wrote. His assurance about the nuclear battlefield was shaken. He saw, he said, that a total nuclear war "would be suicide." Yet he continued to fight for powerful tactical weapons with nuclear warheads. Gavin could not accept the idea that his nation would be willing to risk the lives of its sons and daughters without using every technical advantage.

The next fracas within the Pentagon highlighted more of the inconsistencies of massive retaliation. Quemoy and Matsu are islands, far from Taiwan but near to mainland China. They were Taiwanese possessions and had been heavily armed. The U.S., through its policy of supporting the Nationalist Chinese regime of Chiang Kai-Shek, which acted as if it would momentarily return and recapture all of China, supported Chiang's actions there. Chiang asked repeatedly for men and missiles, a call that found favor with Admiral Radford but rejection by General Ridgway, causing another split among the Chiefs of Staff. Ridgway had taken the precaution of sending an army group to Taiwan to examine the islands' defenses, and the report on its return favored a buildup of missiles and guns. But Ridgway was not convinced that the islands were essential to the defense of Taiwan, for they were isolated and almost in the embrace of the mainland, even within artillery range. Ridgway knew that to defend them, either positions on the mainland should be attacked by air, or a bridgehead established in China to prevent the islands from being shelled by heavy artillery.

But Ridgway reluctantly went along, because the air force planned to station fighter aircraft across the Formosa Strait, in Taiwan. So the army prepared plans to send a 7,500-man antiaircraft and logistics force. But because of fears that Congress would react violently to the movement of men, JCS Chairman Radford ordered the army to send the men without unit designation. Radford had publicly stated that the crisis in the strait would require no additional army units; hence the subterfuge.

Gavin was disgusted and appalled. "To work in an environment such as the Chairman had created was most unpleasant," Gavin recorded, "One never knew when he was being truthful and when not." Gavin was further drawn into a moral dilemma when Senator Stuart Symington, with whom he and Jean had grown friendly, called Gavin to his Georgetown home after hearing testimony by Radford. "He wanted to know what was really happening, since he was puzzled by the testimony," Gavin wrote. "I told him we were sending a mixed anti-aircraft brigade plus a logistics brigade."

Unfortunately, Gavin, believing he was acting in the best interest of his country, was behaving with utter disloyalty according to the standards of his "team player" colleagues at the Pentagon, and the news was soon out that Gavin was a maverick who could not be trusted to toe the line before Congress. It gave Radford a perfect rationale for maligning him.

"Radford saw Gavin as a possible Chief of Staff who would have influence over Congress and the president, and he set out to block Gavin's projects and make his life hell," said General Andrew O'Meara, who worked alongside Gavin with Army Research and Development in the 1950s. Radford also held a strong belief that under the conditions of atomic war, the core of the army—infantry—had lost its function. "You don't need the army, soldiers have outlived their usefulness," O'Meara reported Radford advising.

Instead of bowing to the situation, Gavin went more and more public, making speeches defending the army's continued role. "He went out on the lecture circuit," O'Meara said with amusement. "He was a fabulous salesman," pushing the sky cavalry and midrange missiles, suggesting savings by cutting chemical weapons.

Emboldened by the fact that Ridgway had concurred with his strongly argued opinions against involvement in Vietnam, Gavin decided to concentrate his energies on developing missiles for the army. Missiles were at the forefront of technology, less vulnerable and far less expensive than the manned bombers of SAC. Gavin believed they might solve the army's budget problems with the president and with the New Look cutbacks but still arm the infantry with missile artillery of tremendous power and accuracy.

Gavin had met former Nazi-regime rocket innovator Dr. Wernher von Braun at the White Sands Missile Range in New Mexico. Von Braun had delighted in telling Gavin of German achievements with the V-2 rocket of World War II, the model for the army's Redstone Missile, which had a range of 200 miles. Gavin was highly interested in the Redstone.

Von Braun, usually thought of as an eccentric scientist-for-hire, revealed himself to Gavin's surprise as no scientist at all but, instead, a brilliant and intuitive engineer with an ability to foresee technical problems and solve them. "He referred to his research technique as the 'building block' method," Gavin remembered. "He would test the separate components of the missile—the guidance system, engine propellant system, re-entry nose cone, etc.—until he had developed them just about to perfection. Using computers to simulate missing components of missile systems, he would use actual components of the missiles for exhaustive tests. Finally, when all the systems were tested together successfully, the missile was ready for test firing. As well as he could determine at that point, the missile would certainly go as planned; but experience had taught him otherwise. There was all too often some untoward event in the actual firing that could not be anticipated."

Von Braun had with him 120 scientists who had worked at the German's famous rocket development center at Peenemünde on the Pomeranian coast or at Nordhausen in central Germany. To their great future advantage, American intelligence leaders had realized the vital importance of these men and the quantum leap their weapons represented. The V-1, rushed into action by the Germans June 13, 1944, proved that unmanned rockets could work. The V-1s and V-2s claimed nearly 10,000 lives in Britain in the last months of the war, in spite of heavy bombing attacks on their launch sites. After the war scientists had been given special treatment by the United States and had simply been adopted by the armed services.

Von Braun excited Gavin with farsighted military ideas such as an artificial earth satellite and rockets that could reach the moon. He also considered a satellite an ideal communications vehicle. The army was using the ionosphere to bounce signals long distances, but von Braun felt that an orbiting satellite would be far more workable and secure.

Gavin concluded that the army should back a missile that could both loft a satellite and give the army an awesome striking range of 1,000 to 1,500 miles. Back in Washington, Gavin sold the idea to General Ridgway, and got a further boost when air surveillance photos from U-2 reconnaissance flights over the Soviet Union revealed that large rocket engines were being tested in vast pits at Kapustan Yar. Scientists and strategists reluctantly agreed that the Soviets were readying an intercontinental missile.

During the fall and winter of 1954, von Braun and Gavin kept in close touch over the plans to develop the new army missile with the 1,500-mile range. North American Aviation had already developed an engine capable of pushing the rocket. "The basic problem, which I do not believe has ever been stated in these terms, was that the Army desperately needed the von Braun team if its family of missiles were to come into being. It had developed the WAC Corporal for high altitude research and the Honest John, a 15–20-mile solid propellant missile; and it was beginning to develop the Sergeant, a 75-mile missile, and a new 200-mile version of the Redstone missile. It would appear logical that the Army would ask permission to go up to 500 miles, and some of our scientists recommended that we do so. But if we could attain a height of 500 miles, it would not take a great deal more effort to go up 1,500 miles, which would give us an orbital capability and thus our first communications satellite."

This proved to be the straw that broke the back of Ridgway's term as Chief of Staff. Eisenhower was not interested in a bright and cutting-edge program of new arms but in getting elected. The Republicans lost seventeen House seats in the midterm elections; Secretary of Defense Wilson was proving unable to make the Chiefs of Staff get in line with administration budget cuts. The air force continued to be favored with funding almost twice that ($16.4 billion to $8.8 billion) of the Army. Ridgway, scrupulous and sincere, was the most outspoken, telling Eisenhower he could not guarantee the safety of U.S. troops in Europe, Korea, or elsewhere. Eisenhower had great respect for his former airborne corps commander but found himself in a psychological corner. He only wanted Ridgway to go away.

In the wings was Taylor, fresh from the Far East, eager as ever for advancement. In meetings with Secretary of Defense Wilson and JCS Chairman Radford, he announced that in all ways he would be a team player, though he would soon adopt many of the ideas Gavin had championed under his own label of "flexible response." Taylor vowed that he was a firm supporter of massive retaliation.

Ridgway's days were numbered. "Suffice it to say that the country owes him [Ridgway] a debt that it will never be able to repay," Gavin wrote. "Somehow, despite Secretary Wison and the Chairman of the JCS [Radford] he managed to hold together our Army and to continue to ready it for the nuclear-missile-space age, despite a constantly shrinking budget. Yet, from where I saw the situation, as one of his senior officers, it was not the shrinking budget that was so bothersome. Rather it was those with whom he had to work in the Department of Defense that was most troublesome. He was a stalwart adherer to truth; thus the Army staff officers working closely with him made no compromise with the Army's integrity."

Gavin, after his departure from the army, put it more strongly: "It was plainly not the shrinking budget that was bothersome—for the Army traditionally suffers from fiscal malnutrition in peacetime. It was the deception and duplicity of those with whom he had to work in the Department of Defense . . . Mr. Wilson tended to deal with his Chiefs of staff as though they were recalcitrant union bosses. . . . I have known General Ridgway, after weeks of painstaking preparation, to brief Mr. Wilson with lucidity and thoroughness. At the conclusion, Mr. Wilson would gaze out of the window and ask a question that had no relevance whatsoever to the subject of the briefing. Among his aides it was known as taking the briefer 'on a trip around the world.' It was a studied technique that he used when he had his mind already made up about what you were going to talk to him about."

With Ridgway on the skids, Gavin himself expected to be removed from his important post as deputy. He was now a Ridgway man and an outspoken proponent of new weapons initiatives, completely out of step with the previous four years of the Eisenhower White House.

Though he finally became a lieutenant general on March 25, 1955, his bureaucratic risk-taking set in motion a chain of events that would lead to Gavin's own departure from the army and the ruin of the military career of one of the army's best combat commanders.

19.

FAREWELL TO
THE ARMY

Matt Ridgway retired as Chief of Staff of the Army on July 1, 1955, and Maxwell Taylor, Ridgway's replacement, was fifty-four years old. He had made the most of his outstanding war record, which included Normandy, a daring secret mission to occupied Rome, and Bastogne, and he had avoided controversy. Slightly deaf, due to an army engineering blasting accident early in his career, he was movie-star handsome, thought of as a clever intellectual, fluent in French, Spanish, Italian, and Japanese. Taylor had switched his service arm from engineering to artillery and was far more widely traveled, because of his language proficiency, than most army officers. He had not sought airborne service when Ridgway in 1942 wrote his name down on a short list for chief of staff of the 82nd Airborne, and recruited him to the paratroops. He was good at both staff and field work, and Ridgway knew him from West Point, when Ridgway had been Taylor's language instructor.

When airborne's founding father, Major General William Lee, commander of the 101, suffered a heart attack in February 1944, Taylor inherited the division at Ridgway's suggestion. He had only jumped once, and never in combat, when he took over three months before D day.

The contrast between Taylor, who finished fourth in his class, came from a well-established military family, and Gavin, the man of no background who struggled through the Point, was glaring. Then they arrived on the vast canvas of the European war as leaders of America's two most glamorous divisions. Gavin had a harder, better war, in which he advanced through extraordinary competence, but at the end of it found himself upstaged within the service hierarchy. He had fought to keep his division active and won, but Taylor, the senior man, won the peace with the vital, visible job as superintendent of West Point. Gavin, like Taylor, played tennis, but he was also a boxer and a handball player, and he was fond of brutal hikes. Taylor shunned most sports except tennis.

Gavin had instinctively disliked Taylor from the moment he first laid eyes on him at West Point. While Taylor was cool and distant with his men, Gavin believed in total immersion. Taylor studied *gravitas*, while Gavin deliberately took up a trooper's rifle and used it with relish in the field. Taylor worked from the command post and acted the general officer. Gavin's was the common touch; Taylor's focus was attention to his superiors. Taylor was the new man, the political careerist, the peacetime political soldier, while Gavin was a throwback to a warrior mold now discarded.

Taylor ran into few stumbling blocks during his career and knew well how the army system worked and how it could be manipulated by transfers, friends in high places, and avoiding the displeasure of superiors. One of those he did displease was Douglas MacArthur, who criticized his generalship during Korea, though the lash of that tongue was felt by many, including Ridgway. The antipathy between Gavin and Taylor had deep and long roots, but in the spring of 1954 they were yoked together again. Taylor was senior to Gavin, just as they had been in World War II. And Eisenhower's watchword was teamwork.

With the sure hand of the chess player, Taylor kept Gavin on tenterhooks by not immediately appointing his own deputy chief of staff. His first move, a few months into the new job, was to separate the areas of plans, training, and operations research and development into two staff positions. On September 1, 1955, a new assistant secretary of the army post to handle research and development was created and awarded to a civilian, Dr. William H. Martin. The secretary of the army, Wilbur Brucker, told Congress the new post was created specifically to give a civilian R&D director "stature in order to manage research and development because of its importance." This, of course diluted Gavin's grip on the army's future considerably, since plans and R&D were now separated.

Taylor gave him the choice of "which one I wanted to keep, and I told him I would choose R&D because of its great potential in terms of the Army's needs."

At the same time, Gavin made a bureaucratic countermove. He officially requested to leave Washington to take over the Continental Army Command, a choice plum that would allow Gavin great authority to direct army training. "There I could apply many lessons that I had learned to get the Army ready for the future, which was certain to bring many changes. He thought it was a good idea, but declined to make a decision at the moment."

There was cool calculation on both sides. Gavin, now a controversial figure because of his opposition to massive retaliation and his budget-breaking hopes for new machines and methods, would be off the hotseat as Continental Army commander, but he would still be in line for a fourth star and possibly Army Chief of Staff himself if all went well. Taylor, on the other hand, preferred Gavin at close quarters where he could be closely monitored and his deviations from policy noted.

Taylor quickly consolidated his advantages. Earlier in 1955, Taylor had been brought from his Far East command to meet with Secretary of Defense Wilson and President Eisenhower. The president demanded and got a promise that Taylor would "wholeheartedly accept that his primary responsibility related to his joint duties." This was meant to curb inter-service rivalries. Eisenhower also demanded that Taylor "hold views as to doctrine, basic principles, and relationships which are in accord with those of the President." Eisenhower had a reputation of demanding total fealty from his team. Above all else, he hated what he termed "disloyalty" from military officers.

Taylor and the other Chiefs of Staff were told "the President does not consider them as advocates for the Army, Navy, etc. Though each has a particular service background, they should think and act as a body . . . great harm had been done on past occasions when the Chiefs of Staff were called upon to speak out on individual policy views without regard to announced Administration policy. . . . Subordinates in the services may advance service interests very strongly. The Chief of Staff will be acutely aware of these pressures and sensitive to them, but he must shape them into the larger purpose." The new doctrine, which turned on its head the previous practice, was sent in a memorandum by Eisenhower's military liaison staffer, General Andrew Goodpaster.

In reality, Taylor was no firm believer in the "New Look," the "Bang for the Buck," the "Nuclear Shield" or other nicknamed Republican Party attempts to reduce military spending on the way to achieving a balanced budget. He was, in fact, strongly influenced by the same reasoning that had led Gavin to want the army to arm itself with modern missiles and rockets and fresh helicopter ideas. To make these concepts his own, however, he had to pay lip service to Eisenhower, Radford, and Wilson while he developed the theory of "flexible response," meaning an army that was shaped to fight either on the nuclear battlefield or in a conventional "gunpowder" war against local aggression.

Taylor's formulation of this theory was called the "Pentomic" division, and it created a new formation for fighting units. Taylor chose the idea from those coming across his desk with rapturous haste—partly because it seemed to sound modern and partly because it would indicate army willingness to "be a part of the bigger picture," in other words, budget reductions. The five-part division the name implied was simply packaging that eliminated the regiment and cut colonels out of an important, long-honored job. In any case the Pentomic division proved an embarrassing failure in practice and a few years later was quietly dropped. Taylor seemed to take little interest in the concept beyond its launch.

But Eisenhower's response was unexpected. He thought the idea could save personnel costs and thus supported it for the exact opposite reason Taylor intended.

Gavin was scathing in his opinion: "The staff had been fiddling around with that Pentomic division, and it was really a mess. A five unit division, but they only had something like a battery of artillery or so with each battle group. God, if you've ever had to use artillery, you knew it was grossly lacking in artillery."

The first six months of Taylor's reign as chief were hell. Gavin lost half his responsibilities and was refused a transfer to another post, though Taylor was too subtle to tell him so, keeping him dangling in spite of Gavin's characteristic face-to-face queries and requests. Taylor also found Gavin too valuable to lose, according to colleagues, and sometimes thought of him as a likely successor as Army Chief of Staff. There was little secret that the army thought Taylor a likely choice to become chairman of the Joint Chiefs.

But Taylor's methods, which would eventually scuttle Gavin, were hard on subordinates. Taylor would draw ideas from a staff, try them out in the political winds, and then if they failed to win approval, Taylor would step aside and let the axe fall on underlings. "He was absolutely ruthless," Gavin said.

A growing sense of isolation and a feeling that he alone was fighting for the life of the army seemed to take over Gavin's mind in the winter of 1955. He also puzzled over the relationships he had to maintain between the political chieftains on congressional committees who held the money and the military chieftains competing for a bigger share of it. He had long since come to the conclusion that the established system—the service chiefs and the defense secretary—was seriously flawed, and had been so since 1947 when the department of defense, a civilian agency, was interposed between the heads of the services and the cabinet-level secretary of defense.

Gavin's draconian prescription was to abolish the Joint Chiefs, the top military counsel, and rely on the staffs of the services to present ideas for decision directly to the secretary of defense. In fact, few top military men liked service on the JCS, whatever the glory. After discovering the nature of the job, the endless battles with other chiefs, the military's supplicant role with Congress, even Eisenhower wrote that the job of Chief of Staff of the Army was a "sorry place to light after having commanded a theater of war."

Pointing as usual at a genuine problem, Gavin did not really understand that it was a problem those in power did not want solved. Bureaucracies, for all their waste, duplication and watered-down ideas, function to blunt the force of error as well as brilliance. Politicians find them useful and are always ambivalent about their reform.

Gavin's solution was to have only retired men on the JCS, men who could no longer wield power or give rewards or withhold them within their own service. The "new" JCS would be a "senior advisory body" to the secretary of defense. The chairman of the JCS would be abolished and the service chiefs would directly advise the secretary. "The proposal was too radical a change," Gavin noted. By making it, he put himself more at risk than ever among the military establishment.

In the early spring of 1956, Gavin toyed with the idea of taking his ideas to a more public forum than the quiet offices of the Pentagon. He was asked to attend a series of meetings on nuclear weapons and foreign policy in New York, sponsored by the Council on Foreign Relations, a closely watched policy think tank that often harbored movers-and-shakers-in-waiting, recruited others, and sheltered still others from adverse storms in Washington. Its chairman was John McCloy, one of the best-known Cold War warriors. Anti-big bomb, anti-JCS, Gavin was leery. "I did not think it would do for me to appear publicly in open criticism of the present policy of massive retaliation." So he sent the peppery General Andrew O'Meara, a deputy in his Pentagon office. O'Meara, always blunt, returned in a high state of alarm. He told Gavin that if he didn't get up there and talk to the regular contributors to *Foreign Affairs* magazine, the air force, which had spoken strongly for continued reliance on bombers and massive retaliation, would win the day. Yet almost for the first time, Gavin hesitated for political reasons.

Senator Joseph McCarthy had demonized the State Department; the Council on Foreign Relations sounded exactly like another "fig leaf for Communism" to the senator's followers. Nonetheless, Gavin went to New York on June 12, with numerous luminaries in the audience, including a rising Harvard University government professor, Henry Kissinger, then getting his first taste of participation in the foreign policy elite.

Gavin was not alone. Other military men presented ideas, including General Elwood Quesada of the air force and Rear Admiral John S. Tach of the navy. "I spoke to the problem as honestly as I could," Gavin said. He noted "surprising" support from the scientific community and was questioned closely by Kissinger, who was then preparing the book that made him famous, *Nuclear Weapons and Foreign Policy*, one of the first studies to question the effectiveness of massive retaliation. A dead silence came from the Defense Department and from Taylor. Though there was no criticism, Gavin thought "the meeting continued to add to my reputation as one opposed to the policy of massive retaliation."

Gavin was surprised to find in his mail a few months later, the manuscript of Kissinger's book, sent by Kissinger for comment. It voiced many of the thoughts Gavin had aired at the June conference. "It was a good book and the first to question the effectiveness of the existing policy," Gavin wrote.

Feeling like a lame duck in another administration, Gavin had made clear to Taylor that he wanted to leave. Now he would begin to wage war from within, a dangerous game at the Pentagon.

His Senate admirer and close friend Stuart Symington announced hearings on air power in the spring of 1956, and Gavin sought to be placed on the witness list before a subcommittee of the Armed Services Committee.

Symington, of course, agreed, and there was little the army could do. "I had a theory about air power on which I had been doing a lot of background reading and thought that I could make a contribution that would be supportive of the Army's position," Gavin wrote. "I had many good friends among my colleagues in the air force, especially the troop carrier personnel, who believed that air power in its ultimate and purest form was a big bomb delivered by SAC, and that a few of these would solve all our problems. . . . I believed true air power was that form which moved man and his means to wage war wherever he was needed. For example, early in World War II the Germans flew a band into Oslo Airport and the band got out of the plane playing the Norwegian national anthem. With the help of Quisling and some other Norwegians, the Nazis took over the country without suffering heavy casualties. That was one form of air power and it was certainly far more effective than dropping bombs."

Since the Symington hearings were held in executive session, there would be no news stories. The army feared no embarrassment from what Gavin said. It was his first experience before such a body and it caused him some uneasiness. Symington, then chairman of the Subcommittee on the Air Force of the Senate Armed Services Committee, "somewhat to my surprise . . . swore me in, and I felt uncomfortable about this because there was an implication in the act that I would not tell the truth unless I was duly sworn."

Symington reassured him in private that the swearing was like a safety valve; "that if we did tell the truth and were then taken to task by our Pentagon superiors, we could then explain why we had to . . . this slight inroad into senior officer integrity in the Pentagon was a harbinger of what was to come."

The explosive facts to come out of the hearing were elicited by Senator James A. Duff, (R-Conn.) who asked Gavin about the "number of lives that would be lost" in a nuclear assault by SAC "against Russia with nuclear weapons in such a way where the prevailing winds would carry them southeast over Russia. . . ."

Gavin deferred to "the Air Force or a proper study group to give you this answer" and then went on to give the answer that he knew himself: "Current planning estimates run on the order of several hundred million deaths. . . ."

Gavin had seen a recent Army Corps of Engineers study that put the "anticipated casualties on the order of 425 million," mainly in Europe,

Asia, and the Pacific islands as a result of "current plans . . . to use 20-megaton surface bursts to crater the runways of airfields that might be occupied by the Soviets. This would result in colossal amounts of earth and debris being sucked up into the fireball and scattered downwind as radioactive fallout."

And the study concerned itself only with the effects of an American first strike and did not calculate the possible deadly effects of Soviet response, or those of a Soviet first strike and an American response.

As is the usual case, the Congressional Record printed portions of the testimony, although long gaps were censored. The censor, Vice Admiral Arthur C. Davis, ret., released the fallout testimony about a month later, and the press was quick to pick up on the horrific casualty toll of hundreds of millions. Gavin had touched a sensitive public nerve. The casualty figure made a better argument than anything else about the reality of the nuclear shield, which looked exactly like a nuclear tombstone.

The headlines missed Gavin, who was in Naples on defense business at the time. A telegram from Taylor brought him up short. "He wanted an explanation of my role in the hearings. I was disturbed by the implication of his cable, since what I had done was entirely proper. . . . It seemed to me that the Chief of Staff was protecting himself from Defense Department criticism. I replied to the cable and returned to Washington without delay."

NATO allies of the United States were furious about the casualty figures, which were politically devastating. The United States, the strongest proponent of NATO, was seen protecting itself with millions of European lives while remaining in relative safety behind two large oceans. But the figures, or their equivalents, should not have surprised anyone. All the facts were known; it was simply a matter of mathematical calculation.

The *New York Times* (June 19) front-paged the testimony under the ambiguous headline ARMY FAILS TO BAR BOMB TESTIMONY. The story highlighted the fact that "hundreds of millions of people, including a great many in friendly countries, would be killed in the event of an all-out Air Force nuclear attack on the Soviet Union." The story went on to say that "Army and other Defense Department officials made vain efforts to prevent publication of the testimony late this afternoon."

When he arrived at the Pentagon, colleagues told Gavin that JCS chairman Radford, Secretary of Defense Wilson, and Secretary of the Army

Wilbur M. Brucker (former governor of Michigan and a World War I veteran), were all "extremely angry with me," and the flap had gone far enough that Supreme Allied Commander in Europe General Alfred Gruenther, a close personal friend of Eisenhower, called for a clarification.

An open attempt to undermine Gavin and paint him as an alarmist whose facts were wrong was under way. "I continued to hear from the Chief of Staff [Taylor] and the Secretary of the Army about my fallout testimony," Gavin remembered. "As late as December 1956, the Secretary of the Army had me to his office to tell me once again that Secretary of Defense Wilson was convinced that I had knowingly erred in testifying before the Symington committee."

Did Gavin know he was playing a dangerous game, teaming up with the Missouri Democrat Stuart Symington, a vigorous proponent of more defense spending (at least until Vietnam)? It was through Symington, a member of the Senate Armed Services Committee (along with such other famous national figures as Virginia's Harry Byrd, Texas's Lyndon Johnson, Mississippi's John Stennis, Washington's Henry M. "Scoop" Jackson, North Carolina's Sam Ervin, Jr., Massachusetts's Leverett Saltonstall, and others), that Gavin hoped to get his ideas into play— assuming that they would be heard and judged on their merits. To read the yellowing transcripts now is to see Symington pushing Gavin's ideas about airlift, mobility, even abolition of the JCS, and also to see the relentless opposition of the team of Pentagon witnesses defending the status quo, from Brucker and Radford on down.

Gavin should have known his head was on the block when Secretary of the Army Brucker called him in to tell him that he, Brucker, "was going to bat" for Gavin in spite of the criticism from DOD Secretary Wilson. Everyone in politics has heard the "Jim, I just want to help you . . ." speech, usually while feeling a prickly feeling between the shoulder blades. But Gavin seemed determined to maintain his innocence of the process and its machinations.

Of course Taylor could not simply fire Gavin or remove him. The man was too famous and too outspoken. The wily Taylor preferred to keep him and let the issue die unresolved. Gavin was twisting in the wind and he did not know it—nor did he seem to care. Worse was to come as Gavin resolutely walked out toward the end of the plank.

Eruptions became more frequent. In November, Gavin was informed that there was "little need for the services of the von Braun team" to develop the army's liquid fuel missile program, since the navy had decided to use solid fuels for the Polaris submarine-launched missiles. The navy persuaded Congress that it alone had the mobility to survive and counterattack after a Soviet first strike, and a first strike was the only opening scenario possible under U.S. policy. "This was a devastating blow to the Army and set back all our missile programs as well as our aspirations to launch an earth satellite." The next blow was a JCS altitude limitation of 200 miles imposed on the army's missile development program, into which Gavin had poured time, energy and persuasion. That ended the possibility of a satellite launching and a communications satellite, as well as the 1,500-mile missile.

By this time Gavin knew remonstrating with Taylor was useless. Instead, he tried to save both von Braun's work and the army's missiles by an end run. Because of the secret U-2 spy flights by CIA aircraft begun in 1956, the Pentagon had for the first time excellent photos of vast areas of Russia, photos which would reward hours of skillful study to decode their secrets. (The U-2 scheme would blow up in Eisenhower's face in 1960, when the pilot of one mission, Francis Gary Powers, was shot down.)

But in the meantime the U-2 pictures were an enigma. Gavin asked von Braun to come to Washington to use his knowledge of how missile facilities were set up to decode the pictures. "Von Braun at once pointed out where the hydrogen was stored, the location of the jet fuel and the liquid oxygen, how the gases were moved, where the pipes were, and what their purposes were. He said that the Russians had copied exactly the German rocket installations at Peenemünde."

Gavin's experiment had the indirect effect of revealing that the Russians had advanced rapidly with the development of liquid-fuel rockets. A simple range calculation led Gavin to the conclusion that the Soviets would soon have a missile that could reach the United States.

The warning had little effect on Taylor; however, by this time he himself was under suspicion as a big spender for his "National Military Program," which reminded the country that it might have to fight small wars as well as big ones and use tactical nuclear weapons. Taylor's program died a quiet death. The two men, had they combined their energies and talents, would have made a formidable team. For as Gavin slowly learned the art of politics, Taylor inclined more and more to accept Gavin's ideas of limited war, mobility, and the necessity of better machines to move infantry, still the "queen of battle," on a vastly expanded battlefield.

Gavin was glad to see the end of 1956. The satisfactions the miniwar over Suez and the Hungarian uprising, both of which were object lessons on the slowly evolving theory and study of limited war under the atomic shield, were minor. Eisenhower's landslide reelection ensured a continuation of his stringent spending policies and of the regime of Admiral Arthur Radford. And partly as a result of intelligence about Soviet missile capabilities, Congress grew freshly alarmed about falling behind the Cold War enemy.

New indignities were heaped on. Gavin was ordered to attend congressional hearings with Assistant Secretary of Defense Donald Quarles, Secretary of the Air Force. But in the hearing room, he was directed to a seat right behind Quarles, and beside him were seated "three flag officers, one for the Air Force, an admiral from the Navy—and myself . . . I was very uncomfortable with his [Quarles's] testimony and his answers to questions and I was just as uncomfortable with the impression he left that we three officers were there to back him up." Since members of Congress asked the trio no questions, the illusion was complete.

Gavin was angry and stopped by the office of the secretary of the army to report on the hearing, a customary courtesy. Gavin told Brucker directly that he didn't like "being used to presumably confirm Quarles's testimony.

"Secretary Brucker lowered his head, looking at me rather quizzically over his glasses; then his face seemed to harden a bit as he said: 'General Gavin, you have nothing to worry about. To prove you guilty of perjury, they would have to prove that you intended to mislead Congress, and this they cannot do.' He then spent about half an hour explaining the elements of perjury to me. I had never thought of perjury as a subject of concern to me before. He pointed out that one could pass on considerable misinformation to Congress provided it could not be proven that you intended to deceive."

Unbelieving, Garvin held his tongue. "This was a deeply disturbing experience," he wrote ". . . It shook me a bit at the time, and I realized that it was symptomatic of the state of affairs in which the military was drifting." The lecture about avoiding perjury was a new threshold of Pentagon iniquity, and perhaps a harbinger of the 1960s Vietnam army.

Wilson, Garvin decided, was simply ignorant. "The Secretary was a man who knew little about the Armed Forces. He obviously knew even less about missiles and considered space satellites child's play, not something that senior officers should take an interest in or even talk about," Gavin wrote angrily, "meanwhile the Army General Staff and particularly G-3 and those responsible for the development of new weapons, such as those involved in space, found themselves having to accommodate to situations by agreeing to courses of action that they had recommended against."

Gavin made a decision never again to lend himself to compromising situations. "I would not go along with half-truths and omissions . . . I was going to stay in a proper orbit, serving the Army and my country as best I could, regardless of what consequences might befall me. If the situation became intolerable, which was likely, I would simply leave the service, probably by retirement."

Gavin rode along into 1957 into the calm which followed Suez and Hungary. The military crises resolved themselves, but fresh money problems for the services arose with the White House calling for a 10 percent reduction in Army personnel and no increase in spending. Gavin continued studying Russian intentions and picked up an important clue when they openly published the frequencies over which their first satellite would broadcast. "It did not elicit any reaction and few people seemed to pay any attention," Gavin wrote.

Typically, Gavin sought the countermove. Convinced a Russian satellite was coming, he sent General Andrew O'Meara, his deputy director of research, to von Braun to ask if it would be possible to intercept such a satellite "if the Department of Defense ordered us to do so." He was also laying the groundwork for what he knew would be a nasty public-relations problem if the Soviets launched a satellite first. When in mid-September he met with the Army Scientific Advisory Committee, Gavin asked von Braun to brief the group on the still-active army missile programs and their potential for launching a satellite, which was nil.

Wilson retired October 3, 1957, much to Gavin's relief, to be replaced as secretary of defense by Neil McElroy, a top executive of Procter & Gamble. By chance, Gavin was given the job of acquainting the new secretary with a number of defense installations. Gavin, always at his strongest in one-on-one situations, gave his best shot at pointing out the army's problems and the possible solutions. Naturally, he took the incoming secretary to meet von Braun and his team, who were still at work at the Army Ballistic Missile Agency on the Jupiter missile.

It was there on a warm autumn afternoon, October 4, that Gavin, after a day of touring and talking, was relaxing at the officers' club, at a small party thrown by the post commander, when the news came in that the Russians had launched the world's first space satellite, and it was now circling the earth. The news struck Gavin hard. He put down his drink and walked outside. "I felt that this was a crushing defeat for all of our efforts and for the country. I went outside for a walk and then returned to the party and talked briefly to Dr. von Braun."

Gavin asked von Braun to meet with him and the new secretary of defense before the return flight to Washington. The legendary rocket engineer and the paratroop leader met at the lab at 8 A.M. and lectured McElroy at length. Von Braun told the secretary the nature of the formula that put the satellite into orbit—how heavy it was and what thrust was required to place it there. He stressed the communications role of a U.S. satellite—which would benefit all three armed services. Gavin told McElroy that an orbiting satellite would eventually become the heart of a weapons system of unbounded potential. "It would provide information on targets and continuing surveillance of the target and continuing surveillance of the target area, including poststrike reconnaissance. It could also acquire a capability of detecting launches on the part of an enemy and might serve as the eyes of an ICBM system. . . . McElroy listened patiently," Gavin recorded.

The next day, turmoil hit Washington. The administration attempted to downplay the historic event (James Hagerty, Eisenhower's press secretary, denied the United States was in competition with the Russians, and called the satellite a matter "of great scientific interest"), but the nation's newspapers reacted: RUSSIANS MAY HAVE ULTIMATE WEAPON cried the *Washington Post*. The next day headlines screamed of SPY IN THE SKY. Senator Symington, continuing his battle for more defense spending, called for an inquiry by the Senate Armed Services Committee. The world reaction to *Sputnik*, as the satellite was called, reflected an enormous coup of prestige and propaganda for the Russians.

Taylor called a tense group of the army's top staff together on October 6. "Looking around, he asked, 'What are we going to tell the White House?' Setting his gaze upon me, he then asked, 'What are we going to tell the President?' " Gavin responded, "General, it's easy, just simply tell the truth: the Joint Chiefs of Staff blocked the Army from launching a satellite."

But the chances of Taylor reporting that were slim. "Our staff conference went on for about an hour with a great deal of tense discussion," Gavin wrote. "It all came down to the fact that if the Secretary of Defense had been permitted to get all the information that he needed, he would have understood the problem and could have directed the proper defense agency to orbit a satellite." Thus Gavin again blamed the "two hat" system of the JCS leadership. This time, he was almost gloating over the public scrutiny and the glare of disgrace the services faced. But there was little indication that Wilson, had he known everything about how to launch a satellite, would have pushed the program. From retirement, Wilson told reporters he thought *Sputnik* no more than "a nice technical trick."

At what point Gavin decided he was through with the ducking and dodging is uncertain. From early in 1957, he took a new interest in reassignment, and visited the army director of personnel more than once to ask about his options. This was the action of a man without a protector, since any assignment would have to be approved by Taylor. He called on the personnel director, General Donald P. Booth, again in the fall. Booth had meanwhile made inquiries to Taylor, who indicated that Gavin might be assigned to the army's Continental Command. It was what Gavin wanted, but was customarily the last assignment before retirement for a good, but not a superlative, career officer. But by that point, Gavin would have relished obscurity, anything to be out of policy and back commanding troops. Gavin expected the assignment, and with it, the probable end of his Chief of Staff hopes. He went so far as to visit the service schools and test boards and formulate some ideas about fresh measures for America's home army—and laid them before Taylor, a clear indication of his desires. Though Taylor voiced agreement with Gavin's suggestions for the Continental Command, Gavin heard his superior mention "uncertainty in his mind about what the attitude of the Secretary of the Army might be," a doleful-sounding note in a bureaucrat's ear.

For the first time in his life, Gavin had to face seriously the prospect of leaving the army. After the meeting with Taylor he discussed retirement openly with General Booth. To his chagrin, he found that he would have barely enough to live on. His family life was still entangled by alimony from his first marriage, and he worried whether he could afford to retire. Still he felt that morally he could not stay.

In Washington, he believed, the officer corps was lying to itself, and that he could not tolerate. Having a believer's reverence for the only real society he had ever known, he had idealized its secrets, and when he found them false and muddy, he held up his hands in horror and came to believe even the world of business held to a higher standard than the military.

Meanwhile though, in Washington, heads were demanded, and politicans needed a forum. The public, it was decided, needed to know who was to blame for the simple fact that the Russians had a satellite and America had none. Leading the rush this time was not the sympathetic Symington, but a Texas Senator named Lyndon B. Johnson.

On November 2, the Russians had sent *Sputnik II* into orbit with a dog inside. The Senate Preparedness Subcommittee, moribund since the Korean War, was selected as the forum. Eisenhower disapproved, but Senate Democrats saw in the hearings a good way to turn the *Sputnik* debacle to political advantage. The hearing opened November 25. On December 6 with the hearings in progress a week, the U.S. Navy satellite *Vanguard I* was launched. Smaller than *Sputnik I*, it malfunctioned, exploded, and fell to earth near its Cape Canaveral launchpad.

Gavin was called to the stand to testify on December 13. It did not take long for the questions to "get to the matter of our failure to launch a satellite," Gavin wrote.

"In response to questioning, I stated that the Joint Chiefs of Staff system was not working because of their dual responsibility. Further, I said that the Secretary of Defense should be in a position to receive timely and substantative information about the issues in the defense area. It was because of the failure of this, while the JCS prevented the launching of a satellite, that the United States had failed to launch one." Gavin might have chosen equal truths: that a satellite was not a top priority, while reducing defense expenditures was; that the multiplicity of efforts between the services was wasteful, and this was the result; or that the man most likely to accomplish the feat, Wernher von Braun, had been given short shrift when the navy chose a solid-fuel system for their missile rockets. But he chose his own truth. The trouble with it was that while it ws doubtless true, it jammed a helping of crow directly into the mouths of Radford, Taylor, Brucker—even Eisenhower, who after considering altering the JCS system in 1949, had decided against it.

The newspapers once again made the most of the sensational testimony. Gavin had described a command system that didn't work because it was designed wrong. TOP DEFENSE SHAKEUP URGED, the *Washington*

Post headlined the next day. Immediately, Gavin was on the carpet before Taylor, who, remarkably, asked Gavin why he had testified as he had. Taylor was particularly upset because on the same day Gavin testified before the Johnson subcommittee, Taylor had sat in the same chair and told them that the Joint Chiefs system was working fine and no changes were needed. Gavin reminded his boss of the October 6 staff meeting held in the wake of *Sputnik I* "in which we all agreed that a reorganization was necessary." Gavin had heard that a representative of the White House had called to ensure that there would be no testimony recommending reorganization. Gavin had stepped out of line. It would be for the last time in his career.

December 23 Taylor sent for Gavin again. "After I entered his office, General Taylor wasted no time in getting to the point and informed me that I was to stay another year 'to defend the budget.' " It was the equivalent of handing Gavin a pistol. Unable to accuse him of testifying incorrectly, Taylor had abruptly canceled the provisional arrangements for another command; he'd compounded this by demanding that Gavin stay in the Pentagon and reverse his criticisms. Gavin, Taylor was saying, would come to heel—or else.

The two men faced each other. It was a moment Gavin had savored in his imagination. No one knows what words passed between the two. Taylor has no record of the incident in his memoirs. Gavin would say only "I had thought about this moment a great deal and my mind was made up. I told him at once that I was going to retire without delay." Taylor responded with chilling correctness. Gavin should make his wishes known to Lieutenant General Lyman Lemnitzer, Taylor's deputy chief of staff, and to Secretary of the Army Brucker. Taylor, reported Gavin, said little else. "With that, he left on an extended trip to the Middle East."

Jean Gavin recalled her husband telling her Taylor had first cajoled Gavin, telling him, "Come on Jim, you can do this," and when Gavin remained stony, quickly offered him the Continental Army Command as a reward for "not rocking the boat." Gavin replied he would like the job, but not at the cost of testifying contrary to his beliefs. Taylor waved off Gavin's reaction, sure that this could be worked out.

Within the hour, Gavin had written out his letter of resignation, making it effective March 31, 1958, (thus giving him thirty full years from his enlistment) and handed it to Lieutenant General William Westmoreland, secretary of the General Staff. Then he completed his work day and went home to break the news to Jean. His army career was over.

But his career was not over. Gavin's position as a lightning rod for criticism of the Pentagon and the administration's defense policy made him a dangerous adversary. He was still and would always be the dashing young paratrooper, and he had the respect of powerful politicians, plus the devotion of his men and many officer colleagues. Lemnitzer, "very friendly and understanding," begged him to stay, and suggested he be posted immediately to the Continental Army Command (CONARC). But Lemnitzer knew nothing of Gavin's recent icy meeting with Taylor, and in any case, as a deputy he had no power to do anything decisive. At this late hour, Gavin admitted, "I said [to Lemnitzer] that I wanted to go to CONARC and the Chief of Staff and I had agreed that was what I would do next."

Meanwhile nothing final could be done. Secretary Brucker was on Christmas vacation in Ohio. But the news soon leaked. What with Gavin's wartime fame, the questioning of the Johnson committee, the partisan tug-of-war over defense expenditures, the shock of the *Sputnik* and *Vanguard* launches, it smelled of fresh scandal. Moreover, few in Washington's news-making circle could believe that Gavin, who, at the age of fifty, still seemed to have a brilliant future ahead of him would retire from the labor of thirty years over a mere budget battle, a favorite Washington game. No, they had to find an insider's reason, a bureaucratic Washington reason for such an event. Gavin would afterwards blame the devious mind of Lyndon Johnson. In later years he told others that Eisenhower or his staff had made a decision to get rid of him and to "make him look not too good in the process," according to General Douglas Kinnard.

The news of his retirement created a minor sensation. Jean would write of it: "Within minutes after the news was announced, the telephone started ringing. Calls from friends and fellow officers, from newspapers and wire services. They were official and unofficial, long and short, early and late. For days it was almost impossible to make an outgoing call on our phone; it was always busy. At one point the operator told me she had calls waiting that would fill the next ten hours. Right behind the phone calls came the mail—letters by the bagful from all over the world. Men who had served under Slim Jim wrote wistfully that they hated to lose him. Veterans, long back in civilian life, sent messages of support. People we had not heard from in years, and people he'd never heard of, added their votes of confidence."

But there was silence, too, the army's method of disapproval. To some, Gavin's retirement was simply one overly proud man's refusal to take on an uncomfortable assignment.

Events unfolded slowly to envelop their protagonist. "At 10:30 A.M. on January 6, 1958, I appeared before the Johnson committee," Gavin wrote of those last days. "Senator Johnson explained that they were very disturbed; that Admiral Hyman Rickover, who had preceded me, refused to answer questions, and furthermore, that he refused to allow in the record some of the answers he did give."

"How can I get you fellas to tell the truth?" Johnson stagily asked Gavin.

"He seemed sincere in his efforts to obtain frank answers, and all of the committee members entered into the discussion of the problem. In view of the satellite situation, they were particularly disturbed that military officers would not give them frank answers in a closed top secret hearing."

Gavin was told repeatedly that the hearing was closed—not to be released to the press, perhaps never revealed at all.

Johnson was particularly curious to find out why Gavin had been "demoted" from deputy chief of staff to plans and research. "I pointed out that it was not a demotion. . . . He seemed to doubt that I was telling the truth, and by his questions he appeared to be looking for some rational reasons—rational to him anyway—for my retirement. I pointed out that I was completing 30 years of service in March and that I would not agree to defend next year's Army budget."

Lyndon Johnson was not satisfied. He pressed Gavin on the issue of possible future assignments. He had his own scenario, it became clear, a further twist on a story then circulating that Gavin was bucking for promotion to four stars. Johnson suggested that Gavin was being denied promotion because of his record of outspoken Hill testimony and his most recent statements, suggesting the Joint Chiefs of Staff need be abolished —or at least reorganized.

"Nothing I could say seemed to change his view," Gavin wrote, "But I expected he would entertain some thought of my own integrity."

The hearing ended in a stalemate between the two men, Gavin protesting he had not considered advancement, Johnson suggesting the opposite. Then the press was allowed into the hearing room. It was Johnson, not Gavin, a relative innocent, who had the last word that day. Johnson had prepared and distributed a press release alleging that Gavin "was not being promoted and that was why I was leaving." When Gavin protested to the committee's legal counsel, Ed Weisel, he was told it was too late. The release had already been handed out. It was out before Johnson had finished questioning Gavin.

On the afternoon of January 7th, Secretary Brucker called Gavin in. With Lemnitzer there as a witness, Brucker pointedly said that the proposed assignment was not influenced by testimony before the Johnson commitee on the subject of the Joint Chiefs of Staff. Brucker then offered to make Gavin a deputy chief of staff for research and development, allow him to stay in Washington for a full year, and then assign him to Europe with every prospect of getting a fourth star.

Gavin could not accept any of it, for to do so would be to admit to the theory that he had, indeed, bargained with his retirement for a promotion. Another, hardier or more cynical man would have taken the offer and simply avoided testifying by any of the well-known methods of Washington's official lie. But that was not James Gavin's way.

Brucker continued to press in vain. And it was not all false. Unknown to Gavin until much later was the role that Westmoreland had played. Ever since his first announcement of his retirement, Gavin had held that he had "submitted" his resignation to the secretary of the army. Senators on Johnson's committee had reinforced this point when Gavin reminded them that his retirement was merely a "request," which had to be acted on by the higher authority. What Gavin did not know was that Westmoreland, perhaps out of sympathy, or on Taylor's orders, or from the thought that Gavin was reacting with anger which would be regretted later, had never passed the request along to Brucker. Westmoreland had locked the resignation in his office safe, where it had stayed for ten days. Taylor may have meant only to allow Gavin to cool off. Westmoreland later explained to Gavin that he had delayed the papers, hoping Gavin would change his mind and not retire.

Thus Secretary Brucker—though he doubtless regarded Gavin as a disturbing influence and a foe to his policy—may also have believed some kind of bargain was in Gavin's mind. "General," Brucker told Gavin [according to Jean Gavin] "You do this and a year from now nobody will even know what your name is."

Gavin left Brucker's office saddened. The secretary had issued a statement to the press saying Gavin was "reconsidering." "He clearly gave the impression that I was bargaining with him," Gavin wrote. With Jean, he dealt with the phone calls and tried to think. For once, he was at a loss. A man who had always played by the rules was being beaten. "I went home quite disturbed about the predicament in which I found myself," he wrote of that night. "I had talked to no one in the Pentagon about the unfolding drama. I thought that my testimony, honestly given in a straightforward manner on Capitol Hill, would tell all that had to be told." While he, Jean, and the girls tried to eat a somber dinner, reporters pounded on the front door—they had talked their way onto Fort Myer somehow. Jean argued at the door and was literally shoved aside. Gavin met them in controlled fury. He told them, "I have nothing to say."

But when one shouted a question about bargaining for promotion, Gavin responded. "I replied to the effect that the Secretary may say as he pleases, but I am not interested in a promotion and am not bargaining for one."

Yet the bargain for promotion remained prominent in the papers. With a crushing sense of burden, Gavin began to realize that he had created his own defeat. Like a man in a trance, he drove to Capitol Hill to appear once more before the subcommittee. This time, Lyndon Johnson overtook him in the hall. "Fella, I hope I didn't hurt you the other day," Johnson said, draping an arm around Gavin's shoulders.

Jean Gavin would never forgive Johnson for this bit of false bonhomie: "I told James, 'If I get out of this town without telling that man what I think of him' . . . he absolutely cut it off at the ground. James had no choice the way it evolved."

A brief, subdued hearing followed in executive session. Gavin took care to release his own press statement this time: "Promotion has nothing whatsoever to do with my forthcoming retirement," it read. "I was retiring because I would not stay and defend the budget through one more session of Congress. I would not support a budget that was seriously affecting the combat readiness of the U.S. Army. Furthermore, that I would be happy to serve in the Army if it were the kind of Army that I wanted it to be, in any grade, including that of private."

Gavin took a taxi to the Pentagon, and a phone call brought him to Brucker's office. The secretary took one more try at mollifying Gavin; but Gavin cut him short. "We are simply not communicating," Gavin told him. Brucker reached for the paper on his desk—the retirement request, delivered at last by Westmoreland—and signed it. "I was on my own at last." Gavin remembered thinking, "I was thankful."

20.

A D L A N D

B O S T O N

To a man who had earned his own living since the age of twelve, being out of job at fifty was alarming. He had five daughters, alimony payments, child support, and no home except the army. "I went down to G-1 and got the numbers on my retirement. I found that my retirement pay was unbelievable. I think I had something like 500 dollars a month. And I had been put in another stupid position there, in that not only didn't I want to stay, out of honesty; but I couldn't retire, because I couldn't afford to retire."

From Quarters Seven at Fort Myer, the "lovely old red brick house facing the flagpole," ripples spread from his departure that touched some of Gavin's closest friendships. Many admired his principled stand. But many others who adored, admired, or respected him felt sincerely that he had taken himself out of the battle at a crucial point, that he had surrendered to circumstance, that he should have retreated to fight again another day, in a different way.

One of these was General O'Meara, who wrote Gavin what he (O'Meara) termed a "Say it ain't so letter," urging Gavin to stay on in the high level of command and fight from within. "He looked bad because he lost in the end," O'Meara would comment about Gavin's endgame with the Pentagon monolith, "he could never match power plays with

Radford—or with Lyndon Johnson." Gavin stubbornly refused even to read the newspapers' highly colored accounts of the affair, in spite of Jean's urging.

O'Meara's language was strong and couched in the moral idiom that would strike right to Gavin's heart. "I told him, you know the Bible says what is the profit if you get all the money in the world. And I said but what good is it if you don't do what God put you on earth to do—to be the best Chief of Staff that there has ever been?" Gavin took it hard, never responding to the letter, and from then on relations between the two old comrades were icy.

Jean was everything in those days—arranging a round of visits and dinners to say good-bye to old friends from the Washington years, ended so abruptly, dealing with the calls, the reporters, and the fact that they would have to move again. For Gavin was not ready for retirement, and after all his years of planning, he had not planned what to do. They would linger for a month, leaving only at the end of March when Washington is at its spring loveliest.

Gavin spent hours gazing out to the east, where the Capitol's dome, the Washington Monument and the gothic post office tower swim above a haze of gray-white marble. He thought of some of the men who had lived at the same quarters and seen the same panorama—Ridgway, Bradley, Eisenhower, among others. And there was bitterness that he would not go on in the same way, to the logical next step, to Quarters One. Gavin, trying to come to grips with time, dabbled with his oil paints for something to do, and he painted the scene.

As the buds swelled, there was time to visit with Washington friends. The Symingtons, of course, Joe Alsop (who hosted the Gavins a farewell dinner in Georgetown), Joe's brother Stewart; *Time*'s man Bill Walton, Charles and Louise Collingwood, Senator Scoop Jackson, Tiger Teague, Marguerite Higgins, married to a West Point classmate of Gavin's, and Arthur Hadley, a young writer Gavin had befriended through a series of letters on his book *Airborne Warfare*.

Eventually the momentous nature of retirement came home to Gavin, and he clung to his last days as a general. He wisely asked for retirement —which in the army is an elaborate ceremony—from his heart's favorite unit, the one he came up with, the 82nd.

For this he returned to Fort Bragg, where he was still "Slim Jim" and the greatest of the World War II paratroopers. Today a special section of the post museum is devoted to Gavin artifacts, uniforms and mementos. Washington may have driven Gavin from the service, but Bragg took him home. He was given a residence at Carenton house, by coincidence next door to the very house where Jean and Gavin had first met, back in 1946 when the Zaises, Melvin and Aileen, Jean's sister, had lived there.

Gavin's retirement was heartening. There were the handful of 82nd Veterans who'd served with him and the rest of the division, as smart-looking as ever, turned out for their unit's greatest hero. Senator Barry Goldwater attended, as did senators Prescott Bush and Strom Thurmond; Ridgway flew down. Walton was there and Brucker sent his undersecretary Charles Finnucane, who had become a Gavin confidant. The weather was perfect as the division passed in review, and many eyes misted. At the end of the procession came an Honest John missile and a giant caricature of Gavin with "Good-bye Slim Jim" in bold letters underneath. When it was over, never again would Jim Gavin don a uniform, except in a ceremonial role.

Gavin rented a house in Southern Pines, next to Fort Bragg. "We were starting from scratch," said Jean of those days in the early spring of 1958. Gavin had little savings, nothing to sell, no stocks or bonds. He had only one resource, and he quickly mined it. He contracted to write a book for Harper & Row, which he worked on from dawn to dusk for the next two months. *War and Peace in the Space Age* was an unusual book, a simultaneous autobiography and strategic examination. In it, he told the world a bit of himself, and he defended America's need for the new technology of war. It was Gavin's major statement about the future of the army, his firm belief that in spite of the nuclear shield and the world of the atom, the old world had not changed, and that men would still fight with hand weapons in limited wars. Conventional weapons, he was also sure, would still prevail in the twilight time after the nuclear exchange.

Gavin had the highest hopes for the book. "After much soul searching, I had decided the time had come when I could serve my country better by releasing myself from the restrictions necessarily imposed on the military and telling the American people directly what I thought was wrong with the U.S. defense picture. And there was a great deal that was wrong," he wrote.

The keynote was that in Gavin's view the Russians had eagerly advanced into missile technology while the United States, a captive of the "Big Bomb" theories of a succession of air force generals, had created a "missile lag period in which the Soviets will have a steadily increasing ICBM striking capability which we will be unable to match for several years."

In the meantime, Gavin said, conventional forces had been neglected, as was shown in Korea. "We will be nibbled to death," was Gavin's thumbnail picture of the future.

Ironically, he foresaw the kind of tactics developed in Vietnam ten years later, by which time he had become a fervent foe of that conflict, but he saw them then as the means to victory. And he clung to the idea of tactical nuclear weapons.

His predictions have an eerie fascination to the post-Vietnam reader— for he was so nearly right. "To some, limited war differs from general war only in that general war lasts longer. This is not true. Limited war is limited in the objectives sought, the means employed and, usually, the areas in which it is fought. Limited war may be of such protracted nature as to go on for many years, as Mao demonstrated in China. Furthermore, there may be several limited wars all going on at the same time. In fact, this is the most probable nature of future war. It will start with a slow, almost imperceptible transition from a bad economic and political situation into internal disorder. Arms will be provided by the Communists to the side they choose, and sometimes which side they choose is not even important. They will throw out the original leaders and substitute their own, including their own revolution of the 'proletariat' at the time of their choosing. Thereafter sufficient force will be used until it no longer seems worth the West's effort to continue, or until the West is decisively defeated.

"To cope with a Communist program of this nature requires good, imaginative strategic planning as well as highly specialized tactical forces. The forces must be technically superior to anything that they encounter —decisively superior. Above all they must be highly mobile. But intelligence, communications and missile firepower all require special consideration. All of these subjects, in their relationship to limited war, have been slighted at best, and grossly neglected at worst, in our defense planning in the last 10 years. Hence the dilemma—how to keep from losing limited wars without preparing to meet them. It simply cannot be done."

The book received good notices, and the essence of it was blasted across the cover of *Life* magazine in August 1958 under the alarmist headline WE ARE IN MORTAL DANGER and a full-dress color photo of Gavin, three stars gleaming from his epaulets. Piercing the reader with his hypnotic gray eyes, he looks ruthless, but a ghost of a smile hovers around his tight lips.

Gavin's warnings were pushed aside at the Pentagon as the words of a familiar Cassandra. Without the threat of his own future power as a possible member of the Joint Chiefs, he was simply another outside voice.

As a text for a great debate about the future of American strategy, Gavin's volume failed. But for him, it was a labor, not of love for the army, but of passion and idealism. Then too, Gavin's ideas had an invincible enemy in Dwight D. Eisenhower. In 1958 Ike was still determined to strengthen civilian control of the military. In spite of his deep understanding of military matters, Eisenhower was a prisoner of his time, a direct descendant of the all-fronts, big war theories of Grant and Sherman. In a single package, the atomic bomb combined both. It overwhelmed the enemy with military power, and it definitely waged total war. And best of all it was cheaper than soldiers.

A year later, Gavin's literary effort was upstaged by Maxwell Taylor's own assessment of the problems facing the military, *Uncertain Trumpet.* Taylor's book, which echoes many of Gavin's arguments, had the happy circumstance of also influencing an ambitious and hawkish young politician named John F. Kennedy. Taylor's timing proved exquisite. His book appeared at the perfect time for John Kennedy to use it as the text for a political attack on what Eisenhower had done with the military. The "missile gap" and the condition of America's defenses would play an important role in Kennedy's election.

In the early summer of 1958, Gavin had no occupation and few prospects. He was extremely glad that his girls were out of school and thus would not need new clothes for several months. Jean sold a piece to *Good Housekeeping,* about an army wife's experiences when her husband departs the military.

Then, providentially, the feelers began arriving. Gavin's mail was heavy and varied. He had little sense of what sort of job he could take, but he was determined not to take a "revolving door" job with defense suppliers, as so many of his fellow officers had done, joining the procurement process from industry's side. Many of the jobs he was offered were temporary or decorative, and many were from colleges and universities, which could not add enough to his retirement income for the family to live comfortably. One such came from Henry Kissinger, who remembered Gavin's insights about nuclear strategy. He suggested that Gavin join the Harvard Center for International Affairs. Though Gavin declined (he did become a fellow of the center), the suggestion drew him toward the Cambridge, Massachusetts, area, where he eventually settled and bought his first home, a large suburban house in Wellesley Hills.

One corporate feeler which appealed to Gavin was from Roy Little, nephew of the founder of the research company Arthur D. Little. The company was one of a kind, famous for taking on unlikely challenges, some of them publicity stunts to illustrate their main stock in trade— finding solutions to apparently impossible problems. A legend of the firm's founding genius illustrates Arthur Little's approach to problems. Trying to manufacture artificial cloth in the 1890s, Little created a man-made fabric and went to a banker for financing to produce the product. The banker, a Bostonian, refused to believe that anything could surpass natural fibers, which, he said, were given to man by God. Little returned to the labs and managed to create a silklike fiber out of gelatinized pigs' ears, thus proving his point, that you could make a silk purse out of a sow's ear. The purse is now in the Smithsonian collection. In the 1980s, ADL engineers would create a lead balloon of extremely thin sheeting and launch it successfully. The contrariness attracted Gavin to such a company.

Arthur D. Little was founded in 1886 by a chemical engineer of that name, who had dropped out of M.I.T., impatient at the chemical engineering curriculum there, and eager to try out his own ideas. He developed a firm whose business was testing products, improving products, and eventually helping other firms to develop new products.

Little was faced with a difficult transition in 1958, due to the retirement of a chief executive. The firm's search committee, chaired by Roy Little, nephew of the founder, had hired an industrial headhunter, John Handy. Handy knew of Gavin's reputation as a leader and of his interest in technical innovation, and took the unusual step of calling on the Gavins during the hectic days at Fort Myer in the wake of Gavin's retirement. Handy struck a chord, and the offer of a vice presidential position, a salary of $60,000 plus valuable options and the possibility for advancement answered most of Gavin's immediate problems. He was interested.

But the Little executives were far from sure that they wanted an army general to head their group of scientists and engineers, many of whom were long-haired academics or intense, eccentric specialists. Gavin was summoned to Boston for a look-over by a group of executives. "It was obvious at the outset," Gavin wrote, "that they did not think much of Arthur D. Little being taken over by a general. They started questioning me on my views about everything under the sun, technology as well as management. I found it quite fascinating and rather enjoyable in some ways. I was obviously learning as much about them as they were about me. But I could not quite tell if I was turning out to be more acceptable to them or not. Finally, one of the senior officers present, Dr. Larry Bass, a Yale man and an outstanding biologist, fixed his gaze upon me and asked, 'What do you think of Suetonius?' It happened that I had read this Roman historian of the second century A.D., who is best known for his lurid description of the sexual mores of the Roman emperors."

"Print it in paperback, with a naked woman on the cover and it would be a best seller," Gavin told them. There were no more questions. The meeting resolved all of Gavin's doubts and those of the committee. He was able to spend the next two months at the typewriter working on *War and Peace in the Space Age.* The day after he finished, he went to work for Little at their head offices on Memorial Drive, Cambridge.

From the beginning, the combination of Gavin's gift for galvanizing human talent, plus his unlimited interest in technical innovation proved that Roy Little and John Handy had made a wise decision. Gavin proved one of the best salesmen Arthur D. Little had ever had. As he had with the 505th Parachute Infantry Regiment, Gavin immersed himself completely in the mission of the company, using many of the leadership techniques he had found to work with the often rough, rootless, and self-destructive men who tended to volunteer for the paratroops. Now, he found the same simple practices worked with motivated, and highly educated specialists.

At ADL Gavin would wander incognito through labs, often visiting offices where lights were burning late, without introduction, and ask questions about projects. There was no class of employee in whom he did not seem to be interested.

Just how well these simple management techniques translated into the high-toned atmosphere at ADL is revealed in a letter Gavin received in 1959 from an employee he'd asked to research whether wide reading

helped form better leaders. Gavin, the worker wrote, "set a small confla-
gration" with his questions and interest, convincing his listeners he was
not only interested in the products of their work but "the entire person."

It was very good for business. Gavin had extensive European contacts
and used them to expand the client base of ADL enormously in his years
as an executive there.

He earned the respect of his senior staff and the adoring allegiance of
his younger workers, just as he had with the young men of the 82nd,
though it would have amused the troopers to know Gavin was interested
in "the entire person." What he admired most about the 82nd, as he had
jotted in his 1945 war diary, was that they were "superb, close quarters
killers."

Gavin's daughters were growing, and now in Wellesley Hills, for the
first time he found a stable community, made friends, sent his children
to the best local schools (Beaver Country Day, Windsor School, and the
local public schools) and rejoiced in what Jean idealized as "a steady
normal family life, which we basically had very little of."

General Gavin was given the ultimate accolade, membership in the
Boston Atheneum, the superexclusive club on Beacon Hill. He also joined
the socially elite Somerset Club, Boston's refuge for conservatives. The
army had taught Jean, as well, the value of joining local groups, and she
soon found herself immersed in the brilliant museums, the university
life, the company of professors. The Gavins even joined the Dedham Polo
Club.

It was a charmed time for Jean, and for her husband, a welcome shift,
a gathering of some of life's gentler rewards. He did not bring his work
home, nor did he adopt the habits of a top executive. Gavin, for the first
time in his life, spent hours with his daughters.

Gavin's fame had a way of calling on him, though. Early in 1959 he
received a letter from the ambitious junior Senator from Massachusetts,
John F. Kennedy, who was then making the preliminary moves toward
his candidacy as the Democratic candidate in the 1960 presidential election. The note was formal. "I would like very much for you to have
lunch with me and others in the academic, research and related fields who
are advising me on policy this year. The luncheon will be at 12:30 P.M.
at the Harvard Club in Boston. I hope that you can be there for a talk
about matters both general and specific. I would like to have some discussion on questions of defense, etc."

The two men had met right after World War II when Kennedy was campaigning for his first House of Representatives seat. Kennedy had addressed a reunion of 82nd Airborne vets. It was a casual thing, but Gavin had admired the young former navy man's speaking style and ease. Then in September of 1958, Kennedy spoke at the dedication of a new research plant in Concord, Massachusetts. ADL was involved, and Gavin was there. Gavin was again impressed and took the opportunity to compliment Kennedy, who by coincidence, had favorably reviewed Gavin's *War and Peace in the Space Age* in *Reporter* magazine. "I was impressed by the similarity of our views at the time on fundamental space and defense problems," Gavin noted. Flattering notes flew back and forth between the two men that fall.

But the luncheon opened a new level of intimacy between them. Gavin drove into the city on Sunday, February 15, 1959, to find a glittering group of men who would be, but were not yet, the eyes and ears of the Kennedy advisory group: Walt Rostow, Henry Kissinger, John Kenneth Galbraith, Arthur Schlesinger Jr., Archibald Cox, Lincoln Gordon. Also attending were Barton Leach, Professor Robert C. Wood, and Abram Chayes.

The luncheon was long over and winter dusk descending as the talk continued. Gavin, always impressed by academics and intellectuals, was quite bowled over. "Senator Kennedy's broad knowledge, incisive questioning and careful analysis of the many views presented, some of them quite conflicting, were very impressive. Unquestionably, I wanted to give him my full support in the trying months ahead. This was the man I hoped would be President." For Gavin, who had feared Roosevelt and hoped for a dictator during the depression, who had despised Truman and been ruined by the defense policies of Dwight Eisenhower, Kennedy's appeal was generational, but it was more than that. They were both World War II veterans, and Kennedy, rich, privileged, and glamorous, had asked Gavin for his counsel and help.

Before World War II, Gavin had always been a "die-hard" Republican. He had scorned the Roosevelt approach to government and looked upon "handouts" as un-American. After the war, Gavin became a Democrat who fervently believed government should show responsibility to its citizens. In fact, in his later years many would classify him as a "die-hard liberal" or a "bleeding heart." Yet, this may have been only a reflection of Gavin finding himself.

Over the next year Gavin sent a steady stream of letters, papers and suggestions to Kennedy, building the defense themes to which he was dedicated—deterioration of the army, the need for an army missile program, and for new efforts in weapons research. Kennedy was able to make political use of some of this material in his attacks on Eisenhower's defense policy. From that point on, the two men met occasionally when at the same parties, or dined together.

If Gavin was impressed (his allegiance to Kennedy put him in the doghouse with an older and closer friend, Stuart Symington, who himself sought the Democratic nomination in 1960), Kennedy also immediately liked the flinty-eyed soldier and was sympathetic to the moral dilemma of Gavin's departure from the Pentagon. Gavin was the right kind of soldier and the right kind of character for Kennedy—an iconoclast, a man of action who was also an eager intellectual. Kennedy sought to include him in the campaign by sending him position papers for comment. Gavin responded quickly and always added thoughts of his own. But Gavin held no political hopes. The contacts seemed too casual.

The campaign of 1960 against Richard Nixon was no easy victory for Kennedy. His religion had faded as a negative issue, but business was against him, and his youth (he was forty-three) was a handicap. The lead he enjoyed early in the campaign narrowed. Then President Eisenhower made a strong last-minute effort to help his two-time vice president.

Kennedy was an agile campaigner who had decided to spend hard and run hard to the finish. Gavin knew Kennedy had the ability and the money to rush any new concept straight to the stump or to television. He was, remembered Gavin, "always on the lookout for ideas that might be useful and of assistance to him." Gavin would pitch him a great one, in the concept of the Peace Corps.

On October 18, Gavin was meeting in Manhattan with a committee of businessmen, sponsored by the National Chamber of Commerce, to discuss how to use American manpower and technology to help emerging countries. There was an air of discouragement. America, the businessmen seemed to agree, could not match the Soviet system of exporting training and technicians to tackle specific problems in individual countries, to locate resources and provide solutions, and thus reap political dividends.

"We are wasting our time," one businessman said. "We can never compete with what the Soviets are doing in Africa. They program their young people through school, giving them the necessary technical and language training so that upon graduation they are ready to go to specific countries and deal with specific problems, whether they are petrochemical engineers for Ghana, foresters for Nigeria or petroleum engineers for Morocco . . . we cannot possibly match such a program. Neither the government nor industry would support it."

The negativity galled Gavin, "Yet I could not answer his charges in specific terms. It was most unlikely that American industry would organize and support such an undertaking. It was true, too, that our government had no such program."

The midwife for the idea forming in Gavin's mind was Philip Sporn, board chairman of the American Electric Power Company, a board to which Gavin had been appointed. Sporn thought that, in spite of the natural disinclination of American youth to join the military, the draft was something that the voters accepted and supported. It was Gavin's idea that a volunteer service could be created to match college students' academic training with skills needed in foreign countries. It would be an alternative to the draft and satisfy the requirements of the draft law. Gavin even saw it as a replacement for the draft.

Gavin's idea began to take on a life of its own when he brought it to colleagues at Arthur D. Little on his return to Cambridge. They were enthusiastic and suggested the name Peace Corps—which Gavin promptly vetoed as having "too strong a military connotation." But he could not come up with a better or catchier name.

For a week the idea lay in limbo until October 27, when Gavin was to give a standard stump speech on industry and the space age to a group of businessmen and educators in Miami. He was seated between South Carolina Governor (later Senator) Ernest F. Hollings and Florida's governor-elect, Farris Bryant. Only ten days remained before the election, which was the main subject of conversation among these strong Kennedy supporters. Both of his dinner partners were worried that their states would be lost to Kennedy. When Gavin stood up to speak, he decided to try his idea out. "As I neared the end of my talk, I told the audience that I welcomed this particular occasion because I wanted to use them as guinea pigs. I wanted to try out an idea on them. I then outlined my concept of a Peace Corps and how the idea could be carried out. To my surprise, they broke into spontaneous and quite enthusiastic applause."

Hollings told Gavin, "You really have a good idea there. We have got to get it to Jack Kennedy." Gavin, feeling somewhat discomfited that he had made public property of his idea without offering it for its political worth, decided to take it to Kennedy himself. He phoned author Cornelius Ryan the next day and asked for an interview with Kennedy press secretary Pierre Salinger. Kennedy was crisscrossing the country in a last-minute series of campaign appearances and didn't get back by phone until October 29. Kennedy, it turned out, had also been approached by Hollings. The candidate enthusiastically asked Gavin to put together a briefing on the idea, and by the next evening, a Sunday, Gavin had ready a two-page memo. By Wednesday, Kennedy had the plan and used it in a speech in San Francisco. "Thus it began," Gavin would write later. His friendship with the new President was cemented with something more than mutual recognition—a favor at the right time. When Kennedy won by a razor-thin margin of less than 1 percent of the popular vote— 112,881 votes, it was time to reward every good Kennedy idea, and the Peace Corps was one of the best.

Gavin anxiously awaited returns on November 6, but from a vantage point in Paris, France, where he was attending a marketing seminar— among luminaries like Belgian prime minister Paul Henri Spaak.

Meanwhile Jean Gavin went with friends in the press corps to Hyannis-port's National Guard armory. But when midnight came, the result was still uncertain, and a wave toward Nixon was rolling in from the west. Kennedy told the press he would go to bed at 2 A.M. An hour later, it was clear that Nixon would carry more states than Kennedy and the electoral college vote would be a squeak. Not until the next morning was it clear that Kennedy had won the election.

Gavin's unusual loyalty to Kennedy (for the officer corps is overwhelmingly Republican) drew him inevitably to Washington. His first post for the Kennedy White House was a brief but complete victory over his nemesis Maxwell Taylor.

Taylor, meanwhile, had not been idle. As Army Chief of Staff he fought, as Gavin had, the increasingly parsimonious Eisenhower budgets. The fight over massive retaliation continued, and Taylor announced his retirement from the army in June 1959, taking a job first as a top officer of the Mexican Light and Power Company and later as president of Lincoln Center. Settled in New York by the end of 1960, he pushed his idea of a flexible military strategy in the pages of *Foreign Affairs.* The new president had already set Taylor down in his book of New Frontier wise men, and had used Taylor's book *Uncertain Trumpet* to beef up his own attacks on the Eisenhower Defense Department.

But one of the first calls Kennedy made in the first days after the election was to Gavin. Apparently confident he would not get a refusal, Kennedy designated Gavin grand marshal of the inaugural parade.

Gavin was at first flattered. "Traditionally, the Chairman of the Joint Chiefs of Staff (then Gen. Lyman Lemnitzer) is the Grand Marshal. Later it had been the Chief of Staff of the United States Army," Gavin wrote, "I had not worn a uniform since my retirement in early 1958 and the idea of being Grand Marshal was the farthest thing from my mind." Kennedy also called on Bill Walton, who'd settled in Georgetown and had become a favorite of the Kennedys, as deputy. It would be old times— and Kennedy's own wry joke, for he had heard the story of how Gavin, jumping from the same plane as Walton over Normandy, had insisted that the newsman jump last in the stick lest he freeze and hesitate at the door and keep troopers from making their exit at the critical moment. Now the first man and the last were again working together.

The grand marshal's job turned out to be a nightmare, due to the snowstorm that swept into town and turned Washington into a mess under 8 inches of white. Gavin and his family almost didn't make it to the event, though he had cautiously started from Boston the day before. At one point, they were stuck in a bar in Maryland's Charles County, after their first car slid off the road and the second had no chains.

Gavin walked to a nearby Maryland state police barracks and persuaded officers to drive him to Washington in a cruiser that did have chains, and the family finished the twelve-hour journey to the familiar quarters at Fort Myer at one in the morning.

Though Gavin's post was largely ceremonial, he attacked the snow with a fervor, and with the support of the Military District of Washington, over two hundred pieces of snow-removal equipment were put into action to clear the parade route and access roads.

But everything seemed determined to go wrong that day, as if the fates required Kennedy's inaugural to be stamped in memory. The clergyman giving the invocation, Richard Cardinal Cushing, prayed on and on in the icy winds blowing past the north side of the Capitol; there was a small electrical fire from a short within the speaker's podium; and the poet Robert Frost was almost blinded by the snowy glare and could hardly read.

But the show went on, Kennedy making his memorable "Ask not what your country can do for you" inaugural speech. The real trouble came afterwards. Overplanning, perhaps, or overreaching, or an inability to

disappoint, led to the longest parade in inaugural history—15,000 soldiers, sailors and marines, 10,000 civilians, 40 floats, 32 pieces of military
equipment including missiles, tanks and airplanes, plus much more.

Kennedy had asked for a two-hour limit on the event, but as it wore
on into its third hour, the crowd began to thin and the dignitaries in the
reviewing stand in front of the White House hung on grimly as shadows
reached across Lafayette Park and fell darkly. Shortly after the 82nd
Airborne appeared on the icy pavements, Kennedy called to Gavin so he
could stand beside him to take their salute. "You know, Jim," Kennedy
cracked, "this is the longest two-hour parade I have ever seen."

But the presidential party stuck it out to the end even after Jacqueline
Kennedy left the stands. Kennedy and one or two aides, Jean and Gavin
—and Walton—were the only figures remaining as the streetlights and
floodlights came on. One of the last marchers, a single representative
carrying a large banner reading "Trust Territories of the Pacific" trudged
by. "Gavin turned to Bill Walton and asked him where in the world that
was. Walton replied, "I don't know, but you will be ambassador there if
you don't get this parade over with."

2 1.

FRANCE

Even as the inaugural parade ended, Kennedy had already laid plans to ask Gavin to be ambassador to France. Ironically, Taylor later claimed in his autobiography that Secretary of State Dean Rusk had first asked him if he wanted the post, but he had turned it down to work at Lincoln Center. Sources close to Kennedy, such as Bill Walton, dispute the claim, and because Kennedy believed a president could not afford to be turned down, he always sent out careful feelers before officially offering anyone a job, a practice that suggests Taylor's account of the Rusk approach might have been a parting shot at an old rival. Gavin, though he was now president of ADL, accepted the post.

The problems of Charles de Gaulle's France—insistence on its own atomic weapons program, the "force de frappe"; an anticolonial revolt in its largest possession, Algeria; and France's thorny relations with the rest of the European Economic Community—were all related directly to the colossal ego of the French war hero. Military questions weighed heavily in this balance.

Kennedy felt that a strong, unified NATO was the best assurance of a balance of power in Europe, and America should control nuclear weapons in aid of its allies. De Gaulle's insistence on France's own atomic striking force was diametrically opposed to this. Dialogue had ceased, and Kennedy told Gavin that his top priority was at least to open dialogue, something the State Department had concluded was impossible.

Gavin was regarded as one of the new thinkers of the Pentagon, but the logical choices for the ambassadorship were State Department veterans Charles "Chip" Bohlen and Robert Lovett, both Cold War "wise men." Lovett did not want the post (and also turned down State, Treasury, and Defense), and Bohlen, who did and would get it after Gavin, was resentful. Other political appointees were traditionally rich. A self-made man like Gavin was almost unheard of in such a position.

Gavin was chosen, mostly on Kennedy's intuition and calculation that whatever else de Gaulle might discount about an American, he could not discount the man who had offered his life in the leap to liberate France in 1944. Bravery was a de Gaulle absolute, and Kennedy felt Gavin would prove popular with the Frenchman in the street.

Kennedy also saw Jean—certainly the most beautiful ambassador's wife sent to Paris in the century—as a further stroke of American glamour. After the inaugural, Kennedy reviewed hastily assembled press clips and photos of the presidential party shivering at the reviewing stand. "That woman is beautiful," Kennedy told Bill Walton. "She should be in Paris."

Walton was dispatched to feel out Gavin. He first mentioned the possibility at the inaugural party, then he phoned Gavin. Walton got Gavin to agree to return to Washington. The two men and Kennedy met January 24 to seal the arrangement. Gavin was extremely reluctant to take up a post for which he felt less than perfectly qualified. First, he had no French to speak of besides the smattering picked up in two terms at West Point and in the bistros and countryside of Normandy, and the quiet and shy Gavin was not a good public speaker, even in English. Second, he had no experience as a diplomat and his methods had usually been the opposite of those described as "diplomatic." Third, he was not rich. Gavin was entirely dependent on his ADL salary, and he had not had time to accumulate savings that would allow him to serve in what he knew was a rich man's post.

Nevertheless Walton recalled Kennedy had commented favorably about Gavin's qualifications for the job. "His hope was that, as a man of action as well as intellect, he would be able to establish a rapport with de Gaulle, which had eluded previous envoys. He talked about the quality of [Gavin's] mind, and noted that [he] read books and seemed to be an independent fellow."

Kennedy, the son of a former ambassador to Britain, was no stranger to the strains that had existed between the State Department and the White House—extending, in the case of France, to the deep and insoluble sense of insult that de Gaulle harbored against the American policymakers for their refusal to accept his leadership as France's head of state in exile after the fall of France in 1940.

Gavin got a negative read from Eisenhower's wartime deputy General Walter Bedell Smith. Bedell Smith, whom Gavin trusted, said Gavin should not give up a business career unless he intended to become a career diplomat. But others encouraged him, and Gavin's response belied his reluctance. When he saw Kennedy at the White House on January 24, he promised to begin studying French at once, and even before he left for France, began a daily program with a tutor who insisted on a daily discussion of the French press. To Gavin's money worries, Kennedy blithely gave assurances that there would be no problem. "From the very beginning of his administration," Gavin related, "the President had been determined upon a policy of assigning the individuals he considered best qualified for the post and then seeking such Congressional assistance as might be necessary." Of course Kennedy, who had inherited millions, had no conception of Gavin's penury as a retired general.

Then Kennedy told Gavin of the heart of his mission. "I have given a great deal of thought to Paris and it seems entirely clear to me that the one problem we have is General de Gaulle. No one can get along with him. Our last ambassador [Amory Houghton] left his post four months ago, and we haven't had adequate representation during that time."

He then went over the qualities that de Gaulle might admire in Gavin. "That de Gaulle had been somewhat of a maverick in the Army and had written about warfare, as I had. He reminded me that I had parachuted into France the night of June 5–6, 1944 and this should be very much in my favor with the French people." Kennedy considered the transaction closed when Gavin told him he would still have to make mutually satisfactory arrangements with ADL. He also asked for time to discuss things with Jean.

Gavin hurried back to Boston by late afternoon shuttle and met with Roy Little, whose involvement with the company included a post as chairman of the ADL executive succession committee. Though the company had named Gavin president only a short time before, Little gave him leave with the proviso that Gavin pledge to return eighteen months after the beginning of the appointment. He also assured Gavin that in return for his pledge, the company would continue to support him to the tune of $60,000 per year while he was ambassador. Still, money would be hard to come by. He would have to forgo his army retirement pay because of federal rules against the practice of "double dipping."

Back in Wellesley Hills, Gavin and Jean discussed whether to sell their house or rent it. Kennedy called Gavin, and his first words when Gavin picked up the phone were, "Well, Jim, when are you going to be ready to go?" Gavin sought further reassurance and said he would return to Washington and stop at the White House once more. This time, Kennedy was more forceful. "The President must have sensed a reluctance on my part," Gavin recalled, "he finally said, 'Look Jim, are you reluctant to help me out?' There was but one reply that I could make. 'Of course not,' " he told Kennedy.

Jean took the news that the Gavins would be uprooting yet again with the stoicism of a true army wife. Her only worry was that they might not be able to afford the life and the schools for the four girls, who had so recently settled into Wellesley Hills. But she knew from Gavin's determined attitude that it was time to pack once more.

Though it is questionable whether Gavin affected the long-range policies of Charles de Gaulle, he set a new style for the often lofty and distant, high-society Paris embassy. The symbol of the American presence was the Herrick mansion at 2, Avenue d'Iéna, a residence given to the United States by Ambassador Myron Herrick, one of the very rich men who had held the post.

Simply maintaining the mansion and its famous kitchen, rumored to be the best in Paris, making sure that the dignities of the various government and private visitors were attended to, took a staff of twelve. Dinners were regularly held for forty-eight people. Cocktail parties and receptions dotted the calendar.

Gavin took little notice of the elaborate domestic arrangements, but Jean was taken completely aback, particularly when the head housekeeper for the vast establishment decided she should leave. If anything, Jean's French was worse than Gavin's and was indelibly marked with a deep Tennessee accent.

Jean confronted the enormous house "with the staff all lined up at the foot of the stairs waiting to be presented," with amusement. "The children all wanted to explore the house," she remembered, "they thought the elevator was great fun—and the garden." The house though, was not well suited for entertaining. Then the top two members of the staff, Mme. Simone Blanchard, the overall housekeeper, who really ran the residence, and Mlle. Elizabeth de Canenmont, the social secretary, announced they wanted to leave but would stay on for a couple of weeks— or until Jean could find somebody. "Me, find somebody? I hadn't a clue," she remembered. But the charm worked and they relented. "I knew I had to get the children placed in schools, I had this big crisis, and I knew in less than three months the Kennedys were arriving for their big state visit."

Mme. Blanchard had the unique distinction of having remained at the embassy for all the dark days of the German occupation during World War II, and it was she who answered the legendary phone call, about a week after the Normandy landings, from some soldier who had the wit or good humor to call the embassy and tell her, "We are the Americans and we are here in Normandy. We are coming." She hoisted the U.S. flag on the day Paris was liberated.

Jean's debut as an ambassador's wife was her official call on Madame de Gaulle. "You're invited in, you sit in a formal chair. And Madame says, 'Madame, how do you like Paris?' And you say, 'Oh Madame, I like it so much, it's wonderful'. And Madame asks you if you would like a cup of tea."

The night before Mme. de Gaulle was to call at Avenue d'Iéna was the night of the Challe revolt, the crisis caused when a group of French army officers took over the Algerian government and threatened to send French paratroops to Paris to spearhead a general revolt against de Gaulle because he planned to allow Algerian independence.

Gavin assured Jean, and Kennedy, that the paratroops could not possibly mount such an operation in any numbers. He knew it was logistically impossible. Still it was to Jean's great surprise that Mme. de Gaulle reconfirmed her intent to visit the American ambassador's wife. "*Nous sommes pres de vous dans votre angoisse,*" Jean memorized. *We are with you in your time of trouble.* The two women spent a pleasant visit discussing points of interest. "The de Gaulles went out of their way to be very friendly with us, they were very warm with us, and the word got out very quickly that the de Gaulles liked the Gavins."

Gavin brought Jean into his work more than he ever had before. Her youth and curiosity were valuable. She was thirty-seven, at the height of her mature beauty. She found that her perfect figure made her of interest to all the couturiers of the city. She was loaned clothes she never could have bought; she shone and glowed in the attention and glamour.

Gavin plunged immediately into his task with the same intensity he had devoted to warfare. But first, as usual, he did reconnaissance, reading everything he could get his hands on about the great general, filling several looseleaf notebooks with information he had collected. He concluded that the State Department was largely to blame for the apparent impasse in U.S.-French relations.

Only two days after his arrival, he was face to face with the man himself, and the difference between them was obvious. De Gaulle adhered strictly to the byzantine forms of French diplomatic practice. Gavin was told there would be no handshakes, and to emphasize the distance between the embodiment of France and ordinary mortals, the two men met at a distance of 4 to 6 feet, each making a brief formal statement.

The meeting seemed to signal to Gavin the enormous gulf he would have to bridge to achieve better relations with de Gaulle. Kennedy not only wanted a friendlier France, he wanted a stronger NATO and the first task was a review and analysis of the condition of the Atlantic alliance. Gavin was shocked to find, on meeting with a Pentagon group, that the briefers showed him essentially the same material he had reviewed ten years before when he was Chief of Staff Allied Forces Southern Europe (his Naples post) and later as commander of VII Corps in southern Germany. "The same general disposition of combat divisions . . . was presented, the same reserves to be moved about on a specific time schedule in a manner much, if not exactly . . . the same as [in] World War II dispositions. In the meantime, however, we had developed and placed into the hands of troops tactical nuclear weapons which were certain to change the entire nature of the battlefield," he grumbled.

There was, he noted, no integrated missile defense, a shortage of mid-range missiles, little redeployment of resources that were vulnerable to missile attack. NATO, it seemed, had been in a deep freeze.

American policy, always adrift between administrations, fell back on time-worn theories based on illusions—the chief one being that de Gaulle, unable to solve the Algerian crisis, would soon depart as had all the other failed French presidents since World War II. Kennedy was pushed one way by the State Department, while his inclination was to follow the other.

While Gavin labored to persuade de Gaulle of America's good intentions, Henry Kissinger left the Kennedy White House because the president was so anti-de Gaulle.

But the real problem with Franco-U.S. relations was a complete lack of understanding of de Gaulle. Yes, de Gaulle was arrogant and difficult to get along with, but he was dedicated to doing what he believed was in

France's best interests, regardless of what the United States desired. De Gaulle was never interested in being an ally; he wanted to restore France to world leadership. To do that in the 1960s, he meant to make France a nuclear power. The one thing the United States wanted least in Europe was an independent-minded, nuclear-armed France acting on her own initiative in a region that had been American dominated since the end of World War II. This was the gap Kennedy expected Gavin somehow to bridge.

Gavin's first chance to prove America's friendly intentions came from the crisis in Algeria. Algerian Arabs were fighting a bloody insurgent war for independence. But if de Gaulle granted it, almost a million French colonists, the "Colons," would fight, backed by their families and allies in the homeland. Bombings in France had become commonplace. And what made the situation even stickier was that constitutionally, Algeria was not a colony but a province or department of metropolitan France. To give in to Algeria was, to many Frenchmen, to cede French soil.

The Challe revolt, which threatened to bring down de Gaulle's presidency, happened in April, while Gavin was on an official visit to Bordeaux. A new military government of Algeria, headed by General Maurice Challe, a former NATO commander, had taken over the colony with the intention of clamping down on the Arab revolution and forcing the French government to back "Algérie Française," an Algeria under the rule of France.

Immediately rumors began to spread that the revolt was supported by outside right-wing forces supported by the U.S. Central Intelligence Agency. Gavin felt he should return to Paris. Against the advice of a senior CIA official who was with the Gavin party in Bordeaux (and who thought that Gavin's return would only spark more rumors about U.S. involvement in the crisis), he returned immediately to show solidarity with the de Gaulle government. First, he sought information about the capabilities of the rebels who were threatening to send French paratroops. His search was frustrating and led to disillusionment about the CIA network. "I asked the CIA to find out how many planes suitable for parachute operations they had and what types of planes they were. I asked them to make further inquiries of the U.S. Military Headquarters, all to no avail." Gavin found the CIA could offer nothing but rumors and press digests, and no advice. The intelligence men could get no information from their own military leaders, either at NATO Southern Europe head-quarters, Sixth Fleet, or his own old command at Naples. Gavin returned to Paris on Saturday; Sunday afternoon de Gaulle made a powerful ad-dress to the French people, asking for their support, ending it with the call "Françaises, Français! Aidez-moi!" *(French women, Frenchmen! Help me!)*

This speech, expressing de Gaulle's resolve to master the crisis by staking his enormous political capital, spurred Gavin to action. At 9 P.M. he placed a trans-Atlantic call to the White House, asking that he be allowed to call on de Gaulle to offer U.S. assistance to France, squelching the CIA rumors. Kennedy told him to go ahead. But when Gavin arrived at the Élysée Palace, he was told that de Gaulle, with perfect sangfroid, had gone to bed. But the next morning de Gaulle would thank him, and at a remove, Kennedy.

Further disillusionment with the CIA came Monday when syndicated columnist Marquis Childs visited Gavin to report that French Foreign Minister Couve de Murville had confirmed the story that the CIA was behind the Challe revolt. Gavin quietly told Childs his information could not be correct. Why else would Kennedy have approved Gavin's support-ive call on de Gaulle?

The new ambassador's part in the crisis came about a week after the revolt began: Guest of honor at a luncheon at the Anglo-American Press Club on May 3, he was confronted by a reporter for a London paper, Sam White of the *Evening Standard,* who asked a loaded and provocative question, accusing the CIA of involvement in the Algerian revolution, adding that the French government had confirmed the involvement. Gavin deftly deferred the question to Couve de Murville's spokes-man, who sat nearby. The spokesman refused to reply and flew into a rage. Gavin won favorable headlines in New York for soothing his rage and deflecting the question, avoiding another "U.S. denies" news story.

Gavin learned that far from being unable to solve the Algerian crisis, de Gaulle was determined to resolve it by giving the North African colony its independence and dealing with the results of that decision. If it meant that France would lose its African oil, de Gaulle's reply was "there is plenty of oil in the world." If it meant paying and pensioning every single French-born Algerian for life, he would do that, to avoid the cost of an armed struggle.

"As it turned out, our help was not needed," Gavin wrote. Gavin would never again depend on the CIA to help him with decisions. Nor the State Department, which, he decided, needed to be completely reformed. "What is needed more than anything else today are more Foreign Service Officers so that an adequate number can be kept in school each year. After a period abroad, they should be returned to school to be brought up to date again on both technical and cultural subjects. This should be a recurring event in their service lives, exactly as it is in the armed forces. Along the way, they should be given training of an executive nature, training in making cold and deliberate evaluations of political and business situations, training in reaching sound judgements and firm decisions, training in good administrative practices."

After de Gaulle's firm handling of the crisis had defused the threat of the Challe revolt, Gavin was plunged immediately into a crisis of a different nature, the preparation for Kennedy's goodwill tour to France at the end of May 1961, a prelude to meeting with Soviet Premier Nikita Khrushchev at Vienna. Though ceremonial in nature and overshadowed by the meeting with Khrushchev that immediately followed it, the visit had more than minor importance because it signaled the eagerness of Kennedy to make fresh arrangements with France.

Gavin's record of the event is a catalogue of colors and richness, "The Guard Républicaine, two hundred strong, wearing their colorful Napoleonic uniforms—blue coats faced with scarlet, white breeches, black spurred boots, and crowned by a shiny gold helmet, complete with cockade and flowing horsehair plumes dangling from the top . . . we came into Paris to the shouts of the crowd and the sound of a one-hundred-one-gun salute which was still booming over the Seine River when the Presidents arrived at the Quai d'Orsay."

He noted that Jacqueline Kennedy received as many shouts as the president, and that the Kennedys received a larger turnout than had either Eisenhower or Khrushchev.

Amid the whirl of receptions, state dinners, press conferences, visits to places of great fame, Kennedy dined with the Gavins the night before his departure for Vienna. Gavin, never a master of high-society details, made sure that ingredients were in the pantry for Kennedy's favorite cocktail, but took at face value the assurances of the butler that he had mastered the art of making the daiquiri.

But when Kennedy, as expected, asked for his drink, there was a long and ominous delay in the pantry. Gavin hurried back to find the butler nonplussed. He quickly put the drink together himself.

Kennedy took only a sip or two, and smiled. "Jim," he said, "I think I'll have a martini instead."

Gavin did not want simply to play at ambassador. He found little opportunity to make progress with de Gaulle's sour attitude toward NATO, and in fact, gradually came to agree with de Gaulle, or at least to reach a sympathetic understanding of the old general's desire to keep France independent and strong. He found it difficult to understand why such attitudes scandalized the State Department.

Gavin's most revolutionary idea frightened Washington. So at ease had he become with de Gaulle, that he concluded that it might be good for the United States to help France attain a nuclear weapon. He believed, correctly as it turned out, that France would soon develop its own nuclear missiles anyway, so why shouldn't the United States help in return for France's increased cooperation in NATO and in permitting Britain into the Common Market. Ideas such as this were not well received in Washington.

Gavin soon tangled with Dean Rusk, the Georgia-born Cold Warrior and Far East specialist Kennedy had named secretary of state. Gavin's telegrams from Paris asking for change moved up the line and could not be ignored, for their author was too close to the president. But Rusk could offer little comfort to Gavin and responded with a lecture. No student of European affairs, he was trained in indirection and resorted to tortuous arguments when faced with Gavin's straightforward assessments and requests for action.

Gavin, on April 18, 1961, sent Rusk a long secret message beginning, "I am becoming increasingly convinced that some basic changes are required in our policy toward France" and going on to detail how the information and equipment embargo on nuclear weapons "has been taken over by events" since most information about the technology was freely available in specialist journals. Meanwhile, Gavin pointed out, "Our policy has not inhibited us from furnishing missile technology and from offering [missiles] to another NATO ally, the United Kingdom." He also pointed out that the idea that the United States could limit nuclear proliferation by policy was "not valid" since France had the option of using supersonic aircraft to deliver nuclear weapons on a foe.

Gavin's suggestion that the United States simply drop its embargo on rocket technologies brought an elaborate response from Rusk three weeks later. "Key question throughout, in my view, is not so much whether France will achieve some sort [of] nuclear weapons capability," Rusk telegrammed, "but effect on German aspirations and thus on NATO of U.S. posture of encouraging French nuclear effort. The French will face a most serious resource problem in trying to prosecute a national missile and nuclear program alone. They may well seek German aid at some point. The Germans would not now wish to be drawn into such a venture and would be unwilling to grant aid under present circumstances. But if U.S. signifies it approves French program and helps that program, German resistance to joining it may be greatly weakened. Even possible that, despite Chancellor's desires, Germany might eventually be moved to seek U.S. aid for its own program in this event. Any such German effort [to] create or join in creating nuclear capability would shake NATO to its foundations."

The Rusk telegram indicated a distrust of U.S. allies—and in particular, distrust of de Gaulle (indeed in one part of the three-page telegram, Rusk speaks of the "post-de Gaulle period" ahead). It was clear to a frustrated Gavin that French policy was frozen under the rubric that nothing could be done until de Gaulle went away. Gavin knew that this would not happen during his ambassadorship.

The more Gavin studied de Gaulle and French postwar history, the more he became convinced that de Gaulle's vision of France as the third great power, after the United States and Russia, was unshakable. He came to realize that de Gaulle's ultimate aim was to make France the leader of Europe. Or, as he put it in his 1959 memoir, "the third planetary power, and if necessary [to] become one day the arbiter between the Anglo-Saxons and the Soviet camp."

On December 5, *Washington Post* syndicated columnist Drew Pearson charged that Gavin's summer and fall as ambassador had revealed him as a man who did not understand diplomacy and could not speak French. Then later in the month *Newsweek* dropped the following honeyed poison: "One casualty in the Administration's current impasse with Charles de Gaulle may be James M. Gavin, U.S. Ambassador to France. Gavin's ability is unquestioned but some policymakers here wonder whether, as an avowed de Gaulle fan, he can fight hard enough for U.S. views opposed by the general."

U.S. News & World Report chimed in with a similar report: "Lt. Gen.

James M. Gavin, U.S. Ambassador to France, is expected by his friends to be transferred from that position before very long, opening the way for Dean Rusk, Secretary of State, to appoint an Ambassador of his own choosing. President Kennedy personally selected General Gavin."

Gavin wrote to Rusk on December 28—with a copy to President Kennedy—challenging him: "If I am not being replaced in the immediate future, then the [State] Department should issue an emphatic denial without delay."

Kennedy responded loyally and warmly January 4, in spite of the hectic holiday season. "These rumors are annoying, I know," Kennedy wrote, "but I believe this is a temporary matter. There are so many rumors in the press that it appears as though the reporters pick up the rumors from other reporters.

"You have my complete confidence and the Secretary likewise shares my feeling toward you. We will take every available step to make it clear to the French government that you do have this confidence and that these reports are not true. You are not only a good public servant, but also a close personal friend. . . . You are by far the best ambassador we have had in that post since Franklin."

At the same time Pierre Salinger, Kennedy's press secretary, told reporters "Ambassador Gavin will continue in the Paris post and the President has the greatest confidence in Ambassador Gavin and the work he is doing." The flurry of negatives abruptly dried up. But the long knives were still out at State.

Meanwhile, Gavin traveled throughout France with Jean. There were dozens of wreaths to lay and short speeches to make that would not tax Gavin's rudimentary French. He also kept a wary eye on the long negotiations between Great Britain and the Common Market, and he had early clues that the British would be rejected on their official application for entry into the market in January 1963. "From the outset it was apparent that the British were far more optimistic of a satisfactory formula for entry being found than were the French," he wrote. Gavin had noted that the British had hoped to gain a long period,—perhaps six years —during which both British and British Commonwealth agriculture and manufacturers would have access to European markets. The Europeans, on the other hand, wanted this adjustment period to be as short as possible. Gavin saw this, correctly, as the deal breaker.

Believing his analysis would be helpful to his chiefs in Washington,

Gavin telegraphed the prediction that the British would be rejected for admission. But in the process of drafting the message, seasoned embassy staffers caught its gist and reacted with handwringing.

"I prepared a telegram outlining this general situation in which I concluded that the British would not achieve entry into the Common Market for these reasons in the spring of 1962."

A senior embassy official advised, "a telegram such as that would be very upsetting and I really don't think it should be sent."

This was the kind of advice the ambassador loved to disregard; he later learned that Kennedy's State Department aide Walt Rostow agreed that the British would be rejected.

On the subject of nuclear arms, Gavin could not change the iron will of de Gaulle, nor would his own government alter long-standing policies. The only possible solution to the impasse over the French desire for nuclear weapons and the American desire for nuclear hegemony—and it was only an interim measure—was the joint NATO nuclear force, first proposed by Eisenhower's Secretary of State Christian Herter in 1960 and embraced by Kennedy: Submarines, armed with nuclear Polaris missiles, would be manned by international crews. The French would have no part of it, and the British were dubious. Only the Germans and Italians were enthusiastic, a fact which set up frictions on a different level.

A permanent attitude of suspicion hovered over all U.S. efforts to create the multilateral force. The Europeans did not believe the United States was sincere and thought it was only foisting on Europe another expensive weapons system that they would have to support, but not control. All the elements of stalemate existed and Gavin could not change that.

Gavin thought that a potential solution lay in a true European Common Market, which even then, he was fond of forecasting as a "united states of Europe." "I wholeheartedly agree," Gavin wrote, "with Paul Henri Spaak's observation: 'The three greatest events of the first half of the 20th century, outside, of course, of the two world wars, are the Russian revolution, the end of colonialism and the effort for European integration.' "

This was a concept large enough and sufficiently progressive for Gavin to embrace in the wake of his realization that he could not succeed in moving de Gaulle toward U.S. policies. But the completion of "European integration" would have to wait, he knew.

Meanwhile Gavin played a part in a diplomatic coup over settlement of the Laotian crisis. This Far Eastern sore point was left over from the Eisenhower administration. Eisenhower had regarded the little kingdom, run by Prince Souvanna Phouma and a cadre of corrupt generals, as the weak point on which Communist China would logically exert maximum pressure to hasten the communist conversion of the entire region, including Thailand, Cambodia, and South Vietnam.

American foreign aid had poured into the country, only to disappear, while the generals who stole it did little to stop the infiltration of the Communist Pathet Lao. The Eisenhower CIA had connived with a coup against Souvanna Phouma and the fight over leadership disintegrated into chaos. Civil war threatened when Phoumi Nosavan, a military man backed by the CIA was opposed by another military upstart, the para-trooper Kong Le, who allied himself with the Pathet Lao. When Le's men faced down Phoumi's, the Kennedy administration faced the dire choice whether or not to intervene. Defense Secretary Robert McNamara suggested a half-hearted bombing with surplus planes. The Joint Chiefs of Staff and Rostow recommended 25,000 combat troops.

Kennedy wanted no part of a war in Laos and depended on diplomats and the action of the International Control Commission to avert it. He urged peace talks in Geneva. Veteran diplomat Averell Harriman, mean-time, flew to Vientiane, the capital of Laos, and on to New Delhi, where Souvanna Phouma waited in exile. Harriman was able to convince the prince that with U.S. support he could regain his country and solve the crisis without U.S. military intervention. Souvanna Phouma, in turn, vowed that he wanted a neutral Laos that would ward off the Commu-nists.

Harriman spent long months steering the ICC negotiations to a conclu-sion that was at least satisfactory to the United States. In July of 1962 the major powers and Laos' neighbors all agreed to Laotian neutrality and a return of the Souvanna Phouma regime. Gavin played a guiding role in the negotiations over the former French colony. He carefully nurtured relations with the arrogant and prickly prince Phouma, who owned a house in Paris. Gavin sought out the prince and assured him that the Kennedy administration would respect the freedom, neutrality, and inde-pendence of his kingdom.

Gavin also learned that, unfortunately, the Vietminh were using Laos during the interregnum to move massive amounts of munitions and thousands of soldiers into South Vietnam.

By summer, Gavin began to enjoy his ambassadorship. Most of July (from Bastille Day on) was taken up with a leisurely Mediterranean cruise from Monte Carlo to Rome. With the girls off to camp, this was the longest vacation he and Jean had ever had together. A flying visit from the Eisenhowers began August. On the 15th the Gavin family returned to the States for a month's summer holiday in Massachusetts. Gavin returned to France only to pay a final series of courtesy calls and say good-bye. He left the embassy for good September 26, having served almost exactly as long as he'd said he would. As he had feared, the tour had almost bankrupted him. Jean estimated it took $100,000 per year simply to fulfill social obligations, and they had been forced to borrow.

Chip Bohlen, who would succeed Gavin with no more success but with the approval of the old boy network at State, was already enjoying a round of farewell parties in Georgetown. His appointment was something Gavin could not prevent, in spite of a personal appeal to JFK. By October 10, Gavin was back at work at ADL. "The first fall foliage was in color," he wrote "and our home was a welcome sight."

22.

THE ANTIWAR

YEARS

President Kennedy threw a dinner party for the Gavins a few days after the ambassador's return to Boston, but Gavin met a different Kennedy, an idealistic president trying to respond to American racism. Students had rioted at the University of Mississippi the day before to protest the admission of James Meredith, a black student. Retired General Edwin A. Walker, West Point '31, led die-hard segregationists with combative radio broadcasts proclaiming an "anti-Christ Supreme Court," and he urged his followers to be with him at Jackson "ten thousand strong." Ultimately, General Walker was arrested on several charges, including resisting arrest, conspiracy, and insurrection.

It was a no-win situation politically, and Kennedy was angry at everyone involved. "General, what in the world are they teaching those people at West Point?" Kennedy asked Gavin. He told the president that he knew Walker had "a bad reputation of being far to the right on the political spectrum."

Nevertheless, the dinner went well, and Kennedy even indicated he wanted Gavin to come to Washington and "help him straighten out the State Department."

Gavin would see Kennedy alive only once more, in late October, when the general visited the White House to thank Kennedy for making a film strip for the annual meeting of the Association of the U.S. Army, which had elected Gavin its president. And again the president discussed the problems of the State Department. This time, Kennedy looked forward to a meeting with General de Gaulle, possibly on American soil. "But first, I have to get those people over there [at State] straightened out," Kennedy told his ex-ambassador.

"I told him he was absolutely right, that his problems were not in Paris, but in the Department of State." Gavin went on to outline his own plan for reviving the State Department's training system by adding more foreign service officers to the corps, and then rotating them through various schools for advanced degrees. "I have heard it all too frequently that the problem in Washington is that whenever there is a serious situation, the Pentagon has a plan to deal with it, but not the State Department. . . . This, I believed, was its most pressing problem."

But this plan never took root.

On November 22, 1963, Gavin was at a luncheon of the board of Directors of Arthur D. Little, Inc., in Cambridge. He got word of the Kennedy assassination from a waitress who whispered in his ear. "It was a tremendous shock and if I were to announce it to the board, we might as well end the meeting right there so I continued," Gavin noted. "After the luncheon the same girl told me that President Kennedy had been taken to the hospital and that a priest had been called. That to me meant he was dying, so I told the board what I knew, and in a short time the meeting ended."

Gavin paid his respects the next day, while the president's body lay in the White House East Room, and stayed in Washington through that somber weekend, numbed by the killing. His association with a man who could have helped fulfill his own deep sense of debt to his favorite institution, the U.S. Army, and to his country, had been ended prematurely. Now he was no longer an insider; far worse, he regarded the new chief executive, Lyndon Johnson with deep suspicion and skepticism. Jean Gavin openly detested Johnson and blamed him for the difficulties of 1957 when Gavin was forced to resign from the service on principle. Gavin was also emotionally wounded, for he had idolized the young president, ignoring his flaws and lapses with the uncomplicated devotion of a believer.

Because of Gavin's contacts and ideas, Arthur D. Little was expanding on a large scale into international business, which for the first time brought Gavin the kind of income he needed to make up for years of army pay and the expense of four college-bound daughters.

But Gavin had brought back from Europe a new and distinctly different attitude about America's involvement in Southeast Asia. He was more strongly against it than he had been in 1954 when the French had struggled against the inevitabilities of Dien Bien Phu. The French had clarified things mightily for Gavin: All future thoughts about ADL's participation in the area would be based on business and economic realities. For America's Southeast Asia policymakers, on the other hand, few realities counted, and certainly none of economic significance.

Gavin had reacted harshly to a report by General Maxwell Taylor which gave a firm and upbeat prognosis for America's growing presence in Vietnam. Taylor's involvement there went back to June of 1961, when to shore up the regime of Ngo Dinh Diem, president of Vietnam, Kennedy sent reinforcements to a small U.S. military advisory group and agreed to finance the arming and organizing of 30,000 South Vietnamese troops to fight Communist guerrillas. The move was Taylor's suggestion.

Taylor was then in the newly important role of "military representative to the president" a post handcrafted for him. But he had little to do with the Berlin crisis of that summer, which led to the building of the Berlin Wall between the East and West sectors. On October 17, 1961, Taylor had been sent to Vietnam on a fact-finding mission with Walt Rostow, the Yale-educated aide to Kennedy's hawkish National Security Advisor McGeorge Bundy. Kennedy told the two that he hoped to find a way to avoid committing American combat troops.

Their report stated "There is no need for fatalism that, somehow, Southeast Asia will inevitably fall into Communist hands. We have the means to make it otherwise."

Taylor told Kennedy that sending American troops would be the best and most convincing way to hearten Diem's forces for their fight. Troops were needed on humanitarian grounds also, to deal with disastrous floods then adding to South Vietnam's woes. He said, "The risks of backing into a major Asian war by way of South Vietnam are present but are not impressive. North Vietnam is extremely vulnerable to conventional bombing, a weakness that should be exploited diplomatically in convincing Hanoi to lay off South Vietnam."

Kennedy had moved gradually. He rewarded Taylor with an appointment as chairman of the Joint Chiefs of Staff, a return in triumph after the frustrations Taylor had felt as Eisenhower's Army Chief of Staff. On Kennedy's death, Lyndon Johnson inherited the report and the general.

Gavin thought the report seriously flawed. "Its most glaring omission was a total lack of consideration of the role of China or the USSR. . . . I found myself in a troubled state of mind," he wrote.

Gavin held lingering doubts about soldiers who dabbled in politics. "After I had officially opposed U.S. military involvement in Vietnam in 1954, I did not speak out against it publicly. . . . Professionally, I felt a great deal of concern for the commanding General, William Westmoreland, whom I had known for many years, going back to 1942. . . . As I mulled over the drama that was unfolding in Vietnam, I realized that it was following the disastrous pattern that we had anticipated in the plans office of the Pentagon in 1954."

Gavin, as a civilian and fully occupied with ADL, several board memberships, and his family, was out of the circuit. But as months passed, he decided to weigh into the debate about the war. By the time he went to his writing desk in Wellesley Hills, as historian/soldier General Douglas Kinnard put it, "The dark clouds of Vietnam closed in around the new President." Diem had been overthrown and murdered. Taylor had recommended a continuation of the gradual buildup and had finished his term as JCS chairman. He was now ambassador to Vietnam. When Taylor finished that tour in 1965 he became a special consultant to President Johnson as the war deepened; the marines had landed at Da Nang in front of the television cameras; the 1st Cavalry Division (Airmobile) had triumphed in a bloody battle at Ia Drang. But Vietnam now drew U.S. troops in ever-increasing numbers. The United States was deeply committed.

In November of 1965, Gavin prepared a letter for the *Infantry Journal*, but they found it too controversial to publish, so he sent it to John Fischer, editor of *Harper's* magazine. It was headlined by the magazine as "Gen. James Gavin vs. Our Vietnam Strategy" when published in February 1966.

In the letter, Gavin made the startling suggestion that the United States shepherd its forces, gathering them into "enclaves" easily supplied by sea along the east coast of the narrow country. "We should maintain enclaves on the coast, desist in our bombing attacks in North Vietnam, and seek to find a solution through the United Nations or a conference in Geneva. We could very likely do so with the forces now available.

"Maintaining such enclaves while an effort is being made to solve the internal situation in Vietnam, and in the face of the terroristic war that would be waged against them, poses some serious problems, and the retention of some of the enclaves may prove to be unwise; but the problems that we would then have to deal with would be far less serious than those associated with expansion of the conflict." The places he suggested for the enclaves were not fully sketched in, but would include the obvious ones—Cam Ranh Bay, Da Nang, "and similar areas where American bases are being established."

Behind this minimalist strategy, which Gavin called the "Enclave Strategy," was his belief that enough force to guarantee victory in Vietnam would inevitably bring in the Chinese, possibly with nuclear weapons.

The article was hailed as the first military counterattack on the administration's war plan. Actually, there was no overall war plan except an increase of pressure, reaction to events, and the search for more effective ways to apply force to an elusive enemy. It was Taylor's "flexible response" idea from his book, *Uncertain Trumpet,* in action. The plan was to keep increasing the pain until the North Vietnamese gave up. The trouble was that no certain military objective existed. Gavin's enclave plan at least proposed clear and limited goals. The antiwar faction seized upon it because its author was a war hero and a recognized strategist. Almost immediately Gavin discovered it was distorted into a call for retreat by one side and a recipe for withdrawal by the other. He meant it as neither, but he bears the responsibility for never making completely clear how the enclaves would work militarily. Letters poured in to Congress, to the news media, and to Gavin.

The Pentagon reacted as if it had been stung by an adder; it pulled out all the stops, sending Taylor to the networks to promote the administration line. Taylor did his duty, lambasting Gavin's hastily sketched plan for enclaves as a withdrawal to the coast. He termed it a retreat, a dishonor to the troops; "dig in where it is safest," Taylor threw out.

Gavin hoped to persuade the country to adopt a strategy that would allow "an early extrication of our forces," while still making it possible for the United States to punish the enemy brutally with air strikes, armed reconnaissance, and missiles.

In 1965 and 1966, Gavin's position on Vietnam was still an unpopular one. Most Americans still supported the war. The popular press seemed more hawk than dove, and defeatist dispatches were to be avoided. Still, in February, while *Harper's* was on the newsstands, Senator J. William Fulbright began his televised public hearings on the war. Gavin was called —as were Taylor and George Kennan. Gavin's testimony was prominent. Unfortunately, he fell onto the defensive, thanks to a well-orchestrated campaign of commentary and leaks from the White House and the Pentagon that distorted his proposal and exaggerated it, claiming it would be a retreat and would devastate the morale of the American soldiers.

For example, the day before Gavin testified, February 7, Johnson described those who "counsel retreat" as "belong[ing] to a group that has always been blind to experience and deaf to hope."

The men who testified alongside Gavin were impressive: George Kennan, the principal architect of the Cold War policy of containment, Secretary of State Dean Rusk, General Ridgway, and General Taylor. Taylor, officially retired, was then in an anomalous position somewhat parallel to Gavin's. No longer pulling strings at the Pentagon, he had been ordered by President Johnson to sell the war to the American public, which he did —speaking from coast to coast, often with a chorus of chanting antiwar demonstrators in the background. "Taylor seems often to have persevered by a certain hubris; having sipped the heady wine of White House insidership in Camelot, he still liked the taste of it," noted Douglas Kinnard.

Gavin was suffering considerably the day he testified—not from the pressure, which he rather relished, but from a painful attack of an old man's disease, prostatitis, which brought a fever of slightly over 100 degrees.

Gavin stressed that the United States was reducing its global commitments because of Vietnam but that was not what really concerned him. He was critical of the fact that the war was being run, not with an overall plan of action, but in reaction to the enemy's plan. This he found incomprehensible. "When we begin. . . . to support a tactical confrontation that appears to be escalating at the will of an enemy, we are in a very dangerous position."

Fulbright greeted Gavin's testimony warmly, praising Gavin simply and without the usual clichés of the senatorial introduction. "He is one of the leading military strategists of the postwar period. Although he is now in private industry, he has remained a thoughtful observer and commentator on military strategy in the nuclear age. General Gavin has served his country well and he has a right to enjoy his retirement from the controversies of Washington. We need his advice, for there are few people with his experience."

Gavin related how, as he viewed the increasing commitment of Vietnam, it had seemed to him out of balance, with little thought to cost and alternatives. "My feeling was that we were being escalated at the will of opponents rather than at our own judgement, and I based this as much upon the statement of many officials who have been sent to that war-torn country and who returned with optimistic statements, only to find they have had to change them successively thereafter, which suggested to me that in the very beginning they didn't understand what the requirements were and thus couldn't estimate accurately what the needs might be to meet those requirements."

But the turning point in his thinking, Gavin said, came over the bombing. "I have a feeling as our bombing went on beyond what were obviously military targets such as ammunition dumps, tank cars or concentrations of trucks and military targets, to powerplants and such as that, we were slowly creeping to urban bombing. I wanted to lay this at rest for once and for all time."

His suggestions when he made them were simple, as they had been in the *Harper's* article, now given in slightly more detail: "First of all, what do we have today and what can they do, and I simply stated today we have sufficient forces in South Vietnam to hold areas along the coast where sea and air power can be made fully effective, and then we can use this power as we see fit to do so. I then suggested that we might look at the alternatives very realistically. . . .

"Are we really trying to seal off Vietnam entirely, extending the 17th parallel all across, all the way across to the Mekong River? This has been considered. One could put a *cordon sanitaire* across there at considerable cost. It still would be open ended a bit at the end but it is possible. . . .

"One could extend the security down to the Cambodian border but to me these appear to be terribly costly in manpower and our national wealth, and I use the word 'wealth' to include all necessary material resources. . . .

"So, I finally came to the conclusion, and I think this is very important in view of the charges that have been made about what I have said, and I quote: 'We must do the best we can with the forces we have deployed in Vietnam now.' Nothing more than that. I did not say 'withdraw,' 'retreat,' 'go ahead,' 'attack,' do anything else. We must do the best we can with what we have in hand, keeping in mind the true meaning of global strategy in world affairs today."

So in the end the argument came down to definitions. Gavin meant enclaves to be, not siege positions, but areas of control, "a vast defended area . . . out of which we seek and destroy and link up with other forces in the interior." He tried throughout that long day of often hostile cross-questioning to simplify his concept. Perhaps the closest he came was in an exchange with Senator Clifford Case.

CASE: "Do you have an alternative . . . to suggest by which we may regain the initiative?"

GAVIN: "No; not in this particular theater, I do not have. I would think I would have to be out there on the ground. I do have hopes and this matter has not come up here this morning, that I hope that through a very aggressive research program we might find some technological things that would give us a real advantage in the theater. . . . We cannot afford to pull out. We should not escalate. We can find some advantage."

He went on to push the "sky cavalry" concept of hard-hitting, heavily armed forces that could be sent anywhere in a short time.

When the hearing broke for lunch at 1 P.M., Gavin was exhausted. His physical pain had caused him to bicker sharply with one of his best friends in Congress, Stuart Symington, who relentlessly questioned him about his opposition to bombing, opposition which was a direct result of Gavin's close reading of strategic bombing surveys of World War II. Symington roused Gavin's ire by suggesting that Gavin was among those who wanted to reduce the level of hostilities, in essence to be "fair" to a less technological foe.

SYMINGTON: "They feel some think it better to pursue hostilities primarily on the ground, because there we give the enemy a break, even-Stephen; in fact they have a little advantage, because they have the most numbers of bodies. Do you think that is what we should do, even including full utilization of what you call sky cavalry?"

GAVIN: "Oh, no. Let us understand each other, Senator. I would never give an opponent any break in combat. The best break he can get as far as I am concerned is to be dead. I would not give him a break."

Taylor, of course, did his best to rebut, painting an optimistic picture of U.S. prospects, outlining a mostly theoretical four-point strategy, which included bombing and peace-talk efforts.

He reserved special scorn for what he called the "holding strategy," a direct attack on Gavin's ideas. "To button up our troops in defensive positions and thus to sacrifice their unique attributes of mobility and firepower would constitute the abandonment of our allies on the battlefield and would assign a most inglorious mission to our troops, who, for the present, have a high morale and complete confidence in their ability to cope with the Vietcong in the field. The effect of such behavior on our Vietnamese allies would be disastrous . . . another serious result of such passivity would be the impossibility of obtaining honorable terms at any peace table. The Communists are tough enough to deal with when one has the upper hand. They would never give us acceptable terms if the military situation reflected weakness on our part and a readiness to withdraw."

To Gavin's satisfaction, Taylor tangled acrimoniously with Fulbright and with the irascible Wayne Morse, one of only two senators to vote no on the 1964 Tonkin Gulf Resolution that expanded the Vietnam war. When Taylor told Morse that Hanoi would welcome news of public opposition to the war, the Oregon senator snapped back "that is the kind of answer you militarists give to those of us who have honest differences of opinion with you."

Taylor's views also came under fire from General Ridgway, who proclaimed that the cost in lives of a complete victory would be "completely out of proportion to what the U.S. would gain."

George Kennan also commented favorably on Gavin's "enclave strategy." Gavin later said that he thought the Fulbright hearing was a turning point of doubt about the war. "This was by far the most effective committee that I have seen in operation. Their impact on the Vietnam War showed every promise of being decisive and it may have given us the first step back from the quagmire that was to be Vietnam," he wrote.

But events ground on, apparently self-propelled. The search and destroy missions under General William Westmoreland went forward as did the bombing of strategic supplies and the village pacification plan. The year would end with 385,300 U.S. troops in Vietnam.

Meanwhile Gavin held an important meeting with Henry Kissinger, then at the fringes of the White House advisory group, who had called him. "[He] came by to see me. He wanted to talk about Vietnam . . . now we had gone down the road to full-scale war, and I thought I should talk about how it would appear in numbers. First I pointed out to him that Westmoreland's mission and war was not analogous to that of Eisenhower's in Europe in World War II. Eisenhower's was to land in the continent of Europe, destroy the German Armed Forces and occupy Germany, simple and straightforward. Westmoreland's mission was to bring about conditions of peace in which democracy could flourish in South Vietnam," Gavin wrote of the meeting.

Gavin suggested to Kissinger that three new alternatives be considered for the conduct of the war: Plan A, as he dubbed it, would seal the border along the 17th parallel and defend the coastline and rear areas, requiring, Gavin thought, about 500,000 men. But this, he knew, would leave open infiltration routes via Laos and Cambodia.

More severe was Gavin's Plan B, sealing both the 17th parallel and the Laos and Cambodian borders and the seacoast. "The buildup forces would probably approach something in the vicinity of a million men," he noted, "and we still would not have regained the initiative. . . . It would also be clear that our involvement in Southeast Asia placed Western Europe in considerable jeopardy since we would have difficulty in meeting our requirements in that theater."

Plan C was the "final alternative," Gavin told Kissinger. "Consider the same mission as that given Gen. Eisenhower in World War II. Enter North Vietnam in the Tonkin Delta area, seize Hanoi, destroy all the Communists in North Vietnam, and occupy the country up to the Chinese border." This, he estimated, would take 1.5 million men and would require the navy to take Hainan Island, Chinese territory. "We would go to war with Red China and Red China would very likely open the Korean front again. The results might well be catastrophic."

Kissinger sat in silence, reluctant to offer alternatives.

Gavin had come to the conclusion that even his enclave theory would only prove a prelude to an inevitable withdrawal of U.S. forces. The choices he laid out for Kissinger were designed to force that conclusion on the advisor.

A month after the Kissinger meeting, Gavin was called to Washington to confer with Defense Secretary Robert McNamara and Cyrus Vance, his deputy. This time the request was precise. The two men wanted Gavin to discuss the enclave strategy. "During the meeting, Secretary McNamara asked most of the questions," Gavin wrote. "McNamara wanted to know how we were going to win in Vietnam. I told him that we couldn't win as the situation now stood. He said that couldn't possibly be true, that we had to win. I told him that we would be sure to be defeated if he continued on his present course of action, and I explained why. He could only talk about how to win."

Then early in 1967, as antiwar riots raged, Gavin was recalled to Washington by Fulbright to testify once again. But this was a coda, almost an orchestrated performance, with Gavin speaking more like a politician. For the first time he ventured far out of his realm of weapons and strategy, and spoke to a national audience, not as an expert, but as a man with an agenda. With the help of his longtime friend Arthur Hadley, who had written Gavin letters about his book *Airborne Warfare*, Gavin was planning a run at the presidency. They were even then collaborating on a book intended to serve as a campaign platform and focal point, *Crisis Now*, an attack on America's social and war policies, and Gavin's testimony reflected the views he stated in the book.

This time he told the Fulbright-chaired Committee on Foreign Relations that the domestic programs of the country were beginning to unravel along with the military situation. He had changed his tack in one regard at least—internal problems in China and overt hostility between China and Hanoi reduced the threat of Chinese intervention, which had been the major concern in Gavin's gloomy forecast for the possibility of victory in the Vietnam War.

But even with the Chinese no longer standing behind North Vietnam, nor likely to reopen the Korean front, Gavin still thought radical armed action to end the war successfully would be wrong.

"Our intellectual, physical, and economic resources should be applied as a matter of first priority to the problems of our American society," he told the committee. "It must be a society that uses its tremendous technology and physical resources, and its national wealth, to rid the country of poverty, to raise the standard of living of its citizens, to provide a healthful environment, to provide educational opportunities for all of our people, and opportunities to achieve high standards of excellence in competitive amateur sports . . . and finally, a domestic security for its citizens."

Gavin's opening statement to the committee was far ranging, from foreign aid, a sharp criticism of his old enemies at State ("another agency, which, it seems to me, perpetuates this obsession with Communism"), to handling of U.S. national resources ("we got off to a very fast start in our war against poverty without adding planning, and we have made mistakes"). He updated his view of the way to change U.S. strategy in

Vietnam: "In summary, I recommend that we bring hostilities in Vietnam to an end as quickly and reasonably as we can, that we devote those vast expenditures of our national resources to dealing with our domestic problems, that we make a massive attack on the problems of education, housing, economic opportunity, lawlessness, and environmental pollution."

Gavin knew by this time that far more energetic measures would be needed to change the minds of the pro-war politicians. He began to take a more active role in politics, calling Senator Edward Brooke, then running for a second term from Massachusetts, to urge him to base his campaign on pledges to stop the war and bring troops back. Gavin received bundles of letters supporting his position, which he'd reduced almost to a stump speech in interviews and speeches and at meetings, as the antiwar movement warmed to a new, passionate yet reasonable supporter.

Brooke not only let him down, but soon after his election came out in support of the war, flattered by Lyndon Johnson with an appointment to the Bicentennial Committee and a trip to Vietnam. When confronted, Brooke told Gavin that he had been impressed by what he was told in Vietnam. Gavin, angry with what he called a "complete about-face" was blandly told that Brooke had suggested to LBJ that he invite Gavin to Vietnam as well.

When Gavin received the invitation from Westmoreland, he went, but he was not impressed. "The American presence was everywhere; U.S. trucks, helicopters, sedans, jeeps, and troops, seemed to be all about Saigon. Some of the streets looked like one vast American PX with stacks of American merchandise piled on the street curbs or on the sidewalks against buildings."

Gavin called on Ellsworth Bunker, the gaunt aristocrat who replaced Maxwell Taylor when the latter went back to become Johnson's war spokesman. Bunker had arranged a small luncheon—no doubt intended to disarm Gavin—with Creighton Abrams, who as a junior officer, had broken the blockade of Bastogne in the winter of 1944–45 and since had risen high in the army. Gavin admired Abrams as a fine soldier, but when the older man raised the specter of Chinese intervention in Vietnam, Abrams seemed unconcerned. Gavin was nonplussed.

"Westy" Westmoreland and Gavin danced a stiff dance of official friendship and desire on both sides to develop an agenda. Gavin, already skeptical, pushed to see more than the official V.I.P. tour. Westmoreland, knowing the potency of the older man's judgements, was equally anxious to show only the success stories. Gavin got top attention. Westmoreland and his staff appeared, and Gavin "asked that they not give me a briefing, but be prepared to answer my questions." He'd heard about Vietnam briefings from Brooke. Gavin listened and traveled hard, dressed in a white short-sleeved shirt and slacks, visiting all three corps areas and questioning the three top commanders.

"I left, sad and depressed about the tactical dilemma in which our troops found themselves. I remember when visiting an outpost in the highlands, a grizzled old veteran from Europe came up to shake hands with me, and he said to me, 'General, let us win but one more. We haven't won a battle since World War II.' "

Gavin had to tell him it could not be done.

He returned, more convinced than ever that he was right about the inevitability of failure in Vietnam. He would say later, "The Vietnamese would have been better off if we had never gone in."

The year of the Vietnam summer, 1967, saw his sixtieth birthday. Cambridge was the headquarters for the antiwar groups and the nerve center for over 25,000 volunteers throughout the country. Because of Gavin's stature and the publicity he had received in the wake of the Senate hearings, he had become a "peace" leader, considered part of the nationwide movement to end the war. Few people who wrote him discriminated between his views and those of leaders much further to the left. And to many of them, he looked like an ideal leader. His problem, for the rest of the presidential campaign, was keeping the support of the radical left without being politically destroyed by them.

Gavin launched his brief political career by trying to attract the attention and support of moderate Republicans. Though the radical left still supported him, Gavin's fledgling campaign soon drew doctors, lawyers, and businessmen and -women who wanted alternatives to the increasingly shrill left or the stubborn, bunkered right in the war debate. For them, Gavin's controversial career made sense. They believed that Gavin could present a moderate Republican image to counter the right wing formerly led by Barry Goldwater and now beginning to regroup around California's Ronald Reagan.

But the political professionals of both parties wanted nothing to do with Gavin's efforts.

Gavin felt impelled to move ahead in a fight he knew he could not win.

There was not only Reagan, but the far more likely candidacy of Richard Nixon or upstart motor executive and Michigan Governor George Romney. In fact, Gavin wished only a supportive role. "I am hoping," he said in a much-quoted interview in the *National Observer* at the end of August, "to be able to support a candidate who offers a proper alternative to the administration, but, if there isn't such a candidate, then perhaps I must be one."

Nothing would come of it. Later, Gavin would explain, "It is important to remember the political situation in 1967. Neither Sen. Eugene McCarthy nor Robert Kennedy had as yet entered the Presidential race as anti-war candidates, nor was there any sign of such a candidate on the Republican side . . . in such a vacuum even a nonpolitical individual like myself received a lot of attention. I remember driving home in my car on Storrow Drive . . . and hearing Walter Cronkite say on the radio that in Cambridge I had assembled a 'vast staff' to run for the Presidency. Since all my 'vast staff,' myself and Arthur Hadley, were seated in the front seat of my car, I found this amusing."

Hoping to get some sage counsel from a man he respected, who was widely mentioned as a leading moderate Republican, and for whom Gavin doubtless would have worked as a vice-presidential candidate, he went to see Governor Nelson Rockefeller. Rockefeller, in a boisterous mood, greeted Gavin with a playful punch to the stomach and his famous grin. "Hi, fella," the governor said, "So you want me to open a second front?" But Rockefeller, carefully judging his constituency, would not move to support a firm antiwar position, lest he lose potential votes himself. And he told Gavin emphatically that *he* would be a candidate. He asked Gavin to join in his campaign, as part of the political staff.

The entry of Robert Kennedy into the race ended Gavin's chances. Here was the candidate he was looking for and morally could not work against. "With my long ties to both Sen. Robert Kennedy and more particularly his brother the former President, I now had no further wish to be in the race or attached to some other candidate."

But Gavin did go on to play a role as a member of Rockefeller's campaign staff, joined in the Rockefeller camp by the likes of baseball player Jackie Robinson and political strategist Frank Mankiewicz. The nascent "Draft Gavin" drive died quietly, and Gavin with some poignancy, took it in stride. "I went back to my schedule of making speeches, managing Arthur D. Little, and finishing my book."

The book, *On to Berlin*, was a full account of his wartime experiences and would occupy the next ten years of his life. But for the first time, there was no hurry. Gavin had done what he could—all that he could— to change his country's course, to repay his "Spartan mother" on the Hudson. Except for a halfhearted attempt to gain appointment as CIA chief under President Jimmy Carter, he would not enter public life again.

2 3 .

WHERE DID

THE TIME GO?

Jim Gavin retired from his position as chairman of the board of ADL in 1977 after twenty years with the company, a year before Viking released his World War II memoir, *On to Berlin.* He had approached much of his time at the company idealistically, maybe even altruistically.

Until 1974, when he stepped down as CEO, Gavin was busy all the time.

The consulting firm of Arthur D. Little is a diverse, very close knit (employees tend to be fiercely loyal even when critical of the firm) and unusual company. It has no tangible product to market; it lives and dies by the quality and quantity of its ideas. Its staff is brilliant and energetic, they work on a far-flung array of projects, and, being a very intellectual group, they are difficult to lead. Uniqueness is ADL's trademark, its advantage, and its bane; and it often made Gavin's life uncomfortable. But he did what meant the most to ADL. He used his fame and influence to bring business. His fame also brought him numerous engagements as a lecturer and honored guest across the country, particularly at universities, where he became famous for engaging young students in long conversations so he could "stay abreast of the views of the next generation."

Under Gavin, ADL nearly doubled in size during the 1960s. When the U.S. Olympic team asked for help in increasing its success, it was Gavin who maneuvered ADL into the picture through phone calls to powerful friends, and it was Gavin who accompanied the project director, Bruce Old, to the Tokyo Olympics in 1964 to keep the doors open while satisfying his own fascination with the Olympic team.

Yet Gavin knew his limitations, and he designed his role to conform to his own situation. He left each of the division heads a great deal of room to run their operations, even to the point of financial autonomy, and he kept his guidance as just that. Many people within ADL did not understand the relationship.

During the late 1960s, Roy Little, who controlled the company's trust money and thus the company itself, made ADL public to fend off a buyout attempt by increasing the company's value through a stock offering, and Gavin supported and played a prominent role in the change. At the time, he believed in it because, not only would going public foil the buy out, but the change carried the extra bonus of making it easier for ADL to acquire some small research businesses without paying more taxes. The decision turned out badly, and in 1988, ADL returned to private ownership, but memories of the public experiment linger on.

Then there was expansion, overseas expansion. The 1960s were good for American business, and, like many firms of the period, ADL grew rapidly, but Gavin had a definite agenda for the growth. He believed the world must undergo radical change in the future. He had written *Crisis Now* as a call for America to end the Vietnam War while revitalizing decaying cities and helping the poor, and he had taken his ideas to the office. Gavin worried that the world could not last with most of its population living in poverty, and at ADL he had made this and other issues an increased part of the agenda of a company already moving toward Third World involvement.

Gavin believed the international market was the future, and that ADL should be a major force in it. He established the Management Education Institute (MEI) through ADL, a school designed to train managers for Third World business, and he convinced the state of Massachusetts to accredit it to grant a master's degree. The idea had come from a 1963 visit to Nigeria where ADL was training managers. He concluded then that it would be more effective to bring the Nigerians to Cambridge where training would have the support of all of ADL's resources. The school still lives, and though it has made little money, it is the monument of which Gavin felt the most proud.

The same concerns that drove him to found MEI led him to other projects designed to foster Third World development. He placed Hamilton R. James as vice president in charge of international development, and he made certain James and his ideas received priority at a time when many within the firm thought international expansion nothing more than an expensive luxury. Before Gavin arrived, ADL had offices in Switzerland, Mexico, and Canada. By the time he retired, the firm had branched into Nigeria, Brazil, Argentina, England, Germany, Saudi Arabia, Iran, Peru, Spain, Japan, Thailand, and other countries.

But the expansion held problems too. ADL grew too rapidly. Fast growth meant fast hiring, and fast hiring sometimes meant bringing in less qualified people. Gavin found himself downsizing during the mid-1960s as a result. Having learned the hard way, after that he kept growth to what the company could qualitatively support.

Affirmative action was also a Gavin concern. From his early days in Arizona supervising black soldiers to his experience with the desegregation of the 82nd Airborne, Jim Gavin had never been a racist. At ADL, he set a black headhunter from *Ebony* magazine, Joseph Rollins, to finding qualified blacks, and Rollins located numerous candidates. ADL soon became integrated from the executive offices down. Women in the firm also appreciated Gavin's new priorities because along with black specialists on the staff came large numbers of women.

In the early 1970s, the company experienced a down business cycle and morale dropped. Jim Gavin authorized an outside company to perform a social audit, an examination of the attitudes of employees. They issued an unfavorable report, and the interviews with employees stirred up discontent. A small group of men calling themselves the headshrinkers (the culprits remain officially anonymous), circulated a questionnaire on whether the company was being run properly. Gavin took it personally. He called the entire staff into the executive dining room and accused them of being "fair weather, summertime soldiers." Roy Little got involved. The sacrifice was Howard McMahon, whom Gavin believed could not make decisions dynamically enough to be president. Gavin instructed all section chiefs to bring their business to McMahon's assistant, John Magee, a tall, quiet mathematician, then in his forties, who had been with ADL twenty years.

Gavin made Magee president and axe man, and Magee immediately became unpopular as he fired and reorganized. Gavin wanted to step down as chief executive officer, the real power behind the president, and he named long-term trusted friend Eli Goldston as his replacement without interviewing Magee, who had told Gavin he would like to be considered. Magee felt slighted and passed over, but the two men had very different personalities, and Gavin dismissed the quiet Magee as not charismatic enough for the job. Then, just as he was to take the job, Goldston suffered a fatal heart attack. Gavin searched elsewhere for a replacement and found none suitable. Finally, Roy Little intervened and decided that Magee had grown as president and could now handle the role of CEO. Gavin agreed, and John Magee took over in 1974.

John Magee today expresses his full admiration of Gavin, particularly his ability to lead, and he credits Gavin with having rendered him his fullest support; but others within the ranks of the firm felt Gavin could have been more supportive of Magee, under whom ADL prospered.

Joseph E. Levine was then making the movie version of Cornelius Ryan's *A Bridge Too Far*, an account of the Holland jump, and Gavin served as a technical advisor, though he was critical. He thought Ryan O'Neal, who played him in the movie, was not forceful enough for the part, and Gavin hated the way O'Neal wore his uniform—not up to the immaculate Gentleman Jim's standards. After the movie opened in 1977, though, he thought it an interesting film. However, he decided it was too long and that Levine, who touted it as an antiwar movie, had spent too much time on grisly shots of the dead.

When Gavin stepped down as chairman of the board in 1977, he left behind a company that had grown from approximately 1,200 employees in 1958, generating $16,131,000 in revenues, to a 2,078-employee company in 1977 that generated $106,619,000 in revenues.

He had planned much for his retirement, but the struggle to find his mother remained preeminent. Now, even with all the power and resources a public figure, powerful executive, and financially successful man could muster, the best he could do was gain the cooperation of a Catholic priest in Ireland, a Father Fitzpatrick, who sent him a list of the children born to Matthew Ryan and Margaret Tubridy, his suspected mother's parents, and confirmed that Katie Ryan was probably his mother, saying, "[She] is, I am convinced, the woman whom you are seeking."

He wrote his autobiography, and he made the search for his mother the last chapter. Anguished after having failed in the one thing that mattered most to him, Jim Gavin waxed as emotional as his writing ever got when he wrote, "I find it difficult to accept such a negative outcome after so many years of searching. To anyone who has not lived through an orphan's experience such as this, it is unbelievable. . . . The question today is why punish orphans by denying them information about their own background. They are not guilty of a crime against the church or the state. Sooner or later the orphan encounters a slight. They are often treated as being somewhat less than people who have families to take care of them. Are orphans guilty of some social crime that puts them in a separate category from others? Hardly. Efforts must be made to secure all the information they seek. I believe that the federal government should examine this problem with the objective of providing fair treatment for all of its citizens, orphans and nonorphans alike. Thus my search has not ended, it continues."

But his autobiography was never published. The draft is awkward, and it repeats much that he had already written elsewhere.

In 1982 the Gavins built a second home in Florida. Very soon after, Dr. Paul Gross, a neurologist at the Leahy Clinic in Boston, diagnosed Jim Gavin as suffering from the early stages of Parkinson's disease. By then, in his mid-seventies, other physical problems had come from his active life. In 1975, he had passed out in a taxi in New York while on the way to a meeting of the Board of American Electric Power. Dr. Mirbach at Leahy Clinic had diagnosed the problem as a weakening heart. Gout had plagued him since the 1960s, and his spine, which he had cracked in Holland, often caused him crippling pain. At ADL he had hidden the pain by finding tricks to make it better that only his faithful assistant, Hazel, knew of. He would elevate one foot at a time to equalize pressure, wear a lift in one shoe, and avoid walking great distances. But he couldn't beat Parkinson's.

By 1985, his once tall, youthful frame had been stooped by disease to about 5 feet 7 inches. Walking was painful, and as the Parkinson's progressed, he had difficulty performing even the most elementary of tasks.

Gradually, Jim Gavin appeared less and less in public. The mountain of correspondence that had always poured in continued, but he needed Jean's help in answering it, for he could no longer write. It was the paratroop meetings he still attended, and it was the paratroopers' letters he read over and over again.

James Gavin died at 7:30 on the morning of February 23, 1990.

EPILOGUE

I first met Jim Gavin in 1989, when Professor Harold Silesky (lately of Yale University) and I visited Gavin's home on Cape Cod to see him about the possibility of commencing work on his biography. Jean, his wife, had cautioned us that his Parkinson's disease had become severe, and she had worried that we would be disappointed when we saw what he had become.

That day when we visited his Osterville home, the leaves had just left the trees, and a strong north wind with the first chill of winter blew across the Cape. Still, Jim Gavin greeted us himself, standing in his doorway with Jean. I had always pictured the general as he had been in World War II, young, energetic, and sure. Now it seemed that Parkinson's had robbed him of all that. He no longer stood erect, and he weighed under 150 pounds; his hands shook; and when he spoke, we had to listen closely, because he had trouble forming the words. Yet, the old Gavin was still there too. Shuffling along as best he could, he showed us about his home, and almost with a flourish he held the doors open for us as we moved about. When he spoke, it was with effort, and he experienced great difficulties in swallowing, but he resolutely fought through his ailment to convey what he wished with eloquence; and when speaking of his condition, forcefulness filled his still-bright gray eyes, and he announced that he would be the first man to beat Parkinson's disease.

About his home were displayed the photos and memorabilia of an astounding lifetime, honors that somehow lent credence to that brash assertion. Perhaps it was the mementos that brought the images—for one could not enter his presence in that house without forming them—of the stalwartness at Ste.-Mère-Église, the horror of the Bulge, the desperation of Holland, the nervousness in Sicily, and, yes, of the swank of the ambassador.

On the back porch, with a blanket across his knees to shield them from the wind, he agreed to the book project. In fact, he badly wanted it done.

439

He felt his life had messages he wanted revealed. He made no conditions for the biography. He believed his legacy was there and would come out through the biographer's objectivity. The fact that I myself had been a paratrooper also inspired faith. That was enough, for it made me one of his "crazy characters," one of his children. We questioned him about his past, and in spite of the intense effort it demanded, he sat erect and spoke of Sicily, of Normandy, and of the politics of the Korean War. We left astounded. He was frail, he was aware that he was losing his body and mind day by day, but the same relentless will that had stymied German divisions across Europe remained.

By 1989, Jim Gavin had battled his disease for seven years. He had done so with an unflinching attitude. In December, his old friend Bill Folmer came to Gavin's Florida home for dinner. Gavin greeted Folmer and his wife at the door and announced, "Let the party begin!" Three days later the final disaster struck; he suffered two small strokes and contracted pneumonia, and in spite of his longing to remain at home, he became too much for Jean to handle. His family hospitalized him at Walter Reed, initially; then, in January, moved him to the Keswick Home in Baltimore, just blocks from his daughter Line's house. By now I had begun research on the book, and I went swiftly to Baltimore to visit him. He remembered me when I came through the door to his room, said "Tom," and reached for my hand. Tears filled his eyes. He hated his condition—one side of his body was partially paralyzed, and nurses tended him constantly. He wanted badly to leave the home, and he beseeched me to "help me break out of this place." In holding my hand, perhaps he felt a fellow paratrooper near, the presence of someone who might understand his torture. The hospital symbolized imprisonment to an active man, so he fought it; yet tragically, horribly, and undeservedly, his true prison was his own body—the same body that had once tirelessly taken him through crisis after crisis on the battlefields of Europe. And the same mind that had brought a new vision to warfare now could only focus on the present briefly. It too had been ravaged. Jim Gavin would have gladly fallen in battle, but this was truly his nightmare.

Still, he struggled to answer questions. Fighting for each word, he recollected events of his childhood and the war. Then, drained by the effort and tearful that he could not communicate more, he lapsed into exhaustion. This book was important to him to the final days of his life. It was his last project.

Others visited. Word was out that "Slim Jim" might be nearing his end. Good-byes had to be said. The deputy commander of XVIII Airborne Corps arrived and presented him with a statue of a World War II paratrooper. Salutes are often taken for granted in the army; they are given and returned thousands of times a day, but this salute was different. When the young paratroop general offered it, and Jim Gavin returned it, it was as much with love as respect. Ostensibly, XVIII Corps had come to let Gavin know they still cared and wanted him well. What went unspoken was that all knew that this young general was really saying good-bye to an old legend.

On February 13, 1990, Major General James H. Johnson, Jr., then commander of the 82nd Airborne Division; his aide, Captain Jeffery W. Terhune; the division command sergeant major, William J. McBride; and the NCO of the quarter, Sergeant First Class Gene G. Wolf, also came. For this, we brought General Gavin to his daughter Line's house. Seated in a wheelchair, wearing a sport jacket that hung hopelessly large about his shrunken frame, he braced himself to sit as tall as he could. He knew that this might well be his last appointment.

His family had told him of the 82nd's visit in advance, but one surprise had been withheld. Retired General William T. Ryder, the same Ryder who had shared Gavin's days in the Philippines and helped get him into airborne school, came with them. They gave the legend his last gifts: a poster-sized photo of the 82nd's return drop from action in Panama, a mounted bayonet from the same action, and a certificate of thanks to a man they esteemed above all others. Bill Ryder brought a special present.

Though he and Gavin had not seen each other in two decades, Gavin still recognized him instantly, his eyes misting when his old friend entered the living room. They spoke of old times, and more tears came to Slim Jim's eyes; then Ryder read and presented letters from other surviving airborne pioneers. Gavin's face filled with joy. He had been of the worlds of business and politics, but he was first and always of the paratroops. It was they, above all others, whom he cherished.

Gavin asked General Johnson pointed questions about the just-concluded Panama mission, Operation Just Cause, the mission that had brought Noriega to a Florida prison. Johnson, probably feeling for a moment more like a young captain than a commanding general, answered promptly, and Gavin indicated his approval. He thought the fight had been well made.

After the presentations, all moved to the dining room, lunch came and went, and with its end, General Ryder said his own good-bye. It was not original but it worked. With glass raised, he offered the old Irish toast, which both of them, soldiers and Irishmen, identified with and understood.

May the road rise up to meet you,
May the wind be always at your back,
May the sun shine warmly on your face,
And may the rains fall gently on your fields,
And . . . until we meet again . . .
May God hold you in the palm of his hand.

The good-byes complete, Gavin watched the uniformed young generation depart, longing in his eyes. They were on to places he still dreamed of, and his face spoke of his regret as their departure chilled his bones.

The next day, a last delegation arrived. This one from Special Forces. The commander of 10th Special Forces Group, Colonel Jesse Johnson, and his sergeant major came to the Keswick Home. In a short ceremony, they too presented gifts. They were the last soldiers to see Jim Gavin alive.

The worst had happened. A man who had lived his life with dash and ingenuity had suffered a grievous assault by Parkinson's. He had fought it with all he had, but relentlessly, its ravages had continued. He now had shrunk to around 120 pounds. By the end, he was more skin and bones than muscle. With his last farewell, he made his final command decision. The strokes had been the unexpected flank maneuver. This battle was his last, and he knew it. Yet he would not allow this enemy the satisfaction of total victory. If he must yield, it would be on his terms. If he could not beat his disease, then he would cheat it.

Soon after the last visiting paratrooper had departed, Jim Gavin refused all food and drink. He felt ready now. Death was coming, but he wanted it his way. His resolve never wavered and he died by his own desire, at 7:30 A.M. on February 23, 1990.

The funeral was in the Old Cadet Chapel at West Point on March 6, and the chapel, in a landscape of barren trees and scattered snow, was filled. Paratroopers in rigid ranks stood outside in the calm air. A nephew and a son-in-law spoke over him. They tried to capture the man's spirit, and did as well as anyone might have, given his complexity. His pallbearers, honor guard, and color guard were those he would have wanted— soldiers from the 82nd. Handpicked men from each regiment stood in their ranks, and no soldiers ever looked better than those young men with their maroon berets and their jump boots did that day. They were only a fraction of the division, but nearly every man in General Johnson's command had volunteered to be there.

They had been up practicing even before the cadets took their early rise. The post chaplain had been awakened by a contingent drilling behind his home. Still bleary-eyed, he had asked them if they were not overdoing it. A young squad leader had replied, "Sir, this is not a detail, this is the greatest honor of our lives. We will keep drilling until it's right." Another man piped up, "That's right, sir. We want to be here, and we don't care how long we practice." Their desire showed. It was right. They were perfect, and their "father," Jim Gavin, would have been proud of them. When they marched, their ranks moved in perfect order, they never missed a step, and not a jump boot or a speck of brass could have looked better. Some had tears upon their cheeks as they stood to attention, but none of them moved a muscle that should not have moved.

After the service ended, the procession wound to the grave site. The wind had been calm before the service, but that changed now as the casket left the chapel. Suddenly, from across the plain that Gavin had walked so many times as a young man, a chill blast rippled flags and uniforms. Then General Jim Gavin reached his final home behind the chapel. The desolate sound of taps rippled over the wind, the volleys rang out, and the casket was lowered. Then came other music, then finally, the light strains of "The All-American Soldier." And the words rang through my mind:

Put on your boots, boots, boots,
Your parachutes, chutes, chutes, chutes. . . .
We're All-American and proud to be
For we're the soldiers of liberty. . . .

He had wanted that song played, perhaps because he knew its light melody would give him a soft good-bye.

When the notes carried away upon the wind, the mourners, slowly and singly, as if each felt isolated in his or her own thoughts, ambled past the Old Cadet Chapel and headed for their cars. I remained a few moments more and looked upon the grave. Images like those I had seen in Gavin's home once again filled my thoughts: desperate men amidst the snow and the darkness of the Bulge, the young colonel with the fierce gray eyes at Biazza Ridge, the stooped octogenarian, resolutely proclaiming that he would be the first man to beat Parkinson's disease. Finally, the images stopped and I too turned for my car. Ahead, some of the troopers of the old 82nd, the "Devils in Baggy Pants," shuffled damp cheeked, gray, and lonesome through the trees.

I stopped and turned once more back toward where General Gavin lay. The wind reminded me that my eyes also were damp. I thought of the general's last battle and his decision to end the engagement in his own way. Then words I had learned long ago as a young paratrooper at Fort Benning, the "Parachutist's Creed," came to me, and I uttered them.

I volunteered as a parachutist, fully realizing the hazard of my chosen service and by my thoughts and actions will always uphold the prestige, honor and high esprit de corps of parachute troops. . . .

By my actions and deeds alone, I speak for my fighting ability. I will strive to uphold the honor and prestige of my outfit, making my country proud of me and of the unit to which I belong.

The wind bit through my layered clothing and I too began my exodus through the barren trees.

SOURCES AND

ACKNOWLEDGMENTS

PRIMARY SOURCES

Though the sources used for this book constitute a diverse array of primary and secondary sources, it is largely, as much as it could be, based on the personal papers of General James M. Gavin. The Gavin papers are not presently available for public inspection, though they will become so within the next year; however, Mrs. Gavin generously allowed us to use them for this biography. In content, the Gavin papers are not nearly as comprehensive as the Ridgway papers. They consist of over 3,000 photographs—some of which have never been seen by the public before —documents from Gavin's childhood and West Point years, which include some school essays and his adoption papers, and we have obtained his West Point service record. From his between-the-wars army experiences, there are two diaries, photographs, some notes taken at various times, some articles he wrote for army publications, and some correspondence. On World War II, there is a wealth of information. All of the 82nd Airborne official after-action reports are available, as well as some of the notes Gavin took at various meetings, many of the maps he used, copies of some message traffic, some letters he received, official citations, copies of some historical accounts written by his friends, a copy in draft form of John MacDonald's official history of Market-Garden along with Gavin's criticisms of the draft, two recorded interview tapes, a complete war diary, and his in-print works. In addition to this, we have collected over three hundred letters and many hours of interview tapes from the men who served under or with him during the war. From his Pentagon years, the information is scanty. Much of what he was working on was classified, so he kept no record of it among his personal effects. Some notes he took still remain, as do his appointment books. There is also the written record he made public through his congressional testimony and his published works. Material from his Arthur D. Little days is prolific and largely maintained by that firm. In addition to these materials, there is quite a bit from his time as ambassador to France, and thousands of miscellaneous letters from many different people, concerning a wealth of different issues and business. What are perhaps the true jewels of the Gavin papers are a memoir he wrote but never published and his complete wartime diaries. We used them extensively in the construction of this book because they are the best sources on what Jim Gavin actually thought about the issues of his time and the war.

We conducted several interviews in the preparation of this book with people from Gavin's past. They are as follows: all five of his daughters, Colonel Ben Vandervoort, Colonel Chester Hansen, Jack "Beaver" Thompson, Robert Anderson, Mrs. Jesse Johnson, General Paul Thompson; Vince Bianchi and Mrs. Jacob Bridey (both knew Gavin in his childhood); Hugo Olsen, Buck Dawson, and Barney Oldfield (from his staff in World War II); Colonel Harold "Ace" Elliot (at one point Gavin's bodyguard and driver during World War II); Lieutenant General Hal Moore and General Douglas Kinnard (both from his Pentagon staff); Colonel Walter Winton, Colonel Al Ireland, Colonel Mark Alexander, General Jack Norton (unit commanders or staff members within the 82nd during World War II; Bill Walton (World War II reporter); Arthur Hadley (longtime friend); Hazel Shaner, Dr. Bruce Old, John Magee, Hamilton James (all of ADL); Senator Barry Goldwater and General Andrew O'Meara (both served with Gavin before World War II); the late General William Ryder and General William Yarborough (early developers of the airborne idea and Gavin's lifelong friends); Peter Emerson (contact within the Carter administration and family friend); Mike Tadusiac, Joseph V. Tallett, Joseph Briggs, Ed Pade, Buffalo Boy (World War II paratroopers); Joseph Napoli. We spent many hours reconstructing events with Gavin's wife Jean, whose indefatiguable assistance will always be appreciated. Barbara Gavin Fauntleroy, who furnished his between-the-wars diaries and West Point letters, was also of fantastic help, and her patience will long be appreciated. Many of those listed above who consented to interviews are busy people who were extremely generous with their time. We are grateful to each of them. I would also like to thank all the paratroopers who sent letters or phoned on General Gavin's behalf. Time and funding limited how many interviews we could conduct, but we learned a great deal from your letters. We also thank Don Lassen for his support.

No serious work on Gavin could be complete without access to the Ridgway papers, which are on deposit at the United States Military History Institute at the Carlisle Barracks in Carlisle, Pennsylvania. They fill more than sixty sizable boxes, but they are well organized, and we are deeply indebted to the institute's Mr. Sommers and his staff for their generous assistance. Other papers we found there that were helpful include materials from Mark Clark, William Yarborough, Chester B. Hansen, and an oral history from Maxwell Taylor.

Other primary sources include certain official histories available in the Seeley Mudd Library at Yale University and the West Point archival section of the West Point Library. Dr. John Duvall of the 82nd Airborne Division Museum was also very helpful.

Also of use were copies of *Our Army* magazine, which was a pre-World War II publication, available for research at the Carlisle Barracks. Available in the Seeley Mudd Library at Yale are post-World War II copies of the Command and General Staff publication, *Military Review* —which is excellent for seeing what the army was thinking about during postwar years. Finally, there are articles relating to Gavin and the politics surrounding him in many magazines, ranging from *Harper's* to *Life*.

A final point about the sources we have used is that we have sometimes —particularly for his childhood years—been limited only to Gavin's version of events. This is so because we could not find other sources. Given that most of his childhood friends are long dead, we may never be able to verify some points he made about his childhood. As much as possible, elsewhere in his life, we have sought out alternate viewpoints.

We used many secondary sources, but some books were particularly helpful. World War II has been chronicled substantially. The best general work on Second World War airborne operations in the European theater is Clay Blair's *Ridgeway's Paratroopers*. If the reader is interested in specific campaigns, then S. L. A. Marshall's work *Night Drop* is the best on Normandy, in spite of its having been maligned for errors, though Napier Crookenden's book *Dropzone Normandy* is also good. On Market-Garden, Cornelius Ryan's *A Bridge Too Far* is a fine work, but it is not comprehensive enough in regard to the American effort. On the Battle of the Bulge, the best books we found are Jacques Nobécourt's *The Battle of the Ardennes*, John Eisenhower's *The Bitter Woods*, and John Toland's *Battle: The Story of the Bulge*. On Sicily and Salerno, there has not really been a comprehensive scholarly work yet written. General histories of World War II abound, but Chester Wilmot's history, *The Struggle for Europe*, is one of the best.

The early chapters of Russell F. Weigley's *Eisenhower's Lieutenants* are extremely well done and strongly affected my view of American doctrine at that time—though I have one very strong complaint with Weigley's work. He gave much credence to S. L. A. Marshall's book *Men Against Fire*, which asserted that Americans in World War II were reluctant to discharge their weapons (he said only 25 to 30 percent would do so even in elite units). If that were true, then those 25 percent were firing an amazing amount of bullets, according to World War II supply figures. My own research does not support Weigley's use of *Men Against Fire*, which is a needless slur against the World War II American soldier.

Information on the between-the-wars army is scanty, but there are two fine sources available: Allen R. Millett and Williamson Murray's volume titled *Military Effectiveness* and Forrest C. Pogue's biography of George C. Marshall. The best work I found on the Korean War was Clay Blair's *The Forgotten War*. Three books tower above all others in discussing post-World War II American defense policy: Henry Kissinger's *Nuclear Weapons and Foreign Policy*, James M. Gavin's *War and Peace in the Space Age*, and Maxwell Taylor's *The Uncertain Trumpet*. For a view of Kennedy's Camelot and the origins of Vietnam, David Halberstam's superb *The Best and the Brightest* remains definitive. For a good picture of the development of the Vietnam War, see Neil Sheehan's

A Bright Shining Lie or Stanley Karnov's *Vietnam*. A fantastic view of the development of post-World War II foreign policy is presented in Walter Isaacson and Evan Thomas's *The Wise Men*.

Finally, I would like to compliment Professor Harold Selesky on his lecture and seminar courses on American military history at Yale University. They got me to think about warfare in a new way.

WHAT IS NOT AVAILABLE

After having perused a tremendous amount of World War II literature during this book's preparation, I found that the major figures of American politics and warfare have been overchronicled. Historians, like the journalists who covered the war, have invariably centered all their studies around those who commanded the troops: It was Eisenhower who won the war, it was Patton who relieved Bastogne, and it was Bradley who took the bridge at Remagen. In reality, none of those men did any of those things, and very little or no serious writing has been done about those who did, the troops themselves—other than in vignette form to support the great deeds of the generals. Ultimately, World War II was won by those soldiers who did the dirty work of killing and dying. Somewhere along the way it seems to have been forgotten that the greatest strategist in history, and Eisenhower was very far from that, could not win a battle without a worthy army serving as his implement.

What we have become convinced of from German sources is that the true strong point of the American army on the battlefield in World War II was that it possessed a great deal of leadership throughout its ranks. Germans constantly commented that what made fighting Americans so difficult was that, no matter how many leaders were killed, there was always someone within the ranks who would rally his peers. Given the high casualty rates among lieutenants, and the fact that they were often the least experienced men in their units, one must ask what role the noncommissioned officer played in World War II—particularly when it is the NCOs who do most of the actual troop training? Was it not a minor miracle that the U.S. Army was able to develop as quickly as it did an NCO corps of the scope necessary to hold together one hundred divisions? Unfortunately, there is no serious work available on the soldiers or the NCOs who fought in World War II. That is a shame because the book is conspicuous in its absence and might be worth a great deal to posterity.

THOSE WHO HELPED

In the three years it took to construct this manuscript, many people gave us a great deal of help. Their generous deeds are too numerous to relate, but here is a list of some of them, and to each we would like to extend our sincerest thanks: Jackie Booth, Dr. Joseph C. Booth, Helen M. Booth, Donna Booth, Ken Goff, Mr. and Mrs. Kermitt Jess, Kathy Pompy, Lisa Williams, Mrs. Jesse Johnson, Col. Jesse Johnson, Kris and Kim Valente, the staff of the Big Piney Library, the Visintainers in Mount Carmel, Mount Carmel Public Library, Edie MacMullen, Jeff Doctoroff, Jen Fernandez, Gail Ross, Elizabeth Outka, Melissa Morse, Missy Gully, Blair Wellman, Bob Bender, Col. David Hackworth, Nora Kueppers, Dr. Harold Silesky, Del Marbrook, Robin Moore, Anna and Harry Pappas, Marie Arana-Ward, Dr. Chris Taylor, Debra Glenn-Long, Jim and Lisa McKay, Don Lassen, Dr. John Godfrey; and my children, A.J., Joe, and Andrea, for being so patient. All of you will never know how much we appreciated your assistance.

Special thanks to General Jack Norton, Colonel Mark Alexander, Beaver Thompson, and Jean Gavin for reading the manuscript-in-progress and providing immensely helpful comments.

Soft landings to General William Ryder, who is now with his longtime friend Slim Jim. Soft landings, too, to all the original "Devils in Baggy Pants" who are still with us and those who have gone on. If Slim Jim was your ideal, so too were you his. Long may your sacrifices and stories be remembered.

NOTES

All quotes not otherwise attributed are from Gavin's unpublished memoirs.

1. Eve of Fame—June 5, 1944

The jump scene is derived from several sources but mainly from the recollections of Bill Walton.

PAGE

13   *Bill Walton watched:* Interview with Bill Walton.

13   *Below, the land:* Preinvasion German defenses are discussed in a multitude of sources: the 82nd Airborne after-action report written right after the invasion; James M. Gavin, *On to Berlin* (New York: Viking, 1978), pp. 90–98, are two sources.

14   *more than 1,000:* Official 82nd Airborne Division after-action report.

2. Boyhood

This chapter is based on Gavin's birth documents, Gavin's own unpublished account of his search for his mother and his childhood, author interviews with Mount Carmel residents, and author interview with Jim Gavin one month before his death.

PAGE

21   *"A minor child":* Gavin's adoption papers.

27   *"They are my":* Gavin, 1940 diary.

3. From Panama to West Point

The West Point section of this chapter is built upon Gavin's memoirs, letters between Gavin and Irma Baulsir, Gavin's West Point Service Record, interviews with West Pointers from that era, and a plethora of secondary sources—some of which are listed below. Some information on Gavin's experiences and views on West Point is also available in James M. Gavin, *War and Peace in the Space Age* (New York: Harper, 1958), pp. 32–35. He also spoke briefly on the subject in an interview conducted with Gavin through the Senior Officers' Debriefing Program conducted by the U.S. Army Military History Institute in Carlisle Barracks, Pennsylvania. Many books exist on the history of West Point, but the best available is Stephen E. Ambrose, *Duty, Honor, and Country: A History of West Point* (Baltimore: The Johns Hopkins Press, 1966). It is largely from this that the profile of West Point was developed.

PAGE

34 *Conditions in the Canal:* Interview with Gen. Andrew O'Meara. Much of the information in the following paragraphs is based on that interview as well, and the report of the department commander in 1923.

42 *"I found the studies":* Jean Edward Smith, *Lucius D. Clay: An American Life* (New York: Henry Holt, 1990).

42 *But neither was West Point:* MacArthur's impact on West Point is well covered in William Manchester *American Caesar* (Boston: Little Brown, 1979).

46 *During Gavin's time:* Manchester, *American Caesar*, p. 127–32.

46 *Modern in outlook:* ibid.

46 *MacArthur was a:* ibid.

46 *But most of the faculty:* ibid.

48 *"I am desperate":* Various quotes from letters of Gavin to Irma Baulsir, 1928–29. The collection of near-daily correspondence is sugary indeed.

49 *"They are just":* Howitzer, 1929.

4. Up from Zero

Information on this period of Gavin's life is scanty, but two supremely good sources have survived, his 1931 and 1932 diaries. The rest of the diaries up to 1940 are missing, or unavailable for some reason. As a result, much of this chapter is built upon Gavin's memoir, interviews, and secondary sources. Comments on Gavin's failure at flight school are derived from an interview with Gen. William Ryder, who once discussed it with him, and his own account in James M. Gavin, *War and Peace in the Space Age*, pp. 35–36. Information on the history of the American army may be found in Russell Weigley's *Eisenhower's Lieutenants*, in Part I; and Russell F. Weigley, *History of the United States Army* (Bloomington, Ind.: Indiana University Press, 1984). Discussion of strength of the armed forces in the post-World War I period may be found in Forrest C. Pogue, *George C. Marshall: Education of a General* (New York: Viking, 1963), pp. 205–206; and in Allen R. Millet and Williamson Murray, *Military Effectiveness Volume II: The Interwar Period* (Boston: Allen & Unwin, 1988), pp. 77–81. Millet discusses the preparedness of all the major participants of World War II. A good source on the sparcity of promotions in this period is Douglas Kinnard, *The Certain Trumpet* (New York: Brassy's, 1991), pp. 6–12.

Interviews with Gen. William Ryder and Gen. William Yarborough were of invaluable help in reconstructing Gavin's time in the Philippines, as were interviews with Gen. Andrew O'Meara on Fort Sill, and with Gen. Jack Norton on the West Point period. For the situation at the Infantry School, Forrest C. Pogue's work was again of significant help and there is a great deal on this period in Barbara W. Tuchman, *Stilwell and the American Experience in China, 1911–*

45 (New York: Macmillan, 1970), pp 123–8. For general information on the 1930s, one of the best works available is William Manchester, *The Glory and the Dream* (Boston: Little, Brown, 1973). Information on Taylor's assignments is from Kinnard.

PAGE

51 *"The object seemed"*: Gavin, *War and Peace*, p. 35–36.
52 *"Washington must have"*: ibid., p. 36.
53 *"I hope E."*: Gavin, 1931 diary.
54 *"Throw out everything"*: Tuchman, p.124.
55 *"Stilwell in his"*: ibid., p. 289.
56 *"a genius for"*: ibid., p. 125.
56 *"Cut would be good."*: Gavin, 1932 diary.
57 *"yet I am"*: ibid.
57 *"One cause of"*: Tuchman, p. 130.
59 *"This change proved"*: Weigley, *Eisenhower's Lieutenants*, p. 8.
61 *"not colorful or flashy"*: Interview with Gen. O'Meara.
63 *"If you went"*: Interview with Gen. Ryder.
63 *"I never expect"*: Gavin, 1940 diary.
64 *"is a confirmed"*: ibid.
66 *"so far as I know"*: Letter, West Point superintendent.

5. The Airborne Idea

This chapter leans heavily for its airborne development material upon the fine work of Gerard Devlin in his book *Paratrooper* (New York: St. Martin's Press, 1979). Also of great assistance were Al Ireland, Barney Oldfield, Gen. William Ryder and Gen. William Yarborough. Gen. Gavin's diaries were also helpful, along with his unpublished memoir. The German commander of the Eben Emael assault, Oberst Rudolf Witzig, wrote a fine analysis of the operation. It may be found in Rudolf Witzig, "Coup from the Air: the Capture of Fort Eben Emael" *History of the Second World War*, Part 4, Marshal Cavendish U.S.A. Ltd., 1972, pp. 106–11.

PAGE

74 *"We had lots of enthusiasm"*: Interviews with Gen. Ryder and Gen. Yarborough.
76 *"The vital need"*: James M. Gavin, FM 31–30: *Tactics and Technique of Air-Borne Troops*, (Washington, D.C.: War Department, May 20, 1942), p. 49.
76 *"Because I wrote"*: Interview with Gen. James M. Gavin.
81 *"the first out"*: Interview with Al Ireland.
83 *"The 505th may"*: Clay Blair, *Ridgway's Paratroopers* (Garden City, New York: Dial Press, 1985), p. 51.
83 *"In view of"*: ibid.

6. Sicily

For reconstructing the Sicily drop, we are indebted to several sources: James M. Gavin, *On to Berlin*; Clay Blair's *Ridgway's Paratroopers*; the official after-action report by the 82nd Airborne Division; Jim Gavin's diary for 1943; Jim Gavin's 1943 letters home to his daughter Barbara; interviews with Gen. William Ryder, Ben Vandervoort, Al Ireland, Mark Alexander, and others; and numerous documents from the Gavin papers.

For a description of the British drop, near Primosole bridge, see William B. Breuer, *Drop Zone Sicily* (Novato, CA: Presidio Press, 1983), pp. 170–180. The after-action debate is based upon documents from the Gavin and Ridgway papers, and I am indebted to Chet Hansen for his assessment of the airborne drop.

PAGE
85   *"The type of training"*: Gavin, 1943 diary.
86   *"I was assured by Gen. Ridgway"*: ibid.
90   *"The entire convoy"*: ibid.
90   *"genius for finding"*: Interview with Mark Alexander.
92   *"It is clear"*: Gavin, 1943 diary.
93   *"It is annoying"*: ibid.
93   *"I will never"*: ibid.
94   *"Your priorities are as follows"*: ibid.
94   *"This goddamn stuff"*: ibid.
94   *"At about 10:05"*: ibid.
95   *"They are splendid-looking"*: ibid.
95   *"The DZ's are O.K."*: ibid.
96   *"Seldom in modern warfare"*: Blair, *Ridgway's Paratroopers*, p. 83.
96   *"Soldiers of the 505th"*: Gavin's notes written at the time.
98   *"I think we're off course"*: Interview with Gen. Ryder.
100   *"I'll take care"*: Gavin, *On to Berlin*, p. 25.
100   *"What in hell"*: ibid.
101   *"I wanted to survive"*: ibid, p. 27.
101   *"It was a relief"*: ibid.
108   *"Actually, Colonel Gorham"*: ibid, p. 41.
109   *"If you do nothing"*: Interview with Mark Alexander.
113   *"The usual action"*: Gavin, 1943 diary.
113   *"The only hazards"*: Gavin, *On to Berlin*, p. 45.
115   *"We have learned many"*: Gavin, 1943 diary.

7. Italy

For an overall account of the Salerno landing, see the reprinted version of Samuel Eliot Morison's official account in: Don Congdon, *Combat: World War II, European Theater of Operations* (New York: Arbor House, 1983), pp. 323–55.

Clay Blair also handles the action extensively in *Ridgway's Paratroopers*, Jim Gavin wrote an account in *On to Berlin* and *Airborne Warfare* (Washington, D.C.: Infantry Journal Press, 1947), pp. 19–36. Devlin's *Paratrooper* has a great deal of information, and see William Breuer, *Geronimo* (New York: St. Martin's Press, 1989). The 82nd Airborne after-action report is also extremely helpful for exact numbers, times, and dates. Both the Ridgway and Gavin papers contain a great deal of the official paperwork surrounding the battle at the time. For an account of Taylor's trip to Rome, see Maxwell D. Taylor, *Swords and Plowshares* (New York: Norton, 1972), pp. 56–63. Col. Mark Alexander was particularly helpful in reconstructing the 505's actions in the fight to reach the Volturno.

PAGE

122   *"They're just like animals!"*: Blair, *Ridgway's Paratroopers*, p. 114.
122   *"Opened the recreation"*: Gavin, 1943 diary.
123   *But the place:* Interview with Jack Thompson.
123   *"I went to G-1"*: ibid.
123   *"Our continued association"*: ibid.
123   *"I feel that many"*: ibid.
123   *"There is only"*: ibid.
127   *"Glad to move"*: ibid.
127   *"At this stage"*: ibid.
127   *"At best, however"*: ibid.
128   *"During these conversations"*: Ridgway memo, 9/9/43, "Development of Operation Giant."
130   *"Just before take off"*: Gavin, 1943 diary.
134   *"Put food and ammunition"*: Blair, *Ridgway's Paratroopers*, p. 149.
136   *"As soon as you"*: ibid., p. 151.
136   *"Sir, we are assembled"*: ibid.
136   *"The regiment that had jumped"*: Gavin, *On to Berlin*, p. 67.
139   *"Hell no!"* ibid., p. 68.
141   *"triumphal entry is organized"*: ibid., p. 71.
144   *". . . typical British attack"*: Gavin, 1943 diary.
144   *"It is evident that"*: ibid.
145   *"Tucker doing well"*: ibid.
147   *"He [Ridgway] has recommended"*: Gavin, 1943 diary.

8. Airborne Planner

For an in-depth discussion of the issues surrounding Overlord, see Weigley's *Eisenhower's Lieutenants*, pp. 1–94. For a look at the problems of the 82nd on the eve of the invasion, see Gavin, *On to Berlin*, and Gavin, *Airborne Warfare*. Clay Blair covers extensively the period between Italy and Normandy, when the 82nd refitted in England, in *Ridgway's Paratroopers*. Jim Gavin's diary from this period is fantastically detailed.

PAGE

151   *"Before my departure"*: Gavin, 1943 diary.

151   *"I am aware"*: ibid.

151   *"Talked to him"*: ibid.

153   *"Keep the upper hand"*: ibid.

153   *"The situation regarding Browning"*: ibid.

154   *"I sensed in Leigh-Mallory"*: Gavin, *On to Berlin*, p. 93.

155   *"I wish to hell"*: Gavin, 1944 diary.

155   *"Everyone wanted to discuss"*: Gavin, *On to Berlin*, p. 90.

157   *"The 507 and 508"*: Gavin, 1944 diary.

157   *"That is a tough spot"*: ibid.

158   *"lazy, soft, indolent"*: ibid.

158   *"There will be lots"*: ibid.

159   *"This fast growing habit"*: ibid.

159   *"It is very refreshing"*: ibid.

159   *"Strange thing and one"*: ibid.

160   *"General Ridgway was very badly"*: ibid.

160   *"Val is a problem"*: ibid.

160   *"I have always figured"*: ibid.

160   *"Several near riots"*: ibid.

161   *"I am getting anxious"*: ibid.

161   *"This afternoon General Ridgway"*: ibid.

163   *"Taylor went to London"*: ibid.

164   *"Working with General Ridgway"*: ibid.

164   *"Walked home from"*: ibid.

164   *"I wouldn't call Gavin"*: Interview with Chet Hansen.

165   *"I have never let"*: Gavin, 1944 diary.

166   *"I am still"*: ibid.

167   *"All echelons of the"*: Gavin, *On to Berlin*, pp. 96–97.

169   *"He [Bradley] is still"*: Gavin, 1944 diary.

169   *"I certainly had"*: ibid.

170   *"I want to come back"*: ibid.

170   *"Our landings in the Cherbourg"*: David Eisenhower, *Eisenhower at War, 1943–1945* (New York: Random House, 1986), p. 251.

171   *"When you hear the roar"*: Gavin, *On to Berlin*, p. 101.

9. Operation Neptune

Numerous sources are available on Neptune, but the most exhaustive, famous and controversial is: S. L. A. Marshall, *Night Drop: The American Airborne Invasion of Normandy* (Boston: Little, Brown, 1962). Extremely close checking reveals that Marshall may have had a few inaccuracies in his work, but they are minor, and given the complexity of the Normandy drop, that is understandable. *Night Drop* is a good piece of work. Beyond that, Gavin's *On to Berlin* and

Airborne Warfare are good sources, as are: Blair's, *Ridgway's Paratroopers;* Devlin's, *Paratrooper;* Napier Crookenden's, *Dropzone Normandy* (New York: Scribners, 1976); and many others. Of particular interest for its supply-side view of the Normandy invasion is: John Ellis: *Brute Force: Allied Strategy and Tactics in the Second World War* (New York: Viking, 1990). For a good overview of the invasion, Weigley's *Eisenhower's Lieutenants* covers the issues well. There are also several books by generals who were there, such as: Omar N. Bradley, *A Soldier's Story* (New York: Henry Holt, 1951) and J. Lawton Collins, *Lightning Joe* (Baton Rouge: Louisiana State University Press, 1979). Eisenhower himself gives his view in *Crusade in Europe* (New York: Doubleday, 1948). For specifics on the 82nd Airborne Division, their after-action report is a fine source.

PAGE

176   *"About a half a mile"*: Gavin, *On to Berlin,* p. 108.

187   *"The artillery shells and mortars"*: 82nd Airborne after-action report.

192   *"I got the details"*: Gavin, *On to Berlin,* p. 116.

194   *"Go! Go! Go!"*: Blair, *Ridgway's Paratroopers,* p. 273.

196   *"stretched head to foot"*: Gavin, *On to Berlin,* p. 117.

197   *"I can't hold"*: ibid., p. 118.

197   *"I want you to stand"*: ibid. p. 119.

197   *"no one was going"*: ibid.

198   *"Where are you going"*: Interview with Al Ireland.

200   *"I continued to visit"*: Gavin, 1944 diary.

200   *"That's how close Gavin"*: Interview with Pvt. Mike Tadusiac.

10. Market-Garden

The indispensable source for the airborne invasion of Holland is Cornelius Ryan, *A Bridge Too Far* (New York: Simon and Schuster, 1974), and it is drawn upon extensively here. Other works, such as Gavin's and Blair's books were also of great assistance. Additionally, in the Gavin papers is John MacDonald's original version of the official history and Gavin's comments on it. It too is extremely informative.

PAGE

203   *"These parachutists have"*: Gavin, 1944 dairy.

204   *"He was a person"*: Interview with Ed Pade.

212   *"It was unquestionably"*: Gavin, *On to Berlin,* p. 143.

214   *"The big Nijmegen bridge"*: ibid., p. 151.

215   *"The flak in the area"*: Gavin, 1944 diary.

215   *"General Browning shed"*: ibid.

217   *"They had been through"*: Gavin, *On to Berlin,* p. 152.

218   *"Sir, I just killed"*: ibid., p. 154.

224   *"This encounter with 88's"*: Gavin, *On to Berlin,* p. 163.

226   *"We've come a long ways"*: Ryan, p. 298.

226 *"A highly creditable performance"*: Gavin, *On to Berlin*, p. 168.
228 *"I soon found myself"*: Matthew B. Ridgway, *Soldier: The Memoirs of Matthew B. Ridgway* (New York: Harper, 1956), p. 110.
229 *"I have always felt"*: ibid., 111.
230 *"Get the hell"*: Ryan, p. 346.
232 *"As I arrived"*: Gavin, *On to Berlin*, pp. 175–76.
233 *"No, they're just getting"*: Ryan, p. 385.
233 *"When we reached the top"*: Captain Henry Keep to his mother.
235 *"As we came into the open"*: ibid.
235 *"Nobody paused."*: Ryan, p. 390.
235 *"Many times I have seen"*: Keep letter.
236 *"The troopers fought"*: B. H. Vandervoort, *Nijmegen Bridge*, unpublished.
240 *"I am afraid"*: Gavin, 1944 diary.
240 *"No apparent effort"*: Ridgway to Gavin, October 5, 1944, letter on military courtesy.
240 *"You will at once"*: ibid.
240 *"I am somewhat uncertain"*: Gavin to Ridgway, October 6, 1944.
240 *"I was sure"*: ibid.
241 *"I know airborne operations"*: Gavin, 1944 diary.
241 *"I am getting tired"*: ibid.

11. The Bulge

Numerous sources helped with this chapter. The Gavin materials as listed in other chapters were of great help, and Clay Blair's account in *Ridgway's Paratroopers* was particularly helpful. Some good sources on the Bulge include: John Toland, *Battle: The Story of the Bulge* (New York: Random House, 1959); Robert E. Merriam, *The Battle of the Bulge* (New York: Ballantine, 1947); and John Pimlot, *Battle of the Bulge* (Greenwich, CT: Brompton Books, 1990). Many thanks to Sgt. Joe Tallett of the 505 P.I.R. for his help in constructing the soldier's view.

PAGE
242 *"Troops of the division"*: Gavin, 1944 diary.
242 *"A most enjoyable night"*: ibid.
243 *"No champagne this night"*: ibid.
243 *"they made a good"*: Gavin, *On to Berlin*, p. 203.
243 *"Chaplains are very much"*: Gavin, 1944 diary.
244 *"Get out of the sack,"*: Interview with Sgt. Joseph Tallett.
247 *"I do not think that"*: Maj. Gen. F. W. von Mellenthin, *Panzer Battles* (New York: Ballantine books, 1956), p. 406.
247 *"Of course, from the strategic"*: ibid.
251 *"Things in an uproar"*: Gavin, 1944 diary.
253 *"I felt as though"*: Gavin, *On to Berlin*, p. 219.

256   *"Any ordinary infantry regiment"*: ibid., p. 223.
260   *"After all, gentlemen"*: ibid., p. 379.
261   *"wearing long overcoats"*: Gavin, *On to Berlin*, p. 254; and he made a similar comment in his 1945 diary.
262   *"At that time"*: Gavin, *On to Berlin*, p. 233.
263   *"Rose's 3rd Armored Division"*: ibid., pp. 236–7.
263   *"To my amazement,"*: ibid., p. 235.
263   *"A goddamn Black Irishman"*: Blair, *Ridgway's Paratroopers*, p. 392.
264   *"They can come back"*: Gavin, *On to Berlin*, p. 232.
265   *"By dark the last"*: ibid., p. 237.
265   *"He [Ridgway] had unbounded faith"*: Blair, *Ridgway's Paratroopers*, p. 394.
265   *"This has been"*: Gavin, 1945 diary.
265   *"The fact is that"*: Gavin, *On to Berlin*, p. 239.
266   *"It was a very cold"*: ibid.
267   *"The Panzers came in"*: ibid., p. 248.
267   *"Our Army has"*: Gavin, 1944 diary.
269   *"Undoubtedly the best"*: Gavin, *On to Berlin*, p. 221.
270   *"when Stars and Stripes"*: ibid.
270   *"Almighty and most merciful"*: ibid.

12. The Road to Berlin

PAGE
272   *"The Army's attack"*: Gavin, *On to Berlin*, p. 249.
272   *"It was frustrating"*: ibid.
273   *"How he found the time"*: Blair, *Ridgway's Paratroopers*, p. 419.
273   *"Came close to getting shot"*: Gavin, 1945 diary.
273   *"It is an interesting fact"*: Gavin, *On to Berlin*, p. 250.
274   *"One regimental CO,"*: Gavin, 1945 diary.
274   *"Lieutenant, get off"*: Gavin, *On to Berlin*, p. 251.
274   *"They were shooting"*: ibid., p. 252.
274   *"We finally were allowed"*: ibid., p. 253.
274   *"He had been commanding"*: ibid.
275   *"I was very lucky."*: Gavin, 1945 diary.
275   *"[It] had become so deep"*: Gavin, *On to Berlin*, p. 255.
276   *"I don't think"*: Ridgway, p. 127–28.
276   *"It was a very rough"*: Gavin, 1945 diary.
276   *"To our dismay"*: ibid.
277   *"I proceeded down the trail"*: Gavin, *On to Berlin*, p. 261.
278   *"An army which depends"*: Weigley, *Eisenhower's Lieutenants*, p. 365.
279   *"He began to turn"*: Gavin, *On to Berlin*, p. 263.
279   *"The following morning"*: ibid., p. 265.
279   *"Much of their"*: Gavin, 1945 diary.

280   *"I began to experiment"*: Gavin, *On to Berlin*, p. 266.
280   *"We were delighted"*: ibid.
280   *"If our infantry"*: Gavin, 1945 diary.
281   *"It seems to me"*: ibid.
281   *"190 nurses"*: ibid.
281   *"How in the world"*: ibid.
281   *"Thought it a good"*: Ibid.
282   *"Well, Miss Gellhorn"*: ibid.
282   *"I am so anxious"*: Weigley, *Eisenhower's Lieutenants*, p. 542.
282   *"Under no circumstances"*: ibid., p. 543.
282   *"It was into this"*: Gavin, *On to Berlin*, p. 266.
282   *"I think it is fair"*: ibid., p. 268.
283   *"By mid-1944"*: ibid.
283   *"It was a sobering prospect"*: ibid., p. 269.
284   *"about airborne operations"*: David Eisenhower, p. 716.
284   *"Hold on to it"*: Bradley, p. 511.
285   *"At one point I"*: Gavin, *On to Berlin*, p. 278.
286   *"to harangue the crowd"*: ibid.
286   *"The displaced persons"*: Gavin, 1945 diary.
287   *"Gavin, you're as nutty"*: Gavin, *On to Berlin*, p. 279.
289   *"his first choice"*: Blair, *Ridgway's Paratroopers* p. 490–91.
289   *"I don't see why"*: ibid., p. 493.
290   *"Reached the depths"*: Gavin, 1945 diary.
290   *"I want to get"*: ibid.
290   *"the fields were freshly green"*: Gavin, *On to Berlin*, p. 285.
290   *"We soon overtook him"*: ibid.
290   *"large groups of Germans"*: ibid.
291   *"young and old"*: ibid., p. 286.
291   *"Sir, there's a German"*: ibid.
291   *"looking like any"*: ibid.
291   *"Rather haughtily, I thought"*: ibid.
292   *"The first free Yank"*: *Saga of the All-American*.
292   *"I had no control"*: Gavin, *On to Berlin*, p. 487.
292   *"No, but I know"*: ibid., p. 288.
293   *"One could smell"*: ibid.
294   *"One Jewish boy"*: ibid., p. 289.

13. The Russians

PAGE
296   *"This is it"*: Gavin, 1945 diary.
297   *"Their surprise was extraordinary,"*: Leonard Linton to Gavin.
298   *"I understand why"*: Gavin, 1945 diary.
299   *"so I continued"*: Gavin, *On to Berlin*, p. 291.

299   "It is hard to believe": ibid.

300   "They were fine": ibid.

300   "several days with Martha": ibid.

300   "Talked to Gen. Ridgway": ibid.

301   "In all my years": Gavin, ibid., p. 294.

302   "The Army, from a strength": Gavin, War and Peace, p. 105.

302   "came close to": ibid.

302   "it began to cut": ibid., p. 106.

302   ". . . As the days went by": Gavin, On to Berlin, p. 291.

303   "News of the first atomic": Gavin, 1945 diary.

304   "It was the surprise": Gavin, On to Berlin, p. 299.

305   "A heavy price": Bradley, p. 535.

306   "I noticed that": Gavin, On to Berlin, p. 293.

307   "It never occurred": Jean Edward Smith, Lucius D. Clay.

307   "I found him": Gavin, On to Berlin, p. 293.

307   "The problem was not": ibid, p. 315.

308   "conducted with the utmost": ibid.

309   "when I devote myself": ibid.

309   "Fortunately, I was living": Gavin, On to Berlin, p. 293.

309   "I saw him out": ibid.

310   "the morale of the division": ibid. p. 295.

311   "82nd has participated": Memorandum, Ridgway to Army Chief of Staff.

311   "the outstanding student": Martha Gellhorn, "82nd Airborne, Master of the Hot Spots," Saturday Evening Post, 218 (February 23, 1946), p. 40.

14. Jean

This chapter is contructed mostly from interviews with Jean Gavin and Gavin's own remembrances from his memoirs. Hal Moore's discription of the 82nd right after World War II was also helpful.

15. Peace—at a Young Age

Information on this period of Gavin's life may be found in his unpublished memoirs and his books War and Peace in the Space Age and Airborne Warfare. The latter is a fascinating, farsighted war chronicle that should still be read. David Halberstam's The Fifties (New York: Villard Books, 1993) does a great job of diagraming nuclear developments of the period. One indispensable guide to the political shapers of the period is The Wise Men by Walter Isaacson and Evan Thomas (Boston; Faber & Faber, 1986). William Manchester's brilliant work The Glory and the Dream was also helpful. Jean Gavin's recollections were essential to this period as well.

PAGE

324   *"In those days"*: Interview with Jean Gavin.

324   *"Then, the Allied powers"*: Gavin, *Airborne Warfare*, p. 174.

326   *"As the war came"*: Gavin, *War and Peace*, p. 98.

326   *"One of the most"*: ibid.

326   *"Never again may"*: Gavin, *Airborne Warfare*, p. 170.

327   *"best trained and equipped"*: Gavin, ibid., p. 175.

329   *"Radiating out from ground zero"*: ibid.

329   *"Our backs were turned"*: ibid.

330   *"this rise in Arlington"*: Interview with Jean Gavin.

330   *"I served Gen. John Hull"*: ibid.

330   *"a big vase of flowers"*: ibid.

330   *"Sharpsburg he knew"*: ibid.

330   *"five or six books"*: ibid.

330   *"kind of isolated"*: ibid.

330   *"James sat in grade"*: ibid.

331   *"When I was a cadet"*: Senior Officer's Debriefing Program, Interview with Gen. James M. Gavin, (Carlisle, PA: U.S. Army Military History Institute, Carlisle Barracks, 1975), pp. 73–74.

332   *"We've licked the best"*: Kinnard, *The Certain Trumpet*, p. 26.

16. The Forgotten War

The outstanding work on the Korean War is Clay Blair's *The Forgotten War* (New York: Doubleday, 1988). David Halberstams's *The Fifties* is also helpful in understanding the politics of the time.

PAGE

333   *"been militarily inexcusable"*: Gavin, *War and Peace*, p. 116.

336   *"For better or worse"*: Gavin, *War and Peace*, p. 118.

337   *"I have no doubt"*: Gavin, personal note to William Manchester.

338   *"an elaborate arrangement"*: Gavin to William Manchester, August 17, 1977.

339   *"The preparation of Kimpo"*: ibid.

339   *"During the war"*: Clay Blair, *The Forgotten War*, p. 573.

17. Tilting at Windmills at the Pentagon

During the period, Gavin wrote *Cavalry, and I Don't Mean Horses* (Harper's, April 1954). Gen. Jack Norton worked with him in the Pentagon, and his suggestions were helpful. David Hackworth's book, *About Face* (New York: Simon and Schuster, 1989) is a brilliant description of what it was like to be in the New Look Army. Matt Ridgway's autobiography, *Soldier*, was also helpful. Douglas Kinnard, Taylor's biographer, is also well schooled in this period and tremendously helpful.

PAGE

349 *"number of Airborne officers"*: Interview with Joe Napoli.

349 *"All the soul-searching"*: Gavin, "Cavalry, and I Don't Mean Horses,"
p. 56.

350 *"Memory can become"*: ibid, p. 58.

353 *"sensitive and thoughtful"*: Gavin, essay on Eisenhower, 6/23/81.

353 *"A general simply"*: ibid.

353 *"When he picked"*: ibid.

18. The Indochina Crisis

Gavin did a great deal of writing on the Vietnam War, and his thoughts may be found in James M. Gavin and Arthur Hadley, *Crisis Now* (New York: Random House, 1968), his testimony before Congress, and his memoranda written at the time survives.

PAGE

359 *"series of meetings"*: Stephen E. Ambrose, *Eisenhower: Soldier and President* (New York: Simon & Schuster, 1990), p. 359.

361 *"military consequences of intervention"*: Excerpt from a page of Gavin to Ridgway memo, 1954.

366 *"Radford saw Gavin"*: Interview with Gen. Andrew O'Meara.

366 *"You don't need"*: ibid.

366 *"He went out"*: ibid.

19. Farewell to the Army

PAGE

372 *"wholeheartedly accept"*: Kinnard, *The Certain Trumpet*, p. 40–41.

372 *"hold views as to"*: ibid.

372 *"the President does not"*: ibid.

373 *"The staff had been"*: Senior Officer's Debriefing Program, p. 45.

374 *"He was absolutely"*: ibid, p. 46.

376 *"number of lives"*: *Study of Airpower*, Hearings before the Subcommittee on the Armed Services, United States Senate, 84th Congress, 2nd Session, April 16-June 1, 1956, Parts I-XI, vol. 1, pp. 860–62.

376 *"the Air Force"*: ibid.

377 *"hundreds of millions."*: *New York Times*, June 19, 1956, p. 1.

377 *"Army and other"*: ibid.

386 *"make him look"*: Interview with Douglas Kinnard.

386 *"Within minutes after"*: Interview with Jean Gavin.

389 *"I told James"*: Interview with Jean Gavin.

20. ADL and Boston

For a good account of the founding of Peace Corps, see Coates Redmon's book, *Come as You Are: The Peace Corps Story* (New York: Harcourt Brace, 1986).

PAGE

390   *"He looked bad"*: Interview with General O'Meara.
391   *"I told him"*: ibid.
392   *"We were starting"*: Interview with Jean Gavin.
393   *"missile lag period"*: Gavin, *War and Peace*, p. 6.
393   *"We will be nibbled."*: ibid.
393   *"limited war differs"*: ibid.
393   *"To cope with"*: ibid., p. 129.
397   *"normal family life"*: Interview with Jean Gavin.

21. France

Mr. Robert Anderson of the State Department and retired journalist Bill Walton were extremely helpful in the creation of this chapter. Much is in print about de Gaulle, but Jean Lacoutre's recent release, *De Gaulle: The Ruler, 1945–1970* (New York: Norton, 1991), is extremely good, though of a decidedly French viewpoint. For more on Chip Bohlen, see *The Wise Men*. One of the best books in existence on the Kennedy administration is David Halberstam's superb *The Best and the Brightest* (New York: Fawcett Crest, 1972).

PAGE

407   *"with the staff"*: Interview with Jean Gavin.
407   *"The children all"*: ibid.
407   *"Me, find somebody?"*: ibid.
408   *"We are the Americans"*: ibid.
408   *"You're invited in"*: ibid.
408   *"The de Gaulles went"*: ibid.
413   *"I am becoming"*: Gavin to Rusk, April 18, 1961.
414   *"Key question throughout"*: Rusk to Gavin.
414   *"One casualty in"*: *Washington Post*, Dec. 5, 1961.
415   *"If I am not"*: Gavin to Rusk, 1962.
415   *"These rumors are annoying"*: Kennedy to Gavin, Jan. 4, 1962.
415   *"You have my complete"*: ibid.

22. The Antiwar Years

For a good account of the escalation into Vietnam, see Neil Sheehan's *A Bright Shining Lie* (New York: Random House, 1988) or Stanley Karnov's *Vietnam* (New York: Viking, 1983). The Feb. 11, 1966, edition of the *Denver Post* contains a good summary of the first round of Senate hearings. Gavin and Hadley's *Crisis Now* is a good summary of Gavin's political views at the time.

PAGE

419   *"help him straighten out"*: Interview with Jean Gavin.

421   *"There is no need"*: Report on General Taylor's Mission to South Vietnam, November 3, 1961.

421   *"The risks of backing"*: ibid.

422   *"The dark clouds"*: Kinnard, *The Certain Trumpet*, p. 130.

422   *"We should maintain"*: Gavin to John Fischer.

423   *"Maintaining such enclaves"*: ibid.

424   *"Taylor seems often"*: Kinnard, *The Certain Trumpet*, p. 165.

424   *"When we begin"*: Hearings Before the Committee on Foreign Relations, United States Senate, Eighty-Ninth Congress, Second Session, Supplemental Foreign Assistance, Fiscal Year 1966—Vietnam (January 28; February 4, 8, 10, 17, and 18, 1966, all Gavin testimony is on pages 225–325.

424   *"He is one"*: ibid.

425   *"My feeling was"*: ibid.

425   *"our bombing went on beyond"*: ibid.

425   *"First of all"*: ibid.

425   *"Are we really"*: ibid.

425   *"One could extend"*: ibid.

425   *"So, I finally came"*: ibid.

426   *"a vast defended area"*: ibid.

426   *"Do you have"*: ibid.

426   *"this particular theater"*: ibid.

426   *"They feel some think"*: ibid.

426   *"Let us understand"*: ibid.

427   *"To button up our troops"*: Vietnam Hearings, January–February 1966, Taylor's testimony is on pages 432–560.

427   *"that is the kind"*: ibid., p. 432–560.

429   *"Our intellectual, physical,"*: U.S. Congress. Senate. Committee on Foreign Relations: *Conflicts Between United States Capabilities and Foreign Commitments*. 90th Cong. February 21, 1967.

429   *"another agency, which"*: ibid.

429   *"we got off"*: ibid.

430   *"In summary, I"*: ibid.

23. Where Did the Time Go?

This chapter is built primarily on interviews with Gavin's friends and co-workers. We are indebted to Bruce Old, Hazel Shaner, Hamilton R. James, John Magee, Dr. Joseph C. Booth, and Peter Emerson.

PAGE

437   *"I am convinced"*: Fitzpatrick to Gavin.

BIBLIOGRAPHY

Acheson, Dean. *Present at the Creation: My Years at the State Department.* New York: Norton, 1969.

Agronsky, Martin. *The First Hundred Days of the Kennedy Administration.* New York: Simon and Schuster, 1961.

Allen, Frederick Lewis. *The Big Change: America Transforms Itself 1900–1950.* New York: Harper, 1952.

Ambrose, Stephen E. *Band of Brothers.* New York: Simon & Schuster, 1992.

———. *Duty, Honor, and Country: A History of West Point.* Baltimore: The Johns Hopkins Press, 1966.

———. *Eisenhower: Soldier and President.* New York: Simon & Schuster, 1990.

Appleman, Roy E. *The United States Army in the Korean War.* Washington, D.C.: U.S. Government Printing Office, 1961.

Blair, Clay. *The Forgotten War.* New York: Doubleday, 1987.

———. *Ridgway's Paratroopers.* New York: Dial Press, 1981.

Bradley, Omar N. *A Soldier's Story.* New York: Holt, Rinehart and Winston, 1951.

Breuer, William B. *Dropzone Sicily.* Novato, CA: Presidio Press, 1983.

———. *Geronimo.* New York: St. Martin's Press, 1989.

———. *They Jumped at Midnight.* St. Louis: Zeus, 1983.

Carter, Ross. *Those Devils in Baggy Pants.* New York: Appleton-Century-Crofts, 1951.

Cashman, Sean Dennis. *America in the Gilded Age.* New York: New York University Press, 1988.

———. *America in the Twenties and Thirties.* New York: New York University Press, 1989.

Clausewitz, Karl von. *On War.* London: Penguin, 1988.

Cochran, Thomas C., and William Miller. *The Age of Enterprise: A Social History of Industrial America.* New York, 1942.

Collins, J. Lawton. *Lightning Joe.* Baton Rouge: Louisiana State University Press, 1979.

Congden, David. *Combat in World War II, European Theater of Operations.* New York: Arbor House, 1983.

Cook, Blanche Weisen. *The Declassified Eisenhower.* Garden City, NY: Doubleday, 1984.

Crookenden, Napier. *Dropzone Normandy.* London: Ian Allen, 1976.

Daniels, Jonathan. *The Time Between the Wars: Armistice to Pearl Harbor.* Garden City, NY: Doubleday, 1966.

Dank, Milton. *The Glider Gang.* New York: Lippencott, 1977.

Davis, Kenneth S. *Experience of War: The United States in World War II.* Garden City, NY: Doubleday, 1965.

Devlin, Gerard. *Paratrooper.* New York: St. Martin's Press, 1979.

Donovan, Robert J. *Eisenhower: The Inside Story.* New York: Harper, 1956.

Earle, David. *Makers of Modern Strategy: Military Thought from Machiavelli to Hitler.* Princeton, NJ: Princeton University Press, 1952.

Eisenhower, David. *Eisenhower at War 1943–1945.* New York: Random House, 1986.

Eisenhower, Dwight D. *Crusade in Europe.* Garden City, NY: Doubleday, 1948.

Ellis, John. *Brute Force: Allied Strategy and Tactics in the Second World War.* New York: Viking, 1990.

Ferro, Marc. *The Great War.* New York: Ark Press, 1969.

Flemming, Thomas J. *West Point: The Men and the Times of the United States Military Academy.* New York: William Morrow, 1969.

Fontain, André. *History of the Cold War: From the Korean War to the Present.* New York: Pantheon, 1969.

Frost, John. *A Drop Too Many.* London: Cassell, 1980.

Fuller, J. F. C. *Armament and History.* New York: Scribners, 1945.

———. *The Foundation of the Science of War.* London: Hutchinson & Co., 1926.

———. *On Future Warfare.* London: Sifton, Praed, & Co., 1928.

———. *The Reformation of War*. London: Hutchinson & Co., 1923.

———. *War and Western Civilization*. Andover, UK: Chapel River, 1932.

Gavin, James M. *Airborne Warfare*. Washington, D.C.: U.S. Government Printing Office, 1947.

———. *On to Berlin*. New York: Macmillan, 1974.

———. *War and Peace in the Space Age*. New York: Harper, 1958.

———. "Backdoor to Normandy." *The Infantry Journal*, November 1946.

———. "Cavalry, and I Don't Mean Horses." *Harper's*, April 1954.

———. "Paratroopers Over Sicily." *The Infantry Journal*, November 1945.

———. "The Tragic Mistakes and Bickering That Undermined U.S. Preparedness" *Life*, August 4, 1958.

Gavin, James M , and Arthur Hadley. *Crisis Now*. New York: Random House, 1968.

Geelhoed, E. Bruce. *Charles E. Wilson and Controversy at the Pentagon 1953–1957*. Detroit: Wayne State University Press, 1979.

Greenfield, Kent Roberts. *The Organization of Combat Ground Troops*. Washington, D.C.: Historical Division of the Department of the Army, 1947.

Guderian, Heinz. *Panzer Leader*. Translated from the German by Constantine FitzGibbon. New York: Dutton, 1952.

Hackworth, David H. *About Face*. New York: Simon and Schuster, 1989.

Halberstam, David. *The Best and the Brightest*. New York: Fawcett Crest, 1972.

———. *The Fifties*. New York: Villard Books, 1993.

Harrison, Gordon A. *Cross-Channel Attack*. Washington, D.C.: U.S. Government Printing Office, 1951.

Hastings, Max. *Overlord: D-Day and the Battles for Normandy*. New York: Simon and Schuster, 1984.

Heller, Charles E., and William A. Stofft. *America's First Battles 1776–1936*. Lawrence, KS: University of Kansas Press, 1986.

Horrocks, Sir Brian. *A Full Life*. Toronto: William Collins Sons & Co., 1960.

Isaacson, Walter, and Evan Thomas. *The Wise Men: Six Friends and the World They Made*. Boston: Faber & Faber, 1986.

Karnov, Stanley. *Vietnam*. New York: Viking, 1983.

Kernell, Samuel. *Chief of Staff*. Los Angeles: University of California, 1986.

Kennen, George. *American Diplomacy 1900–1950*. Chicago: Mentor, 1951.

———. "The Sources of Soviet Conduct." *Foreign Affairs*, July 1947.

Kinnard, Douglas. *The Certain Trumpet: Maxwell Taylor and the American Experience in Vietnam*. New York: Brassy's. 1991.

Kissinger, Henry. *Nuclear Weapons and Foreign Policy*. New York: Harper, 1957.

Langdon, Allen L. *"Ready."* Fort Bragg, NC: 82nd Airborne Division, 1986.

Ley, Willy. *Rockets, Missiles & Men in Space*. New York: Viking, 1968.

Liddell-Hart, B. H. *History of the Second World War*. New York: Putnam, 1970.

Lacoutre, Jean. *De Gaulle: The Ruler, 1945–1970*. New York: Norton, 1991.

"Lyndon Johnson Has the Ball." *Life*, January 20, 1958.

McLain, Raymond S. "The Army's Role: A 1949 Perspective." *The Infantry Journal*, January 1949.

Manchester, William. *American Ceasar*. Boston: Little, Brown, 1979.

———. *The Glory and the Dream*. Boston: Little, Brown, 1973.

Marshall, S. L. A. *Night Drop*. Boston: Little, Brown, 1962.

Masterman, J. C. *The Double-Cross System in the War of 1939 to 1945*. New Haven, CT: Yale University Press, 1972.

Merriam, Robert E. *The Battle of the Bulge*. New York: Ballantine, 1974.

Miller, Merle. *Lyndon*. New York: Ballantine, 1980.

Millett, Allen R. and Murray Williamson. *Military Effectiveness, Vol. 2: The Interwar Period*. Boston: Allen & Unwin, 1988.

———. *Military Effectiveness, Vol. 3: The Second World War*. Boston: Allen & Unwin, 1988.

Mitchell, Broadus. *Depression Decade: From the New Era Through the New Deal, 1929–1941*. New York: Rinehart, 1947.

Montagu, Ewen. *The Man Who Never Was, rev. ed.* Philadelphia: Lippincott, 1967.

Montgomery, Sir Bernard Law. *The Memoirs of Field Marshal Montgomery*. New York: World, 1958.

Morison, Samuel Eliot. *History of United States Naval Operations in World*

War II, Sicily-Salerno-Anzio, January 1943–June 1944. Boston: Little, Brown, 1954.

Mrozek, Stephen. *Prop Blast: Chronicle of the 504th Parachute Infantry Regiment.* Fort Bragg, NC: 82nd Airborne Historical Society, 1986.

Nicolson, Nigel. *Alex: The Life of Field Marshal Earl Alexander of Tunis.* London: Weidenfeld and Nicolson, 1973.

O'Neil, William. *American Society Since 1945.* Chicago: Quadrangle, 1969.

Patterson, Thomas G. *Meeting the Communist Threat.* New York: Oxford University Press, 1988.

Patton, George S. *War as I Knew It.* Cambridge, MA: The Riverside Press, 1947.

Pogue, Forrest C. *George C. Marshall: Education of a General 1880–1939.* New York: Viking, 1964.

———. *George C. Marshall: Ordeal and Hope 1939–1942.* New York: Viking, 1966.

———. *George C. Marshall: Organizer of Victory 1943–1945.* New York: Viking, 1973.

Pussey, Mario. *Eisenhower, the President.* New York: Macmillan, 1956.

Rappaport, Armin. *A History of American Diplomacy.* New York: Macmillan, 1975.

Redmon, Coates. *Come as You Are: The Peace Corps Story.* New York: Harcourt Brace, 1986.

Renaud, Alexander. *Ste.-Mère-Église.* Paris: Julliard, 1986.

Ridgway, Matthew B. *Soldier.* New York: Harper, 1956.

Rovere, Richard H. *Affairs of State: The Eisenhower Years.* New York: Farrar, Straus, and Cudahy, 1956.

Rumble, Greville. *The Politics of Nuclear Defense.* Cambridge: Polity, 1985.

Ryan, Cornelius. *A Bridge Too Far.* New York: Simon and Schuster, 1974.

Sheehan, Neil. *A Bright Shining Lie.* New York: Random House, 1988.

Shirer, William L. *The Rise and Fall of the Third Reich.* New York: Simon and Schuster, 1960.

Smith, Dale O. *Cradle of Valor.* Chapel Hill, NC: Algonquin Books, 1988.

Smith, Jean Edward. *Lucius D. Clay: An American Life.* New York: Henry Holt, 1990.

Summersby Morgan, Kay. *Past Forgetting: My Love Affair With Dwight D. Eisenhower.* New York: Simon and Schuster, 1976.

Sun Tzu. *The Art of War.* New York: Oxford University Press, 1971.

Taylor, Maxwell D. *Swords and Plowshares.* New York: Norton, 1972.

————. *The Uncertain Trumpet.* New York: Harper, 1959.

Toland, John. *Battle: The Story of the Bulge.* New York: Random House, 1959.

Tompkins, Peter. *Italy Betrayed.* New York: Simon and Schuster, 1966.

Tuchman, Barbara W. *Stilwell and the American Experience in China 1911– 1945.* New York: Macmillan, 1971.

Urquhart, R. E. *Arnhem.* London: Cassell, 1958.

U.S. Congress. Senate. *Hearings Before the Committee on Foreign Relations, United States Senate, Eighty-Ninth Congress. Second Session, Supplemental Foreign Assistance, Fiscal Year 1966–Vietnam* (January 28; February 4, 8, 10, 17, and 18, 1966, all Gavin testimony is on pages 225–325.

U.S. Congress. Senate. Committee on Foreign Relations; *Conflicts Between United States Capabilities and Foreign Commitments.* 90th Cong., February 21, 1967.

U.S. Congress. Senate. *Study of Air Power.* Hearings before the subcommittee on the Armed Services, United States Senate, 84th Congress, 2nd Session, April 16–June 1, 1956, Parts I–XI, vol. 1.

U.S. Congress. Senate. Preparedness Investigating Subcommittee of the Committee on Armed Forces. *Inquiry into Satellite and Missiles Program.* 80th Cong., 1st and 2nd Sess., November 25, 1957, through January 23, 1958.

Von Braun, Wernher, and Frederick I. Ordway, III. *History of Rocketry & Space Travel*, New York: Crowell, 1969.

Von Mellenthin, F. W. *Panzer Battles: A Study of the Employment of Armor in the Second World War.* Translated by H. Getzler. New York: Ballantine, 1956.

Weigley, Russell, F. *Eisenhower's Lieutenants.* Bloomington, IN: Indiana University Press, 1981.

————. *History of the United States Army.* Bloomington, IN: Indiana University Press, 1984.

Wilmot, Chester. *The Struggle for Europe.* London: Collins, 1952.

Wright, Gordon. *The Ordeal of Total War 1939–1945.* New York: Harper, 1968.

INDEX

PHOTO CREDITS